a bold unflinchin
era and its despe

HELEN MACLEAN—a small-town girl whose driving ambition brought her to Chicago and to "the other apartment" of a married man.

WARREN TAGGERT—a sensitive ex-G.I. who finally sublimated his sexual aberration in publishing and politics.

MARGARET COWAN—rich, careless, she cherished wealth and her father's power, loved neither wisely nor well and much too often.

MARVIN KAUFMAN—hard-working young doctor who rebelled against his parents' bigotry to marry Helen.

ZEEDA KAUFMAN—who walked out on her family into the treacherous depths of Communism

TIGER RUZZUTO—a tough Chicago hood who slugged his way to respectability as an anti-racket fighter in the labor unions.

STEVE WILLIAMS—a talented, intense, successful young writer who had an affair with Zeeda, married Margaret and never knew how close he came to Helen.

"*a blockbuster . . .*"
—Cleveland Press

"*brilliant and solid . . .*"
—New York Telegraph

"*sledge-hammer impact . . .*"
—Indianapolis Times

"*exciting and sensitive . . .*"
—Robert Traver author of *Anatomy Of A Murder*

"*powerful . . . rough and sexy . . .*"
—N. Y. Sunday Mirror

The Crest imprint on outstanding books is your guarantee of informative and entertaining reading

The Side of the Angels

by Alexander Fedoroff

A Crest Reprint

FAWCETT PUBLICATIONS, INC., GREENWICH, CONN.

Member of American Book Publishers Council, Inc.

A Crest Book published by arrangement with Ivan Obolensky, Inc.

ACKNOWLEDGMENTS

O, WHAT A BEAUTIFUL MORNING by Rodgers and Hammerstein. Copyright © 1943 by Williamson Music, Inc., New York, N. Y.

NEW YORK, NEW YORK, words by Betty Comden and Adolph Green, music by Leonard Bernstein. Copyright 1945 by M. Witmark & Sons. Used by permission.

SENTIMENTAL JOURNEY by Bud Green, Lef Brown and Ben Homer. Used by permission of the copyright owner, Edwin H. Morris & Company, Inc.

GRASS by Carl Sandburg, from the volume CORNHUSKERS. Copyright 1918, by Henry Holt and Company, Inc. Copyright 1946, by Carl Sandburg. By permission of Holt, Rinehart and Winston, Inc.

WALTZING MATILDA by A. B. Paterson and Marie Cowan. Copyright 1936 and reprinted by permission of Allan & Co., Pty. Ltd., Melbourne, Australia. Copyright 1941 by Carl Fischer, Inc., New York.

SOMETHING SORT OF GRANDISH by E. Y. Harburg and Burton Lane. Copyright © 1947 by Players Music Corporation, New York, N. Y.

ALMOST LIKE BEING IN LOVE by Frederick Loewe and Alan Lerner. Reprinted by permission of the copyright owner, Sam Fox Publishing Company, Inc., New York, N. Y.

I'M LOOKING OVER A FOUR LEAF CLOVER by Mort Dixon and Harry Woods. Copyright 1927 by Jerome H. Remick & Co. Used by permission of the Remick Music Corporation.

I'M JUST WILD ABOUT HARRY by Noble Sissle and Eubie Blake. Copyright 1921 by M. Witmark & Sons. Used by permission.

TENNESSEE WALTZ. Copyright 1948 by Acuff Rose Publications. All rights reserved, International copyright secured.

GOODNIGHT, IRENE by Huddie Ledbetter and John Lomax. Copyright 1950 by Ludlow Music, Inc., New York, N. Y. Used by permission.

PRINTING HISTORY

First Obolensky printing, October 1960
Second printing, November 1960
Third printing, November 1960
Fourth printing, December 1960
Fifth printing, February 1961

Second Crest printing, February, 1962

Crest Books are published by Fawcett World Library, 67 West 44th Street, New York 36, New York. Printed in the United States of America.

To my wife

1

IONE NELSON HAD ONCE BEEN PRETTY, BUT now her features were puffy with an invalid's fat, and under the pillow-matted hair her round face was scarred with anxiety.

"Danny Maclean!" she shrilled from the window beside her bed, "you go home this minute or be careful of that sickle! Does your mother know a little boy like you is playing with a sickle? Danny, do you hear me?"

In the back yard Danny Maclean turned his small sunburned face up toward Mrs. Nelson's window with a scowl of defiance, squinting against the August sun.

"Up yours, old lady!"

Mrs. Nelson gasped.

"You filthy-mouthed, awful little . . ."

But the boy was gone. Mrs. Nelson gave the curtain a petulant flick of her hand, and sitting down on the edge of the bed, turned to Mrs. Parley, broad and self-righteous in the visitor's chair.

"I'll never get well," she declared.

"They get it from the father, if you ask me," said Mrs. Parley. "That Helen's just as bad."

"Oh, Helen's a sweet girl," Mrs. Nelson said. "Now, now, I know how she looks to people in Charter Oak. But it's because she's so *ambitious* for *better* things. Helen Maclean is never going to settle for less than she wants, and I like that in a girl."

"Oh, Ione——"

"She reminds me of me, when I was a young lady. Oh, the dreams. I guess I'm the only one in Charter Oak who knows why she's put-onish the way she is. I was just as uppity when I thought there was a life ahead of me. . . ." She pulled herself onto the bed again and made a futile effort to straighten the sheet that covered her.

"You were never a bit like Helen Maclean," Mrs. Parley was assuring the sick woman. "I don't care what you say.

And she's not a bit like the really nice girls in Charter Oak. Look at how nice they ran the June bazaar, and the young ladies going all the way over to Grantsville every other Saturday to the orphanage. Nice girls. Swear I don't understand what gets into the likes of Helen Maclean. Now you take *Mrs.* Maclean, she's a good wife and mother . . ."

Mrs. Nelson did not like the word "swear," and her mind had begun to wander anyway. Muttering, she straightened the thin nightgown on her shoulders, drawing a flat, old woman's breast out of sight. She pushed the sheet aside, leaving only her feet covered. "I wish Harry would tell that Danny not to play around the window. I just can't take many more of these hot flashes. Every time—oh, what's the use! Why don't we go sit out on the front porch? Wouldn't it be cooler there? You'll have to help. Harry always has to do everything for me."

"Jesus God," said Mrs. Nelson, "I wonder if I'll ever be the same again."

The porch swing bounced and trembled under the impact, and the rusty chains by which it was suspended gave a cry.

"There!" said Mrs. Parley.

The great trees that grew along the sidewalk shaded the house from the sun, and the glare at the end of the little street, where the line of trees ended, shimmered blindingly. In the early afternoon the street was quiet, but from a distance the summer air bore the muted music of a martial band. The steady thump of a bass drum and the uncertain barking of a trumpet could be heard.

"Ted O'Harra's men," said Mrs. Parley, "Whooping it up for the meeting tonight."

"Oh, yes . . ."

"Harry going?"

"Harry *always* goes," said Mrs. Nelson. "Don't think he'd stay home with me, do you? . . . Here it is Sunday, and where is he? Listening to the baseball game over at the Rooses' —nothing else to do in the world."

"Well, Ione, a man's got to have some entertainment. Everybody's betting on the election, y'know. You registered?"

"I haven't registered in years."

"Well, now, I always like to vote. Then afterward people

can do anything they want, and I always have the right to say I told you so. We're for O'Harra."

"Shush!" Mrs. Nelson gave a start. "Harry says you shouldn't *tell*."

"Why not? Nice young man like that, full of get up and go, not like old Staples and his crew up at Grantsville. If Roosevelt were alive, he'd sure be telling us to vote for the young veterans like O'Harra."

"Do you think Roosevelt would really tell us to vote for a Republican?"

"For a veteran he would." Mrs. Parley nodded decisively. "War may be near over, but we still got to go on to other things, and the men that were *in* the war are the ones who'll know what's best for all of us. Young fellow like O'Harra's got get up and *go*."

"And he *did* marry a Charter Oak girl," Mrs. Nelson considered.

"Oh, everybody's going to come out for O'Harra this election. You oughta try getting down to the rally, Ione. Make Harry take you. It'd do you good to get out of the house for a change."

A rock whooshed through the thick foliage of one of the trees along the street.

"Danny Maclean!" The porch swing trembled with Mrs. Nelson's cry. "You leave the birds alone. I'll tell your mother on you!"

The boy emerged from the shrubbery beside the porch. He dropped the other rock he held, and shoving his hands defiantly into his pockets, the blade of the sickle hooked perilously over his wrist, he walked off down the street.

Where Kenner Street ended at Wilson Street, the Maclean house stood, under the last tree. With each step along Kenner, Danny kicked up the dirt and pebbles that filled the gutter and tried to think of what awful things could befall old Mrs. Nelson practically any day now she was so beat up—until he turned in and walked up the driveway. In the yard between the house and the garage his sister Helen was hanging clothes out to dry in the hot sun. She turned when she heard his step on the pebbled drive.

"Mama wants you," she said.

"What for?" Danny asked.

"How should I know? You left your skates out on the floor in your room."

"Least *my* room don't stink of lotion all the time."

"Cologne!" Helen snapped, putting up a brassière and clamping it deftly to the line. "Wish you'd learn to talk better."

"Aw." He put the sickle away in the garage and came back to where his sister was working. On the edge of the grass plot in the back yard he found a length of string he had dropped before lunch. He picked it up and moved over to sit on the back steps of the house. Settled there, he began to tie the string in knots, betting mutely with himself on which loop would tie exactly on top of a previous one. When the game became automatic, his attention wandered to his thin twelve-year-old legs. He tensed the muscles of his left leg and examined the calf. There hardly was a calf, nothing at all like his father had. Tiring of this pastime, he watched Helen's movements along the clothesline with dispassionate appraisal. She turned to fetch more of the wet clothes from the laundry basket, and when she bent over, Danny could spot her round breasts beneath the top piece she wore. Helen caught him at it and at once stood erect, flushing.

"I said Mama wants you, now go on," she said, tugging nervously at the bandanna that bound her head.

"All right." Frowning, he stood up, threw the knotted string away, and went through the screen door into the house.

2

THE BANGING OF THE SCREEN DOOR MADE Helen start. She clucked her tongue and went back to hanging the clothes, her movements swift. Boys were awful till they grew up, she thought. And they were particularly terrible to live with at her time of life, at seventeen, when so much was going on inside her and nothing at all was happening *to* her, *outside*. Well, by 1947 she'd be nineteen and nothing would bother her. By that time her parents wouldn't mind if she went away from Charter Oak. By then she could get along all right on her own.

Cissy Haller had left Charter Oak at *eight*een. Cissy'd

gotten along fine in Minneapolis and later on in Chicago. Helen knew she was better equipped than Cissy to be a career girl. For one thing, she was prettier. She watched herself better, and there were the magazines she bought every month that had special sections teaching you practically anything. She'd found out about her voice that way, and now whenever she talked to anybody who wasn't in the family, she forced her voice up from deep within her chest. It sounded wonderful and husky. All you had to do was learn the helpful hints like that.

To be like the girls she knew was what she feared most of all: to live locked up in her own petty problems. One day she would marry; she wasn't sure what she wanted her husband to be like, but if she married him, he would necessarily be a man deserving the best in a wife; that was what she was determined to make of herself. To be the finest kind of wife, to be the most admirable kind of mother to the children she would have. To be respected. To be accepted as a contributor to the world. And then, after a while, after she had won the life she wanted, the people of Charter Oak would have forgotten her; and when at last she came back to visit the town, beautiful, sleek, gracious . . .

Wouldn't they be surprised! Even Leonard. Boy, would they be surprised.

She pinned the last stocking to the line, and tossing the extra clothespins into the pan, she took it into the garage. With long, swift strides she passed back through the yard, lifted the empty wicker basket up without a break in her movements, and carried it up the back steps, through the screen door and into the house.

The sewing machine beneath the dining-room windows was purring rapidly, and Mrs. Maclean was bent over it. Her practical, bony hands were drawing bright yellow cloth through the machine, turning and twisting the material as it passed beneath the bobbing needle.

"Is it almost finished, Mama?" Helen asked.

"I'll be able to try the hem out on you in a few minutes," said Mrs. Maclean.

She held the crisp yellow dress at arm's length. It was compete except for the hem, and Helen felt a leap of fresh excitement. She pulled the dress on over her head with eager fingers. She had found the pattern herself in a magazine, and had embellished it with extra touches: cloth flowers down the front and a lot of little bows to give the dress some personality; she had even thought of writing to the magazine to tell them how she had improved the design.

"Mama, it's beautiful!"

"Hold still now." Mrs. Maclean knelt on the floor, turning in the hem of the dress and pinning the material with brisk expertness. "Now turn around."

"Can't I look in the——"

"Slow! You can see yourself later. . . . There, that's fine."

"Mama, it's beautiful!" Helen repeated, studying it as best she could without a mirror. "Honestly, exactly what I wanted."

"Thank your stars it's simple this time," said Mrs. Maclean. "One more set of fancy pleats and you can learn to do your own sewing. Besides, pleats aren't patriotic."

"I'm learning, Mama."

Mrs. Maclean helped her pull the dress off.

Once in her room again she threw herself across the bed in a luxury of satisfaction. In that dress she'd be the hit of the rally, she couldn't *help* it! She'd look so *cool*. . . . "The space between is but an hour," she recited to herself wistfully, "the frail duration of a flower . . ."

There wouldn't be many boys worth worrying about at the rally, but they would all be coming back soon; the duration couldn't go on much longer now only Japan was left. She wondered dimly if she should've followed the war more closely, tried to understand it; they'd want her to understand when they came back. Like poor crazy Jeff Muller that nobody could make any sense of; couldn't hold a job or anything, fighting with his father and giving up all that money. . . .

She hurried through her bath. The last of the daylight would be gone soon, and she did not want to miss a single minute of the hours ahead. After her bath, half dressed, she put on the only pair of nylons she owned, and stepped into the white high-heeled shoes she wore to church on Sunday. She took the pins from her hair, and sitting down in front of her vanity table, began to brush the new curls with increasingly rapid strokes, not counting as she usually did, but with a feverish effort of will, urging the curls into place.

The mirror before her reflected a curious change in her

face as the brown waves, glinting with lighter shades beneath, fell more evenly and more neatly down to her shoulders: the frame they provided softened her aspect. Her features were dominated by the alert and inquisitive gaze of her eyes. They were a girl's eyes, bright, their expressions quickly and constantly changing; but their woman's awareness of what they saw was too subtly penetrating for her glance to be called straightforward. As she studied the mirror, Helen herself noted a warmth in the gaze that was not a child's warmth, but deeper and less reassuring to the person on whom it fell. She began to put on her make-up, not quite sure of the job she was doing, afraid of using it too sparingly to benefit her in the poor lights that would be used at the rally. She painted her mouth to mask the contours that seemed to her too young, and very lightly applied a dab of eye shadow to each tender eyelid.

At last she slipped into the yellow dress.

When she stooped to examine herself in the mirror, she gave a sudden smile of surprise. A *dream*. . . . She checked her teeth for lipstick and reached for the bottle of cologne. She dabbed the cologne on her bare shoulders, her ears, and the back of her wrists. She found a delicate handkerchief and arranged it in the pocket on the breast of the yellow dress. That would show off her figure, she thought to herself. She glanced at her reflection full face. Were there just a few too many flowers on the dress? No. No, it was perfect, perfect. She was ready.

She had only a minute more to pose before her mother called her to dinner.

At the table Helen ate little, and quickly, paying no attention to her father's talk about the war news, centering all her efforts on keeping her eyes open wide to prevent her mother's discovering the eye shadow she had used. She succeeded, and as soon as the chocolate pudding she had made was finished, excused herself from the table.

"Pudding was good, Helen," her father said.

"Thank you, Daddy," she answered.

"Danny . . ." Mrs. Maclean warned. Helen tarried at her place.

"Yeah, Helen," said Danny grudgingly.

"Thank you, Danny."

With that she pushed her chair back into position, crossed

around the table, and hurried off to her bathroom to brush her teeth and put on lipstick again.

On Wilson Street, as she walked along in the deep dusk, Helen could hear more clearly the imperfect but vigorous thumping and rattling of the band from the town square. A number of people were already on their way to the rally, hurrying down the street before her, toward the unfamiliar carnival brightness of the square—an unimpressive oblong of torn grass, dotted here and there with wooden benches. Helen slowed her pace, deliberately suppressing her acute anticipation, determined to give the appearance of bemused enjoyment, the pleasure a worldly woman might take in affecting rustic occupations. A few yards before her Mr. and Mrs. Hennessey came out of the brick bungalow, the newest in Charter Oak. Helen's father had said once that the house was built on blood, and everybody knew that Mr. Hennessey was always playing politics over in Grantsville, but Helen had noticed with disapproval that when the men got together they still laughed and said Mr. Hennessey was quite a card. Helen watched Mrs. Hennessey's jagged walk as the middle-aged woman came down hard on her low heels, loped forward with each step, bounced gracelessly from side to side. She became more conscious of her own movements, and letting the Hennesseys rush on before her toward the square and the blaring band, imitated accurately the stride that Bette Davis used: a step forward and then, just as the foot was coming down, a sudden swing of it to the side, coming down with the heel tilted at a sharp angle outward. It was difficult to do, but the ryhthm was firm and each step made her hips roll sensuously. As she neared the square, the street became more crowded: women in their summer dresses, some new, some faded by the sun, few enough becoming to their wearers; older men in clean white shirts and painted ties, their collars already melting in the heat of the evening.

At the last corner on Wilson Street stood Jim and Amy Cooper, the young couple who had settled in Charter Oak when Jim had come back from the war in Europe. They were the only new people who had moved in for as far back as Helen could remember.

"Hello, Amy."

"Hi, Helen. Nothing's started yet."

"You seen Frances?"

"No, I haven't."

Jim Cooper smiled in the tired way he always smiled, and his faint Southern accent gave a purr to his voice. "Quite a deal for you folks, huh? See them loudspeaker systems they got on the trucks? Got wires strewn all to hell-and-gone."

Two open trucks draped in red-white-and-blue bunting were drawn up onto the grass. On one, the uniformed band was blaring its martial tunes, and on the other, chairs were being arranged for the speakers and the guests. The lights of all the surrounding buildings had been turned on; lanterns glowed from wires strung between a number of poles that had been set up on the square that afternoon, and flags and welcome signs were draped beneath the windows of the courthouse and the firehouse.

"You're all spiffed up, Helen," Jim Cooper said. "Hot doings later?"

"Jim!" said Amy, and smiled commiseratingly at Helen.

"That's a lovely ribbon, Amy," Helen said, with more enthusiasm than the compliment called for. "Blue's wonderful for you—it's always nicer on blondes."

"Thank you. Jim likes blue."

Helen felt increasingly ill at ease with the young couple. They always looked nicer when they were married, and still young. That's what happiness did for you, she thought. You didn't ever have to be tensed up or embarrassed, because you'd found out about everything and everybody knew you did it at least once or twice a week. You could even feel proud of the fact if your husband was as good-looking as Jim Cooper, even if his teeth were a little bucked. They all knew you enjoyed it, even at funny times like in the mornings. Once you knew about sex, you stopped thinking about it all the time, the way Helen realized she did. Once you knew, you could be free to think of other things and do other things. It was like being jailed when you didn't know and couldn't find out; like being crippled before you'd ever danced.

"I've got to find Frances," Helen said.

"Don't get lost now," said Jim.

The sidewalks around the square were crowded with

townspeople, their faces red and shining in the unaccustomed brightness of the lantern-light. Two children, raggedly dressed, ran through the street, noisily imitating the loudest instruments in the band. The faces of the town were cheerful, but to Helen Maclean they seemed to have too many dimensions. Familiar faces she had known all her life seemed somehow curious, misshapen, stubbornly individual and assertive: the hard, vigorous faces of farmers and their wives; the small businessmen; the people descended from the earnest, hard-laboring pioneers who had settled Iowa and Illinois and Indiana, the people weaned on the harshest of Old Testament religion; Helen responded to the phenomenon without knowing to what she was responding. And there were the faces of recent Europeans, second and third generation Danes and Finns and Poles, faces still strongly marked by the meager crops, the bitter snows, the deprivation and antiquity of the lands from which they'd come.

Helen said Hello to Mrs. Watsky and smiled at Mr. Roose when he whistled at her playfully. She strolled on through the standing groups and knots of gossipers, lifting her chin as if she were looking for someone. As it happened, she knew exactly where Frances was to meet her, and the plump red-haired girl was there in front the library, standing beside the wooden steps that led up to the main entrance. She waved and flashed her open-mouthed smile; Frances really had no poise at all, Helen thought, and as she walked up, she noticed with an inward groan that her friend was wearing anklet socks.

"Helen, ain't it the *end?* Oh, listen, the band's stopped. Goodness, I can even hear myself think for a change. . . ."

Helen smiled softly. "Yes, it's pleasant seeing the square so festive." The word "festive" sent a surreptitious ripple of pleasure down her spine, it had come to her mind so easily. She didn't think she had ever used it before.

Frances went on, "Leonard was at the drugstore and said to wait for him. He ought to be here now. Honestly, does he go for you!" Frances tittered and Helen raised one shoulder lightly.

"Leonard's such a child," she said.

"Did you hear where Jeff Muller moved back with his family? Old lady Patterson could've died—he was paying her *ten dollars* for his room. And last night he gave Janice the gate. They were in the Elbow Room; he almost hit her one."

"Maybe he should've," said Helen.

On the truck beneath the bright lanterns the band struck up again with "Oh, What a Beautiful Morning," the bass drum booming a ponderous waltz tempo, and the trumpets squeaking through its unaccustomed rhythm. In her quavering falsetto Frances began to sing the words:

"Oh, what a beautiful morning,
Oh, what a beautiful day"

She broke off abruptly and tugged at Helen's arm.

"There he is!"

"Who?"

"Jeff Muller. But who's that with—*Helen!* Look, he's with Leonard. . . . Well, can you beat that? What's he doing with —Leonard, hey!" The plump girl stood up on her toes and waved violently.

Beside Leonard's clumsy scuffle Jeff Muller looked self-assured, and the sullen expression on his face gave him a mysterious air. Only Leonard smiled as they came up.

"Hi. Hello, Helen."

"Good evening, Leonard," said Helen. "Jeff. How are you?"

Leonard began, "I'm——"

"Just fine," said Jeff, looking directly at her. He was taller than Leonard, and the breadth of his shoulders, the hardness of his chin, the forward thrust of his hips made the younger man look like a child beside him. Leonard caught their exchange of glances and, blushing, turned to Frances.

"Where's Don?"

"Baby-sitting the Coopers' little boy. He used up his allowance Saturday night, and his father won't advance him any."

"Boy, will I be glad when we get called," said Leonard. "Then I'll really have a chance to make some dough. I'm gonna try for O.C.S." He looked to see if Helen had heard him, but her eyes were turned toward the square and she seemed to be listening only to the band. Leonard raised his voice. "Why'd they have to have this on a Sunday? Don't they know some of us've gotta work tomorrow?"

Frances quickly took hold of Leonard's arm. "Let's cross on over, they should be starting soon."

Frances and Leonard went ahead. When they followed automatically, Jeff Muller did not offer Helen his arm. They did not speak, but Helen sensed his gaze upon her, and her heart had begun to beat quickly. They stepped onto the curb and then into the grass, where the soft soil gave way to Helen's heels and threw her off balance. Jeff caught her elbow, but made no comment. His hand, with its long, strong fingers, maintained its grip, and Helen made no move to free herself from it when she regained her balance. His grip softened then, but the hand remained, cupping her elbow caressingly as they walked across the square. The crowd of townspeople was drawing forward with them, and two men in white linen suits had climbed onto the truck reserved for the speakers and guests. Sweating and gasping for breath, a palmetto fan fluttering beneath her chin, fat Mrs. Parley passed in front of them. She glanced at Helen, but without speaking, went on her way. Jeff halted.

"Let's stand here so we don't get jammed up in that crowd."

"All right, " Helen said.

She saw a black limousine, gleaming with polish, turning into the square and drawing to a stop on the other side, beyond the parked trucks. When the door opened, a shout went up and the audience surged forward toward the car. A man not yet middle-aged stepped out onto the grass, waving a straw hat in his hand. The shouting began: "It's O'Harra! Come on, it's O'Harra himself! They're gonna start soon!"

"This sure as hell is an O'Harra town," said Jeff.

"Yes," Helen said, turning to look up at him. His sullen eyes met hers, and a crooked smile twisted his full mouth. Helen turned back in time to see O'Harra shaking hands with Harry Nelson, who laughed and bobbed his head up and down, and Mrs. Thompson, the postmistress, wearing the drab black she had worn since her son John's death at the monastery place in Italy. O'Harra was coming through the crowd with long strides, a big-boned man with dark thinning hair, his eyes squinted by smiling. Helen studied the shouting, gyrating crowd in the middle of the square. O'Harra was sure to be elected, she thought, if Charter Oak had anything to do with it. The bandmaster on the truck bowed in answer to O'Harra's long-armed wave and the band burst into O'Harra's campaign song. Helen didn't know the words, but the singing, stirring melody sounded something like *The Marines Hymn.* That was, she guessed, because the candidate had been in that branch of the service. O'Harra stood before the second, foremost truck and shook hands and waved and, grinning, spoke to people pressing near to him. The men on the truck—Helen recognized Mayor Kenner joining the first two—looked out over the crowd and smiled, nodding their head as if the demonstration were in their honor and they wished to show the audience their gratification. The last-minute arrivals coming into the square pushed past Helen and Jeff, leaving them, in the end, on the edge of the gathering.

"Don't you think it's exciting?" Helen asked.

Jeff did not answer or even look at her. Helen quickly called up the husky tone. "Jeff. Don't you answer people?"

He shifted his weight and shoved his hands into his pockets.

"My old man had the right idea, all right."

"And what was that, Jeff?"

"They drove over to Grantsville for the night to get out from under the racket. Christ, these people act like a bunch of damned kids over that joker."

"You don't like O'Harra? I thought everybody was for O'Harra."

"What's the difference? They're all the same, bunch of damned chiselers."

"Shame on you," Helen chided gently, "you shouldn't talk that way."

His sunburned face would have been handsome had he worn a more pleasant expression. Even the slight knowing sneer was interesting in its way. Helen saw his look follow through from her face to her breasts and then away again toward the crowd.

"You set on staying here for this gaff?" he asked.

"Well—a little while, anyway," said Helen. "We don't really have to . . ."

"Well. Give the joker a chance. See what he's got to offer, anyway," he muttered.

"All right."

The band finished its rendition with a smash of cymbals, and on the other truck Mayor Kenner stepped up to the microphone. He took a deep breath and was about to launch into his address when the loudspeaker began to buzz shrilly. The crowd laughed, and one of the young men who had arrived in O'Harra's car ran over to fix it; the buzz turned into a whine and then, with an ear-piercing squeak, died out. Mayor Kenner waved the laughing crowd to silence and began his speech, smiling down in a kindly way, like a minister who by his kindliness gives you to understand he knows from his own experiences the nature of sin. The crowd began to stir restlessly as his introduction droned on, and some of the women began chattering together to pass the time away until O'Harra himself should come forward to speak. At last the Mayor wheezed into his peroration, and lifting his voice into a hoarse cry, ushered O'Harra forth.

He needed no second invitation, and came forward immediately. The crowd shouted and clapped their hands, and some of the grammar-school boys whistled with their fingers. O'Harra smiled and waved, waiting patiently for the exuberant welcome to subside. When the noise ebbed, he opened his coat, and plunging his hands into his pockets, assumed an easy, genial stance at the microphone.

"Friends," he began. "I've come here to Charter Oak tonight because the last time I came here—I got what I wanted." The crowd guffawed and their eyes turned on one of the women on the truck, in the seats toward the rear, O'Harra's wife. He went on above the laughter. "And I mean to get what I want this time, too." The laughter rose, and then, after a moment, subsided. "But seriously"—there was a hush over the assembly—"all of you good people here in Charter Oak know me and know why I'm here. Over in Washington, in the nerve center of this great country, our government faces some of the grimmest tasks of its history. Please God, the conflict in which we are involved in Asia, in the Pacific, and lately in Europe, may soon end victoriously for the forces of justice and democracy in a free world. When it does"—he lowered his voice to a note of earnest gravity—"when it does, will we be prepared to face the problems that unconditional surrender will leave on our doorstep? Most important of all, will *you*, each and every one of you, be truly represented in that great forum in Washington, will *your* will be expressed by your Congressmen, the representatives endowed with the inestimable honor of being the spokesmen for this great state in the nation's capital? Those are the questions we must try to answer tonight. Let us look at the facts. . . ."

"Shit," muttered Jeff. Helen gave a start.

"Jeff," she whispered.

"I'm getting out, I've had it. Wanna come?"

Helen looked around. The eyes of the crowd were on O'Harra, and she saw her own family up close to the truck.

"Come on," Jeff said.

"All right."

He walked rapidly back across the grass toward the library, and Helen in her high heels stumbled repeatedly on the soft earth as she hurried after him. They crossed the street, and Helen came up beside him as they stepped up onto the sidewalk.

"Please," she murmured, breathing heavily.

"Oh." He slowed his pace then. He took a cigarette from the package in his shirt pocket, and stopping briefly, struck a match to light it. They went on down the street, strolling now, the murmur of the crowd fading behind them and O'Harra's voice over the loudspeaker distorting into an incoherent stream of sound, rising and falling monotonously.

"Let's try the Elbow Room," Jeff said without enthusiasm.

"Nobody will be there, you know, it'll be like a tomb," said Helen. She wondered if she could actually get away with going into the Elbow Inn against her mother's orders.

"That's dandy with me," said Jeff.

They turned off the square at Albany Street and walked down to the door of the Elbow Room. There Jeff stopped and faced her.

"Your parents won't raise the roof?" he asked.

"Why, of course not . . ." she began.

"Never mind, I'll take care of the bartender."

Jeff held open the door and Helen walked before him into the bar. The room was dark, and the miniature lamps on each table along the wall spread no more light than as many candles.

"Let's get a back booth," Jeff said. "Then if anyone comes in, we can get away through the kitchen. Mary'll let us."

Helen slipped into the booth immediately beside the swinging door that led to the kitchen and the alley beyond.

"What'll it be?" Jeff asked, still standing.

"Oh, a Coke."

He went back to the bar, moving with a swinging step, his arms hanging loose at his sides. He stood talking to the bartender, and Helen saw him give the man a bill and nod in her direction. The bartender winked, pocketing the bill. She felt both shocked and flattered. In a moment Jeff came back, a glass in each hand. He slid into the booth beside her.

"Is it really a Coke?"

"Go on, it won't hurt you." He looked at her, and for the first time grinned with a natural friendliness. "You're a big girl, aren't you?"

Helen smiled, but hesitated.

"Go on, liquor relaxes you," said Jeff. "And look at the knots you're in."

"Does it really relax you?"

"Only reason *I* guzzle like I do," he answered.

Helen took a tentative sip that stung her tongue and throat.

"How is it?" Jeff asked.

"All right. Thank you," she said.

"Good girl. . . . You're a nice kid, Helen." She looked straight at her glass and did not answer. "You're a nut to play around with Leonard. He's a nice kid, I guess. But a kid." His chuckle was deep in his throat, hidden. "You know about things like that, don't you?" He lifted his glass and took a deep swallow. He drew her hand down to the seat between them. He was sitting close beside her and the back of her hand was pressed against his hip. She moved her knees very slightly and the one nearest him touched his sprawling leg.

"Now," he said. "Sitting pretty."

They drank without saying more. Jeff lit another cigarette and crushed out the old one in the ash tray before them. He blew a billow of smoke up toward the ceiling. Helen wondered if he thought her very different from Janice. Slowly he pulled her hand up until it rested on his thigh. She wasn't certain whether she should cross him or not. Was he trying to prime her? Was it possible he wanted to go to bed with her? Was he going to try and see if he could? She made no protest. Jeff drew on his cigarette again, his face serious, preoccupied.

"I heard some of the kids are driving over to Lincoln tonight," he said. "They got themselves a club. You know about it?"

"Why, no," Helen lied.

"Thought you might." He offered no more.

"Are you a member?" Helen asked.

"Why should I go in for kid stuff? I know I'm a non-virgin. I don't have to join a club to prove it."

"Is that what it is?" She felt her hand growing damp in his.

"The Non-Virgin Club. They just go over to Lincoln to get laid. Guess they thought with all the goings-on tonight, nobody'd give a damn. Can you imagine a bunch of stupid kids making a club out of it?"

In Helen's chest was a knotted pain, heavy and still. In addition to the pain she felt her own fear of Jeff Muller, but she pushed it aside. You couldn't let yourself go on being afraid of sex. It was silly, she told herself, a childish shyness unworthy of her knowledge. What kind of wife would she ever make if she was going to be afraid of the very thought of sex? Aloud she said, reining the uncertainty in her voice, "Why didn't you go if you're not what you said?"

"Kid stuff," Jeff repeated. "I don't like quick lays. I like a lot of time. You know? That dame Janice, rushing off to Mama like a——"

"You mean Janice and . . ." She stopped, hating herself for having blurted it out. Jeff looked down at her. He gave a short laugh and squeezed her hand.

"Sure." He grinned. "You didn't know? Hell, any girl's gotta break in sooner or later."

"Oh. Sure," said Helen.

"Why shouldn't they? Christ, guys start the first chance they get. No guy afterward can know if you give him the right line. . . . You know the line, don't you?"

"Of course I do." Almost with satisfaction she thought it wouldn't be a line at all with her, it'd be the truth: tennis.

"So what's the worry?" Jeff laughed again and pressed her hand against his leg. "Not Leonard, huh? I never thought so."

Dimly Helen wished he wouldn't talk like that. It wasn't any of his business, and it sounded patronizing.

"You ever try it?" Helen pretended not to hear. "Just as well. It's always better to start with somebody knows what the hell he's doing." Helen began to tremble; she bit down on the inside of her bottom lip, but the tremors went on, as if of their own will, betraying her.

"Hey," said Jeff. "Hey."

"It must be the drink," Helen said, tittering unconvincingly; "it's so cold."

"Want another?" The patron's archness was gone from his voice now, and there was concern in his manner. That was odd, she thought. It was almost as if her trembling had interested him, had made her seem special to him.

"No, thank you," she said.

"Ever try any rum? That's rye you got now. Rum's the stuff, real sweet. I've got a couple of bottles at home." He paused, the twisted smile touching his mouth again. "Why don't we go over and mix some Cuba libres? You wanna?"

Silently Helen cursed her awkwardness in the face of his question. She resented the sudden shame that twanged like a plucked steel cord inside her chest, dissolving the pain that had been there before. She took a deep breath, but the trembling persisted. Her thoughts ran with lightning clarity, in unreal flashes, illuminating the decision before her. If she gave in to him, if she had intercourse with him, maybe thinking about sex would not plague her the way it did now. She would know about it, it would be in its proper perspective. He was good-looking and he wanted her. Real love had nothing to do with it. Real love would come later, maybe much later. There was no reason for her to go on being ignorant and inexperienced until then. Who would tell her it was wrong to give in to him except a lot of pious-mouthed hypocrites? It was the last decision of the evening, she knew, because if she accepted his invitation to go to his house for more drinks, she accepted everything, and halting later would be as mean to him as dishonorable in herself. What would it be like? She couldn't imagine. What would a boy be like, this boy, making love to her, initiating her, what would it be like at last to know the feel of love? She lifted her head abruptly.

"I'd like to try whatever those drinks were you said," she answered. "Besides, you know, there won't be a chance of my parents bursting in like there is here."

The sureness of her voice had now startled her. She wanted him, she admitted to herself. She wanted the knowledge and the passion that was in him.

"Mine, either," said Jeff. "Not at least till midnight. This is paid up, come on. I'll really mix you a batch."

They slid out of the booth and walked back out to the sidewalk. Jeff waved good night to the bartender as they went through the door.

The Muller house was a block farther from the square, on a more sedate street around the corner from the Elbow Room. The front porch was broad and bordered with boxed shrubs. Jeff unlocked the front door.

"Give me your hand," he said, "I don't want to turn on the front lights."

He led her by the hand through the darkness of what she imagined must be the front hallway and the long parlor and the dining room. Helen had never been inside the Muller house before, but even in the darkness she fancied she could see the shining furniture, the spotless floors, and the rich draperies she knew the rooms must contain.

Jeff snapped on the kitchen light.

"There, we'll get that damn thing off in a second," he muttered. "Lights upstairs don't have such a glare. I hate glary lights." From the refrigerator he took a tray of ice cubes and fixed their drinks at the sink. When they were ready, he looked at the half-emptied bottle of rum. "Better hold on to this, huh?" He put the bottle under his arm and handed one of the drinks to Helen. He made a wordless sound in his throat before he spoke. "We can have them in my room; I got it fixed up like a living room so I can entertain my own friends there," he explained to her.

"All right."

He turned out the lights and went ahead to the hallway off the dining room, where a lamp burned to light the stairway. Helen followed him, and they went up the stairs. Jeff's room was at the head of the stairs. Going in, he turned on another lamp; it threw a dim amber glow across the floor.

"Come on in," he said.

Her head had begun to cloud and she made no attempt to take in what she saw. In the half-darkness she was aware of a couch, a desk, a whatnot shelf in the corner. Venetian blinds over the window were drawn closed.

"It's nice," Helen said.

Jeff took her by the arm and turned her toward him. He looked at her in silence.

"The rum drink tastes good," Helen said, "better than whatever I had at the Elbow Room."

"Good. You can put it there on the end table."

Helen put the glass down, and as she turned back toward him, Jeff lowered his head suddenly, pressing his mouth hard against her neck. She gave a gasp, but did not move. He put his glass down beside her own and embraced her, locking his arms about her waist. Pulling his head back, he grinned down at her.

"You drunk?" he asked.

Helen laughed uneasily. "I think so." She hoped desperately that it was so. If she were drunk, whatever impressions came to her might be a little blurred. She would remember them, but she wouldn't have to study and sort them as they came, but could store them up hungrily, and in her drunkenness could hold onto them until it was over and she was away and alone by herself. Please God, she prayed, let me be just a little bit drunk.

Jeff spread his feet apart so that his face was level with hers. For a moment he looked into her eyes, then he kissed her on the mouth, pulling her close against him. Helen put her arms around his neck, a new release rushing through her, her blood warmed and slowed by the liquor. His lips, for all the roughness of the kiss, were tender, and in the kiss there was a reassuring discovery. Forgetting her misgiving, her doubt, the withdrawn and watching shrewdness her mind had guarded her with, she gave herself to the embrace. Jeff groaned and lifted his mouth from hers. Helen tried to smile, but the smile quivered. She was aware of him with a different and deeper awareness that shocked and moved her. Her hands felt his shoulders, and beneath his clothes her fingertips sensed the tension and urgency of his body. This is a man, she thought. This is what a man is like. She had never thought of bodies with so direct a knowledge, and her own seemed, when she thought of it now, flushed and febrile, open.

He kissed her repeatedly in his arms.

"I want you so much, Helen," he said. "Do you know how bad I want you?"

She wanted to answer that she was glad he did, but she was trembling with the richness of all she felt: emotions so new she could not name them, sensations so far removed from what she had anticipated that the dreary speculations of the past were to her now the confused and hollow images of a child, a shapeless little girl, ignorant and pretentious and oblivious of everything that was possible to her. She could not answer him with her voice, but her hands like tongues awakened to a language as appropriate and clear as any words could be. Her hands lifted, tentatively, young in their speaking, slipped down from his shoulders to his chest. Through the shirt her fingertips felt his hard nipples. Jeff drew his breath in sharply, and Helen's eyes met his to find their lids narrowed together. He guided her over to the couch. She sat down, but he eased her back farther until she lay stretched out before him. He sat beside her and kissed her again; Helen felt his tongue on her lips, and with a new shock realized he wanted to put his tongue into her mouth. When she held her lips firmly together, he pulled back. He did not speak, nor did his eyes accuse, but they studied her, following the lines of her eyebrows and the roundness of her cheeks with a singleness of interest that was heated, fanatic, but kind. He lowered his lips slowly, as if they were a gift, until they brushed her own. His hand covered her breast and began to press down upon it, circling, the fingers kneading. She felt a twinge of shame that a moment before she had pushed him in that slight and meaningless aspect aside. She waited now, determined not to offend his urgency again. His breath smelled strongly of cigarettes and rum, and the rankness of the odor penetrated her consciousness like a hint and foretelling of more secret smells, forbidden sensations half-hysterically indulged. She moaned in the luxury of her obedience, and lifting her head when he kissed her again, she drew his tongue in her mouth. Her hips writhed. Jeff's hands reached behind her and tried to pull open the buttons of the new yellow dress. His fingers slipped and he drew his head back. His eyes were on hers again, as if he hated to break the silence, to shatter the tenuous braid of misgiving and confidence, of wonder and need, that bound them. He sat up on the edge of the couch, his hand following along her arm until their fingers met.

"You'd better get them yourself," he said. "The buttons."

"Yes."

They stood up and undressed. Helen thought with terror that it was going to be clumsy. Why couldn't clothes just evaporate? Anybody, anybody at all looked clumsy getting out of their clothes or into them, it would spoil everything; already the spell was cracking. Helen watched to see how much he would take off, and when he dropped his shorts, she threw the last of her underclothes aside. Jeff sat on the couch, one leg crossed under him. In the faint amber light his body was fair, younger than she had expected, despite the matted black hair that covered his chest and ran in a thin line down to his navel, spreading beyond into his groin. The black hair itself was young, and it occurred to her that he was not yet twenty-one. She was glad he was as young as that. Glad that his body was as supple, as fresh, as vigorous as her own.

She wouldn't let the spell be broken, she told herself, hands clenching. While it went on, she'd think about something else, she'd keep her mind far away so that nothing crude that might happen could pierce it. Another part of her cried out in anger: No, no, what would be the sense to it if when it was over she were as ignorant and jailed within herself as she'd always been? She'd face it out. They were safely through the hauling and wriggling of getting undressed, weren't they? No, she'd miss nothing of what was to come, she wasn't afraid, she wasn't afraid a bit. She stood without pretense, looking at Jeff's body, and standing before him, she felt suddenly, rather than shame, exhilaration. Nothing would go wrong, she knew then, or be disgusting or frightening. The still air of the room was cool against her naked flesh, and she had the sensation that if she should dance, it would be like no other dance the world had known, freer and cleaner, lighter and more lilting than the dances of human bodies could ever be. The man's body before her, young as it was, was strong and wise enough to understand her: it sat on the couch, assured, bold, pleased with its nakedness. She went back to him and stood before him.

Jeff brushed a peak of black hair back from his forehead. Over in the square the band had begun to play again, and the regular thumping of the drum found its way over the humid air through the deserted streets of Charter Oak to the half-lighted room where they gazed at one another in a long, soundless study of contours, lights and shadows, flesh and hair, that seemed mysteriously choked with meaning. The bass drum thumped and the trumpets wheezed in the distance. Jeff began to caress the round thigh Helen held nearest him. She swayed where she stood. He reached for her hand, and with a passionate whimper, she threw herself forward to his kiss.

Their actions were by turns tentative and possessed, clumsy and co-ordinated, made fluid in rhythmic sequence as if by an accomplishedness that came upon them, in recurring moments, like an instinct, without their knowing.

When the clock in the downstairs hallway struck eleven and the band over on the square had ceased to play, Jeff was lying stretched out on top of her, exhausted and dripping with sweat. After the long, still silence he stirred. "Hey," he whispered.

"Yes."

"You're all right? I didn't hurt you?"

It was funny, she thought, the concern with which he said it, and she realized how much a part of him concern and gentleness were. "I'm a little sore, that's all," she said. "It's all right, Jeff."

He kissed her forehead lightly. "Good girl. Christ, you're good. I wish we didn't ever have to move. Ever have to move a goddamn muscle again. Hold still. . . ."

Helen gave a cry of pain as he withdrew. Her body was as sensitive as an open wound. For a while he lay still upon her, his fingers tangled in her hair, the weight of him leaden now, but pleasurable in the very force of its pressure, reminding her sleepy, weary mind of his strength and size, the masculine toughness, in their love-making the hardness of muscle beneath his wet and boyish skin. "Baby," he breathed in his exhaustion. "Christ. . . ." He pushed himself slowly up on his fists, and Helen's arms fell to her sides.

"You want a drink, Helen?" Jeff asked.

"No, thank you."

"Okay." He stood up beside the couch, and as he looked down at her, the crooked smile came back. "You're a natural, you ought to know that," he said, his voice still soft, incongruous with the harshness of what he said.

"It's late."

"Yeah."

He lifted the bottle from the floor beside the couch and held it up against the light.

"Almost empty," he said.

He drank from it with obvious thirst and breathed heavily, his mouth open, to cool his tongue and throat. He put the bottle aside. Moving gingerly, Helen got to her feet. Jeff took her arms.

"Do you want to stay?" He squeezed her arm.

"Not all night——"

"For a while. It doesn't have to be over, you know, just because we've had two——"

She broke in quickly. "I've got to go. Honestly."

"Oh."

"Please."

He sighed, and released her arm. "Okay."

Helen dressed while Jeff stood watching her. The business of dressing awakened her a little and cleared her head. She was tired, satisfied, and not sorry. She knew now.

Jeff was lighting a cigarette when she tucked her handkerchief into the pocket of the yellow dress and turned to him, ready.

"You can find your way?" he asked.

Helen had expected him to escort her home. She hesitated. "Well—yes, I guess so." She stood near him and they embraced again.

"I love you," Helen said, and with the words an unexpected sob jumped up into her throat. The words amazed her; they weren't true, she hadn't meant to say them, they were senseless and self-indulgent, and she stiffened at Jeff's scowl.

"Now, none of that crap." He was firm. "Roll in the hay, that's all——"

"I didn't mean to say that," she answered quickly. "It's stupid, it just jumped out."

"Nice party, and nobody hurt. Isn't that right?"

"Yes. Of course it is. I really didn't mean to say anything like that."

But she realized she *was* hurt. In spite of her decision, her conscious act of will, she was hurt. A tardy pride struck her in the face, startling and then enraging her. She kept a rigid control on her expression and said nothing for a moment, then, kissing him quickly, she whispered, "Be good," and went out of the room and down the stairs.

She left the Muller house and walked with rapid, uneven steps down the street away from it. The liquor she had drunk had lost its effect, and she felt disquieted, depressed, and a little sick. Before she could reach home, the tears came to her eyes and the sob that had assailed her before broke in her chest. Well, she'd done it herself, and now she knew. It was perfectly all right—ridiculous to be upset by something perfectly natural. But her feelings still were bruised, and suddenly she hated the insensitiveness of him. If only he had escorted her home, if only he'd taken her to the door of his own house. Anger choked the screaming of her pride, and she began to curse beneath her breath, viciously, blindly striking down the treacherous hurt and bewilderment even while she was convinced that it had no meaning, that it was only a stubborn echo of habit and education and superstition and everything she hated in her life in Charter Oak. They were trying to trap her; now, by making her feel slighted and wounded, they were getting even with her self-assertion, stifling the excitement and the strangeness of what she had discovered on her own, spoiling whatever was good in what had happened between herself and Jeff Muller. Well, she wouldn't let them! She wouldn't listen to any damn conscience; she wouldn't care if he'd dismissed her lightly; it was meant to be light, the whole thing—she'd started into it knowing it didn't mean love or even esteem or affection between them. She had wanted to find out what sex was like, that was all; and she had found out more than she'd ever counted on, more sweetness and fierceness to Jeff Muller than the narrow, hardened, bitter women of Charter Oak ever dreamt of. Jeff Muller would never be her idea of a husband for herself. God forbid. Only fools prattled of getting pinned or engaged or married, all because they wanted—Jeff's words came back to her—a roll in the hay. Maybe *no* one would ever want to marry her—how did she know? Men weren't dependent on marriage the way girls always thought of themselves as being dependent.

She stopped on the dark sidewalk, taking a sharp breath. That was the secret, she told herself: men don't *want* to marry you!

The notion stunned her. She shook her head. Later on she'd think it out, later on she would think the whole thing out calmly. She heard her own voice, and the sudden awareness of the gibbering she'd been doing cut the flood of her thoughts abruptly, mercifully. She repeated to herself once, "Men don't really want to marry you. . . ." And pressing a fist against her rougeless mouth, she started to run the rest of the way home.

3

WHILE THE BAND STORMED HIS CAMPAIGN song into the night air for the last time, O'Harra and his wife, flanked by the campaign staff, and followed by Charter Oak's dignitaries, made their way to the car. Ethel's arm was firm on his, and, as always, she followed along beside him with a sureness of step, a calmness of bearing, that reassured and relaxed him. When he turned away from an exchange of pleasantries with Charter Oak's mayor, she whispered, "Good speech," without looking up at him, but directly ahead, smiling. He pressed her arm nearer to him.

All Ethel ever said was, "Good speech," but for Ted O'Harra it was approval and encouragement enough. Ethel was nobody's fool, and she knew him too well to have to flatter him or lecture him. Without having to disrupt his own thoughts, he shook the hands put forward to him and kept smiling widely. Ethel had breeding, no doubting that, more than *he* could lay claim to, and the calm, assured intelligence which grew from that kind of breeding had stood him in good stead since his return to the States, even as it had before. Sometimes he wondered how different it might have been without her. Would another wife have pressured him, in the inoffensive, undiscouraging way Ethel had pressured, to go after that commission, to assert himself in the Corps, to use what brains and guts he had to advance himself—and not out of an empty greed or fanatic ambition, but because it was only right and proper that a husband of Ethel's *should* advance? And without her, what would the return from the war have been?

At the car door young Mike Wyman held open for him, he shook hands with the mayor again, thanked the chairman of the welcoming committee, and ushered Ethel into the rear of the Cadillac. When he had followed her in and the door was closed, he sat waving and grinning to the surrounding crowd until Mike Wyman climbed in behind the wheel and the car, with a surge of its engine and followed by the staff's three Packards, turning into the street that led from the town.

O'Harra sat back, tugged at the linen trouser legs, wilted

with perspiration, and gave a sigh. Ethel, lighting a cigarette, returned the Ronson to her purse and smiled at him.

"Are you bushed, Ted?"

"A little. It gets easier every time, the preaching routine."

"You work so hard at it, I should hope it would."

"Y'hear what Bob said when I finished? The *s*'s were flawless. Swear to God, he did."

Ethel laughed, softly and warmly. "Home team one."

O'Harra chuckled, and reaching over, took hold of her free hand. They fell silent, and slumping a little in his seat, weary and pensive, he watched the houses and vegetable gardens on the edge of Charter Oak slip by. They had seemed to like him, the people of this town, mostly because of Ethel, probably, but somehow, he suspected, not entirely. Small towns could be cruel when they wanted to, and when they were bent on destruction, no loyalty to a long-absent native like Ethel would deter them. "Human interest," that's what Bob had called it, and human interest did swing votes when the other elements were reasonably accounted for. He was grateful it was the cinch campaign the Republican stronghold took it to be. It meant fewer speeches, less of the frenetic drive Ethel had persuaded him to anticipate. O'Harra wasn't sure he could have stood up to an intensive campaign, not after the years of battle pressure, of uncertainty and fear and sometimes—secretly, though he shared it with a million others, a secret still—anguish; not after the quick unterrifying wound, the nightmare transport, the hospital, and suddenly again the sight of familiar plains and fields and green hills rearing up before him, strange faces welcoming him home, the hysteria and pawing generosity and almost sensual affection of the crowds of people who welcomed him as a symbol of the other men who would be a longer time coming back.

Now, settled back in the car, he did not turn his eyes from the sight of the rich and verdure-bearing earth they were driving past, the summer fields under the hot moonlight, brushed and cooled by the hint of a breeze from the north. He watched it flow past the land he had to represent if he won the election, and what he felt had only a pale reflection in the sentimentalities of the speeches he had to give.

To represent the land: coming from this part of the country, that's what it meant, all right. Not so much the cities, nor the faceless mass of labor, nor industry; the land and those burned, unfamiliar, suspicious, calculating, fair-minded faces he had seen in every town on the campaign route. They were a good people, a noble people, and if they elected him to represent them, he knew he would not take the commission lightly.

Would he win the election? The future seemed sometimes to be so clear cut—a veteran for veterans, a young man for the young, an exciting personality, as Ethel was always telling him—in the end an easy battle, and he was grateful because if ever they were to get in on it, the young, it would be now.

Ethel had helped, he had known he could rely on her, and Bob, and Congressman Campbell Robinson; and once in Washington there would be Judge Cowan to lean on—intelligent people, with minds and sensibilities more subtle than his own. He would need them. Then as the car sped along and Ethel sat silent next to him, his thoughts sank, running glibly one upon another, until there stole over him the feeling of unreality that had dogged him since the others had put him up for office.

Ted O'Harra . . . and what the hell was he doing in politics? What was he for? Let's get the boys back as fast as we can: good enough. Let's not waste the taxpayers' money: fine. But in reality he knew that only his own ambition coupled with Ethel's assumption of his success drove him on in the campaign. If he was *for* anything, he was for being a Congressman who got *re*-elected when the time came, and he knew that this fact alone prompted his self-questioning about his platform. He had as his tools the campaign speeches all of them cooked up together, but he had no rallying cause, no battle cry. He might get elected once on the strength of his war record, but twice?—or repeatedly? For the men who went to Washington nowadays, he was convinced, the old-fashioned shepherding of their constituents' special interests was no longer enough. A Congressman had to create a public image, command attention far beyond his own precincts, if his people were to return him to office again and again. And to do so, he needed an opposite number: a target, a goal to fight toward, a clear-cut battle line. He had none.

His heart sank within him, and his sigh was deeper and keener than usual, and as usual, Ethel pressed his hand.

"What were you thinking?" she asked.

"Whether I'll win."

"Nothing much you can do about it," Ehtel said, pitching her voice so that young Mike Wyman could not hear, "except try your best. . . ." For a moment she was silent. Then: "You do want it, don't you, Ted?"

"Huh?"

"I mean, I don't like thinking I forced you into it, or anything like that."

His laughter was soft. "What the hell kind of line are you handing me? You know damned well you forced me into it."

"Don't make fun of me," Ethel said. "I mean honestly. I should know if you don't want it." She smiled. "Then I can make my needling a little more clever."

"You're great, you know that? Just great."

"Thanks."

He looked out the window again. They had turned into the road that would lead to the capital. Twenty minutes more, at the most. Ethel would fix some supper for him, and Bob would be sitting in the kitchen guzzling coffee, refusing anything else, making him feel like a glutton, pounding on the side of the refrigerator and driving ideals and concepts and techniques into him, sometimes getting them mixed up so that he sounded like he wanted him to be Christ with the brain of a Tartar. And he would listen and try his damnedest to absorb it all.

"I do want it," he said to Ethel. "And if I get it, how do I keep it? How do I ever make the United States Congress aware that I exist at all?"

Ethel had her cigarette half lifted to her lips, but the gesture died in mid-air. She dropped her hand again and looked at him directly, twisting in her seat. She smiled, and in the depths of the finely shaped brown eyes she had the knowledge, the insight, the devotion that had broken and trapped him from the beginning.

"Ted, they say a good German is a dead German. In ten years they'll be saying a good Russian is a dead Russian. At least, if you win, you can help stave off another war, even if it's bound to come sooner or later."

"It isn't bound to, there's no goddamn reason it——"

She twisted further in her seat and leaned forward to him in her earnestness. "Ted, who can be certain about it? When the war ends, who knows what comes next or who's equipped to cope with it? You've got a kind of corn-fed integrity. That at least puts you one rung above most of the others. Stick by Bob and Judge Cowan. They knew what they're doing when they say you're the man for this election. *Some*body's got to be responsible. If I were one of those *hausfraus* in that drab little town, *I'd* go your way. And you want to know why I personally want you to win? It's not because you're my husband, and I can't wait to set up housekeeping in Washington. It's because the years coming are going to be one hell of an adventure. I don't want to miss a minute of it, and I'm going to use you to see that I don't miss it. Doesn't Judge Cowan feel the same way? The only reason the old pukka-sahib doesn't die is he's afraid *he'll* miss something. Ted, the whole damn party needs you, not only me."

She sat back abruptly and sighed. "Oh, God, I hope we win," she said. "I do hope we win."

For a while they were silent again. O'Harra felt remotely hungry. He wished Wyman would drive faster. Campaign nerves, he realized. Briefly he reviewed his schedule. The dinner party the next night, the big Young Republicans *klatch* afterward. The next morning—oh, Christ, Margaret Cowan would come steaming into town to stay with them. Well, she was a sweet girl. She would end up being a barfly, O'Harra suspected. She and her brother, Mike, both would someday, and she certainly would have Wyman down and out in no time. But a sweet girl, all the same. In her willfulness there was something of her father the Judge's impressive strength and fiber.

Beside him, Ethel stamped her cigarette out in an ash tray, neatly, gingerly, as she did everything. He glanced at the plain black pumps she wore, the fine line of her calf, the tan of her arm. Even when eventually she grew old, Ethel would always have that look, he knew, the sleekness of a good race horse, the tension, the unflagging alertness of the brain. A good Congressman's wife, sure as hell. He turned around in his seat; the staff cars were twenty yards behind, their lights glaring.

"What're you looking at?" Ethel asked.

"I was trying to see the town. The car lights are too bright," he said.

4

"CLAUDE RAINS'LL BE WONDERFUL," SAID Frances as she and Helen, with bandannas over their pinned-up hair, set forth to see *Here Comes Mr. Jordan.* "He's so distinguished. I like distinguished men."

"You can talk to them about things," Helen agreed, "and they've read a lot. I wish there was somebody distinguished in Charter Oak."

"There's Jeff Muller. Leonard says he and that Janice made up. That's all right, that match hasn't got a chance. You be patient."

Helen stopped short, fright draining her voice. "Patient? What do I have to be patient about, I'd like to know?"

"Well, you know." Frances shrugged. "It figures like algebra. There's only one unattached girl in town besides Janice, and that's you. I don't count me. There's only one unattached boy in town besides Leonard, and that's Jeff. You and Jeff, you know, it's obvious you should be patient."

"I don't know any such thing!" Helen marched on.

"Helen, it's me. Frances."

"What do I care about anybody and all this small-town gossip?"

Frances laughed. "You're a scream. Everybody knows how good-looking Jeff Muller is. And sophisticated. Why shouldn't you think he's cute? Oh, Helen, you're a scream! Now don't get angry, I mean, but you really make me die."

"Don't you dare!" Helen bristled.

"Honestly, I admire it, the way you can——"

Helen tugged her bandanna into place with a venomous gesture. "I'm not in love with Jeff Muller, and I won't be. It's always the girls and their silly palaver that're always falling in love. *Boys* don't fall in love every time they turn around. You know what I've figured out? Men don't want to marry you."

"Course not, silly, but you can *make* them marry you."

"Why should I?" Helen demanded. "It wouldn't be right."

"What difference does that make?"

"You've got to be right about something, or it's stupid

going into it in the first place!"

"Helen, you *always* think you're right——"

"I guess my brain's as good as anybody else's! It's a free country, isn't it?"

"Honey, there's free and *free*——"

"I thought I wanted to get married and have babies, but I've changed my mind," Helen declared, her chin beginning to tremble in spite of the thin fury in her voice. If she could tell her, if she could tell anybody what had happened, they'd see clearly enough what she meant. But she could never tell Frances or anybody else. "Don't you see?" she argued aloud. "A man wants to have a sex life, he doesn't want a wife and a house and a lot of babies. I'm not going to get married just because I'm sex-starved. I won't do it, I never will. Frances, I'm going to run away."

"Helen. No—how can you? I'd be scared to death."

"I'm not scared," Helen asserted.

"You ought to be!" Frances squeaked. "Honestly, you remind me exactly of Greer Garson sometimes. Be reasonable!"

"I'm reasonable, I'm the only one who is! This is still America, and I'm not going to be oppressed. I'm not going to stay buried here in Charter Oak the way my mother did, there're too many interesting things going on in the world, and I'm tired of waiting!"

As Helen Maclean strode ahead along the tree-darkened street, a swell of history went with her. Often she recalled —and at the moment she was doing so again—the stories her grandfather Maclean had told her of his boyhood in Minnesota: the story about the unreliable gun his father had given him when he'd been ten years old, charging him with providing the family's meat—duck, rabbit, and deer. Their homestead a poor one, ammunition had been precious. Wastage had meant parental wrath upon his return home, failure to provide game for his mother's oven had meant hunger and ostracism. One day he had lost three rounds of ammunition trying for duck, and afraid to return empty-handed, had wandered through the woods, sick at heart, ashamed, and desperate. That day, for the first time, he had killed a deer—an achievement justifying the earlier wasting of ammunition, vindicating his membership in the family, bestowing on him the grace of a hero at the homestead. His eleventh birthday had been still six months away.

Not for nothing had her forefathers, the Macleans, come out from the East to storm an uncharted, sometimes treacherous, always doubtful continent. In wagons they had come, alongside men with spades and hammers and plows—if they could borrow enough money to buy them—and shortly behind them, their women and their children, striking out from the same towns and familiar ways of Maine and New Hampshire, New York and Delaware. Not for nothing had they grabbed the land, put down their seeds into its virgin, waiting furrows, tamed it and nourished it and built new cities and new ways. It was their determination and their confidence, condensed by generations, that gave fearlessness to Helen Maclean's stride as she walked on. Nor for nothing had her mother's people, the Bergsons and the Lyles, and far back the Smithfields, come with their Bibles and their haunting Puritan spirits and their stern demands, besieging in turn the pioneers who had seized the land. The farmers and the preachers, adventurers and prophets—their eternal conflict waged in her veins. She had been created from their violent mating, and the irresolution of that marriage had spawned both the guilty distress in Helen's eyes and the rapacity inherent in the thrust of her bandannaed head.

When they reached the theater, Frances was trembling. Helen waited impatiently while the girl fumbled with the knotted-up handkerchief that held her coins. They bought their tickets and went in. In the dark theater, crowded as usual on a Sunday evening, the Movietone News had just come on. They sat down in the back row, and Helen, now that her decision had been spoken aloud, wept quietly a moment, too quietly for Frances to discover it. There was nothing past generations of her family had done that she couldn't do. She was the daughter of those men and women, and they hadn't been dead so very long at that. If she had a problem, it was there, it had to be met; she'd meet it and she'd win out over it—you could bet your next six dates she would!

She covertly brushed away the last of her tears and lifted her chin resolutely in the darkness. She wouldn't wait, she'd leave Charter Oak with or without permission. You could do anything you set your mind to. Anybody could do anything.

The breadth of the world was open to her, inviting.

5

THE SUNLIGHT THAT ROSE OVER CHARTER Oak on Monday, August 6, found only Mrs. Thompson, the postmistress, dressed in black, on the street. She hurried down Wilson Street toward the square, where the torn bunting and the weary unlit lanterns of the O'Harra festivity the week before still hung, gray and piteous in the dawn. The sun brightened, and its light, spreading beyond Charter Oak slowly to the farms between it and the capital, Grantsville, glistened on the dome of the capitol and moved on toward the hills, dispersing the morning fog, over the range of the Rockies westward to the ocean. When in Charter Oak the men were coming out of their houses on their way to work, the coffee was only beginning to percolate on the kitchen stoves of Oregon and California. The morning papers told of the President's expected return from the Potsdam Conference and the increased efforts on the part of the Pacific troops to press onward to the Japanese mainland.

At Beach Cove, California, only the grocer and the town officials read the Beach Cove *Weekly* instead of the Los Angeles morning papers. The people who lived there either had the paper delivered by Buster Landon or waited to buy it when they went into the city. At seven o'clock Mary Ellen Dwyer's station wagon pulled out from the garage behind the actress's cottage and turned into the road that led up the incline to the highway and on into the city. Half an hour later other cars began to back out into the street, and the salt air of Beach Cove was filled with the smell of exhaust and the hollow, numb conversations of husbands and housecoated wives in the early morning. By eleven the town had eased into normality. Housewives shopped for dinners at the grocery, a typewriter clattered from an upstairs room in David Schapiro's cottage, and the people on August vacations at Beach Cove moved out onto the beach that dropped gently down from the road to the surf of the Pacific.

When the sun had reached the highest point of its progress across the sky over Beach Cove, Steve Williams came out from one of the cottages that lined the shore, spread a blanket on the sand where the beach was still almost level with the road, and lay down on his stomach, folding his long arms under his chin. At twenty, his chest, arms, and legs were well developed, primarily by the exertions of his boot training and the months of active service that had followed; and now, after his hospital confinement, toned by swimming and long walks up and down the beach, he was beginning to harden again.

He was tanned, but where the skin peeled from his bony shoulders layers of whiteness were visible; and his features, straight and regular rather than handsome by common standard, were burned red. Beneath the slight curve of his eyebrows, his eyes, deep blue, were mild and thoughtful. The sensitiveness of his broad lower lip was balanced by the straight, grave line of the upper one. His fine hair, bronze-colored after two weeks on the beach, was cut very short, and his scalp ached under the impact of the sunlight. He lay, unstirring, his gaze turned sleepily and sardonically on the beach below and the people there.

The muscular, lithe young men who were playing down near the surf, apart from the other sunbathers, seemed more an element of the scene than visitors to it. Sons of Beach Cove families, they had been on the beach since nine o'clock, when Steve had first looked out from his cottage to see if the day would be clear. Their hair was the color of sand and their bodies as brown as the still-damp driftwood that here and there had been washed up from the sea. They played with a careless grace, a pagan indolence, throwing two beach balls back and forth—bright-colored balls that in the glare had as little reality as the players. Their brown limbs glowed with a condensed vitality that human limbs did not have. They were like arrogant creatures born of the sand, conscious of nothing beyond themselves and their game. In the heat of the noon, they were, Steve Williams thought, the acolytes of the sun.

He turned his head away and looked up toward the road, seeing nothing, playing the memory game that had occupied most of his hours at Beach Cove. He had only begun to remember things spontaneously the last week or two, and now as he reviewed the mental images his efforts had at last evoked, the details began to fill in, with hardly any effort on his part at all. He could recall Houston quite clearly now, the smell of his father's gas station—but it wasn't his father's? No, it really belonged to the other guy. His ear could re-echo the timbre of his mother's voice, and he noticed that the shouts of the young men down by the surf reminded him of older shouts, the rowdy games on San Angelo Street in his childhood, the gang fights and the futile evenings his mother kept him indoors as punishment whenever he came home with a scratched face or a torn shirt.

The sounds echoed, too, from the later time in high school when he'd lost interest in the games of San Angelo Street; the sounds then would drift faintly in through the window of his bedroom in the late afternoon when he sat writing clumsy short stories, consciencelessly plagiaristic rendering of whatever writers he was most interested in at the moment. His memory could not yet push beyond his seventeenth birthday, but he had no desire for it to do so. The rest was vague and frightening, and now there were only the scars—one on his side, the other on his back—looking like clumsy erasures on a charcoal drawing.

He had written to his parents from the naval hospital, briefly from the separation center, and somewhat more fully from Beach Cove, the first day he'd arrived. He knew he'd have to write soon again, but he wanted to delay, at least until he was quite sure the things he had begun to remember were really accurate. He sighed, reached for a cigarette, and cupping his hands against the breeze, struck a match. He puffed on the cigarette and threw the match out onto the sand. He noticed that one of the young men playing farther down had detached himself from the circle around which the bright-colored balls traveled. The young man stood alone, his hand shading his eyes, looking up at Steve. Then he began to walk forward toward him, edging up the slope of the beach as he advanced.

Steve sighed and drew on his cigarette again. The figure coming toward him was lean, slouched, and the feet scuffed the sand in what looked like a consciously careless way. The young man spoke before he had quite reached him.

"Hi."

"Hi," Steve answered.

"I thought it was you, but I wasn't sure at first. This damn glare blinds the bejesus out of you." The words were friendly enough, but the deep voice held a faint note of antagonism. He stood, looking down on Steve, and Steve realized he had noticed the scar. "Nice tan. Remember me, don't you? From the bar the other night. Christ, you were carrying it."

Steve squinted up at the face above him.

"Your name's Smitty," said Steve.

"That's right." He sat down in the sand before Steve's blanket, his face turned toward the sea. "Vacationer?"

"Yeah."

"Veteran, I bet."

"That's right. Just got freed a couple of weeks ago." Steve guessed the stranger's age at something under his own—eighteen, nineteen. He wondered why he wasn't in; he wasn't old enough to have finished a hitch already.

"Army?" asked Smitty, glancing at him without turning his head.

"Navy," said Steve.

"Good deal. . . . Been celebrating? You sure were the other night. Jesus."

Steve raised himself on his elbows, but he followed the conversation without enthusiasm, running his fingers through the sand beyond the edge of his blanket.

"I'm afraid I don't know many people to celebrate with," he answered. He bit down on his lip as soon as the words were out. They sounded self-pitying, and he flushed when he thought of the impression they gave.

"You ought to get around more," the young man said. "They're friendly here at Beach Cove. If they knew you were a Navy man, they'd turn out in style."

Steve chuckled. "Spread the word."

"Okay, I will. Don't you know *any*body?" The stress he put on the word suddenly revealed the youth in his voice, and the diffident aggressiveness was gone. A kid, Steve thought.

"Nope."

"Y'know the Vergeses?" Smitty asked.

"No. They live here?"

"Got a house up beyond town. Beautiful layout. They entertain a lot. I was thinking because some friends of mine and me are going up there today for a drink. Hilda's got lots of guys up for cocktails, celebrities and everything. Y'oughta come on up with us."

"They don't know me, whatever their name is."

"Verges. What the hell difference does that make? You're a veteran, aren't you? Hilda would go for you. She lays around a lot, she don't care."

Steve frowned, and looked suddenly away. That hadn't started up yet; maybe that was why it was taking him so long to come around. How long had it been? Well, it was no good trying to figure that out. Months. Maybe a girl was what he needed.

"She young?" he asked. He kept his tone casual.

Smitty grunted. "Naw. *I* don't go for her, anyhow." He looked at Steve again. "But there's always some girls there. Studio kids. Wanna try it?"

Steve shrugged. "Well—maybe," he said. "See how I feel later on." He crushed his cigarette out in the sand.

"You're at the place next door to Dwyer, aren't you? Tell you what, we're taking the car, we'll honk for you when we're leaving, if you wanna go. Think about it, the liquor'll be good."

"I'll do that."

Smitty jumped to his feet. "I gotta get some exercise. We'll be leaving about five, okay? Nice tan you're getting." He smoothed a hand over his chest. "I'm going pretty good this year."

"Yeah, swell," said Steve.

"See you later." He turned and scuffed off down the beach. Steve watched him for a moment, then turned over on his back. He smoked another cigarette, and when his stomach began to growl with hunger, he realized he hadn't had lunch. Throwing the cigarette away, he got to his feet, shook the sand from his blanket, and folded it meticulously. Maybe he'd try reading something after lunch, before it was time to get ready for the party: the old couple who had rented him the cottage had left some pocket books on the end table in the living room. A good mystery would take his mind off himself for a while. He walked back up across the road to the cottage, hung the blanket over the railing of the small back porch, and went in to fix lunch.

At five o'clock that afternoon, when the car pulled up in front of the cottage, Steve Williams was the only person in Beach Cove who hadn't heard the news.

When he came out onto the porch in his new white slacks, the collar of his sport shirt turned out over the light summer jacket, the boy he had talked to that noon waved from the open-top car.

"All ready? Christ, you're going formal!"

"First frigging chance I've had to dress decently," Steve answered the laughter of the others, coming up to them.

"Crawl in," said Smitty, opening the door. Steve climbed into the rear of the convertible and settled back beside him. Smitty introduced the other young men, who were of a uniform indiscriminate age, the creatures of the sand. They murmured Hello, and one of them shook Steve's hand. He felt uncomfortable when they pulled off down the beach road in silence, and before they reached the highway, the back of his head was aching with tension. Then Smitty broke abruptly into conversation.

"You think it'll be long now, Steve?"

"Long?"

One of the others half turned to look back at him. "They won't hold out a week."

"Twenty thousand tons," said Smitty. "Jesus, it's like—it's like——"

"Don't let that Cadillac bastard edge you off," said another to the driver. "It's the same stuff that makes sunlight, like the sun falling down on L.A., just like that. Nothing left of the place, not a goddamn thing. Pulverized, that's what they said."

Steve looked at Smitty. "What the hell are you talking about?"

Smitty answered his look incredulously. "You didn't hear about the new bomb?"

"An atomic bomb," said one of the young men in the front seat, whose sun-bleached hair blew about in the wind.

The gusts of wind and the speed with which they flew onward down the highway distorted their words, and Steve could not follow clearly.

"The power of the sun," Smitty shouted in his ear. "Equal to twenty thousand tons of T.N.T."

Steve snorted. "Who told you that?"

Smitty's face was flushed with excitement, an aspect of his youth he had been careful not to reveal before. But the news's challenge to his imagination was not to be combatted with archness or nonchalance, and his eyes shone.

"Haven't you heard anything? It's all they've got on the radio all afternoon. It means the war's over! They dropped one bomb—one little bomb—on one of the big towns in Japan, and *pow!* The town's disappeared. They'll surrender in no time! We could blow up their whole lousy country in one air raid. Science, that's what America's got over them all, know-how! They haven't got a chance——"

Steve looked away, trying to absorb the news. "How many tons?" he asked, hardly audibly.

"What?"

"How many tons," he shouted back.

"Twenty thousand tons of T.N.T.," Smitty yelled. "Jesus! They haven't got a chance."

Steve tried to reckon the force of the bomb, but could not. If it could destroy an entire city—they were right, then, it'd be the end.

Suddenly he was sad. He didn't want it to end, not really. He studied his reaction with surprise. If he had had enough energy to be emotional, he would have been scandalized. War was wrong, a useless mess, accomplishing nothing. He'd believed that, and he still did. Men should live in peace, nothing else had any sense or rightness to it. He was against war. But *the* war.

It seemed different now, suddenly there was little connection between the two. What had peace been like before? No rationing—he told himself, rather than recalled. Business slumps. No uniforms around. Had his father lived for radio news-reports before the war? No more letter-writing or stations or destinations. Peace. Steve made a sound with his tongue against his teeth. It was sure going to be strange as hell.

He had slipped deep into his surprise and puzzlement, losing awareness of the things about him, and he came to with a start as the car turned into a sloping drive that wound up toward a large, sprawling house with a terrace that commanded a view of the highway and the ocean below.

A number of people were on the terrace, and one of them, a woman deeply tanned, wearing a white low-necked dress, was watching their approach. She waved to them, and the young man driving waved back. The woman on the terrace beckoned them to the main entrance of the house, and the car swung around the terrace, rising to the building's level just as they pulled to a halt before the front door. They waited until the woman from the terrace appeared there. She rushed out, carrying a half-finished drink in her hand.

"Darlings, did you hear the news, isn't it wonderful? The whole thing's over! Or at any rate it will be soon. Darling, pull the car over there next to Freddy's, the Buick. Hurry on in, it's a *wild* party, everybody's so excited."

The young men smiled, but their replies were brief and meaningless. They parked the car under the woman's direction and climbed out. Chattering on at a feverish pace, her voice ragged with phlegm, she led them back to the house. She held the door open as they entered, and when she saw Steve, she smiled, but without surprise or curiosity. "Ben's mixing and everybody's on the terrace; there's a delicious breeze. Come in, come in."

The woman went ahead of them through the short hallway and a broad, many-windowed living room out onto the terrace. Steve touched Smitty's arm.

"Don't forget to introduce me, whatever you do."

Smitty shrugged. "Hilda's real informal, she don't give a damn."

The house was richly furnished, and Steve's discomfort increased. He guessed he looked presentable, but he wished there were fewer people on the terrace. When they came out from the living room, no one was introduced, and the young men he had arrived with eased into the groups already formed. Steve stood, cursing his awkwardness, in the doorway. Dance music was playing from a radio-speaker set up in the far corner of the terrace. The woman in the white dress had disappeared.

Avoiding the welcoming eyes of the other guests, Steve made no attempt to move farther into the party, but took out a cigarette and lit it, trying to look at ease. A number of girls were there, sun-tanned and made up too carefully; two older men in brightly patterned sport shirts and shorts, balding and already slightly drunk; near the radio-speaker was a woman of middle age who smoked a cigarette through an ornate holder and held her sandaled, bunioned feet stretched out on the slats of the deck chair she sat in. Directly before him, in an iron garden chair set against the terrace's railing, sat a girl dressed so strangely that Steve's gaze came to rest on her and went no farther.

The others about him gossiped about the new bomb, laughed and gasped, repeated the radio's messages again and again, called into the house for more drinks, rehashed the rumors and planned their celebrating for the unconditional surrender, which was bound to come now.

Steve did not listen. At the feet of the girl he was watching, on the bricks of the terrace, sprawled a husky thick-necked man who steadied his cocktail on one uplifted knee. He wore horn-rimmed glasses like the other older men; he was talking vociferously, his head jerking from side to side, and the girl listened with an intensity of concentration. On her feet were bizarrely patterned sandals, dyed red, and on her wrists and about her neck were pieces of heavy silver jewelry, roughly fashioned and studded with bluck lusterless stones. Matching pieces, thick and aggressively tasteless, hung down from the lobes of her ears. Steve said "Brother!" to himself. The full skirt, the wide leather belt, the peasant blouse and the jewelry—all gave the girl a savage look. Steve thought she might be Mexican, but her delicate mouth, strong nose, and intent black eyes looked neither quite Spanish nor quite Indian. Her coarse black hair was braided, and the braids were joined by a ribbon at the back. The ankles showing beneath the skirt were fragile, of a thin and fine design, and her wrists were brittle-looking, but her body beneath the extraordinary clothes was a body eminently ripe and on the instant desirable. Above the slim waist her breasts stood erect and young, but not virginal, alert and waiting.

Steve put his hands abruptly behind his back. She was small, and in spite of her flamboyance, her face as she listened to the man sprawled out before her had the innocent, solemn deference of a respectful child. Her cheeks had a natural high color, and her almost rougeless lips, shapely and expressive, held Steve's gaze. He gave a start when a voice at his elbow wheezed: "Now what's your name? Tell me all, I'm terribly concerned about you."

It was Hilda Verges. She did not wait for a reply but hurried on. "Have you met Ben? No, of course you haven't, he's buried behind that serving bar in the living room. I wonder what'll happen when Truman gets back. All those talks at Potsdam, I wonder if he told the others about the atomic bomb—after all, the damned thing was going off at the very moment . . ." She did not look at him as she spoke, but glanced from one to another of the little circles into which her guests were formed, assuring herself that everything was going smoothly.

"Smitty just told me about it," Steve said, "I didn't hear any of the news broadcasts."

"Smitty? Oh, *Smitty*," said Hilda. "Well, I couldn't believe my ears, darling. Darling, what's your name did you say?"

"Steve Williams."

"I'm so glad you came. Have you met anybody? Well, that will take care of itself. Oh, for God's sake, where's your drink?"

Before he could answer, Smitty came out from the house with a tray of cocktails. Hilda Verges took one and handed it to Steve.

"How you doing?" Smitty asked him.

"Never mind, he's doing fine," Hilda answered. "Now go away." Smitty lifted his eyebrows and moved on with the tray. Hilda turned back to Steve. "I hated the war, I'm glad it's all over; all those nice young boys, God only knows what happened to some of them."

"Didn't you like their uniforms?" Steve asked. "The dashing look?"

"Only the soldiers, I'm terrified of sailors. My, aren't you clever, thinking of that. You're a veteran."

"Yes."

"I knew it! I can always tell. Medical discharge? Or are you crazy?"

"Wounded," said Steve.

"Shrapnel, they always get wounded with shrapnel; in this war nobody's ever actually shot. I hope it wasn't anything vital——"

Steve laughed. "No, it wasn't, thanks." He had no objection to her fatuousness. She deliberately made herself a figure of fun, with her cropped gray hair and her alcoholic hoarseness, and he liked her.

One of the girls on the terrace, a baby-faced blonde, waved her arms and cried, "Listen to what they're playing, the *On the Town* score—oh, I'll die! I *never* wanted to leave that show—quiet all of you, listen!"

Most of them did so. From the speaker came the opening

lines of the musical, then the sharp, unsettling explosion of the music.

> "New York, New York, it's a helluva town,
> The Bronx is up and the Battery's down . . ."

The blonde sobbed elaborately. "It makes me so homesick!" Others began to follow the lyrics, singing shrilly, laughing, at every opportunity sighing with lying sentimentality. Steve watched, bemused, and drank his cocktail.

> "Manhattan women are dressed in silk and satin,
> Or so the guide-books say . . ."

A young man lifted the blonde to her feet and they began to dance, improvising the lurches and grinds they remembered from the show. Hilda left Steve's side when another car pulled up toward the terrace from the highway. Presently new guests came out to the terrace, gossiping, joking, gasping greetings, and others moved back into the house. Steve circulated about the terrace, avoiding the newly forming groups, wondering dimly what had become of the wild-looking girl with the silver jewelry. One of the newcomers, a woman of Hilda's age, was shouting, "The commentator on the way up said we can expect the Russians to declare war on Japan now. Did you know the Russians *hadn't* declared war on Japan? *I* didn't, for Christ's sake. My dear, L.A. is like you've never seen it, the *talk*—nobody's talking about anything else; it's the first time in history that movie people have managed to forget shop for a minute."

"Sarah," Hilda wheezed, "you've been drinking——"

"Steadily! Ever since I heard! We've got to celebrate. And I want to put in a long-distance call—on your phone—to Rachel Pemberton, to discuss the whole thing. She'll lecture me viciously about being tipsy, but I don't care. To think after all these years I'll finally be through with those goddamned Gray Ladies."

"The war isn't over yet——"

"But it will be, silly, everybody knows that. I never *felt* like a Gray Lady in the first place. I did it for my country, but my heart wasn't in it."

Steve wandered into the living room off the terrace.

The war sounded different when these people talked of it. He felt disoriented, like that summer in the Boy Scouts when he'd studied map-reading and had gotten lost in the woods that surrounded camp. Yet to be disoriented in this kind of company was a feeling not unlike what he supposed Hilda Verges must feel with him, or with all those young, never-really-familiar faces that came into her house. She seldom knew any of them, he guessed, or, considering their own problems, their own viewpoints, their own boisterous ignorance of her, the very reasons for her interest in them.

It had happened so easily, the way he himself had come into the Vergeses' house, and he wondered if this, too, wasn't perhaps something rather new in the world. Hadn't there once been restrictions, a kind of code, even among the citizens of a great democracy? Hadn't there been a fairly stern selectivity, having nothing personal in it, but only the arbitrary separation of class and interest?

Perhaps his Southern training had made him overly aware of this kind of separation; perhaps the formlessness he sensed in the Vergeses' household was a California idiosyncrasy. He lacked, he knew, the exposure to other households that would have made comparison possible.

The living room was deserted at the moment, but the noise from the terrace filled it. Without thinking, Steve wandered on through the long broad hallway of the lower floor, studying the expensive furnishings, the pictures on the walls. Not even in the service, being invited to dinner by well-meaning strangers, had he ever entered a rich family's house before. Highly polished floors, luxurious rugs thrown across them here and there—it was the kind of place he wanted for himself one day, if he were ever talented enough to earn it.

The racket from the terrace faded behind him as he wandered back through the house. A crowd of the guests had come inside before. Steve wondered what had happened to them. Then he heard the music: a woman singing—a thin voice, plaintive, and occasionally the chord of a guitar. He stopped, drank the last of his cocktail, and then went on, following the sound. At a turn of the hallway in the far end of the house he came upon a room with its door open; a dozen of the guests sat in a semicircle on the floor of the room, and in their midst, seated on a low hassock, was the dark-haired girl he had stared at on the terrace.

Without looking at her audience, her eyes cast down, her long fingers falling upon the guitar strings with a careless, strumming movement, she was singing a song that Steve did not recognize.

> "And if my love no more I see,
> My life will quickly fade away:
> Black . . .
> Is the color . . .
> Of my true love's hair . . ."

Steve stood in the doorway, almost afraid to breathe. The girl sang as with a sigh, and among the people on the floor around her there was not a stir or a sound. Gently, softly, the song ended, and the last chord faded into silence. Then all at once the people broke into applause, and the girl, looking up for the first time, grinned at them.

"Gorgeous!" cried one of the men.

"But Zeeda, the strangest damn voice——"

"I love folk songs!" groaned one of the women.

And someone who knew about such things was saying, "There's a much brighter version, you know, Zeeda—from the Peekskill region."

The thick-necked man in horn-rimmed glasses said to someone near him, "Zeeda really feels the beat of the earth."

Steve paid no attention to the remarks, the congratulations, the demands for an encore. He watched the girl, who embraced her guitar and smiled over it at the man in horn-rimmed glasses, who shouted earnestly, "Folk music would be sensational in pictures—now why the hell hasn't somebody thought of it?"

The girl clucked her tongue. "They're the songs of little people, Murray, and little people are the one thing those sonsabitches aren't interested in."

The profanity on those delicate childlike lips made Steve start. The girl's black eyes shone brightly on him then, and she waved her hand. "Hi there, come on in, pull up a rug."

"Thanks," said Steve.

A space was opened for him, and he sat down in the semicircle. Zeeda smiled at him. "What'd you like to hear?" Her voice when she spoke, as when she sang, was rich and lilting.

"I don't know any folk songs," said Steve.

"Sure you do, think back, everybody learns them when they're little."

There was nothing to think back to, but he couldn't tell her that: books he'd read at school, others he'd found on his own when he was older, short stories he had written, little music outside the Metropolitan broadcasts on Saturday afternoons and the Hit Parade tunes that whirled briefly from the radio, associated themselves with scenes, incidents, particular emotions, and then grew into memories; and there were many memories still missing.

"Where are you from?" asked Zeeda.

"Houston, Texas."

"Well, that's no help. What nationality are you?" she pursued.

"Scotch-Irish and French, by way of Alabama. My mother's from Alabama. Does that help?"

"Alabama, let's see. Oh, I know one—everybody south of Jersey knows it." Before she had finished speaking, her fingers fell upon the guitar strings and plucked out a bright, rapid rhythm-pattern. The people around the room fell silent, except for one who gave an "Oh!" of recognition.

"Frog went a-courting and he did ride,
Rinktum bonnamitcha camb-o—
Sword and buckler by his side,
Rinktum bonnamitcha camb-o—"

The song, which Steve was sure he'd never heard before, had many verses. Zeeda sang the first three looking directly at him, then, turning, played the remainder for the others, her laughing eyes moving over the assembly, their gay expression almost covering another more watchful light that lurked deep behind it. Her face and eyes projected the moods and meanings of the song, but within, something else, Steve did not know what, a more objective, more calculating awareness, watched the upturned faces, caught their subtlest reactions, and seemed to be trying to read in them the strength or the weakness the listeners found in her performance.

"Frog jumped up and away he ran,
Rinktum bonnamitcha camb-o—

And that's why he's a single man,
Rinktum bonnamitcha ca-am-bo!"

The song ended, the group broke again into chattering applause, and Zeeda got to her feet.

"Oh, no, you're not quitting——"

"Please, my voice is really awful today, I need much more practice——"

"But Zeeda, darling, so soon!"

"Once more, Zeeda, just a short one——"

The girl smiled and laughed, but could not be dissuaded from closing the recital. One day soon, she assured them, she'd play for them again, when her voice was in decent shape. All the best of the songs went far too high up the scale for her to be able to sing them today.

Some of the couples, getting up, began to drift back through the house toward the terrace. The man who had occupied Zeeda's attention earlier was talking to a small slope-shouldered pot-bellied man who, Steve realized from their conversation, was Ben Verges, his host. Verges had thin, iron-gray hair and a wide-eyed gaze. The other man was considerably taller, big-boned rather than muscular. He stood slumping, his full, mottled cheeks and jowls darkened by his beard's stubble. Steve slipped by the two men and crossed the room to the couch where Zeeda was busy replacing her guitar in its battered case. She looked up at his approach and smiled again, but said nothing. When the case was closed, she lifted it up from the couch. She was so small that Steve made an involuntary move to help her.

"It's all right," the girl snapped suddenly. Then, as if embarrassed by the sharpness of the remark, she chuckled. "I've been lugging this around for all of my twenty years."

"You're not leaving, are you?" Her smallness gave Steve self-confidence again. Looking down at her, at the pert smile and the cautious, almost suspicious eyes, made him aware of his own height, his solidness. It made him feel reliable. He wanted to take her hand then and offer his support, to reassure her of his kind intention and trustworthiness.

"Well, I've got to eat dinner, you know . . ." the girl began in answer to his question.

"The party's hardly begun."

"Do they usually go on long?" she asked.

For a moment Steve did not know what to answer. He had assumed he was the only stranger in the house.

"I don't know," he said, "this is the first time I've been here. Same with you?"

"Yes."

"I've had a good time. Zeeda's an unusual name."

"What's yours?"

"Steve Williams."

"It isn't. Lucky you. What do you do, Steve?"

"Nothing. Nothing right now. I'm recuperating, as we say."

"And when you've done that?"

"I don't know."

"You're not one of the studio kids, are you? There're a lot of them here."

"No. I used to want to be a writer. Maybe I still do, I can't tell. Recuperating is a hell of a lot of work. If you're straining at the bit about dinner, Zeeda, why don't you have it with me? I have a cottage down on the beach I'm renting. It would save you the trouble of rushing back to the city."

"But I came in somebody else's car, it isn't any trouble . . ."

Steve realized she was teasing him. He laughed with her. "Come on, I'll make you some spaghetti," he said.

"I don't trust anybody's meat sauce but my own——"

"Now for God's sake, don't be so hard to get. . . ."

Zeeda grinned with delight. "I'm a girl, I'm supposed to be hard to get."

"Then what the hell am I supposed to do now?" Steve demanded.

Zeeda laughed. "If we go back to the terrace, I can tell Murray I'm staying behind. I came with his crew."

By now the room was empty except for themselves. The others had returned to the terrace. Zeeda put the guitar back on the couch, and apparently not noticing his proffered arm, walked ahead of him from the room. He had not seen her walking before, and the sight arrested his attention: she moved with swift, long strides, on the balls of her sandled feet, the whole of her neat, small body arced. The folds of her broad skirt swung from side to side as she led the way back through the house, and beneath them her legs looked trim. She turned back to him as she walked.

"Some layout, isn't it? A simple, unaffected little mansion, that's what I like."

In the dinning room Ben Verges stopped them and put fresh cocktails in their hands. The man in horn-rimmed glasses came up to them and Zeeda introduced him as Joseph Murray. He looked at Steve with bland dislike; he did not offer to shake hands. Zeeda told him of their dinner plans, and Murray nodded. The three of them went on out to the terrace. The sun was almost gone, and the figures sitting about the terrace were wrapped in the last of the twilight.

The woman Hilda Verges had called Sarah was saying, "Of course Truman warned them from Potsdam, you can't say he didn't. Naturally when he talked about rains of ruin and everything, who the hell knew what he was driving at? And the English thought the V-bombs were bad, God!"

"I wonder what it would be like if we got hit with atoms?"

"We'd start being brave, just like the British."

At Steve's side Zeeda gave a short little laugh.

"Don't you think we would be?" he asked her, keeping his voice below earshot of the others. Zeeda looked up at him. In the deepening darkness he wasn't sure, but he thought her mouth looked hard, almost bitter. She did not answer his question, but turned back as Smitty, sitting next to Hilda, was exclaiming, "Americans are as brave as anybody, look at the servicemen, what they went through——"

"Look at the Gray Ladies," said Sarah wryly.

"And the civilians?" someone else challenged Smitty. "Those fatsos in Washington who think this is a war against fascism?"

"What's *their* percentage of the population?" Smitty snorted. His voice sounded shallow, lacking in conviction. Steve guessed he had not yet indulged in many political talks with his elders.

The voice that had challenged him—the figure was beyond the range of light that spilled out from the living room, and Steve could not identify the speaker—replied at once, "Bigger than you think, young man. They're all soft—one bomb and this country'd go scurrying off with its tail between its legs."

"Oh, I don't think we're as weak-kneed as all that," Sarah put in.

Steve wondered which of them was right. A weak country: sometimes it seemed that way, bungling, stalling off its entry into the war until almost too late. A country torn with opportunism, deals, and bickering. . . . He listened to the voices in the darkness with the uncanny sense that they came, not from the terrace, but on the early evening breeze from all over the country, voices speculative, defensive or contemptuous, untroubled by opposition, and sometimes, he thought, even stimulated by it.

The shrill blonde broke in: "Listen, everybody, they're gonna play *Bloomer Girl*——"

But her attempt failed. One of the young men said "Shh!" in her support, but nobody obeyed and no one bothered to turn the speaker louder. Over the faint music one of the balding men in shorts, seated directly in the stream of light from within the house, continued, "Mark my words, if the Japs surrender, it'll be fine, but it won't be the finish. Those guys with the U.N.O. are peddling everybody in this country a lot of hogwash. What the hell do professors know about things like that? I ask you. The Government can make all the gestures they want, but war is part of the nature of men. We're still beasts, and war's as necessary in the long run as eating and sleeping."

"Who'll be next then?"

"Who d'you think?" he said.

"The Russians?" Steve asked. The balding man looked up at him, squinting against the stream of light. Before he could answer, Steve went on, "We've gotten along all right together through *this* war."

The man whined, "Sometimes you have to get along."

Hilda declared, in her hoarse growl. "When there are new ideas abroad in the world, the smart people don't try to buck them. All we have to do is show the Russians we're friendly and well meaning."

"Like with the Negroes?" Zeeda asked quietly, but without lightness. Steve was the only one to hear.

"Hilda, you're too damn optimistic about those guys——"

"What's wrong with the Russians? I think they're marvelous, hard-working people. Look what they've made of their country in only twenty-five years——"

The man in shorts chuckled. "You always were a Red at heart."

"I'm not a Communist," Hilda persisted, "I'm a Christian. But it seems to me somehow the most amusing people around these days are Communists."

"A hell of a lot they think of Christianity," the man contradicted, "persecuting people——"

"Now they don't really, if you mean in Russia. They just refuse to give them a boost up the way we do."

"Look at the Catholics!" the man said.

"You look at them." Sarah sneered.

Zeeda glanced up at Steve again and shook her head in a gesture of pity for the disputants, smiling at him before she turned her attention back to the conversation.

He'd been right about her, Steve told himself. It was just what he needed. And he would get it. That night, for sure. A beautiful girl, in her dark, curious way, intelligent. He'd never had a nice type of girl before. With the others, sometimes he had tried to call into his mind images of heroines from the books he'd read, women in paintings he'd seen in museums in all the large cities he'd been to during his Navy hitch. But always the whore's ways had intruded—the gross movements, the vapid talk. Then in his heat the more practiced ones had grunted obscenities in his ear. Maybe she'd do that, too, but then it would be different. With a nice girl doing it, really breaking loose when she had her legs around him, then it would be a kick.

His hands began to sweat again, and he followed with his gaze the contours of her body beneath the peasant blouse and the wide skirt. Maybe eventually there'd be something more to it: a strange, vague pain troubled his breast. Would he finally be settling down, fixing up a house for some girl like this, working and raising children? Only not yet. There would have to be more.

He listened no further to the easy conversation that rose to good-humored banter, fell gently down to fair-minded but definite opinions, and rose again on chuckles to a quip from Hilda or a snorting retort from the balding man in shorts. His eyes were on the girl beside him, with her odd, quickly changing expressions and her skeptical, watching eyes. He sipped his drink and wondered how soon he could get her away from the party.

He succeeded within the hour, and after a brief mumbled conference with Zeeda, he went over to Hilda Verges to say good night. But before they could escape the terrace, Smitty came up to them. His eyes were sleepy and bloodshot, and his speech somewhat less than certain.

"I'll drive you back," he offered. "Come on."

Steve turned to Zeeda, who said, "I guess we can risk it. Who wants to live?"

"Okay then," said Steve.

"I'll put the guitar in Murray's car," said Zeeda. "No sense hauling it all over California. I can get it back from him in the city tomorrow."

While she fetched the guitar from the back room, Steve and Smitty walked out to the parking circle to wait for her.

"Boy, you work fast," said Smitty sleepily, drunkenly admiring.

Steve gave him a half-smile. "Dry up," he said.

"Feeling less lonely?"

Zeeda came out from the house, put the guitar into the back of one of the cars farther down the drive, and returned to them.

"Weren't there some others with you?" she asked.

"They're staying awhile longer," Smitty answered. "I'll probably be coming back later on, but I need some dinner before I pass out. Jesus."

Steve thought of inviting him to dinner but quickly dismissed the prompting, and Zeeda said nothing, nor did she look at him. They got into the car and drove off.

They were silent on the road back to Beach Cove. Above them the Pacific night stretched cloudless and filled with stars, and the breeze was cool.

The car pulled up sharply before Steve's cottage, and Zeeda and Steve, tendering their thanks to the half-dozing boy behind the wheel, climbed out.

"See you on the beach tomorrow, if I live," said Smitty.

After the racket of the party, the cottage had a comforting peacefulness about it, and when the lights were on and the door closed behind them, Steve felt more at ease. He'd made the hurdle.

"Do you want dinner right away?" he asked.

Zeeda, glancing about the little room, said, "Not particularly, thank you."

"I'm afraid I don't have any liquor."

"How about some coffee?" she suggested.

"Fine. I'll brew it."

"Let me."

He did not prevent her, but followed beside her as she went into the little kitchen, found the cord switch for the overhead light, and filled the coffeepot with water. From the refrigerator Steve took the coffee, and while the water heated, he prepared the percolator.

"One more," said Zeeda.

"What?"

"One spoon for each cup, and an extra one for the pot."

"Oh." He followed her direction, and they stood together before the stove, watching the flame beneath the coffeepot, not feeling foolish, but at ease with one another, comfortable in waiting for the water in the pot to boil.

"What do you do in L.A.?" Steve asked. "Movies?"

"I'm a dance instructor," said Zeeda. "Actually, I'm an actress, but I haven't done anything in years. I'm from a long line of theater people."

"Really? It must be a lot of fun."

"Oh, they've gone respectable now, my family. I'm the only one who's held on since my grandfather died."

"Who was he?"

"You wouldn't recognize his name. He was an old character actor. Never a very big name, but I thought he was great, and people in the theater all loved him. And remember him. I'm the black sheep now, though. And a failure to boot—in commercial theater, anyway. So I teach ballroom dancing to tie salesmen and office clerks."

"I suppose you hate it, the way you sound."

"Oh, it's not so bad. I kind of like it, in a way. When you teach dancing to those types, you're practically a psychiatrist, and after a while you get to love them. They're all such misfits, and they try so desperately. Sometimes you even succeed with them. They get a little more confident, or they get really het up about music and stop worrying so much about how they look on the floor, and then it's exciting. It's as if you're helping. You know, really doing something for people who can't help themselves. Maybe providing a lot of happiness for them. It takes the curse off the bloody job, anyway."

As they watched the coffeepot in silence, Steve felt deeply moved by her gentleness of character. What she had said revealed this fact about her. Maybe, he thought, that was why she had accepted his invitation so readily. Maybe she thought he, too, needed help. For a moment, smiling, he luxuriated in the idea. What the hell, why not? He could use a little help. It would be a change, anyway, being mothered. This was rich, it really was. And he began to laugh.

"What's so funny?" Zeeda asked.

"Nothing much," he said. He searched for a subject to serve as a decoy. "I was just thinking how wrong I was about something."

"What?"

"Well, history. Once upon a time I would've thought that if great things were going on, wars starting, wars ending—look, it's practically the end of the war now, tonight—you'd think people would feel historical, somehow, and everybody would forget little things; they'd all suddenly stop and be quiet and wait till the history had happened, and then go on again. But they don't. You see? Like you and me, the war ending, God knows what era of history about to begin, and we don't give a damn about it. I'm much more interested in your dancing class, and having a cup of coffee to sober up on, and making a pass at you when you look ready for it."

"That's a hell of a thing to tell me," she gasped.

"You know what I mean. It's funny, isn't it?"

"The coffee's perking."

"Let's go inside and leave it."

He turned the flame lower beneath the pot and followed her into the front room of the cottage. She sat down on the couch beneath the front window, and Steve sat down beside her. He took her hand. For a while they said nothing. When at last he spoke, his voice was low, drawn down to a casual intimacy as they sat together, proper to the musings of the moment.

"Once I was interested in history," he said, "at least contemporary history."

"Not any more?"

"Maybe I've had it in that department. Politics, I don't know—maybe later on I'll get interested in it again. Right now, small things seem so damned important to me. Personal things nobody else cares about."

"Could it be because you just barely missed losing them for good? The small things?"

He turned his head to look at her. She was smiling. Her gaze waited, unquestioning, unanxious.

"It sounds high-flown. There might be something to it, I don't know." He paused. "I don't think I care."

"Let's not think about it," said Zeeda.

"Let's not think, indeed." He kissed her, and she made no move to avoid the kiss. His arm slipped around her, and returning the kiss, Zeeda put her hand up to his cheek. When the kiss ended, Steve asked her, grinning ruefully, "You really want coffee?"

"It isn't ready yet."

"I mean when it is."

"Well—no, I guess not."

"Or spaghetti and meat sauce?"

"Do you?" she asked.

"Not honestly."

"All right."

6

MORE PEOPLE THAN USUAL CAME TO HILDA Verges house at Beach Cove for cocktails on Friday, and Zeeda Kaufman had a large audience in the little room at the back of the rambling house. When she had sung "Springfield Mountain," the song Steve liked best, in her high plaintive voice, he slipped out of the room and went back to the terrace. From the loudspeaker outside a waltz was playing, and some of the young people were dancing. Steve sat down on one of the deck chairs and Smitty pulled up an ottoman beside him.

"Why didn't you wait for us to pick you up?" he asked.

"Zeeda wanted to come up early," Steve answered, "to talk to Murray about something."

Smitty leaned closer. "That guy's nuts."

"He's all right," said Steve. "No nuttier than anybody else around here. And he makes interesting conversation."

Smitty looked at him suspiciously. "Yeah. . . . Well."

Steve was too preoccupied to notice that farther down the terrace, seated in two of the white garden chairs, Hilda Verges and her friend Sarah were talking about him. Hilda's voice was hoarse from drinking again ("The first sign of night air always does me in"), and she mashed her mouth with the back of her hand as she leaned toward Sarah, with tipsy emphasis.

"My dear, he's a dreamboat. Now really, take a look at those long legs, and so slim! All the boys around here are letting themselves get chunky, lying around the beach all day. And that sensitive face."

Sarah puffed her cigarette and exhaled between tightly drawn lips. "Of course, what you see in chicken is beyond me."

Hilda frowned. "Don't call them that. They're nice boys."

"Yes, dear."

"Anyway, it's not just that he's attractive. I think he's intelligent, too, and God knows you don't find many of those nowadays. You know he's read Scott Fitzgerald? Told me so yesterday, while I was pumping him. He might just as well have told me he'd been paging through a diary of mine, it gave me such a shock. Whoever heard of anybody his age being interested in the things we lived through?"

"Maybe he's a garden-variety snob," Sarah suggested.

"Even if he is, I don't mind so much. Besides, he told me straight out he was from nowhere. I like that. I think maybe Ben and I should—*you* know—do something about him. He's terribly well mannered, and I think he's lonely. Yes, I'm sure of it."

"What about the little gypsy number?"

"Darling, that's nothing," Hilda assured her. "The poor boy's got to have some fun, hasn't he? Back from that lousy island fighting, it must have been terrible for him. I think he appreciates coming here. He's not like the others."

Sarah fixed her with a look. "Why do you bother creating a lot of reasons for doing what you're going to do anyway?"

"Don't be difficult. I'm not going to *do* anything." Her face reorganized itself. "He's the first one we've had here who's going to achieve something. He used to want to be a writer—when he was a youngster, before the Navy got him. I'll bet he will again."

Steve remained unaware of their scrutiny. He sat watching the people immediately around him, and as had happened at each of the parties he'd been to, for a terrible moment he felt lost. With nothing but a pleasant face and a conscientious manner to recommend him, he had stumbled into an entirely foreign world of rich Jewish businessmen and the rips who were their wives; his head was still clouded by the abrupt displacement. He held no brief for them—none of them seemed really admirable to him in any way, generous of their acquaintance as they had been to him; but they were an anchor, they constituted a setting which for the moment helped him to focus, and he didn't think they would have any objection to his making this kind of use of them. They seemed to regard him without question as one who belonged among the attractive young people crowding Hilda's terrace every afternoon, but they thought him, Steve had noticed, distinct from the others—to be accounted for in some other way than as a hanger-on. It was patent in the brief, idle exchanges he had had with Ben Verges and Hilda's friend Sarah. Why they should have an opinion of him different from the opinion they had of the beach boys and the contract starlets was a mystery to him. Perhaps, he reasoned, it was only that he was a year or two older than Smitty and his acquaintances, and none of these had been in the war.

I wouldn't last, he told himself. Hilda and her friends, he suspected, were fickle. Easily satisfied, their curiosity not longed-lived, before long they would begin to tire of him—not because he was without accomplishment or without money, but because he was not really a contemporary, and this difference, for all their self-deception, was something they did not in practice ignore. But for the moment their friendship gave another dimension to the reality he was slowly returning to, and bore him along on his journey.

Soon he might be able to work again, to make the decisions necessary before he could return to a life of activity and purpose. He made a mental note to write to his family and ask them to send him his notebooks and the handful of unfinished stories he had written before leaving Houston. He wasn't sure it would be worth anything, trying to write again, but he knew of nothing else he wanted to do. The money he had wasn't going to hold out forever.

What would he write about? he asked himself. There must be material for a story in Ben and Hilda Verges. What manner of story would that be? Ben had been trained in business from his youth by his father, who had been a successful banker. In young manhood he had gone from banking into commodity-market speculation, and had been one of the initial organizers of a life-insurance company that had flourished; he had prospered impressively, and a year before the crash he had abruptly retired and taken Hilda on a trip around the world. His losses had been comparatively slight.

But of the couple, it was Hilda who had the dramatic quality that attracted him to her as a subject for fiction. He wasn't sure how many women there were like her in the world; few with her zany amiability, too many with her sadnesses. They had grown up in the twenties, women like Hilda. The period had marked them for life. And now if they had money, they entertained a good deal and lost a good deal on the horses. You probably came across them most often at parties, Steve thought—two or three graying women who drank too much and got sloppy when they did it, their lipstick smeared a little by the rims of glasses, the cords of their necks stiff with their chattering, their eyes hungry and, in their depths, bewildered and sad. He was certain Smitty had been mistaken about Hilda's sexual activities. She talked an amoral line, but he had seen already the undisguisable deference she showed her husband, Ben. He was strongly inclined to believe that whatever she did about sex was done within the limits and authority of her marriage. But women like Hilda kept young people about them, young men in particular, out of what need? To flatter themselves that they were contemporaries? To pretend to themselves that the blazing of their own youth was not dead at all? To convince themselves that the party had only moved from the speakeasies and the crowded Village apartments and the Long Island cottages to terraces in California and the racetracks at Santa Anita, Hialeah, and Belmont? There was something about the eyes of Hilda Verges, the rigidity of the fingers that held her glass, that reminded Steve of a lost and panicking animal, left behind by her pack, and now defenseless. What would he write about her? What key was there to her that an outsider like himself might be able to turn?

He smiled to himself. As long as he had been sitting there, he'd been able to think without distraction. He had not taken another sip of his drink. Certainly that was good for a little self-congratulation. . . .

Joseph Murray appeared on the terrace and went over to Ben Verges.

"Anything on the six o'clock broadcast?" he asked. Steve looked up at the two men standing near him.

"Not a word," Ben answered, trying to look up at Murray without raising his chin or admitting by any action that he was fully a head shorter than the man in horn-rimmed glasses. "One of the commentators this morning said if the Japs accept the ultimatum, they'll make their reply through the Swiss. It'll all take time."

"Hurry up and wait," Steve put in. Murray gave him a glance, more casual than his glances usually were, and not so patently guarded. He stood with his great lips slightly apart, one pawlike hand jammed into the pockets of his slacks.

"The Japs want to keep their Emperor," he said to Ben. "That's what all the trouble is—can you beat it?"

"Why not let them keep him?" Ben shrugged his sloped shoulders.

"Keep him? The Japs got the way they are because of their Emperor-worship," Murray stated emphatically. "Are we going to indulge them in it? Paternalism, the great ancestor image: I suppose we're supposed to let them go right on drugging themselves with that crap? That's MacArthur for you, he doesn't give a damn about fascism. A war's a war to the generals, the values involved don't mean a damned thing. I tell you, Ben, this country is going to suffer for putting too much power in that man's hands."

Steve said, "It's true I never heard a good word said about MacArthur by the men who fought under him. Real sonuvabitch."

"A fascist bred in the fascist tradition." Murray gestured with his Martini and gave a patient sigh. "Ben, the only sense in fighting a war like this one is that once you get contact with the *people,* you can teach them something else besides the formulas their old leaders kept them hoodwinked with." Ben Verges pursed his lips and continued listening with attention, making no gesture of contradiction. Murray shook his head slowly from side to side. "It's gonna be rough when the shooting's over, I tell you. And I'll tell you one other thing: the minute it really gets urgent for everybody to work together—like what we're all going to do about atomic power—then there are groups in this country that're going to throw their smear campaign wide open. Red-baiters like Hearst, and the *Tribune* people. They'd sell their country to hell to provide themselves with headlines. And if they *didn't* sell it, they'd try to convince you that some other guy had."

Steve wondered aloud, "What kind of headlines can you have in peacetime? It'll be pretty damn dull, won't it?" The only headline stories he could remember from the years before the war were those of the Lindbergh kidnaping and Wrong-Way Corrigan's flight to Ireland.

"Oh, it won't be dull for long," Murray assured him. "With all the work to be done in the world today, you don't think the Hearstlings are going to let anybody get it done, do you?" He shook a finger at him. "Every decent, intelligent, progressive thing you try to do in this country, or in any other country, is going to threaten the Wall Street position. *They* don't want internationalism. Look at the way they nibble away at the U.N.O., the same old mossback psychology that frigged everything up in the first place. . . . I tell you, it's criminal."

Steve watched the big man's face in the gathering darkness. He did not want to admit to himself his dislike for Murray's glibness. There was a lot in what he said. Steve feared people like MacArthur. He had heard and seen enough of the military mind avidly at work not to question its innocence—but Murray's pat phrases annoyed and embarrassed him.

Zeeda came out from the house. She dropped down beside him, her wide skirt flaring.

"I just had an idea, so I stopped playing," she said.

Steve liked her best in those odd, disconnected moments when the childlike spirit came over her and her smile was impish. He knew it was not very sincere, but it brought a warmth to his heart, and it rid her face of its wild quality, stilling the feverish expressiveness of her eyes. Now he smiled down at her.

Zeeda went on, "Do you still want me to spend the week end at Beach Cove?"

"Sure," said Steve.

"I'll have to get clothes from town, but Murray can drive us in tonight." She turned her head. "Would you, Murray, like a dear? Can we drive back to L.A. with you?"

Murray glanced at Steve again. "Sure, if you want."

"We can stay overnight at my place," Zeeda said to Steve, "and come back to Beach Cove early tomorrow. Okay?"

"Fine," said Steve.

Zeeda jumped up and went to fetch her guitar, and Murray turned back to Ben Verges. Steve had not expected her to accept his invitation—she had been morose and distant on their way to the party; and now that she had accepted, he felt a vague sense of dissatisfaction. It would be good having a girl around the cottage all the time through the week end, but he was aware that sometimes Zeeda's burning energy, her violent demonstrativeness in the throes of the slightest emotion, tired him out. In bed she was adept, docile, affectionate, but he had noticed once or twice a rigidity about her. There was much about her that troubled him, small things. Awake, she looked like a child; asleep, beneath the billow of her thick hair, her face appeared strangely drawn and old. Sometimes she spoke to him with rough aggressiveness; at other moments she chattered with giddy superficiality—something like the talk of Hilda Verges' cocktail party starlets.

Before the night came on, they said good-by to Hilda and Ben and went out to Murray's coupe, a tattered unwashed machine with a New Mexico license plate. Zeeda had told him that Murray and his wife owned a ranch somewhere out there. He wondered disinterestedly what sort of wife a man like Murray had. The inside of his car smelled of dogs.

On the ride into town Murray began to talk about New Mexico. He spoke of the desert with affection, and described to them the time he had gotten lost in the Painted Desert just at sundown. When he paused, Zeeda put in, "You're as homesick as I am."

"Are you homesick?" Steve asked, squeezing her lightly with the arm he held across her shoulders.

"This place is doing me in," she answered, "but fast. I don't have anything to keep me busy."

"What about the dancing lessons?" Steve asked.

"Who the hell wants to spend the rest of his life teaching the rhumba to a bunch of ninnies? You understand, Murray. . . . You should see me in New York, I'm different. Isn't that true, Murray? You remember. My voice never gives me trouble in New York. One look at the people out here and I miss the Village and Central Park, and I miss the theater. Well, I'm not the Goldwyn girl type!"

"You might be able to find a play in New York," said Murray.

"You didn't seem to mind the dance studio before," said Steve gently. "How long since you acted?"

"New York's the only place that appreciates *real* people," said Murray, and Steve winced.

The one-room apartment was on the third floor. Zeeda turned on the lamp nearest the door and ushered Steve in without self-consciousness, standing the guitar case upright in a corner.

"You flop down somewhere, and I'll cook dinner," she said. She left him alone and disappeared into the kitchen, hidden from view by a shutter-screen.

Steve wandered slowly about the bare little cubicle, switching on another lamp farther in. There was still little light in the room, but he saw no other switches to be turned. Against the wall was a couch covered with a dark spread and crowded with pillows, and beneath the single window was a desk with books piled on it in disorder.

Picking up a volume, he called toward the kitchen, "Is Karl Kautsky any good?"

"Oh, Kautsky. No. He started off in the right direction, but he gets all fouled up. I'll tell you about him later."

Steve dropped it and sat down on the couch. Another book, this one well thumbed, Lenin's *The Iskra Period,* lay directly before him on the coffee table. Steve had read something of Lenin's before, during that great drinking in of other men's knowledge in which he had reveled unreservedly years before.

He began to leaf idly through it, squinting against the gloom in the apartment. Soon he was reading with sudden, surprising hunger, with no exercise of his critical faculties but a resurgence of his inquisitiveness and wonder—and then dinner was ready.

"This isn't going to be famous," Zeeda warned, unsmiling. "But it'll cancel out some of the gin."

On the coffee table, which she spread ritualistically with a table cloth, she served thick patties of chopped beef, large portions of fried potatoes, a salad, a pitcher of iced tea, and a pan of garlic bread. Zeeda ate hurriedly, but with more petulance than appetite. She did not try to create conversaversation. Toward the end of the meal, without a word having been spoken throughout, she suddenly stopped eating and looked at him. Her eyes were wide and angry. Then she shrugged her shoulders and looked away.

"Anything wrong?" he said.

"I get so damned fed up with myself," she said. "I start talking about New York, and before you know it, I'm thinking of all the hellish things about it. I'm sorry, it'll go away."

Steve paused. "Didn't you like it there?"

"My family," she answered.

He wiped his fingers on the napkin and pushed his empty plate aside. Before he spoke, Zeeda set her fork down.

"I don't want to talk about the sonsabitches."

"Zeeda . . ." Steve began. "Look at things this way——"

"They're Jews," she said. "Real Jews. Vulgar and pushing and stubborn."

"Uh-huh," he said. It was all he could say in his astonishment.

"My father's in the jewelry business. And my mother—Christ, that woman!" Steve hoped she was not going to describe a self-centered mother and a neglected childhood, but he said nothing. "They think with their money they can do anything they want—anything she wants, anyway. They don't know Jews are bound to be abused and laughed at behind their backs because they simply refuse to give up their narrow-minded nationalism and all the earmarks of it that make them sitting targets. Everybody laughs at my father. You don't think he minds, do you? He doesn't know the meaning of pride. Far as he's concerned, the money proves his worth, his 'position,' if you please. He thinks there isn't anything else to it. . . ." She pulled a cigarette from the pocket of her skirt and lit it. Steve waited, a feeling of embarrassment and disappointment forcing him to deceive her by sitting forward in his chair, his elbows on the table, and to assume an attitude of calm attention and impersonal sympathy. He wished she hadn't begun the story, but her manifest need to tell it softened his instinctive antagonism to adolescent woes.

"They don't laugh at my mother as much as they do at my father," she said. "My mother used to be very pretty, and she hasn't let anyone forget what she could get away with once upon a time. She was so pretty, she didn't know what the hell to make of me when I was born."

"How do you mean?" asked Steve.

"I was ugly. I looked Jewish. My mother couldn't believe anyone as beautiful as she was could have an ugly child. I was too dark, my hair was too thick—it was an insult to her own looks; she never looked Semitic. When she was young, she wanted to marry a rich Gentile. I think she settled for my father because he could be led around by the nose, and he did have *some* money, and his own business. She never lost her looks entirely, and she was never anything but vain and selfish and self-seeking. She made me wear a veil."

"A what?"

Zeeda nearly shouted in an effort to contain her simmering emotion. "A veil around my face! Oh, Jesus, let's talk about something else——"

"Look, it was a long time ago, Zeeda——"

"Not as long as that." She stood up suddenly from the table, her body rigid. She caught her breath. "I said let's talk about something else. What the hell does my family matter anyway? They're not the kind of people somebody like you can understand."

She moved to the couch and stretched out full length upon it, on her back. Steve kept his place at the table by the window, silently watching the uneven rising and falling of her breasts as she breathed. It was not what she had been telling him that had excited emotion in her; she was dishonest enough to let him think so, he supposed, but not dishonest enough to create the emotions out of nothing. Something less pat than the veil story troubled her. He had read the novels and liberal magazines. He had been told over and over again, and himself had told often enough, stories of what Jews went through, even in America, in the country their endeavor had helped to make powerful and rich, efficient and profitable, colorful and diverse, as all the races had; but he didn't in point of fact know anything about it. He had known few Jews in his life, and those he had known, he had never thought of in terms of their Jewishness. He had never been witness to oppression or intimate with a regularized, standardized hatred. It must be for them, he thought, as it is for the Mexicans in Texas and the Orientals out here in California. But it had been going on longer with the Jews. It was an integral part of their history and their meaning, and surely that must have made a difference in their make-up.

He could think of nothing to do to comfort or reassure her, and deep within himself he suspected that any comfort coming from him would be patronizing and cheap. Nor could he respond profoundly to the story of her mother; the picture Zeeda had painted seemed oversimplified. It sounded like a dramatized, symbolized picture of perhaps one aspect of a real woman. Yet the hurt the girl had suffered was terrible if it could have this effect on her so long afterward, he thought. Perhaps that kind of wound, unhealed and untended, could cause the strange, illogical, inconclusive behavior he had discovered in her, could after all cause her present distress.

He got up from the table and went over to the bed. He pulled his jacket off and threw it across one of the straight chairs against the opposite wall. Zeeda made room for him on the couch and he lay down beside her, slipping his arm beneath her head and pulling one of the pillows under his own. Her hair was bushy beneath his chin, and during the silence in which they lay, Steve brushed it back under her head, in a slow and reflective caress.

There was no clock in the room to tick, no sound but the distant unassimilated purr of traffic from the city outside. In the half-darkness Steve thought of the girl he held, of her smallness, the compactness of her figure, and some of his embarrassed discontent lingered in his thoughts. She had talked like a foolish child, hurt by a trifle, confused and self-pitying. In a child it would have been all right; in a very young girl it would have excited his pity, his affection.

Zeeda stirred in his embrace, and turned her head. "Well," she said, "maybe sometime you'll see them. . . . Then you'll know what I mean."

Steve grunted a reply. His free hand felt for her slim arm.

"I have an older brother," she continued. "He was always nice to me. His name's Marvin. Med student. The only trouble with Marvin is that not even a medical career is going to pull him out from under the family. By the time he's got his M.D. and starts practicing, he'll be as bad as any of them. But at least he had possibilities."

"How long since you saw your parents?" Steve asked.

"I've lost count. Marvin must be twenty-three now."

"Have you acted very much?"

"Not in a long time," Zeeda said. "The kind of theater

you've got in America doesn't have room for real acting. It's an industry here, not an art. Christ, I never even wanted to be *that* kind of actress. Not many people understand how you can feel that way, you know."

"I thought in New York——"

"It's as bad as out here, for an artist," Zeeda interrupted. "But someday I'll go back to the theater. Maybe not in New York. I'd like to try it in Paris. I might be able to study with Rosay—she was a friend of my grandfather's, I'm sure she'd remember him. But that has to wait until I'm ready. Really ready."

Nimbly she crawled over him and stood up beside the bed.

"I wish we hadn't started talking theater," she said. "Would you like coffee?"

Steve hung fire momentarily. "No, thanks. . . . Are you sleepy?"

"Getting to be."

"I'm bushed."

"Climb in then," she said. She did not smile. Steve sat up on the couch and watched her as she took off her earrings, the thick metal bands that hung on her slim wrists. As she undressed, a frown drew her straight black eyebrows together. Steve threw his trousers and shirt over his jacket. When he had pulled off his shoes and socks and put them underneath the chair that held the rest of his clothes, he turned off the lamps, leaving only the dimmest one burning near the door. Zeeda did not look at him. From the chest of drawers she took a nightgown, pulled it over her head, and dropped her pants from beneath it, leaving them on the floor at the head of the couch. Throwing back the covers, she climbed into bed. Steve turned out the last lamp, but a glow from the kitchen lights seeped through the shutter-screen, marking the general outlines of the furniture in the room. In the darkness Steve lay down beside her. He touched her hip and moved to embrace her, but her back was turned to him. She did not stir or speak.

"Hey," he whispered. There was a pause.

"What?"

"You still upset?" His whisper sounded choked, unnatural. Slowly she turned over until she lay facing him. He tried to lift his arm to encircle her shoulders, but she held it firmly down.

Quickly he tried to find her mouth, but she turned her face away. "What the hell is it, Zeeda?"

"I don't want you to touch me," she answered. "Not tonight."

"All right."

He waited, lying motionless, tensed. His own casual desire did not trouble him, but he knew he would not be able to sleep, not with Zeeda's distress so unresolved, not with so many questions left unanswered. Perhaps something simpler than that had made her put him off; perhaps she only wanted to be pursued, to put up obstacles in his path; had he begun to take her too much for granted? His casualness might have offended her, wounded her. No woman liked being presumed upon. She lay on her back again, but she was not asleep. Her body beside him was still rigid, and he could feel her breathing. When he looked over, nothing of her face was visible in the darkness. He waited, not knowing what to expect.

Suddenly he felt her shift toward him, and then turn herself until her breasts and shoulders crushed against his chest. When he tried to lift a hand again, she held it firmly down beside him. He made no other move of acknowledgment or acceptance. Not knowing what was offered, he was afraid to accept too readily. Zeeda held her face lifted above his own, and he could feel her breath brush past his chin. Her hand was on his waist, and as she began to caress him, Steve became aware of a dull uneasiness. She was not giving in to him, and whatever it was she intended was not born of pleasure or any healthy passion. In the lightless air around him he could sense a harsh and bitter anger, a foul determination, a grossness of indulgence he had not known her capable of. Braced, afraid of what he could not define, he was incapable of responding to the caress; but in the dark it continued, more strongly, the hand stroking his hip, his thigh, slipping about the fleshy inner side of his leg, squeezing with the urgency of the male. Steve's breath caught in his throat. She was urging him, seducing him, as a man seeks on his woman's body the keys that, pressed, will unlock her reticence and release her. She was playing the male, not in sexual desire, not in the eagerness of love, but to get back at something that in no way concerned himself.

The sudden realization that he had no identity to her

jolted his vanity. His natural pride revolted. He had no time to formulate his quick confusion before she fell angrily upon him.

Her passion unleashed; she embraced him, pressed upon him, bit his lips. Her hungry hands raced over him, called on his dependence, his weakness, his welcoming. With a sudden violent rising in his stomach Steve sprang up into sitting position, grabbed her shoulders and pulled her up abruptly against his chest, as if to rip her suddenly out from her own blind aggressiveness. A sound he had never heard, a guttural scream of frustration, sounded in her throat, and throwing her head forward, she bit him, viciously sinking her teeth into his arm. Steve winced with pain when he felt the skin break in the grip of her teeth. Zeeda jumped up from the bed and Steve grabbed at the wound, the palm against his broken flesh warmed with a drop of blood. In his dismay he could not see her anywhere in the room. He wanted to call out to her, to help her, to comfort and tell her that whatever was wrong could be set right. Then, as if ending a nightmare whose meaning he would never fully fathom, the light of the lamp nearest the door went on.

7

ZEEDA STOOD BESIDE THE LAMP, HER HAND still on its switch, gasping for breath. The room was hot, and her eyelids felt heavy with fever, but she was trembling. Steve was bent over the couch, his tanned shoulders and legs suddenly pale and naked in the lamplight. There was a kind of bewilderment in his eyes for a moment, but it went quickly, to be replaced by a questioning that humiliated and trapped her. She fought to control her trembling, waiting for the hysteria to subside within her. She felt ashamed, miserable with the vague knowledge that some mind other than her own had taken hold of her, had made her act the way she had, without will or reason.

Why didn't he say something? Why didn't he ask her what was wrong? Why didn't he at least tell her to go to hell? Steve's eyes looked at her steadily, puzzled, but not angry. It was the lack of anger in him that Zeeda resented most.

Under his questioning, almost sympathetic stare, her sense of shame increased. She started to speak, but decided not to. Instead she went over to where her clothes lay, picked them up, and went to dress behind the screen that masked the kitchen.

When she was dressed, she walked quickly back to the living room. Steve lay stretched out on the bed; he had put on his shorts again.

"I've got to take a walk," Zeeda said.

"Go ahead." There was no reprimand in his voice. He knew her thoughts, knew everything she thought without understanding any of it. He would be gone when she got back.

In the street there was little light, and the air was heavy with night mist. But it was cooler than the room had been, and Zeeda walked swiftly down toward the boulevard, where the lights of restaurants and theaters still beckoned to the dark, smaller streets that branched out from it. As she approached the boulevard she noticed a knot of people congregating around the newsstand on the corner. A man in white ducks ran across the street and a middle-aged couple detached themselves from the crowd and walked away down the boulevard, talking excitedly, their heads bent over a newspaper. It was then that Zeeda heard the news vendor shouting, "Japs offer to surrender! Get the latest on the surrender!"

She turned onto the boulevard and walked toward the drugstore on the next corner. Surrender, hell! she thought. Rumors. The war wouldn't end until the moneybags had blown up every last city in Japan. Stamp out the yellow menace, that's all those fatheads cared about.

The drugstore counter was filled with teen-agers stopping off for Cokes on their way home, and a few crowded the aisle that led to the telephone booths in the rear.

"Hello?"

"Murray? It's Zeeda."

"Hi, Zeeda."

"Have you gone to bed yet?"

"I'll be up for hours. Listening to the news."

"I've just got to talk, Murray. It is nothing important——"

"Come on up," Murray replied. "And don't worry."

The abrupt click the receiver made when he hung up unnerved her, and she rushed outside and hailed a taxi—something she knew she couldn't afford. The taxi pulled off down the bright boulevard. Zeeda avoided glancing out the window; for a moment she wanted to know nothing of what was about her. Her hands made a small tentative movement, as if, like birds in terror, they might take flight from her wrists. She pressed them down on her crossed knees to restrain them. She could not think clearly; her mind flew with a hysterical exhilaration from notion to notion.

Something was about to happen to her—she'd make it happen and leave confusion and loneliness behind her. If something could be made to happen, everyone would find her as she really was—talented, courageous, an inspiration to the people. And the people would know Zeeda Kaufman was to be honored and loved because she deserved honor and love for all her sacrifices (the sacrifices she would make if only Murray would let her). She would get him to take her back into the Party. The dialogue had only to be right: serious, because the situation was serious; desperate, because now she was desperate—the sudden, unwilled upsurging of grief and want and shame within her was enough to make anybody desperate.

The crazy mystics of religion had their visions to draw them out of themselves, but their deliverance was minor compared with what Zeeda knew she was capable of—losing herself entirely in work for the oppressed and cast-aside. They were people she understood and loved more deeply than she could ever love the Steve Williamses she met, because of their very facelessness, because of the unindividualized mass of their need. Her place was with them, giving herself to the only political action that could save them—to Murray, to the Party, to all her old friends. If Murray helped her, she could quit the goddamned dance studio, where these same oppressed and cast-aside assuaged their hurt and bolstered their vanity in aping the rituals of the moneyed people they had been taught to admire—the idiots!

The Party's was the only goal that made sense, hard realistic sense, the only design that held the faintest hope of freeing them. She would persuade Murray one way or another to find worth-while work for her to do. Without that, nothing was worth while. Without the Party, she was dead and useless.

At Murray's apartment house, a corridor led to a small patio in the rear. His apartment was the first to the left. She rang the bell, and Murray opened the door, in shorts and a bright open-necked shirt.

"You got here fast," he said.

Beyond the small foyer there was a long low-ceilinged room with a coffee table, a divan, a desk and chair, and a number of ottomans and bizarre lamps. Piles of record albums stood in stacks around the floor, and she noticed that the doors to his bedroom and kitchen were both closed.

"Like a drink?" said Murray.

"God, no. But I'll take a cigarette."

"You're jittery." He offered her one and struck a match to light it by. When she sat down on the divan, Murray sat before her on an ottoman and picked up his half-finished drink. "Shoot," he said.

"I've got something to tell you, Murray," she said.

"Think I don't know it?" Behind the horn-rimmed glasses his eyes were small, alert, and when they were tired, as they were now, the muscles of his brow drew the usually limp flesh above them upward.

"I've only just realized it. It's something I've tried to hide. From myself. All this time. . . . I've just got to get it out into the open."

Murray rested the sweating glass on his bare broad leg. He drew it upward toward the edge of his shorts and the incongruously fair hair of his leg matted with the moisture.

"You know Steve Williams, Murray."

"That guy!"

"I know. But I can't turn down someone who cries when he talks about the war. Now he's asked me to marry him."

"Christ."

"I got out of *that*, thank God." She paused, twisting her cigarette round and round. The cigarette, its realness, gave her a sense of reality. "I've left him, Murray."

"Good. Now have a drink."

"He's in a state back in my apartment. . . . Murray, I know now why I get into these fixes."

"You do?"

"Yes, I've been rotting, Murray. Someplace way back I stopped being a real *person*. Somewhere in the last few years I lost my identity."

"Career got you worried?"

"Murray, I should be *doing* more. You know what I mean. There's so much to be done. I don't like feeling useless. Today you've got to be *part* of something, and I'm not part of anything—not like I used to be."

"I knew that would start to bother you eventually."

She dashed ashes off her cigarette. "My God, you don't know—what it's like."

"You've done well at the canteens. You've handled yourself well with those idiots at Ben Verges' house."

"The daughter of the United Front, sure. But it's going to be different now. The United Front's had it. I don't want to be left behind now, when the real fight is bound to start."

"How do you think it will be?" he said.

"I don't know." Her voice was eager now. "But I'm a grown woman, Murray. I don't have to be sent to bed any more and let the adults stay up for the good part!"

Murray put his glass aside. The mass of his big-boned body seemed sunk in contemplation. "I never used to think of you as being 'left out.' "

Zeeda looked away. "Maybe not. But—well, it was long ago. One forgets a lot."

"Remember New York?—the Christmas strike, that night on Columbus Circle? It was you who began the singing."

"Only because Ozzie Lubin told me it was a good idea."

"But that's what's important! Look. You were *brilliant*, honey. Every damn Christmas that goes by Vinnie brings it up. As if she had to remind *me*. You started that singing and one by one all those spineless men joined in. You don't think they were scared, do you, with those cops and their goddamned horses. . . . You kept 'em going, honey. You didn't bat an eye."

"I remember that, all right." Zeeda laughed. "I remember Vinnie getting all choked up. She stood beside me and held my hand, listening to all those men we'd started off, hundreds of them. God, it was exciting!"

"How old were you then?" Murray asked.

"Fourteen. Fifteen."

"How old are you now?"

"Twenty." She watched him closely. How to get it across to him. She had learned so much since then: the American Students Union, American Youth for Democracy? How much older than a mere twenty she actually was. "Anybody can lead a song," she said.

Murray shrugged.

"I'm a hard worker!"

"It'll take some figuring," he mused.

"My God, Murray, you've got every starlet in Hollywood, practically!"

"They're different. Their signatures are all we need."

"Write to Ozzie Lubin about it," Zeeda urged.

"His word'd help, all right," said Murray. "Of course you'd have to take the stiffest kind of reorientation course." His eyes warmed with enthusiasm. "We're trying to solidify, getting rid of all the cranks. We've got to be a team—a trained, fit, ready team."

"That's where I belong," Zeeda said.

Murray nodded soberly. "I'll fix it up—if I can, Zeeda. A few meetings, same old get-togethers—except, no outsiders."

"Whenever you can work it," Zeeda assured him. "I'm ready. But you know that."

When the door of Zeeda's apartment closed behind her, Steve got up from the couch, searched for a cigarette, found one, and lit it hungrily. He felt stunned and, somewhere deep in his stomach, agitated. He wondered for a moment if he were going to be sick. For a while he stood looking at the disheveled couch, baffled by its appearance as he might have been by some inexplicable object. Dimly he tried to fathom what it meant, what its uses were, and what had really happened.

He began to dress, slowly, cautiously, and with a sense of drugged awakening. He thought, "Any other time I would have run after her and caught her." And he wondered whether he would ever again be capable of reacting properly to the immediate-demand circumstance. Maybe it would forever after be this way.

Zeeda had been in bad shape, and the realization began to press on him, too late as always. He wondered now whether he should wait, or go to look for her, or in last resort, go back to Beach Cove and forget the whole damned business—one thing he knew he did not want. He finished dressing, except for putting on his jacket, and sat down on the edge of the bed, his head in his hands. In a few months he'd be twenty-one, and he didn't even know where the hell he was half the time. At Beach Cove he'd lie on the beach, drinking too long each day and trying to remember things that had no importance anyway, except that forgetting them made him feel ashamed and incomplete. He didn't want to go back to that. Zeeda had brought about a change in him. She had come into his existence, and no matter how unexpectedly she had left, she would leave behind a mark of her passing. He did not love her, but he wanted to talk to her and reason with her and see if there were anything he could do to help her, as she had in turn helped him. At least in this way, in being worried about her, he was coming more alive toward others, toward the world outside himself.

He felt pity for Zeeda, because she was frail, and something of awe, because for all the women he had had, he had never known one of them very well before, had never lived with them even as long as the few days he had lived with Zeeda. And there was still a mystery about the hidden, suspicious, unstraightforward nature of women that made him unsure of his judgment of them, uncertain even of his taste. But Zeeda was so frail, and so embittered.

Two hours went by, until the cigarettes were all gone, and then a half hour more, while his eyelids grew heavy with sleep and the muscles of his neck ached with the effort of keeping his head erect. Perhaps she didn't mean to come back at all. Or maybe she was out there, across the street, or at the corner, watching the building, waiting for him to go away. It was her apartment, after all. He had no right to stay.

When he found the paper and pencil, he wrote the note hurriedly, in his swift, angular handwriting, folded it once, and scrawling "Zeeda" across the front, propped it up on the coffee table near the couch. He took a last look at the room and turned out the lights.

It was early still, and the boulevard was crowded with people. It occurred to him that a good stiff brandy might jolt his brain awake again, help him to collect himself before the bus ride to the cottage. Around the corner, past the shouting newsboy, he found a bar. The sharp chill of its air-conditioning and its dim lighting eased his nerves. The bar was crowded with servicemen and their women, and everyone talked with nervous excitement.

At the far end of the bar, perched on a high stool, both elbows propped before him, sat a civilian, a year or two older than Steve. In the buttonhole of his jacket lapel was the little gold ruptured duck to be seen in increasing numbers on the street. His face was scarred, and the dark glasses he wore did not hide the tentative tilt of his head, the slight and almost unnoticeable groping in his gesture as he lifted his glass. The man was nearly blind. Steve had seen such men at the hospital. He found an empty stool near the door, and when the bartender came to serve him, ordered a brandy and a pack of Camels. While he waited for them, he tried to take no notice of the people around him, not even the blind veteran. He didn't want to talk, or exchange jokes, or discuss his plans for the peace years ahead. He wanted only to sit silently and drink.

He lit one of the cigarettes first, and then, with a sense of anticipation and a nerve-racked thirst, he took the first sip of brandy. The liquid bit stingingly at his tongue and burned the back of his throat, but slipping down to his stomach, it warmed him immediately, and he felt himself beginning to relax.

He was tired of his body, he thought; tired of watching its reactions, tending it, always preoccupied with the possibility that it might suddenly fail him, that the undependable mass of tissues and veins inside his head might in a crisis desert him abruptly, leaving him lost. It was good he was tiring of it; that meant his interests would be turning increasingly outward, as a man's should, his attention bending away from the battered machine he had to work with to the world around him.

He finished his brandy and ordered another, wryly amused: How often did men have a chance to know their bodies as well as he knew his? Less often than they knew the mechanics of their automobiles. But he had had to know it; to watch it, study it, test its strength, to discover how far he could depend on it for life, how much he could make it do, how steadfastly it could serve him. The thought that he had almost lost it permanently made him queazy with fear. If he had had to live with an incomplete body, he supposed he would have succeeded. Like the blind veteran down at the end of the bar, he would have learned to cope with blindness, or lameness, or impotence. But he was whole. He had been saved, and his wavering mental capacity was slowly but distinctly returning.

Why the hell had he been so gloomy not five minutes before? The hell with gloom, the hell with Zeeda's damned dramatics. He was saved, and the body he had trained, the body he had fought with, the young and vigorous and exuberant body he had led back to health had a great importance now, a preciousness he had not realized until it had been threatened, and there wasn't a damned thing he was going to be gloomy about any more.

He knew then, through the warming fire of the brandy and the smooth fullness of the cigarette smoke that swelled his lungs and steadied his hands and stilled the dull aching of his wounds, what the meaning of it was. The line of his life had been cut, as if in the palm of his hand the slash of a knife should sever the life line; and after the burning of the gash, and its slow healing, the line had to be taken up again, as if for the first time, and followed onward.

That was why his body had been a stranger to him, why its possibilities were only now beginning to penetrate his consciousness. He was not a newly born child. It was more extreme than that. It was as if he were the first of the race of men, knowing nothing, remembering nothing, without a past save the oblivion of darkness and savagery. For all practical purposes he *was* without a past. He might think of going home to Houston, to his family, but—new to the world, to vitality and growth and sensate living—he had no sure knowledge of the past, no memory that moved him or drew him to return. And he knew now that he was more seriously, more profoundly on his own than was to be contemplated within the realm of assistance or comfort from his mother or his father, from the families of San Angelo Street or the loafers around his father's gas station.

They were all on their own, he thought; the blind young veteran with the silly, insulting, unworthy gold duck on his lapel; the soldiers standing near him at the bar; the girls with them; Hilda and Ben Verges; and in her own dark, proud, hurt way, Zeeda; the men he had known in battle, whose faces and names he would never be able to recall; the people at the hospital and the separation center; the rookies in training at San Diego, in Kansas and South Carolina and Maine—the line of all their lives had been cut; maybe the line of the life of the whole damned country, for all he knew.

Between now and the time the peace was signed they would be coming awake, shaken, after the birth pangs of war. It wasn't a myth, it wasn't merely proverbial. America, after the last five years of parturition, was on its own, and all its people were on their own, down to himself and his neurasthenic preoccupation with memories which, once remembered, could no longer serve him. He was alone, fresh-born to earth, untutored and unguided, and he had a life before him to live.

For the moment, he decided, he was going to celebrate the fact. He was going to drink more, laugh more, lay more. He was alive, he thought with an exhilaration that was near febrility. Zeeda could take care of herself. They'd *all* have to take care of themselves for a while; and if anybody was going to celebrate, he, Steve Williams, was going to lead the parade, not in misery or disillusionment, but in joy of himself and the world that was left to him, in power and in potential, in the burgeoning strength of his body, the new understanding of his mind. For there was joy in the first moment of standing erect, full grown, and whole.

"Not forever, but for a little while," Steve thought, "I'm going to get almighty stinking drunk."

8

IN CHARTER OAK, LOS ANGELES, EL PASO, IN all the towns and cities where papers were read, radios listened to, sons awaited, babies fretted over anxiously in the absence of their fathers, throughout the farmlands and industrial circuits, Army posts and commercial shipping centers, stores and offices, the news bulletins of the following days were followed with the absorbed attention of men whose most intimate and personal activities had come to be known, discussed, predicted, and worried about.

Sprague Burrell, a Chicago businessman currently in the Navy, began to organize his interests with a view to returning to business full time. A Special Services captain in New York named Jules Fischel signed a lease on offices in which he would open a modeling agency after his discharge and alerted the younger brother of his fiancée to be ready to go to work as his assistant. The young man changed his name to Ladd Dorn, practiced his new signature, and considered himself ready. On the trains that laced across the country, strangers talked endlessly, but not loudly, of the coming of the end. Army posts bristled with rumors, and letters both to and from the families of servicemen were tense with expectation, painful hope, and a bitter inner conviction that it was all a mistake, that the end couldn't really be coming, that the country was too numbed with exhaustion to exert itself to the task of composing or negotiating or administering the documents and rules of peace.

Peace was something few among the young remembered, and many more could not think or talk about it without misgiving and deep-hidden feeling of delirium. Private Al Gustineo was released from the stockade at Fort Benning, Georgia, and found to his disgust that Tom Henderson, the lieutenant in the Judge Advocate's Office who had been the prosecutor in his court-martial, had been sent to a separation center and was by now probably a civilian. His plan for vengeance evaporated, and he turned his attention to the prospect of being discharged himself and going back to Chicago.

On Thursday, August 9, news had come that the Soviet Union had declared war on Japan. On small-town corners, in the subways and buses of larger cities, on dusty farmland roads, in spite of the heat (and for most, the humidity), men talked optimistically, repeated the news items with excitement, not infrequently unsure in their hearts what they were excited about. When the President's radio address began that night, apartments in New York grew hushed and farmhands in Kansas and Missouri lay, listening, still and thoughtful in their narrow bunks; Cajun fishermen in Louisiana gathered outside the trading store, absorbed in that level, twanging, calmly determined voice without always understanding the American words, but impressed by the hard vowels and the stubborn timber of leadership. The President reviewed the events at the Potsdam Conference and all that had occurred since then. He issued a final ultimatum to Japan, and women sitting with their husbands in kitchens or automobiles or, if they had battery portable receivers, on front porches, mopped the perspiration from flushed breasts and vaguely prayed. A young Jesuit, John Davis, joined his fellow-seminarians around the radio in the recreation room to hear the speech. Les Vernon, an agent for the Federal Bureau of Investigation, heard the broadcast on the radio in his automobile as he was driving through Utah on his way back to Washington. Wynn Bargmeister, who had been given an obscure post in the Department of State the year before, was on vacation in Coral Gables, Florida, and listened to the speech in his hotel room there. In the torrid night babies whimpered, children counted out how many days the war had to end in if it was going to end before school began again. Sailors snickered over the port raids they planned for V-J Day. Everyone waited.

During the next few days people went about their business: Phillip Houghton addressed a young men's business club in Des Moines and warned them of the inevitable return of the Marxist threat to the American way of life. Steve Williams, on the other hand, thought neither of the war news nor of the prospect beyond surrender. For several days he thought very little.

Eddie Maxwell, who delivered the papers to Beach Cove, arrived that Monday with an extra load; they were all sold by nine o'clock. Over her poached eggs Mary Ellen Dwyer wept as she read of the personnel who for long secret years had worked at the development of nuclear fission. This because a special article on page nine announced that the age of the atom had begun, and studying the illustrations accompanying the article, Mary Ellen was sure it had. What brilliant boys they must be, she thought, hustling away and coming up with this incredible new force that had come into life. Probably in a few years Klieg lights would be atomic, she considered, and automobiles and hair driers. Everything would be different now, just as she had always hoped—everything would run smoothly and everybody would be nicer to everybody else.

A little furrow deepened between her meticulous eyebrows when Mary Ellen thought of the war ending. Hal Capbern would be back, and he'd certainly pop up in L.A. the first chance he got. But it had been so long ago. Sweet as he was, this wasn't Murray Hill, and *Panama Hattie* was very much of the past. Besides, everything was going to be different now, she was sure the papers were right—a few really good pictures, maybe another Broadway show where she would really attract attention. Everybody and everything would be different with all these new forces going off all the time.

Drinking her second cup of coffee, Mary Ellen turned to page ten and studied the pictures of Oak Ridge and White Sands. The installations looked stern and efficient, like every place the Government had anything to do with. One of the White Sands candid shots showed three soldiers in a jeep entering the post for the first time, ignorant of the high calling of their destination. They were very cute, Mary Ellen noted, and one had the sort of rough look that even at breakfast made her shudder with a pleasure of anticipation. The caption gave no names, but Mary Ellen could tell the one with the heavy straight black eyebrows was the kind of man who was really sincere and manly and—well, anyway, not like those studio pansies. She finished breakfast, and checking quickly through the rooms of the cottage, found the things she had to take with her to the studio. She asked the maid to be sure to have dinner ready on time for Mr. Kahn, went out to the car, and started off to work. All the way to the studio her thoughts kept returning to the picture of the soldier at White Sands, and she wished she had noticed what his rank was. She should have remembered to bring the papers along.

Other papers carried the same Associated Press photograph that day and the next. The Grantsville *Courier* used the thick-browed soldier in its full-page montage of the personnel associated with the development of the atomic bomb. The El Paso *Register* blew the complete trio up to half-page size, and the issue sold to the men stationed at White Sands for a dollar a copy. Tiger Rizzuto bought six copies. Not only was it the first time his picture had appeared in a newspaper, but it was the first picture of any kind that had shown his corporal stripes. It was a good likeness, too, he considered: his heavy eyebrows were just right, and it was the first picture he'd ever seen of himself that made his goddamn jaw look decent. In the A-Company barracks after duty he put two copies into the large envelope of vital papers he kept at the bottom of his footlocker. The other four he took across to the recreation room in the wooden building that served as Company Headquarters.

Sitting at a desk under the glare of the fluorescent light

in the quiet corner of the recreation room reserved for letter-writing and magazine-reading, he wrote two brief notes. The first he wrote with great care, frequently hesitating over his choice of words:

"Dear Juney:

This is what came out in the paper today. So now you know what kind of work that I have been at work on all this time and why the Army could not send me overseas again. After the news got out everybody was very excited. How do I look? I don't know where they been keeping this snapshot all this time. But I think I have built myself up much better since it was taken. There is still some juice in me yet and don't you let anybody tell you Tiger Rizzuto is finished by a long ways. When I get back to Chi you will see how built up the Army has made me even better than on my last furlough. Well honey it's late and I have got to hit the sack. Let me hear from you when you have a chance. These Mexican women don't make me forget one minute about a nice girl like you who has good sense and morals. The Army life is bad and particularly when I was overseas in Europe, but now that I have my points and everything doesn't get s.n.a.f.u. I will be coming back to Chi soon so wait for me and don't forget that Tiger Rizzuto is a guy with plans and his girl has got nothing to worry about.

All my love,
Robin (Tiger)"

The second note, to his mother and father, he scribbled out hurriedly. The last two copies of the paper he put into envelopes without accompanying messages and addressed them to Mr. Erskine Allender of Kosciusko, Mississippi, and to Sergeant Al Sowalsky of Camp Chaffee, Arkansas. He wrote "Free" on the corner of each envelope, and going out of the recreation room, dropped them into the letter box outside the captain's office. He picked up his pass at the desk, signed himself out, and from the hall called back into the recreation room, "Himbly back there? Hey!"

"He's in the can," a corporal at the pool table shouted.

Tiger left the wooden building and crossed the sand road to A-Company barracks. The latrine was immediately inside, set apart from the barracks by two steps that led down to the chill cement floor. Tiger spoke from the corner of his mouth as he went in:

"Himbly——"

The beefy redhead growled, "Jesus, can't I ever get any peace? Whadya want?"

"You driving into town?" Tiger asked. "How about a lift?"

"Lift, your ass," said Himbly. "Okay, I'll be leaving in a coupla minutes."

"Meet you outside. Don't fall in."

"Fall in, your ass," said Himbly, tugging his bunched shirt-tail forward over his fat hips.

Tiger went back to his footlocker, took out a shoebrush, and rubbed the sand dust from his heavy shoes. The polish gleamed again. He pulled his socks straight, replaced the shoebrush, and found a clean handkerchief. He combed his hair before the mirror that hung at the end of the bunk farthest from the middle aisle of the barracks. His black hair was both thick and coarse, and he combed it carefully, congratulating himself on his fastidiousness—he was one of the few men in the company who refused to content himself with the scalped jobs that never required combing and needed trimming only once every three weeks. Nobody who cared a damn about his appearance would keep his head shaved that way, he thought. Smart guys were careful of their appearance. He pressed a whitehead on his chin; then he wiped it away with his fingers. In the bunk mirror he could not see his body, but he flexed his muscles, jabbed at his belly to test its hardness, reassured himself that, trim and trained, he was as hard as he'd been two years ago, on his nineteenth birthday.

When he was ready, he stood out on the platform at the barracks entrance until Himbly came out. They walked across the company area to the motor pool and picked up the jeep. In a minute they were off the post and speeding down the road to El Paso.

Sergeant Himbly did not like to talk when he was driving, and that night his disposition was more sour than ever. Tiger wondered how a guy got to be that way. He knew nothing of Himbly's private life, except that he was from Boston. He guessed it griped anybody Himbly's age, thirty or thirty-five, to be grabbed off by Uncle Sam just when he was beginning to pile up some cash, deck himself out in some sharp civvies, and get all he wanted from his women because he could afford to treat them the way women demanded to be treated. He guessed it'd gripe him himself. But he did not try to talk. Tiger had learned early that sympathy was a trap. It didn't pay you feeling sorry for anybody. It made you sound like a punk. Take it like it comes, that was his motto. He didn't even look at Himbly, but bounced contentedly in his seat, his eye on the desert around him.

Tiger liked the desert. He never told that to any of the Texas punks. They'd sure as hell never have a chance to tell themselves that Tiger Rizzuto was impressed with their cruddy country; but in the early evening when the glow of the sun lingered in the sand and the mountains rising in the distance changed from brown to blue and pink and finally to the sharp blackness of sundown, what he saw reminded him of the dreams and waking fantasies he had of a country where there were no cities big or small, or houses rich or poor, or factories or farms or even any people outside himself: bare country with mountains in the distance, changing their colors for his entertainment alone, at his command, open desert warm and dry. Population, one.

On the road ahead a gas station came into view, and beyond it the first scattered houses. Tiger straightened up in his seat, running his thumbs along the inside of his tight-pulled belt, touching his tie to make sure it was straight. When they passed the gas station, he saw the steak house he was going to in the distance. He glanced at Himbly and took a deep breath.

"Not many more fucking hauls like this one for me, I guess," he said, talking again from the side of his mouth.

"*Your* orders coming through?"

"This week sometime, they sure as hell should by then."

"Jesus Christ," Himbly snorted and whined at once.

Himbly pulled to a stop before Stella's Steak House.

"What time you driving back?" Tiger asked before getting out.

" 'Leven," said Himbly. "I'll be by the park where the bus stops."

Tiger sneered. "Too fucking early for me. I don't have to be back till reveille. Well, just in case, you can keep a lookout."

Himbly gave what was nearly a sob. "Lookout, your ass. You wanna ride, you be there."

"Keep your shirt on, nobody's gonna chew you out if you're a few minutes——"

"The captain——"

"Captain, your ass," said Tiger, climbing out. "Maybe I'll see you later. Thanks for the lift."

"Okay, Rizzuto," Himbly wept. "Any time, like I said."

He released the brake and pulled off, the sand dust rising behind him. Tiger pulled his trousers straight, and cocking his shoulders forward aggressively, went into the restaurant.

The room was bare of decoration except for the white piqué curtains on the windows and the pictures of mountain landscapes covering the walls. But it was brightly lit, dispelling the purple of the twilight outside, and the white tablecloths shone with a cool freshness. All the tables were taken, and two elderly couples were ahead of him. Tiger took off his cap and pulled it up halfway through his belt. The woman nearest him as he joined the end of the line, a frail, wrinkled old lady with a black straw hat tilted low over her forehead, looked over her shoulder at him with blue eyes filled with fear. Catching her glance, Tiger looked away and tried to suppress a smile. He knew very well how his battle ribbons impressed women. He pushed his chest out and stood straight, his feet slightly apart, trying to look taller. Well, what he lacked in height, he made up for in other ways. Women knew that much when they looked at him, even an old dame. Once they'd had it, once they'd been getting it steady, women never outgrew it. He frowned, drawing his full black eyebrows nearer together, set his mouth in a hard, mirthless line, and looked over the heads into the crowded dining room. The hostess inside noticed him and came forward with crisp, efficient steps.

"One, sir?" she asked. "We have a table you can share, with another soldier, if you don't want to wait."

Tiger gave a sigh: Why wasn't it ever a woman?

"Okay," he said.

He stepped past the old people and followed the hostess toward a table against the window looking out to the road. The hostess was tall, but beneath her black dress her hips rolled voluptuously when she walked. Tiger wondered where it was he'd heard that they trained them to do just that, just to keep the men coming back for more. Tall or not, she had it. With a flick of his tongue he moistened his lips.

At the other tables were the pleasant, curious-eyed families from the neighboring residential suburb. Two or three tables were taken by soldiers, and an officer and his wife occupied one corner, their baby in a high chair between them.

Tiger sat down opposite a T/3, younger than himself, soft featured and well groomed. They nodded to one another, but did not speak. The T/3's blond hair was cropped short, and this brought a brief sneer to Tiger's face, but his head was well shaped. He held himself erect, and Tiger noticed that he handled his knife and fork with assurance. Tiger pretended to study the menu the hostess gave him, but he glanced repeatedly at the stranger, as he always did at strangers, half-consciously preparing his strategy for the encounter. Mild eyes, a straight short nose, a mouth like a baby's but firmly held, a good-looking kid, but undeveloped. Beneath his desert tan his cheeks were pale.

The waitress came up, her pad and pencil poised. She did not speak, but stopped at Tiger's elbow.

"K.C. rare and French fries," he ordered, sharpening his voice against the quaver that threatened it. "And let me have some iced tea, too."

The waitress scribbled the order and moved off toward the kitchen. Tiger lit a cigarette and braced himself to speak. "How is it tonight? Steak good?"

"Yah, sure," the T/3 answered with the beginning of a smile. "It always is here."

They were silent again. Tiger puffed on his cigarette: the guy's voice was smooth, he thought, deeper than he had expected. He looked like a guy with class. There was something about the look of rich men's sons. T/3, and he was still a baby. Well, what the hell, the whole Army was getting fucked up with all the high-school kids coming in. Tiger himself had come in from high school, but he'd had a man's experience, he reasoned. He had been more rugged at eighteen than the slick kids ever got in their lives.

"I was just wondering," Tiger said, "you ain't been in very long, have you? In the service."

"Six months," said the younger man. "Guess you're on your way out, huh?"

"This week or next."

The young man smiled. "Everybody going out, nobody coming in."

"Things'll really start popping when the Japs give in."

"I'm bracing myself," said the T/3. "Christ, I almost wish it'd go on till I could catch up a little. The guys at the separation center aren't going to know what hit them when Japan surrenders."

"That where you are?" Tiger asked.

The younger man nodded. "You'll be seeing me next week to get your job record," he said.

"Say, good deal." The guy was pleasant, Tiger thought, and sometimes it was good to know people like that; if the Army was ever going to fuck you, it'd be at a separation center. "You doing the town tonight?" he asked.

"Small way, sort of." The T/3 shrugged.

"I come in coupla times a week from White Sands. They don't keep you very busy."

"That's good." The T/3 gave a rueful smile. "It's nice to know you can have it easy and still manage to make the atomic bomb."

"Hell, that was all over before I got back stateside," said Tiger.

The waitress brought Tiger's steak and put it before him. He canceled his order of iced tea, called for red wine instead, and asked the younger man to share it with him.

" 'Sgood for you," he said. "Guess I'm a real Ginzo."

"What's a Ginzo?"

"Italian."

"Oh."

They introduced themselves, and when the bottle was brought, Tiger poured out two glasses. He was always curious about people he fell into conversation with, and soon he was questioning the younger man, who answered politely but briefly. Warren Taggert was from Cleveland, but his family were originally New Englanders. He had no plans for after the war.

"I guess I'll go to college. I think I'd like to study languages. Or study for the foreign service."

"College? Yeah?" Tiger echoed. "You're not married, are you?"

"No. But I'm going to get married when I get discharged. To a girl in Cleveland."

"Nice," said Tiger. "I mean, it's nice when a guy don't have to worry, when he can afford to get married when he wants to. Better than laying around, I mean, for a nice clean-cut guy like you." Tiger knew he was being hypocritical. Laying around, ha, he thought. Kid was probably still a virgin, jacking off every chance he got like a high-school kid. He began to feel fatherly toward the boy.

"You got a girl in El Paso?" he asked.

"No," Warren Taggert answered. "I don't."

"You must get lonely."

Warren glanced down at his empty plate, and then out the window, his cheeks coloring. He gave a half-smile, but did not answer. Tiger realized, amazed, that the question had embarrassed him, and the kid was too dumb to try bluffing through. He chuckled inwardly and shook his head, swallowing the piece of steak he chewed before speaking again.

"You're a funny kind."

Warren looked back at him. "Horse-shit," he said.

"Naw, you are. Bet you never even get laid in town. See a movie, get stinking drunk, and never even get laid."

"Sometimes I do," Warren defended himself.

Tiger lowered his voice. "You can pick up a nice piece of tail in El Paso. Even better in Juarez. You oughta try it sometime, it'll loosen you up a little. Look at you, you're so tensed up you look like you got a broomstick up your ass."

"I'm sorry," Warren said.

"Don't tell *me* you're sorry." Then Tiger grinned, and his straight white teeth brightened his face, dispelling the sullenness in his eyes. "You know, you're a good kid. . . . You got a nice way of talking. That's important, when you really know how to use good English."

When they had finished dinner, Tiger offered to show him some good spots arunod town most people didn't know about, and Warren Taggert accepted. They caught the bus into town, getting off at the little park in the middle of El Paso, near the bridge that crossed the Rio Grande into Juarez.

"Sometime you got a Juarez pass, I'll show you around there," Tiger said as they walked down the street.

"Fine," Warren answered.

9

WARREN TAGGERT BEGAN TO FEEL LESS SHY of the tough corporal. Since Bill Hart had been discharged and had returned home to San Francisco, Warren had befriended no one else. He got along well with the men in his office, seldom speaking, but listening with attention to what they said, laughing at their jokes, and performing his duties with a speed and efficiency they usually respected and even mentioned to one another over coffee at the PX. He had had dinner at the PX several times a week with Calloway or Hultberg, and twice he'd been on week-end drunks with Sergeant Fischer from the Judge Advocate's office; but these had been casual acquaintances, and frequently when he was alone, or even in the midst of the barrack's noisy, good-humored chaffing or the endless bull sessions of pretentious, garrulous privates and patronizing noncoms, he had been oppressed with loneliness, an uncertain troubling sense of incompleteness, of undefined, unworded dissatisfaction.

There was little he had in common with the other men. A background of privilege had walled him in from any appeal their companionship might have held for him. The expensive prep school, the acceptedly exclusive character of the circle of friends he had in Cleveland, the elaborateness of the house he'd grown up in—he blamed all of them for dividing him from the mainstream of the men he lived and worked with. What would his father, James Taggert, think of some of the men he was thrown in contact with? Or, worse, what would his mother think of them? She would deplore their manners, and the notion that her only son had to associate with them would be enough to put her to bed for a week with one of her undiagnosed spells. And usually, he knew, he shared his parents' insularity; but now he felt unaccountably euphoric as he walked down the street with the vulgar, swaggering corporal from White Sands: a hell of a type for him to end up with, Warren considered, but a pleasant guy beneath the toughness. His surly talk only half masked his warmth.

They bought a bottle of Scotch from a dealer Tiger Rizzuto knew in one of the side streets off the park, and went around the corner to the bar in the basement of the Central Hotel. The basement room, its greater area given over to a large circular bar, booths huddling in the space left against the walls, was suffused with an orange light. The thick smoke in the air was stagnant. Warren and Tiger took a booth near the bubbling-light juke box and ordered setups. They had time for only one gulp of their drinks before two of the women left the bar and came over to their table.

"Want some company, Tiger?" asked one of them.

"Come on in, Hazel baby," he answered, with a wave of his arm.

The women were both brunettes, one skinny, the other fat. Hazel's plump cheeks were pimpled beneath the layer of pancake make-up she wore, but her companion, a girl with friendly gray eyes and a proud carriage to her bony shoulders, had a fresh natural color in her narrowly petulant features, and the moist greenish shadows beneath her eyes were all that betrayed her tiredness.

"This is Jeanette," said Hazel as she sat down beside Tiger.

"Hi," said the thin girl.

"Hello," said Warren. Jeanette slid neatly into the booth beside him. They had brought their drinks from the bar. There was no need to order more; all four orders would appear on the soldiers' bill. Tiger listened with a smug grin while Hazel chortlingly reported her surprise on seeing his picture in the paper. Her hard eyes shone with a steely brightness behind their greased and powdered lids. When she talked, her lips worked as desperately and disproportionately as the hands of a traveler might in coping with an unfamiliar language. Then she turned the eager dark eyes on Warren. "You from White Sands too, honey?"

"No, Fort Bliss," said Warren.

"Oh, I know lots of guys from Fort Bliss. They all come here. Jeanette knows 'em, too."

The thin girl sat, silent and uncertain of herself, watching the older, fatter girl, as if studying her manner, wondering how to adopt it, what tricks to save and which to discard. Warren put an arm around her waist. Too quickly, as though the movement were prescribed, she leaned heavily against him. Glancing at her, Warren saw that she was fixing Hazel with a stare, seeking approval of her maneuver. No one seemed to want to keep the conversation going, and soon they fell silent. The juke box's anguish was almost deafening, and the smoke stung Warren's eyes. Presently Tiger ordered more setups. From the booth at his back Warren could hear the languorous conversation of two other men from one of the posts near El Paso. He pressed Jeanette's hand, smiled at her occasionally with a successful pretense of knowledgeableness and assurance, and half listened to the droning voices from behind, stubbornly forcing their way over the noise of the juke box.

"The Cards have it in the palm of their hand," said one of those in the next booth. "And the *fourth* straight National——"

"Blow it out, the Giants would've killed them," another voice sneered. "Bunch of lousy southpaws. Know what they are? Bunch of jerks don't know their left from their right."

There was no anger, Warren noted with half his attention, in their dispute. They were either too drunk or too tired, and the argument growled on as if of its own volition.

"And what about Whitey Lockman? Guess the homer was all a magic trick, like a goddam magician er something——"

"I tell you, in the palm of their hand——"

"And what about Dauntless Danny? Up your ass with the Cards, bunch of dumb jiggers . . ."

They could go on like that endlessly, Warren mused. In the barracks there was always, buried away in some corner beyond the bunks that flanked his own, a continuously stubbornly groaning conversation, plowing on day after day and, with the seasons, from sport to sport—always the same tone, and it seemed sometimes the identical voices, week after week. How the hell could they stand it? He knew he couldn't take *any* subject of conversation and spin it out without end, with an infinite lack of variation, no matter how fascinating. Occasionally, it was true, they changed mental positions and talked of women, but women provided only an intermission, and then their voices were more subdued and the talk took on a subtler cast. The most loquacious and the loudest of them all might sometimes grow reticent then, the older ones particularly, with a strange boyish shyness, and sit back and listen, smirking but silent, until the subject of an athlete, a team, a particular event should intrude itself and rescue them.

The contents of the bottle before them dwindled as the voices from the next booth did. The ash tray before them filled slowly with cigarette butts and ashes; once Warren said "Ouch" when the girl beside him groped him with too much enthusiasm, and by the time the bottle of Scotch had been emptied, the two soldiers were grinningly, excessively drunk.

"Excuse me." Warren burped.

"All right, honey," Jeanette said soothingly, patting his leg.

There was a movement under the table when Hazel nudged the younger girl. She grinned at Jeanette and nodded toward Warren with a wink.

"He's cute," she said in an elaborate whisper.

Jeanette did not answer, but smiled emptily. Hazel turned to Tiger. "Jeanette and me are staying together now."

"Oh," said Tiger. Then to Warren: "Objections? Any objections? Speak now or forever hold your peace."

Hazel brayed at the pun, and Jeanette gave a giggle. Warren was confused for a moment, then he shrugged.

"No objections," he said.

They paid the bill, Hazel told the bartender good night, and they went out through the opposite entrance to the lobby of the Central Hotel. Hazel's room was on the second floor. They passed the elevator and went up the thinly carpeted stairs. At a turning Tiger stumbled and Hazel lifted him to his feet again.

"Honey, you aren't going to be able to get it up with a balloon," she taunted him.

"I'll be all right," Tiger laughed.

They found the room and went in. Tiger said "Jesus" and went into the bathroom, Warren immediately behind him. Warren turned on the light for the corporal, excused himself to the women, and closed the door. He held Tiger's shoulders while the corporal vomited into the sink. The young Italian's frame felt small to Warren's hands, and it shook convulsively. Warren turned on the cold water and Tiger, scooping it up from the faucet, splashed his face. He groaned and lifted himself erect with an effort. Both of them were swaying dangerously when they went back in.

The lamp in the room had been turned off. The women's slips shone in the light that spilled out from the bathroom. Tiger and Warren, reeling, fell onto the bed, and Hazel and

Jeanette sat on either side of them. Tiger, pushing his head back, began to sing loudly—something incomprehensible in his drunkenness, but sounding vaguely operatic—and as much as Hazel tried, she could not silence him. He sang with relief and exuberance and the delight, Warren suspected, of being off his feet and flat on his back in the dark and fetid room of two whores who were not pretty, but straight-forward and funny and fond of him. The more Hazel snapped at Tiger, the louder he sang, and finally the fat girl was laughing, "This guy's the limit!"

"That's me," he crowed, "I'm Tiger Rizzuto and I go and I am the limit! I love you, Hazel, and I love your pancake goop and your dumbness and your swell and fancy establishment here, which I can't even see in all this goddamned dark, but I love you!"

"Dry up," said Warren, "you'll get us thrown out!"

"Don't throw us out," Tiger cried to the ceiling, "and especially don't throw out my eager-beaver acquaintance here that rests at my side. He's a good boy, boss, and he's happy where he is."

"Shoosh," said Hazel hopelessly. Their remonstrating accomplished nothing, but a return of his queasiness did. He turned on his side, growled weakly with a drunken, sickened petulance, and was silent. Hazel cooed over him and stroked his black hair. At Warren's side Jeanette sat helplessly for a moment; then leaning forward, she kissed him on the mouth, taking him somewhat by surprise, but distracting his muddled brain from the troubles of the corporal. He put a listless but agreeable hand on the thin girl's knee, then moved it up her leg, pulling her slip awry. Tiger groaned from his side of the bed. "Baby, this is hopeless."

"Lay still awhile," said Hazel. "I like you, you know there ain't no hurry, just so long's you keep your big mouth shut."

"Any other time——"

"C'mon, I want it, baby"—mechanically, efficiently—"c'mon, you know how bad Hazel wants it." She began to undress him, and Jeanette, meek and businesslike, followed her example. Tiger slid gently off the bed onto the floor, and Hazel followed him; when Warren rolled over to the vacated side of the bed, Jeanette, pulling off her slip, lay down beside him. In his witless drunkenness it seemed to Warren they were surrounded by pieces of assorted clothing, male and female, and he wondered how they'd find anything afterward. But he did not care. Unable to see clearly, his chest aching with whiskeyed breathlessness, he began to care less and less. For all her thinness and awkwardness, Jeanette was warm beside him. He pawed the girl and kissed her again. She lay on top of him, rubbing herself in a slow circular motion against him, until the sweat between them began to make small popping noises. They turned and twisted, locked together. Mounting the girl, he did not think of her as sharing his fornication. He was aware only of the stimulation of the vaginal contact; her womanness remained apart from him, and his consciousness even in his drunken state drew back with distaste from the possibility of seeking it out. He heard Tiger sigh from the floor: "The hell with it." A moment later he was aware that Tiger's silhouetted form was leaning against the bed, and the corporal was trying to tap him on the shoulder with an undirected, leaden-weight hand. "Hey. I'm moving the hell out."

"Wait a minute," Warren spat at him, without stopping.

"Come on, come on. We're moving the hell out."

The corporal began to coax him to his climax, and Warren, furious, tried not to hear him. Now it was easy not to hear, or see, or know anything of reality. . . .

When his orgasm was complete, he collapsed upon her, and lay exhausted for what seemed an endless time before Tiger slapped him loudly on his wet buttocks and cried, "C'mon, home!"

Warren opened his eyes. He felt sleepy, but comparatively sober. The girl beneath him was rigid now, material and relentless. For an instant revulsion for her overcame him; he felt tricked, disarmed, and unclean. He would have to face it down; forget it, not admit it; and perhaps then the others in the room would not see that when it was over, he could hate and condemn what had occurred.

They washed, dressed, paid the women, and staggered out. On the way down to the lobby Warren suggested they find a pro station, but Tiger snorted and waved a hand of dismissal. On the street the night had grown cooler, but it was still early. Warren walked with Tiger to the bus stop at the park, relieved that the women were left behind, sleepily pleased to be alone with the corporal. They found a bench and sat down to wait for Himbly's jeep to arrive. Tiger, smoking a cigarette, dropped his free arm around Warren's shoulders, and after a moment, the tune wavering and sour, he began to sing:

> "Gonna take a sentimental journey.
> Gonna set my heart at ease.
> Gonna take a sentimental journey,
> To renew ole memories . . ."

Warren joined in and the melody staggered into another key. They sang carelessly, their heads flung back, listening with dreamy eyes to the effortless rolling of their voices.

"Los Angeles

Dear Marvin,

I guess after not hearing from me in so long you'll be surprised I should suddenly pop up on the horizon again. But I was talking to some friends of mine the other night about you, while telling them something about the whole family, and afterward I got to wondering how things were going with you.

For myself, I've been doing fine since I came out to California—not that I'm very fond of the place, but I have an all-right job and a fine little apartment. But naturally I wonder sometimes how all of you are. I can't write to Momma, because it would only upset her hearing from me, and if I wrote to Poppa he'd certainly be sure to tell her I had, so it's got to be you. That is, if you're still on speaking terms with me. I realize only too well I didn't even send you so much as a card for your twenty-third birthday. Hope you had a grand time celebrating it anyway. I can't figure it out exactly, but you must be nearly finished med school, aren't you? What plans do you have for afterward? Will you be staying in New York, do you think, or taking off for far, exciting places? I sort of hope you will take off. It seems a shame to spend your whole life at home when there are so many wonderful places to see. Like California. Why not come out and practice in California? I know *plenty* of sick people I could introduce you to.

Not having much to say, this is a pretty silly letter. But I did want you, at least, to know I'm still alive, and to wangle some news out of you about yourself. So write to me, tell me everything you're doing in school (and I know you must be doing as brilliantly as you always did) and all about New York. I miss you, and if I ever get back there, or you come to California, it'll be wonderful getting together again. In the meantime, be sure to write. And take good care of yourself.

Love,
Zeeda"

Marvin Kaufman read the letter through again as he sat at the big mahogany desk in his father's den. He had brought the letter home from the hospital because he wanted to read it in the atmosphere, among the rooms and the furnishings, where he had known Zeeda best. The sterilized air of Bellevue made her seem unreal, her letter, a fantastic communication from the dead, and he had sought the familiar sight and scents of the family apartment. He knew he would have to steel himself not to mention his receipt of it to his mother, as Zeeda had asked. It wasn't easy not letting her know Zeeda had written. Sometimes, he knew, she felt wounded and depressed by what seemed to her her daughter's callousness. Marvin knew well enough how little calloused his sister was, but it was no good trying to explain to his parents. They hadn't ever understood her, and Marvin knew they had never given her the attention, the love, the pride they had given him.

The qualities Zeeda had were not what his mother and father appreciated. She hadn't been brilliant in school. She hadn't been much sought after by rich boys, as her mother would have wished. She had been raucous and inconsiderate, with the high-spirited thoughtlessness of a young animal; but deliberately cruel she had never been. That's what they would never realize. She hadn't run away out of spite, but out of desperation.

Marvin knew intimately the promptings she must have gone through. In the depth of his heart he was a little ashamed that he had never been able to break away. But Zeeda had had it easier in that respect: she had had no loyalty, to the family, and no need for loyalty, no obligation, as he did. When they'd discovered she was gone, there had been tears and recriminations, hysteria and a frantic search to find her and demand her return. But none of it had gone on for long.

His mother had been morose and uncommunicative for a few days, but then her day to receive the bridge club had come up, and that was the end of it.

Only his father, though he said nothing, seemed affected by it. His silence betrayed him. There was the listlessness with which he moved about the apartment for weeks after her disappearance. Often he would not hear when he was addressed; and his interest in articles and newspapers, usually so rapacious and healthfully irritable, became perfunctory, a thing of habit. In his grief there had been more bafflement than hurt. As in his simple, faithful, happy-minded way he had never understood his wife, so Zeeda to him had always remained a mystery. Marvin suspected the old man was a little afraid of them both: uncertain in the face of their strength, intimidated by the beauty of the older woman and the fiercely opinionated character of the younger. Poor Poppa, Marvin thought, he'd certainly chosen the wrong family to be the head of. . . .

From the living room his mother called, "Marvin, will you have a cocktail with me before dinner?"

He looked up from the single page of the letter to answer, "In a minute, I just have to write a note I want to get off."

"I'll have Bevey mix them now. You want a Martini?"

"Yes, sure, Momma. Anything."

He put the letter to one side, and taking a sheet of blank paper from the desk drawer, took up his father's pen.

"Dearest Zeeda,

I can't tell you how delighted I was to hear from you after so long. I miss you, too—all of us miss you, and I wish to God there were something I could do to make it possible for everything to be set right for you. But I guess it's none of my business—a fact you often pointed out to me—so I'm following your instructions and not telling Momma or Poppa anything about your letter. But I'm so glad you wrote—I've thought of you over and over again, hoping you weren't dead or starving or just plain unhappy.

There is little news I can give you. New York is all in a swat about the unconditional surrender, and things at the hospital have been more disordered than usual the last few days. I am interning now at Bellevue, still living at home, though, and looking forward to setting up practice in a couple of years. I'll probably go in with Dr. Kassal. Poppa's bent on it, and I'm too fond of New York to let him down, particularly after all he's given me, and considering what high expectations he has for me. So it looks like California's out for me, at least for the time being.

As I started out to tell you, New York is pretty much like Los Angeles must be. After the false alarm on Sunday, everyone's been very tense. We got the news just before I left the hospital this afternoon that the Japanese have accepted, now that Hirohito is going to stay put. On the way up to Seventy-sixth Street from Bellevue everybody seemed very excited, and I guess tonight the celebrating will break loose. One of the guys from the hospital and I are going to go down to Times Square to take a look at it—so we'll have something to talk to our grandchildren about. Myself, I'm a little depressed I wasn't in it. I guess I should be grateful, but once or twice there I could have torn my eyes out of their sockets for what they were doing to me. (My glasses, by the way, are half an inch thicker since I last saw you, and thanks to the hospital food, I am fifteen pounds heavier, which I can ill afford.) But anyway, I keep trying to convince myself it was all for the best, and that it's to the country's benefit that this brilliant, important, incomparable brain of mine is intact. Well, I don't want to sound ungrateful. It's just something that occurs to me once in a while.

Everything is pretty much as usual here at home. Momma and Poppa are both well, and I'm sure they'd really like to hear from you. Why don't you try writing them? It can't do any harm to try, and you never can tell what might come of it. In the meantime, though, I'll keep my promise and not mention your letter.

Now that I've written, you've got to promise not to drop completely out of sight again. Let me hear from you, and I'll promise to be quick about answering. Take care of yourself.

Love, M."

From the pigeonhole before him he took a fresh envelope, and folding the letter, stuffed it in and sealed it. He did not address the envelope, but together with the letter from Zeeda, stuffed it into the inside pocket of his jacket. He got up from the desk, replaced the chair precisely in its position to avoid bumping into it the next time he passed it, and leaving the den, went through the little hall to the living room of the apartment. His mother was sitting in the middle of the sofa, a game of solitaire played out on the coffee table before her. She looked up as he came in, the deep-set, wide blue eyes coyly solicitous.

"Ready for your Martini, Marvin?"

"Any time, Momma."

At the farther end of the room Bevey was fixing the cocktails, her frail black hands deft and practiced, her fresh uniform stiff with starch and brilliantly white against the deep brown of her mouselike, preoccupied face. She mixed the Martinis unsmilingly, absorbed in the business of measurement and stirring, intent on maintaining the proper balance of ingredients so that her employer and her family should have no need to flinch at the peculiar bitterness of too much gin or the musky sweetness of too much vermouth. Bevey had mixed cocktails for the Kaufmans every day for two years, but it was her favorite duty, her greatest pride in the day's unvaried regimen, and she pursued it with the conscientiousness of a virtuoso. Marvin smiled to himself and looked away as he threw himself down in one of the two large chairs that faced the sofa.

"*Don't* bounce, dear!" his mother said.

"Sorry."

"Going out tonight?" She leaned forward over the last moves of her game of solitaire.

"Don Biel's picking me up later," Marvin said. "We thought we'd go down to Times Square."

"Times Square? You wouldn't catch me in Times Square tonight, not on your life."

"We figured it might be something to tell our grandchildren."

"Let them see their own celebrations," she advised blandly. "Your life won't be worth a dime."

Mrs. Kaufman played her cards out briskly, hesitating now and again over a decision. The cut of the flowered-print dress she wore prevented her leaning forward with any freedom, and the tautness of the cloth as she moved to play a card betrayed the slight roll of fat above her girdle. Marvin turned his glance away to the string of pearls she wore about her throat—a powdered throat, the flesh withering in spite of all her care—to the once-pretty face, distinguished by the straight, small nose and the uncommonly large eyes, painted cautiously and cleverly to produce an aspect still handsome in encroaching age, strong and arrogant, with a fullness of mouth that was more vain than sensual. Her hair was worn neatly bobbed, combed in waves back from her face, very gray and touched with a bluish tint. Her shoulders were straight and broad, and Marvin suspected that in the slimness of youth she must have been even more imposing than she was now.

He thought of the letter in his pocket, and frowning a little, wondered whether after all it would not be better to tell her. True, she'd be shocked at first—the surprise of hearing from Zeeda after so long would be too sharp to give her pleasure—but afterward she might be pleased; and when she read the letter, as she would have to, she would see Zeeda's concern—"it would only upset her," Zeeda had said—and perhaps some of her old hurt would be assuaged. The excitement the letter would cause might even heal the break between them. She might herself write to Zeeda, urge her to come home, confess that she had been wrong, that she was eager to correct everything that was amiss between them.

He sighed, watching his mother's hands as she played out the game of solitaire. Could those taut, brisk, sure hands write a letter like that? Those hands with their rings, with their scent of powder, had been loving enough to him. Had they to Zeeda? They had always knotted in anxiety, he knew, whenever new friends of his mother had had to have Zeeda presented to them. Maybe it was better that Zeeda was out of her life. If his sister was able to subsist on her own in California, maybe her independence and his mother's forgetful, serene briskness of disposition were too valuable to be disturbed by the letter in his pocket, shaken and scarred by a reunion that would probably in the end be abortive. He would not tell her, he decided. Things were all right as they were. The woman playing solitaire had no need of her daughter, no wish for her; she had never had anything of the kind. . . .

"Were they excited at the hospital?" his mother was asking.

"A little," said Marvin. "Some of the patients."

Bevey served their cocktails. Mrs. Kaufman lit a cigarette

before taking hers up from the coffee table, and shuffled the pack of cards together again, turning to put them on the edge of the end table beside the sofa.

"What about the nurses?"

Marvin smiled.

"I don't like nurses. I don't think you can trust them."

"We have very good nurses at Bellevue, Momma." His mother's primness made him smile, as most of her affectations did. He was grateful for that, he knew. It was preferable to being embarrassed for her, and it helped him to overcome his annoyance whenever she was downright stupid. There were times when she would run on with perfect idiocy about things she knew nothing of, but this had never greatly bothered him. The energetic confidence with which she displayed her ignorance touched him instead, rid her performance of meanness or guile. She meant well, he thought, but then he caught himself out in his own patronizing. In the depths of his heart he wished she were different.

When the door out in the hall opened to admit his father, his mother rose from the sofa and went to greet him.

"Have a nice day, Joel?" Her voice was getting sharper, Marvin noted, and the insincerity in her question was patent. She had asked it too often, greeted her husband's homecoming with too much regularity, without alteration or diversion. That was what she liked, probably—the certainty of his arrival home every afternoon, the undisturbed knowledge that he looked forward to it, that he thought of her as he read the evening paper on the subway train.

But such regimen had taken its effect. On her part she was stodgy now, had all but lost her curiosity, had become irrevocably set in her ways. Soon, he suspected, she would become irritable, dissatisfied with middle age, nostalgic for the youth she had lived so self-indulgently, without bringing from it anything except his father and his father's income to enrich her existence later on. Time would find her increasingly querulous, he was afraid, and in the end her vanity would be unendurable. At the hospital he had seen so many like her, not as fortunate. Bellevue patients did not often have furs and jewelry and an apartment as lavish. But they were just as narrow of mind, just as nearsighted and snobbish and materialistic. They were never happy women.

And their husbands, when they visited the hospital, were too often like his father. . . .

Mr. Kaufman's seersucker suit was stained dark with perspiration, and his round plump face was flushed with excitement. The flesh around his small speculative eyes was discolored by years of overwork, and the eyes met his son's welcoming look with an expression of dismay.

"They almost killed me," he said.

"Who, Joel dear?" asked Mrs. Kaufman.

"The people on the subway. My God, you should've seen them, you wouldn't believe it. Good evening, son. Good evening, Bevey."

"Poppa."

"You aren't going out tonight, are you?"

"Why, yes," said Marvin.

His father grabbed his arm. "You might get hurt. They are all drunk, drunk and screaming——"

"Have a cocktail, dear. Bevey——"

"Aren't you excited the war's over, Poppa?"

"Of course. I'm glad, I'm glad. But not that excited about it. Myra, they are all crazy, you should see them. To David Weiss I said, 'David, they will all be killed, there are so many of them.' David tried to get a taxi to take him to the Bronx, already the taxi couldn't get out of that part of town. I walked to Lexington and got the subway there. You should *see* the people!"

"What about the shop, Poppa?"

"Extra guard," said Mr. Kaufman. "Not easy to get, but I got him, extra guard for tonight. Those hoodlums, thousands of them, I emptied the display window and locked everything up like it's never been locked before. Mr. Golden is staying at his shop himself tonight. It is terrible. Thank you, Bevey." He took the cocktail from her, his face still flushed, his fingers trembling.

"Sit down, Joel," said Mrs. Kaufman.

As he did so, he asked, "How was it at the hospital, Marvin?"

"The same old story."

Mr. Kaufman lifted his thin eyebrows.

Marvin sighed. "They had to give some of the patients shots to quiet them."

"You gave them shots?"

"No, Poppa. The nurses gave them."

"Why not you? You're a doctor, aren't you? David Weiss' boy Jacob gives shots. Michael Muller gives *me* shots whenever I go to him."

"Poppa——"

"So why can't you give shots?"

"We have other things to do," said Marvin.

"Oh." A moment's pause; the old man sipped his Martini. "But you *can* give shots if you want to."

"Yes, Poppa."

"Oh. All right. I just wondered. I know you're a good doctor, Marvin. Isn't he, Myra? I told Davis Weiss——"

Mrs. Kaufman sat beside him on the sofa. "Did you get your price for the necklace? From Mrs. Stone?"

"I told you I would."

"You're sure you got it, Joel."

"Yes, of course I got it."

"Good. We've got to get Leah a nice wedding present, but I didn't want to without that sale."

"Myra, there's plenty enough——"

"Never mind. Drink your Martini."

They talked more of the shop, his mother inquisitive, his father diffident, and with relief Marvin turned from them to get a cigarette from the box on the mantelpiece. As he lit it, he wondered how his mother would feel once the wedding was over and Leah had gone off to Chicago with her new husband. She had wanted Leah for him, he knew. She had plotted and schemed unscrupulously to throw them together. A Gentile daughter-in-law might have pleased her more, but Leah's family had more money than the Kaufmans, and Leah was as intelligent and as well educated as Marvin himself. Too intelligent to fall in love with him. When she had announced her engagement, Marvin had been filled with a sense of relief. Leah was beyond his mother's reach now, but he would feel more comfortable about it when she was actually married. It was unwise to underestimate the miracles his mother could accomplish. Above the flat exchange of voices behind him, he remembered briefly his father's dim suspicions; in his unsophisticated, family-proud anxiety, the old man had watched him for days after Leah's announcement, afraid there was another girl he had not told them about, a nurse at the hospital, perhaps, an intern's younger sister, a Gentile girl. If it had been a Gentile his father would never have forgiven him. Perhaps it wa the one position he would have maintained against th domination of his wife, if it had ever come to the drawin of positions.

What Gentile, Joel Kaufman reasoned, could know the patterned, almost ritualistic emotions that bound them together, could appreciate the long years of inhuman industry he had endured—not for his ambitious wife's sake, but for his son, for that part of him which would live a different life than he had known, a life less hard, the life of a native American, educated in American schools, boasting an American medical degree, tending America's sick. What Gentile girl could know how long and how deeply he had dreamed of it for his son Marvin, how many humilations he had faced up to proudly so that Marvin could rise in the world as a symbol of what Jews in America could be? None. A nice Jewish girl, sweet and talented and pretty, could understand; could appreciate and esteem him; could honor Marvin, as a son so brilliant, so hard-working, and with a future such as Marvin's deserved to be honored. No Gentile could.

Marvin turned back to them.

"David Weiss' nephew in Germany," his father was saying. "They had a letter, three weeks old. Things were terrible over there before, he said, worse than we were ever told about. David Weiss' nephew is going to stay over after his discharge. To help. Marvin, what do you think?"

"I don't see why not."

"Isn't America good enough for him?" Mr. Kaufman asked. "Shouldn't American boys be at home where they are needed?"

Mrs. Kaufman put in, "A stay in Europe will educate him, Joel."

"It is wrong." Mr. Kaufman was sure. "Those people over there, soon enough they will be able to take care of themselves, without the help of David Weiss' nephew. An American boy should come home."

"Maybe you're right, Poppa."

Mrs. Kaufman stood up and walked back to the kitchen. Mr. Kaufman glanced after her, then, turning to Marvin, beckoned him nearer.

"Your mother thinks Europe is everything," he said when

Marvin sat down beside him. "That's because she wasn't born there. It is glamorous for her."

"I know, Poppa."

"You stay in New York, Marvin. It's the greatest city you'll ever find, and if you want to be famous and wealthy, a great doctor, this is the place to do it." He spread his hands. "Look what I have done for myself in New York."

"I've thought sometimes, a place less crowded with doctors——"

"Are they as smart as you?"

"Most of them."

"Nonsense! How many of them are working in the hospital at your age? How old are your classmates?"

"Probably I will stay in New York, Poppa. I wouldn't want to leave you and Momma."

His father sat back, and for a moment said nothing. He looked at Marvin, and presently his little eyes watered and sentimentality drew his hand forward to pat Marvin's knee.

"I know that. I know what a good son you are, how lucky your Momma and I are. You stay where you belong, you'll be a better doctor than any of the others. You will make Momma and me proud of you. Prouder even than we are now. When you're getting old as quick as we are, it's important we should be proud of our son."

Marvin did not answer. With a galling sense of guilt he remembered the letter stuffed into the pocket of his jacket. How often had the old man thought of Zeeda, he wondered, how often asked himself what had become of her, why had she turned irrevocably against them? And he wondered most of all if his father ever thought to blame his mother, if he were capable of hatred.

Throughout the meal Marvin sat silent, trying to look as if he heeded their conversation, trying not to follow his train of thought through to its logical conclusion. He was part of this old man, and part of this woman, and no amount of personal feelings provided him with an excuse to forget that fact, or neglect it. He was bound to them, to their lives, because they were his family, and he had to answer to them. It was a commitment that brooked no evasion. Zeeda had broken free, but she would suffer. He knew that without the family, for all her prized independence wherever she was, it must be harder. They had offered her precious little comfort or security, but it was something. People like Zeeda and himself, Joel Kaufman's children, did not desert with impunity.

He left them immediately after dinner, and after washing his face and putting on a fresh tie, went out to meet Don Biel. Don was waiting for him in the lobby when he came out of the elevator.

"I was just about to come up and find out if you'd fallen in," said Don.

"Dinner took longer than I expected. Sorry you had to wait."

"It's okay. Come on!"

They went out into the street and started walking west toward the next avenue.

Don Biel lacked Marvin's height, and beside Marvin's bulk he looked spare and sickly. His cheeks were scarred with acne, and his eyes, deep blue beneath the neat dark eyebrows, had the unnatural brightness and sharpness that only benzedrine could give them. He walked swiftly, nervously, moving on the balls of his feet, and hurrying beside him, Marvin felt plodding and awkward, sadly lacking the grace of Don Biel's catlike leanness.

"What's today?" asked Don suddenly. "What's the date?"

"Fourteenth," said Marvin.

"Fourteenth! I meant to remember it: Christ, it's great! You know what I did on my way out of the hospital today? I kissed old Hatchet-Face Rowan, kissed the old bitch right on the kisser, I got so carried away! Come on, come on, get the lead out."

"Look, it's great, I'm all for peace, but I'm damned if I'm going to run from here to Times Square."

"Aren't you hopped up about it? This is history, man!"

"I don't like running."

"Fourteenth! Tuesday, August the fourteenth, nineteen hundred forty-five! You realize how important that date is gonna be?"

"You've had a couple," said Marvin.

"Benny. Had to, I was out on my feet." Then Don grabbed his arm as they got to the other side of the avenue and walked with hurried, long strides down the dark street westward. "A great day, Kaufman, doctor, sir! Once this is over, this whole damned country is going to open up wide, like it should've done long ago, a country of wolves hot to slaughter one another, competition like you've never seen before. Me, I'm gonna make a mint. You, too, my friend, if you'll use your head for what God gave it to you—achievement, advancement, accomplishment! After a little rest, a little setback, this country's going to bust out with more damn vitality than you ever dreamed. You think we're going to lose the peace? Like shit we are—we're going to be the lords of the manor, 'cause there isn't anybody in this country that's going to stand for less. It'll be our day, boy, and this is the beginning of it! Tuesday, August the fourteenth, nineteen hundred forty-five! V-J Day!"

"You *sound* pretty victorious."

"Don't make insinuations. You mean just because I wasn't in it? Is that any reason I should get left out now? The hell with that—in six weeks nobody'll give a damn who's a veteran or not, and that's the way it should be. My fault nobody wants me? Who the hell's *ever* wanted me?"

"I love you, Don. Don't feel lonely," said Marvin.

"Screw you." He released his arm and plunged his hands deep into his pockets. "No, I mean it, this is a goddamned great era we're going into. It'll be the jazziest time. So what if it ends in the big bust? You think *I* care if this country's decadent? Sure it's decadent, and that's the way I like it —its richest, hottest, greatest time—and I'm gonna be in on *all* of it! You won't see me for my goddamned dust."

Don Biel babbled on, half intelligibly, feverish with a real stimulation that gave body to the manufactured drive loosening his tongue and lengthening the strides with which he walked. Marvin envied him in a way, envied him his confidence, fake as it was, his hopefulness. Beside people like Don Biel he felt himself inconsequential, an overgrown bookworm good for nothing but study and the least imaginative kind of work, nobody to cut a swath in the world, nobody to create or even partake of history. A plodder. Well adjusted, reasonably happy, and dull. He knew his own dullness and condemned it without knowing what he could do about it. It was the way he had always been; the Don Biels he had known, he had always admired and befriended but had never been able to imitate. He was regrettably, he knew, the salt of the earth; and now the earth would be for people like Don, their speed, their meat. Well, it was nice to be friends with Don, anyway; it gave him a vicarious position in the present, and might even rescue him to some extent in that future world that Don was determined to midwife into being. No scientist, no idealist, no prophet could be found in Don; but that curious kind of ambition that made him likable and popular and would one day make him rich —Marvin did not in his heart esteem it, but he wished he had a large share of it himself.

The streets lightened as they moved, first westward, and then south toward Times Square, and the broad avenue filled with people as they approached what was sure to be the center of the celebration. From somewhere Marvin could hear a band playing, and radios blaring, and they began to pass drunken parties that laughed and shouted and waved to them. Don Biel would shout a greeting back to each, and when they passed a girl who was alone, hurrying homeward from some errand, he yelled, "Merry V-J Day, baby!" to her, but she did not reply, or even glance at them.

"Scared shitless," Don said. "They'll all be scared, the virgins, anyway. There aren't any of them going to be safe on the streets tonight. We'll find something in Times Square, bound to, they'll be throwing themselves all over the place."

Marvin did not answer. He took a breath and tried to keep up with Don Biel's pace. The crowd thickened, and soon they could no longer walk together. Marvin fell a step behind him, and struggling for breath, trying not to bump into too many people with his beefy arms, his clumsy strides, he fought to keep up.

"Happy V-J Day, honey," a feminine voice said.

In the crowd a girl with skin as white as paper took Marvin's arm, and when she smiled up at him, her skin cracked and creased. Marvin started violently and without a word pulled himself loose. The girl released him without objection, and he hurried on, desperately afraid of losing Don now, terrified by the crowd as a child is terrified, furious with himself that he should behave so unreasonably—as big a lug as he was, frightened by a streetwalker. He passed a knot of people who, stationary, bisected the flow of the crowd, and looking down over their heads, saw in the center a girl, younger than the one who had tried to stop him, and two sailors, kissing one another indiscriminately, sloppily, delirious and drunk. The girl screamed something and the crowd about them laughed. She screamed again, but her cry was stifled by one of the sailors, who grabbed her to him roughly, and bending her back, kissed her clumsily. Everywhere there were servicemen, uniforms of every branch, faces of every shape and color and mood, old couples whose presence in the throng startled and dismayed Marvin as he rushed headlong behind Don Biel—they'd certainly get trampled by the crowd, they hadn't a chance. Younger couples, young fathers with their children sitting on their shoulders, surveyed the scene with wide, amazed eyes. The rushing, the shouting, the strong odor of liquor that swelled from the mass of people about him made Marvin giddy, and he began to laugh—the slightest tittering, but he could not control it. He tried to concentrate on the back of Don Biel's head.

In the steady thickening of the mass they both were forced to slow their pace, but Don was dodging, thin and catlike, through the couples and small groups, avoiding the long lines of young people holding hands, stampeding through the street in writhing courses, like snakes rampant. A bespectacled soldier and a woman Marvin took to be his wife because she was so plain clung to one another at one corner, weeping copiously. When Marvin looked back from them, Don had disappeared.

"Don! Don! Where are you? Wait for me, for Chrissake!"

Frantically he searched the crowd ahead, but he could see no sign of him. His cheeks were flushed, and his perspiration made his glasses slip down on his nose, leaving him momentarily blinded and outraged until they could be readjusted.

"Don! Where've you gone! Don!"

He pushed headlong into the mass, but it did not give way, and he bounced back, sweating with frustration and anxiety. Then he saw Don at last, hanging from a lamppost, waving and shouting back. The din drowned his voice, but Marvin, hysterical with gratitude, plunged toward him. A few feet away he could hear Don's voice again through the surrounding roar, "Come on, we got a vantage point! This thing can hold you, too! It's Tuesday, August the fourteenth, nineteen hundred forty-five! Marvin Kaufman, you are born!"

"Get the hell down from there, you wanna get hurt?" Marvin shouted up at him, desperately grabbing at his ankles.

"Watch the hell out, you stupid sonuvabitch, I'll fall!"

"You're damn right you'll fall, come on down!"

"I can't, I suffer from agoraphobia!"

"Don, please, for *me!*"

"You put it that way, Marv, I can't resist you. Watch out, here I come!"

He jumped down and threw his lean steely arms about him. "Marv, you dumb sonuvabitch, why can't you be happy?"

"Why can't you act civilized?"

"I wanna drink," said Don.

"Christ, yes, I need one."

A blonde passing on the edge of the sidewalk flow threw them a glance of large brown eyes, heavily outlined in pencil, and Don grabbed her around the waist, shouted "Hiya!" and kissed her. Marvin instinctively glanced away, at the same time cursing himself for a prude. When Don released her and the girl stepped back, Marvin, with an off-balance over-zealous effort, reached out for her, but with a laugh she eluded him and disappeared again into the turgid river of hysterical, flushed faces. Don slapped him heavily on the back.

"Well, so you're making a trial anyway, old man. Good for you!"

"Drop dead," said Marvin.

"Nothing wrong with a trial, is there?"

"It's a celebration, isn't it?" asked Marvin.

"You're so right!"

From the square before them a girl screamed; they turned toward the sound, but could not see where it had come from. "One more down, seven million to go," said Don Biel. "Come on, there's a bar over there, let's get a drink." As Don led the way, shoving, bowing, repeating "Pardon" with every step, Marvin followed, his fingers always on Don's coat, and as he moved forward, he looked over his shoulder toward the living mass that filled the streets as far as he could see, gyrating sluggishly, some scaling the walls of buildings, some leaning from the windows of offices and hotel rooms. It was breathtaking. He wanted never to forget the inhuman frenzy and the willful abandon of it. The hordes of servicemen, the showgirls here and there, the prostitutes, the ordinary family people who had come out from cold-water flats in little bands, tourists in their strangely cut clothes, instantly recognizable, businessmen in the windows of the Astor Hotel, waving to the crowds below, throwing out showers of newspapers hurriedly torn into pieces, crowds beneath the theater marquees, crowds unsteadily watching the news bulletins that ran in jerking, lurching lights around the Times Building, crowded restaurants whose patrons pressed with febrile faces against the windows like urgent suitors pressing toward a beloved in the crowd outside—they jostled and shouted and cried and drank, but most of all they drank and kissed one another and, in the protection of the crowd, sought out the bodies nearest them for a body young and whole and rejoicing in the victory.

On the corner of Forty-fifth Street and Seventh Avenue Clay Harrison of Nevada held his wife's hand and in his free arm supported his five-year-old daughter.

"You see, Nettie, I told you you should come to New York with me. You wouldn't want to miss this, would you?"

"It's grand. It's just grand."

"Didn't I tell you? Didn't I tell you, sister?"

"I'm thirsty," said the child.

"I was afraid it might be unpatriotic," Mrs. Harrison pointed out, "for us to come. That was all. I'm glad we came with you."

An empty liquor bottle crashed into fragments at the feet of Eleanor Stacey as she stood wedged in, trembling but exultant, against the door of a phonograph shop at Forty-third Street and Broadway. In eighty years Eleanor Stacey had seen more than her share of celebrations, but never anything like this. Of course in Montana nobody ever celebrated like this, she understood, there'd never been so many people, and then they had never got so drunk and wild as this—not that she remembered, anyway; but even the last war, Armistice Day, which she'd also seen in New York, hadn't been this way. Wild, of course, and at fifty-some-odd it had unnerved her, but this was better, much better. She supposed it was because she was older and her senses didn't work so quickly or so accurately as they had that it seemed so much more jumbled and nervous and exhilarating. She wished her granddaughter Lenore could be with her to see it. Her frail, withered fingers clutched her purse against her, but her rheumy blue eyes gazed with a lively smile at the thousand isolated scenes and faces in the sea before her. It was a smile of youth, and Eleanor Stacey herself marveled at the fact that she was still there, after all this time, and still in a way as much in on things as she had been in her girlhood. Oh, it was wonderful, but the bigger and the more terrible the wars, the bigger and noisier the Armistice. It was really a shame she'd miss the next one; that would *really* have to be sensational; but of course it was sinful thinking that way, you should be grateful it's over and hope and pray it never happens again. Eleanor Stacey gave a short sigh of impatience. She was always thinking sinful things, as long as she could remember, she had warred against that vicious barbarian demon within her that delighted in everything awful, that could thrill to terror and lose no vigor in facing up to death. She wished to God she could be a good woman, all her life she had tried to be a good Christian, as well as industrious and busy and polite to people, but it was no good; at heart she was a sinner. She supposed she might as well accept the fact and thank her stars that the sinner in her at least gave her the support of audacity when things were seriously bad. She distracted herself from her momentary conflict by turning her attention—fiercely, if only to escape her inner doubts—upon a trio of men a few feet from her who, huddled together, arms on one another's shoulders, were loudly singing "It's a Long Way to Tipperary." Eleanor Stacey thought it was pretty silly—that song didn't really apply any more—but it was a nice tune and she knew the words—oh, yes, she certainly knew the words—and she began to bob her head in rhythm with the singing and at last broke out into the song herself, her ancient voice so weak that no one heard her, but her gnarled old sinner's heart strong inside her chest.

"Goodbye, Piccadilly—
Farewell, Leicester Square. . . ."

Dead, they were all dead, all those people the song brought to mind. She stopped singing and clucked her tongue, thinking, "But damn it all, everybody else is alive; you don't give up just because you want to." And tightening her shrunken, still stubborn jaws, she started to sing again.

Newsreel cameramen stood atop the theater marquees flanking the junction of Broadway and Seventh Avenue. Through the densest part of the crowd at the foot of the

Times Building, Marvin Kaufman squeezed his way, Don Biel behind him, clinging to his jacket as Marvin had before, both having drunk too fast in the bar, both uncertain of step and carried away in the delirium of the celebration. Marvin's glasses kept slipping down on his nose, and with a muttered oath he would set them in place again. He narrowed his eyes, trying to focus them in an attempt to choose a destination, and saw before him the uniform of a naval officer, he did not know what grade, the precise white cap, and a face that smiled and said, "Jesus, what hit *you?*"

"Not a thing, friend," said Marvin. "Only some bad Scotch. Meet Don Biel."

"Hi."

With him was a Navy pilot and between them, two girls. Marvin nodded elaborately. "Good night," he said.

"What d'you mean, good night? Here, have some."

The pilot thrust a bottle into his hand, and Marvin drank.

"Thanks," he said, returning it.

"My name's Don Biel."

They gave the bottle to Don, laughing, pressed close to one another by the stirring of the crowd, kicked and badgered by people trying to get past them.

"I'm Frank, this is Dave, this is Peggy, this is Jean."

"Got any friends?" Marvin asked the girls.

"Sure, we got some. Don't we, Jean?"

"I think so. We'll see later."

Frank said, "We're going to a party as soon as the bottle gives out. Wanna come? No sense being lonely a night like this." The naval officer's eyes were bloodshot. Instinctively Marvin tried to think of a prescription, but his medical knowledge lay closeted somewhere beneath the reeling of his brain, and he could not reach it.

Dave, the flyer, proffered the bottle again. "Have some more."

"Thanks."

"Which is Peggy?" asked Don, hanging onto the shoulder of the flyer.

"I'm Peggy."

"Hi, Peggy."

"He's cute," said the naval officer.

Marvin watched the girl named Jean. In her thin face her mouth was full, its lipstick long since smeared on the mouth, the neck. He did not look at her in curiosity, or very much in desire, but contemplatively, pleasantly, wondering who she was and, remotely, how she would be in bed. But then he reminded himself that she was taken, and he chided himself for his forgetfulness. He'd gotten drunk awful damn quick. Excitement, excitement did it. He wished he'd stayed sober, it would have been a lot better, but he knew that sober, he would never have picked up with strangers this way. He'd never done that before. He guessed before the night was over he would have done a hell of a lot of things he'd never done before. It was great, fine, marvelous. The others, he realized, were all laughing about something, but he had missed the joke. Don must have told it, because Don was looking smug again. Marvin thought, "God Almighty, it'll be wonderful with it all over and done with. Everybody will be civilians. Not just beat-up guys like me and draft-dodgers like Don. Everybody will be civilians. It'll be the best thing ever."

Then he realized that another girl was standing with them and everybody was talking to her. He noted the dark hair, the small suspicious eyes, the hard line of the jaw. Her dress was damp with perspiration and it clung to her in a way that was both repugnant and alluring. The naval officer introduced him to her, and she smiled the practiced, ready, meaningless smile of invitation, her eyes resting on him a moment longer than necessary. Don Biel moved as if to join her himself, but Marvin put a hand on his chest and held him back.

"Up yours," he said with satisfaction. And his other hand, big and clumsy, fumbled until it found the new girl's waist. Don Biel could damn well take care of himself. He had a girl for the night, by God. Marvin Kaufman had a setup.

10

THE WARM WIND OFF BEACH COVE SHIFTED to the south, and a spray of sand persuaded Steve to change his position. He lay facing Smitty now, his eyes close to the even bronze of Smitty's thigh. He rested his aching head on his arm.

"But why so much, if you can't take it, huh?" Smitty demanded. "Why drink so much? Jeez. You had Hilda Verges scared shitless."

"Didn't mean to. It's just not being able to remember, that's all."

"Battle fatigue," Smitty serenely diagnosed.

"That's right."

"Battle fatigue and that Commie tail you was carrying the torch for."

"Zeeda had nothing to do with it. On the contrary."

"What on the contrary?"

Patiently, lifting his head in an effort to make his point: "She started me feeling things."

"You can say that again."

"Fuck you. Before, I never *felt* anything, good or bad. Like liking somebody, or hating somebody. Now I do. I'm getting better every day. I hate your guts: I'm getting fine."

"Yeh. Huh," Smitty grunted.

It was true he'd been drinking too much. For the two weeks since V-J Day he could remember no sober moment beyond the sickening first hour of hangover each day. Some days there had been no hangover. On those days he had reeled out of bed fully as drunk as he had fallen in. But in spite of liquor, he knew he was improving. His scrupulous study of his own reactions convinced him of it. He wished he could control his drinking. He wished he could decide what to do with his slowly returning energy, but he had not yet rediscovered the faculty of decision. Should he have another cigarette now, on the beach, or wait till he was inside the cottage? He'd be going in soon, naturally. It was almost time for lunch. He would wait for it, smoke it while he mixed the tunafish salad.

Smitty proffered his package. "Smoke?"

"Sure."

He took it and lit it. What was so important about a cigarette? Only through the twisting glass of sickness did something like a cigarette take on dimensions and meanings not its own. Deciding to shave or not to shave. Two drinks before dinner or three? Should he try writing a short story about Hilda Verges, now that he'd gotten to know her so much better? It was so difficult, searching out the raveled ends of a suddenly broken life line. Struggling to splice the segments. He would invent exercises for his will. Small unpleasant tasks he would force himself to do. Pleasantries he would forego. Masochism?—screw that. It might be his only hope. He pressed his newly lit cigarette into the sand.

"I'm going in, Smitty. I'm baked out."

"Sure. See you."

"Be good."

He pulled the edge of the blanket from under Smitty's rump, folded it with careful, scrupulous tidiness, and with deliberate promptings of his will, forced his legs to carry him up to the cottage.

The folding of the blanket and the exertion of his will to walk drained off the cream of his energy. He reached the cottage too exhausted to fix lunch. He filled a water tumbler with bourbon and sat down in the wooden armchair that was drawn up to one of the front windows of the cottage.

On the window sill next to his elbow was the large manila envelope the mail had brought that morning, propped up beside his empty coffeecup, unopened. He took a swallow of bourbon, lit another cigarette, dropped the spent match onto the edge of the saucer. He picked up the envelope. The postmark read, "Houston, Texas, August——" He could not make out the date.

He wasn't sure how important it was to live in one way as opposed to another, by one fixed standard as opposed to the endless numbers of standards and ethics and formulae the civilized world had to offer. But it *was* important to live. He could not have said why. He could not have defined his reluctance to think of that dark mapless realm that lay beyond the world of starless night and cloud-grayed day that had inhabited his mind for what seemed a substantial lifetime.

Dimly he knew that to live was more. Once not long before he had held in his arms a dying boy whose will had held up to the last instant of his blasted life. In the moment before his head fell forward, lifeless, against Steve's chest, Steve had seen in his eyes the decision to release the tendons in his neck that held his dying head erect. The dying saw and felt and judged. To live was more than the forming of judgments, or even decisions. To live was to exert. It was the last, and the most terrible, of his steps back to normality, because he had no proof that he would ever be able to accomplish it. And not to accomplish it would be to have won nothing, never to have returned.

He opened the manila envelope and pulled out the manuscripts. Cheap paper. It had already turned brown along the edges. How many years? He could not quickly estimate. Not many. Not very many.

"2,000 words
Steven Williams
640 San Angelo Street
Houston, Texas

THE MEXICAN
and
TEXAS

I never saw Madeline Fenner-Athcot without wondering why anyone would marry her, but four grown men had. . . ."

Steve laughed out loud: Madeline Fenner-Athcot! He, Steve Williams, while sound of mind, had made up a name like "Madeline Fenner-Athcot"! But after a moment the sound of his laughter died away. He sipped his bourbon and flicked ashes from his cigarette. Would he be able to write any less poorly now? Was even that small unborn talent dead, remembered only as dead days of childhood are recalled in unfamiliar climates, in distant and unreasonable occupations? No, O please sweet Jesus, no, let it be still alive. Let Steve be capable.

He got up and walked up and down the room. He pulled off his bathing suit and, naked, jumped up and down, goading the circulation of his blood, wrenching his muscles back to vitality.

He pulled on his bathrobe. The sand-dust of the floor gritted against the toughened soles of his feet. He picked the manuscripts up from the floor. He searched for a pencil, found one, and sat down again in the wooden armchair, propping the pages against his raised knee. He turned the topmost page over on its face and poised the pencil over the blank surface.

The cottage was soundless. From the beach came the shouts of the boy Smitty and his friends. Steve clamped his teeth down on his bottom lip and printed across the top of the empty page:

THE ACOLYTES OF THE SUN

Then even the shouts faded, and but for the drum-rolling of the surf, there was no sound. Nothing happened. His hands sweated. The pencil-point wavered and then fell down across the page as his arm dropped, the lead leaving behind it a dying trail.

How did a man learn to write? He was a memory returned to mufti; the separation center had made a ridiculous blooper to merit retelling for years to come: they had honorably discharged a ghost.

It is important to live. To live is to make something, to exert, to create. Every man creates; it is all that distinguishes him from the dead. Later, maybe, find out why. At the moment, it's important only to live, to make yourself do it, not to let life slip away.

In high school he had spent long hours copying out the work of his favorite writers in longhand, a kindergarten exercise. Had it helped him then? Would it now? Blind mechanics, to rid his fingers of their strange heaviness, to lubricate his knuckles, to bruise his skin against the pressure of the pencil until it calloused, until the sensation of writing down words was no longer foreign?

If the time came when he remembered this moment and felt ashamed of his presumption—in that moment he would give up life without whimpering. But now he would give it a try.

Firmly now he began again: "I never saw Madeline Fenner-Athcot without wondering why anyone would marry her, but four grown men had."

The pencil felt clumsy, but he continued his copying. The sentences did not make sense. He did not try to read them. All his effort went into keeping the pencil steady in his stiff fingers, and moving on.

On September 7, 1945, Tokyo, the last of the enemy capitals to be occupied, was entered by American troops. The flag that had been flying over the Capitol in Washington on December 7, 1941, and had since been seen against the alien skies of Rome, of Berlin, of the sea on which the battleship Missouri floated the day Japan surrendered—the same flag, not yet weary of triumph, climbed another staff to flutter over the headquarters of Douglas MacArthur in Tokyo. Three days later Vidkun Quisling of Norway was found guilty of treason, sentenced to death, and shot. Restrictions on fraternization in Germany were abandoned for the most part, effective October 1.

The news bulletins from abroad came thick, came fast; and if newspapers were not studied as intensively as they had been two months before, perhaps the reason lay in their sudden lack of drama, urgency, the easy glamor that could feed a vulgar mind. No battles now (guerrilla action here and there, who could care about a mopping up?), but committees and monthly reports and statistical averages and investigations. Private individuals, most of them, saw in these the tiresome, sunless routines of administration, could assign no greater value to them, could find in them no meaning bearing on the immediate drama of return, of waking up, of seeking out their places in the unfamiliar world of conquest. Already the Veteran—gone beserk, or fathering twins, or robbing a loan office—had snatched the public interest. The New Orleans *Item* biographed him, the Chicago *Tribune* analyzed him, the Cleveland *Plain Dealer* quoted, recorded, and interviewed him.

That October day's issue of the *Plain Dealer* lay folded on the foot of Warren Taggert's bed. Already read by his father, his mother, and Mrs. Wade, who kept house for them on Hillman Road in Shaker Heights, the paper had been brought to Warren's room on his breakfast tray at ten o'clock. He had not read it. He could not identify himself with others' triumphant returns or apprehensive slinkings-back to civilian life because he had no concept of himself as "veteran." In the same way he had been unable to create an image of himself in his own mind as "soldier." He had been Warren Taggert, moved by impersonal forces from place to place, wearing clothes that belonged to someone else. He was still Warren Taggert, and about the house, in the workless days he was allowing himself, his interests were the same as they had always been. That morning, after breakfast, he bathed and shaved and dressed himself in the pants, sweat shirt, and sneakers, stained with deck paint, he had used to wear on the Jensens' sailboat. Sue Jenson had knitted the thick-ribbed socks herself. Dressed, he went to seek out his mother, only to discover from Mrs. Wade that she had already gone out.

"Gone out?" Warren frowned. "I thought she was so darned sick."

"Oh, your mother was sick," said Mrs. Wade, "very sick. The poor thing, she simply had to force herself to get up. There's another committee meeting of the U.S.O. Nobody seems to know what to do with the U.S.O. now."

"And Mother couldn't resist a committee meeting if she were halfway in her grave. I know."

"But she *was* feeling ill, really. It's your mother's heart, Warren, and all she's been through . . ."

"What's Mother been through, Mrs. Wade?" Warren asked straightforwardly.

"Your being away and all——"

"*I* was in the Army, Mother wasn't. I never got within sniffing distance of harm and—oh, what the hell. I know. Mother worries just the same. Forget it."

He went downstairs and drifted into the alcove off the living room that was his father's study. How long had his mother been a chronic palpitations-and-hot-flashes case? Since before he could remember. Two of the bookshelves on the right of the broad window in the study were his own, and he drew a chair up near them. With no particular purpose he took down two of the textbooks he had used in his senior year in high school. He turned the pages slowly. The hieroglyphics scribbled in the margin were indecipherable now. He returned the textbooks to their places and took down the tight little *As You Were* of Alexander Woollcott. His mother had sent it to him at the induction center, and he had brought it back home, dog-eared, its binding broken by travel, on his first furlough. Paging through desultorily, he stopped on

> "Pile the bodies high at Austerlitz and Waterloo.
> Shovel them under and let me work—
> I am the grass; I cover all . . ."

The dull bite of discontent made him stir in his chair, but prevented his turning the page. What was the nature of it? Why should stray lines of Sandburg's bring it on?

> "And pile them high at Gettysburg
> And pile them high at Ypres and Verdun. . . ."

He was a stranger to all those lines implied. Was that the reason they disturbed him? A dim guilt that his Army career had been without serious challenge, as ordinary as the life of a clerk in his father's brokerage office? He did not think so. He did not envy the opportunity to display courage in battle given to someone like the tough young Italian corporal he had met that night in El Paso. What *did* he envy? What did he want?

It couldn't be a matter of desire. Wanting to be made love to was reprehensible enough in the weakling dependency it implied, and he had fought the inclination back whenever it had made its presence known; but worse, the corporal with the Italian name had been crude, uneducated, a half-step removed from a thug.

From the hallway he heard the ringing of the telephone, and presently Mrs. Wade appeared.

"It's your father, Warren."

He hesitated before he got up to answer it, knowing what his father had to say. Would he have lunch with him in town today? Warren had gone to lunch with his father two days before and could feel no enthusiasm for a repetition of the experience. But he knew there was no way out. He was a veteran, wasn't he, a grown man? It was presumed he and his father would automatically have more to talk about now that official records proclaimed him an adult.

He answered the phone and made a date to meet his father at the Klieberhaus at one.

The restaurant was crowded with businessmen, but Warren and James Taggert sat at their table as in a locked cubicle, the noises of the restaurant distant from them, the cubicle only as wide as the white tablecloth that separated them. Martinis stood before them, and they took their first sip with a silent toast, an awkward, half-made gesture of the glass.

Warren had inherited his mother's features but his father's coloring. Jim Taggert's hair, blond and worn long, showed those discolored streaks that are equivalent to graying. Younger-looking than his fifty years, his face nonetheless had the slight swollenness resulting from a lifetime of good Scotch and a meat-and-potatoes taste in food. What hardness there was in his face was in the expression of his eyes. It was the glance of these eyes, blue, unblinkingly perceptive, that intimidated his son—and his hands. They were heavier by far than Warren's hands, muscular hands, guiltless of grace, unthinking, powerful hands. As soon as Warren put his glass down, he hid his own hands beneath the table.

"Good Martinis here," Jim Taggert said.

"Yah, very good," Warren said. Maybe Mrs. Wade was right. Maybe his father *was* still a young man, able to be befriended as an equal, but under his scrutiny Warren himself was still a ten-year-old, trembling before his father's inquisition.

"Paper said Pierre Laval's gotten his," his father commented. "In Paris, a firing squad."

"Oh," Warren answered. "I'd almost forgotten about him. Laval. That was so early in the war, it's hard to remember."

Jim Taggert hesitated. "Yes, I guess so. . . . He tried to take poison first, but they caught him at it. Guess you read it in the paper this morning."

"No, sir. . . . I don't read the papers much," said Warren.

"No? Oh. . . . Don't guess you have any ideas about the atomic bomb then."

"The bomb?"

"What we're going to do with it," his father explained. "I mean, how we're going to handle all this new power."

"No, sir, I can't say I have." God, and they hadn't even ordered their lunch yet, he thought. Just then his father leaned on one arm of his chair, and for a while Warren was able to breathe freely with his father's gaze piercing some other object out in the sea of the restaurant around them.

Jim said, "Always like to keep up with things myself. You understand. Means a lot in the market."

"Yes, I guess it does. . . ."

Silence fell again. At length Warren broke in: "I told you last night, didn't I? About Dean Schaeffer? Everything's all right for the February term."

Jim looked up with pretended brightness. "Oh, really? Fine, son." Then lamely, "Yes, I think you did tell me last night."

"I thought I had."

"Did you tell your mother?"

"Yah, I did," said Warren.

"That's good. I'm sure she'd want to know."

"Oh, sure," Warren said.

And again the conversation mired in vacuity. Warren took

out cigarettes and offered one to his father. Exhaling, he sipped his Martini and waited for his father to take the initiative this time. He resolved not to take it himself again. Damn it, he could sit in silence through the whole lousy lunch if he had to.

But his father asked, "What're you going to major in, son?"

"I thought—I mean, I'd like to major in languages," Warren answered.

His father snorted. "Languages? French? Don't see what good that's going to do you. What will you be able to *do* with it?"

"Oh, a lot of things," said Warren. "I don't know what the setup is, but I thought later maybe I could look into the chances of the diplomatic service——"

A louder snort. "Diplomatic service! For Christ's sake, who put that idea in your head? Your mother?"

Warren felt the blush stinging his cheeks.

"Mother said she thought it would be fine," he conciliated. And then more argumentatively: "As important as the United States is going to be now the war's over with——"

Jim Taggert interrupted by leaning forward with elaborate patience.

"You can't make money out of the diplomatic service, or any other kind of nance poppycock like that." Warren suppressed a start; he had never heard his father use a word like *nance* before; the presumption of understanding, the assuming of equality between them in that kind of reference, shocked a deep-rooted sensibility in the younger man. No reference, however farfetched, to anything sexual had ever passed between them and, Warren knew, never could. Warren emptied, without too much suddenness this time, the Martini glass before him.

"I'm not interested in making money," he said. "It's not as if we were poor or had to make something of ourselves or——"

"Nobody's so all-fired rich with today's taxes to pay. And we'll be a lot less rich when the money gets split between *two* households, when you get ready to marry Sue Jensen. *If* you ever marry Sue. . . ."

Warren could not tell what his father's suspicions were. How did you read the mind of an other-world creature? What would his father think of his son's thoughts if he could really know them, not only guess? What, Warren wondered, would his father think of that night in El Paso, the two girls in the bar, the drunken young Italian? What particle of himself, of Warren, could be understood by a man with eyes like his father's, hands like his father's hands?

"What do you mean *if?*" Warren asked, and his voice shook despite his effort to steady it.

"Just that," said Jim Taggert.

"Sue and I are fine," said Warren. "I'm—I'm seeing her tonight. Some of the kids are getting together at her house."

His father interrupted. "Have you ever tried to . . ." But he stopped. He gave a sigh. "We'd better get our order in," he said, lips tightly drawn.

Halted at the border of the unacknowledgeable terrain, they turned their backs on it, in as much frustration as relief.

Jim Taggert, too, finished his cocktail. But it had been said, and each of them knew it had been too close for comfort.

The playroom in the Jensen house occupied half of what had once been the cellar. On the paneled walls hung hunting prints of Sue's mother's careful choosing. The chairs and couches were all deeply built, well worn, and comfortable. One corner was given over to a small bar and another to the phonograph. The ping-pong table and the dart set had long since been moved out, and cluttering the room now were record albums, a chess set, books, and a table piled with anagram blocks.

The party had begun in earnest at eight o'clock, but it had grown larger than anyone had expected because some of the young people brought additional friends, and others, as the racket grew feverish, called up college classmates indiscriminately and invited them over. Some of the young men were in uniform, either of the active services or the R.O.T.C., others in the demobilized khaki trousers or shirts that stated their veteranhood.

"The Army of Occupation, that's for me, boy," said one. "The *fräuleins,* the mademoiselles——"

"The grand tour, and it won't cost us a cent!"

"I've had it. I'm going to live out my days in Shaker Heights and the hell with the rest of the world."

Some drank beer; others, whisky.

From one corner a knot of young men began to sing above the jive of the phonograph:

"Once a jolly swagman
Camped on the billi-bong
Under the shade of the Koolibah tree
And he sang as he watched and waited
While his billy boiled
Won't you come waltzing, Matilda with me?"

Under Sue Jensen's direction Warren Taggert and Mel Anders carried a new tub of beers precariously down the cellar steps. On every side as he and Mel staggered with the tub through the dancers Warren heard snatches of talk about engagements, honeymoon plans, accelerated courses and numbers of credits, the G.I. Bill of Rights. From the talk he could not tell how many were fresh out of uniform, how many near to induction.

An incoming phone call announced there was another get-together at the Mixons' house. Should they come over to the Jensens or would Sue rather bring her guests there? No coherent plan was made. Some couples appeared from the Mixons' party, a number of Sue's guests went over in exchange. Gradually the situation resolved. In ragged handfuls the young people, to Sue's relief, made their way over to the Mixons, and Warren and Sue were left with only Mel Anders and Boofy Clinton, the playroom a happy shambles.

The four friends toasted their privacy with new highballs.

"I'm not going to pick up a single ash tray, glass, or beer can until tomorrow," Sue declared. And archly to Warren: "Furthermore, we haven't had an uninterrupted dance together all evening."

"Jitterbug?" Mel Anders asked from the phonograph.

"Anything, but anything but jitterbug," said Sue.

The danced smoothly to a Harry James recording while Mel and Boofy looked through the scattered albums for new choices. Warren danced somewhat uneasily to the music, thrown off balance by the sudden quiet of the playroom, wondering vaguely how the party at the Mixons' house was going.

". . . And we can fix our schedule so we'll have free time

together," Sue was saying some minutes later, her brown eyes bright with planning, her hair—blond as Warren's—shining in the room's muted lamplight. "Warren, there're so many people you have to meet. Boofy and Mel are just about the only ones from the old crowd I ever see. Everybody's gone drifting away someplace."

Warren was aware of the young perfume she wore, had always worn; it put him in mind of snowing nights, on the way home from high-school dances a couple of years before, of summer excursions, of the thousand times he and Sue had danced together: that happy, almost sexless comradeship. As though in deference to that old relationship, he held her lightly now. At his own age, nineteen, Sue was as pretty as ever, and her hair was no longer crimped with permanents as it had been when she had been following the fads of her years in high school. But in the time he'd been away, had there been no ripening, no maturing on her part? Warren could see no evidence of it.

Mel Anders raised his red head above the rampart of record albums on the floor.

"Drink, Warren?" He raised his empty glass.

"Help yourself."

"No, I mean you and Sue. Join us?"

"I'll get them," said Warren. "You can help if you'd like."

Releasing Sue, he took their glasses to the bar, and Sue joined Boofy by the phonograph.

At the bar Mel busied himself with the ice cubes.

"You and Boofy know where you're going to live after the wedding?" Warren asked.

"My grandmother's house," Mel said. "She's opening up her country place again; we'll have the house in town to ourselves."

"Good deal."

"What about you two?" the redhead asked. "Any late news bulletins?"

"That's some time off yet," Warren hedged.

"Hell, you're not going to wait till you're finished college, are you? Hell, that's too long." A glance over his shoulder assured him the girls were occupied with their own conversation. In a whisper: "Making out any?"

Warren shrugged.

"Your age," said Mel judicially, "you shouldn't wait too

long. Only makes for trouble later. Sue's nobody's fool, you don't have to worry about accidents."

"I know, I know."

"Butting in? Sorry."

"Everybody's so goddamned interested in my sex life all of a sudden."

With a laugh Mel clapped him on the back. "Hell, aren't *you?*"

From the pile of record albums Boofy looked up. "That was a dirty laugh: what are you two talking about?"

"Nothing, baby," said Mel. "Just kidding around."

Another set of records was started on the phonograph. As though by prior arrangement, without a question, the two couples separated: Mel and Boofy to the sofa against the wall nearest the stairs, Warren and Sue to the couch in the opposite corner. The records—soft sweetnesses, all of them—played on, unheeded but for an occasional accompanying hum from Mel Anders. Sue sat back in Warren's arms. For a long moment no one spoke.

"It'll be funny," Warren said to Sue softly. ". . . You'll be a junior, thanks to acceleration. I'll be a freshman. Be kind of funny around the campus."

"Everybody'll know you've been in the Army, Warren," Sue said.

"Who're some of the friends you have now, people you see? Tell me about them."

Softly, unhurriedly, Sue described the new crowd. Warren did not listen with attention. They would be the same as everybody else he knew in Shaker Heights. Sue's conservative taste in friends would take care of that. He studied the clinch Mel and Boofy were locked in now across the room. Warren felt a shudder of dislike. Was it brazenness, callousness? There was something repulsive to him in the blatant petting sessions other couples regularly indulged in. They were all engaged, of course, they would all be married couples in a year or two. He had known Sue and Boofy and Mel from childhood; why was he no longer able to be comfortable with them?

Sue allowed her monologue to die, and after a moment, turned her face to him. He kissed her lips: a lingering, casual, heatless gesture. What would she think if he went no further? Impossible: it was the thing everybody did, you couldn't sit like a stick all evening without somebody getting suspicious. He kissed her again, and mechanically, without desire, moved his hand from her waist to just beneath her breast, squeezing her body closer because it was expected. Sue lay in his embrace, relaxed and passive. She never reacted passionately to his caresses. Warren suspected they did not interest her, that she resigned herself to them as prelude to the wifely role she had been trained lifelong to play. The dull beginning of his erection neither excited or dismayed him—an animal reaction to the nearness of another body, it sought no definite object, projected to no particular goal of satisfaction. They would sit here another hour, he knew, as the phonograph records played themselves out, Sue polite and acquiescent at his side, himself play-acting the amorous groom. Dull, that was the only word for it, he told himself, stupid and dull and pointless. Sue, himself, their friends, living out the stale old patterns. A whole damned war had happened, but this hadn't changed. Two dull people necking, two dull people announcing to dull listeners their engagement, assuring the dull world they, too, were playing the game. All their dull friends—the nice little girls would become the nice little wives in nice little houses with husbands holding down nice little jobs in nice little insurance companies and brokerage houses and banks (neat little suburban deal; decentralization, that's the train you want to ride from here on out). Dull! said the shouting inside his head.

Warren supposed the friends of his haphazard choosing were no duller than some of the men he had lived with in the Army. But in the Army he had known at least it must someday end. Here, he was committing himself for life, signing up for permanent membership with the Mel Anderses and the Boofy Clintons and the Sue Jensens. And Sue. . . . What would it be like later, when they were married? As mechanical, as polite? Would his erection then awaken in Sue an answering need, would there arise in their coupling a meaning, a drive they neither of them felt now? Or would it be an endless history of well-bred acquiescence on Sue's part, of fulfilling expectations on his own?

The phonograph played:

"Gonna take a sentimental journey,
Gonna set my heart at ease . . ."

His lips immediately against Sue's ear, Warren whispered, "Sue. I'll stay after they leave. No one will bother us down here. Sue, can I stay?"

Sue whispered back, "Baby, what is it?"

"Sue, do you want me? Say you want me. . . ."

Softly crooning, a still-mechanical response: "Baby, baby . . ."

"Do you? If you only did, I could——"

"Dearest, isn't this enough?" She stroked his cheek. "I mean, anything else would be silly, if we're going to wait so long to get married. . . ."

"Okay," said Warren. His embrace loosened perceptibly.

"Warren. . . . You'll see it my way, dearest. You know I'm right. . . ."

"Yah, sure," Warren muttered. "You're right, Sue. . . ."

11

HE NEVER ASKED HIMSELF LATER WHY HE did it. Why he proceeded to drink too much, why after leaving the Jensens' house he went to wander the night-club streets of Cleveland. It was one o'clock when he came into Club Monaco.

A narrow dim-lit room, the bar filled its length except for a minute deserted bandstand at the farther end. Warren took the bar stool nearest the entrance and gave his order. By the time the drink was before him, his eyes had adjusted to the dimness, and he saw that the room was almost empty. At a table next to the bandstand a girl and boy his own age held hands and whispered, heads close together. Two stools down from his own a young man with thinning tan-colored hair hunched over his drink.

Warren knocked back half his drink, and searching his pockets for coins, went over to the juke box. He read the title-slots and chose one. When he pressed the buttons the machine shook itself alive, the mechanism whirred the length of its runway to the chosen disk, drew it forth, and conveyed it to its altar. The dance band blared into the nearly empty, silent room.

"Gonna take a sentimental journey,
Gonna set my heart at ease. . . ."

Warren climbed up to his place at the bar, searched for a cigarette, found and lit it.

What, he wondered, almost aloud, had brought him here, what had he expected to find? Nobody he knew would be out tonight, certainly not in this place. He smiled openly. Wouldn't it be funny if he ran into some of the guys he had known in the Army? But he hadn't known anyone from Cleveland. . . . Still, wouldn't it be funny if just suddenly he bumped into that young corporal? Where had he said he was from? Chicago. . . . Chicago wasn't far away. He might someday take a trip to Chicago, maybe look up—— But he couldn't remember the corporal's name. Something Italian.

The smile curdled on his lips. Reeling, his mind tried to steady itself, to focus on the knot of unhappiness drinking always brought up into his chest.

The night at the bus stop in El Paso, the corporal had sat with his arm around him, all unaware of how that gentle pressure had felt to him. He had tasted the impossible longing almost as far back as his memory reached: the yearning for the strong and gentle arm. Guarding. Bearing up. Comforting. What good would it ever do? He was as he was, for some reason he never hoped to understand he had been cast to play out his life in hunger and alone. Oh, there was the perverts' underworld, he knew: one poor queen had given him a blow job in the last row of a movie house one night in his sophomore year in prep school; boys he had known in adolescence had gone on to the orgiastic world of the unnatural. But that was furtive and filthy—he shrank from it at the same time that it slyly drew him. If he should give in, if he should ever join those hidden ranks—not hidden really, there were always plenty of people who could point them out—the penalties were too great. Among the prominent, moneyed families making up the texture of his environment, the penalty of ostracism was complete. It was not a rare occurrence: family lines grow old and blood runs dangerously thin. He had too much pride ever to make himself a sacrifice to the majority's intentions. The corporal had been a momentary gift, now taken away. You found a home in the Army! "Pile the bodies high at Austerlitz and

Waterloo. Shovel them under and let me work. . . ." Only silly queens were left to be his brothers.

It wouldn't be easy getting away, he told himself. But if he went after it right? A few weeks' trip to fill his idleness: he could probably persuade his father to give him the money. If worse came to worse, he could enlist his mother's persuasive power. Where would he go? Chicago, New York, some smaller place. . . . A lot of talk would be caused, and talk would sting Sue's sense of conformity unbearably. But oh, she would be patient and sympathetic. "Now, dear, you're just having trouble readjusting from the Army. Everybody goes through it, read any of the authorities. We'll just have to grit our teeth and see it through, Warren. . . ."

Away from Cleveland he would himself go on conforming, but the pressure on him might not feel as great; the watching and the estimating of eyes that knew him too well. It would be rough on Sue, but nothing compared with what it would be if he stayed any longer. Away from Cleveland, slowly postponing his return from day to day, he would get her used to the idea. It could be handled gently, without pain to anyone.

In anticipation he could taste the freedom of it. He could never satisfy his hunger—not and face himself as well—but he could see his objects here and there, look at them, not touching, content to imagine what it might be like. Often on the street he would see a man, not much older than himself, a clean-cut of feature, a bold and self-possessed stride. His eyes would hold the picture unless the stranger chanced to intercept his stare. Then quickly he would look away, but he had seen. Walking with Sue, an occurrence of that sort would rack him with guilt for days thereafter. But without Sue he wouldn't need to endure that aspect of the agony, he realized—only the hunger, and the hopelessness.

He decided he would tackle his father with the idea of a trip tomorrow. He would go to lunch again, and this time they would have something to talk about. He paid for his drink and got up. But turning toward the entrance, he stopped suddenly, and what he saw there made him stagger back a step, knocking his stool against the bar. In the doorway, eyes unhappily wide with puzzlement, fall coat pulled close about her slim young figure, was Sue Jensen.

She took a step forward.

"I was worried about how much you were drinking, Warren. I followed you in Dad's car." Another step nearer and an emphatic whisper: "Warren, nobody we know goes around drinking like this in bars. We just don't, Warren."

In Cleveland soon thereafter the first snow fell. The trees, like much-applauded burlesque girls, gave up all hope of dignity and bared themselves to winter. In November President Truman, Prime Minister Attlee of Great Britain, and Canada's Prime Minister Mackenzie King were with tentative fingers feeling their apparently united way to a proposal about the future of the atomic bomb. No good purpose, their meeting concluded, would be served by releasing to the world the methodology of producing the palm-sized chaos that had been loosed to end the war. The gentlemen stated, in decent accord with their governments' diplomatic commitments, that it was absolutely necessary that the bomb and other weapons of gigantic destructive capability be internationalized immediately upon establishment of "effective, reciprocal and enforceable safeguards acceptable to all nations." Newspaper readers felt a shock of understanding. The United States was looking with misgiving eastward, beyond dead Germany, to Russia. The statement of the men at the meeting clearly demanded that the Soviet Union, if it wanted to know how atomic power had been harnessed to practical use, resolve to work with and place its battered, calloused-over trust in the United Nations Organization.

By the nation-wide press services, news of the meeting of the prime ministers appeared simultaneously in Cleveland and in California. In California, as in Cleveland, it was in the following month eclipsed by news of the beginning of the postwar strike. Labor, in uncertain harness through the war, its bridlings unfit for patriotic sympathy, rejoiced its vigor in the sensation of victory.

In December, at the Barlum Hotel in Detroit, Driscoll Mills was one of the two hundred representatives to the Congress of Industrial Organizations' United Automobile Workers who cast their vote for a total production stoppage at the General Motors Corporation. It was Driscoll Mills' last act as a union member. Next week he was going to join Tom Henderson on the staff of the Demo-Socialist Party in New York.

The country could not be expected to demonstrate convincing indignation in the face of labor's pressure. It was a sign, some of the Jim Taggerts thought, of returned normalcy, however painful. Walter Reuther observed with a grin, "Almost like old times, isn't it?"

But Steve Williams had given little thought to the strike, and on the evening he went to have dinner alone with Ben and Hilda Verges, uppermost in his mind was his gratitude that they were offering him a decently prepared meal.

"A quiet dinner alone with Ben and me," said Hilda Verges that evening. "That's what you need, that's what we all need." Taking note of the long-sleeved dress she wore and how it softened the impact of those ravaged features and the shock of cropped white hair, Steve followed her into the living room. In the fireplace logs burned not so much to warm the room as to lift the spirits against the drizzle outside. In one corner of the room a silvered Christmas tree glowed with the blue lights strung through its painted branches. "Ben, Steve's here at last. Sit down, Steve, sit down."

"Steve." Ben wore a Hawaiian sport shirt as though in defiance of the dripping windows.

"Evening, Ben," Steve said, shaking hands. "I'm sorry to be late, I had to hitch a ride."

"Why don't you get a car?" Hilda demanded.

"No money."

"Now, Hilda," said Ben.

"We already have our drinks. There's a pitcher of Martinis on the table over there. They're very mild."

Steve poured out a Martini for himself and looked at her over his shoulder.

"Quiet dinner? Mild Martinis? What's up?"

"You won't like it," Ben intoned.

Hilda gave her husband a look. "It's for everyone's good," she said. "And it won't do you and me a bit of harm."

While Ben stirred the logs in the fireplace, Steve joined Hilda on the long sofa before it. His back to them as he bent over his work, Ben said, "She's on a campaign, Steve. That's why she put on such a demure kind of dress—to soften you up."

"I'm flattered." Steve nodded to Hilda.

"Hear me out," she said. She waited to see if Ben would sit down, but he was still busy with the logs. She went on,

"You've turned out three or four good stories recently—not really good, but promising."

"Thanks. Cheers." Steve sipped his drink.

Without breaking her speech, Hilda lifted her glass an inch. "And in spite of that air of offhandedness I think you mean to try to make a living at writing. Fine. As far as I can tell, you haven't a friend in the world except Ben and me, so I'm making myself responsible for laying down the law. You drink too much."

Steve gave a start, tipping a brief stream of Martini into his lap.

"And whose liquor is it mostly?" he returned.

"Well, you won't get any more. At least not as much. It's bad for you, Steve, it's lousy for anybody with a thinking job. Writing is very, very hard work, everyone says so, and for hard work you've *got* to keep your health."

Steve's wry glance drank in her own battered face, the permanently bloodshot eyes.

Ben returned to the wing-backed chair nearer the fireplace. "We met Scott Fitzgerald at Antibes once, and Hilda never got over it."

"That's bickering, and you know it," Hilda defended herself. "I'm not a literary type at all, but I think Steve needs guidance and I don't have an earthly thing else to expend myself on. Now Steve, you really must cut down on the helling around. The war's over and you've had your binge and you've written some very nice stories about it, but it's time to get on. I got you an agent."

Steve jumped again. Listening to Hilda was, he thought, like driving on a corrugated road. But now he put out a hand to stop her.

"An agent? What do I want with an agent, Hilda?"

"It's the first thing a writer wants." Hilda spread her hands.

"Can't I mail my own scripts to the magazines?"

"Mailing them doesn't sell them. This is a very good agent."

Steve shook his head. "You beat everything."

Hilda laughed. "I knew you'd be delighted. She's an old friend, a really marvelous woman, Rachel Pemberton, and you'll be crazy about her when you meet her. I sent her your stories, that's why I haven't returned them yet."

"Figures."

Hilda unfolded her legs from under her, and getting up, fetched two envelopes from the mantelpiece.

"She wrote you one letter and me another. Do you want to read mine first or yours?"

"Good God, Hilda——"

"I know it's all come in a rush, but I'm getting older every day and I haven't time to lose. I'll read you mine first." She flopped down on the sofa again, tossed him the unopened letter addressed to him in care of herself, and pressed out the other letter on her knee. "She writes: 'Dear Hilda,' blah, blah, blah, . . . 'we haven't seen one another for years—' and so on and so on, '. . . and *this young man*—has a decided flair, a feeling for language; flairs and feelings never sold anything, but they are a healthy indication. I am writing to him about these stories. To you and Ben I can only say that if you want to encourage him in your friendship and worldly wisdom, you could do much, much worse. And be practical; a literary apprenticeship can take many years, and young writers have gluttonous appetites. If Mr. Williams is without connections in California, you and Ben would be very sensible as well as generous to see about arranging employment for him that would keep him alive and yet not put too much pressure on him. He will get enough pressure from me if he's interested in my handling his work. Write to me again about this young writer and your personal feelings about his progress.' There. Now you read yours—it was all I could do not to steam it open today."

The impact of Rachel Pemberton's letter to Hilda was still on him, and Steve could not answer. He sat, looking at the envelope he held, his cocktail forgotten in his other hand. He did not know whether to be pleased or angry with Hilda. He had been concentrating diligently on writing in spite of the boisterous interruptions of his return-to-life binge, but it had been private endeavor. Or rather he had thought he was not yet committed. The letter unopened in his hand was the symbol of commitment, however he might disclaim responsibility for it and blame Hilda's well-meant, flattering meddling.

"One thing at a time," he said. "I have to digest yours first." Her look was eloquent.

"All right, Hilda, you win." And at least opened and spread

out, the letter looked less formidable. He read her the pertinent passages quickly and without feeling. " 'I feel a great sensitivity here in these pieces. There's an appreciation—if not a command—of structural technique. But, above all, you have a style that is your own. . . . I don't believe I can sell them. Not yet . . . but I believe that if you keep at it, you may soon find the particular channel of writing and thinking that suits your own individuality. You should be a novelist.' " He didn't read her advice to send her everything he wrote, good or bad, and not to make the mistake of expecting an early financial success. Enclosed was a list of her authors. There was hope.

Hilda said, "Now, you see, you've *got* to put the screws on yourself. It was weeks ago you gave me those stories, and ever since you've been running hither and thither to every party you could get an invitation to and making a nuisance of yourself in barrooms when you couldn't. You couldn't have gotten a stroke of work done!"

Steve started to answer her back, but stopped himself in time.

"Nothing much," he agreed. "Some notes."

The truth of the matter was that he had that afternoon finished typing the final draft of a new short story. But he dared not mention it; the story was the one about Hilda, and although it was sympathetic, it was not entirely complimentary. For an instant he feared his momentary hesitation had betrayed him, but Hilda only looked at him belligerently for a moment and then went on berating him until she had to go to check things in the kitchen.

Ben poured fresh Martinis out and came to sit by Steve.

"I'm no place with this literary routine, Steve," he said, "but Rachel Pemberton is no fool. What she says about a job makes sense, it seems to me."

"Thanks, Ben."

"How's your money holding out?"

Steve shook his head.

"I'm owed favors by Fred Isaacs, and it'd add another one if I found him a man with brains. Ever meet Fred here?"

"I don't remember," said Steve.

"He's come up during the war. Expecting great things of him in the next couple years. He's a major appliance wholesaler up and down the Coast, and he pays well."

"How would I fit in?" Steve asked. "What could I do? I couldn't sell anything if my life depended on it!"

"You've never tried. You're attractive. You've got poise. You'd be a cinch in the appliance business. Besides, the writer in you'd be seeing a lot of California life you wouldn't otherwise. I'll get you and Fred together for a talk."

"Can I think about it?"

Ben gave a sigh of reminiscence. "There's nothing like being on the bottom of the ladder. The damnedest people are just dying to help you up."

"Does Hilda know the Fred Isaacs possibility?" Steve asked.

"God, no! You keep your mouth shut or she'll get Fred on the phone. She'd have you made a vice-president on the spot and you'd never have time for writing! Hilda may act like a lush, but she's a power!"

The next day Steve reread the story he had written about Hilda. It looked far poorer than it had the day before. He decided that if he were going to talk with Fred Isaacs about a job, he'd better get with it, and he called Ben Verges to tell him so. Ben made an appointment for the three of them to meet in Los Angeles the following Monday. In the intervening days Steve worked tirelessly on the story about Hilda. On Friday and again on Sunday he dined with the Vergeses. Hilda nagged indefatigably to be told what he was working on, but Steve continued to evade her questions. On Sunday night, coming back to his cottage, he read over the fresh-typed pages of the story, and unresolved about his own opinion of them, put them back into the desk drawer, swearing he would not look at them again until a week had passed.

His interview with Fred Isaacs went well, and he agreed to start work in the warehouse sales office the following week. He would spend two weeks breaking in with the firm's more experienced men and would then be given his own territory. He'd be on probation, naturally. The starting salary was a hundred dollars a week.

After Ben dropped him at the cottage, Steve threw his jacket on a chair and went into the kitchen to pour himself a drink. He had a twinge of guilt all over again about Hilda. It really wasn't fair of him to expose her that way. Perhaps he ought to tear it up. There were plenty of other things to write about, for God's sake. He went to the desk and pulled open the drawer. The story was not where he thought he had left it. He searched the drawers of the desk. The story was in none of them. It was gone.

12

CHRISTMAS FOUND FAMILIES REUNITED WHO had not spent the holidays together for three years or more; in many houses the fathers and husbands were still absent, and grumbling demonstrations of the servicemen's impatience were beginning to break out in Berlin, in Paris, and in Tokyo. As the January snows crept southward across the face of the country, so did the strikes. The General Motors strike was insoluble, and a nation-wide walkout of some two hundred thousand electrical workers occurred. Then, within the space of a single January hour, the C.I.O.'s United Steelworkers accepted and the United States Steel Corporation rejected the compromise wage offer suggested by the President. Lewis Clark, president of the meatpackers' union, called out his men. The cattle pens of Chicago stood empty. In Chicago, too, young wives and babies stayed on with grandparents, many in the smaller outlying towns, while their demobilized husbands crowded into furnished rooms to look for work. In the icy nights less lucky veterans huddled together where they could, newspapers pulled up about them as their only shelter against the snow-flecked wind.

Tiger Rizzuto had been fortunate. He had found a furnished room that rented for five dollars a week. Its yellowed wallpaper was featureless.

The whistling of the January wind through the cracks on either side of the curtainless window pulled Tiger awake one morning before the alarm clock sounded. Dead air, stiff with cold, hung in the cramped room, and Tiger watched the vapor of his breath dance its small jig above the edge of the quilt that covered him. Beneath the covers he stretched himself, luxuriating in the self-generated heat trapped beneath the sheets. Then he relaxed, and lay wondering whether his fingers would drop off, frozen, if he tried to reach for the cigarettes on the bedside table. He turned over on his side, maneuvering his arm so that his darting hand would not be exposed to the bite of the morning chill any longer than necessary. There. Cigarettes and matches in one sweep. Two cigarettes left. But he'd be outside before he needed a third. The empty ache behind his ribs cried out for coffee, thick with cream.

He turned over on his back.

By cupping his hands close to his chest he could strike the match with only the tips of his fingers showing outside the quilt. The leaping flame almost scorched its sateen edging, but then the cigarette was lit.

Today was not fair. The windowpanes were covered thickly with soot, but on a fair day at least if the sun slanted in at the right angle he had a view. He could sometimes make out the smoke-stained tawdry buildings of South State Street. Not today. It would snow again.

The washstand at least answered back with a bald brightness. Tiger himself scrubbed the washstand with Dutch Cleanser daily, and the little mirror above it. Smart guys kept an eye on their appearance, Tiger knew.

It was the way you looked to people that counted, and you couldn't trust some jerk of a buddy to tell you. Not even Juney was reliable in that department. A mirror—that you could trust.

With a sharp intake of breath he bounded up, naked, into the icy air. He grabbed his bathrobe and pulled it on, but it was worn too thin to warm him. The crummy radiators weren't on, but he was pretty sure there was hot water left in the building: too early for the shiftless crud who lived there to have used it up. He turned on the faucet, and presently the steam rose. He plunged his wrists into the water. The heat would warm his blood at the pulse, he reasoned; the blood would carry some part of the heat through his veins to the rest of his body. Some little part of it, anyway.

Shivering uncontrollably, he pulled on his clothes. He hesitated when he picked up his shirt from the back of the straight chair. Could he use it another day? The collar and cuffs were already soiled, but only against his skin. The showing surface was not really clean, but it'd have to do. "Shit!" he said aloud, hanging it on the chair again. He should have changed shirts before going out last night, and saved this one to job-hunt in. For the first time he remembered the night before.

He took his green glass cup from its hiding place in the chest of drawers, dropped in a less-than-level teaspoon of powdered coffee, and filled the cup at the hot water faucet. He would need to shave as soon as he'd had coffee. He turned the water off.

Last night, as on most nights, he had stood around Bilkey's with the more sociable members of the 52-20 Club. Outside, the snow had continued falling, and the wind was rising. But Bilkey's, sour and smoke-filled, was roaring hot. With Sammy he shot a few games of pool and had a beer with Midge Perrino. Midge was the only one in the neighborhood who still wore his ruptured duck, but he had been back less than a month. Midge was always whining about the housing shortage.

"Didja see the Mauldin cartoon today? It's *me,* Tiger! . . . You get ready to come out. You think, Boy, I want out! Anything I wanna eat or drink, time on my hands. And what've you got? Some dumb broad you was stupid enough to marry when you was eighteen and now a coupla kids you gotta keep stuffing food in their mouths. I could rot away in that sonuvabitch stockade. I'd be better off!"

Al Gustineo was another alumnus of the stockade, but when later that evening he came into Bilkey's, he looked like a man prospering on freedom.

"What kind of deal you got?" they asked him. "What's the pitch?" And he would only laugh. But at least a few of them prospered, like Al, and came to Bilkey's only occasionally, to keep in touch with old, less favored friends. Army careers had sharpened the wits of these few. In some cases Army time had first taught them their trade.

Tiger wondered if he was yellow, if that's why he hadn't cashed in as they had. A word in the right ear at the right time—hell, no, he wasn't chicken. He was as tough as any of them, tougher. Tiger Rizzuto kept in trim. You had to hand him that.

Al had approached him once before with a proposition, a tempting one. But Tiger had his plans, and as long as the separation money had held out, he'd been able to stick to them: find the right job, get some cash ahead—enough to help Mamma a little—then marry Juney, settle down, get respectable, make something of yourself. The war was over, the easy times were dead. Weren't they?

Tiger finished shaving, put his shirt on, and pulled his tie—already knotted, as it had been for a week—over his head. His sports jacket covered most of the dingy parts of his shirt. He recombed his coarse black hair, pulled the quilt up over the bed, and going out, locked the door of the room behind him.

He called the Malone apartment from the coin phone in the hall.

"Hello?"

"Juney. Hiya, baby."

"Tiger!" A warm, small laugh of welcome, enriched with loving concern. "I thought you'd call last night, even if I wasn't going to see you. Are you all right? You didn't get too wild last night?"

"I told you and told you about questions, baby," he cautioned her, without impatience.

"Oh. Yes, I remember. No questions. Can I ask how you feel this morning?"

"Great, just great!" Tiger assured her. He covered the mouthpiece at the sound of a toilet flushing loudly in the bathroom down the hall. Cautiously he lifted his hand again. "I'm hitting the old sidewalks again today. And today's my lucky day, baby, there's juice in the old boy yet——"

"Oh, Tiger, I *hope* it happens today. Where're you going?"

"Ain't even seen the papers yet, Juney," he said. "If I hit it today, a big celebration, huh? Blow the goddamn lid off!"

Juney laughed, trusting and sure. "Except you should *save. . . .*"

"You know me, Juney, I'm your open-handed boy."

"Good luck, dear. . . . I'll pray for you. Will you pray for me, Tiger?" The voice on the phone sounded suddenly distant and unclear.

"Wha' say, baby? Pray for you for what, for Christ's sake?"

He could hear her draw breath. Her voice was clear again, and soft and calm. "Oh, that we both have a good day today."

"Sure, baby," said Tiger. "I'll call you later. Right away if I get something."

"I—I love you, Robin."

" 'Bye, baby."

He hung up, his small supply of cheer exhausted. He turned from the phone and tried to readjust the set of his jacket. The Army sweat shirt he wore next to his skin bunched in his armpits, making a decent fit for his jacket impossible, but without it or a topcoat he knew he would freeze all day in the sunless streets of the Loop.

He was at the door of the first employment agency on his list before it opened for the day. With a dozen other young men he stood reviving himself in the warmth of the hall, wishing they were dead and where the hell they got off with clean shirts! One of them, older than the rest, hadn't even shaved this morning, but his goddamn shirt was clean. Tiger with a casual air repeatedly pulled the lapels of his sports jacket closer together. He tried to tighten the knot of his tie, but it was already rigid from uncountable tightenings.

At nine a woman opened the door. The spearhead of unemployed surged forward. Expertly, unruffled, the woman herded them. "Form a line by this window, please," she called, indicating the aperture through which the firm's receptionist, dull-lidded, successfully employed, looked out. "Form a single line now! And when you get your card, fill it out over there at the long table!"

"The Army!" Tiger muttered, and presently he received his card from the receptionist. He threaded his way through to the long table at which five other applicants already sat bent over their cards. Tiger sat on a chair at the end of the table. He was about to begin a perusal of his card with emphasized casualness when he noticed the others filling in theirs with pens. A trick, a goddamned trick! He'd used a pencil at all the other agencies. He didn't have a pen. The agency wasn't offering any, either, a trick to see if you came prepared! He cursed himself vehemently for wasting his time. He should've seen from the ad this place was too lah-de-dah for him. Your own pen for Christ's sake! What did they think you needed work for? He leaned forward and nudged the elbow of a pimpled boy in a freshly ironed, freshly shining blue tropical worsted suit.

"Hey Mac," he said softly. "Borry your pen a minute when you're through?"

The boy did not meet his look and shifted. "Sure, sure."

Nervous as I am, Tiger thought. Why? A pimply kid, what responsibilities did *he* have to worry about? Probably made good marks in high school. Oh, Jesus, he wondered suddenly, do these ritzy agents telephone your goddamned *high* school?

"Here y'are," the boy said.

He accepted the pen with a smileless nod and bent his attention to the card he held. Its edges were already smudged by his sweating fingertips. Quickly he filled in his name, address, and social security number. Then the awful, empty aching of the last two weeks struck him.

"Previous experience:

Please describe in detail your last position; in the next section, the position you held before that; in the third, the position you held before that, and so on to your earliest employment. . . ."

Sweating afresh, Tiger studied the first space and wrote: "U. S. Army. Infantry."

Hell, Chicago needed lots of infantrymen, didn't it? The one thing I need, Mr. Armour said to Mrs. Armour only the other night, is a carbine marksman. Carefully covering the period after *Infantry,* he made it *Infantryman.* Something about the sound, he thought.

Second space. Worse. He tried to think back. Nothing you could call a position. He had told the other agents about odd jobs in high-school days: delivering for the flower shop, helping Marto from the Euclid Bakery deliver bread. The hours about dawn, the pungent, aphrodisiac smell of bread in the broken, wheezing truck. Way back: how did they deliver bread nowadays in those far-off tiny neighborhoods? He had been up at dawn a number of nights. He hadn't seen a really old-time bakery truck in years. Big vans, transports, sure. What Mr. Armour really needed was somebody who knew about old-time bakery trucks. . . .

He left the second space blank.

With a twist in his throat he realized there were five new people at the table with him. Starting, he turned to look for the one he'd borrowed the pen from.

"Here. Thanks, Mac."

Tiger got up from the table, delivered his card to the receptionist, and went to wait, standing against the farther wall.

One slow look around the room told him the nature of his competition. Younger men, mostly, a few girls in bright winter suits. Their faces announced "business school" or "six months assistant bookkeeper with the So-and-So Co., Inc." Cruddy bastards. . . .

He decided to think on constructive lines. They would say, "Exactly what kind of position were you interested in, Mr. Rizzuto?" What would he answer them? He knew there was nothing he *could* do, nothing he really knew outside the Army. If only there were something he could be really enthusiastic about. He knew it would be apparent to anyone who interviewed him: there was nothing in business that Tiger Rizzuto really wanted to do.

He shook himself and sternly called his spirits to attention. Hell of a way to impress an employment agent. Okay, okay, you're going to get a job; what if the choice if yours? What would you *pick* to do? . . . A cloud grew over his vision. Distantly, distantly, he heard the dreamer's sounds: "Mr. Rizzuto, Los Angeles is calling. . . . Mr. Rizzuto, the polka-dot tie for your conference with the President? . . ." Vaguely glory-filled, that's what the job would be; pretty secretaries around in bright woolen suits, a lot of wavy white material on the front of their shirts. A telephone he'd pick up: "Rizzuto speaking." No, better still: "Rizzuto here!" Why shouldn't it be like that someday? Hadn't Chicago given America some of its greatest people? And *he* was a product of Chicago as much as they had been. Jane Addams, the founder of Hull House; Cardinal Mundelein, as far as Tiger knew the only democratic Red Hat the damned Church ever had; Colonel McCormick—nuts, maybe, but maybe you had to be a little nuts to be a great man!

The voice of the receptionist sharply recalled him: "Robin A. Rizzuto, please!"

The fantasy was gone. What kind of a job had he had in it? What kind of actual duties? What kind of company had he been working for in his dream? In what field had he in his imaginings been so accomplished? The knowledge beat a sickening tattoo inside him: none, none, none, none. . . .

The thick-waisted man waved him to a chair as he came in and turned at once to read Tiger's card. As he read it, Tiger studied him as though he were a strange and treacherous animal into whose cage he had deliberately and knowingly walked. He tried to swallow, but the moisture in his mouth had evaporated.

The interviewer was not yet forty, but his niggardly mustache, the spread of his body, the unamused weariness with which he read the card in his hand, these aged and soured him. Humorless? Not quite. An unpleasant smile was even now rallying itself on those unfriendly lips. Tiger felt his fists knotting automatically in his lap.

"Well! Not exactly years and years of experience behind you, eh, son?"

Tiger flinched.

"No, sir," he muttered. Come on, come on, he thought, jump in, be confident, toss it off, show the sonuvabitch you know you're good! "Not exactly."

The interviewer was direct as anyone could wish. "We don't have a hell of a lot of stuff going on at the moment," he said. "Maybe with some background. . . . What'd you study in high school?"

"High-school stuff." Tiger squirmed. "Nothing special."

"No special courses in the Army?"

"No, sir."

"Hmm. . . ."

Tiger swore to himself he wasn't saying it, it was saying itself, against his will, against all judgment. "Look, mister, I used to work with a guy delivering bread."

The interviewer's eyes widened perceptibly. "Bread?"

"Way back, of course. You know the little neighborhood groceries, how they used to keep the bread boxes out on the sidewalk?"

"No, I don't, exactly——"

"Sure, they used to keep the bread boxes out on the sidewalk. He'd deliver the bread to the bread boxes 'cause it was so early, the grocery store people hadn't gotten there yet. I mean I can drive a truck, and—and I used to make out tickets and things for the grocery stores. You know, delivery tickets, kind of invoices?"

The interviewer scribbled on the card.

"Now, for truck drivers——"

"But——"

"We don't have such work in our files, you understand, but from time to time we hear of things——"

"No, that ain't it," said Tiger. "Isn't. I mean—I guess I run off at the mouth 'cause I'm nervous, you know how it is."

"Of course, son."

The flinching shook him again, and somewhere far beyond his nervousness, hot anger flowed into him. His voice hardened suddenly. "I'm not interested in no truck driving. I——I'm just out of the Army, y'understand. A career, what I need's a career. . . ."

Over the already lightless eyes came the instant professional curtain.

"Well, thank you so much for leaving this information here with us," the interviewer said. "You understand all those people out there are looking for some job *you* want. We'll call you if anything comes up. Oh—you don't list a phone."

Tiger was on his feet. "No. S'long, Mac."

The next awareness he had was of the comparative chill in the hall outside the agency.

Truck driving! He laughed as the elevator descended to the street. Sure, unskilled labor, anybody could get a job that way! Money, ready money, and what could you do with it? A *future* you needed: if you settled for money from manual labor, you were stuck with it, you'd never better yourself, the rest of your life it'd be the work gangs. Didn't he have his own damned father to set him an example? As an example it was a beaut: his father (who had told him faintly in the far long past?) had wanted to be a musician; Italian music was in him, poured out of him. And marrying too soon, he had had to go to work. Oh, music would come, sure. You couldn't take music out of the blood of a Ginzo! But the work on the gangs had taken the Ginzo out of his blood. Or tried to. Two years, ten years, and his father had grown to hate his own Italianness. Music wasn't what you wanted in America, you wanted ideas, learning, drive, to be smart, smarter than anybody else, hard and figuring! The Italian music had crescendoed, climaxed, wavered once and died, but no American moxie had succeeded it. A manual laborer: it wasn't his father's *trade,* Tiger thought. Lacking Italy's music, lacking America's moxie, manual labor was his father's *nationality*—the only one he had.

A future! You had to get yourself a future! You had to learn something, anything. Even if you didn't know what it was, that was what you needed.

The card at the second agency that morning, when he had filled it in, was not so bare of background. In Space Two he wrote: "Allender Co., six months, shipping clerk and mail-room." He laughed as he invented the company: what was old Erskine Allender up to today? and how were careers shaping up in Kosciusko, Mississippi?

Why *not* invent? he asked himself when momentarily his native wariness warned him of danger. He had lost track of the number of agencies where he'd left applications—none of them had come through for him. There was Juney to face, wasn't there? You bragged about what a big shot you were. Did you expect her to go on waiting forever for you to hit the jackpot?

At the third agency it became: "One year, superintendent shipping department, file clerk and typist." Another agency and then another. As the hours passed and his stomach ached with hunger, he began to grow lightheaded. His eyes played tricks on him when he tried to fill in the blank spaces on the applicant cards. The whole frigging situation was getting to be funny, he began to giggle to himself as his lie grew. He *had* to have a job before the day ended, at least some kind of prospect; he couldn't face Juney with another day's failure, another day's offhand explanations of dismissal. But the anxiety receded as giddiness came back. He'd sell 'em, he vowed, by God if it was experience they wanted, he'd sell them a line they'd choke on!

The fifth agency specialized, the legend on the glass door plainly told him, in clerical help. His head light with walking the Loop, his fingers numb from scribbling with borrowed pens before his hands had thawed from the cold of the streets, Tiger wrote in Space Two: "Allender Co., 1 year, secretary and typist."

"Allender Company?" said the crone with the steel bird in her blue hair. "An unfamiliar name."

"That was in El Paso, Texas, ma'am." It was past two o'clock. Drunk with lack of food, Tiger could smile the blatant lie.

"You say secretary and typist," the interviewer read. "Am I to assume this means you take dictation?"

"Yes, ma'am," Tiger said.

"What's your speed?"

How fast *did* secretaries take dictation? Fifty words a

minute, seventy-five? In his lighthearted euphoria the way out was easy. "I haven't taken a speed test in some time," he said. "The guy I used to work for was pretty fast."

"Mmm," and the steel bird bobbed in its nest. "I don't know whether they would consider a young man, but . . ." She was writing on a slip of paper. "Go over to this address on South Dearborn. We've sent a number of people over already, but nothing's decided yet. I'll call the receptionist to expect you."

Then, playing it out to the purposeless end, Tiger smiled and thanked her and strode out confidently. Alone in the hallway he let his mask drop and slumped against the wall. He stood still for a long moment before, unaccountably, a sob rose suddenly in his throat. Hold it, you're losing your grip, he ordered himself. No food, that was it. If he went by his mother's apartment, he could get something. But he knew he couldn't go there again, not till he had some cash to take with him. Too exhausted from the round to feel anything more than a dulled and impotent anger, he slowly crushed the slip of paper the woman had given him and let it fall to the floor.

He walked the snow-clogged mile back to his furnished room. Locking the door behind him, he found the room warmer than it had been in the early morning. He threw his jacket aside, pulled off his tie, still preserving its petrified knot, and stretched out full-length on his bed.

There might be some scarcity of work, he thought, but that was not the real reason he still had no job. What was it? He lit a cigarette, and in its idle smoke as it climbed the draft from the cracks around the window he sought the corridor that would lead him out of his fix. At the first agency that morning he had wondered what he would do if he had his pick: accountant, engineer, salesman? The trouble, he told himself again, was that there wasn't anything he *wanted* to do, except earn some money. He gave a groan in his hopeless sterility. Other guys had aims in life, impossible things, maybe, but something they dreamed of. Not Tiger Rizzuto. He felt his cheeks flush as the thought came: Just like your old man. No! he answered, not like him. What the hell was the sense in having kids, in bringing them up, one generation after another, if they were all alike? A by-product of screwing some dame you had the hots for, an accidental return on a semen investment? The hell with that. It was because each son could rise a step higher than his father, be a step better off, if he had any balls, be a step finer as a human being—only a little step, maybe, but not the same dead, pointless weight.

He drew too deeply on his cigarette, and a sudden spell of coughing racked his lungs. He turned over on his side, and as the coughing subsided, lay still, feeling the faint throbbing of a headache beginning behind his eyes.

That, he began to realize now, was why he hadn't been able to stand living with his parents any more. They were dead people. People alive had customs, ways, traditions that identified them. His parents had wanted to stop being Italians, just like that. Don't talk to other Italians, do like the Americans do, don't cling to what's old and behind you—throw it away. But they hadn't become Americans, either. Like the slang-burdened language they spoke, their efforts had never managed to ring exactly true. That was the crushing backload of the slum dwellers, Tiger thought. *Not poverty, but emptiness of heart. . . .* He writhed to think of the words occurring to him. Sentiment, a crock.

But in his inmost mind he admitted he believed it. This much he had thought out for himself. No priest, no teacher had told him, no wise guy had passed the word. Tiger Rizzuto himself had looked at his miserable stinking life, and the look had given him a thought! His heart began to pound abruptly, irregularly, and he lifted himself up on his elbows. Like the first ape to pray, he had conceived an idea independent and original! He laughed aloud and sat up in bed. "How about that?" he exclaimed to the walls. "I'm a goddamn philosopher!"

But his momentary excitement evaporated when he remembered that he was just where he'd been this morning. No kind of *thought* was going to put money in his pocket. Out of money and out of hope, that's what he was—one big hairy flop, a joke of a big wheel, Tiger Rizzuto, the noisy nothing. He fell back on the bed and rammed his fist into the wall beside him.

The temperature of the room began to drop as the afternoon waned. Maybe he'd go around to Bilkey's and sponge a beer. A beer would stop the growling in his stomach. He was on the point of getting up when a knock sounded at the door.

"Yeah?" he called.

The man's voice from beyond the door was muffled. Tiger opened the door on Al Gustineo.

"What the hell are you doing at my goddamned pigpen?"

Al gave his usual moist smile. "Came in for a talk," he said. He moved in slowly, fastidiously.

Tiger closed the door. "Don't tell me," he said. "Let me guess what I have that you want."

Al's thin eyebrows lifted.

"A clean record?"

"You don't sound overly friendly, Tiger. I like you. I'm friendly toward you, if you was smart enough to know it. Always been real fond of you, Tiger."

Tiger laughed. "Take a seat. Anywhere you like. Any one of the thousands of chairs I got."

As if the two straight-backs might have dust on them, Al sat quickly at the foot of the bed.

Tiger pulled up a straight-back and sat on it defiantly. "And I was just about to go over to Bilkey's and cadge a drink off you."

"Out of dough again?" Al asked.

Tiger shrugged. "I manage."

From an inner breast pocket of his suit Al drew out a rolled gold cigarette case. He offered Tiger a cigarette, took one himself, and with a deft flip of his rolled gold Dunhill lighter, lit them both. "I'm making out, myself," he said.

"Just give me time. Just give me time," Tiger muttered.

"Course, being older than you, I know more of the ropes," said Al.

"Show me," Tiger challenged.

"That's in the cards, too."

"I'm a quick learner!" Tiger was indignant.

"I think you are, too, Tiger. That's why I'm here."

Al would have looked great on Cagney, Tiger thought—the same patronizing half smile, the same cold all-seeing gaze.

"I got more specific ideas this time," Al continued. "And you're hungrier."

"If I was you, I wouldn't trust some guy who's hungry."

"I known you since fifth grade at Saint Joseph's, don't I? I known your mamma and your poppa and Juney and everything there is to know about you. You wouldn't never cause me trouble, Tiger—even if you ain't interested."

For a moment they were silent. Tiger wished the sleek

bastard would go on talking. He didn't want to think, not right now. He didn't even trust himself enough to let Al state his case. He got up from the bed and walked to the window. He was trembling.

Al followed Tiger's movement to the window. "There ain't much you don't know about me, Tiger. I'm penny ante, I admit it. But I buy myself sharp clothes so I don't walk around in January in no fucking sports jacket."

Tiger threw him a glance of admission, but said nothing.

"You're a loudmouth lots of ways." Al was good-humored now. "But it so happens to be my personal opinion you got brains. Brains don't have to cadge drinks—or put off marrying some piece of tail if they don't want to."

Tiger turned. The words had caught him by surprise.

"Thanks for the compliment. Anyway," he muttered. "But don't let's talk about Juney. Not that kind of language, Al. Thanks anyway. I don't hear much about my brains. Not these days."

Al leaned forward confidently. "I like you, like I said, Tiger. I got an opening in my business. See? . . . It's yours, Tiger."

Tiger's lips felt parched. He wet them with the tip of his tongue. "Look . . ."

"Your move, Tiger."

He hesitated. Al was right. He *was* a loudmouthed punk. For all his swaggering, he didn't know his ass from business like this.

"I'm green, Al. You know that——"

"So ripen up—like I said, Tiger——"

"Can you—can you tell me something about it? . . ."

Al Gustineo studied the ash tray beside him on the bed.

"You gotta give me a clue, Al. . . ." The silence was oppressive.

"My uncle with the garage," Al said after a time. "We're partners in this setup—temporarily, anyway. I ain't gonna share-alike with that sonuvabitch forever."

"Cars?"

Al nodded." You can learn the pitch." He shrugged. "There's nothing to it. I pay you ten per cent of whatever you bring in. If it's worth two grand, you get two hundred. Worth that much to *me*, that is. Little more or a little less, *you* get a little more or a little less."

"There's others?" Tiger asked.

"A couple. I ain't naming."

"How does the setup work?"

"You bring 'em to the garage. My uncle goes over 'em with his file and his paint, and we send 'em out of the state. We got an outlet."

"I get paid when they're sold?"

"No. When you bring 'em in," Al said. "You'll have to take my word on their worth, far as your percentage goes. Not as much as if they were legit, you know. You got overhead. How much you clear in the long run's up to you. Your time's your own."

Tiger gave a low whistle.

"Easy enough for you and Juney to get married. She won't even have to know. You got the garage for a front." He shifted on the bed. "If it's your future you're thinking about, don't. Who says we gotta stop with penny-ante stuff? This penny ante will give us capital, and with capital we can work our way into the real money. You know where that is, Tiger?"

"The rackets."

"Nah, kid. The labor unions."

"Unions?" Tiger frowned.

"You bet your life. There ain't no end to the goddamn possibilities. And this kind of start—hell, kid, it's a cinch! I can take you over to see my uncle tomorrow."

Tiger rubbed his palms on his trousers. Great men Chicago gave to the world, he thought. There were greats and greats, who the hell was to say one was better than the other?—nutty McCormick to old Samuel Insull? And Dion O'Bannion and Al Capone and Nitti the Enforcer! How far from Jane Addams to the Everleigh Sisters? Boy, *there* was Chicago's gift to the world all right: the ritziest whorehouse in America. But you had to be tough and quick. You had to grab at your future when you were given the chance. They didn't hand that out at the employment agencies, you snatched it from the air and ran.

Tiger came to sit at the head of the bed. "It'll be okay with your uncle?" he asked.

Al waved a hand of dismissal. "Personnel? That's *my* department."

"Then if I said Yes, it'd be as good as fixed?"

"I'm sitting here and waiting, buddy. That's all."

"I asked because—well, I don't have to kid you, Al. I owe rent on this hole, and—and there's other things I'd like to do—for Juney. I wondered whether—an advance—"

Al made a face. "Tiger, Buddy. What's the problem? I'm good for an advance even if you wasn't in the business." He stood up, and from deep within the folds of his overcoat drew out a billfold. "How much could you use?"

Tiger hesitated. "A hundred?"

"Don't *ask. Say,"* said Al patiently. "You're sure a hundred's enough?"

The ease of it brought Tiger's lightheadedness back again. He wavered to his feet.

"Oh, sure. That'll take care of everything fine," he said. "You can take it back out of the first money I earn from you."

"Good deal. Eleven tomorrow morning? I'll be at Bilkey's. We can go over to the garage from there. Okay?"

"Okay." Tiger put out his hand. "And thanks, Al, for thinking about me."

With a wave, Al Gustineo was gone. When he was sure Al would have had time to get out of the building, Tiger ran down the hall to call Juney.

"Baby?" he shouted into the telephone. "I got a job!"

13

AT SEVEN-THIRTY THAT EVENING TIGER brought Juney into the double cocktail lounge of the Palmer House called Town and Country. Tiger tarried in the entrance to give customers a chance to see his girl. His pride was not misplaced. The mild blue eyes and shining black hair would have been becoming even to a plain girl. In Juney Malone they were coupled with the translucent complexion that Irish girls are sometimes heir to and the features that, though irregular, are attractively pert. Her bearing reflected a shy, uncertain temperament and the clothes she wore were stylishly simple—an evidence of modesty that was for her highly becoming. She rested her fingertips on Tiger's arm with true dependence. Her other hand proudly carried the flowers he had brought to her.

"Town or Country?" Tiger asked. "It's your pick."

"Oh, Tiger, I don't know. That's the Town room, the one all brown?"

"Yep. This one with the white iron stuff's the Country."

"All right," she decided. "I say Country."

They took the first vacant table from the entrance and Tiger ushered Juney into her chair. They ordered Manhattans, and when the cocktails were brought, Tiger offered her a cigarette. The girl smiled and shook her head and Tiger lit his own.

"So what did you do after I talked to you?" Juney asked.

"Went by Mamma's to tell them the news, bring them a little something," Tiger said.

"Please tell me about the job again."

Tiger hesitated. "Just a garage job. But it'll bring in something, and a garage—a garage can always *grow*."

"And you'll grow with it." Juney nodded. "That's the best thing can happen for any workingman."

Tiger covered her hand with his. Tough as he wanted her to think him, when he was with her, he could not hide the tenderness her presence filled him with.

"Juney, there's things I want to do with the money," he said. "Mamma and Poppa first, and lots of things I'm going to need. You know, a couple of suits and things. But soon there'll be enough for us to get married on. I mean, soon enough so we can plan on it now."

"You really think so?"

"I know so," Tiger answered.

Juney frowned. "You don't know yet how the job will work out. You might not like it, or—oh, a hundred things can happen."

"They won't, baby."

Juney started to insist, but stopped herself. There was a momentary struggle before the first threatening tears welled into her eyes. She bit her bottom lip and blinked them away.

Tiger leaned forward. "Juney, honey, what's wrong? Don't cry, for Christ's sake!"

"I'm sorry," she whispered. "I'm just getting excited, I guess."

Tiger waited silently while she collected herself. He sipped his Manhattan quickly.

"Try some of yours," he said. "It'll help."

"Thank you."

Juney lifted the glass gingerly and sipped. She put it down again.

"There," she said, "that's better," and she smiled at him.

"Now what was that all about, baby?" Tiger asked quietly.

"Nothing, really nothing."

"Irish kids don't know how to lie, no more'n Ginzos. That's why you and me get along so well. Now what was eating you? Tell me, Juney."

"I can tell you later," she said. "It's upsetting and I—I don't want to spoil our celebration." With a smile she lifted her glass to him and sipped again.

"You want me to stew about it the rest of the night?" Tiger asked.

She made a clicking sound with her tongue. "You're just like all men. You can't bear not to know something, can you?"

"No."

"Tiger, please——"

"So I want to know why the hell a date of mine starts crying. Besides, you aren't the crying type."

"Just let's forget about it."

"Your family saying things about me?"

"No. Tiger, now please——"

"You don't want to marry me?"

"You *know* that's not it, what a terrible thing to say, why to think that——"

"Don't try no counter-offensive," Tiger warned. "I know your tricks like a book."

"I've missed," she said. "Twice."

She did not look at him when she said it. Her face, expressionless, was almost in profile to him, and her gaze was on the glass she was holding steady with both hands. Tiger was aware that somewhere music was playing; nothing but that and the knowledge of what the girl had just said penetrated his consciousness. They were silent. Tiger tried unsuccessfully to swallow; he took another quick drag on his cigarette. His hand sought hers again and closed over it.

"Juney," he said. "Say."

Still she did not face him. Her voice was a whisper. "I didn't want to spoil your evening. And I don't—I don't want you marrying me except because you want to. And——"

"How many times?" he asked.

"Twice."

"That ever happen before? I mean, some girls miss and it doesn't necessarily mean anything."

"Not twice, Tiger."

"Look, look, don't be miserable. I'm just getting used to the idea. Jesus! When will you feel life?"

In spite of her misery, Juney laughed. "Oh, Tiger, not for months and months."

"Have you been to a doctor yet?"

She shook her head. "I thought you should be the one to decide which doctor I'd go to."

The realization broke on him. "Jesus! We can't let the little sonuvabitch be a bastard. Nobody's going to call no kid of mine a bastard!"

Juney faced him quickly. "No, I don't want you rushing into things just because I'm pregnant. I don't care. I just don't want it that way."

"Are you nuts? If you had a miscarriage tomorrow, I'd still marry you. But we have to think about *him*. What—what if the poor little sonuvabitch grew up and wanted to be a priest? You know he couldn't be a priest if he was illegitimate? Christ, I don't know. There's no telling what they won't let him be if he's a bastard."

"Tiger, stop cursing——"

"*That's* not cursing, it's a word."

"Well, it *sounds* like cursing." She put a hand to her eyes briefly and unnecessarily smoothed her hair. Her chin gave a tremble. "I wish I would," she said finally. "I wish I *would* have a miscarriage."

Tiger grabbed her hand and squeezed it tightly.

"No, no, don't *say* that, Juney! It'll be our kid, it'll be—oh Jesus, things happen fast. What do we do first? A doctor, that's it. I don't know any doctors."

"My sister, Bridget, has her babies with Doctor Tharp."

"Okay. He'll be okay. When do you want the wedding?"

"Let's not talk about it till after the doctor. Things happen. Maybe I'm not pregnant at all."

"*Sure* you are!" Tiger squeezed her hand again.

Juney looked at him incredulously.

"Tiger Rizzuto, you're just as pleased as punch with yourself, aren't you?"

"Baby, I'm pleased with *both* of us!"

"It's my own fault. I know right from wrong. I should never have let you talk me into it. I knew I shouldn't——"

"Juney!"

"I don't blame you, Tiger. I blame myself. You don't even feel the same way. I know that. I should've had more sense."

"And lose out on me?" Tiger asked.

Juney looked at him straightforwardly then, confident.

"You wouldn't have thrown me over for telling you No, Tiger," she answered gently. "You're a better man than you think you are."

Tiger beamed.

"Oh, I wish we were someplace you could kiss me!" she said.

"I been thrown out of better places." He leaned forward, and taking her chin gently in his hand, kissed her lingeringly.

"Is anybody coming to tell us to stop?" Juney glanced nervously to either side, and Tiger pretended to survey the length of the room.

"Nobody batted an eyelash," he said. With a grin he raised his glass. "Pretty hilarious, somebody with a cute little Irish pan like yours being called Mrs. Rizzuto!"

Just then a thought struck him, and he fell silent. Married, could he keep her in the dark about the kind of work he was doing? Could he prevent her finding out about Al Gustineo? . . . For a while, maybe, he thought, long enough for him to get a little money ahead and get out of the deal. Sadness squeezed his heart: love might get her into his bed when she knew it was wrong; no degree of love would make her swallow the fact he was a thief. One night less than a week from now he would have to slip by darkness into somebody else's car, its unfamiliar odors accusing his intrusion. He would jump the ignition and pull away. Could Juney suspect already? He looked at her quietly.

"You're a million miles away," he heard her saying. She was smiling at him. "Hey. Wake up. We're on a date, remember?"

Tiger forced a smile. One thing he knew: his Juney couldn't lie.

"How's about dinner?" he suggested. He felt suddenly exhilarated. He paid the check as a young woman was coming in, alone. As they got up, Tiger said, "Cripes, what's that? There's a masquerade ball around here tonight?"

Juney tapped his arm. "Tiger, don't be mean," she said.

Helen Maclean brushed past the young couple, and stopping immediately inside the door, caught her breath. Well, here she was. She'd made it.

There was only one vacant table in the room. Helen went to it with her Bette Davis stride, sat down, and told the waiter, "My date's in the lobby, he'll be here in a minute. I'll have a Cuba libre, please." She didn't know how long the deception would work, or whether it was necessary at all, but she wasn't going to let the fact that she had no escort spoil her first evening in Chicago.

Ordinarily Helen's eyes were brightly expressive, but now their light was masked by thick false eyelashes, her eyelids weighted by painted shadow. Her brown hair was under control, but its elaborate styling robbed her aspect of its fresh youth. The shoulders of her suit jacket were padded, and the suit's wool was unimproved by the large rhinestone earrings she wore. On her head was a broad-brimmed hat with an open crown, and beneath it her cheeks were flushed with excitement.

Her drink was put before her. She gulped at it once, lit a cigarette, and leaning back in her chair, surveyed the room. With one hundred dollars in her purse, her last three months' earnings from the hardware store, she could not give herself much of a vacation, but she had promised herself one wonderful day. She had had no reservation, but for a one-night stay, the Stevens Hotel on Michigan Avenue had been able to accommodate her. Alone in her room, she had laughed aloud and hugged herself because the room had a view of the lake. She took a bath. The blue wool was her only presentable suit. She put it on, and having gotten directions from the desk clerk, walked up Michigan Avenue to Monroe Street, and over to the Palmer House. Her father had once told her about the double cocktail lounge called Town and Country; he had been there on a visit to Chicago for a small-businessmen's convention.

Helen studied the other women in the place and gritted her teeth with uneasiness. None of them was wearing false eyelashes, as far as she could tell. She considered the picture she presented, as she had last seen it in the dresser mirror at the hotel. Maybe she had made a mistake; the women here weren't dressed as well as she was (simple little winter dresses, not a whole suit in the place except her own), but somehow they *looked* better. Perhaps if you lived in Chicago all the time, you didn't go to so much trouble just because you were going to Town and Country. Suddenly her heart chilled: did she look like a hick to these other women? Beneath her make-up her flush heightened to a burn. She decided immediately to go back to the hotel. The lashes would have to go, probably the earrings, and some of the eye shadow. Then maybe she would take a long walk in the biting wind along Michigan Avenue, and if there was a foreign movie at the Globe, she would go to see it. The reward she was giving herself for running away from Charter Oak would last even into the next morning, because she would order an enormous breakfast from room service and eat it in bed with the whole broad scope of Lake Michigan all to herself outside her window. She'd stay in her warm bed until late. She had the whole afternoon in which to find a furnished room and a nice job somewhere.

14

AFTERWARD HELEN NEVER CLEARLY REmembered the hectic days that followed. A rental agency located a young woman of her own age who wanted to share her apartment: three rooms in an old house in the suburb of Austin. Her roommate, Lenore Stacey, who preferred to be called Stacey, a plain, friendly girl, offered to inquire about openings at the Brach Candy factory, where she worked; but Helen wanted to find a job in downtown Chicago. Her parents called her, and in a conversation of contrition on all sides, forgave her for running away and wished her success, and her father told her he would send her additional money until she found work, as much as he could manage.

The next week she was hired to work behind the soda fountain of a drugstore on East Lake Street. When in her second week of working she was put on the morning shift and was free for her own pursuits at two o'clock in the afternoon, she went at the first opportunity to the public library. She found the circulating department in the rotunda on the third floor, with its stained-glass dome and mosaic friezes.

Biting her lips against embarrassment, she sought out a librarian and presented her case.

"I'm a high-school graduate," she stated precisely. "I'm not able to go to college because I have to work, but I'd like to read enough to educate myself. Now—what would you suggest?"

The librarian, a gray-haired woman with a complexion in color and texture like the pages of the books in her care, blinked rapidly for a moment.

"Were you—a good student in high school?"

"Not especially. But I got by."

"I see." The librarian sighed. "Oh, my. Is there any *field* you're particularly interested in?"

"I'm interested in all of them," Helen answered. "That's the whole point." Suddenly she was afraid the woman would not want to help her. "This is a public library," she asserted, "and I can read any of the books I want to, can't I?"

"Yes, yes, of course."

"Suppose I start with the books they give you when you first go to college?"

"But in what subject, my dear?" the gray-haired woman asked.

"Any subject. Subjects sophisticated people talk about."

"There's really so little to go on," said the librarian vaguely.

"Do you have books on Cromwell? In a movie I saw, Katharine Hepburn talked about Cromwell—it wasn't at a party, but kind of at a party. The things people talk about when they're well educated. Couldn't I start with Cromwell—or Shakespeare, maybe? Something like philosophy?"

The woman did not answer, nor did she seem to hear the question. Instead she regarded Helen with eyes suspicious of her own leaping hope. When she spoke, her hesitation to believe was in her voice.

"This is no joke," she observed. "Am I mistaken? You want to give yourself a good general education, is that it? A sound cultural background?"

Helen spread her hands. "Why else have I taken the boring job I have? Because it's near here, and now I'm off in the afternoons."

The librarian's jaw set. "Suppose you try the hundred great books," she said.

"Which are those?"

"Books that make up the complete course of academic study at the university. They are the original works of literature from which most modern thought derives."

Helen smiled. "Straight from the horse's mouth!"

"One might say." The woman nodded. "Perhaps you'd do better to start with imaginative literature. Do you like fiction?"

"If it's not too silly," Helen answered.

"Suppose we start with fiction then," said the librarian. "It will give you a good base, and it won't demand too much application at first."

Helen was provided with a list, and in red pencil the librarian checked off six titles. Helen looked at them.

"I've read *David Copperfield* and *A Tale of Two Cities*," she said. "*Those* are part of a hundred great books?"

"Yes, they are." The librarian smiled. "You see, you already have a head start."

"Well! To think I've already read them."

The librarian took a breath. "You make me feel bold: let's add Stendhal, *The Red and the Black*. Here it is." She checked it off on the list. Helen had never heard of it nor of the others the kindly woman suggested: Defoe's *Moll Flanders*, Flaubert's *Madame Bovary*, Tolstoi's *Anna Karenina*, and Voltaire's *Candide*.

The librarian stood up. "I'll help you locate these and issue you a card. When you're through with them, let's talk about it again and see where we go from there."

The process of cramming herself with the contents of the books was not pleasant for Helen. Frequently she did not understand what she read, and often what she understood bored her. Except for the action of the final pages, *The Red and the Black* did not come to life for her. She wept in frustration, trying to organize the multiple Russian names in *Anna Karenina*, and she thought Madame Bovary was a jerk. She considered skipping to be cheating, and having skipped much of Stendhal's book, she attacked it a second time one night at home when Stacey had insisted on cutting her hair for her. The shoulder length of the war times had had it, Stacey said, and even at its height could not have been very becoming. Stacey wasn't prepared to argue the point, and Helen meekly submitted, and when it was over, she felt strangely released, and even Stendhal seemed to make more sense.

Eventually she finished all the novels, returning them to the library one morning during her midmorning break from the soda fountain. While she was waiting for a new group of books to be checked out by the librarian, Helen noticed a man in a Homburg and overcoat standing nearby. Within earshot of the stranger, and with a humiliating clarity of delivery, the gray-haired librarian said, "Kant, Plato, and Marcus Aurelius' *Meditations*: take your time and see what you can do with them. *The Education of Henry Adams* will tell you some interesting things, and I'm putting in Plutarch's *Lives* to start you on history. Will you remember something? Reading a great book once won't do much good, not as fast as *you* read them. Go back and reread them as you find those that appeal to you most. Read them over for the rest of your life. Will you remember that, Miss Maclean?"

Too embarrassed to follow the librarian's comments, Helen could think only of the man near by. "Yes, yes, I will," she murmured. Her mind vaguely noted he was tall and his clothes looked expensive. He carried a cane, but did not seem to need it. In one hand he lightly held a thin and ancient-looking book. "Thank you very much," she added, and gathering the volumes to her, she scurried out.

At the drugstore she hung up her coat in the pharmacy in the rear and put the books on a shelf underneath the counter of the soda fountain, protecting them from splashes by bolstering them with the supply of paper-napkin packages. She had served hot chocolate to the only customer at the counter when the door from the street opened and the man with the Homburg and cane stepped in.

He stopped momentarily just within the door, and Helen realized with a sudden flush of color that he was looking directly at her. He had followed her from the library. He came up to the soda fountain. Helen presented him with a mask of impersonality.

"Yes, sir?"

"Black coffee, please."

He was not, Helen saw, as old as his conservative clothes made him look, and when he took off his Homburg, she realized he was handsome. She was thankful when he broke off his stare and seemed to take no further notice of her.

She served his coffee and returned again with a glass of water, noticing the gray speckling of his dark brown hair at his temples.

"That's quite an ambitious reading list you have," he said then.

"I beg your pardon?" she said blankly.

"I was next to you at the library," he said. "I'm sorry, I wasn't really eavesdropping."

"Oh." Helen looked away. "That's all right." She smiled but did not return his gaze, busying herself with straightening the potato-chip rack near him.

"You're a student?" he asked.

"Oh, no. I just read a lot." Her glance indicated the book beside his cup. "You must, too."

"Indian lyrics," he informed her, picking up the volume. "A translation I just heard about for the first time, although it's very old. Do you like poetry?"

His enunciation was exact, and his voice, beautifully modulated, had a roughness of male texture that made Helen faintly uneasy.

"Yes, some," she answered. "I don't know much about it."

The man's eyes were large and brown and heavy-browed. They were beautiful eyes, Helen thought, and there was a faint twist of sadness in the deep lines of his smile. "Ask the librarian to recommend some to you," he said.

"I imagine she will eventually," Helen said. "I'm reading one hundred great books."

The man blinked, and a broader smile enlivened his broad face. "Really? And you're not at the university?"

"Oh, no, I work here. I'm educating myself."

"Good for you," he said with amused interest.

Suddenly shyness overcame her, and in her fumbling she almost overturned the potato-chip rack.

"Excuse me," she blurted, and going to the other end of the counter, pretended to return to pressing tasks.

It was with both disappointment and relief she saw him get up from the counter and pay the cashier at the door. But he walked back to where she was working. He leaned over the counter, one hand gripping his hat and stick.

"I only wanted to introduce myself," he said. "My name is Burrell, in case we meet again. Sprague Burrell. You have very good coffee here."

15

IN FEBRUARY THE FIRST BREAK CAME IN THE nation-wide epidemic of strikes. The Ford Motor Company agreed to an eighteen-cent wage increase for the United Auto Workers. The Chrysler Corporation followed its lead. Eighteen railroad unions and the railroad companies of the nation agreed to submit their case to arbitration. Back into Government-seized plants went the C.I.O. packing-house workers.

Among most Americans the sense of relief was little affected by the growing difficulties in the United States' foreign relations. With March came Winston Churchill from England, and from his speech at Fulton, Missouri, came the first rifle-crack of open anger: "Nobody knows what Soviet Russia and its Communist international organization intend to do," he said, "or what are the limits, if any, to their expansive and proselytizing tendencies."

The United States, having pictured itself as a peace-loving referee, found itself a contender. Daily the men were being discharged from the services, returning home, and no one looking for a party to crash had much trouble. The bars of every large city were crowded to overflowing, first by reunited friends, increasingly by those who, uneasy in an unaccustomed home life, sought out a reminder of the careless companionship of the barracks. The older fighters, tired out, were glad to return, but younger men, their nerves tuned to the high pitch of war, felt dismay and chagrin that the circus had suddenly closed down. Occasionally old faces reappeared at long-accustomed positions: John Erlberg plowed again, and Mark Antony Cusimano was again behind the butcher counter with his father. Out of uniform, guitarist Lindon Adler raised enough money to provide a series of folk-song recitals for himself at the Rejoicing Tabernacle Annex auditorium in Los Angeles.

One member of a small party attending the opening night of the recital series was Zeeda Kaufman. Joseph Murray, who was to have joined them, had been detained, but they were to meet him at his apartment after the concert. Mary

Ellen Dwyer, an incongruous flash of manufactured femininity in that company, was escorted by her producer, Henry Kahn. Two studio writers, one shaggily Lincolnesque, the other foxlike in the hypertensive attention he paid to everything about him, completed the group.

Murray had not returned when they reached his apartment half an hour after the concert, but Zeeda opened the door with the key Murray had loaned her. The lamps she turned on inside revealed the long ottoman-crowded room, with its strewn record albums and reproductions of modern paintings. From the small kitchen beyond Zeeda brought an ice bucket and set it on the floor next to the serving bar.

Mary Ellen Dwyer sat on the divan, her platinum-fox scarf wrapped loosely around her hips.

"A hell of a host if I *do* say," she bridled. "Not even here when he invites us. Look, honey"—turning to Zeeda—"did he say what *time* he might pay us the honor to put in an appearance of his fat face?"

"He'll be along," Henry Kahn interrupted, presenting her glass. "Henny and Art, you can pour for yourselves, you know where everything is."

Zeeda brought her glass of claret to the ottoman at the end of the long glass-topped coffee table.

"You in the industry, honey?" Mary Ellen asked.

"I'm an actress, but I'm not active out here," Zeeda answered.

"Zeeda's a very fine folk singer," the shaggy writer named Art put in.

"Like that guy tonight? Listen, hon, is he on the level? I mean all that fa-la-la, that stuff, the public don't want that. I mean it seems to me the public wants some life, some livin' it up."

"It's nice if you like folk music." Zeeda shrugged. "I don't know that Adler intends to appeal to the general public."

Mary Ellen went on to diagnose the current trend in American popular music while Henry Kahn moved about the room, idly studying the reproductions on the walls, momentarily examing a vase here, a cigarette box there. Presently he stopped at the desk against one wall, on which lay a thin sheaf of typewritten pages, stapled together. He lifted the pages and scanned the first paragraph.

"Say, this must be the petition Murray was telling me

about at the studio," he said. He brought the pages with him as he came to sit beside Mary Ellen. Reading on, he exclaimed, "Now here's something with some muscle to it!" He went on reading as Mary Ellen chattered about popular music. A number of times he nodded gravely over the pages as he read, and at the end slapped them down on the coffee table.

"Hell, I'll sign this any day! Where's my pen?"

"What is it?" asked Art from the bar.

"A petition from independent citizens demanding that we do something about sharing atomic secrets with the rest of the world."

"Oh," said Mary Ellen Dwyer.

Kahn offered his pen. "Come on, sweetie, you sign, too."

"Honey, do I *have* to? I told you——"

"This is a good cause——"

"Hymie's getting nervous about me signing things. He's told me and told me——"

"Look, I'll handle that shyster of yours if you want me to——"

"I don't think I really oughta sign anything more, Henry, honest. You're always wanting me to sign things."

"I'll sign it," said Art, taking the pen from Kahn. "It's high time we *did* something to let the Government know how we feel."

The foxlike Henny followed him. "If we can't trust our own allies with the knowledge we have, what's the sense of trying to make any U.N.O. work successfully?"

"Petitions like this may not accomplish much," said Zeeda, "but at least Washington'll know the liberal-thinking people in this country aren't asleep. If some damned warmonger like Churchill can come over here and try to get us into another war——"

"Oh, but I *like* Churchill," said Mary Ellen. "I mean, in terms of this is a great, great *man*. We'll fight 'em in the street, we'll fight 'em in the hills——"

"Sure, you can admire what he did in the war," said Zeeda. "Christ, that doesn't make him perfect, does it? And Mary Ellen, you don't mean to tell me *you* want to support war-mongering after what this country's been through."

"Well, no, not me, I should say not——"

"The best way to prove it," Kahn informed her, "is to lend your support to efforts like this here of Murray's."

"But Hymie don't want——"

"Oh, screw Hymie."

As Henry and Art contributed extravagant praise of the petition's strong wording, Zeeda studied the fox-scarfed blonde. Silly bitch, she thought, what does she know about this kind of thing? Never had a thought in her vacuous little life except about the ants in her pants. We'll get her. We'll get her yet. I could handle her, wrap her around my finger. I wonder if Murray knows how heavy-handed Kahn is? Sure he knows, that's why I'm here, isn't it? If Kahn can't get the silly bitch's name signed, *I* sure can.

"Maybe so," Mary Ellen was saying, "but Hymie says this is no good time to be signing my name to things. I got a career to protect, remember."

Zeeda and Kahn exchanged a glance and Art cleared his throat. Mary Ellen put her drink down on the coffee table and asked, "Where's the little girls' room here, honey?"

"I'll show you," Zeeda said. A slight gesture from her told Kahn to hold his horses. She led Mary Ellen to the bathroom at the back of the apartment.

"Go ahead, you first," she said as she closed the door of the bathroom behind them. Zeeda stood before the mirror over the washstand and put on fresh lipstick while Mary Ellen unhooked her stockings from their girdle supporters and rolled them carefully down over her knees.

"Nylons," she said to Zeeda's glance as she sat, "you can't be too careful, even now."

"Isn't it the truth."

"That Henry," the starlet complained. "Sign this, sign that! I'm on five different committees, for God's sakes, and I never been to a single meeting. They don't even *have* meetings, all those committees. Honey, what would you say if I said I thought Henry was a Red?"

Zeeda chuckled. "Oh, you can be interested in these problems—any good citizen is—without being a Red." She waited a moment before she went on. "Of course I don't know Henry very well——"

"No? I thought you and him were big buddies in all this petition-signing business."

"No, we've only met a few times. But from people in the industry, I hear he's a shrewd producer."

"Oh, he's all right. I got no complaints, God knows."

"Maybe it's for your own good he wants you to take an interest in things like this new petition."

"Listen," said Mary Ellen. "First it was denouncing the goddamned Finns, and Lillian Hellman *still* didn't give me a part. One thing after another——"

"You know, it's going to be tough in pictures now, tougher than ever."

Mary Ellen looked up, arrested. "How do you mean, hon?"

"The dumb-bunny starlet is a thing of the past," Zeeda said. "*You* know that, you're no fool."

"Oh, sure. Sure I know. What d'ya take me for?"

"The studios want the world to know their contract people are responsible *adults,* willing to go to bat for what they think is right. Those are the ones who're going to be on top from now on in, the intellectuals of this country. Now you and I know there aren't many really intelligent young actresses around Hollywood——"

"They're all in New York," Mary Ellen pointed out, "that kind."

"So it's up to the rare ones like you to *represent* the profession where adult matters are concerned."

"You really think so?"

"The studios expect it." Zeeda opened her hands. "Expect, hell, they're going to be demanding it."

"But Hymie——"

"Hymie's a lawyer, not an artist. No one but another artist understands these things. That's why *I'm* able to understand how you feel about this."

"You do? Well . . ."

"It doesn't cost anything. And don't forget, it's a long, cold fall from a seven-year contract."

The men's conversation stopped when the two young women returned to the living room to find their glasses refilled. No one mentioned the petition, and Zeeda was free to seek Mary Ellen's candid opinions on the intelligent topics of the day, which she did exhaustively, with sensitive fingers controlling the flame beneath Mary Ellen's indignation about the injustices of the world until she was fairly boiling with righteousness. By the time Zeeda referred to the petition again,

Mary Ellen was in no mood to be told what she should or should not do by shyster lawyers who fed on the inhuman capitalist system which had victimized her and frustrated her artistic yearnings her whole life long. She signed her name with a "Humph!" and made Henry Kahn fix her another drink.

It was one o'clock when Joe Murray arrived. He did not apologize or explain his lateness, but the stubble of his heavy beard and the Tartar-like twist of his eyes showed his tiredness. Mary Ellen reminded Kahn of the photographer's sitting she had to face in the morning, and presently everyone but Zeeda had gone home.

Murray sat back on the divan, his legs stretched out under the coffee table.

"Hope you didn't mind supervising things tonight," he said. "I've been with Ozzie Lubin."

"Ozzie!" Zeeda cried. "Ozzie's out here?"

"Just for a day or two."

"How is he? How're things in New York? What's the news?"

"We didn't have time to gossip."

"Oh." Zeeda nodded, subsiding.

"Talked a lot about you. I told him you're getting to be quite a whip at some of these sessions. He's delighted, of course."

"Did he say anything else, Murray? Bigger things, something more important for me, maybe?"

"They also serve who only get Dwyer's signature where it's needed."

"Anybody can do that," Zeeda said. "Ozzie knows I need a real challenge to do my best work, I've always been like that——"

"He knows, he knows."

"Then what did he say, Murray? Haven't I got a prayer?"

"Ever been to New Orleans?"

For a moment Zeeda did not answer. She had succeeded, she realized. At last they were accepting her without suspicion, without reservations, knowing they could trust her.

"I passed through there once, that's all," she said.

"You're moving there."

Zeeda leaned forward. "When?"

"As soon as things are organized there."

"I see, all right. What else?"

"We're pretty active in New Orleans, but the organization isn't tight enough. That's not your problem, you understand, just background." Zeeda nodded, every syllable she heard branding itself on her memory. "There are two arms there. The labor force, especially on the docks. And the French Quarter, the Bohemians. They're our best bet for overt liberal action."

"Agitation."

"That's an ugly word," said Murray.

"Lenin wasn't afraid of it——"

"Lenin was a Red. *You* are a liberal."

Zeeda bit down on her lower lip, then nodded.

Murray went on, his eyes closed, his head back against the divan.

"Roughly, it'll go like this," he said. "I'll send you to an officer of the Port of New Orleans Bank and Trust Company. He'll handle the rest, which will be opening a leather-goods shop somewhere in the Quarter, on money from the bank. Take it easy, get to know some of the younger people around the Quarter as you naturally would. Your income, because you won't make a hell of a lot out of the shop, I don't think, will come from me, personally. Advances from a loyal friend."

"I see."

"And you wait."

Zeeda hesitated. "As indefinite as that?"

"We want somebody reliable *on* the scene when the time is right." The Tartar eyes opened and pinned her. "You scared of this?"

"Not for my own skin, of course not," Zeeda asserted. "I just hope I can do a good job of whatever it turns out to be."

"Nobody's going to demand the impossible of you. You're being picked because you fit the job."

"I know, I trust you and Ozzie. You know what you're doing."

"Don't disappoint us."

Zeeda laughed. "When I've got something really important to do? It's what I've dreamed about: it's like getting born again, Murray! I just worried for a moment, just getting my bearings—I won't disappoint you!"

Zeeda Kaufman left Los Angeles on a Greyhound bus four days later.

A fine drizzle had been falling since sunrise, and it continued through the day, spending itself out toward evening. The road to Beach Cove was slick with wet as Steve Williams drove homeward through the sunset mist. He did not heed the fact. Recurring in his memory at the moment was the surprise he had felt at the silence and shame with which Hilda Verges had borne his tongue-lashing all those months before. December, sometime near Christmas. The sky had been dry and star filled that night. As they had driven to a cocktail party being thrown by friends of the Vergeses in one of the houses on North Cañon Drive, Steve had berated her unrestrainedly.

"What the hell do you think I am, a goddamned escort service for you when your husband doesn't want to have any truck with you?" he shouted. "He said he could've killed you for breaking into my house, and I wish he had. Talk about unmitigated gall! So all right, if you stubbed your goddamned toe on that story, it's your own fault. I was going to burn the goddamned thing."

He had to stop long enough to check his directions, and Hilda said, very quietly, "You and Ben are right to be mad. And I've said I was sorry. Curiosity killed the cat."

Her docility soothed his rage.

"Oh, for Christ's sake, Hilda, I'd rather have hanged myself than have you read that story."

In her fingers Hilda turned the paper cup that held her drink. "It's the best thing you ever wrote."

"I should have had more sense than to . . ." He stopped.

"What?"

"It is. The best thing you ever wrote."

"You're just saying that so I won't hate myself for writing a lot of bull-shit about you."

"You wrote honestly," Hilda insisted. "I was—thrown off balance for a minute when I realized whose dialogue you were lifting without so much as a by-your-leave, but that didn't stop me for long."

"All right, there's nothing really I can say." Steve sighed. He gulped quickly from his own paper cup and gingerly balanced it against the back of the seat once more. "Except I wish you'd cut my heart out."

"You'll want to cut out mine when you hear the *whole* truth."

Steve braked the car suddenly to a lesser speed. His paper cup shuddered but did not overturn.

"What do you mean? God damn it, if you *dared* to——"

"Well, I did."

"Hilda!"

"I sent it to Rachel Pemberton at once, before I had a chance to lose my courage. I knew you'd never let me if I asked you——"

"You're goddamned well right I wouldn't have! It wasn't even finished! Hilda, this has got to stop, this whole meddling, nose-sticking, presumptuous——"

"I know, I know, you can take me home if you want to. We don't have to go to this party."

"I'll take you to the goddamned party," he moaned.

"I realize you'll want to see less of Ben and me after tonight. . . ."

"Oh, Hilda. . . . Why couldn't you just have minded your own business? Well. Well, it's my fault. I *am* your business, I've let it get that way."

Hilda denied it quickly. "You're perfectly right to be angry. Just because I'm your friend doesn't permit me to mess about in your private affairs, certainly not your career. I guess—I guess if you know me well enough to have written that story, you can understand why I get into this kind of jam every once in a while."

"Yes," said Steve, and he remembered what he had thought of Hilda at one of their first meetings. He had so described her in the story: a packless animal, lonely and frightened, clinging for life to the elusive young.

For the rest of that evening they said nothing more about Hilda's housebreaking, and in the following days Steve was too occupied with his new job to call on the Vergeses.

The initial training that Fred Isaacs, Ben's friend, had arranged for him was intensive. With one of his senior salesmen he drove out each day from the warehouse to visit outlets in the neighboring farm and vineyard sections. He was dismayed to think of himself acquiring an aggressive bonhomie like the men he went out with. Their knowledge of the intricacies of the refrigerators, gas ranges, and water pumps seemed to him encyclopedic. But he found compensation in the folk who lived in the backwaters they traveled through, and soon he was looking forward to being released on his own. The people in the farmers and vintners' outlets were friendlier than he had expected to find them, readier to meet him as a more-or-less welcome visitor rather than an intruder. And the details of country living fascinated him. Returning to Beach Cove each night, he would write copious notes on the novel things he had observed during the day, and soon the notes were so many he had to start entering them in a bound journal in order to keep his desk reasonably free of clutter.

During his training period with Fred Isaacs' company, Steve received a letter from Rachel Pemberton about the Hilda story.

"You would have been happy to see my excitement [she wrote] when I finished reading this story. I almost called you long distance, and now I regret I didn't. I'm not certain I can place this story. Obviously, it does not fall into a familiar popular pattern. But with your permission I would like to sound out a few of the editors about it. I will proceed to do that as soon as I have a note from you authorizing me to represent you in this matter.

Mind you, I am not prepared to take back the reservations I had about your work when I first wrote to you. There is an uneasiness of style in this story that may prevent its selling, or that you may be able to correct after a while. But I feel it represents a considerable step forward in your development, and wanted you to know my feeling.

I'll look forward to receiving your permission to show this story to some of the editors whose opinions I believe will be valuable to you.

Sincerely,

Rachel Pemberton."

Steve wrote the note of acceptance hurriedly and sealed it in an envelope. He would mail it in the morning, but he wanted desperately to forget what Rachel Pemberton had said about the story. He knew how easily the slightest hope of income from his writing would delude him, reduce him to sweating out from day to day a check that might easily never appear.

But in the following days the letter was almost continuously in his mind. He did not know what magazines paid for stories, but surely if anybody bought this one, it would be a considerable help to the growing predicament of his finances. For one thing, he needed more clothes for his job—more than he could bring himself to buy out of his salary. The couple from whom he sublet the cottage could return at any time, and he would be forced to find a new place to live that would be almost certainly more expensive than this one. His accounts at three different liquor stores had run into figures that made him queasy. But again he suppressed the prayer. He had made his own difficulties. He had run up the liquor bills of his own free will during his celebratory binge. He would not be such a fool or a weakling as to complain about it now.

He had begun to correspond with his mother and father in Houston—at first awkwardly, then more warmly as he was able to tell them news of his selling job, his writing, and older news of what had happened to him in the Navy. They implored him to come home to Houston, if only to visit, and he began to want to see them again. As his rehabilitation progressed, the wish grew keener. Twice he called them long distance, and the sound of those ever-familiar voices had made him weep. Hoping to sell enough to earn a round-trip visit to Houston, he threw himself determinedly into his work.

As the weeks passed, discouragement overtook him. All his salary had to go to current bills. He could not get ahead, much less consider trips to Texas or a larger wardrobe. He began to wait for word from Rachel Pemberton. She had not written in two weeks, and that could only mean that *someone* was still considering the story. He read articles in writers' magazines and began to try to estimate how much he might be paid.

His increased efforts for Fred Isaacs rewarded him little. Much as he needed money, he found himself continually developing too personal an interest in people he met rather than in his job. After a few determined remarks about appliances, he would find himself talking with them about their work, their families, their stores, and sometimes they would invite him into their homes. On more than one occasion he forgot entirely to mention appliances again until he realized an hour had passed and he was late for his next call, and once a dealer in farm equipment had to avert his hurried exit in order to find out how much value Steve would give him on his stock of old model gas ranges if he bought ten new ones. His volume of sales became progressively worse and the realization made his cheeks blister with shame. The only thing that prevented his being fired was Fred Isaacs' friendship with Ben Verges.

In March he was no better off. He turned from the wet-slick highway into the Beach Cove Road and shortly pulled up before his cottage. He sat at the wheel, without moving, exhausted and discouraged. During his lunch hour that day he had written three pages of notes about a buyer he'd spent the morning with, and now in his head he carried enough impressions of his afternoon prospect's family to fill another page. But he had sold nothing.

"Oh, those days happen to all of us," one of the other salesmen had told him when he checked in at the Isaacs warehouse at five. "Not often, but they happen." Steve was well aware that to date no fewer than a dozen had happened to *him*.

"Try hitting the road earlier in the morning!" he encouraged. "Seven to nine are the golden hours in the farming areas."

At home he dragged himself from the car, found his latchkey and opened the cottage door. His heart stopped when he switched on the lights.

Under his left foot was a letter. It bore Rachel Pemberton's return address. He took one breath and snatched it up, hurrying over to the couch to sit down. He ripped open the envelope, tearing an edge of the paper in his haste. But then he stopped himself.

For the first time he realized how he had been counting on the information in this letter. Was there a check neatly stapled to the page of letterhead? Or was the page a polite, warm-voiced notice of regret? Of a sudden he had no strength to drag the letter from its envelope. He had hoped too much, too far forgotten the chances that no check would be inside. He must face the possibility—the *probability*—of that being the case, and brace himself against the stabbing disappointment.

Taking another breath, slowly he drew the letter out.

The scent of new springtime in the larger cities brought art lovers out as though from hibernation. Zeeda Kaufman found the sidewalk exhibits beginning in New Orleans when she arrived there, the paintings and charcoals propped against the old iron fence of Jackson Square. And far away in Chicago on that bright afternoon, a harassed schoolteacher herded a dozen of her pupils through a museum tour. Resentment sprang up in her chest at the sight of a couple smiling at the trouble the children were making for her, but it receded when she noted what a good-looking couple they were. A tall and strong-featured man escorting a slim young woman whose clothes, though simple enough, had a look of elegance. The schoolteacher studied her for the instant her charges were quiet: the young woman's hair, worn straight and brushed to a gloss, framed her face as with a delicate gesture, but it was her posture that made her clothes look expensive, which the schoolteacher decided they weren't. The young woman had beautiful posture, and she moved with an easy grace as the man with her led her out of the museum.

Helen Maclean and Sprague Burrell had been most of the afternoon luxuriating in the fresh warmth of the first clear day of spring, and stopping off at the museum for half an hour had been an impromptu part of their schedule. They went on to an early dinner at a new restaurant Sprague had heard about, and afterward they sought the quiet of the apartment Sprague kept on Lake Shore Drive.

When they had first become lovers, Helen had known little about Sprague Burrell, and in the interim had learned little more. During the war he had had a desk job with the Navy and had remained in Chicago throughout his term of service. He managed no business of his own, but had an interest in half a dozen companies in Chicago. He commuted daily to the city via the "North Shore haul," except when engagements made it more convenient for him to stay over at the apartment. He and his wife had been estranged for many years, but they still lived together in the same house. Helen gathered that together they maintained a certain social position, but Sprague did not say so. He had no intention of divorcing his wife as long as their relationship remained reasonably cordial. He had told Helen nothing more about her.

When Sprague's man Joseph had mixed drinks for them

and left the room, Sprague went to the desk and brought out an opened envelope.

"I've something to show you, Helen," he said, drawing a chair near to hers. "I wrote to these people to see what it was all about, and they sent me this brochure."

The pamphlet put forward the advantages of studying at a secretarial school teaching the accepted accomplishments of typing and filing as well as a method of shorthand called Speedwriting.

"It may have been something they developed in the war, I don't actually know," Sprague commented. "It sounds very useful."

"I should think so," Helen said. "Why did you write off for it?"

"Well, you don't want to go to college, and I don't think you want to go on working behind a counter. Look at yourself, the very idea is ridiculous. For one thing, you can't earn enough money that way to support yourself properly."

Helen's cheeks flushed. "I think I'm doing perfectly fine——"

"Of course you are, Helen, I didn't mean anything critical." Sprague hastened to palliate. "But I have a plan. You shouldn't be behind a counter, you should be in the business world. You'd do well at it, and I think you'd like it. You're intelligent, you're exceptionally efficient, and you have an impressive amount of energy. I've discovered that much in the months I've known you. If you want to get into business, this would be a quick and direct way of doing it."

"Do you really think I'd make a good secretary?"

"Of course you would," Sprague said. "Helen, it could make all the difference in the world to you. The social orders are changing. And every time the old orders break down, new ones form. You'll want the assets necessary to take your place in the world as it's going to be now; a successful business career can give you those assets. Look, it's the heart of your plan to pull yourself up by your bootstraps, you've been learning a great deal about the fine things—as much as I've been able to teach you, at least. How can you enjoy that knowledge without the wherewithal to exercise it? This is a sound first step, and I could help you to it."

"Sprague, I couldn't quit my job, I have to support myself."

"Let me support you," he said.

"What?"

"You need capital to tackle the world the way you're trying to do, and I've got capital. I've had young friends before whom I've helped. Pride is a wonderful thing, but it can play you false."

"But how do I know I'll ever make good in business?"

"You should see some of the women who have," said Sprague. Then: "It would be a nuisance for both of us if you were to live month to month on presents from me. This would be an outright grant, enough for a year, which is more than you're likely to need. I offer it because I believe in you. I think your determination and your ambition are exciting things, and you deserve the chance. The money would be in your own bank account, you understand, the whole sum. It wouldn't be affected in any way by our relationship. I mean, if you tired of me or found someone else——"

"Don't say that——"

"It's always possible, my angel."

"Would you let me think about it?"

"Of course. Take your time. Keep that brochure and look it over."

"I know right now I couldn't do it unless you'd let me pay you back."

"All right. Pay me back when you've been launched. I won't give a damn if you don't, or aren't able to, but I'll agree if you'll accept my plan."

Helen looked at the brochure and then at Sprague again. "You're so good, Sprague," she said. "I wish I could show you how much I appreciate this."

Sprague took her hand and kissed her lightly.

"You do," he said. "Every time you look at me that way."

16

TWO WEEKS LATER HELEN STARTED HER classes at the Speedwriting school. Excited by the prospect of more lucrative endeavor, she brought to her courses an enthusiasm that her instructors found impressive. In addition, she realized that she had a distinct aptitude for the work, and the surprising discovery of talent in herself—of any kind of talent—was stimulating. At the end of the first month she was able to tell Sprague, "Mr. Dakin—he's the one who places the graduates—he says if I keep up as I've been doing, he'll be able to place me at an absolutely top salary for a beginner."

"Good for you," Sprague said. "Don't commit yourself to anything too soon. There's someone I want you to meet. A friend of mine named Irene Lister."

"Oh? Who is she?" Helen asked.

"A lady who likes her career more than her social position. When she divorced her husband—oh, that was years ago—she opened an agency. An agency for night-club entertainers—that was her downfall socially, not that she ever gave a damn about it. I suppose I'm the only friend of her youth she still sees, but we're very fond of one another. I think you and Irene would work well together."

When Helen was nearing the end of her course, Sprague arranged for Irene Lister to join them for dinner one evening. She was not a beautiful woman, but she had the attractiveness of a quick mind and a warmly cordial manner. In the beginning of their discussion Helen said little; Sprague took it upon himself to tell Irene Lister about her, and Irene in turn told Helen about the agency.

"Actually it wasn't the first business I went into," she said. "At first I started a dress shop, but it was profitless and I cleared out in six months. The night-club business didn't really attract me, but the profits I heard about did. The first year with the agency was ghastly, but ever since we've been thriving. I have half a dozen assistants and clerks; if the work interested you, we could always make room for one more. Suppose we were to put it on a trial basis: you see if you like the work and we see whether we like you."

"That sounds fair enough," said Helen. "You understand I'll be even more uninformed about the field than you were when you started."

"You'll learn fast enough." The older woman smiled.

"If I don't," said Helen, "I wouldn't want you to keep me on just because of . . ." She hesitated.

"Because of Sprague? I wouldn't, I promise. I couldn't afford to."

Sprague put in, "What are Helen's opportunities in the future, Irene? Can she go very far on your staff?"

"As far as Louise," Irene said. She turned back to Helen.

"Louise is my personal assistant, one of those gems you hear about. She'll be a great help to you in learning the business. The highest that leaves for you to go is handling some of the clients yourself, especially the younger and newer ones, finding new talent that you can attract to the agency."

"I'm already excited about it." Helen grinned.

"Call me when you've finished the Speedwriting courses. If reports on your achievements there are still so glorious, I'm sure we can work something out."

That summer was the summer of shortages. Meat shortages, housing shortages, liquor shortages. As though reverting to ancient folkways in time of challenge, the people of the United States found themselves bartering like the wiliest of early Yankees. A car could get you an apartment; an apartment, a car. If you bought wine or gin or rum in sufficient quantities, you might be able to get a little Scotch out of the dealer. Willingly or not, many people ate venison as they schemed their trading schemes, and of every neighborhood islet the butcher was the lord. Mark Antony Cusimano, back at this father's meat counter, broadened the base the peacetime fortune he intended to make by selling meat by the piece rather than by the pound; and no one dared complain except with rueful humor.

From the summer of shortages, the nation went reeling into an autumn of surplus. But it was not the joyous abundance the goddesses of plenty might have thought. Millions throughout the world still had to hunger and wait until it was decided how to handle the vast overload of grain. U.N.R.R.A. was dying. In the daily newspapers the overgrown responsibilities of an unready, too-simple people informed each headline, and in many voices was a nervous awe when the daily events of Government were talked about. In the never-alleviated tension of Washington it was felt by many that scandal at high levels must eventually break out. It did so resoundingly.

Henry A. Wallace was the Secretary of Commerce when Roosevelt died and Harry S. Truman became President. Of men it was a curious juxtaposition. Facing the stubbornly practical empiricist, the lifelong student of the business of government, was the idealist whose optimism, hope and naïveté drew strength from, and could not be comprehended outside of, the concept of the soil of his country. In March President Truman had appointed Walter Bedell Smith United States Ambassador to the Soviet Union, and Secretary Wallace had written to the President:

"The events of the past few months have thrown the Soviets back to their pre-1939 fears of 'capitalist encirclement' and to their erroneous belief that the Western World, including the U.S.A., is invariably and unanimously hostile. I think we can disabuse the Soviet mind and strengthen the faith of the Soviets in our sincere devotion to the cause of peace. . . ."

These sentiments came to the hand of the man who in the face of repeated ill will and intransigence on the part of Russia had told his Secretary of State, James Byrnes; "I do not think we should play compromise any longer. I'm tired of babying the Soviets." The President dismissed the note from the Secretary of Commerce.

Henry Wallace did not remain silent through the summer, but though the views he publicly expressed were at variance with the President's known policy toward the Soviet Union, they were patently the feelings of a sincere and honorable man. On September 10, Secretary Wallace, who had been away from Washington for a number of weeks, spoke to President Truman for fifteen minutes, primarily on the business of the Department of Commerce. On September 12, he said, he was to deliver a speech in New York, and briefly indicated he would plea for an American view of the current international situation as opposed to the customary anti-Russia, pro-England sympathy of many voluble Americans. At this time James Byrnes was at a meeting of foreign ministers in Paris, engaged in the most delicate negotiations with the representatives of the Soviet Union, negotiations which the least hint of imperfect support from Byrnes' Government could irreparably disrupt. In this climate Henry Wallace delivered at Madison Square Garden his speech—a violent and unequivocal attack on the Government's foreign policy. The reaction throughout Washington and in Government offices abroad was explosive. Was Wallace openly breaking from his superior? Was the official American policy about to take a new direction as outlined by Wallace? In Paris the situation of James Byrnes had become intolerable. To the President he sent the message:

"If it is not possible for you, for any reason, to keep Mr. Wallace, as a member of your Cabinet, from speaking on foreign affairs, it would be a grave mistake from every point of view for me to continue in office, even temporarily."

From Wallace the President managed to extract a promise that no more speeches would be delivered until after the Foreign Ministers' Conference. Acting Secretary of State Will Clayton repeatedly conferred with the President at the White House. From Paris no further word was forthcoming. On the morning of September 30, the President called Henry Wallace at his office:

"I am sorry, but I have reached the conclusion that it will be best that I ask for your resignation."

"If that is the way you want it, Mr. President," came the answer, "I will be happy to comply."

The outbreak of conflict within the Government heightened the growing fear that Russia would soon develop its own atomic bomb and be in a position to use it against the West. The resolution and terrierlike persistence of the President could not alone unite the nation in a determination to assume the responsibility of initiative in the world's complex dealings. The Department of State split over the matter of United States policy in China.

The daily-repeated shocks and confusions of the political world moved counterpoint to a nation-wide drama of torrential flux and disorganization. The mobility of masses of the population showed no sign of slowing down. In the nightmare shell game of shortage and surplus, sudden, elusive prosperity touched some. Others, seeking it, hunting it, kept on the move. In circles of friendship everywhere new faces appeared and old ones faded out so quickly that, twice meeting, individuals had the impression they were devoted companions of long standing. There was not much time to ask questions about the new face at the party, the new family next door. They came from Somewhere; they were seeking Roots. They might, just might, stay for a while, might on the other hand suddenly move on their way. Before he had time to inquire about them, a young father found his own quest taking him off to distant cities and his progress shifting him abruptly from one social level to another.

That summer the radios played songs from Irving Berlin's *Annie Get Your Gun.* The sales of folk music record albums rose, and the gangling new generation studied the ground and wondered where its roots might be. On November 13 the hungry the world over were worrying about what was to become of the vast surpluses of food, and on the same day the Atomic Energy Commission, with David Lilienthal its chairman, met for its lead-off inspection of the plant at Oak Ridge, Tennessee. That same week people who had read the previous week's issue of *The New Yorker* magazine discussed a story in it by a writer no one had heard of.

By the time the magazine appeared, Steve Williams had put the story from his mind. As his first published effort, it had personal meaning to him, but not in any other way. Even in Hilda Verges' mind it had receded to its proper position as a magazine tale one might read and perhaps someday read again—it was no longer the painful examination of her own character it had at first been. Too much had happened to them both since *The New Yorker* had bought the story. Steve had written half a dozen more stories and Rachel Pemberton had sold two of them. Only yesterday he had received a check for a third. Embarrassed by exploiting Fred Isaacs' friendship for Ben Verges, he had resigned from his job with the appliance dealer at the first opportunity. With the money he received from the first story sale, he had paid off the bills at the village stores and bars and had returned an old loan to Ben. The couple from whom he had sublet the beach cottage came back to Beach Cove, and for a few weeks he had been able to rent a relatively expensive apartment in Los Angeles. He had disliked the arrangement, and he had leaped gratefully at the opportunity when the Vergeses had asked him to come and live in the unused playroom on the first floor of their house overlooking the village of Beach Cove. Another check had come from Rachel Pemberton's office, and he had bought himself some clothes. Still foremost in his mind was the plan to go home to Houston for a visit, and when still another check arrived and his bankbook showed he had enough to live on for a year or more if he lived sensibly, the plan extended itself in his thinking to a longer sojourn with his family.

He had been working in his room since nine o'clock that November morning, except for half an hour's lunch with Ben, and by two o'clock had completed yet another revision of a troublesome sequence in the novella he was currently working on. His room, on the opposite side of the house from the terrace, overlooked the graveled parking area and its blinding glare in the afternoon sunlight. He left his desk and went to sit nervously in the armchair by the windows.

Rachel Pemberton was coming to see him. He had an hour before her arrival. At his elbow was the thermos of black coffee he had brought back with him from lunch, and he poured out the last half-cup and lit a cigarette. The sun's brilliance on the gravel of the parking area drew his eye. It had been earlier in the year the first time he'd come to the Verges house. August: the end of the war. To Steve it seemed long ago. That day he remembered well. The house had been overflowing with people, fully half of them unknown to the host and hostess, a meaningless carousel of drinking and talk. There had been no such parties there in many months now. Steve's friendship and Steve's work had given Hilda's life a spine it had not had since her youth, and the noisy, hungry, callous young people had been cut loose.

For his own part, Ben Verges was relieved, and grateful to Steve for the change. He had made a point of telling Steve so. He had indulged Hilda's need even if the young people had cared nothing about her, but the atmosphere always had saddened and disturbed him. The return of quiet to his house, according to Ben Verges, was a blessing.

That first day, Steve reflected, he had himself been miserable with timidity, aware of the contemptuous glances of the older people. It was not to be wondered that they—unlike Hilda—had at first grouped him with the other shouting, drunken kids. He *had* been one of them. He drew on his cigarette and exhaled the smoke into the room. The Vergeses contemporaries still came to cocktails or dinner from time to time, but now, thank God, they accepted him as one of the family—the only family, for that matter, that Ben and Hilda had. They still were not much interested in him, but they were gratified for Ben and Hilda's sake that his work, which Hilda had made so much a part of her emotional life, was beginning to succeed, to pay back the convictions Hilda had had in the beginning about the curious young man who came to her parties and drank too much.

So long ago, Steve thought. At least now he could think in kindly and familiar terms of the few friends Ben and Hilda still entertained. Ben and Hilda?—they were friends dearer and closer to him than any acquaintances of his own age could have been. He did not ask himself why this was so. He accepted it, as he accepted with gratitude his presence in their house.

He drained his coffee cup, stood up, and moving to the center of the room, started to do exercises to loosen the muscles cramped by his hours at the desk. Two minutes of exercises nowadays sufficed, and he stretched out full length on the floor till his breath came back.

In this same room he had first met Zeeda Kaufman. What had become of her, he didn't know. He remembered still—not romantically, but because her very vividness was not easily forgotten by anyone—the first words they had exchanged. The first hours alone together in the cottage on the beach. It was almost difficult for him to believe now that he himself had been that disoriented, miserable, self-preoccupied mental case. So much had changed. No trouble with his memory now, no anxiety about his income, no sick grasping after love. All his troubles had resolved themselves into his work, his friendship for Ben and Hilda, his excitement in anticipating the gratifications and challenges of the career ahead of him. Hadn't they? He wasn't misleading himself, was he? How many men supported themselves by the work they were really interested in? He had won the chance, and that good fortune organized his life so that the rootless pain and terrors dripped away. Fortune wouldn't turn back on him again, would it? No, it wasn't possible, once you were in, once you were on your way. . . .

There was the crunch of wheels on gravel from the parking area outside. Steve jumped up and went back to the window. He could see Hilda hurrying out from the house as the car pulled to a stop, wildly waving a welcome. Rachel Pemberton climbed out from behind the wheel, and the two women embraced one another with loud incomprehensible cries of glee.

Rachel Pemberton was in no way what he had expected.

A neat, round little woman, from the distance of his window she looked—he hesitated at the ludicrous concept—motherly. He had expected an agent to look sharp, hard, shrewd. Rachel Pemberton could be all these things, Steve knew, but she did not look the part. Her gray hair, faintly blued and loosely curled, was cut short. Her face was plump, and her smile as she stood chattering with Hilda was of a radiant sweetness. Ben came out and took a suitcase out of the back of her car, and the three of them started toward the house.

Steve went into his bathroom, threw cold water on his face and ran a comb hurriedly though his hair. Then, leaving the room, he walked quickly down the hall.

Hilda and Rachel Pemberton were sitting on the sofa, the excitement of their reunion not yet abated. "Here's Steve!" Hilda cried. "Steve, this is Rachel!"

Near at hand she was even more maternal-looking, and her eyes had a birdlike brightness of expression. Her voice when she spoke, however, had the flat ring of the experienced businesswoman. She stood up and took his hand.

"Steve, how nice meeting you face to face at last," she said. "What a good-looking young man you are. From the stories I couldn't form an impression. Not that it's the sort of question I dwell on."

"Did you have a nice trip out?" Steve asked.

"Fine, thank you."

"Sit down, both of you, sit down," said Hilda.

Ben had deposited the suitcase in the guest room and was now returning. "Something for the dust in your throat, Rachel?"

Rachel Pemberton sat down again and Steve took the chair nearest her.

"Water I would love. Nothing else. I'll wait till cocktail time."

"Steve? Hilda?"

"Let's have some Martinis," said Hilda. "I feel festive having Rachel back after all these years. Rachel, how's Hank?"

"In Europe, the louse. I would've gone with him but there was too much for me to do out here on the Coast. Guess who's on the boat with him? My brother!"

"No!" Hilda laughed.

In explanation Rachel turned to Steve. "My family are

Orthodox Jews, and when I married Hank, there was a practically irreparable breach. In Jewish families, you know, they have a funeral service for a daughter who marries a Gentile. Of course, with the years they grew reconciled to it, and we got back in their good graces, more or less." She turned back to Hilda. "But my brother and his family moved to New York two years ago, and he and Hank have gotten to be great buddies. It's an unexpected joy to my old age. But how are *you?* Ben looks wonderful, too."

"We're all in transports here this week since *The New Yorker.*"

"Happy about it?" Rachel asked Steve.

"Yes, certainly. And thanks to you."

"I wrote you about the *Cosmopolitan* sale?"

"Your office sent the check yesterday," Steve said.

"They're looking forward to seeing the novella. How's it coming?"

"Another month or so should finish it," he answered. "A draft of it, anyway."

Ben served the Martinis, and they toasted Rachel's health.

"Oh, by the way," she said to Hilda, "don't let that suitcase scare you. I brought something to change into for dinner, but after dinner I have to drive back to Los Angeles."

"Oh, Rachel——"

"I'm sorry, too, but it's important."

"Can you manage to come for a day or two before you go back to New York?" Ben asked.

"I'm certainly going to try."

Ben asked after mutual friends of theirs, and Rachel and the Vergeses fell to exchanging news of shared acquaintances. The talk was relaxed, nostalgic, and amiable, and Steve knew he had no place in it.

"Odd," Rachel said, when Ben and Hilda had left them alone. "I'm so glad to meet you for the first time in some place that isn't my office. You've never been there. It's really quite attractive, but there's a kind of—oh, ritual about it. I never wanted it that way, but I've been forced to develop it through the years simply as a means of carrying on business with some effectiveness. Out here I'm high and dry."

"You mean flanks of secretaries a guy has to get through?"

"Oh, no," Rachel laughed outright. "Much more fiendish." Her twinkling eyes lingered on the middle distance as she pictured it for him. "I have a chair that fits my desk. It's rather erect. Anyone coming to see me sits in a very beautiful sort of 'lounge' chair I brought back from Sweden one summer. The poor visitor is much lower than I am, so I have an overpowering effect that a five-foot-two woman seldom has." She laughed again. "I really didn't plan it that way, but when I saw how the chair worked, I decided I'd be foolish to change it. And then, when young writers come to see me—I'm fond of all of them, you understand; I've always loved people who had the courage to go into writing as a lifetime profession—very often they're shy and tongue-tied, so I've developed a trick of talking endlessly. Oh, I'll be thinking of important things—of them, for instance, or whatever work of theirs I'm trying to market at the moment—but from me there's never a moment of silence. Here, in Hilda and Ben's lovely house, miles from the nearest publisher's contract, there *can* be a moment of silence. There will be. I'll shut up."

"Oh, please, no," said Steve. "This is a hell of a lot of new territory for me, I like hearing about it."

"You've never lived in New York?"

"No, I haven't."

"And I don't think you've ever had another agent?"

"No," said Steve.

Rachel smiled again, this time with an inner warmth that had nothing of business practicality about it. "You told me in one of your letters you'd been writing for ages. What have you done with what you wrote?"

"Nothing. I got early into a habit of writing things, I guess, but they were about as accomplished as a schoolboy's love letters. I wrote a lot when I first was in the Navy—you know, new experiences, new impressions. Then I was taken ill."

"What about that? Hilda's referred to it. It crops up once in a while in the stories."

"Little to tell," said Steve evenly. He downed the rest of his Martini. "A wartime incident, and my memory kind of went back on me for a while."

She was watching him then, and all her faculty for discernment was in her large maternal eyes. "You *lost* your memory, you mean?" she said.

"Only temporarily."

"Tell you what," she said brightly, "this room doesn't tell me anything about you. Would you show me where *you* live?"

Steve stood up. "Sure. Would you like some more water?"

"No, thanks, I'm fine. Lead on."

When he opened the door to his room, Rachel stopped just across the threshold. Without awkwardness, she stood quite still, observing the gray of the walls, the three of four Van Gogh and El Greco reproductions, the desk, the bed, the chest of drawers. Then she saw the chair by the windows, and going directly to it, she sat down. Steve pulled up a straight chair and sat facing her, putting his Martini on the window sill.

It was in the act of entering his quarters and sitting in his favorite chair that Rachel Pemberton had suddenly become once again the businesswoman.

"A very nice room," she said briskly. "I hope you're satisfied with the job I've been doing on your stories. And my staff, of course. I must tell you that my wonderful assistant, Lisa Bowen, sold the last story very much on her own."

Steve avoided her gaze. He did not like her sudden switch, and he felt uncomfortably on the defensive.

"How long have you and Hilda and Ben been friends?" she asked.

"Since the end of the war," said Steve. He offered nothing more, sensing a gambit.

Rachel leaned back expressively in the armchair. "We've known one another for years—they're delightful people. I hope you realize what a contribution you've made to their lives. I could hear it in their letters, I could see it when I arrived today."

"I think I know about Hilda's life, yes," said Steve. "Ben's been a good-natured sonuvabitch about it, but I hardly think my existence has meant a great deal of difference to him."

For a moment there was something about Rachel that made him regret having used "sonuvabitch," but then the directness of her glance froze him. "I'd have thought you'd have realized how much he loves her," she said.

Steve blushed.

"Sure—sure, he does." He gestured, but it was not enough. "I liked the books you were kind enough to send me," he said, going over to the bookshelves on the wall in front of her.

"It was interesting to see what other writers—kinds of writers—you represented." It was a move of desperation. She must have known, yet she said nothing.

Steve drew on his cigarette. Under her scrutiny, the room, he felt, was growing quickly airless. It was his room, after all. He looked at her, angrily, now; and when her gaze refused to be unbent, but continued bland and undeterred, surveying him, Steve smashed his cigarette out in the nearest ash tray.

"*I* know why you're a success!" he shouted, turning away from her. "You're a merciless bitch!"

Rachel laughed gently at him—a warm and soothing sound. "Good boy," she said. "You're no fool."

"I'm damn scared by your letters. I always was. You know that." He turned to face her full on, and she shifted in her chair with an air of composing herself.

"Okay, Steve," she said. "Go ahead."

"Ben and Hilda were so glad to see you, and you seemed so nice. But when you put on the professional smirk—these sales, for instance."

"Yes?" she said.

"What's happened the last few months, Rachel, it doesn't mean anything." Rachel's eyelids lowered briefly. "There's something flukey about it. It scares me. I want to be a writer, but I have to support myself. When I get scared, I've got to know whether I'm starting at a shadow or not."

"I see," she said.

"Well, that's all. I'm asking the truth, and it's important as hell to me."

He had done, and Rachel studied the round little hands in her lap for a long moment. Then, without looking at him, she cleared her throat and said, "I don't know anything to tell you except, yes, there's something very flukey about the few sales we've made." She paused. "Let me put it this way. The stories we've sold at least had originality. And luck was with you in the choice of subject matter in that story you wrote about Hilda."

"About Hilda? That story wasn't at all about——"

"Shut up, Hilda told me the whole deal," Rachel said easily. "But you're not yet experienced enough as a writer to pull it off consciously, deliberately, in story after story. You'll learn that eventually as you develop, if you study hard, but—well, I think you may have a number of years still in which you'll have to do something besides writing to provide yourself with an income. Not continuously, necessarily, but from time to time."

Steve sighed. "I was pretty sure that would be the case. I had to hear it from somebody else before I could accept it."

Rachel leaned forward suddenly in the armchair. "Don't let it discourage you, Steve."

"Oh, it won't," he answered. "Writing's a habit with me now, I wouldn't be able to live with myself without writing, even if it shouldn't pay."

"Good," said Rachel.

Steve sat down again in the straight chair. "There's another thing," he said. "I'm planning to visit my family in Houston soon. I haven't seen them since I got out of the Navy, and—I don't know, I think I need to see a lot of things again. Not just my folks, but a lot of people and places around home. Things I knew when I was little."

"I see."

"I've been thinking—I may spend some time writing about some of those things. What I write won't be of much interest to anybody else, I don't guess, but I have a feeling it may be of value to me in a personal way."

"I think I understand," said Rachel, "but permit me to be the judge of what will interest other people. Can your family support you while you're there?"

"Oh, no," he answered. "I'll get a job so I can hold onto what I've earned so far. I wouldn't mind spending a year writing things that couldn't be sold, if they were important to me in some other way. But maybe you would mind."

"Me?"

"I mean, handling a non-money-making writer."

"Don't be foolish," said Rachel. "I think making money's fine, but at your age the most vital thing for you, and for your writing, in the long run, is to grow and develop the best way you know how. If there's something about yourself you're trying to find by going back home . . ." She stopped. "Is that more or less the direction of your thinking?"

"I guess," Steve frowned at the floor.

"Then go ahead and do it. Don't rush yourself. No career is as important as personal happiness. Believe me, I've been a career girl a very long time, I know."

"Fine, then," said Steve.

Rachel stood up, and Steve followed suit.

"I want to bathe and change for dinner," she said. "I'll leave you alone now." She went to the door, but stopped with her hand on the knob. She looked at him a moment over her shoulder. "You might write some quite good things about your life in Houston. Childhood's a rich soil for a writer, as everyone damn well knows."

17

AT SIX O'CLOCK THE FOUR OF THEM HAD a drink together and then went in to dinner. Hilda had decorated the dining room by grouping small cactus plants in the middle of the large Spanish refectory table and arranging gourds and apples on the sideboard; the sweet heavy smell of the Mexican candles hung in the air. Through the meal Hilda led the conversation with vivacity.

"Of course some wonderful young writers have come out of the war, but will they last, that's what I ask myself. What do you think, Rachel?"

"Some of them will, I'm sure," Rachel said. "But I don't think they're the important element to look to. The Southerners' vogue is going to go on a long time. I don't know why so many of the younger Southern writers do better work than their counterparts in other parts of the country, but I'm beginning to feel it's not them, it's us. The reading public is growing hungrier every day for a substantial *folk* literature, and the Southerners supply it. By the ream." Her eyes met Steve's, and she smiled. "Whether Texas qualifies as *South,* I don't quite know."

"But of course Texas is South!" Hilda objected. "Isn't it, Ben? Steve can write the pants off those other Southern people——"

Ben cleared his throat loudly. "Team loyalty," he murmured to Rachel.

By the time dessert was served, Hilda had cut to ribbons every talented new writer the other three could call to mind. "Did you tell Rachel about visiting Houston?" Hilda suddenly asked. "I don't know why that name doesn't stimulate my imagination more, but it doesn't. Not nearly as much as New Orleans, Charleston, Atlanta——"

"It's because Texas *isn't* the South," Ben put in mildly.

"Perhaps," said Rachel, "Steve will make it more appealing to us in his stories." Then to Steve: "You should be able to write quite a lot of them, Steve, if you stay there a considerable length of time."

"But I thought you'd just . . ." Hilda began. She stopped, mystified. "How long *are* you going to stay there, Steve?"

"I haven't made up my mind one way or another—whether I should plan on a longer stay, or just a week or two with the family."

"I see." Hilda nodded. "Well. . . . How about out having a brandy in the living room? Everyone ready?"

They adjourned to the living room and were served coffee and brandy. Ben told Rachel of a recent encounter he'd had with a mutual friend of theirs, and Hilda sat silent and thoughtful while he talked. Later she said to Rachel, "Rachel, do *you* think going back to Houston in a big way might be good for Steve in the long run?"

"I don't know," Rachel answered. "I think it's his own business." She gave Steve a glance. "I think his decision will be a wise one."

Hilda studied him a moment.

"Well. Maybe it would be, Steve. Your mother and father must miss you terribly, God knows. Maybe you should've gone back before now."

Steve answered as gently as he could. "No, it wouldn't have been good before now. Either for the family or for me. I told Rachel this afternoon—I was thinking that staying there awhile might help me get my bearings again after all the changes that've been going on in my life the last three years."

"Yes . . ." said Hilda. "God, but it's going to be dull around here."

Steve noticed that quite unobtrusively Ben had managed to be at Hilda's side. He put a quiet hand on her shoulder now and smiled at Steve.

"You'll come back sooner or later, won't you, Steve?" he asked.

"Of *course* he will——"

Ben interrupted her calmly. "Young people have to go their own ways, Hilda. We can't cling."

Mercifully Hilda's vanity asserted itself with a violence they could laugh at. "Cling! I've never clung to a pair of pants in my entire life. Isn't that so, Rachel?"

"Yes, dear."

"Steve, that woman's got a dirty mind, look out for her."

"I will," Steve nodded, his throat constricted.

They were able to chat desultorily then, and in an hour Rachel Pemberton took her leave.

After the car had driven out of sight, Hilda went off to bed and Ben and Steve mixed a nightcap for themselves. They sat down at opposite ends of the sofa to drink it. They were silent several minutes before Ben spoke.

"You've got to get tough with yourself if you feel bad when—events take you away from us."

Steve, troubled, blurted out, "Ben, I'll be back."

Ben made a patient quieting gesture with one hand. "Sure you will," he said. "I only mean, sooner or later your life will take you away from here, maybe for good. It's been wonderful for Hilda, this writing adventure. But she's got to step aside—for your family, for a wife someday. She's not going to resent that, or let it get her down. So don't you, either. I have a feeling this has done something for her that —what I mean is, what it's done is going to last. Almost as if she'd had a son to be proud of, instead of a friend we're both proud of. I feel it in my bones, Steve."

Steve said nothing because there was nothing he could think of to say. To his humiliation he felt his eyes smarting suddenly. He gulped at his drink. He searched for words that would not embarrass Ben.

"Then on the other side there's *my* account," he said. "Knowing you and Hilda. Having you be my friends. I guess I can't say I don't deserve it because you're not such a fool as to give so much of yourself to somebody who's not worth it, Ben." He took a breath and the words rushed out. "The minute I'm married I'm gonna knock up my wife and have twins, a boy and a girl, and name them for you and Hilda."

He was on his feet spontaneously, not looking at the balding little man. "See you at breakfast," he said. And he hurried out of the room. At the other end of the dark hall, at the door of his own room, he stopped, wondering whether he'd been too abrupt, whether or not he should go back. Then in the quiet of the house he heard Ben Verges humming contentedly to himself and rattling the ice cubes in his glass.

The new isolationism championed by Henry Wallace, and its unreserved opposition to the foreign policy of the Truman Administration, attracted a following that disrupted and divided political alignments and relationships in the passing months of the winter. Aggravating this situation was the fact that the Administration's foreign policy was not a policy at all, but a mode of behavior toward the Soviet Union; faced with the divided sentiments of the nation, the Administration had made public no firm over-all attitude toward the erstwhile ally. Circumstances now made a manner-of-conduct blatantly inadequate.

Since the withdrawal of German troops in September of 1944, Greece had lain in a ruin of starvation, dissension, and apathetic leadership. Poland and her neighbors in Eastern Europe had become the colonial Soviet Union by virtue of occupation by Russian troops. Yugoslavia, Bulgaria, and Albania formed the southern frontier of that camp, and immediately to the south of them Greece breathed with difficulty. Her only deterrent to the encroachment of Communism was the presence on Greek soil of forty thousand British soldiers, her only hope for continued freedom, the advice and encouragement of the British Government. To this bulwark was added the aid and counsel of Paul Porter, former United States administrator of the Office of Price Administration. He headed an economic mission to the beleaguered country, and his arrival there in large part made possible the stunning alteration of the face that his own Government presented to the world.

On February 3, 1947, the United States ambassador cabled from Athens of the talk that England intended withdrawing her soldiers from Greece. Only incredulity could meet such a report: if Greece were left as open as a sleeping virgin to the assault of Communism, it would mean the establishment of the Soviet Union's empire at the eastern end of the Mediterranean Sea. Once the ravaging power had embraced the Greeks, Turkey, free for the moment, would be left an indefensible island in the raging of the Russian tide. On February 12 Ambassador MacVeagh pleaded with his superiors to supply immediate aid to Greece. Nor, the President knew, would stopgap handouts serve: $250,000,000 for Greece, $150,000,000 for Turkey, and that was the price of only the moment's holding of position. The price was being exacted, moreover, from a country with a distaste for foreign obligations bordering on the pathological, whose traditional abhorrence of such obligations had been in the main but dimly lessened by the experience of the war. On Friday, February 21, the Department of State learned officially from England that that country would withdraw its troops from Greece no later than April 1; England had, however her allies might pale, found it impossible to fulfill her commitment there. The Administration faced the one alternative of letting Greece and Turkey, free and independent nations, stand alone to meet the deluge. On the other hand, a decision to come to the aid of these two countries would commit the Administration to an unchangeable position of defiance toward the desires of the Soviet Union, not to mention subjecting it to the outcries of the unlearning and unteachable within the ranks of American citizens. No decision of this breadth could be made by the President without the consent of the House of Representatives, and the Democratic Administration faced a Congress no longer in its intramural control.

Midmorning on February 27 President Truman, in his office, presented the case to the Congressional leadership as represented by Barkley, Connally, Vandenburg, Rayburn, Bloom, Eaton, and Speaker of the House Martin. The specialist officers of the Department of State were set to work determining the particular extent of action the United States Government must take to meet the crisis in Greece. On March 7 the President thrashed out the implications of the crisis with his Cabinet. On March 10 he again met the Congressional leaders. On Wednesday, March 12, he was scheduled to address a joint session of the Congress and, through innumerable radios, the waiting nation at whose head he stood.

At one o'clock on Wednesdays the stores in country towns are often closed because their employees must be on hand to serve the farmers who come into town to buy and barter all day on Saturday. In the city offices you will frequently find a receptionist or a bookkeeper whose miniature radio brings her soft recorded music while she works. All these individuals were available for the broadcast. In many houses an address by the President is sufficient cause to turn the radio on at an unaccustomed hour, to postpone the racket of the vacuum cleaner, to tell the organizer for the Red Cross you will call her back. In Washington, D.C., there was nothing in any way unusual about a large and complex household falling to silence so that the broadcast might be heard with concentration. Such was the case at the house where Judge Ellis Cowan lived with his grown son and daughter.

Judge Cowan, a lean man of stately height whose thinning white hair relieved the sharpness of his long, fatless features, sat in his study alone, the Magnavox tuned to receive the broadcast from the joint session of the Congress. The household staff listened to their radio in the kitchen quarters. Michael Cowan was not at home, but Margaret Cowan, in her room on the third floor of the house, turned on her bedside radio and sat brushing her hair methodically while the hushed voice of the announcer introduced the broadcast.

No one in the Cowan house failed to register the new steeliness of the President's speech.

"I believe that it must be the policy of the United States," came the measured words, "to support free peoples who are resisting attempted subjugation by armed minorities or by outside pressures.

"I believe that we must assist free peoples to work out their own destinies in their own way.

"I believe that our help should be primarily through economic and financial aid which is essential to economic stability and orderly political processes."

Judge Cowan of course had known for several days what the intent of the address was to be. He listened now not only to the words of the President, but with a bemused expression to the silence behind it: before the rostrum in the House of Representatives the Congress sat listening. Was there an unaccustomed depth in their silence, a particular tension in their attentiveness? Judge Cowan wished he were there. What a moment, he thought, for that ill-tempered nobody.

"One way of life," the President continued, "is based upon

the will of the majority, and is distinguished by free institutions, representative government, free elections, guarantees of individual liberty, freedom of speech and religion and freedom from political oppression.

"The second way of life is based upon the will of a minority forcibly imposed upon the majority. It relies upon terror and oppression, a controlled press and radio, fixed elections, and the suppression of personal freedoms. . . . The seeds of totalitarian regimes are nurtured by misery and want. They spread and grow in the evil soil of poverty and strife. They reach their full growth when the hope of a people for a better life has died. We must keep that hope alive. The free peoples of the world look to us for support in maintaining their freedoms. If we falter in our leadership, we may endanger the peace of the world—and we shall surely endanger the welfare of our own nation."

What, Judge Cowan wondered, was Vito Marcantonio thinking now? And he turned the radio off.

Judge Cowan's dinner guests that evening were Senator O'Harra and his wife Ethel. The O'Harras had changed since coming to Washington. Secure in the recognition her husband was accorded in Washington as an able and conscientious young man, Ethel had lost a certain tautness of manner she had developed during the last months of the war. Her calmness and intelligence coupled now with the essential femininity of her nature to make of her one of the more attractive Senate wives. O'Harra on his part had smoothed out; his almost humorless sincerity set him apart from many of the complicated, overbred people who made up his circle of acquaintance within the Republican Party, but he wore his dinner clothes with assurance now, and his boisterous energy was emphatically controlled by a maturing sense of deportment.

Through dinner they talked of the effect of the President's address on the Congress, and O'Harra verified Judge Cowan's feeling about the special attentiveness the President's audience had given him.

"Whatever we thought of it, we knew it was a vital step he was taking," said O'Harra. "I saw Jim Forbes later, he referred to it as 'the Truman Doctrine.' "

They were not joined for dinner by the younger Cowans,

and after the meal, Ethel moved with the two men to the drawing room, where Judge Cowan gave them a liqueur and the maid served coffee. Before the fireplace was a coffee table, and surrounding it were a number of unusually low-built, sprawling upholstered chairs, covered with a material palely imitating the color of apricots. O'Harra and his wife sat near each other while the Judge settled down opposite them.

Ted O'Harra asked, "What do *you* think of sending aid to Greece, Judge?"

Judge Cowan puffed on his cigarette.

"Privately or politically?"

"Both."

"Privately I think the money would be wasted. If we are going to be an imperialist nation—the possibility has a certain appeal to my temperament—there are clearer and firmer ways. My experience of Russians hasn't indicated that they appreciate anything that isn't both clear and firm, not to say heavy-handed. Politically, I support the other leaders of the party in defending the bipartisan character of foreign policy. I can say that sentence so trippingly because I don't feel it and I've had to memorize it."

"Is that what you would advise me to do?" O'Harra asked. "Keep supporting bipartisanship?"

"Yes, I think I would. But I'm more interested in knowing what your own instinct would be to do."

O'Harra held a lighter to his wife's cigarette.

"I don't know. We're a rich country, but I can't see throwing money away. Don't get me wrong"—he raised a temporizing hand—"I've got no use for the isolationists in the Republican Party or for people of Wallace's stripe. And I can see that we're in a position now where we've *got* to take on the responsibility—and that means money as much as it does morals—the responsibility of leading the free countries. But hell, what's going to become of any money we send to Greece? You know as well as I do it's going to be burned up in a factional fracas within the country that doesn't have anything to do with Communism. I don't think the Europeans figure Russia is that much of a threat; they're still fighting the same theoretical squabbles they've *been* fighting for fifty years. I'm not against foreign aid that works, but I don't see how I'm going to bring myself to vote for prodigality."

"You'd better drink your coffee, Ted," Ethel soothed. "You know how talking makes you thirsty."

"I'm sorry," O'Harra said, "but I've been stewing about it all afternoon."

Judge Cowan said nothing for a moment. When he did, it was to offer them another liqueur. He filled the glasses and sat down again.

"I understand there's a measure of relief," he said, "about our new policy among some members of the diplomatic corps."

"I'll just bet," said O'Harra.

Judge Cowan raised his eyebrows and asked with a half-smile, "Is the diplomatic corps also getting your goat?"

"Well."

"Come on, Ted, out with it."

"I know you have a lot of friends among those people. . . ."

"Indeed I do," said Judge Cowan. "But you are also a friend of mine, you don't have to watch what you say in the privacy of my house."

O'Harra studied the Judge a moment. "The diplomatic piss me off," he admitted.

"Ted!" said Ethel.

"Well, they do, sir." He was on his feet then, fists plunged into his pockets, pacing the tiles in front of the fireplace. "I haven't been thinking about this today, I've been thinking about it for months. Maybe you'll say it's personal prejudice, but I think it goes further than that."

"What is it, Ted?" Judge Cowan continued.

"The diplomatic guys have inherited a protocol and a way of thinking from their European counterparts. Europeans have been in the business for centuries, and their way of doing things developed in an era of kings and emperors. The same values are being held today by our foreign service people. But the United States isn't a country of kings and emperors. It's a government of the people, and the people of America are by tradition honest and forthright. I think that in fact most of them are. It seems to me the people who represent us in other countries should reflect that."

"Thus trampling on all available toes?"

"If necessary, hell, yes! We're not the stepchild of Europe any more, why should we ape their standards?"

"You believe our men practice—duplicity? I presume that's what you want me to infer as the opposite of *forthright.*"

"I do." O'Harra stopped in his pacing. "I know one of our men who was educated abroad, whose oldest and dearest friends are with the diplomatic services of other countries. Countries we haven't always been friendly with. They're a goddamn fraternity, Judge; they grew up together; they've had friendships among themselves that have gone on through the years no matter what policies their countries went through toward one another. That guy who's trying to get our backing for a Romanian government-in-exile: he's a *known* unreconstructed Nazi, and he spends his weekends at the house of an important member of our own State Department. Maybe you don't think a friendship of long standing counts for so much with a man. I do."

Judge Cowan chuckled. "I can hit you even closer to home. My own son Michael counts as one of his intimates a young man who was an officer in Hitler's Elite Guard."

"That's what I mean, Judge," said O'Harra. "We *fought* the Nazis, and those of us who did the fighting didn't think it was a joke. And today we don't think Communism is a joke."

Judge Cowan nodded. "I can see that you would be very perturbed. I can't say that *I* am; I've been in politics too long—I lack the kind of sincerity you have that makes real indignation possible."

O'Harra sat down near Ethel again; he was calmer now, but his broad forehead under the dark hair was still marked with his frown.

"Much good any indignation of mine is going to do," he said. "I'd give my eye teeth to make the State Department an election issue instead of harping on the corruption of the Democrats the way everybody else is going to do. But I'm hamstrung by the bipartisan idea. Not only that, I don't have a dramatic hook to hang on to, a definite fact about the State Department I can make voters understand, impress them with."

Judge Cowan sipped at his liqueur.

"I'm not sure it wouldn't be too extreme an issue even if

you did," he said. He crossed his legs and put his glass down on the coffee table before him. "There is a lot of apathy in the country. People are tired of patriotism, tired of the war, and bored by all the juggling we've had to go through with the Soviets. They want to have fun."

"Fun!" O'Harra snorted.

"Yes, and do you know what they're doing increasingly? They're looking to *our* party as a symbol. To a lot of them, especially to the young, Republicanism spells the prosperity and partying of the nineteen twenties."

"But that's the most hairbrained, irresponsible——"

"You think I don't know it? Ted, I *am* the Republican Party, I *know* how hairbrained such a notion is. But I also know the facts. Look at my own children. Privilege, of course, a rich man's children, but not so different for all that from the common run of young people in America. How interested do you think *they* are in this vicious expansion of Russia's?"

O'Harra was soon to see for himself, for presently their conversation was interrupted by an explosion of noise and laughter in the entrance hall as a number of young people poured into the house, the men in dinner jackets, the girls in a swirling, giggling bouquet of evening dresses.

Judge Cowan stepped to the archway leading to the hall. "Margaret?"

"Daddy, I thought you were being out tonight!"

Margaret Cowan blew into the room, pulling her father with her. "Ethel, you're just the one I wanted to see! Oh, Ted, sit down, sit down! Daddy, we were at the *dullest* imaginable social thing, but nobody's hungry for dinner so we're going up to my sitting room and listen to records. We won't make a lot of noise."

Judge Cowan smiled with indulgent affection on the lovely bright-eyed girl. "I'm sure you won't. I'm also sure you will none of you even touch my liquor supply."

Margaret laughed and leaned her cheek against his shoulder. "In two hours there won't be a drop left in the house!" she assured him.

From the hallway came one couple's voices singing,

"Thou art sweet, thou art sort of grandish,
My outlandish
Cavalier . . ."

And a lone baritone competed with:

> "Maybe the sun gave me the power,
> For I could swim Loch Lomond and be home in
> Half an hour!"

"I'll get them upstairs at once!" Margaret promised. "Ethel, make Ted bring you upstairs when Daddy's finished boring him with politics. Daddy, did Michael come in yet?"

"I haven't seen him," said Judge Cowan.

"He's got a marvelous Argentinian, found him at the party. He said they'd meet us all here later. Well, tell him where we are if he shows." She stood on tiptoe to kiss her father's cheek. "And not *very* much noise, I promise you!" She started back to the hall, calling; "You people go on up, the elevator's right there off the side hall; I've got to drum up some ice. Hurry now, and be quiet till you're up there, it's the third floor!"

And she was gone. The voices of the young people faded, and presently they could hear the elevator starting up. Judge Cowan sighed and came back to the O'Harras, his smile lingering on his lips.

"Worried about Russia? No, I don't think they are," he said.

Perhaps Ellis Cowan was correct in thinking so of his own son and daughter and the circles in which they moved, but their apparent levity of interest was not in fact universal. The Truman Doctrine was discussed in the succeeding days by people of every age, and as vociferously in Amarillo, Texas, as in Washington, D.C.; with as much enthusiasm or misgiving in Tampa as in Chicago. In Chicago it occupied much of the conversation of the guests at the birthday party Helen Maclean gave for Sprague Burrell.

When Helen had first joined the staff at Irene Lister's agency, Sprague had persuaded her to move into the apartment he kept on Lake Shore Drive. Lenore Stacey had urged her not to do it, but in the end Helen acceded to Sprague's wishes. Sprague continued to stay over at the apartment only two or three nights a week, and encouraged Helen to treat the establishment as her own. One of the bedrooms was given over to her exclusive use, and she and Joseph together redecorated the kitchen.

At the agency she had fared well. Starting as a junior clerk, she had quickly been promoted to secretary, in this capacity assisting Irene's second-in-command. Then recently two of Irene's younger clients, a dance team calling themselves the Shermans, had been given to her to handle. When Irene had passed on to her a portion of the percentage the agency earned through the Shermans, she had decided to give the dinner party to celebrate Sprague's birthday.

It was a small party. Sprague did not have many friends close enough to him to be apprised of Helen's position in his life and devoted enough to him to lend it their approval. In addition to Irene Lister she had invited John Hyland, a small-parts manufacturer whom Sprague had originally helped to put into business, and his wife Albione, and as Irene's escort, Jim Markus, a quiet, watchful man with a fat, friendly face who had been an assistant of Sprague's for fifteen years or more, intimately involved in virtually all Sprague's business interests.

For the occasion Helen had decked the living room in flowers and repeated the same colors in the new dinner dress she wore. Under Irene's guidance, experiment and observation had begun to lend to her appearance the disciplined perfection of detail that marked her as a successful young businesswoman; but she had not let it spoil her freshness. Art emphasized the spontaneous quality of her youthful attractiveness and did not enamel it. Her decorousness, however, was no weapon with which to deflect the political conversation of John Hyland and Jim Markus. For an hour they had been monopolizing the party in their fervor to condemn the Truman Doctrine. Sprague listened to them with an air of detachment, and when this air had persisted beyond a certain length of time, Helen knew that something was wrong.

Helen and Irene Lister had learned each other's ways well in the time they had worked together, and feeling herself beleaguered, Helen was able to summon aid from the handsome china-featured woman with a glance. Irene threw herself into the conversation unashamedly and in a matter of minutes had led the attention of the two outraged Republicans toward other matters. Helen made her way unobtrusively to Sprague's side.

"Is everything all right?" she asked beneath the flow of conversation in the room.

Sprague answered, "It's wonderful, Helen. I'm very touched you arranged all this for me."

Her apprehension increased. Party panic, she counseled herself; but it did not convince her.

"Maybe you're feeling tired, Sprague," she said. "Dinner will be ready soon."

"Please don't worry," Sprague said. "I'm enjoying myself. Really."

"Good. All right then, I won't worry."

Helen slipped away from him and took Irene Lister's glass to refill.

"May I help you?" Irene asked.

"Oh, thank you, but it'll be a minute or two—I want to get more ice from the kitchen. Joseph's busy with the buffet."

She went out to the kitchen, and passing the small dining room off the hall, saw Joseph busy there. In the kitchen she began to fill the small ice bucket with cubes from the larger one. Alone, she considered the reasons for her apprehension about Sprague. Something between them was changing, had begun to change weeks ago, and she could not be sure what it was. In the first weeks after she'd gone to work for Irene Lister he had followed her progress with interest, had listened, amused, by the hour to her office chatter. She had been promoted and given a raise in salary, and Sprague had shared her excitement as she learned her new duties. Soon thereafter—she was not certain whether there had been a distinct occasion or a gradual process—his enthusiasm had cooled. He listened to her still when she discussed her business day or her after-hours studying, but she found herself less and less inclined to do so, his distraction of mind communicating itself to her. In the past he had stayed overnight in the apartment more or less regularly; of late he had stayed less often; and for the last two weeks, though he came to visit her or take her out to dinner, he had departed chastely. If he was growing tired of her, she did not understand why he hesitated to tell her. They had never pretended that either was committed to the other, had they? They enjoyed sleeping together, but as fond as they were of one another, they knew they were not in love; well, didn't they? Why shouldn't Sprague feel free to tell her if he wanted their sex life to come to an end? Why did he want to leave her doubtful and unsure of herself?

She had half-filled the small ice bucket when the swinging door opened and Irene Lister came in.

"They're back on politics," Irene explained, "but Albione's in there trying. May I keep you company?"

"Sure," said Helen, erasing the expression of concern from her face. "I'll have that refill for you in a second."

"Don't rush."

Irene perched on the stool in the corner nearest Helen so that they were able to face each other.

"Even with the political element, the party's a great success, Helen," she said.

"Do you mean it?" Helen asked. "Are they all enjoying themselves?"

"I was watching carefully, I've never seen you stage-manage a dinner before."

"And it's all right?"

"Perfectly."

"What a relief." Helen sighed. "I've been on edge all day, it's the country girl in me. I guess I'm still not exactly used to Sprague's friends."

"Don't tell me this crew scares you." Irene laughed.

"Not any more, it's just a shadow of what I used to feel. I fought for weeks when he first wanted to introduce me to friends of his. I wasn't afraid to meet them because of—anything about Sprague and me. He explained they were good friends and understood and accepted it——"

"Damn nice of them."

"But—I was trying so hard to live up to what Sprague kept telling me I was. I was doing well at the office, and I didn't want to jinx it. I wanted to meet the interesting people he knew, but I was afraid I'd embarrass him in front of them."

"How?"

"Gaucherie. That's a word I learned from Sprague, and boy, does it ever describe me. I could just picture myself going panicky with his friends and starting up the grand manner all over the place to hide the fact. Sprague would've hated that."

"I daresay he knew you well enough to know you wouldn't let him down," said Irene.

"He's a brave man." She filled Irene's glass with fresh cubes and splashed Scotch over them.

"It's a damned shame you're stuck in that office of mine," Irene said.

"Hey, now . . ." Helen stopped suddenly in her work to look at the woman directly.

"No, I mean it," Irene pursued. "Soda for me. That's the trouble with Chicago, the opportunities are limited."

"Opportunity isn't ever limited," Helen put in. "Unless you limit yourself."

"Have you ever thought of moving to New York, Helen?"

The drink and the ice bucket were ready, but the question was so unexpected, Helen stopped in her task.

"Why, Irene?" she asked. "Are you having misgivings about my work?"

"Far from it, that's why I asked about New york. You know yourself you've gone just about as high up at my place as you can. I don't want a partner, and I couldn't give up Louise if my life depended on it."

"Of course not."

"Also, Louise is healthy and change of life is far off for her yet. So there's no hope for your future there. On the other hand"—she smiled—"I don't want you setting up on your own in competition against me——"

"Irene, you know I never would do such a——"

"I don't think so either. But the temptation might someday get overpowering. Frankly, I think you'd beat the pants off me."

Helen laughed, and in her fondness for the woman was able to answer, "You know, I just bet I would."

"See what I mean?" Irene spread her arms. "I can't afford to take chances with you and your positive thinking." Irene sipped her drink, and balancing the glass on her crossed knees, looked aimlessly toward the door to the hallway to avoid Helen's stare. "I took the liberty of talking to someone about you," she said.

"Really? Who?" Helen asked.

"Jules Fischel."

"I don't think I know——"

"He's an old contact of mine, a nice guy. He opened a model agency in New York after the war; it's doing very well. Modeling is a somewhat nicer field than the night-club business. Not much, but somewhat."

Helen paused. "You go to such elaborate lengths to fire somebody. Why should you take all this trouble over me?"

Irene held her look, then a cool smile touched her mouth. "You're an interesting type of girl."

"Type?"

"Yes." Irene held her ground. "I enjoy doing something that will help you prove yourself, help you progress. There's no need to psychoanalyze me about it. I simply find it an amusing thing to do, and you shouldn't ask so many questions. The opportunities with Jules Fischel are endless—Jules doesn't yet have a Louise in his life as I do—and I think the two of you would get along."

"Irene, I don't want to leave you——"

"Thanks, but I'm hedging my bets," said Irene. "Think about it. He said he wants to meet you while he's in Chicago; that's easily done."

Helen looked away.

"But I don't think I could. Not yet."

"How come?"

"Sprague," said Helen.

Irene hesitated a moment, then cocked her head in puzzlement. "Sprague?"

"Oh, I don't mean he'd object to my going to work for someone else, or even moving to New York. Things aren't—like that, quite—"

"I know." Irene tried to put her at her ease.

Helen pulled a chair up to the table and sat down before her. She said thoughtfully, "I'd want to be caught up a little more."

"Caught up with what?"

"I owe Sprague a lot of money—it's not half paid back yet."

"You mean for that secretarial course?"

"Primarily," said Helen. "And a lot of other expenses."

"Helen, Sprague doesn't expect you to pay back what——"

"But he does——"

"Listen," Irene Lister asserted, "I've known Sprague Burrell a lot longer than you have. The dough he's spent on you doesn't amount to a pack of cigarettes in his thinking. But if you want to pay it back, New York makes more sense than ever. Look at it this way: Jules Fischel can pay you much more than I can; you'll be able to pay back whatever you figure you owe Sprague in no time flat."

"But maybe—in some way—Sprague would be disappointed if I moved off to New York."

"Oh," said Irene.

That was all she said, but the change in her voice snapped Helen to attention. She looked up; Irene was not drinking her Scotch.

"Come on, we'd better get back inside," Helen said.

From the time she had gone to work for Irene, Helen had been severe with her budget until she could pay Sprague the money she had accepted from him. The books she read still came from the public library or were borrowed from friends if they recommended something, and she bought clothes with the greatest of care and seemingly endless bargaining. The one luxury she allowed herself was Billie. Billie came on Wednesdays to do the general work of the apartment and on Sundays to make Helen feel hedonistic. If there had been people in on Saturday night, she straightened away the debris, and usually woke Helen with a breakfast tray.

The morning after the birthday party, Helen awoke ahead of time to find a sunstream coming through the Venetian blinds of her bedroom and dimly heard Billie humming at her work in the kitchen. She was not yet fully awake when the young Negress, with a knock on the door, came in bearing the breakfast tray.

"Good morning, Miss Helen."

"Good morning, Billie." She sat up in bed and fixed the pillows against the headboard. Billie put the breakfast tray across Helen's knees, and going to the windows, adjusted the Venetian blinds. The room filled with a more general light.

"Nice party last night? Everything copacetic?"

"Everything what?"

Billie laughed her wide, bare-gummed laugh. "What everybody's saying, Miss Helen. Everything's copacetic: I learned it from my friend the other night. The front section of the paper's there on your tray, I didn't have room for all them other sections. I'll just get them for you now."

"Thank you, Billie."

With her coffee she smoked a cigarette and desultorily glanced through the paper. When the cigarette was finished, she pushed the breakfast tray aside and got up. She bathed and dressed leisurely, and it was almost noon when she sat down at the dressing table to complete her make-up. She was putting the last touches to her hair when there was a knock on the bedroom door. When Billie did not appear immediately, Helen said, "Yes? . . . What is it, Billie?"

The Negress' eyes were scrupulously veiled.

"Mrs. Burrell," she said, "is here to see you."

For an instant the blood stood still in Helen's veins. *"Mrs. Burrell?"* she said.

"Yes, Miss Helen."

She turned away to avoid Billie's stare. "The—the living room's straightened up?" she managed to say.

"Yes, Miss Helen. Pretty much."

"Thank God." Helen nodded. "Thank you, Billie," she said. "I'll be with her in a moment."

Billie went out, closing the door soundlessly behind her.

Helen sat down heavily at the dressing table. Mrs. Burrell. . . . What was her first name? Of course, Nancy. . . . In a way Helen had never really admitted the woman's existence to herself. The concept of Sprague's wife: it was a fact, perhaps, but an abstract one. She had never tried to picture what she must look like, she was a faceless idea. Now Nancy Burrell was here.

Panic momentarily gripped her and her senses closed tight against reality. She couldn't, she couldn't be here! How had she found out the address, how had she learned about Sprague and herself? Or had she known all along? Sprague had had the apartment for years before Helen had come to live there; perhaps his wife had known where it was—and probably what it was—from the very beginning. Her stomach turned sickeningly inside her.

What did Nancy Burrel want?—to cause a scene?—to denounce and vilify her? . . . But she had not yet turned the knob on the door to the back hall—the other way out—when she pulled herself up short.

No. Running was no good. Sprague was her friend. Apart from bed, apart from everything, he was her friend. Slowly she drew herself up, smoothed her dress down over her hips, and stepping out into the hall, walked toward the living room.

"Mrs. Burrell?" she said.

Nancy Burrell was short and trim, not more than forty, and she had stood up on Helen's salutation. As a girl she must have been pretty, and she had by no means lost her prettiness to age, but her mouth now had a pinched, almost sardonic look. Her clothes were beautiful, the informal garb of a rich suburbanite, and she wore her hair in the suburbanite's casual style. She was totally unlike anything Helen would have expected.

"It's no good my apologizing, I realize that," Mrs. Burrell said.

With the greatest of care Helen kept her voice in its normal register. "Please sit down," she said.

"Thank you."

Helen drew a straight chair up to the coffee table. "May I give you something?"

"Have you any Pernod?"

"I think so. Let me tell Billie."

Helen was aware that every gesture was being studied, but with tightening jaws she refused to be ruffled. With unhurried steps she started toward the kitchen.

She was startled but not surprised to find Billie waiting in the hall immediately outside. Helen firmly closed the door behind her. The maid's glance was not veiled now; her eyes were wide in wonderment.

"Billie, would you fix a Pernod for Mrs. Burrell and myself? On the rocks, I think, and a dash of bitters."

"Yes, Miss Helen. . . ." Billie turned and streaked down the hall.

"Billie!" Helen hissed. The maid braked suddenly and turned back, eyes staring from their sockets. "There's no blasted hurry, Billie! Now, remember who you are."

She went back into the living room where Nancy Burrell waited.

"I told Billie with bitters and on the rocks, I hope that will be all right?"

"Perfectly. Thanks."

Helen sat down in the straight chair, and an unease of silence fell. At last Nancy Burrell gave a sigh. "I had a fine head of steam up when I decided to come here, but it's evaporated."

"I assume you had something you wanted to say to me."

"Sprague has given more of his time to you than to any of the others. I don't know, but I sense it. Maybe it was convenience on your part. Anyway, today I thought I had a weapon."

Helen stiffened. "Sprague's friendship with me may not be very conventional, Mrs. Burrell, but, as you say, it isn't the first. He told me the arrangement between you was quite amicable——

"Did he?"

"Yes. Isn't it?"

Nancy Burrell's gaze clouded. "I knew the minute I walked into this apartment today that the shadows I was boxing defeated me years ago."

"You don't mean you're still in love with him?"

Nancy waved a hand, and let it drop heavily into her lap.

"But Sprague *told* me—I thought you were no more faithful to him than he's been to you——"

"You probably don't know much about people like us, Helen," she said.

"There's not so much difference in our ages," Helen said defensively.

"People like Sprague and me are the end product of generations of good breeding. We're thinned out, overcomplicated. Do you follow me? If I weren't weak, I would have finished with Sprague long ago. I can't help myself, though, and I know it. No more than he can help his attachment for his protégés."

Helen looked away. "I didn't know. It wasn't anything definite Sprague ever said——"

"But he allowed you to believe."

"Yes."

Billie came in with the Pernod, and Helen turned her stricken face away until Billie had left the room again. She faced Nancy Burrell then. "Sprague's never really loved me, you know. Not in any romantic way."

Nancy glanced at her. "It doesn't make much difference," she said, "but thanks for trying."

"Were you going to tell me Sprague has a new girl?" Helen asked quickly.

Nancy Burrell sighed.

"I knew . . ." said Helen.

"Irene Lister has arranged a job for you in New York, hasn't she? I don't mean to dazzle you with my knowledge of the details. There's a lot I don't know about Sprague's activities away from me, but I think Sprague is hoping you'll take that job."

"I see."

"I've never known Sprague to bring a relationship to an end on his own initiative." Nancy Burrell rose to her feet. She paused. "I'm sorry about it for your sake. I changed my mind about telling you, you know. I suspect you have a real regard for Sprague. Unlike the others."

She was gone before Helen could say more.

Nancy Burrell had driven herself into Chicago that morning in the Chevrolet she used for ordinary errands when her chauffeur was busy at other tasks. Coming to the meeting with Helen Maclean, she had not wanted the ostentation of the town car. She had parked the Chevrolet in a side street a block and a half off Lake Shore Drive, and she hurried back to it now as though once inside it, she could forget the pain and embarrassment of the past few minutes.

She opened her purse and rummaged for the car keys. They were not there. She swore beneath her breath in brief annoyance. In her nervousness she must have forgotten and left them behind in the car. She walked more quickly still.

When she reached the corner, she stopped short with a gasp. The space where she had left the car was empty. She hurried forward to it. Perhaps she was mistaken, perhaps she had parked on the next street. But she knew she hadn't. She recognized the white convertible immediately ahead of the space her car had been parked in. She looked up and down the Sunday street. No one was in sight. From one of the apartment buildings she heard a radio playing.

Tiger Rizzuto drove through the streets in a sweat of caution, ferociously braking his instinct to speed, to escape the scene of the theft as quickly as possible, to be rid of the car before its owner could raise an alarm. Rush Street, Huron, La Salle, zigzagging south, take your time, take your time, with the rigid self-discipline he'd had to master. His head throbbed with a hangover, and his eyes were gritty. Sunday morning, and he didn't even know what he had been doing in this part of town.

He had been roaring drunk, his head and his eyes told him that much, and half an hour before he had stumbled out of the pink and yellow duplex off Lake Shore Drive. Coming across the car had been providential. He had walked aimlessly away from the duplex, hoping his head would clear and his stomach settle. He hadn't been out for business; but then the angle of the car's wheels showed it had been parked hurriedly, and he had glanced inside and seen the keys still in the ignition. Not a soul on the street, only the sound of a radio somewhere, tired-sounding, as though it had been left on, forgotten, after a Saturday night drunk. It was a pushover.

Easy, easy, there were more cars on the street in this part of town. He blinked against the grit in his eyes. In all likelihood the bag he had left behind in the duplex was still asleep, and Juney would be on her way to church if she'd found someone to keep the baby. Well, she didn't have any goddamned right expecting him home on a Saturday night; what kind of guy knuckled under to a broad? He *had* to blow up every once in a while: it wasn't as if he could talk to Juney, confide in her.

Everything, every damned thought that came into his head had to be studied, sifted, revised before he could talk to her. It choked you, it built layer by layer a growth inside your head till you couldn't hold it any more and you exploded, letting the booze rush like a cooling river down your throat, erasing everything you knew and felt about yourself. Increasingly he had been blacking out, at first not being able to remember how he'd come to be in this bed, this room; then not remembering where he had met this blonde or this brunette; and now not remembering anything of the previous night beyond the first quick priming shot of booze.

He shook his head to recall himself to reality. A red light shone ahead and he drew to a stop. The idling motor sent a tremor through the steering wheel into his sweating hands. The hell with it: what did he know or feel about himself that had to be driven out, that he couldn't live with? The way he made his money? What else was he good for? Some decent job, some little corner where you sold the rest of your life for forty bucks a week and went home at night to your loving wife with a clear conscience and an uncomplicated lech to bang her and take your shower and sleep soundly like the just? That was the shit you learned in your catechism, he told himself, and then with a start he found himself nearing the garage. The big doors were open, and he pulled into its black and yawning mouth.

In the gray wet light of the garage slack-mouthed Uncle

Piertro Gustineo came hurrying out from the office cubicle, recognized Tiger, and without a word led him with motions through a maze of legit cars far to the back of the garage to the foot of the ramp. The more specialized tools for the job were on the second floor. Tiger got out, the sound of his footsteps ringing on the cement.

"Al around yet?" he asked.

Pietro nodded toward the office, jumped in behind the wheel of the Chevrolet, and pulled off smoothly up the ramp. Tiger walked back toward the office, rubbing his sore eyes with his fists.

In the office Al Gustineo sat conjuring with the wads of paper slips and cash that crowded the steel box containing the entire records of his numerous enterprises. His eyes were sunken and his face yellow-pale with tiredness after his Saturday night. Tiger suspected he had been pimping the last few months. He looked up as Tiger came into the cubicle.

"Hi," said Tiger.

"You look like hell." Al greeted him sourly.

"At least I got an excuse. *I* got decently crocked."

"Juney called," said Al, closing the steel box and twisting the miniature safe-lock.

Tiger made a noncommittal sound in his throat and sat down.

" 'Bout half an hour ago," Al elaborated idly. "She didn't sound worried none. I told her you was out on a spot repair."

"Shit, she knows I wasn't working last night. Well, thanks for the try."

"Sorry, kid." Al shrugged.

"I feel sick," Tiger said.

"Whatsa matter?"

"Nothing, fuck it." He stood up. "I'll be around tomorrow. Afternoon."

"Okay," said Al.

"That Chevy was a deal. I didn't even have to jump it, the keys were in. S'long."

He walked wearily out of the garage and on the street turned in the direction of his apartment.

Tiger hated the apartment because it was the kitchen you first came into. The kitchen with its prewar stove and chipped, yellowed icebox and the glaring newness of the metal table and chairs he had bought for Juney when they were married. The grease-gray window opened on an airshaft, the inexhaustible source of every sickening odor you could name, heavily dominated by cooking cabbage. The narrow middle room, little more than a passage, contained the baby's crib and an unsteady small set of bookshelves where the baby's clothes and feeding paraphernalia were kept. The front room, overlooking the street, held their double bed, and in one corner, which Juney had futilely tried to make look like a living-room area, were two easy chairs and a table-model radio. It wasn't poverty that made a place like this, Tiger knew. They weren't wanting for money now. It was one-part the housing shortage and one-part something in themselves. They had tried to make the place nice. They had put thought and money into it, but whatever they attempted had only underlined the awkwardness and ugliness.

When he walked up the three long flights and let himself in, Juney was at the stove heating a can of baby food. She stopped when he came in, and after a moment's glance, she smiled at him.

"Morning, darling. Got the job finished? Al told me you were out on one."

"Hi." He kissed her—briefly, to spare her the odor of his breath. He did not bother to answer her question. She knew damned well he didn't go to work in his best flannel suit.

From the next room came the baby's whimpering.

"How's Hot-Shot?" he asked.

"She's teething," Juney said. "And ready for her lunch. Sit down and I'll get you some breakfast soon as I can."

"Tell you what," said Tiger. "Suppose I feed her and you can get to work on some bacon and eggs."

Juney gave him a doubtful look over her shoulder.

"Are you up to it?" she asked.

"Sure I am," Tiger said.

He was sick from his hangover and the additional shaking up he had taken in clouting the Chevy. But whenever he came home, he knew he had to raise a double guard. Juney was no fool, and she knew his moods well; the effort the deception exacted of him doubled this tension so that an unhealthy, strained wakefulness widened his swollen eyes and speeded his heartbeat. He went into the middle room and picked up the baby. Her trembling smallness made him grin with proprietary pleasure, and he held her close against his shoulder. He felt the wetness of her diaper seeping through his shirt. He called into the kitchen, "Should I change Her Highness now or after?"

"Oh, now, please, Tiger, if you don't mind doing it," Juney called back. "I'm fighting a war against diaper rash."

He took a diaper from the topmost of the bookshelves, and letting down the side of the crib, gently dropped the baby onto the ammonia-reeking sheet. She rolled over onto her hands and knees and bucked happily, stinging gums forgotten, while Tiger struggled to strip off the sheet and dry the rubber pad beneath. He was shaking and sweating from the effort by the time he had managed to manhandle the squirming infant into the fresh diaper. A new defeat awaited him.

"Goddamn it, Juney, the goddamn pins are too rusty to go in."

"Wipe them through your hair," Juney called from the kitchen.

"What? And put 'em on her? That's unsanitary!"

"Tiger, don't be silly, that's what everybody does. Your hair gets oil on the pins and they go in."

"Why the hell can't we get new pins? All right, Hot-Shot, lay still, can't you?"

With an explosive sigh he finished and picked the baby up. She looked like Juney, but her thick black hair was his, coarser than Juney's hair. Her fists against his chest, she pushed herself back and stared with wild wonderment about her as he carried her into the kitchen and sat down with her at the oilcloth-covered table.

He had fed the baby more often than he had changed her, and he handled the meal with a practiced, if unavoidably mush-covered, hand. While he carried on the feeding, Juney fried bacon and eggs and they desultorily discussed the baby's development and comparative normality for seven months of age. Juney wore her slip. In her hurry to get the baby fed and Tiger's hangover appeased, she had taken off her Sunday dress and put nothing else on.

Tiger did not mind. The birth of the baby had broadened Juney's hips, but not very much. At the cost of great discomfort and greater sentimental frustration, she had used formula bottles from the start, and her breasts were still as firm and round as a virgin's. Tiger watched her movements with an eye that was, after the previous night's carousing, more appreciative and affectionate than lustful. When his breakfast was ready, Juney took the baby from him and returned her to the crib with a freshly warmed bottle. She put the breakfast before Tiger and sat down opposite him at the table with a cup of coffee for herself.

"Did you get to Mass?" Tiger asked, wolfing the bacon and eggs.

Juney nodded.

"Mrs. Kleindorf kept the baby for me. Poor Tiger, you're starving."

"All right," he said.

"All right, all right. . . . But don't give yourself heartburn. Mrs. Kleindorf says we're going to have another war. But she says Mahatma Gandhi is going to start it. Her husband doesn't trust Mahatma Gandhi."

"How can he start a war? Gandhi's a pacifist."

"Are you a pacifist, Tiger?" Juney asked.

"You bet your sweet life I am. Gandhi's got the right idea. *He* doesn't fight anybody, *he* doesn't answer no roll call. He just sits there an doesn't eat and everybody runs around like their heads was chopped off."

"Your grammar's getting worse," Juney observed vaguely.

"Well, you know what I mean."

He ate more slowly as he came to the end of the breakfast, and nourishment loosened his knotted muscles. When he was finished, he pushed the empty plate to one side. He lit a cigarette and sat back, his eyes closed.

"Come on, lie down," said Juney. "I'll take your shoes off for you."

He mumbled a word of appreciation. Juney followed him into the front room and waited while he stretched out on the bed. He was aware only of the sensuous relief when Juney pulled off his shoes and stripped down his socks. Lifting himself briefly on his elbows, he unbuckled his belt, pulled it off, and undid the waist button of his trousers. He sank back down upon his stomach gratefully, his senses swimming into slumber. He felt Juney sit down on the edge of the bed beside him, her hand gently on his back, her voice soft and sweet in his ear, rich with the love she felt for him, purer if not more true than his for her.

"When I went to Mass, Tiger," she was saying quietly, a hint of crooning in her voice, "I prayed to Saint Jude. You know why? Because he's the Patron Saint of the Impossible. I prayed to him—not that you'd love me, I know you love me—but that you'd be content with me. Someday. Sometime before I get old. . . ."

Sorrow and despair strove mutely with his enclouding sleepiness. He'd made her unhappy, time and time again; she'd never done him anything but good, and over and over again he'd hurt her, discouraged her, crushed her. Maybe it was the best way; maybe preoccupied with his screwing around, she'd never have time to think about his income and how he made it. That would be worse for her, he knew—a lot worse. Sorrow flowed into his bones, dissipating its sharpness, making way for the clouds of sleep. The clouds presently drew over him, enfolded him, and he felt nothing.

In midafternoon he awoke, and the light in the room was already thin and colorless with the passing of the late-winter sun. Slowly, his arms and legs stiff with torpor, he pulled himself over onto his back. There was no sound in the apartment. He strained his hearing, but caught no hint of Juney's presence, or the baby's. He knew she had probably taken the baby out for a walk after her nap so that he might sleep undisturbed.

His hangover was gone, but in its place had come worse, much worse, the sickening knowledge that in his life there was nothing he wanted—under the present circumstances, not even Juney. He knew that if it weren't for his stealing, he wouldn't need so much to go around banging other women, damning Juney to a wordless apprehension and doubt. Except for his stealing, he knew, he wouldn't *need* to prove he was just the high-living sport, smart, tough, the whole thing a goddamned lark. How did the others do it? The others, didn't they manage to fool themselves that that's what it was? They must manage it—they went year in and year out living the same way, into prison for a stretch, out of it and nothing changed. At the thought of prison, damp fingers closed quietly around his heart. He stumbled back to the deserted kitchen. He never really regretted not having been a book-reader before, but now he did. Maybe it still wasn't too late. Maybe somehow he could teach himself. He'd have to get some books.

He found the pack on the table and pulled out a cigarette that felt damp, a moist reminder of his big night on the town. He lit it and moved more slowly, puffing on it leisurely, back toward the front of the apartment overlooking the street.

Maybe somehow the others managed to fool themselves, maybe Al Gustineo really believed he was the great hot-shot. Tiger knew he hadn't convinced himself. You had to tell yourself, over and over till the words deafened you, that you were smart, in the trim, one of the best, plenty of life in you yet. But you got older and the words sounded faintly sillier. When did you grow old? In the Army? Tiger smirked to himself. Hell no, in the Army he'd been the cock of the walk, nobody knew the score like Corporal Tiger Rizzuto. When he married? Oh, the day!—the whole damned world was his because he was marrying his girl and she was lovely and nice and not cheap and she loved him.

When do you grow old and the songs you sing to yourself, the inward rallying songs, when do they start sounding tinny and thin?

When little Hot-Shot got born. . . .

Something in his head slowed as he stood by the thinning sunlight of the window, smoking his cigarette and watching the Sunday afternoon movements in the street below. Elizabeth Margaret Malone Rizzuto. . . . The smooth-cheeked, blue-chinned doctor, the nurses on the hall impatient with his presence, the embarrassing hairiness of his baby compared with the other infants in the window of the nursery. His own black coarse hair all over her; his mother and Juney telling him over and over too nervously it was just baby hair, it would all rub off with her first few baths at home. Still, the day they left the hospital she had been the prettiest of the babies in the nursery window; not because he was her father, no, he wasn't that much of a jerk, she *was* the prettiest; even red-skinned and oiled and swaddled round in blankets she looked like a girl, unmistakably feminine—the other people at the window said as much.

Tiger turned abruptly away from the window and threw himself down into one of the armchairs in the corner, sprawling one leg over the arm. He knocked the ashes of his cigarette into the tray on the table that held the small radio and drew deeply on the cigarette again. There was a little of his money stashed away; too much of it had gone on liquor, too much on feeding and taxiing the broads around town, but there was some put by. A little more, a very little more, and he could get out of the hole. How? A course, he could learn a decent trade, they had all kinds of courses, didn't they? He had seen the ads in the horny men's magazines: plumber, electrician, you could write away and you could learn to be practically anything. All right, goddamn it, he *wouldn't* get to be another of Chicago's gifts to the world, but he could support Juney and the baby without being ashamed of how he did it, couldn't he? He wasn't making any fucking fortune clouting cars for the Gustineos, was he? What the hell was wrong with a decent trade except the smart-ass ideas of a lot of punks and misfits on the streets off the Loop? Nothing: he could work cleanly with his hands even if he didn't know anything about mechanics or pipes or cathodes or all the rest of the mumbo-jumbo: he could pay them to teach him. Maybe then he'd start reading up on things he didn't know about. He could even learn something that would help him fix up their cruddy apartment, redo the wiring, get the goddamned can working right once and for all: only one more catch for Al would make all of it possible. One final clout. . . .

The afternoon wore on in a haze of cigarette smoke and dreaming idleness. There is a chapel in the mind of the young, and in it the altar is sanctified to an endless hope. Beaten, unhappy, directionless, the most disoriented of the young can still worship there, won over to or seduced by the cruelest religion men have, the sweet hope that has no terminus.

His optimism grew. It gathered force and power in the waning day, stirring him to wakefulness and energy, carrying him through his shower and his shave; it hurried him into his clothes, provided with a marvelous inventiveness the words he said to Juney and the crooning love sounds he left with the baby, buoyed him up in his determined journey across town to a possible lode field, informed his hands at their work when he had singled out the catch, raced his heart as the first revving of the motor sang the prelude for his liberation. Then, in an instant while the world heaved over once, it exploded into death.

He sensed rather than heard the wordless babble behind him in the lamplighted street.

Then: "Hey, that's *my* goddamned car! Stop him! Stop him!"

Every cunning he had ever known flew out the window and he gunned the car down the street with a screaming violation of the gears. His mind registered frantically, inaccurately, the bumper pulling into the intersection. His foot jammed down on the pedal, and in a shrieking gesture he rammed the car into the other in his path. A blaze of light, an asinine crumpling of metal like cardboard, the sharp pitch of the wheel into his chest, and blackness.

Nothing. An echo of an unbelieving crying out, and nothing more.

In his numbness, the familiar comforting after-taste of hysteria, he was aware of the booking room. Aware of himself giving the carefully memorized replies, the knowing answers, the co-operative words that gave no quarter and traded no rights. A long new blackness, and there was Al Gustineo and a precinct tout and a haggling session with legalities. But you do not feel like listening carefully to human beings' words when you know you're dead.

The tide of dying carried him, unprotesting, unbitter, beyond sorrow.

Hours later they sat in a diner having coffee.

"You're a first offender, they'll rig a suspended sentence," Al was saying proudly. "We got influence, 'cause we pay off. You won't even have a record, thanks to me. We'll have that file pulled by the week-end."

Tiger tore bits off a piece of toast without enthusiasm, beyond appetite.

"Yeah. So," Tiger muttered.

"Right now, our boy and the D. A.'s office, between them, they've fixed it up. Unauthorized use. Crazy young kid gone joy-riding in a car, nothing too serious."

"Juney will know," said Tiger quietly.

" 'Course you got to get out of town," Al said, "after this blows over."

Tiger shrugged. There would be no way of convincing Juney that the charge of unauthorized use of a vehicle was legitimate. Even if, as Al said, the records were cleaned out, she would look at their apartment, their furniture, the things he'd bought for her, the baby's clothes: she'd know all about it. She couldn't go back anyway.

He stuffed bread into his throat and pushed it down with a cramping gulp of coffee. "I'll get a room," he said. "Some neighborhood I won't run into Juney. She damn well won't want to be running into me. Al, could you get my clothes from her?"

"Sure, Tiger."

"A letter. I'll write a letter you can take to her for me."

"Sure, kid," said Al. "Giagharelli's in New York."

"Giagharelli?"

"I was thinking of after," said Al.

"So?"

"Weingard's in New York, too," said Al. "You can go see them."

"Al, there's Juney. There's the baby."

"I thought you wasn't going to be seeing them any more."

"We'll be in the same city at least—for a while."

"Shit. You got obligations, Tiger. You got to pay off."

"I made you plenty, Al," said Tiger, the blackness drawing about his mind again. Still, Weingard took care of his boys. That was his reputation. "I met Weingard," he nodded hopelessly.

"Let's go," said Al.

Tiger went home with Al that night and wrote his letter to Juney.

"Do not try to find me, baby," he scribbled out, "because I do not want you to get hurt any more. Al won't tell you where I am, but he will bring my stuff to me if you give it to him. There is some money saved. It is in the steel box in the bottom of the bedroom closet. It is our savings and you can use it now. The key for the box is stuck under the table with the radio with Scotch tape. I can't ask you to forgive me because you will not be able to now. Maybe later you will be able to forgive me. I am not sure of the laws, but later you can sue me for desertion and get your freedom. It would be nice for Elizabeth Margaret if you could fall in love with a good steady guy who is a plumber or electrician. Not somebody who is just a blowhard. Maybe you could fix it with the church. I love you. If I did not love you, I would not be doing this. Love, Tiger."

18

After endless bartering the charge of unauthorized use of a vehicle was withdrawn. The case didn't even come to court.

In the weeks devoured by the bargaining, Juney did not attempt to communicate with him. Repeatedly he was forced to fight back the temptation to phone her, repeatedly his nights were tortured fantasies filled with the sound of the baby crying and the shredding frustration of his inability to go to her and still her need. The night of rain he left Chicago, he walked first down the street where he and Juney had lived. here were no lights on in the windows of the apartment. It occurred to him that he didn't even know whether she and the baby were still living there or not. She might have found a smaller place, she might have gone back to the protection and security of her family. Alone in the rainfall, unseen in the darkness of the streets, Tiger blew a kiss up toward the dark windows of the apartment and, turning, hurried away. He had only twenty minutes to get to the New York bus.

The weather cleared in the course of the bus' run to New York, and hard-eyed with sleeplessness Tiger counted, without really seeing, the towns and villages falling past. New York: he had never been to New York before. . . . Again and again he started awake at the imagined sound of Elizabeth Margaret's crying, and in the shaded region between rationality and the living dream his aching, exhausted muscles out of long habit stirred and tensed themselves to rise to the baby's demands. Once, coming abruptly to consciousness when he was already on his feet, he fell back into his seat with a single tearless sob of despair, and the old woman next to him, annoyed and nervous, got up and went muttering in search of another seat farther back in the bus.

New York: a new city for him, a strange land. . . .

When in New York he had checked into a hotel he found two blocks west of Times Square, he did not try to locate Giagharelli or Weingard. He knew first he must sleep; it was ridiculous to think he could discuss business successfully the way he felt now. The neon sign outside the window of his hotel room beat an unrelenting tattoo of light against the walls of his room.

Blowhard . . . blowhard. . . . He had described himself that way to Juney. Because it was the truth. *When things are really serious, you've got no patience for anything but the lousy, unflattering, soul-twisting truth. Blowhard. . . .* This way, that's what he'd always be. If he went to see Giagharelli and Weingard? A blowhard. If he got himself tangled into whatever sleazy deals they were up to? A blowhard. All his worthless life before him: a blowhard.

He pulled down the crack-fibered window shades, but the pulsing of the inexhaustible light could not be wholly cut off. He put his suitcase on the floor of the closet, his coat on a hanger there, and pulling off his shoes, the laces unmanageable in his nerveless fingers, fell back across the bed. The skin of his back registered each lump of the chenille bedspread, and his ears, their hearing unhealthily quickened, caught each separate one of the million individual noises that composed the enduring, uninterruptable roaring of the city around him. His eyes unblinking, their fire-edged gaze on the ceiling, he lay motionless for fifteen minutes. Lying there forever would not bring sleep, he knew, and with the small strength his stillness had restored to him, he pulled himself up. From the closet he took his coat and pulled it on. He pushed his swollen feet back into his shoes, and moved out into the hall, locking the door of his room behind him.

Half a block from the hotel he found a liquor store, bought a fifth of blended, and walked back through the momentarily baffling flurries of a first snowfall. The temperature had dropped abnormally. He stopped for a moment beyond the entrance of the hotel, letting the flakes fall on his feverish, upturned face, then going in, he mounted the worn and debris-strewn stairs to his room. He locked the door again. Leaning against it to steady himself, he opened the fifth, and lifting it, drank deeply. He gagged and choked, coughing some of the liquor up into his nose, then put the bottle on the table beside the bed and pulled off his clothes. Dropping them into a heap at the foot of the bed would ruin his suit, he knew; he couldn't care any more.

Naked, he pulled back the chenille bedspread and threw it over the pile of clothes on the floor. He lit a cigarette and stretching out in the bed, drank again from the bottle. He luxuriated in his nakedness as though the skin of his body, covered and bound by his clothes for two days now, could at last breathe freely and deep, drinking in the easing air as he was drinking the easing flow of the whisky. The beginning of relaxation smoothed his taut muscles, and drawing on his cigarette, he began gently to caress his genitals, soothing and comforting himself, knowing that nothing related to passion could be stirred from the deadness of his body. He sighed; the caressing slowed and then stopped; his hand cupped his genitals tenderly; he put his cigarette down in the ash tray, and his eyes at last were able to close. His free hand groped for the fifth, but before it could seek out the promising neck of the bottle, he had fallen asleep.

He awoke, blinking against the light of the bedside lamp. He turned his head and sighed and lay unthinking, not fully aware of where he was or what was familiar to him about the dusty smell in his nostrils. A little while, and then he knew. New York. A dump on the West Side, and not much left in the way of money. But what was familiar? His eyes opened wider, and he saw the drably papered walls of the room—the ugly furnished room he'd lived in until he married Juney. The pungency of furnished rooms and cheap hotels, of yellow-lighted hallways and dust-feathered, grimy carpeting, of threadbare lives. The same room; the same fix. A little more than a year (what month was this? April?) and he had come full circle. Or perhaps he had never moved at all. . . .

And now? Find Giagharelli and Weingard as Al had ordered—not right away, of course. Get himself a berth. Get himself some cash. Or start over again from the same room and the same fix and try a different route this time. He'd been starting again in a stupid half-assed way when they'd caught him. Hadn't he? Yes. He remembered: learn a trade, drop Al's deal, sleep easy, wrapped around your girl. . . . It was the same room, the same fix, and he didn't have a fucking thing to lose. See about a job, try again, you're still a good boy, there's a lot left in the old boy yet. . . .

For the first time in his life, Tiger realized that maybe Al Gustineo had taken him and Juney for a ride.

In the bathroom at the end of the hall he shaved, took a shower, and dressed. In a fresh shirt and tie, his suit still woefully wrinkled from its night on the grimy floor, he went down to the street. A tobacco store with a short-order counter huddled in a corner of the building on the next street in the direction of Times Square. With some of his remaining money Tiger bough a pack of cigarettes and ate the biggest meal he had had in weeks: orange juice, grapefruit, sausages, griddlecakes, coffee, scrambled eggs, coffee, toast, coffee, coffee, coffee: there was no end to his hunger, no crimp in his appetite. He lit a cigarette, paid his bill, and walked out into the windy street. He looked about him at unnoticing buildings, cousins of Chicago's bleak façades, and suddenly smiled at them as if he were still a swaggering Army corporal and the dingy buildings were old ladies titteringly aware of him. With breakfast in him he did not shy from earth-shattering decisions: this coldly appraising new city would show him a way to get Juney and his baby back one day. He looked east toward the vast reach of the sooty concrete city, and for a moment he felt strong enough to blow the whole structure apart, confident enough to pull its toppling buildings to his breast. Find Giagharelli? Find Weingard? Whoever heard of them? Who gave a damn about them and Al Gustineo who said that he, Tiger Rizzuto, was obligated? Who were they that Tiger Rizzuto should waste his life on them? Tiger Rizzuto was in New York; Tiger Rizzuto was through with the part of him that had been a blowhard and a jerk; Tiger Rizzuto was going to find his life again.

For three days Tiger hunted jobs. When he'd found one, he told himself, he'd present the city with somebody who was already on his feet, already part of the respectable world. But the money ran lower. Then it was gone.

He moved out of the hotel and checked his suitcase in a locker in Grand Central Station. In the alcove that housed the lockers he fell into conversation with a bent and shabby old man and asked him where people without rooms could sleep in New York. The old tramp recommended the Salvation Army, but when Tiger pressed him, admitted that those who were hardy enough could sleep unmolested by the police in Union Square. Tiger got the directions and walked to Union Square; that night he slept there.

His first day without food he did not mind very much, except that it frightened him. In Chicago he had had to go hungry a number of times, but his family had been there: if hunger had ever grown into a serious threat, he had known his parents could feed him something rich with tomato paste, and filling; but now they were half a country away from him. The second day without food was harder still, but when night came, he found a restaurant owner on Fourteenth Street who let him work four hours in the kitchen in return for the least expensive of the house's specials. The food was not good, and the sickness that undermined him as he worked to pay for it infuriated him.

By midnight he had escaped the rank odors of the kitchen and was making his way to Union Square. Shivering with cold, he stopped before a building he had not noticed in that neighborhood before. The building was dark and did not appear to be either an apartment house or a shop; there was an institutional look about it. What arrested his attention was that the foyer before the glass doors leading inside was both deep and wide, an estimable shelter from the bitter wind. One arm clasped across his stomach, which was still in revolt against the food he had eaten, he staggered up the two stone steps and into the protecting brick arms of the foyer. On the glass door was a number painted in gilt; nothing else indicated what the place might be. An old building, soot-complexioned and ill-kempt, comfortable. There had been no snow that day, but rain, and the air was chillingly dank and the wind heedless of hiding places. Still, it was better than the openness of Union Square. Tiger found a fat dry wad of newspapers in the refuse bin five or six yards down the block; these he spread on the floor of the foyer and lay down in its comforting darkness. No streetlights sought out his cubbyhole, and the roar of the city for once seemed kind and muted. He tried to fit his body into the unrelenting tiles of the foyer, but could not do it. The tiles would not give, and neither would his bones.

It was all just punishment, he thought; what comforts did a thief demand? And that was what he had done: been a thief, knowing what it meant, without excuse except cheap ones he'd sold himself on because nothing was going right, nothing was as he wanted it to be. Did it go right for anyone? and not everyone else turned thief. Only him. He yearned without hope to be able to give back to the men who'd owned them the cars he'd stolen. None of them had been rich men's cars, he didn't have even that flimsy delusion, little as it was worth when he faced his contempt of himself; they had been cars that ordinary guys owned, most of them, guys whose loss must have been horrible when you thought of the months and months of payments probably still due, the preciousness of a car to most of them. And he could never make it up to them. Not even knowing who they were, if he lived a hundred years he could never atone. . . .

His sickness of a sudden in the cold redoubled, and pushing himself up, he staggered out to the sidewalk to vomit the indigestible dinner he'd worked for into the gutter. Wiping his mouth and trying with exaggerated exhalations to rid his throat of the taste and odor of sickness, he regretted suddenly that he had been sick in front of the kind and ugly old building. With a little more effort, he thought, he could have made it down the block a little way, or even to the gutter across the street. In his heart he murmured an exhaustion-colorful apology to the old building and plunged back into the foyer to lie down again on the newspapers, which were already drinking in the moisture of the night. . . .

It was one of the most generous and loving faces he had ever seen. For one thing, it was strangely large, bending over him, and in the rich chocolate of the face the eyes and teeth were brightly yellow, as if in their kindness they were more sensible than to gleam at him whitely, scaring him or at the least hurting his worn eyes. At first, blinking up at it, surrounded as it was by uncertain daylight, he was not sure it was the face of a woman, he only guessed the fact because the bulging yellow eyes were so kind and the big-toothed grin so confident, the look a mother has, watching her baby come awake. He made a sound in his throat, but he could not be certain it had been heard beyond the dull reverberation of his own eardrums. The brown face blinked back and breathed.

"I can't open the door with you across it," the large yellow smile made plain.

Grunting painfully with the effort, he pulled himself,

rigid with the cold of the previous night, up to a sitting position, leaning back against one of the glass doors, dragging his legs out of the way. The brown face reared up, receding infinitely far away, and he saw that it was indeed a girl; a broad-framed Negro girl in a red raincoat with a pink bandanna pulled over her head and tied under her chin.

"That's the wrong door," she said. "I'm sorry, I still can't get in."

Tiger tried to roll over out of her way and found he could not; rebellious sinews refused to stir at the prompting of his will and he collapsed back against the same glass door.

"Are you all right?" The girl bent over him again.

"I'm sorry. I'm sorry to be in your way."

"Are you all right?"

"I'm . . . I don't know," he managed to murmur.

"Drunk?"

"No."

"Just poor," the brown face nodded, familiar with the phenomenon in the neighborhood of Union Square. "Goodness. Well, gracious. That's too bad. But I've *got* to get in."

"Yeah. A minute. Just a . . ." He tried to breathe with some regularity, but his senses knotted their fists and hit him in the head again. His head rolled foolishly on the strengthless stalk of his neck until he could brace it against the glass panel of the door again. He cocked an eye up at the patiently waiting, mildly concerned chocolate face.

"You live here?" he asked.

"Boy, I work here. And what's more, if we can't get you moved over an inch, my boss is going to be coming along and finding out I'm late. The radiator's on inside. You hear me? If we can get you moved, you can come inside where the radiator's on."

The concept of the radiator stormed his whirling senses and momentarily made it that much more impossible for him to move. He winced to thank of what a derelict he must look to the girl. For a moment he breathed, while the girl waited.

"Sure. A minute. Just a little. *There!*"

Pushing himself up on the heels of his hands, he had catapulted himself out of the way.

"Thank you," said the girl. "You're not sick?"

"No. Just . . . thank you. I'll be gone in a . . ."

"You don't look like the usual," she observed. "When you had something to eat last?"

"God. Last night."

"Oh."

"You don't know the worst."

"I saw," said the girl, briefly closing the rich brown lids over her kind big eyes. The eyes opened wide again, yellow and gentle. "I have a coffee fix inside, you want to come in."

"Huh?"

"You heard."

Again he thought of what a repulsive picture he must be presenting.

"Me? You don't want me to . . ."

The girl shrugged. "As you please," she said. "But it's there."

She put her key in the lock, turned it, and pushed open the door. What her beseeching had failed to do, his own sense of good behavior effected: he dragged himself to his feet to hold the door for her.

The girl stood back.

"If you'll come in, you better go first, 'cause I think you might damn well fall down."

"Thanks," Tiger said. "Okay."

The girl in her red raincoat led him into the shocking warmth of the building. From down the hall he heard the gratifying, splendid, generous hissing of the radiator. The hall was broad; on the left were frosted-glass doors to offices, on the right, clear-windowed ones, which now the girl threw open and through which, taking a solicitous step back, she ushered him.

Inside, Tiger said, "But hell, it's a bookstore, is that it?"

On her own battlefield at last, the girl was too busy to reply beyond an affirmative grunt. Half the room was set apart by a low wooden fence, and behind this was her desk and a small switchboard. Pointing the direction to a chair near the gate to the sanctum, she seemed to take no further notice of him. She stripped off her raincoat and hung it on a wooden tree in one corner. At the switchboard she went through a magical rite of buttons and plugs and wires, the mystical gesture of the beginning of day, and then, without a glance at him, she disappeared behind a screen that stood near the front windows of the building.

There was the sound of crockery pieces knocking against one another, the snort of hot water through a faucet, the clanking of a spoon inside a cup, and then the girl reappeared. She came forward, through the wooden gate to the chair he sat in, the stout cup steaming in her hands.

"Ersatz coffee, but better than *you've* had in some days." She grinned, putting it into his hands.

Discomfort came over him for the first time that this stocky, big-featured, sweet girl should be black. He said nothing, but frowning, drank the hot brew, feeling his blood awaken to the thrust of the coffee's heat through his system.

The girl said, "I'd put milk in, but the water from the tap isn't hot enough, the milk would make it lukewarm. You could have milk separate, ersatz milk, too. Could you stand that? Canned milk?"

Tiger felt the tears welling in his eyes, and decided he didn't give a damn whether they did or not. He looked up at her and nodded.

The girl nodded back and specified, "Now? Or after your coffee?"

Tiger gulped from the cup. He caught his breath. "Later. Thank you."

Satisfied with his state, the girl turned, and going back through the gate, moved around to the other side of the desk and sat down. From a drawer she took some papers and arranged them beside the covered typewriter, but Tiger felt her eyes on him. He waited.

"Cigarette?" the girl asked casually.

"When do we canonize you?" Tiger smiled. "Now or when the weather's warmer?"

She grinned, but did not answer. The cigarette pack was extended toward him. He took one, and the girl, leaning forward over her desk and the fence, held a match for him. He drew on the cigarette lingeringly, as though it would be his last pleasure on earth and was to be savored with reverence.

Still the dark girl watched with her good, bulging eyes.

"Why the heck aren't you home in your bed?" she asked.

Tiger swallowed. "I don't have one." But as he said it, his gaze leveled at her, honestly, directly, without embarrasment.

"Gracious."

"Where do *you* live?" he asked.

"Brooklyn."

"I've never seen Brooklyn."

"You're new in town?"

"From Chicago." He nodded.

"Now isn't that nice. I don't mean for Chicago. . . ." And an ecstatic giggle broke from her.

Presently the giggle was done and she sobered herself to study him again.

"You just fancy our front porch here?" she asked.

"It was out of the wind. On the other hand there was Union Square."

"Jesus. On as nasty a night as last night?"

"True." Tiger nodded.

"How come? You maladjusted?"

"What?"

"Something I'm studying."

"Oh. Well, I ain't. I'm job-hunting."

"Disoriented," the girl said. "First one I met since I started my course."

"What?"

"First boy who's disoriented. I mean, aside from what's obvious. Disoriented means you feel like hell."

"Not me. Not any more." He toasted with the cup. "Thanks to you."

"Shoo." The girl smiled. "Job-hunting? What're you looking for?"

"Anything. Anything. Believe me, God, I mean it. Anything."

"Mmm. But nothing just unskilled, huh?"

"Why the hell not?"

"No, you wouldn't." The girl shook her head and turned inside-out her prodigious bottom lip.

"Wouldn't what?"

"Like janitoring."

Tiger hung fire. "I don't know anything about janitoring."

"Long hours, but no pressure," the girl pointed out. "My name's Edith."

"Hi, Edith. What the hell're you talking about?"

"I'm talking about your being janitor here. You notice the radiators all on when we came in? That's because we got no janitor. He beat up his wife again and she brought charges. Disoriented family if I ever saw one. So I leave the radiators on. I wouldn't be a bit surprised but what we're all going to be blown up any minute."

"What *is* this place?" Tiger asked.

"In here, a bookstore, and me. Upstairs, the library. Over there, just over the hall, some people renting."

"And the rest of the building?" asked Tiger.

"The rest?" Edith drew back. "Classrooms, of course. Boy, don't you know where you are?"

"No."

"You're sitting in one of the most famous and highly thought of schools in the world. Boy, this is the New York Labor School."

Her name, he learned, was Edith Mackey, and of her multiple duties at the New York Labor School, the dominant one was acting as secretary to Mr. Shagley, the school's president. The school, she informed him, was not an accredited formal one, but an old and respected center of informal adult education. Its teachers and lecturers were professor on the staffs of the city's universities; prominent political or economic writers; professional politicians, usually of the Socialist or Demo-Socialist parties, but frequently of the Republican or Democratic. The chief interests of the school were politics and economics; its orientation, socialist and liberal. The student body was variegated: many working people, graduate students whose field of specialty found rich nourishment in the school's more esoteric courses of study, younger members of the labor movement whose unions or political parties (notably the Demo-Socialist Party, which rented offices on the third floor of the school) were providing advance education in this field of endeavor or, finally, private individuals attracted to the stimulation and emotional satisfaction of adult education. A stronghold of socialism, the school had for long decades been fighting a constant battle against infiltration of its staff by Communists, who recognized an invaluable audience for their proselytizing in the politically minded, liberal-tending student body of the school. Tiger knew little of the formal history of the labor movement, but Edith's enthusiastic exposition quickened his interest; it was reinforced by the possibility of work being available to him here, if it were only the menial business of janitoring.

At nine o'clock the president of the school, Mr. Shagley, came in. To Tiger's eyes he looked more like a racing buff than someone engaged in adult education. With his sports jacket and flannel trousers he wore a dark blue shirt and a florid four-in-hand. His shoes were the creamy tan color Tiger associated with cheap salesmen.

Edith followed Mr. Shagley into his office. She would be telling Shagley about him, recommending him for the janitor's job. He wondered if he should tell them what he'd done back in Chicago. Would they hire him if they knew? It wasn't anybody's business but his own, was it? And there wasn't any reason they would ever have to find out. He wouldn't tell them; he would keep it to himself.

He could hear their muffled voices in discussion, and presently Shagley came to the door again. He looked Tiger over briefly, and Tiger, in his discomfort at the examination, found enough strength to get, however shakily, to his feet.

"Edith tells me you're interested in this janitor job," Shagley said. His voice was unpleasantly high-pitched and nasal in quality. Behind him Edith's black head appeared, nodding vigorously at Tiger.

"Yes; yes, I am," Tiger answered.

"Any experience?"

"No, sir. I think I could learn to be good at mechanical things, fixing things, and things like that. And I don't mind hard work, like the cleaning and so forth."

"Where you live?"

"No place, sir. I'm flat broke, I had to move out."

"There's living quarters with the job. Down in the basement here. Not so damn much, but you don't have to pay for them. Y'really want this job?"

"Yes, sir." He took a step forward, his heart pounding unnaturally under the stimulation of the coffee he'd drunk.

"Guess you'll be temporary," Shagley said, "young guy like you. But if it helps you out of a hole, there's nothing lost, and we can use you, if only temporarily." He turned to Edith. "Okay, he's your baby. Show him the place and his room downstairs. Better draw an advance."

And he disappeared into his office, closing the door behind him. Edith stood facing Tiger, grinning broadly.

Tiger said, "Christ. *That* was quick."

"Mr. Shagley doesn't waste his time," said Edith.

"What was that he said about—advance?"

"He's crazy on the subject," Edith answered, returning to her desk. "Mr. Shagley can't *stand* seeing people with no money at all. That's why he's a socialist, in my opinion. Now. How much we need to get you started?"

Tiger drew a small sum against his first salary. It was enough to pay for a large lunch, but somewhere in his days of hunger his ability to eat had sharply waned, and a bowl of soup was all he could manage to get down at noontime. He fetched his suitcase from Grand Central Station and moved into the cramped, musty rooms assigned him in the basement of the Labor School. In midafternoon Edith made him lie down to rest, and on the gas ring in the closet that served as his kitchen heated more soup for him. He slept until five o'clock and awoke with a demanding appetite. When he went out, he returned to the neighborhood lunch counter and ordered the first full meal he'd had since the gargantuan breakfast of his first morning in New York. Feeling as though he had recently recovered from a long, grave illness and walked afresh in the ranks of living men, he returned to the school and sought out Edith at her desk in the bookshop.

"I'm cutting my class tonight so I can show you around," she said. "How're you feeling?"

"Great, thanks," said Tiger. "I want to find out how my job works."

"You will. Don't you want to find out about the school itself?"

"Sure I do."

"Good." She nodded. "Maybe we'll educate you as well as find work for you. You look more intelligent now you've eaten."

Tiger snorted. "Thanks a lot."

"Come on, we'll tour the joint before the crowd gets here."

He started in on his duties the next morning, and in the evening, led firmly by Edith, he sat in on a psychology lecture. On the following day he learned there was to be a round-table discussion on the current adventures of the labor movement and that Norman Thomas would be one of the speakers. He had heard of Thomas in Chicago, primarily as a figure of fun due to his repetitious nominations for the Presidency on the Socialist ticket, but in this persistence there was an aspect of character that appealed to Tiger. It made him keener than ever to hear the renowned man speak.

The discussion proved to be all he had hoped for. Meeting Edith afterward, he offered to by her coffee before she went home to Brooklyn, and they sat for an hour at the lunch counter in the next block while Tiger asked her questions about the history and nature of the labor movement. Edith told him about the school's library. He should check out a few books on the subject the next day, she said. It was past midnight when she went off to her subway.

The library of the New York Labor School owned the most extensive assemblage of labor-movement literature in the United States, an invaluable treasury for research workers, students, and people professionally active in politics or the unions themselves. At either end of the dimly lit vaulted room was a wide balcony where the pamphlet collections were stored; and in its center, on a tiny lamplit island, isolated in a dark surrounding sea of modern political history, sat the gray-haired little spinster who kept the library's glass-paneled doors open from three o'clock in the afternoon until eleven o'clock at night.

Tiger began to spend his evenings there. Reading was hard for him at first, but he forced himself and soon it seemed that the words were coming to him easier. Besides, it was ideas that he wanted. The fundamentals of socialism had an irresistible appeal for him, and he began auditing classes that Edith would recommend. It wasn't long before he was pestering the librarian, and as many of the students as would tolerate his persistence, for her and their ideas: What was *their* story? Why did *they* decide to attend the Labor School? Had they tried practical ways to put their beliefs to work?

Long ago, as a child, Tiger's imagination had been struck by the idealism of Catholicism. It had been lovingly explained to him by the more sympathetic nuns he had been taught by. Yet he had spent all his adult life repudiating the trappings of formal Church practice and had in this way suffered what seemed to him now the severe loss of the real Christian's aspiration of spirit. In the socialists he met now he found this same spirit, sternly tempered by life histories that had been harsh teachers, giving little of comfort and less of privileges. These were tough men who talked to the

Labor School's classes, reared in a demanding and serious business; but the spine of their convictions was an intelligent and rational dream, and the dream drew Tiger's awakening curiosity and understanding toward it.

There would be dying bouts of winter in the northern states, but spring had substantially arrived, bringing with it the ageless signal to begin new endeavors, to start out afresh, to review one's standing and decide to be satisfied or to break out for uncertain goals and dreams of bright achievement. The same road that a week before had led Tiger Rizzuto to New York carried Helen Maclean eastward, her back turned calmly upon the recent past, her mind set with enthusiasm toward the work awaiting her. These were two of many, the young adults, the incompleted beings driving toward destinations they never doubted existed.

Wynn Bargmeister, a clerk in the Department of State in Washington, threw out the textbooks on aeronautics he kept in his small apartment and determined anew to consecrate his attention to his future in the foreign service. Aeronautics had its allure, but only a fool could think it more important than what was going on in the hallways and private offices of the building he worked in. He followed what was going on as closely as he could, and was the first one of his rank to know by what name they were calling the new aid plan in, first, the confidential conferences, then the washrooms, and soon thereafter in the more expensive cocktail lounges of Washington.

As one of the war's victors, from the outset the United States had chosen to travel, not the road of exacted reparations from the vanquished, but, as was characteristic of its people, the road of restoration for both the defeated nations and its sorely damaged allies. This approach was not shared by its ally, the Soviet Union, whose pragmatic attitude toward nations lately whipped to insensibility, as well as toward friends suggestively intimate to her doorstep, altered the aspect of American's filial passion to hold erect an aging Europe. The hymn of rehabilitation became America's martial tune of essential security.

George Marshall was the Secretary of State. As head of the enormous armed forces of the United States during the war, he had become intimate with the administrative life in

Washington, and he knew well the strength of the Congress in deciding upon vital issues and the answers the nation would propose to them. His desire for a stable peace, his knowledge and his well-known perspicacity, so great a contradiction to the popular conception of the military mind, was at this juncture an asset of the greatest value. To the view of the majority of Americans he was everything that Douglas MacArthur was not, and this belief lent still greater weight to his words in matters of primarily civilian character.

His staff had labored with difficulty to design a plan of his that would bring about the rehabilitation of Europe and at the same time provide an incentive to the disorganized and stricken nations to help themselves; it remained for George Marshall to comprehend fully the implications of so vast an undertaking.

The American people heard of this plan for the first time not from George Marshall but from Under-Secretary of State Dean Acheson, in the town of Cleveland, Mississippi, on May 8. Acheson's remarks on that occasion were given full development by himself at Harvard University on June 5. The graduating class of that institution heard an address that was unusual in its simplicity and directness:

"It is already evident that before the United States Government can proceed much further in its efforts to alleviate the situation and help start the European world on its way to recovery, there must be some agreement among the countries of Europe as to the requirement of the situation and the part those countries themselves will take in order to give proper effect to whatever action might be undertaken by the Government. It would be neither fitting nor efficacious for this government to undertake to draw up unilaterally a program designed to place Europe on its feet economically. This is the business of the Europeans. The initiative, I think, must come from Europe. The role of this country should consist of friendly aid in the drafting of a European program and of later support of such a program so far as it may be practical for us to do so."

That June morning it was nine-thirty before Tiger Rizzuto arrived back at the Labor School and got to work. The third-floor offices of the Demo-Socialist Party claimed his attention first. There had been a meeting there the night before, and the conference room was a sea of littered papers, soggy paper coffee cups and heaped ash trays. He cleaned the place out thoroughly, mopped the floor, and for good measure rewaxed the long conference table, though Wednesday was the customary day to spend on furniture upkeep. It was eleven before he could in conscience turn to his favorite task—sweeping and dusting the bookstore. The school was generally deserted until midafternoon, but in the bookstore there was Edith to talk to, and when the dusting and sweeping out were done, she invariably invited him to join her for coffee and a cigarette.

"The problem," said Edith when he sat down to the steaming cup she had placed on the edge of her desk for him, "is what the D.S.P. is going to decide *it* thinks of the Marshall Plan. You know what I think? I think if you've got two socialists, you've got a disagreement. You ever notice that?"

"Hell, I think that's fine," said Tiger. "At least they're thinking."

"Sooner or later somebody's gonna have to compromise."

"Not till the other guys win 'em over. *I* never would," he bragged.

"What would you do when the chips were down, get out of the D.S.P.?"

"You're damn right I would. Wouldn't you?"

The brown brow wrinkled. "I don't know," Edith said.

"Edith," said Tiger. "How come you're tied up in all this? I mean, everything about you, with your heart and all—not just your political opinions."

"Oh."

Quickly. "You don't mind me asking?"

A grin. "Course not." Her full lips came together thoughtfully. "The job here, I guess. I didn't know anything about it till I just got this job the summer I finished high school. Somebody told me about the opening. Then, when I got here—well, I was prepared for anything. You know, you have to be prepared for anything."

"You mean, being a Negro?" Tiger forced himself to ask.

"More or less."

But then he was impatient. "What the hell do you mean, 'more or less'?"

"I mean *yes*," Edith snapped. Then she was shamed by

her nervousness and took a breath. "Well, I had the job. And I noticed how everybody was to me: I mean, Mr. Shagley, and the teachers, and all the people coming to the classes. Nothing I had to worry about or feel bad about at all. So naturally I liked that. And naturally after a while I got intrigued by all that's going on around here." She paused. "Maybe that's why I don't know exactly what I'd do if I had a real serious difference of opinion with the Demo-Socialists. Just drop them? . . . Course that's what they did to the old Socialist Party when they disagreed. But don't you think that's a shame?"

"A shame? No, I don't see why it's gotta be," Tiger challenged.

Edith's eyes lighted with excitement.

"It used to be a real *party*, candidates and all that. That's why Mr. Shagley and all the others, the original ones, that's why they left Mr. Thomas and *his* people. They figured the New Deal had done what *they'd* been yelling for. They didn't want to be Democrats because that would've meant their being hitched up with a lot of stuff they didn't have any use for, but by and large they figured there wasn't any more sense to being a party. The D.S.P. doesn't even want candidates any more, it just gives its support to whatever Republicans or Democrats it likes the looks of."

"That's not the big thing, Edith," said Tiger. "The big thing, as I see it, is it uses its prestige to advise the unions' political-action committees. *That's* the big thing."

"And boy, have they got prestige. I just think it'd be more fun to be a real party with rallies and conventions and all. You know, smoke-filled rooms?"

"Have you seen the third-floor office some days?" Tiger asked.

Gleeful laughter broke from her. "We could put Mr. Shagley up for President—or mayor of New York, anyway."

Tiger leaned back in his chair, stretching his legs out before him.

"Edith. How many guys exactly does the D.S.P. have on its staff?"

"Why are you asking?"

"Wondered."

"I don't know. Real salaried ones, maybe six or seven."

"Where do they all come from? They all educated?"

"How should I know where they come from? Mr. Henderson, he came here from the Army, I know that. He and Mr. Mills are lawyers; I don't know how much school the others got. Come on, why are you asking that?"

Tiger leaned forward conspiratorially. His whisper dispersed the steam rising from the coffee cup just beneath his chin.

"Edith. Do you think I might ever get a job with them?"

Edith sat up abruptly, amazed.

"With the D.S.P.? Gawd, *I* don't know." She thought about it. "I don't see why not."

"What about—you know—fact that I'm the janitor here right now."

Edith crowed. "My Lord, you think anybody cares about that? They see you in class, they know what kind of questions you're always pinning people down with. They know you aren't any janitor. They know it even better when the plumbing breaks down."

"If I went on studying, I could learn enough to be some use to them maybe," Tiger suggested. "I could—I don't know—be a go-between man with the political-action committees, maybe something like that—something not *too* responsible. Help with fund raising, maybe, or the routine office work—

"Why don't you talk to Mr. Henderson?"

For a moment Tiger paled. Then, with a shake of his head, he stood up. He paced the open area around Edith's desk. "No, not that way. First I want to attract their notice. In a good way, I mean. If I learn more, if I really *knew* more, I could speak out more in some of the forum sessions. They might notice me then, Edith."

She faced him. "You want them to, Tiger, they will. You want some helpful tips from a smart girl? The D.S.P. isn't any party any more, maybe, but it's political as all hell, and important. Don't try to fool anybody about anything in your past. Do you have a record?"

"Record?"

"Yes, I just had a feeling . . ."

"Oh, I don't have a record, exactly. But I did come close and I'm clean now and I'll stay that way," he said.

"I don't think that makes any difference, but Jesus, Tiger, don't be a jerk. Keep it in mind. Don't just forget it happened, if the time comes." Her dark cheeks were moist with her embarrassment. "Tiger. Nobody's gonna do anything but admire you and give you a boost up, so long as you swallow what's true and don't kid yourself about it."

He had stopped in his pacing. Now he turned away from her. He walked around to the rear of the switchboard that flanked Edith's desk. He crossed his arms on the top of it and leaned his chin briefly on his arms.

"I've swallowed it," he said. "I don't mind your knowing. Or anybody around the school here knowing. Christ. I never any time till just these last few weeks thought that could be true. It's like what . . ." He stopped, his face flushing.

"Like what *I* said about when I came to work here," Edith finished for him.

"Oh, Christ, Edith, it's the damnedest world."

She chuckled. "Every once in a while, it sure is."

And if he could work his way into the D.S.P., he thought, even with his past openly admitted, was there anything impossible? Was it possible he could get Juney and the the baby back? A family man: could a guy like himself really hope to be a family man one day?—settled, respected, head of the kind of loving family that lonelier people flocked around, hoping to warm themselves at the glow's edge? Could Tiger Rizzuto come through muck and end up a substantial, taxpaying, vote-casting family man? The idea of a vow came to him. If ever he did, he and Juney were going to have big celebrations on holidays, he promised himself, no matter how trying things might be for them at the moment. When Thanksgiving or Christmas or New Year's Day came, they were going to have a turkey—three turkeys in two months, what the hell, live it up—and no holiday would pass without them finding someone who had no family and who would enjoy sharing their holiday with them, warming at the edge of the glow.

He turned his mind to the problem of attracting the notice of Driscoll Mills or Tom Henderson. He caught his breath and whispered, "I could, Edith. And if anything could happen with the D.S.P., I could get my wife back."

Edith looked up at him sharply. She said nothing, but waited.

"I could," he repeated. "Don't you see? If I was doing something that looked like it might lead somewhere eventually, something I liked and *knew* I could be good at someday, then I know I could get her and the baby to come back to me. If—if I could get the place downstairs fixed up, I might even ask her to come out from Chicago ahead of time. She could help me study and get ready—Juney's smart, you don't know . . ." He stopped. "Edith, you think it could be possible for a girl to not mind living down in the basement rooms if she knew it wasn't going to be forever?"

Edith held his gaze levelly. "I don't know. You could fix it up, maybe."

"You look funny. What's wrong?"

"I didn't know you had a wife and baby."

"Oh, I guess not. Sorry, I thought you did, Edith."

"Yes," Edith said.

"What's the matter?"

She pursed her lips in annoyance. "It's nothing to *me,*" she explained. "None of *my* business. But—it's different. I mean, an unmarried girl like me talks to a boy—it doesn't mean anything, I mean she's not after him or anything like that—but the way she talks to him is different than the way she'd talk if he was a married man. When you talk to a married man, you're talking to the whole *couple*. Disconcerting—that's what it is, just suddenly finding out."

"Gee, Edith. I'm real sorry. I never thought."

"Well. You were saying about fixing the place up downstairs?"

"Yes!" Tiger answered, excited again. "Fix it up really nice, I bet I could do it without very much money. I'll write to her, I know she'll be glad to hear from me if—if everything's going to be different now. I'm sure she'd be glad. . . ."

Doubt dimmed his excitement suddenly then. He stood looking at nothing, uncertain of anything now that he was faced with the possibility of winning her back.

"You won't find out till you try," Edith murmured.

That night Tiger did not go to class. He sat in the library for the three hours it took him to write to Juney and tell her where he was.

19

TIGER READ THE NEWSPAPERS AVIDLY. MUCH that he read he did not understand, but much that in the past had either been vague to him or seemed downright foolish was now becoming clearer in the light of his studies. One of the school's activities that had especially drawn his interest was the forum discussion on foreign policy. Moderated by Mills and Henderson of the D.S.P., these free-for-all debates had taught him much. As yet he had not himself contributed to the usually violent exchange of opinions, and though Mills and Henderson knew him as the building's janitor and an almost constant part of the library scene, they had had no personal contact with him. Tiger knew that after each of the forum classes Mills and Henderson went out to have coffee somewhere together. He longed to follow them and eavesdrop on their talk. The possibility of his ever knowing them and being made a part of their after-hours group was impossibly remote.

The forum on foreign policy was held in Room 32, and when Tiger came into the classroom on the following Thursday night, the air was already beginning to fill with cigarette smoke. The school kept forum classes small, and only the first three rows of student desks were filled. Each alternate desk held a battered and shallow metal ash tray, of which Tiger washed dozens every morning. Tiger carried the stenographer's pad Edith had given him to keep his notes in. He let himself in quietly, and went easily unnoticed by the generally voluble people sitting in the student desks. He sat alone in the rear, near the door, in case someone should have to call him to tend to something amiss in the building's functioning. Sitting down, he opened the pad, and out of childhood habit flicked the point of the lead pencil with his tongue and wrote down the date at the head of the blank page.

Presently Mills and Henderson arrived and climbed up to their places at the plain wooden table on the dais facing the class. Tom Henderson was the younger of the two, not yet forty, a broad-shouldered, bull-necked man whose sensitive face belied the aggressive forward thrust with which he carried his head. Driscoll Mills, a self-exiled Southerner, was gray-haired and scholarly-looking; his contemplative calmness of manner offset Henderson's energy.

After a few disorganized nods and wavings of hands to silence the class, Mills pulled his straight chair forward, cleared his throat against the fattening strata of cigarette smoke, and blinked against the glare of the bare overhead lights. "Since the end of the Second World War," he said, "the United States has sat at the council tables of the world timidly."

He waited. Tiger watched his eyes as, without haste, they moved from one face to another of those before him. These forum sessions were always excited. The difficulty was to keep the students in line until the introductory remarks had fully outlined the area to be discussed—this much Tiger had learned. He admired the firmness with which Mills, usually lethargic, confronted the class.

"It is not surprising that we have," he went on. "We are inexperienced on the international scene, beyond the personal force of an occasional Benjamin Franklin or Franklin Roosevelt. Other nations do not know what to think of us, what to expect of us in the powerful new role that, whether we like it or not, we've been given. We have been on trial, and we have looked like it."

He drew a breath, and Tiger knew Mills could sense the kettle boiling in the class. Almost explosively he concluded, "All this is changed, and now we have the Marshall Plan. Okay, what the hell do you think of it?"

The babble was immediate and deafening. Mills and Henderson exchanged a knowing glance, and each waved his hands for order. From the confusion at last came the voice of a poorly dressed and aging white-haired man, speaking in a thickly unaccustomed English. "It is the beginning of America's maturity!" he croaked.

Some applauded, some hooted—the usual response of the class. On one side a swarthy fat woman stood up. "But what about the Jews? Do the people running all that money care about the Jews?"

"Many of them are," snapped someone else.

In the middle of the room a man laughed with suspicious harshness and drew the class' attention. Tiger did not recognize him. "What the hell is the Marshall Plan anyway?" he said. "A fake gesture of pseudo-good will on the part of a sick and dying way of life. So let the money-bags soothe their guilt feelings and tell themselves how goddamned Christian they are. They can't stop the obvious uprising of the real people!"

"Commie!" someone yelled.

"Screw the Commies!" jeered another.

"And *you* can screw George Marshall and the rest of those poor red-assed monkeys!"

"Kremlin crap!"

"Guy's gotta be a Commie 'cause he talks sense?"

"Listen, you dumb jerk——"

Over the tumult Tom Henderson bellowed, "Quiet down, all of you! Any opinion gets heard in this classroom, understand? Any opinion at all. You don't have to like it, but you have to live with it. All of us have to live with it anyway, inside a classroom or out!"

Gradually the racket subsided, and a few wonderfully polite hands were raised now in a bid for the floor.

A sober-faced young woman was recognized. She did not stand up, but leaned forward, gripping the edge of her student desk. "I look at it this way," she said in a clear and sharp-toned voice. "Russia has been steadily extending herself during the time when we were feeling shy and clumsy because all of a sudden we had grown into a being a great, great, big, big boy. Now we accept the fact that we are, and the Marshall Plan is proof of it." There was a mild threat of snorting from others of the class, but still others sharply shushed it. "Now that at last we're *doing* something, I think the Russians will settle back and stop making with so much army-rattling and——"

It was at this point that Tiger said, "Oh, no . . ."

His voice came loudly from the rear of the class and had therefore a special compulsion for the others in the room. The young woman speaking stopped abruptly, and she, together with the others, turned to look at him. Tiger felt the color flooding into his face. Oh, God, why hadn't he kept his mouth shut. What did *he* know about it?

The young woman ended limply. "Well, that's what *I* think."

But the eyes were still on him, in surprise and curiosity.

Henderson had done too good a job of reminding everyone present to mind his manners, and Tiger felt himself drowning in an attentive and cordial silence.

Through the awful quiet he heard Henderson's voice. "Well, *why* don't you think so? You. I'm sorry, buster, I don't know what the hell your name is."

"Tiger. I mean, it don't matter. Doesn't."

The world for him was turning grayish blue on the edges, and the overhead lights were taking on an intensity that was unnatural and threatening. Tiger felt sweat break suddenly on his forehead and on the sides of his neck and in his armpits. Nobody was saying anything. Everybody was waiting, because apparently Mills had given him—him, Tiger—the floor.

"I mean—" He tried to uncross his legs and found that they had gone to sleep, but at least he had found a shaking imitation of his voice. "I mean I don't think they will, the Russians. Settle back—settle down or anything."

"Why not?" Mills asked, and still there was silence. The faces, inexplicably, had not turned away.

"Well. I agree with this young lady about the Marshall Plan and proof and all that. But hell, what you said before, Mr. Mills, about how we've been timid and nobody knows how we're going to act and all that. Well, hell, it's worse than that."

He didn't know why, but they were still listening. The cigarette smoke itself seemed to have arrested its drift in the air. No sound came to his ear. They all had seen him at classes. None had ever heard his voice before. Maybe that was it. Maybe he'd better shut up.

"Worse in what way?"

This time it was not Mills but Henderson. The haze was receding, and Tiger's eyes were able now to register the individual faces turned to him. As he went on, he got to his feet, and as he had been taught to do in grammar school, he stepped around to stand behind his desk.

"The Marshall Plan's fine, shoot, sure it is," he said, still hesitant. "But the Russians have a whole world to look to. Back before, in the old days, I mean through history and all that—well, every goddamned time we dealt with anybody, it was the European nations. That made sense then, I guess. But I don't think it does now. I mean, the countries England

and France and them own, or run, like all over Asia and Africa—those are *countries*. With other people living in them and all, I mean countries. They aren't England or France or Holland."

Still again he stopped. He was about to sit down, but no one as yet tried to speak. He saw the Commie looking at the floor, his back turned to him, and one other person making a note in a book. Everybody seemed still to be looking at him as though they understood he had not quite finished. Then, at last, ease came to him. He realized he was saying these things because he believed in them; it was true he belived them only because the writers he'd read had convinced him of their truth, but that just damn well had to be good enough. Enthusiasm, like a shot of liquor, warmed through him. He held to the back of his student desk, but he knew now he had the floor.

"There's not two worlds," he pointed out. "There's not Europe and us. Or the democracies and the Commies. There's three worlds. That's what I don't think the government has got through its head." He choked briefly: "I don't think they're moneybags, the government. I'm sorry, I don't; but I'd sure as hell *like* to think that everybody I don't like is a moneybags. They're not. They're, I guess, hard-working slobs like everybody else, who keep making a mess 'cause they don't know any better. One thing I think they don't know, or maybe just haven't digested yet—in their thinking, you know?—is that whole other part of the world that's not Europe and not us either. Like India, Burma, them Arabs, the countries in Africa. I don't hardly *know* what countries there are in Africa. And I think the government's in pretty much the same kind of fix as me. They're there. Okay. What do we say to them? You shake hands with a guy, how do we shake hands with all those countries we hardly know? How do we let them know we're nice? The answer is, so far we don't."

He hesitated a moment, and then sat down heavily. A pause, and someone asked a question. Another answered it. Discussion was reborn and the air thickened with ideas, voices, calumnies, and insincere threats. Tiger sat in a bated-breath closet of embarrassment—the janitor guy, too ambitious for his brains, monopolizing. He put his hand over his eyes and tried to concentrate his attention on what the others were saying now.

After he had died afresh a number of times more, he became aware of Mills making what sounded like closing remarks. He looked up, but could barely distinguish the figures on the dais through the cigarette smoke. He lit one of his own cigarettes. A moment more, and the class was clearing, people pulling on raincoats or tightening bandannas or stretching of chattering in groups of two or three. At first he felt he could not move. Vast tiredness weighted him, and it needed effort to get at length to his feet.

The first of the departing students had opened the door to the hall, and with sluggish steps he guided himself toward it.

"Hey. What the hell *is* your name, by the way?"

Tiger looked up. Tom Henderson, a bulging file folder in his hand, was holding the door open for him. With a clumsy pirouette Tiger tried to take the door from him and usher him through, but found himself being propelled into the hall. Over his shoulder to Henderson he answered, "Tiger Rizzuto."

"Oh, yes, I thought it was something like that."

Tiger started down the flight of thin, worn marble stairs and Tom Henderson fell into step beside him, his overlarge head bent forward and down like a charging bull's.

"That was very interesting about the Asiatics and Africans," Mills said.

"Thank you," Tiger murmured, coloring.

"You seem to take quite an interest in this forum class. Although the notebook didn't get as much of a workout tonight as usual, I noticed. Where're you from, Tiger?"

"Chicago."

"Been in New York long?"

"No, sir."

A turn of the stairs and they were nearing the ground floor. Driscoll Mills came up behind them. "Coffee, Tom?" he asked.

"Sure," said Henderson. "I just want to pick up a memo Edith said she'd have for me. She's working late tonight. Won't take a minute."

"Good night, Mr. Mills, Mr. Henderson," said some of the students ahead of them as they headed out toward the street.

"Good night."

"Good night."

Tiger saw Edith come out of the bookstore. She stopped when she saw them approaching."

"Coffee, Tiger?" asked Henderson.

"Huh?"

"Join Mills and me for coffee down the block?"

"Oh. Sure, hell, yes . . ."

As they came up to her Edith said, an unaccustomed softness in her voice, "Tiger, there's a long distance call for you."

Tiger stopped short, momentarily baffled.

Edith explained, "She says it's Mrs. Robin Rizzuto." Then she grinned and forced herself to laugh. "Lord, Lord. You never told me your name was Robin."

The national response to Marshall's statement of his plan was not unanimously favorable; abroad, reaction was similarly divided. While Ernest Bevin of Great Britain and Georges Bidault of France enthusiastically invited their neighboring countries to join with them in a conference to draw up such a program as Marshall had suggested, the Soviet Union rushed forward with a maneuver designed to embarrass the United States into committing itself to a certain exact figure of dollars in aid before the most skeletal agreement could be reached among the Europeans.

The climate of fresh endeavor descends swiftly from the councils of the grave to the preoccupations of the frivolous. In Paris that summer there was a reborning spirit: at the conference tables, at the gatherings of intellectuals, in the petulant guerrilla warfare of the press. As was inevitable, the excitement made itself felt in the salons of the fashionable and the ateliers of the *couturiers*.

The work of the latter was already causing upheaval in the United States fashion industry, and the American people, through the syndicated columns of their newspapers, began to read of one designer in particular, Christian Dior. His name was soon to be adoringly caroled by workers in the garment district of New York, and just as soon to be vilified by husbands everywhere. The New Look he introduced rendered the women's dress of previous seasons irreparably outmoded; this fact would in the coming fall season enrage those who had paid for last year's dresses, but would be the delight and inspiration of the thousands of Americans who earned their living in the world of fashion.

On a certain afternoon that summer, an informal conference was held in the offices of the Jules Fischel Agency, in the Graybar Building on New York's Lexington Avenue.

Only three people were involved in the meeting: Jules Fischel, his promising new assistant, Helen Maclean, and a fat, colorless young man with froggish eyes named Ladd Dorn. Ladd Dorn's real name had a more Baltic timbre to it, but in his profession it was a sensible convenience to adopt a name more agreeable to the ear. He and Helen Maclean sat in chairs before Jules Fischel's desk and waited while the owner of the agency completed a telephone call.

To Helen it was plain that Ladd was still nursing his hangover; if he had had anything to drink at his lunch hour, it apparently hadn't helped much. She was afraid that would make things difficult. When he was feeling unwell, which was often, Jules' brother-in-law and first lieutenant could be waspish.

Jules put the telephone down and, leaning forward, gave a preparatory pat to his small, dark mustache. His deep-set tired eyes, penetratingly black, glanced from one to the other of his employees. "Did you bring that folder, Helen?"

"Yes, right here, Jules," she said.

She handed him the leather portfolio, and he put it down, unopened, before him.

"We've talked a great deal about the new Dior silhouette," he began, addressing himself primarily to Ladd Dorn, "and Helen has come up with a thought. If there's anything to it, it will affect our work here at the agency."

"Aren't you the beaver?" Ladd smiled at Helen unpleasantly. "And what have you thought up now?"

Helen looked to her employer for a cue, and he nodded. She shifted in her chair to face Ladd.

"I got to thinking about the more well-known models, the expensive ones at the expensive agencies. A friend of mine in the art department at Y. and R. helped mock up some pictures to show what I mean." She could not keep her enthusiasm out of her voice. Her fingers were trembling when she picked up the portfolio from Jules' desk. She leaned nearer to Ladd Dorn and opened it. The portfolio contained a dozen full-length photographs of the most sought-after fashion models of the past season, and convincingly superimposed on their images Helen's friend had painted approximate versions of the new Dior line.

"As far as anyone knows, this is what the Dior silhouette will be," Helen said.

"Recherché, recherché, I've said it from the beginning," Ladd declared.

"What do you think of the pictures, Ladd?" Jules Fischel asked.

Ladd made a humming sound through pursed lips. "Very cleverly done, quite clever. Who did you say your friend was, Helen?"

"I didn't, and that's not the point. Now look, I know I'm not a wheel around here like you and Jules, but I think I've got something that can help the agency. Look at those models, Ladd. *You* know all about models. Doesn't something strike you about them in these clothes?"

"Pam Dillard's aging about the eyes," he observed.

Helen pounced.

"Is she? Is she, Ladd? I *knew* I could count on your genius for pinpointing the important point. You saw her spread in the spring things in *Vogue?*"

"Brilliant photography, that's what that was."

"Ladd, *I* think Dior's clothes make her look old."

"What?" He looked wildly at Jules, but the older man was watching Helen closely and gave no sign of his own thoughts.

Helen pursued, "Pam Dillard's the archetype of the models we've been seeing for years. Manicures, enameled—hard."

"Fashion models *have* to be idealizations, darling." Ladd clucked his tongue.

"Do they?" She flipped the pages over. "Look at Rena in this one." Helen grew expansive. "These dresses have a freedom, a flair to them. The popular fashion models won't do, a *new* kind of model is needed for these clothes. The china dolls lack *flair*."

"If it's flair they'll need, I assure you they'll find it in themselves to produce it."

"But it's a chance for *us,*" Helen pointed out. "The highest priced models are beyond our reach. Let's face it, we're strictly second echelon here. Jules, don't hate me for saying that——"

"Go on," Jules Fischel intoned. Neither of the others could tell what his reaction was. Helen plunged on.

"But as a second echelon outfit, we've got younger models and less, well, hard ones. They're pliable. And our prices are pliable. I think with proper handling our girls can beat Conover—anyone—out at their own game."

Ladd Dorn stiffened; his hangover was bringing perspiration out across his lineless forehead. Fleetingly Helen felt sorry for him, but the business at hand was more important; Ladd's sickness would have to wait for a later cure.

"What do you feel about all this, Ladd?" Jules asked.

Ladd pretended to study the photographs. Helen silently cursed Jules' reticence. She knew Ladd was afraid to take a stand one way or another without knowing his superior's views. If Jules would give the slightest hint of interest in her theory, she knew the fat boy would jump to agreement.

"Well, Helen," Ladd began patronizing, "you're a wonder to have gone to all this trouble—such an elaborate presentation——"

"The *idea,* Ladd, what do you think of it?" Abruptly she changed approach. "After all, I'm green at this. *You're* the one who'll have to tell me whether the theory can be implemented practically. You're the only one able to follow through."

Her sugared arrow seemed to hit its mark!

"Not at all, not at all, Helen. It is *your* idea, after all." Ladd simpered with pleasure. "You're such an efficient secretary, I'm sure you've already got hundreds of plans for implementing your project."

He left it in the air as a question, but Helen withheld an answer. As though suddenly struck by an entirely foreign thought, she sat back in her chair and slowly readjusted one of the small combs that held the curls back from her face. Presently she said, "I know all the best photographers think the world of your creative opinion, Ladd. They're the ones who'd have to be sold on this approach—and the manufacturers' people, if you think that would strengthen your position."

Ladd shifted uncomfortably. "I daresay, yes, the manufacturers, by all means," he temporized.

"You know if we go ahead, if there's any minor way in which I might be of help——"

"That's very generous of you, Helen, and——"

Jules Fischel gave a loud sigh and lit a cigarette. Apparently he had listened long enought, and now he spoke with energy.

"I think Helen may—*may,* mind you—have something," he said. "There's money available for some expansion of activity right now; we can invest in a strong campaign to get this agency up out of the—the second echelon, I believe you said."

Helen winced, but she knew a small wound would not deter Jules from racing reality.

He concluded, "I think we should give Helen her head."

Ladd Dorn looked from one to the other in slight mystification.

"In what way did you have in mind, Jules?"

"I wouldn't be able actually to——" Helen began.

"Oh, I think you would," Jules interrupted. "I propose," he stated, "that Helen handle this, at least in the beginning till we see how it goes. If it looks good then, it will need concentration from all of us, of course."

"Of course." Ladd Dorn nodded. "Oh, my poor darling Helen, but the *burden.* I mean, on top of all your secretarial duties——"

Jules was quick. "There won't be a question of secretarial duties."

"Naturally not!" Ladd exclaimed loudly. Then more quietly: "Of course not. Far, far too much responsibility for one person to have to carry."

"I'll want to think about details further before I bring you two in again," Jules said, standing up. He glanced at his watch. "It's four o'clock. Both of you get out of here, and Ladd, for God's sake go have a Martini someplace before your heart fails."

Ladd made gleeful noises as he got up. "Oh, Julie, believe me, after a day such as I've had today, it's all I can do to keep it beating at all."

Jules' reply was sour. "Today has nothing to do with it. Stay out of the bars and maybe *you'd* have a thought or two about the Dior line."

At the door Helen tried to pretend she did not hear the

exchange. Ladd was pale, his face dripping, when he opened the door for her. In the hallway he clucked his tongue. "It's this heat; I cannot *support* New York in the summer—not even the air conditioning does any good."

Helen was direct. "I'm sure Jules didn't mean a word about my taking on any new responsibility. I think he was just being mean to you, and it's hateful of him."

"Thank you, my dear." He mopped his cheeks.

They had reached the door of Helen's cubicle. She put a hand on his arm.

"Lookit, the air conditioning is like the Arctic at the Revere Room. Would you come have a cocktail with me? We *both* need it, and I think I owe you one for unintentionally handing Jules a brickbat."

"You're an angel," he said, "and I'd love it. Get your hat."

"I don't have one, I'm all ready."

"Good. So am I. *What* is the Revere Room?"

"At the Lexington. Three blocks, and the Martinis are gems."

"Thank God."

Helen had stayed at the Hotel Lexington when first she'd come to New York, and had on that occasion become attached to the Revere Room. Its quiet ease was a comfort, and the bold styling of the Paul Revere murals appealed to her without attracting her high opinion. Few people were in the place at four o'clock, and Ladd Dorn surveyed the bar without enthusiasm. Helen munched a pretzel until their Martinis were put before them.

"Good luck with our new program," Helen said, "if it materializes."

Ladd smiled thinly and gulped half his Martini. He fastened a cigarette in his ivory holder and lit it. Helen lit one of her own for herself.

"I'm sure you have an apartment, Helen?" he said.

"Forty-sixth Street, between Second and Third."

"Off Third?" Ladd drew out the marveling syllables.

Helen overlooked the thrust. "It's a converted cold-water walk-up," she continued. "The rooms are tiny, but there are five of them. Gives me a feeling of being substantial and doesn't cost any more than a one-room utility would."

"Snug," Ladd conceded. A calmer sip of his Martini, and

he sat back from the table comfortably. "I'm terribly impressed, I can't tell you, about how you made such a production to sell your little idea with. All those mock-ups and all. God knows one never finds a secretary in New York willing to go to all that trouble."

Helen looked at him. "Ladd."

"Yes?"

"I'm going to be candid with you, and I wish you'd do the same. You just sound silly when you lie."

The frog eyes widened, and the colorless eyebrows rose.

"Open any door in a New York office, Ladd, and you'll find a secretary with delusions of being vice-president if the head of the firm is a nice guy, and president if he's a louse."

"I didn't mean——"

"You meant to put me in my place," Helen stated flatly. "But will you get something through your head, for my sake? I am not—repeat, not—after your job."

He gazed, wounded, out into the room.

"That *is* what you thought in the meeting with Jules today, isn't it?"

There was a betraying hesitation before he answered. He gestured to the waiter across the room for another round.

"I wouldn't want to mislead you, Helen. I admire your ambition and energy but—good heavens, you're no threat to *my* job. I've been with Julie from the very beginning."

"Then do you have to try so hard to strap me down? *Let* me advance myself a little with this Dior idea. I can't possibly do you any harm."

"All right, relax, I won't put the fritz on it. But if ever the day comes when I think you *have* become a danger to me——"

"Now tell me why on earth I should do that?" She hesitated, then added flatly, "As one girl to another."

Only one eyebrow lifted now.

"Aren't we the sophisticates, though," he said as the waiter put new Martinis before them. Ladd Dorn ejected his cigarette from its holder, screwed in and lit another. "Helen?—you're exactly like all the other thousands of versions of you around New York, and let's eschew the all-the-girls-together bit, if you please." He went on. "You're no more a woman than I'm a man."

"Ladd, I . . ." The weakness in her voice astonished her.

"You're one of those bloodless careerists," he continued bitterly. "And because you're not a human being, no human being can trust you. Ruthless? The word has no meaning to your kind. Competitive? One can't apply it to you as an adjective, because it's the most basic part of your make-up."

He swung on her. "Don't you ask yourself why?" he demanded. "Aren't you fascinated by the horror you are? If you want to know the why of it, I can tell you: an ignorant little girl from the Midwest, scared to death at a tender age by some cock with a hard on, and afraid ever since of the fact that you're a woman and nature doesn't give a damn about you *except* that you're a woman."

Ladd let out his breath in an explosive breaking of his tension. His shoulders collapsing, he put his head in his hands.

For a moment Helen hadn't believed what she was hearing, and she sat erect and rigid, trembling from the shock of his attack. She did not trust herself to speak, and she had a strong compulsion to run out and away. But perhaps Ladd sensed this, too, because before she had the time, he lifted his head and calmly drew on his cigarette.

"Well"—he sighed—"it's a mean business." He turned and looked at her over his crumpled shoulder. "And besides, I'm sick, I tell you." The bulging eyes, of no certain color, were veiled.

"Yes, I can tell," she said quickly. "It's all right. Really. Don't worry." She made up her mind once and for all that she'd settle for love henceforth. No substitutes.

"Let's finish this," he said. "It's a bitch's game you're in, my dear Helen, and I'm an accomplished player."

"That's fairly evident," she said wryly and left it at that. Maybe I'll get married to a stevedore, she thought incongruously. She watched coolly as he sipped his drink. She thought he would leave her then, had almost hoped he would, but strangely enough he made no move to go. Well, he'll never do that to me again, she told herself.

More people had come in, and now as Helen looked about her she realized what a fool she'd been with Sprague in Chicago. She vowed she'd never again be a convenience of any sort to anyone. Her talk with Ladd had made that fact eminently clear.

By the door leading in from the hotel lobby she noticed a

young man. He looked down the length of the room as though slightly disoriented and then headed for the bar. He did not reach it. Ladd Dorn suddenly straightened up beside her.

"Shades of the proctoscope!" he shouted. "Dr. Kaufman, of all people! Dr. Kaufman! Marvin! Lookee, over here!"

The young man turned and came toward them with an easy, almost weary stride. Watching his approach, Helen felt an old clumsiness coming over her, a sudden threatening of her poise that happened seldom now. She did not know why this young man with his easy smile and lackadaisical saunter should affect her so. He was tall, but Helen thought he looked somewhat overweight. His features were broad and strong. Mediterranean, in spite of the light brown of his hair and his palish complexion, and he wore the thickest eyeglasses Helen had ever seen outside of those sometimes affected by eccentric villains in the movies. Still, his gray suit hung on him with grace.

"Hi, Ladd," was all he had time to say.

Ladd quickly escaped his handclasp.

"Sit down, join us, do!" he simpered. "Helen, this is Doctor Marvin Kaufman, my very own physician. Sit down, Marvin."

"I'm sure it would be—I was only calling on a patient of mine in the hotel, I thought a quick Martini——"

"Exactly what we're having—it'll make everything so simple for the waiter."

Helen put in, "Please join us, Doctor Kaufman. I'm Helen Maclean."

He held her glance for a fraction of a second, and behind his glasses Helen saw that his eyes were blue. She further felt that her first impression had been right: he looked tired. When he had given the waiter his order, he lit a cigarette.

Ladd Dorn was bubbling. "Helen is hardly old enough to vote, but she really has more talent than you would think possible in a newcomer in the business. She was *born* with a creative knack, flawless. I've just been berating her horribly, but that's simply my ego—I'm wildly envious of her. Helen, do you forgive me?"

"Of course, Ladd."

"And, Marvin, that last little trouble I had has simply vanished Vanished!—since you took care of me. Anything you get, Helen my dear—and you know how things happen in

New York—but anything, just you take yourself to Marvin. I wouldn't be alive without him."

The young doctor twisted uncomfortably in the face of the questionable flattery.

Helen searched a moment for what she might say to put him at his ease. "I hope your patient is better? The one here at the Lexington."

"Oh, I think she will be, thank you," Marvin Kaufman said.

"I'm very glad to know a doctor in New York. I haven't had to go to one since I moved here, but I guess you can never tell."

"Where are you from, Miss Maclean?"

"My dear Marvin," Ladd interrupted, "you must call her Helen. Helen's only a child."

Marvin threw Ladd a look of sharp annoyance. He said quietly, "Miss Maclean would think me a boor, and she'd be right."

Helen smiled. "That doesn't sound like something someone from New York would say. Are you an all-round doctor or do you specialize in something, Marvin?"

The waiter put his drink down in front of him and went away.

"I'm a G.P."

"Confess. You're boning up on a specialty on the side."

"No. G.P. is what I want to be."

"But everybody is specializing nowadays."

"I know. That's the trouble."

"If I guess right, I'm going to buy you a drink—are you dedicated to old-fashioned values?"

"You owe me one drink." He chuckled.

"I couldn't be happier," said Helen.

"I prefer treating the whole man, I suppose. And his whole family—when I'm lucky."

"I like that. Yes. I hope it's not cocktail banter. I'll tell you a secret: I don't know cocktail banter when I hear it."

"It's not banter." He smiled.

When he had finished his drink, the young doctor stood up, murmured polite sentences, and shook their hands and left.

As she paid the bill, Helen said, "Why don't we send you home in a taxi, Ladd? I think you're still ill."

"I'm worlds better, darling, really," he answered, uncertainly ushering her toward the street. "Besides, I'll be having dinner someplace. I shall take you home."

"Oh, for heaven's sake, Ladd, I'm just around the corner." She offered her hand, and the fat young man accepted it distractedly.

"You're an angel to ply me with liquor," he said. "I'll say that now. I don't promise it's the same thing I'll be saying in the morning."

"Fair enough. You're sure you're all right?"

"Oh, yes, certain of it."

"Good night, Ladd."

"Night, darling."

Helen turned and walked down Lexington Avenue alone.

At the agency the following day there was no opportunity to discuss the matter of the New Look models. Ladd was busy on a currently pressing project, and Jules Fischel put Helen to work at once gathering prospects together for a magazine spread that Chester Gibson was photographing. Gibson, an admirer of Helen's acumen, booked the three models Helen suggested to him, and that afternoon she looked in at the Gibson studio to see the progress they were making. Set-pieces of iron grillwork and carnival banners of every color cluttered the large room. The spread was to tie in with the New Orleans Mardi Gras in the coming February, and Gibson intended to take his time perfecting it.

He kept his word. Three weeks had passed before the final photographs were ready. The magazine staff took them over and copy writers set to work on the accompanying captions and story. A certain amount of discussion took place about the possibility of including the spread in a secondary capacity in the January New Year issue. Helen spent four sleepless nights. If the spread came out in January, it would be the same old story with the Fischel Agency girls in a second-rate place in the magazine. The work Chester Gibson had done merited more than that, Helen was certain. In the end it was decided to time the layout more pointedly, and it was scheduled for the February issue, in a prominent position in the magazine. For both Chester Gibson, who was not in the first rank of the city's fashion photographers, and Helen, whose models were less experienced than those usually appearing in the magazine's pages, this was a considerable achievement.

Winter, a hard winter of blizzards and record-making traffic disruption, came to the Eastern states. The Mardi Gras spread, appearing at last on the newsstands in February, attracted favorable comment from many knowledgeable people in the business. In New Orleans it caused some mild amusement. The process backgrounds of New Orleans scenes were authentic enough, but the studio properties in no way suggested the look New Orleans had in the living eye.

Steve Williams smiled to himself, remembering the pages he had idly turned during the airplane flight from Houston to New Orleans. The street he walked on now certainly did not look like the fashion pictures, and the beauty of a few women he passed had had a Latin richness that fashion models, he imagined, would shudder to think of owning.

It had rained an hour before, and the narrow French Quarter street was still wet. A few drops fell from the balconies overhanging the sidewalk, but above the clustered buildings the sun shone. The bright yellow air was still soft with damp, and to Steve it seemed the decay of the buildings he passed was as much related to mildew as to antiquity. The tone of the shops within them was anything but old: except for a few antique dealers, the majority of their windows were filled with modern fashionably imaginative objects. He passed one shop crowded with unusual mirrors, another displaying leather goods at extravagant prices, a small art gallery, a patisserie, and a coffee shop whose walls, visible from the sidewalk, were hung with the paintings of its frequenters. Steve walked with a step lightly anticipatory, and a block nearer than Jackson Square he found the guest house and restaurant he was looking for. Cousins of his in Houston had told him of it, and their description made his heart lift as he came to the door of Thaisa Chapman's House.

There was nothing ostentatiously prepossessing about the place. Two narrow half-glass doors, which rattled, led from the sidewalk immediately into the restaurant—a large square room filled with tables on which were checkered tablecloths and the expected overdripped candles. Steve was astonished to see a garish juke box in one corner; how had the place developed its fashionable reputation in the face of that? Across the room from it, faintly accented by a spotlight angled to strike the wall area immediately behind it, was a grand piano. Along the wall opposite from the street entrance ran the bar in a wide semicircle. At one end of the bar swinging doors led to the busy, noisy kitchen, and beyond it, through screen doors to a patio. The three farther sides of the patio were created by the guest house, Steve was later to discover, and all its rooms opened onto the balconies surrounding this casually kept garden and its iron furniture.

In seeking to determine the appeal of Thaisa Chapman's House, Steve was mistaken to look at the décor. The place was, by popular-hotel standards, shabby, nor did it contain more charm than he could have found in any dozen of New Orleans' innumerable houses. The attraction of this one was Thaisa Chapman herself, and Steve's eyes fell on her as he closed the street door with a clatter behind him.

Thaisa Chapman was behind the bar. More exactly, she was within it: if its shape was semicircular, so was the front half of Thaisa Chapman. Her girth as she perched there on a high stool almost filled the space, so that she seemed to be wearing a mahogany apron. She wore rimless glasses that were at the moment low on her short, retroussé nose, and a mass of blonde hair was piled on the top of her head into a bird's nest that was held in place, unreliably, by the three long pencils skewered through it. Her features were small and strikingly pretty, and the soft ballooning of the rest of her failed magically to detract from their appeal. Her bright button eyes looked up at the noise Steve made with the door, and she adjusted her glasses.

"Hi, hon," she called out, an effortless warmth in the casual greeting. "The rain stopped. Isn't that nice? Come sit down."

At that hour of the afternoon the restaurant was deserted, and Steve moved up the aisle between the tables toward the bar. He put down his suitcase and heaved himself up onto a stool.

"Hi," he answered, already grinning with pleasure.

"Just got here? What's your name?" smiled the friendly, enormous woman.

"Steve Williams. From Houston."

"*You* didn't write for a reservation," she chided.

"No, I didn't——"

"Honey, don't you know this is the absolute middle dead-center of the Mardi Gras season? Nobody in the whole town's got space available unless they're charging highway robbery for it. Now why—*why*—didn't you write to me ahead?"

Steve could not make up his mind how to deal with her directness. "I'm just a jerk," he said.

"It's the God's truth. What'll you have to drink? If I can't give you a room, I can at least give you a drink."

"Scotch and water, and thank you."

Reaching out in various directions around her, without moving from her perch, Thaisa Chapman found a glass, ice, a bottle of Scotch, and the water tap. Steve noticed with gratitude that she served a generous shot.

"I *am* sorry about the reservation," he said. "Some friends of mine in Houston told me how wonderful your place was——"

"Oh? I love Houston. What's their name?"

"Reed. Cousins of mine."

A smile of embracing brightness broke over her face. "That little couple last summer? I saw she was pregnant even before she told me."

"That's right——"

"Oh, what a shame they didn't tell you to write ahead. Wasn't so hard taking care of them, August. But now, well . . ."

"I never know exactly ahead of time where I'm going to be. I'm a writer, and the way I drift around is kind of disorganized."

Thaisa cast her eyes to heaven and gave a groan.

"You're a writer?" she exclaimed. "You don't know what you're doing to me. Look, you're a single, aren't you?"

"That's right," said Steve.

"Drink your drink," she waved a hand.

With the other hand she slapped a bell, and in a moment there appeared from the kitchen a thin little Negro girl in starched uniform who turned half-fearful, half-worshipful eyes on her employer.

"Shirley, what's the pitch with seven?"

The girl whispered something to her.

"Luck!" the employer crowed, striking the bar with a fist. "I've got a good single and bath!"

Steve wondered if he'd heard aright.

"It was once part of the slave quarters." Thaisa poured herself a drink to toast the victory. "It's the building on the other side of our patio. I suppose you're not so used to the way we work in New Orleans?"

"Not a bit." Steve smiled.

Thaisa lifted her glass briefly toward him and sipped.

"A lot of these houses in the Quarter," she explained, "had quarters in back for the slaves. Now if you make a guest house out of the whole business, the slave-quarter rooms have a desirability all their own. Quiet, for one thing. They're far away from all the traffic noises. They're smallish, but they're not terrifically expensive, if you like to keep that in mind."

"It always helps," said Steve.

"Seven's on the second floor, so you can jump down here for your breakfast."

"You're very kind to go to all this trouble——"

"Honey, if I didn't put a nice young writer in seven now, some Mardi Gras drunk would appear on the horizon later, and I'd have to take *him*. You enjoy your stay. Don't run around too much. Mardi Gras goes to some people's heads."

When he had finished his drink, the Negro girl showed him through a corner of the steaming kitchen to the patio and led him up the wooden stairs to the balcony and the room that would be his for the few days' stay he planned. He tipped the maid and put his suitcase on the foot of the bed. The quarters were cramped, but the wall was freshly papered and the view from his doorway of the patio, the restaurant opposite, the mottled roofs of the French Quarter beyond, delighted him. He turned back to the suitcase and started hurriedly to unpack.

That evening at dinner Steve learned how crowded the guest house was. Thaisa introduced him to a number of his fellow visitors at the bar; the tables of the restaurant were filled with the others. From those who knew New Orleans he learned in the following days more about the pageantry of Mardi Gras. The Mardi Gras balls had been going on every night for weeks—since the opening gun of the Twelfth Night Ball. Near midnight each night debutantes turned up in a select number of bars and night clubs in the French Quarter. They were either on the arms of white-tied young men who had been on the floor committee of the ball of the evening or with dinner-jacketed young men who had been maskers in the krewe in their own right or were attending in the stead of their fathers. That first evening Steve observed the good-looking, vivacious youngsters, but met none of them. On his third evening in New Orleans, having dined late at Arnaud's, he came back to Thaisa Chapman's and sat at the bar, drinking a cognac and listening to the juke box. The songs of Edith Piaf were enjoying their first popularity among people with comparatively sophisticated tastes, and at the moment the blaring lyrics of *Fanon de la Legion* competed with the chatter of the patrons.

Steve was ordering a second brandy when two young couples in formal evening dress came in and sat down at a table near the piano. One of them, a short overweight girl in a beautiful dress of white satin, stepped to the bar to speak to Thaisa.

"Thaisa! I've got a catch—one of my house guests plays the piano divinely! Could we shut off that juke box thing? He's really good. Please?"

"Sure, honey, I'll have it taken care of."

As she turned, the girl glanced at Steve with fleeting interest. She bounced back to the table, crowing, "Mike, Thaisa says it's all right! You can play!"

"Oh, Linda, for God's sake . . ." the young man began.

"You promised!"

"I've had entirely too much to drink," the young man said. "Sit down and mind your manners."

"Alcohol makes you play better. Doesn't it, Margaret? It does me. I'll never go out with you again if you don't."

"Let's have a drink first, shall we?"

But by the time the drinks had been brought to them, the juke box had been turned off and people at the tables nearby were calling out their encouragement. Obediently, if with reluctance, the girl's escort took his drink to the piano, and although he had indeed been drinking. Steve noticed that he moved with a boxer's resilience and energy. Tall, neatly good-looking, the man's fingers fell on the piano keys with authority, and the room filled with Jerome Kern. Steve turned a little on his bar stool to get a look at the second young couple of the party and realized with a shock that they were looking directly at him. He turned quickly away, feeling the blood rush to his face.

In a little while the plump girl was calling, "Thaisa, stop

working and come have a drink with us. I want you to meet my guests from Washington!"

Thaisa moved ponderously from her position behind the bar, and Steve ordered a Scotch from the waiter who took her place. An assortment of young people, attracted by the songs, were gathering around the piano, and presently a number of them were singing the lyrics loudly. People at the tables applauded the numbers and the crowded room, filling rapidly with cigarette smoke, began to take on the excitement and clamor of a raucous night on the town when Thaisa called over to him from the table, "Steve! Steve, come over here, honey!"

He did not know whether the young couple who had been discussing him had engineered it or whether Thaisa herself was up to something. Pretending he had not understood her, he forced Thaisa to repeat the invitation. Then he gave a nod, and a smile of acceptance, took up his drink, and walked over to the table. Thaisa reached out and took his arm, guiding him to her ample side.

"Steve Williams, meet some nice young people," she said. "This is Linda Fuselle, one of my very own children. And these kids are visiting her folks for Mardi Gras. Margaret Cowan and Wynn Bargmeister. That's Margaret's brother, Michael, playing the piano."

They exchanged smiling "Hellos" and Margaret Cowan, without rising, pulled up a chair between herself and Thaisa, and Steve sat down. The young man named Wynn Bargmeister, taller and thicker-featured than Michael Cowan, although of the same general stamp, was not quick enough to help Margaret with the chair.

"Thaisa was telling us you're a writer." Linda Fuselle laughed. "Have you known Thaisa for ages?"

"All of four days, I think it is, but I can hardly believe it," Steve answered.

"Isn't it the truth! Thaisa, how do you do that to people?"

Steve did not hear her reply. Beside him Margaret Cowan asked, in a voice not much louder than a whisper, though in no way conspiratorial, "You're visiting for Mardi Gras, too, Mr. Williams?"

"Yes, I am," Steve answered. "Maybe a little longer than that."

He had not gotten a clear look at the girl before. She

looked slightly more mature than the plump Linda Fuselle, and her manner bespoke extensive social experience. She had none of Linda Fuselle's nervous jollity. Her eyes were deeply blue, shaped with a generous hand, and within the golden-brown frame of her long hair her complexion was flawlessly creamy. The décolletage of her ball gown enhanced the delicate slope of her shoulders and not very considerable swell of her breasts. Steve could not remember ever having been near a young woman as beautiful.

"How I wish I could stay longer," she was saying. "New Orleans is such fun, and I've never been here before. God knows when I'll get here again."

"What's Washington like?" Steve asked, matching her pitch of voice so that the others at the table were successfully left to their own.

"Oh, I hate it"—Margaret shrugged easily—"but the friends I have are very nice. We're what you call a political family, and that gets so bloody dull, you could scream. We came to New Orleans to do the screaming."

"Cowan? Cowan?"

"My father's a judge of something or other—*was,* rather—but what he mostly does is be a mother hen to the Republicans. *I'm* going to vote Prohibition next year, so help me."

"Revolting against the parental inclinations?"

"Revolting against every last slob I've ever had to make chitchat with."

Steve grinned. "That include me?"

Margaret's broad smile seemed to throw a loving light upon him. She nodded emphatically. "You're the best thing that's happened to me this evening."

She turned her head away for an instant, for no apparent purpose, and when she turned back, her smile seemed to have gone slack. Steve wondered if the drinks had hit her unexpectedly. She sat back suddenly to include Linda and Wynn Bargmeister in her audience as she said, clearly enough for everyone to hear, "Why don't you join us, Mr. Williams, for what's left of the evening? I won't let Wynn make a pass at you."

Steve gave a start.

"Margaret!" Wynn Bargmeister snapped.

Linda Fuselle gasped, and Thaisa, clearing her throat gently, looked away. The escort faced Steve uncertainly.

"Margaret's fiendish sense of humor," he murmured. "That's what good schools do for a girl."

"The man's a writer." Margaret spread her arms, her voice unattractively loud. "Writers *see* things. Do you see things, Mr. Williams?"

"Shut up, won't you?" Wynn returned. "Why the hell did Michael persuade me to take you on the town anyway?" Where's the rest of our gang?"

"Cruising, my dear," said Margaret unsteadily. "Aren't you jealous?"

Thaisa propelled herself to her feet without delay and included them all in a vague flap of her hand.

"Now you children play nice, and I'll see you later. I have to get back to work."

She moved back to her place at the bar. Someone else had taken over the playing of the piano—older songs than the last—and in the midst of a Romberg medley Mike Cowan came back to them, swallowing the last of his drink as he walked.

"Hello, hello." And pointedly to Steve, with a lift of strongly drawn eyebrows: "And how do *you* do?"

Margaret Cowan said, "Steve Williams, my brother Michael Cowan, a much-sought-after piano-player."

Steve offered his hand and found it taken in an embarrassingly lingering clasp. He withdrew it firmly and Mike Cowan sat down with them.

"I was just wondering," said Wynn Bargmeister, "where the others were."

"And *I* already said cruising," Margaret reported to her brother.

"Oh, God, you're drunk again," he said.

"Mike, she's behaving *horribly!* Mother would die if——"

"Oh, Linda, close your mouth," Margaret drawled. "I was only kidding."

"They were supposed to case a place called Quatre Chevaux," said Mike.

Margaret suddenly leaned forward.

"Let's go find them there!" she said. "Better still, call them to come here! Which, which? Steve, come with us? I want *masses* of men to lead me through the twisting streets!"

Steve grinned. The crowd in the restaurant had been steadily increasing; they stood now three deep at the bar, and couples were trying futilely to dance in the space remaining between the bar and the piano. Meanwhile, Margaret Cowan's intense exhilaration did not abate: no one at the table except Steve escaped the fusillade of her remarks. Yet another guest pianist had taken over, and he was banging out an unidentifiable boogie-woogie. In the uproar everyone was shouting to make himself heard, and in the fore Margaret Cowan shouted across the table to Wynn Bargmeister, "I know you don't mind if I try to pick up Steve, because you're bored to death toting me around. Now don't deny it, you great big future Secretary of State, you!"

At this Mike Cowan blanched and shouted back, "Margaret, if you breathe a word, I'll——"

"Darling Michael, Steve is a rock of trustworthiness. Can't you *see?*"

Mike leaned quickly toward Steve. "Believe me, Steve, nothing personal but——"

"They're just being stuffy beyond imagining!" She laughed, taking Steve's arm in an impulsive movement. "Steve, Michael and I are at the Fuselles' house, but a huge bunch of the boys are at the Saint Charles Hotel—most of them State Department. Frightfully conservative!"

Wynn Bargmeister banged his glass onto the table. "God damn your chattering teeth, Margaret! Mike, you're loony to——"

Without understanding his instinct, Steve leaned past Margaret and grabbed the young man's wrist. His grip was harsh, but the expression of his face stayed calmly sympathetic. "Miss Cowan is extremely indiscreet, and I can understand your taking offense," he said, aiming his voice sharply under the general noise in the place. "Please don't be disturbed on my account." The anger facing him faded to bewilderment and thence to appreciation. Steve released the wrist and turned to Mike Cowan. "I apologize for my presence. Maybe I should just——"

"Oh, no, stay!" Margaret cried. "We'll all go to Quatre Chevaux. We'll have loads of fun!"

Mike Cowan murmured something abashed and polite. Steve went on, "I haven't been there, but the impression I've received is that the Quatre Chevaux is pretty conservative as gay bars go. College kids on dates, so on. The after-ball people. You might like it."

Mike began, "If I thought I dared introduce Margaret into it with her most favorite targets waiting there like lambs about to be hatcheted——"

Margaret folded her arms on the table and drove her face into a thunderous pout. "No," she said. "Absolutely no! You three go on, do what you will, dishonor shall be humor, but I won't set one foot near the State Department queens again. I'll stay here."

Wynn protested, "You're drunk, and you're not responsible for your own——"

But Mike interrupted, "Maybe we should ditch her? It's what she's begging for."

"My own brother."

"But Mike, what will I explain to Mother?" cried Linda.

"That she went out shopping early. Your mother doesn't get up till noon," advised Mike Cowan.

Margaret drew herself up exaggeratedly. "I didn't say anything about not coming home."

"Oh, the hell with it!" Wynn snapped. "Look, Margaret. Stay here as long as you like. We'll check back before we go home. And if you get bored——"

"The Quatre Chevaux," Steve put in.

"The Quatre Chevaux."

"Margaret, baby . . ." Linda Fuselle was not used to the pace of Washington, and Mike stood up.

"Have you got mad money?" he asked.

"Masses."

"I'll take care of the drinks here," he said.

"But I want assurance that nice Steve at least won't leave me in the lurch." She smirked.

Steve said, "Nobody's leaving you, you cluck. You're resusing to go."

"Oh," Margaret said. "That's right."

Steve looked up at Mike. "I don't have anything pressing. I'll keep an eye out till you get back."

"You'd better, if you know my sister," was the answer.

Belatedly Linda Fuselle tried for graciousness as she stood up. "Perhaps we'll see you later, Steve? I do hope so. So nice meeting you."

"Thank you. Wynn, good night. Good night, Michael. Don't worry about your sister's spending her mad money."

"Very kind," said Mike Cowan. "Yes."

And in a stumbling, embarrassed maneuver, the three young people got themselves through to the bar to pay their bill and from there to the street.

Steve heaved a sigh and sat down again. He was startled to see that all of a sudden she was sitting straight and pretty at the table.

"Hey!" Steve said, bewildered.

Margaret smiled her brilliant, infectious smile.

"Well, I got loose from them," she said, her voice sober and smoothly civilized again. "Please don't consider yourself trapped. I'm eminently capable."

Steve laughed at his own astonishment. "I think you're capable of just about anything."

"You know there's nothing seriously hush-hush about Wynn, or any of the rest of Michael's crew. It's their own pompous fault if I blab about them."

"Don't you think you shouldn't?" Steve suggested. "To me, anyway."

"If I don't, you'll just think I behaved abominably, and you'll never understand why I did it." She was obviously sincere in wanting him to understand and not think ill of her. "Michael and I came to New Orleans to visit the Fuselles, and before I knew it, all our friends were joining the entourage. We all drove down together. They weren't invited to the Fuselles', you know. That's why they're staying in hotels. Most of them—not my brother, thank God—are young fellows in the State Department, and in Washington they have to be really horrifyingly cautious about what they do and whom they see. Why New Orleans should be different, I don't know, and I think they're ridiculous to risk it, but there you are."

"What exactly do they risk?" Steve asked, more out of politeness than interest.

"Oh, they drink too much and make spectacles of themselves. It's just blowing off steam, but they go whole hog when they give themselves a break. They consort with the worst kind of people, and they'll practically have a nervous breakdown if one of that kind looks them up in Washington a month from now. I was so bored with them all. I really was. I was desperate.

"Linda's been an angel to us, but my deep, abiding friendship for her exists entirely in Daddy's head. Well, you met her, I don't have to blacken the record further. Are all New Orleans girls so slow to grow up?"

"I shouldn't think so," said Steve. "Furthermore, I thought she was valiant, considering she let it be known she'd ever seen you before in her life—the way you were acting then."

"Ow. But you're mean." Margaret drew back offended.

"Not really." And both of them smiled again.

"No, but I really was desperate. I like Michael, and I don't mind his friends—our friends, actually—but you get tired of a steady diet of faggots. Do you know what I'd like to do? I'd like to go stand by the piano like all those other people."

"All right," said Steve.

She hesitated. "You really wouldn't hate it?"

"You'd be amazed at how few things I hate," said Steve. "Come on, if you're not a contralto. If you are, keep your mouth shut and just listen to the purest light baritone in Houston, Texas."

"I'm a soprano!" she cried. "We're made for each other!"

They jumped up and joined the others. Playing was a cadaverous young woman in a woolen suit whose untended cigarette burned at one end of the keyboard. The crowd was singing lustily to her accompaniment, and Steve and Margaret joined in.

"I'm looking over a four-leaf clover
That I overlooked before . . ."

The young pianist played two more songs, and then bowed out. Margaret's disappointment was obvious.

"Don't you play the piano?" Steve asked softly.

She looked at him hesitantly.

"Come on. Give us a sample."

"All right. I'll try."

Margaret sat down, adjusting the position of the bench to leave room for Steve.

"What shall I play?" she asked.

"A ballad? Why don't you?"

"A ballad. . . ." She looked at him, and a soft, sweetly romantic smile touched her lips. "Oh, I know a ballad you'd like. This will be just for you. Forget about the other people, Steve. This will be *our* song—forever after. . . ."

And then she exploded:

"Oh, the object of my affection can change my complexion
From white to rosy red! . . .
Every time he holds my hand
And tells me that he's mine!"

Her laughter bubbled up through her singing of the song as she watched Steve's open-mouthed surprise. The others around the piano took up the singing.

"You ought to be spanked—" Steve shouted.

To the crowd's delight she went on to play other popular songs of the early thirties, and they all found themselves reaching for lyrics they had not heard sung since their childhood. When she was tired of playing, Margaret grabbed his hand without warning, pulled him up, and hurried him out past the bar into the patio.

The night was too chill for the patio to be in use, and the only light came from the slave-quarter rooms on either side. Before he could catch his breath, Steve found Margaret Cowan in his arms, her lips raised to his. He kissed her, neither politely nor passionately, as though tasting something attractive but unfamiliar.

Margaret bent her head back from the kiss and smiled at him.

"Happy Mardi Gras," she said.

He kissed her again, more forcefully this time, tightening his embrace, and Margaret responded warmly. When Steve lifted his lips from hers at last, she stepped back from him and turned to look up toward the lighted windows.

"Which one is yours?" she said.

"The dark window in the middle there."

"I see." She offered nothing more.

"Would you like to see it?"

"Do you want me to? Would you carry me across the threshold?" Her dancing eyes teased him mercilessly; he could not tell how serious she was.

"It would be fine with me, carrying you across the threshold," he said. "You're nice, for a bad little girl."

Margaret laughed and moved away from him into the

deeper shadows on the other side of the patio. He did not follow her, but spoke softly into the darkness.

"You make up your mind fast, don't you?" he asked her. "Or haven't you made it up?"

"That's for me to know and you to find out," she answered from the shadows. Dimly he could see her white dress gleaming, and the milkiness of her neck.

"You don't know a goddamned thing about me," he pointed out.

"Neither do you about me."

"You're a girl."

"You're a . . ." She stopped. Then more softly still, a thin urgency in her voice: "Steve, come kiss me. Over here in the dark."

He came forward unhurriedly. Was she playing him for a fool again, the way she had done before at the piano? She did not move. Even when he reached her, she said nothing. He took hold of her arms, pulling her against himself, but as his lips were on the point of touching hers, she laughed suddenly and ducked out of his grasp.

Spinning around as she stepped past him, he reached out and caught her angrily, gentleness gone from his voice. "What the hell are you up to?"

"I was only—" Her laughter was already dead.

"I hate prick-teasers."

"Steve!"

"Isn't that what you are? A real cute, real hep-to-yourself, real experienced prick-teaser."

"Nobody's ever dared to——"

"I'll bet not."

She was frightened now, and patently sorry for what she had done. Her hands took hold of his.

"I'm *not* that kind, Steve. I just didn't realize how—I'm sorry, my timing just stinks. Don't be mad with me. Please don't."

He hesitated between resenting and accepting the ludicrousness of his position. "Well, forget about it," he said. "Let's go inside."

"I know what!" Margaret cried, her spirits abruptly lifted. "Let's go find Michael and his crew!"

"But you said you didn't want any part of——"

"But they're loads of fun, Steve. Won't you go with me?

I'm sure we can still catch them at the Quatre Chevaux: it's Mardi Gras!"

"Look, do you have to be so goddamned mercurial? I'll take you, I just wish you'd make up your mind."

Margaret laughed again and, grabbing his arm, pulled him back into the restaurant. Thaisa had put Margaret's coat behind the bar for safekeeping. She gave it to Steve when he signed the bill, and they hurried out to the street.

At two o'clock in the morning the week before Mardi Gras the streets of the French Quarter are still alive, and music blares forth from the bars and night clubs lining Bourbon Street. Its din drifted toward them faintly as they scurried along St. Peter Street to the center of post-midnight activity. The chill February wind bore the uproar toward them like the cacophonous song of a hundred sirens. They bent themselves against the cold and ran.

"What are you doing on Mardi Gras?" Steve yelled above the racket. They had reached the garish lights of the pub belt.

"Linda says anybody with an ounce of honor has to mask and wear a costume. What are you going as? I'm going as a clown."

"I hadn't thought about it," Steve said.

"Go as a pirate. Oh, please, you'd look wonderful as a pirate!"

"Maybe I won't even see you——"

"They say it *is* awfully wild and crowded and everything."

The crowd in the street had thickened, and they were forced now to thread their way through the parties of people coming from the opposite direction. Margaret went miraculously ahead of him, weaving and dodging in her ball gown through the strolling groups. Steve shouted after her, "You have a date already?"

"What?"

"A date for Mardi Gras day—you've already got one?"

Margaret halted at once and Steve came up beside her, out of breath.

"I have kind of a date," Margaret answered. "But not a very serious one."

They were blocking the narrow sidewalk, forcing passing couples out into the street to avoid her wide skirt, but she seemed oblivious of the fact.

Steve spoke hurriedly: "How do you mean, not serious? Something you could get out of?"

"I could if you're the one asking me. Linda has a local debutante's delight lined up for me, but I'm sure he'd be overjoyed to learn he didn't have to go through with it."

"Will you let me take you?"

"Will you go as a pirate?" she demanded.

"Promise," said Steve.

"Then it's a deal." And turning, she was off into the crowd again, calling back with a toss of her head, "Hurry up, Steve, or we'll never catch up with them!"

20

IT WAS NEAR DAWN WHEN THEY CAME BACK to Thaisa Chapman's House. Once reunited with Mike Cowan's party, Margaret had maintained her high spirits for no more than five minutes. Then she grew distant and sulky; she drank her drinks too quickly and had talked not at all. Steve had not been able to persuade her to leave. She was, like a willful child, determined to sit out her misery and get blind drunk in the process.

She was walking unsteadily when Steve led her through the patio, but her sullenness had lifted. In one respect her inebriety was a relief to Steve; no overt word had had to be said about her coming home with him. She made no objection and showed no surprise. Steve groped his way through the darkness of the patio to the stairs leading up to the balcony of the slave quarters. He was not sure Margaret would be able to make it up the warped and aged wooden steps. Bracing himself for the effort, he lifted her up into his arms. She was a lighter burden than he had expected. Her arms slipped about his neck, and smiling, she laid her head against his shoulder. Steve carried her up to the balcony, to the door of his room. He set her down easily, found his key, and unlocking the door, pushed it open. His fingers found the light switch immediately inside. He flicked it on and stepped back to allow Margaret to precede him.

"Won't you come in?"

Margaret smiled but did not move.

"Oh," Steve remembered.

He took her hands and drew her away from the stream of light coming through the door. In the shadows beside it, she came readily into his arms and lifted her mouth to his. He kissed her passionately, and his hand moved up to cup her breast.

"You're beautiful, you're so beautiful—" His whisper broke off. Beneath her coat he found the zipper holding the top of the ball gown fast about her. He pulled it, and the bodice eased forward from her body. He drew out one of her breasts and bent his head to kiss the nipple. Margaret gave a gasp, and Steve, taking hold of her hips, pressed her close. He felt the imperative surge of his own passion rising beyond his control, and quickly he lifted her up and carried her into his room. He set her down on the bed, and going back to the switch by the door, turned out the light. In the darkness he heard her stand. He stepped over to her, and as he did so, he heard the soft movement of her coat as it dropped to the floor.

In the coming of Carnival time there is a change in the character of the city that one senses rather than observes. A week before the last climactic day of street masking and costuming a fever begins to burn beneath the surface and grows steadily more intense as the days progress toward their festive height. On the broad reach of Canal Street, the reviewing stands and their bunting of green, gold, and purple appear. The very street lights masquerade in clown heads and motley or in the woolly bark and crowning fronds of palm trees. The tide of strangers coming to the celebration rises, and each night's parade of floats and bands finds a larger, wilder throng applauding it and contesting for the trinkets the float riders throw out into the sea of arms and shrieking mouths lit by the dancing flambeaus.

In the untheatrical light of Saturday morning, the schoolchildren of the city have their inexhaustible pageant, childish faces incongrously painted, children's featureless bodies dressed in blazing colors of sateen and tarlatan and chintz and cheap metallic braid—the king of their parade, a boy in the white, traditionally medieval dress of an imaginary monarch. His name is Nor, the letters of which are his essence: *New Orleans—Romance*. The Saturday sidewalks are impassable in the press of envious school fellows and searching, apprehensive, proud, delighted, worn-to-a-frazzle parents and strangers to the city who, trapped by the crowds, watch, bemused and patronizing, the children of Carrollton and Mid-City and the Garden District and Back-o'-town and the Quarter and Gentilly and Metairie, the loud, large bands from the schools of Saint Anthony of Padua and Saint James Major and Mater Dolorosa and Beauregard and McDonough Number Nine and Crossman. These strangers, not knowing how long the spectacle runs on, at first patient, are then bored; and finally, while the blockade of endless floats go past bearing the smiling, waving, masquerading, parading, screaming, strutting, painted children, the only place for a stranger to find comfort is the nearest bar on whichever side of Canal Street he happens to be stuck. The bars are soon filled with people. They stay crowded long after the Nor parade is over, and the Carnival fever rises with each passing toast.

The neon lights go on early on Bourbon Street on this particular Saturday night of the year. The jazz bands strike up in the night clubs, exhorting the too many people and the too many faces outside to frenzy—the pressing, pulsing crowds in which identity and its demands drown on the crest of a roistering wave.

On Sunday there are parades everywhere. They are discussed in the morning paper, but how to get to them? They are varying in quality (ask ten natives for an opinion), and it is almost impossible to find the strange neighborhoods where they will be held.

Sunday night in the French Quarter is wilder still. More out-of-towners have either arrived or have just learned that the French Quarter is where Carnival lives after sundown.

On Monday there is a gesture at the carrying on of business in the city, but no one takes it seriously. Tonight is the Proteus parade and there is the old rueful cry, "It *always* rains on Proteus." Rain or not, everyone will be there, drenched, hysterical, feverish, laughing at nothing, loving indiscriminately.

It *does* always rain on Proteus. The drizzle began at four o'clock, and Warren Taggert, working at the Port of New Orleans Bank and Trust Company on Carondelet Street, looked up from his bookkeeping-machine to note the ominous graying of the light in the windows and the first spattering of the drops along the panes. He remembered he had not brought a raincoat with him to the bank that morning and groaned to himself when he realized further that he was wearing his best flannel suit. Perhaps he'd be able to buy a plastic slicker when he got off work, but he would still have to make it through the rain to the drugstore on the corner to find one. He put the concern from his mind, and went on posting checks to the accounts in the ledger tray beside him. D'Antoni, Davidson Albert, Davidson Robert, Davidson Wilma Mrs., Dawson, Debeque . . .

Warren Taggert's young features had taken on a new firmness of line since he had left Cleveland, and now at the age of twenty-one he presented a picture many regarded as typical of clean-cut American youth. Like many of his contemporaries he still wore his blond hair cropped short as he had in the Army, and the monthly remittance he received from his parents together with the salary he earned was enough to provide him with well-cut clothes in only the most acceptable styles. After leaving Cleveland, he had settled in Philadelphia, where some of his mother's people could keep a protective eye on him. Philadelphia had been the scene of his long, anxiety-ridden break-off from Sue Jensen. She had struggled against his attempt to let her down lightly, and in the end the engagement had suffered a bitter and anguished destruction. He had given up his job in Philadelphia and had drifted south, living briefly first in Charleston and then moving on to New Orleans. In New Orleans he had found work easily and had rented a *garçonnière* apartment behind a house on Fourth Street in the Garden District off lower Saint Charles Avenue.

Then he made his mistake.

His mother wrote to give him names of two or three old friends she had in New Orleans ("all good families, people you'll have something in common with"), and sent him letters of introduction to present to them. He did so at a time that proved to be the very beginning of the debutante season in New Orleans, and he had promptly been caught up as invaluable escort material. After his name had been added to one or two lists and his appearance had won the approving attention of potential hostesses, the invitations came thick and fast. He escorted the daughters of his mother's friends and in turn the daughters of *their* friends to cocktail parties and dinners and dances. His mother generously supplemented his allowance to take care of the additional expenses. His reputation as a personable young man spread quickly through the debutante circle. He became indeed, if ever anyone had been, a debutante's delight.

For a time Warren enjoyed himself. He felt comfortable with the New Orleans people; they were a gentler, easier version of the Cleveland families he knew, for whom he occasionally felt homesick, and the dating of many different girls gave him time and opportunity to re-examine his emotional dilemma. At first, whenever he felt it would involve little enough risk, he tried to leave his mind open to the possibility of a direct sexual attraction occurring toward one of the young women he took out. If only, he reasoned, he could find someone who was not Sue Jensen, someone to whom he was not in any way committed, someone from whom he could flee if necessary at any time without complete disgrace, perhaps then a physical appeal would have the climate it needed for its growth.

But no sexual urge struck him, even in the intimate presence of the loveliest of the season's girls. He talked with them. He danced with them. He took them out to dine and to the more acceptable night clubs. He was liked for his ability to listen to other people and admired for the effortless perfection of his manners, but passion did not touch him. It was fortunate that his training in good manners cloaked him, because he was gripped by a graceless fear of the other young men of the city's social world, and when he found this fear translating itself into an ungovernable sexual hunger for a certain one of them, he endured a panic that almost wrecked him.

Garrierre, Gilly, Glech. . . . His sweating fingertips, as he recalled that time, left dark smudges on the ledger sheets he put into and took out of the clattering machine.

To fight back his panic, he had thrown himself into the business of amusing and distracting with a desperate urgency the girls he had dated. He had chattered, he had joked, he had flirted, anything, anything to prevent his attention from wandering toward the other crew-cutted and white-tied young men at the season's social events. He had begun to affect ultra-conservative tastes, and the snobbishness his idealistic standards had previously kept in check blossomed grotesquely in his duress. He eschewed the midnight sorties of the other young people into the bars of the French Quarter, sneering at that section of the city as the lair of Bohemians and misfits. He found himself making jeering references to the ways of known eccentrics, attacking the defenseless to bolster a public image of his own nonexistent morality.

The campaign had exhausted him. Abruptly he had retreated from it, defeated. His retreat was total. For the past three months he had accepted no invitations, seen no one, gone nowhere after his day's work except back to the emptiness of the *garçonnière* on Fourth Street. There had been one exception: a longstanding invitation arranged by the husband of one of his mother's friends. He had not been able to escape it. He had served on the floor committe of the Twelfth Night Revelers' ball. But he had done so as an outsider, with no feeling that he had ever been part of this social scene, with the strange, coldly comforting sensation that he had only just come to the city and his guilty past of treacherous temptations and struggle had never been. He had gone home early from the ball, vowing to make friends with catastrophe, swearing an oath that he would find in loneliness a pattern of existence that would render, as far as was possible, commerce with the quicksand world of human relationships unnecessary.

Kammer, Kaufman A. B. Mrs., Kaufman Zeeda Miss, Krantz, Kuntz . . .

He kept his vow. Only silly queens could be his brothers, he told himself, and his pride forbade his accepting himself as one of them. Masturbation was his only physical outlet, but he fought against the furtive habit, his will power deserting him in only-occasional violent revolutions of his body against the merciless strictures of his continence. He began to collect phonograph records, first expanding his already considerable library of favorite orchestral works, then going, with the spinsterish whirling of his involvement to its vortex, into the collection and cataloguing and endless interrelating of rare recordings, bizarre examples of musical errata, futilely esoteric performances of obscure compositions, the eternally multiplying accessories of a one-track interest. Every evening in the living room of the *garçonnière* he would put a number of records on the phonograph, spread out other records in a great circle on the floor around him, and spend hours cleaning them, refiling them, rearranging the stout albums on their shelves, noting on file cards he kept for the purpose particular curiosities of the performances he listened to. There were records everywhere in the apartment: symphonies, concertos, operas, albums of English music hall songs, American folk ballads, German lieder. No acquaintance was ever admitted to a sharing of his activities with his collection. A young woman in one of the apartments in the main house between the *garçonnière* and the street called him one night on the telephone to ask for the name of a certain string quartet he had been playing at the moment, but after giving her the name, he discouraged further conversation and put the phone down too abruptly when he had said good-by. She did not call again. The record collection was his friend, his lover, his family, to the exclusion of all others. Lost in his preoccupation with it, he passed the evening hours in narcotic quietude of spirit, and began to find that even during the working hours of the day his specialization engaged his mind so that his relationships with his co-workers at the bank faded to vague morning salutations and no more than automatic good nights at five o'clock.

Five o'clock struck now, and the row of bookkeeping machines shook and jumped as subtotals for the day were taken. Warren checked his balance against the adding-machine tape, rebound the paid checks in their rubber bands, and standing up from the machine for the first time since three o'clock, gathered up the materials that would be stored in the office vault until Wednesday.

On his way to the vault one of the assistant bookkeepers fell into step beside him.

"Big night on the town, Warren?"

He smiled uncomfortably and tried to quicken his step. "Not likely," he said.

"Rest up for tomorrow? Not a bad idea. But not for me. Mardi Gras comes but once a year, and I'm not going to bed at all tonight"—his elbow nudged Warren's arm as he laughed—"except maybe in somebody else's. Got a date for tomorrow, Jim?"

Another young man was rolling a ledger tray into the vault and turned to answer the question. Warren seized the chance to escape the encounter and hurried ahead into the vault. He had no plans for the great day of masking beyond staying close to his apartment and his record collection. But the young men about him, coming and going in the vault, checking their supplies and locking their ledger trays for the holiday, talked loudly of their plans, the costumes they were wearing, the dates they had, the drinking places they planned to hit in the course of the day's carousing. Their excitement vaguely troubled Warren; the fever of Mardi Gras was in the air, and feeling its heat, he could not so easily persuade himself of his contentment with his hermit-like existence.

"Got a date for tomorrow, Taggert?"

"What're you going as, Warren?"

"Hell, me and Shirley are gonna shoot up every joint on Bourbon Street."

"You know where the action is tomorrow? Decatur Street! Just bring a gun with you is all!"

"Masking tomorrow, Warren? Where all you gonna be?"

"Got a date for tomorrow, Taggert?"

The fever burned in upon him from every side, and his heart was beating heavily when he fled the vault. In the men's room he washed his hands and face, retied his tie, and put on his suit jacket. He hurried out and found himself caught in the stream of bank employees rushing out to the streets. Mardi Gras was come!

"Have fun, Warren!"

"Night, Taggert!"

"Don't get too boozed up, boy!"

"See you Wednesday if I live!"

"Good night!"

"Good night!"

On the street the rain had stopped and only a misty drizzle fell. The sky over downtown New Orleans was black with threatening clouds, and the streets were dark with a premature twilight. But the crowds of people hurrying homeward or off to a night on the town laughed and cried out to one another and exuded the festive spirit relentlessly. Let it rain on Proteus, who cares? It *always* rains on Proteus!

Warren bent close to the buildings and hurried along to the drugstore on the corner. There he bought a plastic slicker, and pulling it on over his flannel suit, went out and made his way through the rush-hour traffic toward the corner where he would catch the St. Charles streetcar.

The streetcar when it drew up was already filled, and an aggressively competitive crowd was pushing and shoving its way through the clumsy folding doors. Warren hesitated on the sidewalk, reluctant to involve himself in the steaming, rain-drenched, odorous mass of people. He glanced up, and the street lights on Canal Street, under their masks and palm-frond crowns, were coming on. The color and light of festival was transforming the city again from a center of commerce into a massive torchlit realm of Carnival. Warren found that his pulse was racing and he was breathing quickly, carried away unthinking by the tide of excitement in the crowded street.

"The hell with it!"

He turned away from the streetcar and walked swiftly now to the corner and down Canal Street, hurrying, racing, with an indefinite feeling of guilt, not actually knowing where he was going, and suddenly not caring. It didn't have to be such an all-fired big blowout, but he had money enough, hadn't he? And time? Why shouldn't he give himself a good dinner out, a private celebration? He could do that much even if he *was* alone. Arnaud's—a few Martinis—a steak béarnaise—hell, you had to make *some* kind of gesture in recognition of the holiday. What harm could it do? He was sick and tired of having to hole up in his apartment like a criminal who did not dare to appear on the streets of the normal world: for once, just for once, he was going to give himself a break.

Perhaps it was because of this gesture that the city that care forgot gave him that night the temporary boon of his own forgetfulness and assuaged if only for a while the gnawing grief he lived in.

He was early enough to find an empty table in the small grill room at Arnaud's, a location he favored above the large central dining room of the restaurant, and the people at the other tables seemed in general to be decorative. A lively chatter filled the room, and alone at his table, Warren felt himself vicariously warmed by the others' enjoyment of themselves. At one of the large round tables in the middle of the narrow room a party of patent out-of-towners exchanged outrageously inaccurate descriptions of the behind-the-scenes working of the Carnival.

"All the parades," said one of the women, "are put on by secret organizations like the Ku Klux Klan, and you know all the men bid against one another—oh, up into the thousands of dollars—so the girl friend of the highest bidder can be queen. Not his wife, mind you, his *girl* friend."

"Now, mother," said her husband, "if you believed everything you hear——"

"Well, what's the truth then, Mr. Smarty Pants? Winnie, is that *bourbon* you're drinking? Oh, I can't stand the stuff."

"The queen is the *daughter* of one of the men in the krewe," her husband went on. "They spell it *k-r-e-w-e,* no reason, just carrying on—and her *father* has to bid for her to be queen."

"How much does it cost?"

"Oh, I guess he shells out about ten thousand or so."

"So much!"

"Then that's what the krewe uses to build the floats and put on the dance and all."

"I heard it different," said another of the men.

"How did you hear it, Ralph?"

"The Johnsons told *me* they hired the queen from out in Hollywood, one of them starlets. It's a great honor for her, with her career and all and—well, there's more to it than meets the eye."

"What, Ralph?"

"Now, now——"

"Oh, Ralph, tell us——"

"Aw, come on, man——"

"Well, it's true, so help me, the Johnsons said." He bent forward confidentially, but Warren could clearly hear his whisper. "They said the king gets to spend the night with her—he's got special chambers of his own off someplace where the ball is held—and he gets to spend the night with her and that's why it's such a big secret who the king *is,* so his wife can't ever find out!"

Scandal exploded at the table and the insect buzzing of the women sounded throughout the room. Warren, who had learned the traditional and very conservative methods by which entirely respectable young women were selected to reign as queens of the various balls, was hard put to control his laughter. Feeling more cheerful than he had in weeks, he downed his Martini and ordered another. He considered he could have a wonderful time simply by eavesdropping on the tables around him all evening long, with no need of any other diversion.

He ate his steak béarnaise unhurriedly and finished dinner with a brandy and a demitasse. He smoked a cigarette while he sipped at first the glass and then the cup, and when the cigarette was finished, paid his check and went out into the street.

A flurry of people went laughing and running by as he stepped out onto the sidewalk, and he knew it must be nearly time for the parade to turn into the Quarter on its way to the auditorium for the ball. Through the light drizzle he followed the throng over to Royal Street, but there the sidewalks and balconies were both filled to overflowing, and the remainder of the crowd fell back into the side street. A display-windowed shop at the corner had an entrance recess on the side street, and here Warren found, with a little judicious maneuvering, a niche from which he would be able to see the parade clearly. Already a few blocks away he could hear the brash march song of the first band, and the yelling and applause of the crowd grew in intensity as the parade drew near. Warren gave an involuntary gasp of awe as, following the first band and the beautifully costumed dukes on prancing horses, the enormous float that carried the king hove into sight. Proteus in sudden masked majesty appeared above the heads of the human crowd, waving over them the trident-like scepter whose brilliance multiplied in the dancing, whirling lights of the flambeau-carriers. Proteus rode high above them all as his float went lurching and quivering past, and the crowd called and waved to him even when he was past their view and they could see only the papier-mâché ocean wave that cascaded, glistening, down the back of the float. The floats of maskers came then, and the crowd yelled till they were voiceless: "Throw me something, mister! Throw me something, mister!" They fought one another for the penny trinkets; fathers held children high aloft to catch them, experienced fathers dipped into previously filled-up pockets for throws they could pretend they had just caught for their young ones. Some of the thousand snatching the souvenirs from the air would shout their thanks and blow kisses to the waving maskers, and always the deafening noise subsided a little as one float passed only to rise up to a shattering new height as the next one came thrusting and heaving into view.

Warren watched it all in awe-struck silence from deep in the heart of the crowd. Observed objectively, the spectacle in the narrow, torchlit street, flanked by tiers of balconies filled with waving, shouting parties of spectators, was an impressive experience. Away from the Mardi Gras, in the bitter Olympus of his lonely life, he might have lingering reservations about the moneyed middle class he came from; but now, on the scene, he could not but lose himself in the passionate excitement of the pomp and ritual, intrigue and color, hilarity and pridefulness, that this city's privileged class provided entirely for the pleasure of others, not once but repeatedly, night after night, each a magnificent pageant, not in one year only, but decade after decade.

Float after float and band after blaring band marched past the frame of his vision, and with the last flambeaus and the passing of the drab undecorated truck that carried the parade's designers and craftsmen, Proteus' spectacle was done.

The crowd dispersed reluctantly. Some moved off to the automobiles they had had to park many blocks away, others, in the direction of the nearest streetcar or bus lines; still others drifted back from Royal Street to the circus loudness of Bourbon Street, and Warren was among these. A sense of unexpected liberation from drabness and dullness effervescing in him, he moved aimlessly, happily, along with the other strollers. On Bourbon Street he decided he wanted a drink, but since he had assidously avoided the French Quarter before, he did not know which bar to choose. Some, he knew, could be dangerous, and certainly many of them were unrelievedly sordid. He drifted along down the street, borne by the movement of the crowd, idly studying the neon signs and spotlighted photographs of piano-players, M.C.'s, stripteasers, and crooners. He was taken by surprise when a voice immediately beside him said, "Excuse me, would you by any chance know where I can find a place called the Quatre Chevaux?"

Warren looked up, stopping. A dark-haired young man, somewhat taller than himself, was smiling at him.

"No, I'm sorry, I don't," he answered.

"Are you a stranger here, too?"

"I live in New Orleans, but I don't know this territory down here," said Warren.

The young man looked up and down the block.

"I know it's somewhere right in here—I was there the other night, but I seem to have forgotten. Do you mind if I walk along with you?"

Warren hesitated, but then shrugged. "Not at all." They moved on. Warren felt himself unsteadied by a mixture of shyness and a sudden gust of concupiscence.

"Out for a post-parade slug?" the stranger asked.

"Yah," Warren said. "I was just wondering what place to go to. As I said, I don't——"

"Why not come to the Quatre Chevaux with me? If we can find it, that is."

"Oh, I'm sure you'd rather——"

"Hell, no, I'm alone, nobody to meet—I'd be grateful for some company. Being from out of town, you know."

"All right, then, I'd like to," said Warren. "If we can find it."

"My name's Michael Cowan, by the way. From Washington."

"Warren Taggert."

They shook hands as they walked along. Warren shrugged off his own hesitation about taking up with the good-looking young man; strangers in any town at the time of a carnival may be dubiously motivated, but Mike Cowan's manner of speech commended him to Warren as clearly as a letter of introduction would have done.

Presently they found the Quatre Chevaux. Going in, they were constrained to stand blindly in the doorway until their eyes adjusted; the crowded room was lit very dimly, and even this little light was much negated by the thick stratum of cigarette smoke in the air. The bar ran the length of one side of the room, and there were tables and chairs set against the opposite wall. This wall, like the others, was painted a dark blue, and four winged white horses, rendered in tufts of silk, pranced across its plane. The ceiling was also blue, and dotted with sequined stars. The place gave the impression of striving for the look of such fashionable intimate spots as New York abounded in; the dense shadows rendered the effect inoffensive.

Mike and Warren threaded their way through the standees toward an empty table far to the rear. Warren pulled off his slicker and folded it over the back of one of the chairs. They sat down and ordered drinks from a red-jacketed Negro waiter. Mike turned to him with a relaxed smile that revealed well shaped teeth of a gleaming whiteness.

"Do you go to school in New Orleans?" he asked Warren.

"No, I work," said Warren. "At nothing in particular. Except getting used to being on my own and enjoying being quit of the Army."

Mike gave a doubtful frown. "You've already been in the Army? You hardly look old enough."

Their drinks were set before them.

Warren said, "Happy Mardi Gras."

"You have a rousing one, too," said Mike.

He was idly surveying the room when he asked Warren, "Did you say you'd never been to this place before?"

"No. I haven't. I don't come down here to the Quarter very often."

While they drank, they exchanged information about themselves, the exploratory questions and answers of new acquaintance. They found they were both fond of music, and laughed to discover they shared an addiction for folk singers. It was all the common ground they needed. They argued about their favorite versions of particular ballads; they recommended various performers and recordings to one another; each was able to tell the other of a song he had not heard before.

In the middle of the lightly rolling conversation an astonishing thing happened. Beneath the table Mike's leg, as though relaxing its posture slightly, leaned over and came to rest against Warren's. Warren stiffened in surprise, but made no move. A flush of warmth suffused him as Mike's physical proximity both threatened and seduced. He could not move away because that would imply he sensed in Mike's nearness some impropriety. He sat rigid and tried to keep his hand from shaking when he lifted his glass. He drank deeply, and the harshness of the whiskey helped momentarily to steady him.

"Have you heard any of Pete Sibley's records?" Warren asked.

"Pete Sibley? I don't know anything about him," Mike said.

The quality of his voice made Warren pause. The remark was inconsequential, but there was something incongruous in the smile that accompanied it and the sharpness of his gaze, as though while he conversed, his thoughts were elsewhere. He seemed for a moment to be studying Warren intently before he spoke again.

"You've really never heard of this place before? You don't know what kind of place it is?"

"Kind of place?" Warren echoed. Then, with a shrug: "It's a French Quarter bar is all I know."

Mike's eyelids, lowered slightly, veiled his glance, but the mysterious half-smile still lifted one corner of his broad mouth. Beneath the table his leg moved away from Warren's and a hand dropped gently on Warren's knee.

Warren felt the blood rushing into his face when the leg on which Mike's hand rested gave an involuntary tremble. Mike's eyes were still on him, still gently smiling. Warren smiled back at him uncertainly, and the warm, gently pressing hand moved slowly but without hesitation up to his thigh. For a moment Warren thought his heart would burst inside his chest. He could not believe what was happening. This was a clean-cut, well-spoken guy, patently of a background as privileged as his own, whose demeanor bore no trace of the soft or the effeminate—not even such hidden inclinations as Warren's did. It was incredible that he should know the same hunger Warren knew, should delight in his manhood, in prep-school antics. By all rights, anyone who looked like Mike Cowan should be as satyric a ladies' man as any of them, a sports buff, a swaggering young father, a leader of men, not a lover of them. But the pressure of his fingers on Warren's thigh was not imaginary, and his smile now was not a thing of mystery.

"You like that?" Mike murmured.

Warren did not look at him. "I'd move if I didn't, wouldn't I? . . . How did you know I wouldn't knock your head off your shoulders?"

"I didn't. I had to take the chance. I'm still not altogether sure."

"Don't worry."

"You're a good-looking guy. I'm lucky tonight."

"Lucky? I was thinking the same thing myself," Warren said. "In a different way from you."

He felt his blush at last subsiding, and a feeling of sickness came over him. He recognized that what had happened had given him a nervous shock that the drinks he had had could not allay. He waited for his mind to clear before he spoke again, in a whisper, again looking out into the room rather than at Mike Cowan.

"What do we do about it?" he asked. "Anything? I'm not what you might call adroit about——"

"I'm staying with friends here," said Mike. "You could invite me to your place."

"All right."

"Is that the invitation?"

"Yes."

"Hey. Warren, are you all right?"

"Not exactly," he answered.

"I know. Head reeling? It'll pass," said Mike.

Warren was grateful for the noise in the crowded bar. Without it, he felt, the pounding in his temples would surely be audible.

"We could take a bottle up with us," he suggested. "It's a *garçonnière,* up in the Garden District. Is that all right?"

"Any place is all right," Mike said. He grinned again. "You're what's important."

"Look, I——"

"Yes?"

"Nothing. Nothing important. Do you want another drink?"

"Hell, no. Let's get that bottle."

Warren started to stand up. "I'll get it from the bar."

Mike pulled him down again. "You wait here, I'll get it. I don't want anybody stealing you." He stood up and moved off to the bar.

Presently he returned, the package under his arm.

"We're all paid up. Ready to go?"

In the street the drizzle had thickened, but Warren did not put his slicker on again; he crammed it into the folds and carried it in his hand. They caught a taxi and Warren gave his Fourth Street address. They rode in silence to Royal Street, up Royal to Canal, and from there along the deserted, trash-littered parade route to Lee Circle. When the taxi pulled into St. Charles Avenue and picked up speed as it headed uptown, Mike reached over and took Warren's hand in his. Neither of them spoke, but exchanged a glance of straightforward tenderness. Warren secretly told himself however long he lived, he would never forget this silent taxi drive; his grief and guilt were for once washed from him, the endless, damning, inward chant was still. A nice guy wanted him; a nice guy wanted him. . . .

The taxi turned into Fourth Street and pulled to a stop before the vine-masked white house. The couple who lived in the first-floor apartment of the main house had put a Gilbert and Sullivan opera on their record player, and the lilting music tripped out into the street; he heard the couple singing happily together:

> If we're weak enough to tarry,
> Ere we marry,
> You and I,
> Of the feeling I inspire
> You may tire
> By and by . . .

Warren paid the fare and showed Mike the way back along the side of the house through the back yard and up the long flight of steps to the *garçonnière*. The music from the main house faded away. Warren unlocked the door, and turning on the lights of the living room, ushered Mike in, closing the door behind him.

Mike looked about the room.

"Christ, you *do* go in for records. It looks like you've collected as many L.P.'s as seventy-eights."

"Hand over the bottle and I'll pour us a shot," said Warren, discarding the crumpled slicker. He led the way through to the kitchen. He turned on the ceiling light and took an ice tray out of the refrigerator. At the sink he mixed the drinks, and handed one to Mike.

Mike took a sip and set the glass aside.

"What does that window look out on?" he asked.

"A brick wall," Warren told him. "The side of the house behind us."

"Good." Mike nodded. With a smile he came up to him. Warren put his drink down. Mike made no move to embrace him at first, but bent his lips to Warren's and kissed him gently. For a moment they searched each other's eyes, and then they were embracing with a hungry ferocity. Their hands explored each other's bodies hurriedly, greedily, until Mike gasped out, "Come lie down. The drinks can wait."

In the bedroom they undressed and lay down together. Warren laughed aloud in a sudden upsurging of happiness and vitality, and Mike clasped his arms tightly around him.

"Laughing? Hold still," he said, "let me kiss you again."

About them in the darkness, a breath from palpable, were the last guardians of caution; they drew back and off, unwelcome, unwanted. The dizzying release of the passion pent up in Warren for so many years choked his brain, blinding his senses to everything but the young and vigorous masculinity of the body beside him. In his receipt of Mike's love-making there was no restraint, and his frenzied response whipped the dark young man to still greater intensity. At the bursting of the moment, the explosion that gripped them as if it would tear them limb from limb, pulverizing them both so that their bodies' pieces would never be able to be separated or distinguished one from the other—at that moment Warren's joyfulness and power, like a walking ghost, stretched its full height and screamed to heaven. A guttural shout tore through their chests and threw them, bound together, into insensible blackness.

Gradually their bruised senses stirred and awoke, first to the dim light coming in through the kitchen door, then to the wet, gently pulsating heat of their own bodies. Warren was stretched out on his stomach, his arm still thrown across Mike's broad hair-matted chest; he sighed.

"Warren."

"Yah."

"God . . ."

Warren turned his head over to face him, and smiled. "You don't know the half of it, buddy," he said to Mike.

"That drink. Where'd I leave it? That drink you mixed."

"I'll get both of them," said Warren.

From the closet he took a dressing gown he had recently bought for himself. He was about to put it on, but changed his mind, threw it over to Mike. For himself he took out an older one. Tying the sash, he went to fetch their drinks from the kitchen, and shortly came back to the bedroom.

Mike had put on the dressing gown and was lighting two cigarettes. One he gave to Warren, and taking his drink, sat down on the edge of the bed. Warren, feeling unaccountably reserved now, sat in the straight chair against the wall at the foot of the bed. They smoked their cigarettes in silence a long moment.

"Warren. This ever happen to you before?"

"No," Warren admitted.

"Didn't think so."

"How can you tell?"

"You can, buddy, you can," said Mike. ". . . It's a bonus for me, I'm here to tell you."

A pause. Then Warren shifted in his chair, puzzling out the proper words. "It's funny, I never thought it was possible that somebody like you—I mean, you're a nice guy, you're no creep, I never thought——"

"Somebody like me could be gay?" Mike finished.

"Gay? Yah. That's what I meant."

Mike turned the ice in his glass thoughtfully. "You must not get around much."

"I don't."

"The Quatre Chevaux is a gay bar."

A new thought occurred to him, but he did not know how to express it. Silence quivered in the room until he forced himself to speak. "Mike," he asked. "Did you ever fall in love with another guy? I mean, not just playing around?"

"Love? Why do you want to know that?"

Warren did not answer. He put his glass down on the floor and stood up. Moving slowly, almost cautiously, he went over to Mike. He knelt down on the floor in front of the dark young man. Mike seemed to understand. He put his hand tenderly on Warren's back and drew him forward to his kiss. They kissed lingeringly, affectionately. When the kiss ended, Warren sat back on his heels, his breathing strained.

"Drink your drink and I'll fix us another," he said, getting to his feet again. "I thought maybe I'd put some music on."

Mike stood up. "Suppose you be doing that while I do the honors on this round."

He disappeared into the kitchen, and Warren moved into

the living room. He chose a recording of a string quartet playing Vivaldi and put it on the phonograph, turning the volume far down. He lit another cigarette and sprawled out in the armchair, relishing the draining of his physical tension, the soft warmth he felt throughout his body. If there were others, he thought, if other men could live like this, there was hope for him, wasn't there? What was tragic or ugly about Mike Cowan? Nothing. He was acceptable to the world by any standard.

Mike came in, humming the melody the quartet was playing, and handed Warren his drink. He carried his own glass to the sofa against the opposite wall and sat down. He seemed in no way embarrassed or perturbed, but at ease, contented, listening to the music from the phonograph.

Presently Mike asked, "Why don't you mask tomorrow?"

"I hadn't planned to. Why?"

"You could come out with me. There are friends of mine in town, from Washington like myself. I'll be walking around with them. You'll find them *simpatico,* we'll have a lot of fun. Why don't you? It'd make me very happy."

Warren thought. "I don't have a costume——"

"A pair of pajamas?"

"Why, yes——"

"You can go as Sleep." Mike spread a hand.

Warren laughed. "You don't think they'd arrest me?"

Mike's forehead furrowed. "From what I'm told of *some* of the costumes you see, I think an arrest unlikely. Of course we'll be in the Quarter mostly—you said you didn't care for that——"

"Oh, forget it," said Warren. "I feel more kindly toward the Quarter now. I've reason to. Sure, I'd be delighted to go with you tomorrow."

"Good."

"If we're going to get up tomorrow at all, we'll have to get to sleep. Do you have to go back to—wherever you're staying?"

"The Fuselles'."

"Oh, Christ, the Fuselles as in Linda Fuselle?"

"The same, as a matter of fact. I could go there, but I don't have to." He grinned.

"Would you like to stay here?" Warren invited. "I think

I'm stocked up on razor blades. Hell, I just thought, I've got a new toothbrush, even. I haven't used it yet. You could."

Mike leaned his head back and laughed. "I wouldn't pass up an invitation like that for the world."

As they went on talking desultorily, Warren followed two streams of thought at once. The first concentrated on the good-looking young man across the room, who had erupted without expectation into the view he had of his existence. The other was more devious a stream. If this were not simply an accident, he thought, a unique and unexplainable living-out of fantasy that happened once and never occurred again, there was no demand for decision made on him; but if it were anything more, wasn't a new and fuller life possible for him? What were the others of the homosexual world like? The young men at the Quatre Chevaux had not looked notably depraved; any number of debutante's delights Warren knew in New Orleans could appear in their ranks without a look of incongruity, and conceivably, it occurred to him, did so. Were they happy? Was it possible to give rein to the fantasies that had possessed him all these years and find in that license a contentment that other, sterner demands of living would not shatter? Across the room Mike was listening quietly to the music, his gaze on the glass he held. Warren bit down hard on the inside of his bottom lip. Why shouldn't it be possible? For God's sake, he pointed out to himself, you're a privileged character, a healthy sane American with every possible advantage of education and breeding. Why shouldn't you build a life for yourself that you can stomach? All right, damn it, you might not contribute much to the population of the world, but you never will in any case, will you? The Sue Jensens will always send you running, won't they? At least this way you'd have in your life some gentleness, some companionship, some feeling of acceptance; if tonight were possible . . .

He broke with a start from his thinking when he saw Mike standing before him. He looked up at him.

"Yah?"

"You haven't touched your drink."

"Just thinking. Listening to the music."

"Shall we put another one on? The quartet is out for coffee."

"Would you like to hit the sack?" Warren asked.

"I'm willing to listen to music," Mike offered. "Hell, as fond of records as you are, I'd feel like a bastard not to."

"Who needs records?" Warren countered. "I'll mix a nightcap for us." He paused. "And I'll see you in bed."

Steve finished putting on his rented pirate's costume at seven o'clock Mardi Gras morning, and sat smoking a cigarette while he wondered whether he had the nerve to go outside in this get-up. He understood that almost everyone on the streets that day would be in costume and masked, but at seven o'clock in the morning—he gave a shiver. Still, Margaret's instructions had been specific: be at the Fuselles' house on Palmer Avenue at seven-thirty sharp. Perhaps he'd feel better when he had his eye mask on; at least people who saw him (and laughed—he was certain they would laugh) would not recognize him on some future occasion and associate him with this deplorable damned childishness. He put the eye mask on, opened the door to the balcony, and silently thanked God that none of the staff of Thaisa Chapman's House were in the patio. He slipped out and made for the coldly wind-whipped street as fast as he could.

Within two blocks he found a taxi and gave the Palmer Avenue address. He sat back gratefully in the obscurity and comparative warmth of the back seat. Few people were on the street this early, but he noted several groups, already costumed, drinking their breakfasts of Bloody Marys on the balconies of the apartments overlooking Royal Street. At Canal Street there were more people, setting up stations with camp chairs and thermos bottles and boxes of sandwiches. Hawkers of masks and kewpie dolls were readying their display boards and change-aprons. On the farther side of Canal Street the taxi passed a family unfolding its camp chairs; the children were all costumed and masked, but the grownups were not; Steve groaned aloud.

"You're smart to get uptown early, Mac," said the driver. "Little bit longer, ain't none of us cabs gonna be able to *get* across Canal."

"I'd feel better if I were dressed like a respectable adult," Steve answered.

The cabdriver laughed appreciatively. "You'll feel better later on. I'm not taking my kids out till this afternoon—we always catch Rex right at the end of the parade route. Me, guess what the hell I'm going as?"

The question startled Steve, who replied with genuine interest, "I can't. What as?"

"An artist!" The cabbie laughed afresh at the incongruity of the choice. "It's so I can change fast after I'm through hacking. Got me a smock and a tam fourteen, fifteen years ago; I'm still wearing 'em."

"You people really go for this stuff, don't you?" Steve realized for the first time.

"Hell, Mac, that's New Orleans. If you gotta put up with the fucking *summer*time in this town, y'gotta right t'enjoy Carnival."

Along the broad avenue they traveled were more family groups forming, then larger gatherings of costumed grown-ups, clustered on street corners, waiting for the latecomers among their numbers. It was still the uncertain gray of early morning, and it looked to Steve as if there would be rain. They passed an open truck decorated with multicolored paper streamers and a flowered arch to which balloons were tied; a quarter of a mile and they came upon another truck, similarly bedecked, pulled up at the curb. A group of young people—perhaps two dozen—all dressed as angels, were climbing on board; one of the many groups whose trucks would follow the daytime parade in endless number, groups made up of members of a particular fraternity or business organization or family or informal social club—the Krewe of Orleanians. Some carried with them a small jazz combo, hired for the occasion. Some, Steve had learned, were formed when a particular couple wanted to have a truck and put an ad in the paper inviting others to join them in the cost of the venture. Often they met for the first time on Mardi Gras morning as they climbed aboard the truck, strangers to one another. Out of habit, Steve began to weave in his imagination a fictional situation in which hero and heroine should meet in such a way. From the taxi he saw at another corner, not a truck, but a decrepit banana wagon and horse, both gaily bedecked with crêpe paper streamers. The taxi pulled off the avenue and in a moment came to a stop before the Fuselles' house.

Steve paid the driver and got out. The humiliation of being on a public thoroughfare in broad daylight in his pirate costume overwhelmed him again; he fought against his vanity. The house was set back from the street; a semicircular flagstone path led Steve to the front steps and the semicircular portico with its prim columns.

He pressed the bell-button and shortly was admitted to the entrance hall by a white-uniformed maid. A broad staircase led upstairs from the checkerboard marble of the entrance, and on his right was a large rectangular living room. The maid ushered him into the living room and asked his name.

"Steve Williams. I'm calling for Miss Cowan," he informed her. The maid hesitated as if she would say something but wasn't certain she should. Steve realized his eye mask was still on. "Oh," he said, pushing it up onto his head. The maid grinned.

"Yes, sir," she confirmed his realization. "I'll tell Miss Cowan you is here."

She withdrew. No one seemed to have come down yet, but Steve imagined he could feel the house vibrating with the excitement of the morning's activity. He hoped fervently they would all be in costume when he met them. The smell of frying bacon drifted from somewhere in the house. Presently there was a clatter on the stairs out in the entrance hall and Margaret calling, "Steve! Steve!"

She bounded into the room, her face alight and bare of make-up. Steve caught his breath at the sight of her beauty. He had seen it unadorned by make-up before, but the circumstances had been of a different character. The wide-standing collar of the clown costume she had on gave her head the look of a flower, and she wore her eye mask pulled down so that it covered her chin: as though the flower peeked out at him from beneath the partial cover of its leaves. She took his hands and kissed him fleetingly.

"Breakfast is ready," she hurried on, "but the others aren't down yet, and I'm starving and Mrs. Fuselle says we should go ahead since it's buffet anyway."

"Maggie, I feel ridiculous in this outfit."

"You look wonderful! I told you you'd make a heavenly pirate, and I was right!"

"I missed you last night," Steve told her. "God, Maggie, but I missed you."

"I'm glad!" She laughed. She put on lipstick, standing before the large mirror over the mantelpiece. "But honestly,

Steve, it was *much* more sensible of both of us to take the night off so we'd be fit for the doings today. One night of the whole holiday, after all." She pulled him toward a door at the farther end of the living room. "Come on, breakfast!"

The table in the dining room was set for twelve. Who the others might be besides the family and Mike Cowan, Margaret and himself, he did not know, presumably Linda Fuselle's escort for the day and other friends. At the moment Steve and Margaret were alone. They served themselves from the sideboard. The maid who had admitted Steve came in with coffee, and Margaret asked her to fill the cups at two adjacent place settings. They sat down beside each other, and the maid went out.

"Is Mike up and about at this hour?" Steve asked.

"Sh!" Margaret grabbed his hand and squeezed it. "I don't even know if he's come in yet. It's a scandal. I suppose he's found a local trick. There wasn't a sign of him last night." Another, briefer squeeze. "I can't eat with my left hand. See you later." She released his hand and started in on her breakfast, Steve joining in with an appetite, now that there was another costumed adult in his company.

"Did you work last night?" Margaret asked him.

"I couldn't," said Steve. "I was thinking too much about you."

"Silly. I mean really."

"Yes, a little," he said.

"The story with the Houston setting?"

Having bitten off half a biscuit, Steve struggled for coherence, but could only manage a nod.

Margaret hurried on, "Oh, Steve, it must be terrific *doing* something like you're doing. You wouldn't understand. I'll bet there hasn't been a day of your life you weren't doing something."

Steve swallowed. "Ha."

"Or thinking about it. You know what you are? Creative. God but I envy you. I don't mean creative-arty. I mean if you were a bricklayer, you'd probably have thousands of children."

"I mean to anyway," said Steve.

She stopped eating and looked at him—not coyly, but in estimation.

"I'll bet you'd like to," she said, more to herself than to

Steve. "I could tell because when you're about to—" She stopped abruptly and went on with her scrambled eggs.

"About to what? Or were you about to shock me?"

"Yes," she said.

"Oh." He did not pursue the matter.

"What's the weather like?" Margaret asked.

"Bleak. Cold as hell."

"Lord."

"Maggie. Are we spending any of the day with Mike and his crew?"

"Why? Would you rather not?" she asked.

"It's for you to say, whatever you want." Steve shrugged. "We don't have to see them if you'd rather not."

"I'm not being stuffy or anything . . ." Steve put in.

"I know." She took his hand again. "You're just a man, that's all. What joy!"

She grinned at him, and to his amusement Steve noticed that she was not aware of the pieces of biscuit dough between her teeth. On previous mornings she had been more scrupulous, and more designing, about her appearance.

Footsteps sounded on the stairs again and Mrs. Fuselle came hurrying into the room. Steve stood up.

"Don't stand, please don't, have your breakfast! I wish we'd had grits this morning, it's *freezing* outside. You're Steve Williams, aren't you? I'm so glad you're sensible enough to come for Margaret early—before the real horror starts on the streets!"

It was difficult for Steve to answer with equanimity because the short plump woman who stood facing him across the table was dressed in a fantastic, somewhat Oriental regalia, topped by an extraordinary number of colored wooden-and-glass ropes of beads. Her round face was plastered with stage make-up approximating Eastern features.

At the sight of his dismay she laughed. "I'm a Chinese."

Margaret asked, rather tenatively, "And all those beads? . . ."

Mrs. Fuselle nodded vigorously. "I'm a *Creole* Chinese. Do go on with your breakfasts," she said, moving to her place at the end of the table nearest the door to the kitchen. "And hurry. The other apparitions heading downstairs are going to be worse than I."

Soon Linda Fuselle came in, rendered globular by the fuzzy

rabbit-suit she wore. The doorbell began to ring, and the first arrival was Linda's escort, a haphazard and asthmatic idea of a Bedouin. Linda's father appeared briefly, in a cardinal's robes, found his orange juice, and went looking for a little gin to add to it. More people arrived, some to have breakfast, others only for coffee and an exchange of laughter about costumes, still others to make plans for meeting later in the day.

Opposite Steve and Margaret at the table later were an American Indian, in full ceremonial dress, and a Venetian page boy; they were discussing real estate with unblinking sobriety. The Venetian page boy scratched his balding head through the cloth of his blue-silk feathered cap and said, "Once they've zoned the damned neighborhood I'll feel better about the possibility of a commercial development there."

Steve spilled coffee into his lap in his effort to get his cup back to its saucer, and catching his eye, Margaret began to giggle.

The American Indian put his toast aside with a judicial air and said to the Venetian page boy, "Mark my words, the zoning people aren't going to have any choice. The suburban shopping center is the new way of life—the growing population demands it."

"Steve, they'll *see* you." Margaret was choking.

"I can't help it." Steve gasped in the pain of suppressing his laughter. "I can't believe that on any other day of the year—Maggie, it's eight-thirty on a perfectly plain chilly weekday, and I've just had indisputable proof with my own eyes that I've lost my mind!"

Margaret was chortling behind her napkin. "We've got to get out of here, we'll disgrace ourselves if we don't. . . ."

They murmured polite words to the company, more careful ones to their hostess, and getting Margaret's fur coat from a rack in the side hall, hurried out to the sidewalk. There they broke into helpless laughter, and arms about each other, ran down the street until they were out of sight of the house.

Across the way a party of maskers—harem girls and two sultans—were coming out of another house and piling into an automobile at the curb. Margaret was gasping for breath when they reached the corner.

"Where? Where do we go? How do we get there?"

"We get a taxi at St. Charles Avenue, if we can," said

Steve; "streetcar, if not. Into the center of town as far as any vehicle can take us, then walk. Maggie, I love you! This is a glorious day!"

And the spirits of Mardi Gras, who attend, nodded and noted two new victims.

At nine-thirty they were settling down at a table in the restaurant of Thaisa Chapman's House. No other table was occupied, but Steve could hear Thaisa directing the traffic of the cooks and waitresses back in the kitchen.

"It's a prosaic beginning," Steve said, "but I swear I don't have any other ideas."

"What time is it?"

"Nine-thirty."

"Lord," said Margaret. "Well."

"Well. What do we have?" asked Steve.

"I don't *know,*" Margaret admitted. "I mean—it's Mardi Gras and that should be fun and games. But it's also nine-thirty in the morning."

"Why, you're not the tired old roué I thought you were." Steve smiled.

"I'm a healthy red-blooded American girl, and I can't help it if I feel peculiar about drinking anything till the sun's over the yardarm."

"Do they make 'em all so conservative in Washington?"

"All right, go on, you know *lots* of girls who drink the sun around."

Steve realized she was seriously disconcerted. He laughed. "Never met one. I thought you might be It, but ah, now I see I was deluded by a scheming convent girl."

Beneath the table Margaret kicked his shin, not very gently.

Through the doors from the kitchen came Thaisa Chapman. She hoved to beside their table. Thaisa was dressed (there was no sanity left, not anywhere, thought Steve) in a bathing suit of the tights-and-puffed-sleeves era, her black ruffled bathing cap not completely hiding the pencils that were still skewered through the knot of blonde hair on the top of her head.

"Steve, I *heard* you going out this morning, I thought my clock had busted. Hello, honey, aren't you *cute* in that outfit. How y'all like mine?" She did a mincing and enormous pirouette. "Where you going today?"

"We don't know," Steve confided. "We don't even know how to begin."

"Oh, honey," Thaisa sympathized.

Margaret said, "Tell us, how do you *have* Mardi Gras? We just don't know—all we know is we love it."

Thaisa thought seriously. Before she could answer, Steve asked, "For instance, we've had breakfast. Okay, it's almost ten o'clock and we're sitting here; do we have a drink, or do we have coffee?"

Thaisa clucked her tongue. "A drink?" She wagged her head back and forth. "Steve, you two children have to remember you've got the whole day to get through. What you have is a little coffee. And a little drink to go *with* it."

Thaisa laughed her fluting laugh when the couple responded to the joke. She pulled out a chair and sat down, beckoning to the waitress as she did so. They gave their order to the girl, who then disappeared in the direction of the kitchen.

"Now after this little coffee and drink," Steve asked, "then where do we go? Where is Mardi Gras going on?"

"All over, honey." Thaisa invited him with a spread of her arms. " 'Specially in the Quarter; the best costumes are always here. You'll want to walk down to Canal Street, too, for the parade. Not to see the parade so much as to see the Queen. The Queen of Rex," she added, insupportably meticulous. "Did you see her picture in the paper this morning? She's lovely."

"Where does she hang out?" Steven wanted to know.

"She'll review the parade from the Boston Club balcony. Probably wearing a white suit—you can't miss her."

"Where's the Queen of Comus?" asked Margaret.

Thaisa answered with asperity, "At home, taking it easy, if she's got any sense. Nobody'll know who she *is* till tonight."

The waitress served their drinks and cups of coffee. A burst of people in elaborate costumes crashed through the rickerty glass doors from the street, and Thaisa rose to greet them. Alone together, Steve and Margaret toasted one another smilingly.

"Happy Mardi Gras," Steve said.

"You won't get much work done today," said Margaret.

"I didn't expect to."

Margaret sipped her drink. "How much do you work usually?" she asked after a moment. "I mean when you're not in New Orleans at Mardi Gras time?"

"I'm not certain, if you mean numbers of hours. I work all the time."

"What ambition you must have."

"Not by a long ways," he answered. "I'm miserable when I'm not working. I don't tip cabdrivers, I push people out of the way at grocery stores; I'm really awful."

"Have you ever been in New Orleans when it wasn't Mardi Gras?" Margaret asked.

"I've never been here before at all. Why?"

Margaret looked at her glass. "We're supposed to go back tomorrow."

"Christ, don't talk about it. I know," said Steve.

She looked at him soberly a moment. Then she smiled. "I'll bet places to stay are easy to find once the Mardi Gras crowd is gone."

"I'll bet so, too. What've you got in mind?"

"Nothing."

"Oh."

"No, I meant I thought I might stay over a few days," she amended. "See what the city is like aside from all *this* razzmatazz."

"I bet you'd like it. So would I," said Steve.

"Don't jump to conclusions."

"Wouldn't think of it."

"You're going back to Houston?" The voice was small. Steve felt the blood rush from his head into his hands.

He answered casually. "Not right away. No definite plans, except burning candles for your health at the cathedral after you've gone."

"What time is it?"

"Ten-fifteen," said Steve.

"Everybody will be showing up on the streets."

"We can be late and make a grand entrance."

"What are you talking about?"

"If you're looking for a lodging, ma'am, I have this nice slave quarter that I'm sure would suit your pleasure."

Margaret sat back abruptly. "Steve, at this hour?"

"Pirate suits are easy to get in and out of. Clown suits are easier, I'll bet."

Margaret grinned at him. "Just why I chose it."

A pause. Steve said, "Maggie. *Will* you stay over? Let Washington do without you a little while longer?"

"Who wants me to?"

"Don't get coy with me, you everlasting——"

"Okay, okay. I won't. I remember. I won't forget." For a moment she looked really frightened of his displeasure.

"Mayor DeLesseps S. Morrison wants you to," he said. "Thaisa Chapman's House wants you to. The ghost of Huey Long wants you to. And—" However lightly spoken, however frivolous the scene, they were words of commitment, and, Steve knew, such commitment as was not to be washed away by circumstance. For a moment the muscles of his face were rigid and his eyes drank from each feature of the lovely, lighted, smooth, clown-collared face before him. "—And I want you to."

As the trucks and banana wagons of the Krewe of Orleanians were filling, Warren Taggert and Mike Cowan, dressing-gowned again, were having coffee in the living room of the *garçonnière* on Fourth Street. The record player was silent, and the room was chilly against the efforts of the heater's radiants.

Warren drew on his cigarette and through the smoke watched Mike gazing into his cup.

"Where are you going to meet them, the people you were going to meet?" Warren asked.

"At the St. Charles. They're staying there," Mike answered.

"If I'm going as Sleep, what are you going as?"

"I was supposed to go as George Washington, but my costume's at the Fuselles'! Got another pair of pajamas?"

"Wouldn't fit you," said Warren. "You're broader than me in the shoulders."

Mike sat forward and put his cup on the coffee table. "Say, how are you fixed for coffee? Is there plenty in the house?"

"A fresh pound, as a matter of fact!"

"Suppose I call the fellows I'm supposed to see today. Suppose—if I can reach them in time—and for God's sake tell me if this is an imposition—suppose we have them come here for coffee. I'd like you to meet them, if you're willing. While they're on their way here, I'll buck up to the Fuselles' and get my costume . . ." Warren's eyes widened, but Mike waved a palliating hand. "There's a back entrance and I know the way through it to my room. No one but me will ever know I haven't been sleeping there all night."

"Okay. Go on."

"I can be back here before Wynn and his crew arrive, if they can come. You'll have a chance to—well, see what you think of them. And if they can't come, the hell with them. I don't want to share you anyway."

"It's fine with me," said Warren.

Mike made the necessary phone calls to the hotel, but only Wynn Bargmeister was still there. The others had already gone out. Wynn agreed to meet them at the *garçonnière* in an hour, and Mike sped off.

While he was gone, Warren got into the costume that was supposed to represent Sleep, crisply fresh blue pajamas. Over white tennis socks he wore sandals that were necessarily incongruous but would be comfortable for the endless walking Mardi Gras entailed.

Mike was back in his George Washington disguise in time to greet Wynn Bargmeister when he arrived. The three of them shrugged off coffee, toasted Mardi Gras with a drink, and discussed their plans for the day. Wynn was to meet Linda Fuselle and her escort at the Friars' Club, but the rest of the day he planned to keep to himself, roaming the streets to see what Mardi Gras would bring his way. He invited Mike and Warren to join him for the drink with Linda, but they were quick to decline.

With the smoothest lack of offense Wynn was able to learn from Warren, in the course of their easily rambling conversation, how long he had been living in New Orleans, where he worked, and what prep school in Cleveland he had attended. Warren had the impression he had met with Wynn Bargmeister's approval. The three young men finished their drinks and went off in search of the Mardi Gras.

When they reached Canal Street, Wynn left them.

From a vendor Warren and Mike bought eye masks and put them on. They had drinks in a number of the bars along Canal Street, and as they drank, poured forth to one another their histories, each absorbing the other's with attention, as though they were compelled by circumstances they did not understand to simulate a vintage acquaintance they did not possess. Warren found himself talking freely of the Army, of Sue Jensen, of Philadelphia, and of the Port of New Orleans

Bank and Trust Company. In turn he listened with steadfast curiosity to Mike's stories of life in Washington, of Judge Cowan, of his own lack of occupation, and of the friends he had, the brilliant and promising young men of the State Department who opened their circle to a rich idler because he was amusing, attractive, and could with his own income indulge in gestures of grandeur such as they anticipated for their old, and rewarded, age. In the exchanging of stories there was an underlying feverishness, and driving attempt to learn as much as they could about each other, to love one another in the sparse hours ahead of them.

On Decatur Street they found a liquor store, bought their own bottle, and made their way through the rapids of the disguised and hell-raising populace back to the center of festivity, along Canal Street from Royal Street outward, to see Rex parade. While the first of the bands was marching past, they sought refuge in a shop doorway and limbered up the bottle they had bought.

"What do we do after the parade?" Warren wanted to know, taking his second swig and feeling the earlier drinks catching up with him.

"The Quatre Chevaux?"

"Okay."

They drank again. When the floats of the Rex parade came near and the escorting bands were blaring, they pulled themselves free from the sanctuary of the shop doorway and joined themselves to the cheering crowds pressing forward toward the floats. With the crowds they shouted, they waved at the masked men parading, they cried out for throws, they laughed and let the crowds pummel them, and staggered at length back to their base, their exhilaration suddenly doubling the effect of the drinking they'd been doing.

"Where's that bottle?" Mike demanded. He tilted it up, gurgled, and made a face at Warren. "Next best thing I know to you."

"Mike, for God's sake, you're in public. Come on, come on, pass it over." He took the bottle.

"I've got something important to say to you later," Mike confided. "Much later. After today."

"What? What are you talking about?"

"Later, I said. You know what I love? Guys with crew cuts from Shaker Heights."

"And I love young drunks from Washington. Especially in white knee breeches. Especially on Mardi Gras day."

"Hello? Yes. Who is it?" Mike shouted into the phone, trying to breast the tumult of the barroom.

"Michael? Rex has already passed."

"Margaret? God. I *know* Rex has passed. Where are you? How did you ever get me on the phone in *this* place?"

"We ran into Wynn. Headlong."

"Who's we? Margaret?"

"I'm here. Steve, of course. That's we. Michael, can you hear?"

"Yes, yes, Margaret. Do you need help? What is it?"

"Michael, I'm not going back to Washington with you. I'm staying a few days more and——"

"Oh, God! Margaret, listen, baby, you don't know what you're doing——"

"Just a few days more than you, Michael. I thought I'd better let you know, because of the car. Now don't worry about——"

"Oh, Christ on a stick. Margaret, what the hell d'you think I'm going to tell Dad if you——"

"I'll call him before you reach Washington. Oh, Michael, I love you, and I wish you joy——"

"Margaret! Now can the Elsie Ferguson and tell me what the hell——"

"Nothing's what the hell. Not now, but we can always hope. I was afraid we might keep missing connections, like this morning, so I thought I'd better try to find you. To confirm. To confirm cancellation of reservation, or whatever the hell one does with one's own father's car. I wish you love, Michael! Bye-bye!"

21

WARREN HELD TIGHTLY TO THE EDGE OF the bar, hoping his head would clear. Out on the streets while the Rex parade was going on he and Mike had finished off the fifth of whiskey, a number of swigs having been doled out to passing strangers. In the dank coldness of the out-of-doors he had not noticed the effect of the liquor beyond an expanding mood of hilarity on his part and a disposition on Mike's part to keep his arm around Warren's shoulder; the stifling heat and darkness of the Quatre Chevaux, however, had forced him to recognize that he was roaring drunk. He felt his face perspiring under the eye mask while he waited for Mike to come back from the phone. He pulled it down off his face. The room was packed beyond capacity, and it was with an effort that Warren made space for Mike at the bar when he reappeared.

"It was Margaret," Mike said thickly, shrugging. "She's staying over instead of driving back to Washington with us."

"Is that bad? Maybe she's enjoying herself."

"It'll make for a peaceful trip for the rest of us, that's certain," he considered. "But it raises a certain point of——"

"How long have we been here?" Warren asked.

"Two hours, about," Mike said. "You want to go someplace else?"

"No, let's have a drink. What point does it raise?"

"The point'll keep. Same for you? Bartender!"

Of the crowd filling the Quatre Chevaux almost everyone was masked and costumed, and everyone by this time was drunk and shouting. Watching from their station at the bar, Warren and Mike pointed out to one another, with whoops of laughter, a costume here or an incident of behavior there. In the volume and rhythm of the noise, Warren felt a danger. The place was roaring in Carnival spirit, but he had the sensation in the smoke-filled darkness that at any minute the activities of the close-pressed maskers would take a sudden turn for the bizarre. Unsteady as he was feeling, his heart beat rapidly both with misgiving and with a lust to see how abandoned the place would get as the hours passed in clouds of cigarette smoke and bar-whisky fumes. Music, raucous and nerve-racking, blared through the place, and at the moment three tall, heavy-featured women were elbowing their way through the darkness. The first was immediately in front of Warren before he realized they weren't women but men. The second one, passing him, simpered at his astonishment through a muddy application of lipstick and absurdly thick false eyelashes.

"But you're cute!" the bass voice bellowed at him.

Suppressing incredulous laughter, Warren could not answer.

"And so are *you*," Mike snarled contemptuously at him.

"Ooo! We're touchy today! Don't worry, darling, I won't steal him." And with a haughty toss of his ringletted wig, he pushed on through the crowd, his companions crowding close behind.

"Drink up." Mike shrugged.

They ordered another round.

"If they're all queer in this place, why aren't they all dressed up like women?"

Mike narrowed his eyes in intoxicated sagaciousness.

"Only the fools do that," he said, pointing a warning finger at Warren's chest. "If you want to attract a guy who's gay, the first principle to keep in mind is that he likes men, not women. Why go around aping the very thing that's distasteful to him? That's why I hate the flissy types, and why they're usually so miserable."

"Mike."

"Yes?"

"I never thought about it that way but—what type am I?"

Mike laughed. "Worried about being flissy?"

"I'd be disgusted with myself if I were. Drunk, all right. Depraved, that's fine. But flissy, never."

"Don't worry, your wrists are as firm as any guy's. That is one of the many, many reasons, Warren Taggert, that I like you so much."

"Oh, Christ, look at that. Now there's one who's going to get arrested, you can bet."

"Who? Where?"

Through the crowd was edging an apparition. A tall and muscled young man, naked except for an arrangement of cloth of silver to cover his genitals, his body painted a rich brown, silver sandals on his feet, moved silently and with great care toward them. Towering above his head was a Cocteau-like headdress of silver wires, its branches hung with sparkling necklaces of every color. The upper half of his face was covered by a silver eye mask. The crowd opened to watch his approach, and the air rang with hooting and whistling, to which the young man responded with a smiling turn of his head and a scepterlike movement of his arms.

Mike whistled through his teeth in amazement. "The hell

with getting arrested," he pointed out, "the jerk must be freezing to death."

"It's hot in here. Maybe he just runs from bar to bar."

"Or flies," Mike suggested dryly.

The young man passed through and in a moment had reached the three drag queens, who surrounded him. Coarse laughter issued from the circle from time to time and slowly they maneuvered until they were huddling in the far corner of the room. Warren watched, mesmerized by the glistening contours of the naked painted body.

"What are you thinking about?" Mike asked.

"He's beautiful. Jesus. A damn fool, but beautiful. Isn't he, Mike?"

His breathing had gone suddenly shallow, and now his heart thudded against his chest. Two of the men dressed as women were standing close together, their backs to the room. The young man with the headdress was leaning against the wall, his arms spread out on either side, and he was looking straight past their shoulders to Warren, grinning arrogantly. Warren could not see the third drag queen, and felt suddenly faint with shock when he realized what activity the other two were screening from chance observers.

Reeling from the impact of his discovery, Warren turned his back to them.

"Mike," he croaked. "Do you see that?"

"Sure I do."

"Mike, she's—he's going down on him! Right here!"

"It's Mardi Gras!" Mike laughed, as though in explanation. "Just wait, the place will get wilder still in a little while. Another hour and they won't bother hiding it. By midnight they'll be doing it on the bar unless I miss my guess."

"But Mike, the goddamned proprietor——"

"The proprietor is at the moment kissing the bartender."

Warren looked up at the sound of shrieking laughter and applause down toward the middle of the bar. Behind the bar the proprietor and the bartender, both swaying drunkenly, were locked in a charade of an embrace. Warren downed his drink with a gulp. He struggled to catch his breath.

"I'm just not used to it."

Mike leered at him jokingly. "Does it get you—all in a swivet?"

Warren opened his mouth to answer and Mike kissed him,

with his free hand pulling him forward to his chest. Warren began to lose his breath and had to break away. He realized he was near to passing out.

"I'm scared," Warren said. "It scares me to be this drunk——"

"Want me to take you home?"

"How the hell are we going to *get* there? We'll never be able to push our way through that mob on Canal Street."

"Listen. We can walk to the St. Charles Hotel. One of the gang is bound to show up there sometime this afternoon. We can use one of their rooms. We'll feel better after a nap, I can take you out for a slam-bang dinner."

Warren groaned. "I'll never make it. I'll never . . ."

"Warren, I'm *leaving* day after tomorrow," Mike reminded him, suddenly serious.

The force of the point brought Warren up short. He gave his head a violent shake and forced his eyes to focus on Mike's face.

"Oh." He nodded.

"We can make it to the St. Charles, can't we? Come on. Come on, boy, I'll steady you."

He could not stagger; there was no room for staggering. He felt Mike burrowing a passage for them through the crowd; at length they reached the door to the street. Beside it stood a masker of surrealistic imagination; an aspect of the costume was a long train studded with rhinestones and sequins. Warren realized he had stepped on the edge of it and hastened to murmur, "Oh, I'm sorry, excuse me."

The masker, face shining with cosmetics, looked down his nose.

"That's all right, doll," he bridled. "Just watch it."

The street was as shrill as the bar had been. A drizzle fell, but no one seemed to care about it. Warren lifted his face to the revivifying icy drops. Maskers were dancing in the street, and on a balcony across the way a jazz combo belted out music for them. Those not dancing showed a jumpiness in their movement as they walked along, as if they could not keep under control the frenetic energy the enormous masquerade released in their flesh. Arms around each other, Mike and Warren pushed through the crowd as far as Canal Street, but there they met with defeat; caught up in a chain of costumed young people who ran zigzagging and shrieking through the crowd, they were carried, helpless, half a block out of their way. Eventually they broke loose from the hysterically slithering snake of human beings, only to meet with one obstruction after another as they tried to get across Canal Street; it was four o'clock before they reached the sanctuary of the hotel.

They found one of the young men from Washington crossing the lobby. He gave Mike the key to his room, and without waiting to be introduced to Warren, hurried off to an appointment. Mike and Warren took the elevator up to the room. Once inside, they fell onto the twin beds with twin moans of exhaustion. In thirty seconds they were asleep.

They awoke at eight, showered and dressed again, necessarily in their costumes. Because it was long past sundown, they left their eye masks behind, and Mike discarded his Washington wig. They went down to the lobby.

"Where for dinner?" Mike asked. "Are you hungry?"

"Starving," said Warren. "What about the dining room here?"

"Is it good? This is, you know, a highly special meal."

"I guess it's good enough, but that isn't the point. I don't think I could get to a restaurant without taking bites out of innocent bystanders along the way. The dining room's over this way."

Warren led the way across the lobby. The waves of people coming in and going out had perceptibly thinned, but the air of celebration had not. The masks were gone, but the majority of the people in the lobby, except for the hotel personnel, were still in costume. A few clowns and pirates and savages were sprawled on a lobby sofa, either exhausted or drunk; here and there were people in evening clothes bound for the Rex or Comus ball. Everyone still seemed to be rushing, driving hard now to fill with activity the fading hours of the Carnival.

The hotel dining room was not crowded (a couple in motley at one table by the windows, a party of people dressed for a ball at another in the center of the room). Warren and Mike found a table against the side wall, removed from the ones that were occupied. They ordered and devoured an unusually large dinner; they were so hungry, they did not take time to talk until the entree was gone. Then, while they waited for dessert to be brought, they lit cigarettes and sat back with spine-shivering sighs.

"That's better," said Mike. "Sorry we missed the Comus parade tonight."

"If I hadn't gotten some sleep, I wouldn't have been able to see it anyway. Christ, I was drunk."

"I wasn't far behind you," Mike reassured him.

Dessert was brought, and again they fell silent until they had finished it. The party of people in ball clothes left the dining room, and only the couple in motley remained, far on the other side of the room.

Over coffee Warren asked, "What time are you leaving Thursday?"

"Earlyish. No definite plans made."

"I see."

"Do you have to go to the bank tomorrow?"

"Yes," said Warren.

"Damn."

"That's what I was thinking." A pause. Then: "Do you absolutely have to get back to Washington, Mike? I mean, right away?"

"I'm afraid so."

"You don't have a job to get to, do you?"

"No," Mike said. "But stuff. You know how it is." His glance was tender and commiserating. "I'm glad you hate this as much as I do, my having to leave. Lookit, you wouldn't be interested in a few days in Washington, would you?"

"You bet your sweet life I would. But it's out."

"The job?"

Warren nodded.

"Hell. I was thinking: Margaret's not going back with the rest of us; you could take her place in the car—there'd be plenty of room——"

"Yes, I know. Well. Tough."

"Warren . . ."

"Yah?"

"Warren, what if it weren't just for a visit?"

"What?"

"What if I were asking you to come live with me?"

Warren sat back. "You're pulling my leg. . . ."

"No, damn it. I'm asking you."

He hesitated. "To—to live with you? Be lovers?"

"Yes. There. Now I've done it."

Warren shook his head incredulously. "Mike. I can't just —pick up and——"

"Would you want to, that's the important thing." Mike pinpointed the issue. "Would you? A lot of people do it, you know; live together."

"Guys like us? Just as if they were married?"

"Practically as if. Look, you'd like Washington. I could help you find another job there like a shot. . . . Do you think you'd like living with me?"

"Oh, Christ, would I," Warren said.

"Then come back with us."

"Mike, I can't casually——"

"It's all settled then——"

"Mike, wait."

Mike spread his hands, only half-jokingly. "You've got an entire day to get cleaned away here. If you're short on cash, I can take care of that until we have you fixed up in Washington——"

"That isn't what bothers me; I've got some income from my family besides the bank job."

"Good, you can keep *me* then——"

"I don't know, I just——"

"Say *yes*," Mike urged. "Come on, quick, before you can think about it. You can pack enough for the trip in no time."

"What about the heavy stuff? I'm up to my ass in phonograph records."

"Get a friend to put them in storage for you if you don't have time to do it tomorrow. We can have them shipped later."

"I don't have any friends I could ask to do that," Warren objected.

"Then I'll get Linda Fuselle to see about it. Linda's trustworthy, and as efficient as anybody else would be——"

"She'd hate you for it."

"What do *I* care? She'd do it. Answer me, you jerk! Are you game?"

"All right," he said quickly.

Warren sat stunned by his own decision. Could you get away with such a thing? Could you actually take off from a place on a moment's notice with a guy you'd met only the night before? He felt faintly dizzy at the prospect. The hell with it, he told himself, why shouldn't he do as he pleased? He wasn't under any obligation to anyone else, there wasn't anything to hold him in New Orleans if this impetuous, wonderful, lovable guy wanted him to come to Washington. Mike covered Warren's hand with his own—briefly, but long enough to steady him.

Mike smiled, calm and unblinking, when Warren looked at him.

"On that we can have a drink," he said.

The next day Warren was too busy to allow himself to consider what he was doing. Immediately after breakfast he called the chief bookkeeper at the bank to tell him he would not be back, and asked that whatever salary was coming to him be mailed to the Washington address Mike had given him. The rest of the morning he lost himself gratefully in the details of packing. At eleven he telephoned the owner of the building he lived in, explained that his rent was paid through the month and that a friend of his would turn the key over to her as soon as his effects had all been moved into storage. The owner hoped he would enjoy Washington and trusted he had not found New Orleans disagreeable. At noon Mike called.

"Linda Fuselle says where have you been all these months and can you come up for a drink before dinner tonight?"

"Is she mad at you?" Warren asked. "For asking her to take care of storing my stuff?"

"Not at all. She says now Lent's here, she won't have anything *else* to occupy her mind."

"Mike," said Warren. "Look, this *is* Ash Wednesday. You're still serious about all that, the things we talked about last night?"

"Sure. Aren't you?"

"I already called the bank."

"Good boy," Mike said.

"I just thought, in the cold light of Ash Wednesday morning——"

"What do you take me for?"

"Well, I wondered."

"What about Linda, what shall I tell her?"

"Tell her I'd enjoy coming by for a drink," said Warren.

"Good. All the crew will be there; we can find out what *they* were up to on Mardi Gras."

"God, in front of Linda's father and mother?"

"They're not joining us, Linda says. It's all very quiet, being Ash Wednesday, when decent people shouldn't be entertaining at all. The exception is being made because it's our last day here. See you at five or five-thirty?"

"Looking sweaty, but I'll be there," said Warren.

"Okay. Well. See you, buddy."

"Thanks for calling."

"See you later," said Mike.

"Yes. Good-by, Mike."

At five Warren hailed a taxi on Saint Charles Avenue. The streets he was driven through seemed singularly quiet, drained of excitement by the Carnival. The Mardi Gras flags in front of the houses of past kings and queens of the Carnival were gone, the houses themselves were still. The taxi passed a church, and Warren noted the sedate and reverent people going in to receive the customary cross of ashes on their foreheads. Dust thou art and unto dust thou shalt return. . . . Not me, Warren thought, not now; I'm just getting born.

22

THE DAYS OF LENT WERE STILL, AND brought with them the crystal yellows of spring, the green burgeoning of the city. Linda Fuselle, after Mike Cowan's and Warren Taggert's departure for Washington, delighted herself by escaping the responsibility of arranging for the storage of Warren's possessions; she informed Margaret Cowan of the vacancy of the *garçonnière* on Fourth Street and Margaret took custody of the record collection as well as the apartment for the few months she intended to prolong her visit. It was with difficulty that she prevented Linda's discovering the fact that Steve Williams was actually becoming the rentor. Steve checked out of Thaisa Chapman's House two days before Margaret was due to move out of the Fuselles' house; to the owner of the *garçonnière* he explained that his wife was selling their place in Houston and would follow him in a day or two. To her father Margaret wrote that mail should be sent to her in care of Steven Williams, and gave the address. "This is the person I'm subletting from," she explained to her father, "and God knows how long it will take the postman to find out that *I'm* here temporarily. Mr. Williams' mail will be accumulating while he's out of town, so I can't very well take his name off the delivery box." With Steve she laughed over the contortions of deception involved in the explanation, but Judge Cowan's next note indicated no misgiving, and Margaret felt decidedly relieved.

The sunlit days of Lent passed drowsily for them in the *garçonnière*. Strangers in all but love, they were able for hours to spread their reminiscences out, each guiding the other through the maze of memories, incidents, and people that had led them to this moment and this place. Margaret told Steve of her childhood, her boarding school, her father, detailing for him richly the panorama of a life as foreign to his own background as any Asiatic potentate's might be; yet it seemed to him a milieu eminently suited to Margaret. Preoccupied entirely by her company, Steve did no writing. At the moment, he told himself, Margaret was the only important thing in his life, and his attention was focused on her hungrily, to the exclusion of any other business. They dined from time to time in the restaurants whose names they had heard before, but otherwise went out very little. In the evening they would listen to some of the records they had inherited from the *garçonnière's* previous tenant, and marvel at the curiosities they found in the meticulously numbered and catalogued albums. When the music was done, they would lie down together, not always in the storming mood of desire that had begun their relationship, but more placidly now, in confidence and security sharing their lust as well as their affection. Morning would come, and at first desultorily, over the second cup of coffee, the conversation that built up for each a detailed knowledge of the other's past would begin anew. Margaret had more to tell than had Steve; her life had contained more that she thought worthy of reporting. Steve on his part felt that Margaret could only be bored by more than the sketchiest picturing of his early life in Houston and an occasionally indulged dwelling on one or another small aspect of it. She evinced a livelier interest in the time he had spent in the Navy and his friends, the Vergeses, who had done so much for him. Steve willingly told her of these, but not at length; he wanted to know about Margaret, and Margaret unwearyingly complied.

The only substantial amount of time Steve spent alone was when Margaret went each afternoon to the market to buy their dinner. He learned that she liked cooking, and if she concentrated on rather complicated, not altogether appetizing specialties, he put it down to a desire on her part to please and impress him. Margaret returned from her trips to the market as though she had been gone for days, and Steve had the impression that she really was miserable away from him.

"I want to spend the rest of my life talking to you, and only you, and having you look at me the way you do," she said.

"What way?"

"Worshipfully."

"Oh, come off it, Maggie." Steve would squirm.

"Well, you do. And that's what makes me happiest."

Often she would plead with him nervously to come to the market with her, but without clearly knowing why, Steve wanted to cling to the hour or so he had to himself daily; he did not realize that the degree to which he gave of himself to Margaret exhausted him, and he could be replenished only by solitude. When from time to time she insisted and he balked at it, she would burst without warning into passionate tears, and Steve, baffled by her inexplicable cavorting from one extreme of emotion to another, would hate himself for having wounded her.

On a certain day in the middle of March, almost a month after they had moved into the *garçonnière* Margaret went out cheerfully to do her grocery shopping, and Steve sat down to write to his mother and father. He wrote such letters slowly and with care now, an extension of the conscientiousness with which he worked on pieces of fiction, and the hour passed quickly in his occupation.

He looked up from the almost-completed letter with a start when he heard Margaret bounding up the outside stairs of the *garçonnière* and yelling as loud as she could, "Steve! Steve! It's out! You didn't tell me!"

She burst in upon him wildly, waving a slick-papered magazine, the bag of groceries spilling out of her arms. Cans crashed to the floor and rolled across the rug and Margaret staggered through them, the magazine still clutched in her hand, to throw herself into his arms.

"It's out!" she cried. "I almost had a heart attack!"

"What are you talking about?"

"Why didn't you tell me, Steve!" she demanded, beating on his chest. "Oh, I'm so proud! I almost yelled the news out in the drugstore, I ran all the way home with it!"

"Maggie, stop this and talk sense," he directed.

"Your story!" she shouted. "It's in this magazine and your name is on the cover! Oh, God, I've got to sit down!"

Gasping for breath, she threw herself full length on the couch, and Steve caught up the magazine from her hand. The glossy brightly colored cover announced that it included a new novelette by Steven Williams. Steve chuckled. "I wonder what they mean by a 'new' novelette? It's my only novelette, so far."

Margaret bolted upright.

"You beast, how can you be so calm? I went in to get some—some things I needed at the drugstore, and there your name was staring me in the face from the magazine rack: I almost fainted!"

"Maggie, you knew I was a writer."

"Well, yes, certainly, but I mean I've never actually *seen* your—your by-line before. The neighborhood must think I'm a madwoman." She gasped for breath. "I let out a whoop, grabbed the magazine, threw a dollar bill in the direction of the cashier, and ran all the way here!"

"One guess: your forgot whatever it is you were going to buy."

"Oh, my God. Yes, I did. Oh, Steve, my darling, my wonderful—" She jumped up and threw her arms around him. "I'm so proud of you! I'm so excited for you! Here I've been being the next best thing to being your wife for weeks and weeks now and—I just never got it quite clear that you're a *writer*, a real one and—Steve! You've written hardly a word since we've been living here."

"More important things to do." Steve smiled down at her.

"Nothing's more important to a man than his work."

"Shall I start naming things that are?"

"Not really," she reasoned, "*those* things only seem so

momentarily. Steve, you *must* get back to work. I'll help you: oh, how I'll adore living with a writer, being in on everything from the very beginning, and seeing the fruits of all our work come out on the newsstand with your name simply plastered all over the cover. Steve, please let me help—it'll be the first really useful thing I've ever done in my whole life."

"Sure." Steve shrugged. "Can you type?"

Disappointment, keen and humiliating, broke in her eyes.

"Oh. No, I can't." She grabbed his arms. "But I could look things up for you, and tell you how to spell things and——"

"Maggie, I know how to spell. Most of the time."

"Don't you need research done?"

"Not at the moment, I'm afraid; the next couple of things I plan on are just stories about San Angelo Street, where I grew up. I got the research for that done when I was in grammar school."

"Steve, you're mean!"

Her cheeks flamed with resentment. She turned away from him and sat down petulantly on the couch, chin quivering. Steve sat down beside her and folded his arms around her; they leaned against the back of the couch. He kissed her hair and her cheek as she grew slowly calmer, but did not speak. A shuddering sigh came from her at last, and she was relaxed and pliable in his embrace.

Steve said, "I didn't mean to be putting you off. I was just——"

She whispered, her voice not yet free of the threat of tears, "Isn't there *any*thing I can do?"

"Plenty. You can love me, and run the apartment for me, and cook for me, and be always the loveliest, brightest, happiest thing I've got in my life."

"Would you—would you talk to me? About what you're writing?" she asked. "So I can feel part of it?"

"You *will* be part of it," he assured her.

"That story you were finishing when we first met: did you finish it?"

"Yes."

"Is it sold yet?"

"Not that I've heard."

"I'm sure it will be——"

"I'm not," said Steve. "I started selling magazine stories

pretty early; I think it's been a kind of fluke, and I keep waiting for my luck to run out. I didn't think that novelette would get sold, for instance. My agent keeps waiting for the same thing to happen. So far, thank God, the editors apparently don't know what we expect. But the time will come."

"No, it won't. I have faith in you, you're staggeringly talented."

"You haven't the faintest idea whether I am or not, Maggie."

"I can tell," she said. She turned in his arms until she could see his face. For a long moment she studied him. "You're awfully fond of girls, I know that. But me especially, Steve. Do you love me especially? I don't want a love scene, I want an accurate answer."

Her look was grave, and Steve believed her.

"I think I do," he said.

"Think?" She frowned.

"I say that because I'm not always sure what I feel is real or dependable. . . . As far as it's been given to me to know, I love you, Maggie. That'll have to serve."

Margaret kissed him lightly and jumped up. "We're having a drink to celebrate," she said, and disappeared in the direction of the kitchen.

She returned in a few minutes and put the icy glass into his hand. Sitting down beside him on the couch, she lit a cigarette and handed it to him. Steve twisted self-consciously.

"What's with the service?" he asked.

"It's because you're so wonderful, and I'm so impressed I feel sort of scared of you. In a good way, you understand."

"Oh, sure. You're *real* easy to understand," Steve teased her.

"Drink your drink." He did so. "Steve, don't you have copies of your other stories I could read, the ones you've published before this?"

"I'm afraid I don't. My parents probably have copies put away."

"Damn. I want to read them. I'm sure every writer on earth keeps copies of his stories but you."

"I'm a transient here in New Orleans, you remember. I could get Rachel Pemberton to send me a copy of the typescripts for you to read."

"Who's Rachel Pemberton?"

"My agent."

Margaret's eyes opened wide. "A literary agent. What fun! She must be terrifically clever——"

"She's a good agent, I think," said Steve.

"But the intrigue, the internecine warfare, the big motion-picture contract cinched over a couple of cocktails . . ."

"A glamorous impression." Steve nodded.

"I'll bet it *is* glamorous—oh, I'd be in seventh heaven if I were Rachel Pemberton!"

Steve looked at her, puzzled and curious. "You really think it's glamorous? You? You're the personification of glamor yourself——"

"Steve, what a nice thing to say."

"Don't bat your eyelashes, damn it, I mean it. But I'll shut up before I give you any big-headed ideas."

Margaret looked askance a moment. "You mean Washington, Daddy's dough, all that? By glamorous?"

"And yourself—you. Just the thought of an unsophisticated Texas boy." Steve shrugged.

"Bull," said Margaret. "You may have been born on San Angelo Street, but there are an awful lot of other places you've been. But the literary world. That's really exciting, it seems to me. Oh, Steve, I can't *wait* for you to start back to work!"

Thereafter there was less time available for the sharing of life histories. Steve started back to work in earnest and Margaret began to have the time of her life providing what she took to be the proper atmosphere for him. She made pot after pot of strong coffee whether Steve felt he needed it or not; she sharpened pencils continually; she begged him to read to her in the evening what he had written that day. Steve was both flattered and amused by the fierce intensity of her new interest in his occupation. The lonely nature of his work, he knew, was not subject to correction, but Maggie's presence in the same room with him, as well as her devoted ministrations, considerably lightened the burden of his mental isolation. The new pattern of their daily life together was broken of necessity when, in April, warmer weather came and the clothes Maggie had brought with her to New Orleans were no longer suitable. She went shopping for her spring wardrobe for three consecutive days, and left alone in the *garçonnière*,

Steve had opportunity to realize how suddenly painful it was not to have her close to him there. He bore it for two days, but the third was more than he could contend with. His hour's solitude each day when Maggie went marketing had been refreshing, but Maggie's absence for the greater part of the day was different. Silence filled the place. From the kitchen in the morning came no sound or scent, from the bedroom no *tap-tap* of heels as when Maggie straightened up. In the living room where he worked, he heard no sound of her breathing or the crisp turn of a magazine's slick pages as she read. Distracted by the unaccustomed quiet, he could not concentrate, and soon an indefinable sense of oppression came over him. He paced restlessly, returning again and again to his pages, only to find himself incapable of going back to work. At last he gave it up, mixed a drink for himself, and stretched out on the couch in the living room. He lit a cigarette and lay watching the curling of the smoke against the sunlight's glare at the window.

It needed little introspection for him to realize what it was that troubled him. He was convinced he was capable of making a sound marriage, able to sustain a permanent relationship of love, particularly in regard to Maggie. But why should he be thinking of marriage? he asked himself. He had Maggie here; they were content as they were; wasn't that enough? Conventions had never mattered a damn to him before, had they? And Maggie had certainly never indicated that she paid them any heed. But conventions are not born of whims. Steve recognized the skeleton of purposefulness in convention, and in the light of that recognition saw now why he wanted—yes, he did, there was no sense kidding himself, he *wanted* it—to marry Maggie.

The reason was obvious: he could lose her too easily. Perhaps it was the sharp and unexpected restlessness he was experiencing in her unaccustomed absence—for the third day now, as she did her shopping for spring clothes—that had brought the idea up into his waking thoughts. The consideration of how easily he could lose her made him shudder: one moment of anger, one attack of boredom, one sufficiently possessing distraction (and Maggie readily flew to new ideas, new interests), and she would be packed and gone. There was nothing to hold her, nothing to make her even hesitate. As a matter of fact, he pointed out to himself, she would into the bargain have the comfort of knowing she was putting an end to a situation of which the world at large did not approve.

He deliberately put from his mind the notion of her leaving him. Jesus, if he was in *this* state when she'd gone out shopping for a few days in a row, what would it be like if ever he lost her for good? He drank deeply from the glass he held and sat up on the couch. What would she have to consider from her own viewpoint?

That she loved him, Steve didn't doubt. She wouldn't have been with him this long now (six weeks, had it been? two months?) if she weren't in love with him. Money? His income was a pittance compared with what Maggie had been used to at home, but she seemed happy living by his own standards. The clothes she was out buying now would be the first things she had paid for herself since they'd moved into the *garçonnière*. He felt confident of being able to support her decently if their desires were not extravagant. But the world she lived in when she was not shacking up in a New Orleans apartment, half in earnest and half as a lark: the specialness, if not the money, of that world gave him pause.

Not that he himself would stick out like a sore thumb in it. What Maggie had said once before was true. He had known many kinds of people, had never noticed that he had any difficulty dealing with them amiably. A professional writer, too, had his way smoothed in more exalted circles by the regard in which people of cultivated tastes held his occupation. But the cocktail parties of Washington were as far removed in spirit as in geography from the quietness and solitude they had shared in the *garçonnière*. Distractions there would come by the carload: could he hope to hold Maggie's interest, could he hope to keep her satisfied with his love and his concern in the face of whatever feverish activities made up her life in Washington? As far as money was concerned, it was ridiculous to imagine he could support the cost of the kind of entertaining that would be expected of her when she was married and the mistress of her own establishment. Would she countenance having to forego that social position, to settle for being a writer's wife rather than the daughter of a very prominent figure-on-the-national-scene?

Steve drained his glass and crushed out his cigarette. He

didn't know the answers. He was unable to so much as guess at what they might be. There was no choice for him but to keep his mouth shut, or to find out the answers from Maggie. He knew he couldn't keep his mouth shut now.

"Have you heard anything from Mike since he got back to Washington?" he asked that evening.

"Not a word," said Margaret.

They had finished dinner and were having a drink before tackling the dishes in the kitchen. Steve sat in the easy chair in the living room and Margaret, wearing the first of the dresses she had bought that afternoon—a full-skirted tight-bodiced affair, as bright and as spirit-lifting as the spring itself—faced him from the couch. She sat like a girl, with her feet tucked under her and the skirt of the new dress billowing around her. "I imagine he's too busy regaling all his friends with tales of his Mardi Gras conquests."

"And I guess he's got a hell of a lot of friends," said Steve.

"In Washington? Of course. We both do."

"Yes," Steve replied vaguely. "Ready for a second drink?"

"I've still got some, thanks."

Steve studied the ice in his glass.

Presently Margaret went on. "I wish you knew some of my friends. I miss them." Steve's eyebrows went up. "Not boy friends, silly, just people I know. Like the Tylers and the Knudsens—she was Peggy Putnam. And Eileen and Archie—so many of them. You'd like them, Steve."

"They wouldn't think much of your hanging around a writer nobody ever heard of, who on top of it has no social position."

"Oh, Steve, it wouldn't be like that at all."

"Well, it doesn't matter." He shrugged. "The problem's not apt to arise."

He got up, drained his glass, and went back to the kitchen to fix another, uncomfortably aware of Margaret's blue eyes following his exit. When he came back, she lit a cigarette, and she smiled at him casually when he sat down. For a moment neither spoke. Then Margaret gave a chuckle.

"Speaking of social position," she said, "you should meet Charlie Knudsen, Peggy's husband. He's an angel and everybody loves him, but unfortunately he's from Baltimore, so there can't be any vagueness about who his family are—I mean, being right on the scene, so to speak."

"A self-made man?" Steve asked, as though with negligible interest.

"Not yet, he isn't. They're terribly poor."

"And they're still friends of yours?"

"Steve, what a lousy thing to say——"

"No, I didn't mean it that way. I meant if you still see them and—have them to parties at your house and all—it must be kind of difficult for them to reciprocate."

Margaret considered a moment. "I dare say it is," she answered. "But the Putnams have masses of money. I guess when the social obligations pile up enough and they have to throw a real humdinger, the Putnams help out considerably."

"Does Peggy go for that?" Steve asked, taken aback.

"For what?"

"For having her family support her instead of her husband doing it."

Margaret laughed a warm and sympathetic laugh, as though she pitied him his lack of understanding.

"Oh, my darling, they're not supporting her. Charlie brings home the meat-and-potatoes money. What the Putnams come through with is just ice-cream money, presents for them to have fun with while they're young and before Charlie makes his fortune. A lot of couples I know are in the same fix and manage to solve it the same way without getting their pride injured."

"Would you like to have a marriage like that?" Steve asked.

Margaret blinked at him. It was a moment before she had digested her surprise.

"Why, come to think of it, I don't know. . . ." She scrutinized her hands, frowning. "I'd want to do whatever my husband thought best," she said. "I don't think having a lot of money has much to do with happiness. And, you know, it's an odd thing, I've noticed it with friends of mine. Girls who've grown up with a lot of advantages have a kind of self-confidence that makes them valuable wives to guys just starting out. They don't panic when the bank balance gets a case of the staggers."

Steve laughed at the surprising phrase. It was patent, he thought, that at least Maggie would never panic. His laughter ended and neither of them spoke. Steve saw that her glass was empty, and he got to his feet to take it from her.

"Steve . . ."

He stopped. "Yes?"

Margaret flipped a hand and looked away. "Nothing."

"No, tell me."

"No, really nothing," she repeated.

"All right. Was the last one strong enough?"

She turned her eyes up to him again. "It was perfect, thanks."

Steve refilled the glass in the kitchen. His hands trembled in reaction to the effort he had had to make to sound casual. Could they conceivably get away with it? he asked himself. What Maggie had said reassured him about the problems he had mulled over that afternoon. If a great deal of money wasn't important to her, if no one would care too much about where he'd come from or what his father did and his grandfather before him, if, most important of all, Maggie was willing to share his life and be satisfied with what he alone could make of it . . . He hurried back into the living room.

Instead of returning to his chair, he sat down beside her. He touched her waist within the billowing of her skirt. "Maggie . . ."

She looked at him with quick attention. Steve knew his struggle and his doubts now showed plainly in his eyes. Margaret looked deep into them, and her gaze melted into a dawning smile of uncertainty.

"Yes, Steve?"

He could not speak. He held her gaze, and before his mute scrutiny, Margaret's face underwent a gradual shifting of expression. As she read his countenance, uncertainty gave way to incredulity, and this at last to joy. Without his having to speak, he heard the small gasp of happiness escape her.

"Oh, Steve," she said. "Steve, I would, I want to——"

"You knew what I was thinking?"

"I know now!" she cried. The bottom of her glass hit the table and her arms went around him, locking tightly. "I will, Steve, if you really want me, if you're really sure. . . ."

He laughed aloud into the softness of her hair, returning her embrace. "Oh, Maggie, am I sure! I'm sure we could do it and be the best damned married people that ever lived!"

"When, Steve, when?" She sat back, her face shining as she searched his own.

"Any time. Right away?"

"What about Daddy? Would you want me to do anything about him?"

"Do anything? Like my asking his permission?"

"I thought you might like to, but it doesn't matter to me."

"Hey. Now that I think of it—yes, I do want to: it'll make us a real proper marriage, the whole tribal ritual. We could go to Washington so I can meet him and ask him for your hand."

"Oh, darling, that'd be wonderful!" Margaret cried. "Could we be married there?"

Steve hesitated. "A big wedding, you mean?"

"Not if you wouldn't like that," she hurried to assure him. "As far as I'm concerned, two people marry each other, they don't need any frills to accomplish the act. As far as I'm concerned, I'm already your wife in every way that matters."

He pulled her to him and kissed her, as if to solemnize the compact in the gesture. When he released her, he saw that her eyes were brimming. She laughed and stood up, dabbing at them quickly.

Steve said, "If we know that, if we both realize that's how a marriage is made, then it doesn't matter a bit even if you do have a big wedding."

Margaret turned to him, smiling at the temptation. Tentatively she suggested, "It might be fun. . . ."

"Jesus, you'd look gorgeous as a bride! Oh, hell, yes, I want to see you as a bride," Steve declared.

"Then you will, my angel!"

From the table beside the easy chair, she picked up his glass and brought it to him. Kneeling before him, she retrieved her own and touched it gently against his.

"To us and joy," she said.

"To loving," said Steve.

"Will you be demonstrating the Signatelli products for the rest of the week, Miss Maclean?" the salesgirl asked her as they were making their way to the street through the sheeted aisles of the department store half an hour after closing time.

"Yes, I will," Helen said. "Saturday's my biggest day, of course."

"It's a shame you can't stay longer and get to know New Orleans a little."

"When they hired me for this tour as a demonstrator, I wish I had specified two weeks in New Orleans. But there's an awful lot of territory I have to cover; Mobile, Atlanta, Raleigh—sometimes I feel as if I'll never see New York again."

On the street the salesgirl's bus was just coming to a stop. Helen said good night, and turning aside, started toward the hotel where she was staying.

She hated every part of it: the skimpy salary, the inexpensive aging hotels the Signatelli people had booked her into, the smugness of the department-store shoppers for whom she had to perform the deft tricks that demonstrated the special features of the Signatelli electric products. But it had been the only work she could find, and there had not been adequate time to investigate possible opportunities with model agencies other than Jules Fischel's.

She should have been able to foresee it, she told herself. When her plan for exploiting the youthfulness and pliability of the agency's models had begun to show a really important effect on the agency's income, Ladd Dorn had gone to work. His sister, Jules' wife, had brought to bear every possible pressure, and in the end, though hating it, Jules had turned the entire enterprise over to Ladd, returning Helen to her previous status of private secretary.

Helen had revolted. "It's my project, but let Ladd have it if he wants it. In return I want the freedom to develop other projects I can see through to the end, and I want equal standing with Ladd, and an equal salary."

"Helen, I'd do it like a shot; the agency simply can't afford to have both of you in a——"

"The agency can't afford to have your wife's flissy brother in a position of such responsibility."

"I know, Helen, I know——"

"Jules, I'm resigning. I don't have any other choice."

He had fought against her notion, cajoling, storming, making promises for the future. Helen would not be moved; she knew that if she gave in to him at this point, there would be no hope for her future, and she half-suspected that if she made good her threat, Jules would in the end accept her demands. She had walked out. For three days she did not leave her apartment, but sat by the telephone waiting for Jules to call her and tell her to come back on her own terms. The call never came, and finding herself in urgent need of money, she had taken the first job offered, traveling as a demonstrator for the Signatelli Company.

At the hotel there was no mail for her, and her mood of depression grew acute. Before leaving New York, she had arranged that she would meet one of the agency's office workers in the lobby of the Graybar Building. When she did, she let it be known that if anyone wanted to reach her, they could do so through Signatelli's New York offices. Throughout her tour she had waited daily for a note of surrender from Jules. None had come.

She decided against having dinner. She could use the money she would save thereby, and she felt tired enough to be able to sleep twelve hours. She turned from the hotel desk and started toward the elevator.

Now that the time had come for leaving New Orleans, Margaret wanted to buy presents to bring back to her closest friends. From Washington, Mike sent instructions for the shipping of Warren Taggert's possessions, and while Steve tended to that task, Margaret went off on a tour of the shops in the Vieux Carré. Dressed in the prettiest of her new spring suits, her hat girlish and her hands white-gloved, she walked down Royal Street with an air of buoyant well-being that attracted as much attention as her loveliness. In one antique shop she found a brooch of unusual design for Peggy; in another, a Lowestoft bowl for the Tylers, who were currently much taken with porcelain; and in the window of a leather-goods shop she discovered an assortment of handbags, sandals, and brief cases so exotically tooled that she stopped to study them.

Greenwich Village, she thought. Arty, but kind of cute. She turned and went into the shop. The front room of the establishment was small and ill lit. A wooden door from which hung bunches of elaborately worked belts presumably led to the working quarters of the place. Her sight had not fully adjusted from the glare of the street when at her elbow a young woman said, "May I help you?"

Margaret turned with a start. "Oh. Yes, thank you. I need

half a dozen things, gifts for friends, male and female both, and I thought——"

The appearance of the young woman made her halt abruptly. In the flat-soled sandals that the girl wore, she was an inch or two shorter than Margaret. What arrested Margaret was the strikingly wild beauty of her face. The silver-and-onyx earrings that she wore, and her thick black hair pulled neatly back into a knot tied with a scarlet ribbon, gave her the aspect of a gypsy.

Margaret found her voice. "I thought I might finish up the whole list here, you see."

Studying the customer, Zeeda Kaufman instinctively raised all her memorized prices by a dollar.

"Won't you step over here?" she asked, leading the way to the display counter at one side of the room. "This is just a selection of the most popular items we have, but perhaps it'll do for a start."

"They're really very attractive," said the young woman. Rich, Zeeda thought; obviously a tourist. "Where on earth do you get them?"

"We make them," said Zeeda.

"You do? You yourself?"

"Some of them. There are two of us."

"I like those bags. Four of them should do, I guess."

"Four? Well, fine."

"Those over there are men's sandals, aren't they?"

"Yes." She stooped down behind the counter and brought out two pairs. "The red pair is the women's model. A complementary design, you see. These I *did* make myself."

"But they're wonderful. You'd better let me have two of each. And that, heaven help me, finishes my shopping list in no time flat."

"Anything else I can show you?" Zeeda smiled. "Something for yourself?"

"Thanks, but one of the bags is for me," the customer answered, picking one up from the pile Zeeda had assembled on the counter.

Zeeda packaged the lot and made note of the shipping instructions the young woman gave her. She was relieved to see the order would be paid for in cash. Filling out the sales slip, she mentioned the total, put the money into the cash box behind the counter, and presented the receipt.

As the young woman turned to go, Elaine Crosley came in. The sallow-skinned girl, with rougeless lips and dank unclean hair, carried a heavily smudged manila folder in one hand. With an "Excuse me," to the customer and the briefest of glances at Zeeda, she went through the belt-hung door into the back room of the shop. The opening of the door revealed for a moment the presence of three others in the back room. Zeeda looked quickly to see whether her customer had noticed, but she was busy fitting the bag she had been carrying into the larger leather one she had bought for herself.

"Thank you for being so helpful," the young woman turned to say.

"Come back and see us." Zeeda smiled with convincing cordiality.

The young woman left the shop and walked briskly up the street. Moving to the door, Zeeda watched her progress away from the shop. Damn near a hundred-dollar sale, she thought. They don't appreciate what they have, the rich. A pity. She was a lovely creature, with those huge eyes and that shining hair. Almost aloud, Zeeda said to herself, "What a happy-looking girl she is!"

Then she turned and started back to the rear of the shop. On the knob of the door hung with leather belts her hand stopped suddenly. She needed a moment to collect her wits before facing the meeting that she knew was about to take place. Of Murray's plan, part of which she had been assigned to execute, she knew many though not all the details. The people inside, engaged with her in carrying out the project, knew far less. Most important, the essential idea of the plan had been kept from all those inside the shop's back room except Elaine, who had worked closely with Zeeda in the last several months. It was essential that Zeeda in no way betray the existence of her more intimate knowledge of the project. She was not even certain that all the others were members of the Party. They professed only "interest" in the cause of Communism, and as far as Zeeda knew, might have allegiance only to the Progressive Party. They were, as was she, members of the Special Committee of the Democratic Amity Association; nothing more. Good enough for the work Zeeda had assigned them, but a possibly dangerous shortcoming if they ever discovered the project's real purpose. Setting her features in an expressionless pattern, Zeeda went into the workroom.

Elaine and the three others were already bent over the papers in the manila folder, but broke their formation as Zeeda closed the door behind her.

"I'm sorry to keep you waiting," she said. "There was a customer."

The room was filled with tables of all sizes on which were cluttered pieces of leather, tools, patterns, and piles of scrap material. A place had been cleared at the central table, and here the group had assembled. Besides Zeeda and Elaine there was a thin middle-aged woman with untidy gray hair, a young businessman impeccably dressed for his work at the Port of New Orleans Bank and Trust Company, and an older man, short and round and thickly bespectacled.

Elaine handed Zeeda the three papers from the manila folder.

"This is a carbon. Where's the original?" Zeeda asked.

"Johnny said the Invitation Committee would hold on to it," Elaine explained.

"Get it from him and bring it to me. We can't have copies lying around all over the Quarter."

"You want me to go over to his place now?"

"No. Wait till we're finished here." To the others she said, "The Invitation Committee has drawn up a list of a hundred people we'd like to have present at the reception for Doctor Garner. As far as we know, all of them are independent voters. The list is divided into three sections: French Quarter people, artists and so on; academic people, students and faculty-members both; and business people. This Special Committee's job is to extend the invitations—verbally, preferably on a casual basis—to the people listed. Almost all the people will be known to at least one of us on this committee or other members of the Democratic Amity Association. If not, we have a few days to establish the contact so the invitation can be extended convincingly. I believe that some of the very important men involved in the Wallace campaign are going to be keeping their eyes on this project. It's up to us to bring it off, for the sake of the entire third-party cause. We can't bring it off without the utmost discretion. We have to use discretion, you will understand, because we have so much prejudice and inertia to overcome in this part of the country. Now. Have you all had time to at least glance over the three sections of the list?"

The others nodded.

"I'll be responsible for inviting the Quarter people; together with Elaine, I think I know most of them by now." Of the gray-haired woman, she asked, "Do you and Elaine have Tulane and Loyola covered?"

"Oh, yes. And Newcomb. There are only eight or nine faculty members on that list, but I know them all. Elaine will help me cover the student body."

"Frankly, I don't expect much from the Loyola student body," Elaine put in, "but there's a contact who's willing to do what he can. I'm pretty sure of the people from Tulane and the L.S.U. Medical School."

Zeeda lit a cigarette as she studied the names on the list. To the two men before her she said, "You two will have the toughest job, getting business people to come to a party like this."

"I don't know half the people on the businessmen's list," said the younger of the men. "Just what kind do you want us to concentrate on?"

"The fence-straddlers," said Zeeda. "The liberals who are still voting Democratic. Make it clear that the party is in honor of a distinguished Negro, so we don't get overloaded with unsympathetic types who could never be won over. Also, there'll be Negro college students there in full force, since it's Doctor Garner."

The older man asked, "And the party itself, Zeeda? What exactly are we trying to accomplish?"

Elaine gave him a contemptuous and impatient glance, but Zeeda was quick to respond with the air of answering a reasonable question.

"This party, if everything goes right, will bring together a cross-section of liberal, educated, sophisticated New Orleans people. Some of the Bohemians, a lot of the college students and veterans of voting age, as many people in the business world as we can get. The more articulate they are, the better. The more influential in their own spheres, the better. The party has to be a purely social one, that's vital. But Doctor Garner as guest of honor will have the chance to speak. Have you ever heard Doctor Garner speak?"

The heads before her shook, except Elaine's. Elaine said nothing.

"He's brilliant, and moving," Zeeda told them.

"What's he going to talk about?"

"It'll be Doctor Garner who starts the ball rolling for the Wallace campaign in this area."

Comprehension lighted the faces of the group, and the gray-haired woman gave an approving nod.

"But don't let the people you invite know that," Zeeda went on. "We don't want to scare them off. We want to win them over. The picture you must paint for them is that this is a group of Doctor Garner's friends who want to give him the warmest possible welcome to New Orleans. Tell them it's at Elaine's apartment because she's got more room than any of the rest of us. If you want to, just mention we'll have some folk singers and plenty enough drinks going around. Friendly and casual, that's the point."

She took up the papers and separated them from the staple that held them. Each of the pages she turned over to the one who would be responsible for extending the invitations.

"Okay, let's get with it," she said. "You've got the date, time, and address clear? Fine. Don't hang onto your lists any longer than you have to. Get rid of them."

They pocketed the sheets of paper, and with an idle exchange of remarks, the meeting broke up. Standing and mopping his forehead with a rumpled handkerchief, the short bespectacled man observed, "We're going to have a hell of a lot of work this summer to really strengthen the Progressives' position in New Orleans."

"How else are you going to begin but this?" the middle-aged woman answered, tapping the pocket where her list was stored. "Zeeda, I think I can assure you my entire list will be there."

"Fine, wonderful."

"Good-by."

"Good-by, Zeeda."

"Keep your reports coming in here, remember. If you hit any real snags, let me know."

"We will, we will."

"Good-by."

Zeeda opened the workroom door, and they straggled out. Only Elaine remained behind. Zeeda watched them depart.

On the sidewalk they told one another good-by, and the two men went off in one direction, the woman in the direction opposite.

Zeeda shook her head, a half-smile of contempt and pity on her face. "The jerks. They really love these hurried little meetings, don't they? . . . And all the big secrecy about the campaign not having any connection with the reception for Doctor Garner. It makes them feel oh-so-conspiratorial."

Elaine asked, "Which of 'em do you think are with the Party?"

"They're all Progressives," said Zeeda, looking at her sharply. "That's all we need to know."

They moved forward into the shop, closing the door of the workroom. Elaine cupped her cigarette mannishly in her broad hand.

"Zeeda, is Garner in on the real pitch? The raid?"

"As far as I know. But there's always the chance he might not be. Nobody else is but you and me. And the Oliver character."

"How reliable is *he?*"

Zeeda herself had wondered. She knew little about him. He lived in an apartment across the street from Elaine's place. He was an alcoholic and a disbarred attorney. Zeeda hadn't handled the contact herself, and she hadn't heard from Murray who had set it up. She presumed, too, that the police were set up for it, but she would never know for certain. *No* one was ever apprised of the whole picture but Murray. All she knew was that at the height of the party, ex-lawyer Oliver would complain to the police that whites and blacks were having a drunken orgy across the street and demand their arrest. There would be a raid staged, and they would all be hauled off to jail—the college students, the sober businessmen, the artists. Public prejudice would do the rest. The fascism of the South would get the chance of a lifetime to dramatize itself openly, complete with police brutality, a mossback judge, and the public wrecking of reputations. It was a precious opportunity to do some really heavy fund-raising; and in the teeth of the scandal, the Wallace campaign would get rolling in earnest. The bitterness of the injured parties, the anger of educated people at the stupidity of the police and the city administration—these would open the way for the Wallace workers in social areas untouched before. Areas with money that could be easily tapped if they succeeded. The Progressive Party, Zeeda guessed, would loudly support the fight for a reversal of sentence and public apologies to those arrested, and the fight could be prolonged until election time with negligible effort. Wallace wouldn't win the Presidency, perhaps, but the Democrats and the Republicans would both suffer from the pressure that a strong third party would be able to bring to bear, the disruption and confusion the very existence of a strong third party would mean to the established houses.

To Elaine's question she replied, "Oliver will be reliable enough."

Elaine went to fetch the carbon copy of the lists from the chairman of the Invitation Committee. In half an hour it was in Zeeda's hands, and Elaine went off again.

No more customers appeared in the shop that afternoon. Few ever did. The shop itself was obscurely situated, crouching as it did between a large antique dealer's establishment and a gaudily façaded art gallery. More than once the landlord had given voice to his wonder that Zeeda was able to keep the place open at all. At six o'clock she turned out the lights, locked the door to the sidewalk, and made her way homeward in the dusty half-light of spring dusk.

The furnished housekeeping room she lived in was in a rundown building on Dauphine Street, three blocks away. She walked the distance unhurriedly, and by the time she let herself into the building, it was night. From the ceiling of the vestibule a yellow light gave a feeble glow, and its reflection through the soiled frosted glass of the front door had been the only illumination provided for the lower hallway since the light bulb there had burned out half a month before. The lower hallway was still; the downstairs apartment had been vacant for some weeks, and there were no other quarters on the street-level of the house. Zeeda climbed the wooden stairs to her housekeeping room on the second floor. Silence still. On this floor there were two other rooms, and Zeeda supposed they were currently occupied, but she seldom saw the inhabitants. Both men, they did not come home at the end of the working day, but long after midnight, and then they stumbled drunkenly up the stairs. One morning Zeeda had almost tripped over one of them who had failed to make it as far as the door of his room. She was indifferent to her neighbors; they never bothered her.

She let herself in and turned on the two iron standing lamps with their dented shades. She lit the fire on the campstove in one corner of the room. At the washstand, which was also open to the room, she carefully washed her hands and, having dried them, started to fix her supper of canned soup and lettuce salad.

She moved almost listlessly, drained by what she had accomplished so far, and feeling now in that tenuously balanced state of mind that always preceded the violent emotions of a project's climax. She was certain Murray would be pleased with her work.

Having opened the shop, she had made it her business to form a wide circle of acquaintance among the denizens of the Quarter, none of them members of the Party as far as she knew or could tell, but people of a certain vague and spineless liberal inclination as they argued over their coffee cups and cans of beer in the Quarter haunts they patronized. Zeeda had gone the plans one better and included in her circle a number of undergraduates from Tulane, Loyola, and the L.S.U. Medical School. What proselytizing she had done among the apparently readier ones had been of the subtlest kind. She had memorized well her role as a liberal, not an identifiable radical. Every effort had gone into shaping the people and the circumstances that would culminate in the disgraceful and scandalous arrest of teachers, bank tellers, painters, and medical students in an interracial drinking party.

Putting aside her anxiety for the success of Murray's strategy, she ate her dinner, undressed, and lay down to study the carbon copy of the list of friends.

At ten o'clock the next morning Elaine Crosley, whose classes at Newcomb were all scheduled for afternoon, stopped by to tend the shop while Zeeda went down to the Coffee Pot to get containers of coffee for their midmorning break. It was while she waited at the counter for the order to be filled that she saw Mrs. Boulemay and her twelve-year-old daughter at one of the tables against the wall of the narrow steam-filled restaurant. This, she considered, was probably the trickiest name on her list. She hadn't gotten to know the Boulemays very well. She stepped over to them.

"Hello there."

Mrs. Boulemay raised watering green eyes and blinked, a crescent of black coffee staining her upper lip.

"Zeeda. Good morning, how's the shop?"

"No business yet today. Hi, Nana."

Nana was a thin colorless girl with troubled brown eyes, awkward in her novice womanhood, but appealingly gentle of manner. Zeeda felt a twinge of wistfulness and sympathy every time she saw those lean, curveless arms, those uncertain breasts, the appeal of the veiled but questioning eyes.

"Hi, Zeeda," she answered softly.

"Mrs. Boulemay, it's a wonderful thing, running into you," Zeeda went on. "I was going to call you later. An old, old friend of mine is coming to New Orleans, and I want you to meet him. Doctor Garner. I'm sure your husband knows about him as a remarkable Negro writer and lecturer and all kinds of things. All his friends in New Orleans want to give a party for him—at Elaine's house—and I especially want him to meet you and Mr. Boulemay." She smiled archly. "I figured if your husband invites him up to see his paintings, I might get included, so it isn't entirely impersonal on my part. *Will* you come?"

"Why, we'd love to, sure, I'll tell Ralph."

"And would you let me know? Bring Nana, too. Would you like to come, Nana? A wonderful experience for Nana, meeting a man like Doctor Garner."

"Oh, yes, it would be," Mrs. Boulemay hastened to agree. She had the look of a woman who didn't understand how she'd got into this mess—not the immediate one—the one that had been going on for over seventeen years. "I'm sure Ralph would love to meet him, and of course it *would* be very exciting for Nana. Wouldn't it, Nana?"

"I'd love to come to a party of yours, Zeeda," said Nana.

"Bless you!" Zeeda stooped and gave her shoulder a quick squeeze. She turned to Mrs. Boulemay. "Check with Ralph and let me know. It's next Saturday night, eight-thirtyish, and you know where Elaine's place is."

"Oh, yes, we'll certainly be there. I'll tell Ralph as soon as we go back to the studio."

Regularly through the next several days, reports from Zeeda's Special Committee came into the leather-goods shop. The party showed every sign of being well attended, and soon Zeeda and Elaine found themselves overwhelmed by the details of preparations—cleaning the apartment, haggling with liquor dealers for favorable prices based on a quantity purchase, putting up the kind of imaginative but inexpensive decorations one expected to find at a party given by intelligent young people with little money to spend, borrowing highball glasses and ice buckets and serving trays.

In her fine fervor of activity Zeeda was happy; and when, at last, the day of the party came, she was overcharged with anticipatory energy, as though an almost religious transport of feeling resulted from her dedication to the vital, if lower-echelon, work of agitation. She did not open the shop that day, nor did she hurry to leave her housekeeping room after she had had her breakfast. Instead she sat up in her bed, propped with pillows, and as she savored her second cup of coffee, thick with chicory, she savored, too, the satisfaction of knowing how much she would be accomplishing tonight, how proud Murray would be of her when reports reached him. They would all love her and admire her. She had at last really proved herself as an adult member of the Party, a worker to be trusted, an agent to be valued.

Her youth itself, she thought, was of value to them. Looking as young as she did, she fitted with ease into the picture of the university set as well as that of French Quarter Bohemians. She could talk as convincingly to either group. When necessary, she was actress enough to fit whatever role she was called upon to play. Didn't they see what a versatile instrument she was for them to use? Well, they would now, she was convinced of it.

As she crushed out her cigarette in the ash tray she held in her lap, she had a fleeting thought about her mother and father. The latter might be a shadowy, inconsequential figure to her, a foolish and pitiful little man—Jewish nationalism in the flesh—but the image of her mother's conventionally pretty face leaped to her mind as a symbol of the enemy—the accepted, the herd, the spoiled, the useless. Leeches! It would have been so easy for her to be just a little gentle, just a little bit kind. . . . Zeeda thrust the sentiment from her mind with a vicious effort of will. She got up and started to dress.

The greater part of the day was taken up in meeting Dr. Garner's train and seeing him installed in the Mouldin family's house on Esplanade Avenue. Late in the afternoon Zeeda came home again to rest for an hour, then bathe and dress for the party. She sat for some minutes before her mirror, wondering which arrangement of her hair was most suitable for the occasion. One of the most trustworthy tools she possessed in her chameleon life, as thick as it grew and as long as she wore it, she liked it best parted in the middle, pulled back from her face, and gathered softly into a net at the back of her neck; but she often wore it in pigtails to enhance the childlike manner she sometimes affected, or in a tighter knot at the back when an ascetic air was needed, or arranged on top of her head for sophistication. Only her most intimate friends saw her hair hanging loose, a rich black mane.

She decided on her favorite arrangement with the snood. It was not too juvenile, it was not harsh. It would astonish no one at the party who might have met her before in a more particular role, and it gave her confidence. Confidence, Zeeda thought, would be important to her tonight. She went to work with the stout ivory comb and the brushes.

At six-thirty, wearing sandals, a wide colorful skirt, and a peasant blouse with embroidery that gave it a party flair, she rang the doorbell of Elaine Crosley's apartment.

Elaine, her now-excited face still scrubbed and sallow, her hair still lank, was wearing the only dress she had that seemed to her suitable for the party. Zeeda suppressed a small stab of pity when she saw her. It was a dress bought when Elaine had been a teen-ager, pale blue and trimmed generously with yellowed machine-lace. The skirt was full, and it reached just below the calves of her sticklike unshaven legs. On her feet she wore white anklets and thick-heeled brown pumps.

"Hi, come on in, glad you're early," she gasped. "Do you think the place *really* looks all right? I was looking it over again just now, and I swear I don't know. I don't know what the hell I can do about it at this point."

"It looks fine, Elaine. Everything all set up? You have enough ice?"

"Plenty to start, some of the committee are bringing their own ice trays, the ones who live near by."

Elaine's panic in the face of giving a party, a responsibility she had seldom borne, communicated itself to Zeeda, and Zeeda felt the palms of her hands growing damp.

"Where's my guitar, by the way?" she asked.

"Over there on the day bed," Elaine indicated with a twitch of her elbow.

"I'll be getting it tuned up. Look. Why don't you mix yourself a drink?"

"I don't trust stimulants," she said in a little gasp of terror. "What if nobody shows up for the goddamned party?"

"They will."

"The Mouldins are bringing Doctor Garner? Or is he coming by himself?"

"They're bringing him," Zeeda said.

Zeeda took the guitar from its case, sat down on the day bed, and began to tune the strings, while Elaine walked back through the large high-ceilinged rooms to assure herself for the tenth time that the place would pass muster.

At eight-thirty Dr. Garner and the Mouldins arrived, and a moment later the first of the French Quarter contingent. As though frightened of the chairless, rugless space of the apartment, they huddled close together near the improvised bar, loudly chorusing their welcome to Dr. Garner, an impressively tall Negro whose bland eyes from behind their thick-rimmed spectacles surveyed the flushed and nervous faces wearily. More people arrived—the white-haired frail committeewoman with two of the university professors and their wives, followed by a handful of people from the businessmen's list—and the knot of people at the bar, growing unmanageable, broke up into smaller groups, ready now to assimilate the newcomers who by quarter to nine were coming in through the front door in an unbroken procession.

Arming herself with a watery highball, Zeeda moved through the crowd unhurriedly, her senses straining to catch what tone and flavor the party was taking on.

"Now, you see," one of the young men from the commercial district was saying to his wife, "that wasn't bad at all. I told you and *told* you it would be just like shaking hands with anybody else."

And in another group, a student from Newcomb College for Women, whose colorless hair was pulled back into a Grecian knot, was gushing self-consciously. "Naturally *I* don't mind, I mean what could possibly be the difference? If only my *Daddy* could see me here, though, he'd have a conniption fit. Look over there, do you think Elaine really *knows* all those colored people?"

"Just think what the Negro has *contributed* to our culture," one of the slacks-and-sandaled men was saying. "Our entire musical idiom we owe to them, don't we?"

"How can people who dress like that afford this kind of Scotch?"

"But actually, tell me, who is he, this doctor?" a student asked.

"*Darling,* did you see that great stevedore type over there with the goatee. Isn't he divine?"

Slowly the party's separate elements began to mingle. Zeeda began introducing people she herself did not know. The bated-breath girl from Newcomb she turned over to a bookkeeper's wife, and the bookkeeper to a fat motherly Negress who wore steel-rimmed glasses. Surveying the results of her work with approval, she elbowed through the tight-pressed little circles toward the day bed and her guitar.

Zeeda excused herself to a pair of tie-and-coated pre-med students and pulled the guitar out from behind them.

"Oh, are you going to play?" asked the younger-looking of the two.

"What else?" the other snorted.

Zeeda smiled at them imperturbably; they were going to look lovely in the clink.

"Do you like folk music?" Zeeda asked.

"Which ones do you know?"

"All of them," said Zeeda sweetly.

"Let's hear something real stirring," the older smirked.

"Here, sit down."

"Thanks."

"Hey, you people, listen——"

"No! No, don't say anything. It's more fun to let the music pull them in slowly. Watch this."

Softly, with no apparent bid for attention, Zeeda strummed muted, plaintive opening chords. When she began to sing, it was at far less than her usual volume.

> "Oh, the praties they grow small,
> Over here, over here. . . .
> Oh, the praties they grow small
> And we dig them in the fall,
> And we eat them coats and all,
> Over here, over here. . . ."

The groaning mournfulness of the song was almost lost in the noisy chatter that filled the room, but three or four people standing near stopped talking and turned to listen. Zeeda winked at the more amiable pre-med student and with knowing control let the strength begin to flow into her voice. More people turned to listen.

"How I wish that we were geese,
Flying high, flying high. . . .
How I wish that we were geese,
For they live a life of ease
And they live and die in peace,
Eating corn, eating corn. . . ."

The attentive silence spread, and at the end of the song most of the party was applauding with enthusiasm. Zeeda acknowledged the applause with a smile and began on another song. At the end of the second she loaned her guitar to a rawboned young man in blue jeans and paint-spattered tennis shoes who took up the recital. Zeeda made her way through the crowd to Elaine. She had just reached her and was about to speak when the doorbell rang.

Her lips shut firmly and she held Elaine's gaze. The doorbell rang again.

"Come on," she whispered.

They maneuvered their way to the front door of the apartment and Zeeda opened it. In the hall was a policeman, a stout man of less than average height, a bored expression veiling his little eyes. In the shadows behind him two others lingered.

"Yes, may I help you?"

"You-all got a party of some kind goin' on here, sis?"

"Yes, we do. Would you like to come in? You're welcome to."

"Huh?"

"I said, would you like to come in?"

He was too late to prevent himself instinctively glancing back in puzzlement to his assistants. Muttering something incoherent, he shifted his feet uneasily.

Zeeda's gaze burrowed into him. Was this the one, the one she knew they must have somewhere in the police department? Or some dupe suckered into handling the raid? She could not tell. If he was the one, he was too convincing to be guessed.

"You can come in as friends, but not as policemen," Zeeda said. "This is a private home, I mean. You're not here to cause trouble, are you?"

"Well—maybe, sis, if your friends could keep the noise down some."

"Noise?" Zeeda laughed. "This is an extremely sedate party. See for yourself."

With the smoothest of movements she stepped aside and let the door open wide enough to give him a clear view of the room. The crowd inside was quiet, it was true, listening politely to the young man singing and playing the guitar. But with carefully concealed amusement Zeeda watched the policeman's jaw drop as he registered the other aspect of the party. She was sure now that he was no plant of Murray's.

"Jesus," he breathed in honest bafflement. "What you doin' with all them black bucks in there?"

Zeeda tittered. "Who knows what the evening will bring?" She spread her hands with broad-drawn suggestiveness.

The policeman took an involuntary step back. He swallowed.

"Well—just so's you keep 'em quiet."

He turned on his heel and left, taking the other two along with a jerk of his blue-capped head.

"But wait—" Zeeda took a step after them, but they were gone. "Now what the hell's the idea?" She turned back to Elaine. "What's gone wrong? They're supposed to . . ." She stopped herself. "If something's gone wrong . . ." Stiffened, she closed her eyes. It *couldn't* go wrong, it couldn't. She had counted on it too much; she could not now bear to envisage failure.

Elaine came quickly to her. "Oliver. Could he have fallen through on us?"

"How the hell should I know?"

"Maybe they're not the right cops, maybe they're just the beat-walkers in this neighborhood."

"I was sure they were all ready to raid, I tell you I could *smell* it on them. Damn. Shit." She bit down on the edge of a fingernail and viciously tore it off. "Oliver." She turned and hurried to the front of the house, Elaine close behind her. They came to a halt on the front steps.

In the humid night the street was still. On the second floor of the building across the way, light shone in the windows of the disbarred attorney's apartment, but they could see no movement and in the damp air could hear nothing but the voice of the balladeer at the party concluding another song. The sound of his singing died out, and from behind them they heard the party-chattering resume.

"There's got to be a wire crossed somewhere," Zeeda snapped. "I can't believe the cops could put in an appearance here and then be the wrong cops."

"Maybe they got another complaint," said Elaine, "besides Oliver's. A real one they were following up."

"We're not making that much noise," Zeeda objected.

"Everybody on the block could see who was arriving tonight. Any of those biddies might have felt it her duty to call the cops when she saw Negroes and whites going to the same party."

"Maybe you're right. But if the right cops don't show up soon, the damn party's going to be breaking up."

"Come on, let's get back inside," said Elaine.

They returned to the apartment. "I'll keep as many of them as I can herded in," said Zeeda. "You concentrate on not letting anybody make any damned introduction speech for Doctor Garner. Once he's talked, the party's *sure* to break up. I hope to God he knows enough about this not to start giving a speech."

Back inside the apartment they went to work in earnest. The two pre-med students Zeeda had been with when she started to sing came up to say good night, and she was unable to restrain their departure. She redoubled her efforts in the face of this setback, and half an hour later only one more guest had managed to slip away.

It was at that time that the police came back. A different squad, blank-faced and authoritative, calm and mechanical in their movements.

"Okay, folks, down to the precinct. Blacks and whites both, every one of you."

"What are you talking about?" Zeeda demanded. The larger number of the guests gathered around her in astonishment.

"There's been a complaint about disturbing the peace."

"Are you kidding?" Zeeda challenged him. And over her shoulder to the others: "Did you hear that? Disturbing the peace!" Then, facing the uniformed man again, her dark eyes ablaze: "This is the noisiest neighborhood in New Orleans," she cried, "and inside it we're having one of the quietest parties anyone could ask for. Now what's the *real* complaint?"

"People have been complaining, the noise and all——"

"This is outrageous!" Zeeda snapped, and the guests rallied to her predicament.

"Officer, I can't say that I know my hosts very well, but I assure you there is nothing whatever out of order here."

"It's unimaginable that——"

"Wouldn't you know the bigots would——"

"Let's just see what they dare to do!"

"Officer, I don't think you realize what people you're dealing with here——"

"Come on," said the policeman, "I got plenty of help here if I need it, but you're all under arrest."

Zeeda turned on the nearest of the guests, aghast. "What kind of Hitler movement goes *on* in his town? Do you *let* your police force get away with this kind of outrage?"

"Absolutely not!" the guest declared defensively. "They've far exceeded their——"

"I can't believe that in this day and age decent people can't——"

"All of you!" the policeman yelled then. "And right now. Come on now, whatever the hell your color is. You'll all be in the same cell whether you're white or black. That oughta make you feel real comfy."

Bellowing her indignation, whipping the others into a unity of outrage, Zeeda led the parade of her guests off to a night in jail.

23

SIXTY PERSONS WERE BOOKED FOR DISTURBance of the peace, and the child, Nana Boulemay, was sent to a home for delinquent children. The cells they occupied that night stormed with the fervor of their anger and their gradually heightened lust for vengeance. Even the precinct personnel grew uneasy as all through the night the political harangues and the impassioned singing went on. The scandal spread throughout the French Quarter that night, and when the Times-Picayune appeared the following morning, the knowledge was city-wide. In the morning men no one seemed to know turned up to bail out the martyrs to Southern fascism, and throngs of anxious friends and stunned relations greeted the crew when they came out into the blinding sunlight of the street. The scene was horribly incongruous in the light of day. Recriminations snapped in the air, and in one or two places in the growing crowd tears gushed out with abandon. And everywhere were the shouted political slogans, the jeering of French Quarter hoodlums who had come to watch the spectacle, and the angry and unrestrained taunting of the police by some of those who had hurried to the scene to make known their support of anyone willing to buck the prejudices of the cretinous authorities. Standing with Elaine Crosley on the steps of the precinct station, wincing at the sudden glare of midmorning, Zeeda noted with gratification that she had succeeded. Among the guests at the party for Dr. Garner had been only a handful of radicals. Their number seemed to have swollen appreciably through the night.

The Case of the Sixty was to be brought up in night court that evening. All day Zeeda was busier than she had expected to be, organizing the Protest Meeting of Independent Citizens and the Progressive Party's Committee of the Sixty, and scotching as best she could the efforts of horrified parents of some of the college students to hush the affair up. Throughout the afternoon her work went on, while, in the Quarter, among the bewildered housewives shopping on Canal Street and in the corridors at City Hall, open meetings were held, anthems sung, and above all, violently emotional speeches made in support of Henry Wallace for the Presidency of the United States.

The Case of the Sixty was handled briefly and with intense embarrassment by Judge Simmons that night. The prosecution painted an image of a drunken orgy involving the two races indiscriminately, and the defense concentrated on the fact that Oliver, the prosecution's truculent witness who had complained to the police, was an alcoholic attorney long since disbarred. The sixty individuals were sentenced to pay fines for disturbing the peace, but pronouncement of the sentence was almost totally drowned by the shrill demonstrations going on in the courtroom, the hallways beyond it, and on the streets outside the courthouse.

At midnight Zeeda, with Ralph Boulemay and his wife and daughter Nana, stood in the crowd outside the courthouse, listening to Dr. Garner prophesying to the throng with blazing conviction the certain doom awaiting the tyrants and hypocrites of the traditional political parties. The attention of the shifting mass was snatched away from him by a fanatical young man in a shredded T-shirt who stood on the hood of a parked automobile to harangue his audience. A third—a woman this time, sharp-featured and haggard, the cords straining from her neck—addressed the crowd, and unanimous shouts and cries affirmed that in the morning a demonstration would be held to demand redress for the Sixty.

The gathering broke up, and people headed off toward streetcars and busses and taxicabs. In the milling of the crowd, Zeeda found herself holding little Nana Boulemay's hand. She turned to look for Ralph and his wife, but in the gyrating, disorganized mass, she could not find them. She called out their names, but no one answered, and no one seemed to know which way they had gone. Holding to Nana's hand, Zeeda made her way against the predominant flow of traffic to the steps of the courthouse. From the steps she could see across the crowd and perhaps find the Boulemays. At any rate they would be more likely to see Nana and herself in that position. They reached the steps and mounted them.

"Do you see them, Zeeda?" Nana asked. "Are they still here?"

In a moment Zeeda did see them. On the opposite sidewalk, at the farther edge of the crowd. They were quarreling bitterly, and Nana's mother was sobbing without restraint. The caprices of seventeen years had at last, Zeeda thought, reached too great a total.

"They must have gone on, Nana," Zeeda said, hurrying the girl down the steps into the dispersing ranks of people again. "I'll take you home. They probably figured I was doing that anyway and so they just went on without us. They know we'll catch up."

Zeeda searched momentarily for Elaine Crosley, but not

seeing her anywhere, started out with Nana on the hike across the center of the city to the French Quarter.

Half an hour later they were turning off Rampart Street into the comparative darkness of the street where both Zeeda and the Boulemays lived.

When they turned the corner, uneasiness settled over her like a cloak dropped with unexpected suddenness about her shoulders. She stopped, taking hold of Nana's hand again.

"Zeeda? Is anything wrong?"

"No, Nana. Nothing."

But the silence and the darkness of the street were unnerving. Four yards farther on they had left the light of Rampart Street behind them, and the shadows of alleyways and vestibules were impenetrable. The house where the Boulemays lived was on the next corner; Zeeda's own house, midway in the block. Ahead she could see the sickly yellow light burning feebly in the entrance to her own building. Moving slowly now, her grip on the child's hand viselike, she proceeded through the darkness with that dim glow her object. Once there, it would not seem so far to the beckoning street light at the next corner. Hardly breathing, she reached it.

"Nana," she said. "Your parents may not be home yet. You come upstairs to my room and I'll get you some coffee. Then we can telephone so they'll know where we are and so *we'll* know they'll be home when we get there."

"All right, Zeeda."

She walked up the three dirty marble steps to the vestibule and stopped, her heart pounding in her apprehension. It was natural for it to be so quiet, she told herself. The apartment on the first floor was vacant, so there wouldn't under any circumstances be any sound coming from there. The two men who occupied the other rooms on her own floor were doubtless out drinking, as usual. Still, the silence frightened her. She distracted herself by searching in her purse for the key. She found it, and opening the door, ushered Nana in.

She had already closed the door behind her when she saw the hoodlums.

There was no light in the hallway, only the faint yellow reflection through the frosted glass panel of the front door. Zeeda saw them and froze where she stood, Nana's hand unfelt in her paralyzed grip. There were three. In the dim light Zeeda thought they looked young, but they were terrifying in their arrogant size and their leering ease. Zeeda could not move, and at her side Nana was rigid with fright. The biggest of the three shuffled forward from the shadow cast by the stairway, and Zeeda could see he was drunk. He was young, but tall and thick-muscled, and his drunkenness gave his mouth a cruel twist.

"What do you want?" Zeeda managed to ask in a strangled whisper.

At her side, stunned by terror, Nana was speechless.

"She's the one," he said to the others, smirking. He took a step toward her. "You. You're the one fucks coon, ain't you?"

The other two were moving slowly forward, flanking the first.

"How did you find this place?" Zeeda demanded.

"Don't you read the papers? Everybody's address is in the police-reports column today. 'Sides, we live around here, we know the pitch."

From Nana came a convulsive movement, and Zeeda heard the voice spit, "Get her!"

In the incomprehensible moment of violence and terror, Zeeda was aware of the child being torn from her and herself pinned by the iron arm of one of the hoodlums, his thick glovelike hand clamped over her mouth. The tallest, the first who had spoken, snapped, "Inside."

They had broken the lock on the door of the vacant apartment, Zeeda realized as she was dragged through the door into the deserted room. She kicked and tried to bite, but her opponents were experienced: her heels flailed in frustration and her teeth sought hopelessly for flesh. No light burned in the apartment, and Zeeda could see nothing, could sense only the concrete movement of bodies about her. The darkness, the scuffling, muted sounds of struggle, made her nerves scream, and her horror on the child's behalf ripped like a spike through her brain. She heard a thud then, and a sighing groan.

"The kid's out. Anybody like chicken?" one of them said.

Somewhere then in her firing senses Zeeda hit on calm. Deliberately she let her body grow lax in the grip of the one who held her. She struggled no more. Frantically she searched for some hint of their intent. Were they going to beat her up? Were they after money by some remote mischance? The silence around her, the silence throbbing now in the blackness of the deserted room, held the answer. Rape. The tension of their hesitation made it obvious, and her thoughts, like trapped mice, darted hysterically about for an exit. There was none, she realized. But it was better to get it over with than fight hopelessly against it. The hand clamped over her mouth prevented her speaking, she did not know how to communicate her willingness to comply peacefully. Relaxing, she allowed herself to lean back into the embrace of the one who held her. The grip softened, but only slightly.

Close to her ear she heard, "Oh? Giving up, huh? I guess if you like coon meat, you don't mind anything, do you?"

In an instant that brought a sob to her throat she realized her mistake. They didn't want her to give in. These dirty, cheap young cutthroats, they *wante*d to force her, to subject her to their animal use and at the same time punish her because she was a traitor, an outcast, a nigger-lover. Her brain convulsed with anger: all right! If she couldn't escape, she'd give them the show of their lives, she'd turn their brutality to her own uses. They knew where she lived because of the newspapers, didn't they? The bigots of the South weren't content to put you in jail for mixing with Negroes, they published your name, your occupation, your address, so every crackpot in the city would know where to find you. What a story: she exulted as the possibilities unfolded in her imagination. She bit down with all her might on the palm that covered her mouth.

"Ow! You will, will you——"

"What's the matter?"

"The cunt bit me!"

"Let me have her!"

She felt herself thrown into another pair of arms: those of the biggest one, the one whose smirking strength had terrified her in the hallway.

"Where's the kid?" someone rasped in the darkness.

"Conked out. She's okay. She ain't hurt none."

Zeeda renewed her fight, but the ringleader's arms pinned her into immovability. She could smell the thick garlic and wine odor on his breath. His voice rapped out in the blackness: "Okay. Flashlight."

A flashlight went on, and Zeeda saw the bare mattress on the bed against the farther wall. Kicking as much as she could, deliberately and venomously enraging the thug who held her, she felt herself being pulled toward the bed. He threw her down on it and fell with all his weight on top of her. She took care not to try to scream, not to call on help before the right moment, but with her violent struggle to feed the imperious passion of her attackers. One of them focused the uncertain beam of a flashlight on the bed, and twisting her head, she could distinguish on the edge of the circle of light Nana's little body, crumpled unconscious in the doorway to the bathroom.

"Come on, hurry up," one said.

"She's fighting me——"

"Knock her teeth in——"

"All three of us, one right after another, hurry up——"

"Don't knock her out, it's no good if she's knocked all the way out."

"All right, for Christ's sake, one of you guys help me strip her."

The hands fell on her, tearing at the light skirt and blouse she wore. She let herself relax for an instant, and the ringleader stretched out beside her on the bed. Momentarily forgetful as he unzipped his fly, he moved his hand from her mouth. Praying the insult would work, she gathered saliva in her mouth and, with a thrust of her head, spat it into his face.

The fist crashed into her teeth.

She felt the pain of the succeeding blows and tasted blood in her mouth; unwilled prehensile tears rushed to her eyes, but in the midst of the tortured forcing of her body there was a sanctuary in her mind that contemplated with grim pleasure the newspaper stories that would appear the following day.

The next afternoon members of the Progressive Party and the Democratic Amity Association held their demonstration on behalf of the Sixty in a hired meeting hall, and the ferocity of the oratory was dramatically capped by the appearance on the stage of Zeeda Kaufman. In small and trembling voice Zeeda described the source of her bruises, her swollen eyes, her broken lips, and announced that little Nana Boulemay had been hospitalized. It was their need to be at Nana's side that prevented her parents from being present at the meeting. "If the newspapers controlled by the bigoted rich," she told the horror-silenced audience, "hadn't published the addresses of those of us who were arrested, the mugging wouldn't have happened. Those madmen knew where to find me because my address was published in the newspapers. They told me as much. Do you understand that? Without the newspapers the rich put out, it never would have happened." In the next three days there was a rush of contributions to the Henry Wallace Campaign Fund of Lousiana.

News of the success of the Progressives in New Orleans spread from one stronghold to another of the Party. Versions of the tale differed widely, but were always effective in stimulating the campaign's workers to greater effort. A spasm of sympathetic ire was felt in New York's American Labor Party, the Vito Marcantonio organization supporting the Wallace campaign; and in Washington, Wallace's steadily growing strength across the nation, especially among younger people who would vote for Wallace if they never voted for anybody else, caused misgivings among both Democrats and Republicans.

"More among the Democrats than ourselves, I should say," said Judge Ellis Cowan. "After all, the people who vote for Wallace, young or old, misguided or knowledgeable, none of them could be expected to vote Republican in any event."

"Like me," his daughter, Margaret teased him. "I think I'll vote for Wallace just as a way of snubbing the Trumans."

"Cut her off without a cent," Mike Cowan advised his father. "New Orleans has irreparably corrupted her."

The three Cowans sat in the sitting room of Margaret's suite on the third floor of the house. Margaret had been unpacked for two days, but the presents she had brought back for various friends were still spread untidily about the low-ceilinged sunlit room.

"You missed a fearful amount of activity, staying down there among the mint juleps so long," said Judge Cowan.

"Poor Daddy, have you been working horribly hard?"

Judge Cowan waved a deprecatory hand. "The trouble with our growing position in the world," he said, "is that there are too many areas to keep up with."

"I should think the election coming up would keep you hopping," Margaret observed. "I almost broke my neck tripping over people in the downstairs hall this morning."

"You haven't seen the worst of it yet," Mike put in.

Judge Cowan went on, "Not only the election, but the gravest kind of trouble everywhere. Last month the Russians started putting the screws on us in Berlin, demanding to inspect freight shipments from our occupation zone to our sector in Berlin. And they're getting more audacious every day. The Arabs and the Jewish nationalists are doing their best to drag us into their squabble, and the many—um—sympathizers in New York are not making things any easier."

"Didn't I read Israel's becoming a nation of its own now?"

"Just," said Mike.

"What with that and the Russians and Governor Dewey and Mr. Stassen, you can understand why I've hardly had a moment to welcome you home in the last two days."

"Don't you worry about it, darling," said Margaret. "Which one are we running, by the way, the Governor or Mr. Stassen?"

Judge Cowan shrugged. "Day before yesterday they had a radio debate out in Oregon."

"A debate?" Margaret giggled. "Just like boarding school."

"Not exactly. Governor Dewey's point was that to outlaw the Communist Party as subversive would drive them underground. Mr. Stassen feels that to continue their legal existence would be to encourage their campaign to overthrow our form of government. We'll know day after tomorrow which point of view Oregon is going to support in the national convention."

"Oh, dear." Margaret sighed. "Maybe I shouldn't have come back at all. It's obvious I'll never get to see you. Which reminds me, did I tell you about my landlord in New Orleans?"

"Mr. Williams? What about him?"

"He turned out to be a dream," she said. "He arrived back in New Orleans three days before I was planning to leave, but he wouldn't hear of my going to a hotel, he insisted I keep his place for the last few days and not pay any rent. He put up at a friend's house."

"How very hospitable," remarked Judge Cowan, with a dryness Margaret's ear did not register. She was distracted by Michael's staring, deliberately blank-eyed, at something invisible out in the middle of the room.

"He's terribly good-looking, too, and a writer, I think,"

Margaret babbled on. "But the astounding thing is that he's a friend of the Knudsens. Of Peggy's, anyway. Isn't that astounding?"

"Yes, it is," said Judge Cowan. "Well, if he knows the Knudsens, he might come visit them sometime and you could renew your acquaintance with him."

"As a matter of fact I think he mentioned something about doing just that sometime this summer. He travels around a great deal. Getting material, I suppose."

Mike cleared his throat pointedly, and Margaret decided she had done enough planting of the seeds.

"Daddy, wouldn't you like something to drink?"

"No, thank you, my dear."

"Michael?"

"I think I need something." Getting up, he headed, face averted, for Margaret's serving bar. As he did so, the telephone rang and Margaret picked it up.

"Hello? Oh. Yes, just a minute please. For you, Daddy. Senator O'Harra."

Margaret made room for him on the small sofa, but Judge Cowan took the phone without sitting down.

"Yes, Ted? No, that's all right. What?"

The sharpness of the question made Margaret look up. Her father's thick brows were drawn tightly together.

"When? No, not a word. Yes, I will. I'll call you back. Thank you, Ted." He hung up. "Well, damn," he said.

"What is it?" Margaret asked. "What's wrong?"

"Apparently more irritation in Berlin," said Judge Cowan. "It's getting worse by the hour—they're deliberately provoking us. Excuse me, Margaret, I'll have to go down to the study to make some calls. Let Henry know your plans for dinner, will you?"

"Yes, Daddy."

He left the room abruptly, and Margaret turned her attention to her brother.

"I hope you're proud of yourself," she commented, with little rancor. "Why didn't you titter outright?"

Mike laughed. "I was only being amazed by your ingenuity." He shrugged. "You should be grateful I called you off when the story was getting thin."

"Don't you think Daddy believed what I told him about Steve?"

Another shrug. "If he didn't, he'd never tell you anyway. You know perfectly well anything you do is fine with him." To this remark there was the subtlest edge of bitterness, but Margaret, familiar enough with her brother's reservations about their father, was able to overlook it. "Is Steve in Washington?" Mike asked.

"He's arriving by plane this afternoon."

Her eyes fell on his drink. "I need one of those," she said, standing up, "now that *that* ordeal is over."

She walked over to the serving bar. Mike said, without turning to look at her, "Margaret. Exactly, and I mean exactly, what's the pitch?"

The ice cubes in her hand poised in mid-air. "I'm going to marry him," she said, and dropped the cubes.

Mike whistled through his teeth.

"At last, last," said Margaret, making her drink, "you'll have a brother."

"Spare me."

She looked at him. "I'm serious, buster, and don't you forget it."

"Oh. Oh, well, that's different. Really serious?"

Margaret came back and sat on the small sofa. "Deadly."

"Well," said Mike, shrugging, "felicitations."

"A bad end, you're thinking?" Margaret asked sharply.

"What's it matter what I think?"

"You're a man."

"Thanks."

"Oh, Christ," said Margaret, "no, I mean it. I mean, you're a man and you're my brother, and if God were in His heaven, you'd be able to tell me that I'll make some guy a wonderful wife."

Mike pursed his lips a moment. "I will hope," he said slowly, "that this individual will make you a good husband."

"Mean sonuvabitch, that's what you've always been."

"No, *mon chou,* just curious."

"Why?"

"Why? Oh, my baby, what kind of a dolt are you?" He did not, as Margaret was afraid he might, come near her. He sat in the tufted chair, glass restfully in hand. "This Williams guy, fine fellow I daresay, and he's marrying all the world in marrying you. I'll bet he's crazy about you. You are youth and glamor and breeding and a modicum of brains to someone like him, and for you he'll give everything."

"Of course. That's why I want to marry him."

"What are *you* giving?"

"Huh?" asked Margaret, putting her drink aside.

"What are *you* giving?"

She spread her hands. "I'm marrying him," she pointed out.

"So much?"

"What the hell are you talking about?"

"If you want to know how to make a husband happy, ask a queen. You're very well advised, Margaret, to consult me."

"Well?"

"He'll admire you till he wakes up, if ever, but you'll be miserable because you'll be winning his adoration under false pretenses. You'll be miserable in any case, because you're like me, and we're not much good for anything quite so bourgeois as love and marriage."

Margaret stood up, bristling.

"Out of my room," she said. "Out right this minute."

"I won't because you don't convince me you mean it." Mike smiled and sipped his drink.

"I love Steve."

"You love his loving you," said her brother.

Margaret dropped back onto the sofa petulantly. For a moment neither spoke. Margaret lit a cigarette and tried to suppress her burst of temper. After a while she was able to resume their conversation with more calm.

"Ah, Michael," she mused. "Such a wise brother to have. Now let's say nothing more about it, shall we? . . . I meant to ask, but forgot. How is the phonograph-record fiend?"

"Warren? Peachy." Mike smiled his defiance. "And no longer a phonograph-record fiend."

"Discreet enough for you?"

"Not entirely. Young, and new to all of it. If there's going to be a wedding, I don't know what I'm going to do about him; let him off altogether, I guess; he's dead-set against ordinary society—fed to the teeth with it. His background is quite all right, did you know that? Shaker Heights, and allowances from Mama, et cetera."

Margaret wrinkled her nose with distaste.

"You've got no room to sniff," said her brother. "I recommend the most sympathetic attitudes betwixt your plight and mine, doll."

Margaret was about to speak, but before she could, her eyes fell on her wrist watch.

"Oh, Jesus!" she cried, springing up. "I'll never get to the airport on time, and Steve'll think I'm dead."

"Can't you call him?"

"With Daddy on every extension line? Don't be silly."

"What about dinner?"

"With the Knudsens," Margaret told him, plunging out of the suit she was wearing and into a fresh one from her closet.

"I'll tell Henry for you."

"Thank you. Michael, you will help with Daddy? About Steve?"

"Sure I will. It's the only wedding there's ever going to be around here."

"Michael!"

"That's the truth, isn't it?" He was holding the door open, on his way out.

"Oh, God, but I hate the world!" Margaret exclaimed, fighting the zipper on her skirt. "Yes, it's the truth, I guess. Oh, Michael, it's a wretched world."

"Yes, dear." And he was gone.

An hour later, arm locked in Steve's, she stood with him, waiting for the luggage to be unloaded from the plane and studying his smiling face voraciously, as though in the few days they had been separated he might have lost his good looks or changed in some subtler way. She talked rapidly to prevent herself from dwelling on the possibility . . .

"I told Peggy about it at once, and she and Charlie are delighted. They're waiting for us at their house now, and you're to stay with them until you meet Daddy."

"Couldn't I put up at a hotel?"

"You'll be much more comfortable with the Knudsens."

"But I don't even know them, Maggie."

She patted his arm. "Darling, don't be difficult. These are my *very* closest friends—they'd be hurt if we went through this whole conspiracy routine with Daddy and they weren't allowed to help out in it."

"I thought Charlie Knudsen was the one without too much dough to throw around."

"Oh, don't worry about that. They'll let you foot your own expenses while you're there. See? I've thought of everything for you. Don't you think I'm clever?"

Steve smiled down at the childlike gaze and tightened his grip on her arm. "Smart as they make 'em."

Margaret laughed as though to relieve in laughter the pressure of her happiness. "Oh, it's so wonderful having you back, my darling. You don't know how *bored* I've been. Daddy hardly knows I'm alive, he's been so busy. I privately suspect him of juggling world events just to give us an edge in the election this fall."

"He shouldn't bother. Truman will win."

"Steve! Darling, *promise* me you won't say anything like that in front of Daddy. He *loathes* the man, and he's convinced we'll get back into the White House this time."

"Poor guy," said Steve.

"Why should anyone want to vote for Truman? I ask you."

"Americans love a scrapper. Truman is very much a scrapper."

"You don't mean to tell me *you're* going to vote for him?"

"I think so."

"Oh, God. This is going to be a sticky summer, I can see it now." She turned to him. "Steve, seriously——"

"Don't worry, I won't embarrass you in front of the wicked reactionaries."

"I don't know why you talk about them that way—they're not like that at all. How do you expect to make friends with my friends if you start out with that kind of attitude?"

"You're so pretty when you're scared," he said.

"Oh, Steve."

"I'm not up here to get to be big buddies with people out of my class. I came to meet your father and ease him into the idea of my asking for your hand. After the wedding, an inexpensive dugout in New York and some high-powered typing."

"But everybody needs friends——"

"I'm sure we'll find some," Steve acknowledged. "And anyone with your stamp of approval has a head start. But marrying me is going to change your circle, Maggie, don't you see that? It's inevitable. For one thing, we won't be living in Washington."

"All right," Margaret said, "all right. Just try to be nice to the people you meet here. A lot of them could be very important to you."

"Oh, baby . . ."

"I *know* you don't care. But I do. I'm thinking of the future."

"Okay," he said.

"Look, here are the bags at last."

The porter preceded them.

About the airport, Steve noticed, were an unusually large number of servicemen. Soldiers and sailors singly, in pairs, a few of the classic trio. He wondered briefly if it was because this was Washington that there were so many of them; then he remembered the new draft law everyone was talking about —Universal Military Training. A sergeant passing, duffel bag on his shoulder, reviewed Margaret appreciatively and glanced with unmasked derision at Steve. People talked about the draft law, he thought, but it was already accepted as a normal part of life. Your boy graduated from high school and sandwiched in his service time between that and college or work. Were the Reserves a better idea? Wouldn't it be better if he took his freshman year of college first, perhaps give him a taste for it? It had been so different with the mobilization during the war.

Dimly Steve recalled the irate mothers of San Angelo Street, the drama of boys going away and returning on furlough as men: smoking, drinking, accepting the patronizing of the older men who had ignored them before as squeaky-voiced embarrassments; it was the stuff of drama then, extraordinary and foreboding. Now they were all bearing, he thought, the burdens the other great nations had had to bear through America's suckling. The men, without much fanfare, trained and made themselves ready and were displayed around the world in their readiness. How changed, how far removed from what had passed.

They reached the car, and shortly, settled in with Steve's two suitcases and portable typewriter, set out for the Knudsen house in Georgetown, Margaret at the wheel. Margaret expanded on the theme of her delight in having him back with her, and in Washington, but it was with difficulty that Steve pulled his mind back from its wandering. It was no problem, he knew, to carry on a conversation with her when he was distracted. She did not demand a continuing flow of encouraging cues, and on this occasion she was, if anything, oversupplied with lighter news. Steve found himself wondering, beneath the pleasant and undisturbing rippling of her laughing voice, why he had felt no fuller pleasure in their reunion here. The first sight of her at the gate, waving frantically, had stabbed him with a sharp delight, and the feel of her in his arms, when he embraced and kissed her with the force of several days' accumulated erotic thoughts, had reassured him about the purpose of his appearance in Washington. But soon thereafter (waiting for the bags? when they had stumbled awkwardly on the issue of the election? somewhere) a letdown had occurred, and with it, a chilling mood of pointlessness had overcome him. Was it that Maggie was talkative and he himself in silence? Was it the city's strangeness to him, its familiarity to Maggie, that separated him vaguely from her? He looked at her as she guided the car expertly through the heavy late-afternoon traffic, and the glance was enough to rob him of objectivity. The delicacy of her beauty, her shimmering youthfulness, the very grace with which she handled her body, coltlike as it was, the angle at which her chin was so frequently tipped, the trimness of every part of her: his hunger for these, insusceptible of appeasement however often he knew her sexuality in bed, twisted his heart. No, there was no mistake, no misunderstanding; this girl he wanted for the rest of his life.

She pulled the car as expertly to a stop in front of the Knudsens' house as she had managed it in the drive from the airport, and with a light sigh of having finished well a tiresome task, took his hand and squeezed it.

"Here we are."

Peggy Knudsen greeted Margaret with a conspiratorial crow of delight and himself with a warmly cordial shaking of both his hands. Plain of feature, Peggy had the self-confidence in her appearance he had noticed in Maggie. Her hair a crop of loose curls, her spring dress not easily fitting her rather squat frame, she wore them both with vivacious conviction.

Throwing the door wide open, she led them into a small and dim-lit drawing room. "It's dark as pitch in here, because I'm experimenting with keeping the house cool the way they say you should: curtains drawn all day. Charlie will be here in no time, and we can have a party. What can I get for you to drink now? Steve?"

Steve looked at Margaret.

"Let's wait for Charlie," said Margaret, "If he's coming right on."

Peggy gave a speculative click of her tongue against her teeth. "You two want to be by yourselves," she concluded aloud. "That's fine, 'cause I've still got work to do. Come out in the garden—it's at its best this time of day."

She led them out through the hallway to glass doors opening into a small garden. The garden was hemmed in by the neighboring buildings, but the bright sunlight gained entrance through an opening between them, and Steve led Margaret toward a white-painted iron garden bench in the pool of light. With a hurried pleasantry Peggy disappeared into the house.

"Do you like her?" Margaret asked Steve.

"Very much," said Steve. They were standing near to each other. He drew her into his arms and kissed her lingeringly. When he released her, Margaret sat down on the bench and with a tug at his hand pulled him down beside her.

"There," she said.

"Maggie, how soon do I get to meet your father?"

"A few days to make it clear to him we didn't plot this," she answered.

"How long before I ask for your hand?"

"A couple of weeks."

"Then look, after I meet him, how about my finding a place of my own?"

"Why? Don't you think you'll like the Knudsens?"

"Of course I will, but—well, you won't want to sleep overnight here, will you?"

Margaret laughed, and lifting his hands, kissed them lightly.

"Oh, darling, aren't you sweet: will you really miss me that much?"

"No, damn it, I'm not *going* to miss you. I'll simply find a place of my own and then we can——"

"Steve?" Her laughter died and she faced him with eyes grave and anxious. "Would you hate me if we didn't?"

Steve tensed. "What do you mean, Maggie?"

"Well, there's going to be so much going on," she answered with a vague nervous shrug of one shoulder. "Aunt Hermione will be throwing parties for us all over the place, and if we're to get married in a hurry, I'll be like a one-armed paper hanger, buying clothes and——"

"And you'd rather not have to worry about sleeping with me?"

"Not *worry,* darling. It's just that we'll both be so busy and I thought it'd be simpler just to not . . ." She stopped, and took a breath. "Besides, I want to feel like a bride."

"Oh, for Christ's sake," moaned Steve.

"Is there anything so terribly wrong about that?"

"Maggie, it's childish. You'll have a great big wedding—okay, fine with me. But a few weeks of continence won't make you a virgin again; I'm surprised you're even concerned with such an idiotic, kindergarten idea of——"

But already her wheedling had undermined his purpose. Softly she said, "Please, Steve." The large blue eyes filled with her appeal, and Steve found himself unable to withstand them.

On May 21, 1948, all Oregon's twelve seats in the Republican National Convention were won by Thomas Dewey, and Judge Ellis Cowan was seen by his two children to experience a decided sense of relief. Having conferred with unnamed people in New York, he flew back to the house in Washington that day. Finding both his children out, he called one of the more reliable young women at his seldom-visited office to start her on the search for them with instructions that, barring vital engagements, he expected them to dine with him at home. This was a course Judge Cowan rarely pursued, and both his children, out of a well-trained deference that brooked areas of disagreement or lack of day-today contact between themselves and their father, responded: Michael in black tie and Margaret in one of the more frivolous dresses she had bought in New Orleans.

Margaret spent dinner on edge, awaiting the moment her father learned that the Knudsens' friend from New Orleans, Steven Williams, was visiting them. Through Margaret's machinations, the announcement came from her brother, and she was able to express a mild gratification at the news.

"Well," her father said blandly, "you must ask him over, Margaret, since he was so kind to you down there."

"Oh, I'm sure the Knudsens will be dropping by with him

sooner or later," said Margaret. "I wouldn't want him to get the idea I had any special interest in him."

"Have you, Margaret?"

"Only as I explained to you before. He *is* awfully nice. I think writers are fascinating, don't you?"

Her father nodded slowly.

At nine o'clock a servant opened the door to the Knudsens and Steve Williams and led them into the drawing room with the information that Miss Cowan would be in from dinner presently.

It was a room, Steve thought, as he surveyed it leisurely, that spoke of Maggie, even if she had had nothing to do with arranging it. Deep yellows and dull, quiet golds seemed to predominate in it; around the area in front of the screened fireplace were low-built sprawling chairs, their tailored covers the color of pale apricots.

As it happened, Mike and Margaret appeared at the same time. Rushing forward to him, Margaret threw her arms around him and lifted her lips for his kiss. The kiss was broken when Mike stepped forward to shake hands with a reserved good will.

"Good to see you here, Steve."

"Daddy's stuck on the phone," Margaret said, "but he's coming in later. Sit down, Charlie. Peggy. Steve, come sit over here by me."

"I'll call Henry to come tend bar," Mike Cowan said, and disappeared into the hall. In a moment he returned with Henry, a wan thin man with expressionless eyes whose white jacket was rigid with starch, except across the crook of the arms, where the cloth jagged in broken lines. Henry took their orders for drinks and went off to a far corner of the room where the serving bar stood. Margaret and Peggy were gossiping—somewhat nervously, Steve thought—and could not be interrupted until, shortly after Henry had served their drinks, Judge Cowan came in.

He greeted the Knudsens with courtly grace and turned to have Steve presented to him.

"Daddy, this is the kindly old landlord I told you about. Steve Williams, my father, Judge Cowan."

Steve shook the hand the tall, lean-featured man offered him. His handshake was vigorous and brief, and his acknowledgement of the introduction, disarmingly gracious.

"I must thank you for your kindness to Margaret in New Orleans, Mr. Williams. Is it Steve?"

"Yes, please, sir," Steve said, surprised by his own ease in meeting so formidable a man as Maggie's recounting had made her father seem.

"Margaret's done her share of traveling, but I don't think she's really very sure of herself when she's on her own. A kindness can mean so much when you're alone in a strange city. Please sit down. Henry, I think I would like a brandy, please. Peggy, I was speaking with your father only this afternoon. He told me your mother is out of the hospital at last. I'm very glad she is."

Mike Cowan brought a straight chair forward for his father and Judge Cowan sat down. He went on speaking, not out of garrulity, Steve took note, but with an unhurried flow of small talk, putting the younger people at their ease. Steve liked the man at once. Judge Cowan turned to him unexpectedly.

"Peggy's father's office is working day and night over all our troubles in Berlin. We're introducing a new mark there, you know."

"No, sir, I didn't," said Steve.

"The Russians have been bouncing the mark's value around like a shuttlecock. It's almost worthless now."

"Why should they do that, Judge Cowan?" Steve asked. "It must not endear them to the Germans very much."

Judge Cowan pursed his lips in consideration. "On the other hand, their ideology can't hope to thrive except in a situation of uncertainty and deprivation," he elaborated. "We are under the obligation of protecting the Germans in our sector, that's why we're putting out the *Deutschmark* to replace the old *Reichsmark*. Naturally the Russians are furious. Therefore, as you've noticed, all this transportation hampering we're having now."

"I see," said Steve. He cleared his throat. "I'm afraid I have to admit I'm not as well informed about current events as I'd like to be, Judge Cowan. It's a privilege to hear about them from someone like you, who lives with them so intimately."

Judge Cowan chuckled. "Spoken like a true Southerner." He nodded. "Thank you, Steve."

Margaret put in, "You're probably the first person I've ever introduced to Daddy who can talk intelligently with him. All of us are what Daddy calls frivolous."

Charlie Knudsen began, "Now hold on there——"

"Except that as I said, I don't actually know anything about——"

"You've been rather busy with other things, Steve," Judge Cowan hastened to point out. "It must be difficult keeping abreast of the forties when you're having to be so occupied with the twenties."

"The twenties?" Margaret asked, the pitch of her voice rising with sharp anxiety.

"Your story, you remember, about the sad old woman who had been young in the twenties and longed for them?" Judge Cowan reminded him.

"Daddy!" Margaret cried, "you've *read* Steve's stories?" And the Knudsens exchanged a panicky glance.

"Of course I have, Margaret." Judge Cowan remained calm. "Good heavens. What a question."

Mike Cowan, Steve noticed, finished his drink in a rolling-eyed gulp.

Margaret fought for speech, and gasped out at last, "You didn't *tell* me. Of all the——"

"Naturally I recognized Steve's name at once when you sent your address from New Orleans," said Judge Cowan. "Although it's been some time since *The New Yorker* published that particular story." To Steve he parenthesized: "I read it at my club, you understand. I don't keep *The New Yorker* around the house."

The leg-pulling in the remark was apparent, but Steve felt dimly there was a larger joke somewhere. Had Judge Cowan seen through their charade? Was he aware of a great deal more about Steve than he was prepared to have them realize? At his side Margaret's drawn-bow tension exploded when suddenly she jumped up and headed for the bar.

"Anyone for seconds?" she called over her shoulder with a strained gaiety. "Henry's deserted us, we'll have to do our own."

Charlie Knudsen joined her, Mike Cowan came around the opposite sofa to lean against the mantelpiece, and the conversation became more general as Judge Cowan turned his attention to Peggy and Mike engaged Steve in some situation-masking conversation about the restaurants and night clubs in Washington and anecdotes of the currently competing hostesses of the city. Henry reappeared to call Judge Cowan to the telephone.

"And I'll probably be on it the rest of the night," said Judge Cowan. "Come back and see us soon, Steve. Peggy, Charlie." He bent to kiss Margaret's cheek, and gave a pat to her arm. "If you decide to go out later, my dear, look into the study before you leave. To say good night. Good night, everyone."

And he was gone. Mike Cowan sighed with a whistling through his teeth, downed his drink, and excusing himself, hurried out, explaining as he went that a friend of his had expected him half an hour ago. Steve and Margaret settled down opposite the Knudsens.

Charlie Knudsen, freckled and grimacing, was occupied with earnestly examining the political issues of the day, as if he had forgotten that his own wife was the only one listening to him. He ran a forefinger between his thick neck and his shirt collar. "Every poll in the country gives the election to the Republicans, especially if Taft doesn't get the nomination. Either Dewey or Stassen can do it, if you ask me."

Steve caught enough of the one-sided conversation to ask, "Don't you expect the Democrats will be putting up quite a fight, Charlie?"

"What good would it do them? They've never been in a bigger mess. Look at the strikers going out right this minute: all over the country there's labor trouble the Democrats spawned in the first place, and people are sick of it. People in business feel exactly the same way Vivien Kellems does."

"Who's Vivien Kellems?" Margaret asked.

Peggy laughed. "You haven't heard about it? She owns a company—in Westport, Charlie?"

"I think it's Westport," said Charlie. "She's put her foot down and refused to pay any attention to the withholding tax regulations. Hell, she's right—why should she spend her time being a collection agency for the Government? Course she's tied up to here in legal actions about the whole thing, but by God I'm back of her. Anybody in business would be. And it's a symptom of the way the whole country's feeling about this Adminstration."

"Look," Margaret pleaded, "I've got enough politics in my life. Tell me what's been going on while I was away."

Peggy had readied a further selection of current gossip, and the four of them talked desultorily for half an hour more. Then the Knudsens started to organize their departure.

"But Steve can stay a while longer, can't you, Steve?" Margaret asked. "I'll drive you home later, or you could take a taxi."

"A taxi will do fine," said Steve.

Charlie asked, "You've got the key to that side entrance to the guest room?"

Steve checked his pockets and found it. The Knudsens took their leave, and in a moment Steve was alone with Margaret.

At the serving bar he mixed a fresh drink for each of them while Margaret moved about the room, turning off a few of the lamps. In a dimmer, gentler light she went back to the sofa before the screened fireplace.

"I wish there were a fire," she said, taking the glass he brought to her. "This room is always its most beautiful when the fire's burning. . . ."

Her fragile features were weighted with melancholy. Steve sat down next to her and took her hand.

"Are you going to be sad, leaving it?" he asked. "You'll be trading it for some pretty unimposing diggings in New York."

"It's my home, Steve; I've lived here all my life. Don't you think it'd be very strange if leaving it didn't make me sad?" She squeezed his hand, and turning suddenly, pressed her lips against his cheek. Steve moved his head until his mouth found hers; he kissed her ardently. A moment, and Margaret retreated from his kiss, astonishing him by burying her face in his shoulder and shuddering violently when a sob shook through her throat.

"Maggie——"

"Oh, Steve, you've got to love me more than any man has ever loved a woman. *Will* you, Steve?"

"Maggie, I——"

"Tell me. I mean it: *will* you?"

Steve hesitated, confused. "I love you with everything I have," he said. "Is that enough?"

"I don't know!" she cried out into his shoulder. "I'm

frightened. How do I know how much devotion from you is needed to get me over being scared?"

"Maggie, stop it, darling . . ."

She was weeping openly now, in one of the startling plummetings into depression Steve knew she suffered. He held her tightly while she cried, and felt for the first time an awesome misgiving. If there was so much about Maggie's moods that mystified him, could he be sure of how useful a husband he'd be to her?

The question brought him up short as he held her. He had not before looked on this idiosyncrasy in Maggie's personality as a really serious problem. He was not certain now that it was. Her gusts of impatience or despair frustrated and exhausted him. Nothing he could do or say seemed to help, and returning just as abruptly to the heights of well-being and vigorous optimism, she exacted of him a degree of devotion he was not certain he could provide. He felt at these times an ineffectual stranger to her, and the thwarting of his need to aid or comfort her wore him out.

Still, the occasions were not frequent, and between them he had in the past easily forgotten his chagrin and his misery. But now it came to him that perhaps this lovely, bright, amusing girl was too complicated, too unpredictable, too erratic, ever to be satisfied by anyone as direct and, he thought, as prosaic of nature as himself. In her weeping he continued to hold her tightly, void of everything but his helpless longing to remove her momentary fear, or rather, he suspected, the deep wellsprings of unhappiness that masked their spoutings with the mists of an actually unrelated reason for distress. Maggie herself would not know the real origins of her recurring, unfathomable despondency; how could he expect himself to be able to discover them, let alone circumvent their effect on her? He held her in his arms, knowing that at any moment she would come back to him.

As he had known it would, the sobbing ran its course, and with a shuddering breath Margaret set up to brush the staining tears from her cheeks.

"Darling, I'm sorry," she said, "I don't know why I'm acting like such a fool. I've been so much on edge, getting you introduced to Daddy."

There it was, the unrelated reason, the euphemism Margaret was always able to provide. Steve sighed, relieved that the outburst was over.

"Feeling better now?" he asked.

"I'll be all right now." Margaret smiled reassuringly. "Really I will."

24

SHE DID NOT BURST INTO TEARS AGAIN, neither that evening nor in the following days, but her tension did not lessen. She did not dare to let it lessen until she had been seen around Washington with Steve often enough to make the announcement of their engagement seem convincing in terms of the fictions they had woven about their relationship. Steve urged her to give it up and let him make his wishes clear to her father.

"I don't think he's fooled one bit," he reasoned. "Nobody who read that story of mine would remember my name this long afterward, wouldn't remember it at all without some other very good reason, and I don't think your father makes a habit of reading the women's slicks I've been selling to since then. He found out, somehow or other, and he investigated. That's what I would have done in his place. I don't know what your father's connections are, but they're bound to be formidable. And diverse. I'll bet he's found out everything there is to know about me." But Margaret was adamant. Her father would be horrified if she said she wanted to marry him when to all intents and purposes she barely knew him. He would think Steve a social climber; he would accuse him of being after the family's money; and if ever he found out that Steve and she had been living together in New Orleans, there would be no hope of their ever marrying with his approval.

"Goddammit, do we *need* his approval so much?"

"Of course we do," Margaret insisted.

"Why should you want it if it means going through all this crap?" Steve asked. "If you don't mind lying to him at every turn, why should you care about whether he approves of us or not?"

"Because we'll *need* him afterward——"

"What? Look, Maggie, I've come through a number of years without even having heard of your father's existence. *I* don't need him. And I don't like having to act like my sex life was too lurid and revolting for him to know about. For God's sake, I don't even *have* any sex life this way."

"Steve, a few more days, please."

In the end she won his grudging agreement, but two days later she begged for another postponement. Steve refused to promise anything. The next day he was to take her to luncheon, calling for her at the Cowan house at noon.

At nine o'clock he telephoned Judge Cowan.

"I'm supposed to pick Maggie up at noon, Judge Cowan," he said. "I wondered whether you might be free to see me if I came there at eleven."

"I'd be delighted, Steve," Judge Cowan answered. Was there a breath of relief in his smooth and measured delivery? "There's to be a meeting of some people here at ten, but they should be gone by eleven or a few minutes after. How was the Tylers' party last night?"

"Why, just fine, sir."

"I'm glad. I'll look forward to seeing you at eleven. Good-by, Steve."

The meeting Judge Cowan had spoken of was being held in the drawing room, and Steve was led to the study to wait for him. The leathery masculinity of the book-lined room had obviously been defended with success against any encroachment by feminine members of the family, Margaret or her mother before her, and its tobacco-and-brandy flavor put Steve at his ease. He was about to sit on the leather divan against the heavily curtained windows overlooking the street, but changed his mind and chose instead the straight and slump-resisting armchair placed at an angle to it. For this damned interview, he told himself, any slumping would have to be done by the Judge.

He lit a cigarette, and before he had half finished it, heard the drawing room doors sliding open and the babble of voices as the Judge's meeting broke up. There were felicitations and good-bys in the hall for a few minutes, and then Judge Cowan came in.

He moved with briskness but an undisguisable dignity, coming forward to shake Steve's hand and wave him back to his seat. He himself sat on the sofa—erectly, Steve noticed.

"Yes, Steve, what was it you wanted to see me about?" he asked.

"About Margaret and myself, Judge Cowan. But I imagine you've guessed that already. Judge Cowan, we want to get married."

Margaret's father did not answer, and for a moment Steve wondered if he had heard. He repeated, "We want to get married. I don't go in much for old-fashioned methods of doing things, but I do want your approval and permission."

The white eyebrows went up a fraction of an inch, but Judge Cowan showed no greater astonishment.

"You sound like you've been rehearsing that, which shows good judgment on your part," he said. "Are you very nervous?"

"A little," Steve said, but he did not smile.

"When I went through this with my father-in-law—and he *was* old-fashioned—I kept praying he'd offer me a drink, and the mean old scoundrel refused to do it." He was on his feet. "Let's have a drink."

For a moment Steve gaped, then his heart turned over in his chest. No one had ever impressed him as being quite as extraordinary as this wry-humored, generous man. He followed him to the liquor cabinet on the other side of the room.

"Blast it," the Judge was saying, "my children have been robbing me again. Will Scotch and soda be all right? I can always call Henry for something else."

"That's fine, Judge. Thank you."

Judge Cowan mixed the drinks and handed one to Steve. He raised his glass. "Now let's talk about it," he said, and drank. Steve followed suit, and they went back to their places.

"Old-fashioned customs are incongruous with a girl like Margaret," her father said, sitting down, "but I have a certain regard for them. I'm glad to know you feel the same way, Steve. You want to be married soon, I take it?"

"Yes, sir. Maggie says she wants the whole circus, and I realize that takes time. But comparatively quickly."

"No pressing need for hurry, is there?" Judge Cowan asked.

Steve gave a start, but answered, "No, sir."

Judge Cowan looked at his drink as he went on, "I've always tried to prevent myself from nursing any illusions about my children, Steve. And I'm active enough in the world to know young people's standards for their own behavior these days. I didn't know whether Margaret's adventure in New Orleans would lead to any serious decision in her life, but I made inquiries out of a natural concern for her safety and happiness. The impression I received of you was a favorable one."

"Thank you," Steve said. He hesitated then, but forced himself to go on with what he'd been thinking. "I didn't know for certain whether you'd caught on. I'm sorry if you were hurt by our feeling that we had to conduct this charade rather than tell you where things stood."

Judge Cowan shrugged. "Margaret is fond of me, but I don't think she has much confidence in me."

"Oh, I'm sure she——"

"No, she doesn't. And it's not of any importance. Children rarely have that kind of confidence in their parents, and as far as I'm concerned the psychiatrists are wasting their breath on the subject. Have you two thought where you'll have your honeymoon?"

"We'll go straight on to New York. We expect to live there for a while. We won't really have enough money for a trip anywhere, what with the cost of setting up an apartment—furniture and all the rest of it."

"But that's a shame." Judge Cowan frowned. "Couldn't I give you the trip as a present?"

Steve took a breath. He cursed himself for letting the subject embarrass him, and swallowed some of his drink.

"That's very kind of you," he said. "I guess I have to make myself clear from the start. Maggie wants a big wedding, and I've agreed. You'll be giving her that. Beyond that, I want her to learn to live on my income. I know you've got a lot of money and Maggie will inherit it someday, but I want to earn my own diversions—through writing, if my work goes on well. If my wife is being supported by her family, I won't have much incentive to do that."

Judge Cowan nodded thoughtfully, and did not speak for a moment. At last he said, "I see. Well, the theory must be that you're either a clever kind of fortune hunter or you're not one at all. I swear I know of no test to prove which it is."

Steve flushed angrily, but he kept his voice firm, if not calm. "I'm no fortune hunter," he stated flatly.

Judge Cowan looked at him appraisingly. "I don't think you are. And it's an ugly subject to have to run into. Inevitable, as I'm sure you understand."

"Yes, sir. There's another inevitable problem. I'm not in any way any kind of social wheel."

Judge Cowan spread his hands. "You haven't been around," he countered.

"I mean, my parents aren't either."

"I don't think that matters a damn any more, Steve," said Judge Cowan. "You have all the manners a man needs today, and Margaret has kept up her social position in New York to the point where anyone she marries will automatically be accepted, if you give a hoot."

"I'm afraid I don't. I'm going to be busy with work for many years to come, and I certainly don't expect to be making enough to keep up with any social whirl."

"You must take care to keep Margaret's mother's family at a safe distance, then. They're in Boston, as I suppose she's told you."

"Yes, sir."

"You'll have enough to contend with in my sister, Mrs. Pierce, here in Washington. Have you met Hermione?"

"Yes, day before yesterday. We called on her."

"Then you understand what I mean." Judge Cowan finished his drink but held the glass idly in his hand. The white eyebrows drawn together, he said, "I don't know what else to say, Steve. In the long run I could never deny Margaret anything she was really determined to do. You strike me as intelligent, so I imagine you are aware that Margaret has been spoiled more than a little bit by me and the rest of the family. She is, I think, lacking in real wisdom, and she takes a delight in behaving outrageously on occasion. Those will be your problems, as they've been mine."

"I'm aware of them," Steve answered. "Do you think perhaps some of them are due to the fact she's young, and that she hasn't had much to keep her occupied and out of trouble?"

"It may be. For your sake I hope so." He looked at his watch. "You'll be wanting to let Margaret know you're here." They stood up, and Judge Cowan shook his hand. "This is all very hurried, of course, but I'm glad if you and Margaret feel you can make a happy life together. You have my approval and permission, and thank you for the courtesy of asking for it. You and I must take pains to get to know one another better these next few weeks. It would mean a great deal to Margaret, I think."

"Yes, sir," said Steve. "And Judge Cowan—I can't thank you enough for being so candid with me. I guess we'd better go whole hog. I'm voting for Truman in November."

Judge Cowan smiled. "Are you, Steve? Well, we *will* have a lot to talk about."

They went into the hall when they heard the elevator coming down from Margaret's floor.

After his swim in Duncan Baring's pool, Mike Cowan dried his hair, and spreading the overlong towel beside the pool's edge, stretched out on it, propping his chin up on his fists. The sun on his back was searing, but swimming had cooled him, and he regretted only that he had left his sunglasses behind in the dressing room.

Warren was still in the water, swimming the length of the pool with slow, long, easy strokes. Warren's swimming was beautiful to watch, he thought. Duncan in his grisly prurience had urged them not to bother with trunks since there was no one in the house but themselves, but neither Mike nor Warren had either the locker-room indifference to each other's naked bodies or the salivating womanishness that motivated plump, pendant-breasted Duncan. Now Mike was almost sorry. He watched the clean, ease-stroking progress of Warren's body in the water, and the trunks he wore seemed to bisect what should have been a flawless, pure-lined entity. Warren reached the end of the pool and hauled himself out of it. Snatching his towel up from where he had dropped it, he came around to where Mike lay and sat down with a gasp before him. Legs scissored, he dried his hair.

"Wow," he said in his breathlessness, and Mike knew it was not a cue for a reply. He studied the dripping young body before him. It was odd how he could forget its look, awakening to its appeal afresh whenever it was presented to his eye in a new scene, a new situation. The hair on his chest was blond and sparse, the hair on his legs a light brush of glowing sunlight over his deep tan. Wand-straight as was his back, like that of a boy, his shoulders had an angular strength and his chest a depth that suited his lean but masculine construction.

"Wow," Warren repeated, his breath returning as he stretched out, head-to-head. "Where did Duncan go?"

"The telephone rang. More about the party at Fritz's I daresay."

"You still want to go?"

"We can't, Warren."

"Jesus, Mike, we go to enough other parties."

"Do you want like hell to go to this one?"

"I think it'd be fun. There's never enough fun in Washington."

"Not for anybody who has a twenty-four-hour-a-day appetite for it."

"Don't talk like a bitch," said Warren. "*I* know it's all new to me and I get carried away sometimes. What the hell's wrong with my getting carried away if I want to?"

"Nothing," said Mike, "except I can't do it with you, and you, thank God, don't want to do it without me."

"Of all the fucking self-confidence——"

"Do you?"

"No," said Warren.

"There are places we can go, Warren, but not all of them. I'm known around Washington because of Dad, and I'm known to have a lot of friends in State. It's the prison of discretion, but there it is."

"Yes." Warren sighed.

They were silent, and the contact—the delicate, endlessly shifting, impalpable contact between them—was broken. Like the snapping of a twig, Mike thought; and a bud of gall burst in his stomach. Bittersweet. All his affair with Warren was bittersweet, and he hated bittersweetness.

"Have you met the Knudsens?" he asked, trying anew for easiness of tone.

"The Knudsens? A married couple? No, I haven't. No thanks."

"Charming in their way. Charlie Knudsen is from not quite anywhere, but Peggy comes from——"

"Look, Mike, don't gossip," said Warren softly.

"What?"

"It makes you sound like a woman."

"Warren, for God's sake——"

"I'm sorry." Warren scowled, regretful but impatient. "It just does."

Mike held fire a moment. "I was only building up to the joyous news that there's going to be quite a lot of social life going on—including the Knudsens. My sister's getting married. To Steve Williams, a guy she met in New Orleans."

"Oh, really? Are you glad about it, Mike?" The impatience had drained away, and Warren was looking at him softly again: a boyish, gallant concern that made Mike catch his breath.

"More or less," he managed to say evenly. "Very attractive guy, though I don't know how happy Margaret's going to make him."

"Nothing's expected of *me*, I hope," Warren said.

"Not if you want out."

"Jesus, yes, please."

"But it'll keep *me* busy as hell."

"I'll tend to my tatting while you're busy," said Warren.

"Now who sounds like a damned woman?" Mike demanded.

"I apologize. Well, screw it. Want another jump in the pool before we go in?"

"I don't guess," said Mike.

Warren started to push himself up, but hesitated halfway in the movement, poised half-lifted on his fists.

"The wedding will keep you busy. If I did anything on my own—indiscreet parties, as you say, nothing serious—it would be bad, wouldn't it?"

Mike looked at him in pain, flicking the salt sweat off his upper lip with a darting of his tongue. "Yes, Warren. If it's too much for you to stomach, I'll understand. Christ knows it won't be anything new. Warren——"

"Mike, I won't disgrace you," said Warren. "Don't worry. I'll lay low till the damned wedding's over. But I'll be lonely for you. Come on, let's go in."

Mike rolled over and sat up, his back to Warren. "Let's make the drink with Duncan quick, and go to your place. A feast of temporary farewell!"

Hermione Cowan Pierce had been readying herself for the task of supervising Margaret's wedding ever since her niece had first gone off to boarding school; and because she was widely known in Washington, her plans were formidable. They were not subject to simplification by so unimportant a fact as that the wedding was to take place in less than six weeks; she merely compressed her schedule, without allowing circumstances to hack away at the complex structure of its multitudinous details. Steve and Margaret found themselves riding a train of engagements and appointments with the unconvincing picture of their married life as a destination and no stopovers on the way. Younger people took them to luncheon, older ones, to dinner, friends of the family gave elaborate parties for them, and the Republican Senators and their wives who were still in Washington at that season of the year vied aggressively for available opportunities to entertain in their honor. Margaret enjoyed each occasion as though it were a unique experience and would leave behind it an unmatchable memory. Steve at first found the parties stimulating and amusing; he was flattered by the interest so many distinguished people showed in him, and eagerly appreciative of the chance to meet intelligent and experienced men intimately connected with the business of government; but in the third week of festivities he found himself listening to the same men again and again, being becomingly attentive to the same women, and he realized that but for the hastiest exchange of words and an occasional frantic conversation over the telephone, he had seen little of Margaret. It occurred to him fleetingly that she was too distracted in celebrating the occasion of her engagement to give any consideration to his need for her; it was for her a moment that would not come again, and he could afford to wait.

At the end of the fourth week Hermione Pierce gave her own party in their honor, and when Steve delivered Margaret to the door of the Cowan house at two o'clock the next morning he said, "Maggie, we've two weeks to go. Isn't there going to be a single evening we can have alone together before the wedding?"

"Poor darling, are you exhausted. You must be fed to the teeth with all these people who don't interest you——"

"No, that isn't it. I've met some wonderful people, and I'm grateful for it. But I miss you: I don't want to find myself facing a stranger at the altar. Damn it, Maggie, I want an evening for us to be alone together."

"There will be, darling, I promise you."

"When?"

"Oh, I can't think, Steve, let me see—no, not a night this week, I'm certain——"

"An afternoon?"

"Steve, I haven't got *half* my shopping done yet. Oh, don't be angry. I know what a bore it must be for you . . ."

"When then, Maggie?"

"When are your parents arriving?"

"The Monday before the wedding," said Steve.

"Oh, I can't wait to meet them, I know I'm going to love them so much——"

"What night for us, Maggie?"

"I know! There's nothing this coming Thursday, is there?"

"I've lost track, to tell you the truth."

"There isn't," she affirmed, "nothing we can't get out of. And your parents won't have got here yet, so you won't feel bad about not looking after them. Thursday, my darling, for just you and me."

"Promise? No last minute changes?"

"Promise. I want our evening alone myself, you know. Just as much as you do."

He took her in his arms. "All right, then," he breathed. "God, I'll be glad when its over."

"It'll be over in no time, darling, and we'll be off to New York and by ourselves and writing story after story. But all this will be so wonderful to look back to and remember. Believe me, Steve, it will."

Being able to look forward to the coming quiet evening smoothed out the knots of tension that had built up in Steve's temper through the weeks of party-going, and he was able to present as affable a picture to the people entertaining them as he had in the beginning. He made his plans carefully for Thursday night. From Charlie and Peggy Knudsen he learned the name of an excellent restaurant not yet discovered by fashionable people generally, a place where they would be unlikely to encounter anyone known to them. He reserved a table at another place where they might dance for an hour or so after dinner, and feeling he was doubtless beginning to hope too much for Thursday night, reserved under another name a room in one of the large hotels where anonymity would be possible even for Margaret.

Steve arrived at the Cowan house at six on Thursday evening, and Henry ushered him into the drawing room. He fixed a drink for himself at the serving bar as Margaret had asked him to do whenever he had to wait for her to come down, and spent ten minutes desultorily leafing through an over-size slick magazine whose name did not penetrate his consciousness. All his capacity for awareness and response was concentrated on the evening he had planned.

He stood up as Margaret came in. She wore a dress he had not seen before, and her smile was radiant. She came forward quickly and kissed him.

"Maggie, you're beautiful," he said. "I feel like I haven't seen you in a year."

"Do you like the dress? I got it this afternoon, just for tonight."

"It's fine. You're fine. Are you ready to go?"

"Finish your drink, darling. At least for once we can take our time. I'll have one with you."

"Let me get it."

"No, you sit down," she waved, walking away.

He did so, and in a moment Margaret was back with her drink. She sat down beside him, and he took her hand.

"What did you do all day?" he asked.

"Spent as much of Daddy's money as I had time to." She laughed. "Oh, and guess what else happened. Oh, I *do* hope you'll be happy for me, Steve, even if you don't know the people yet. . . ."

"What're you talking about?"

"The Fergusons: Daisy is one of my dearest friends, a marvelous girl, and all the family just got back from Europe, just this afternoon. They've been in Germany for ages and ages, but her father has some kind of new post now and so they'll be here for the wedding. Oh, I want so much for you to meet Daisy, you'll love her."

"Sure, sure I will."

"She called this afternoon, the minute they got to their house, and begged us to come over this evening. All my friends are going over to welcome her back and hear all about Germany—but of course I told her no dice."

"Good girl."

"Oh, I almost wish we could go. I can't wait to see Daisy."

"She'll be at all the other parties we have to go to, won't she?"

"Of course, darling, but you know it's not like the first night when somebody's really fresh back in town. . . ."

"Do you want to go?" Steve asked.

"Darling, I couldn't do that to you, you know I couldn't."

"What about yourself, Maggie?"

She lifted her chin. "Or myself either. We have this evening for ourselves, and that's the way I want it." She looked away. "But—oh, Steve, I'm so glad I'm going to be married to you, I'm just awful on my own—but the truth of the matter is I sort of bollixed things up on the phone. Steve, you're going to hate me."

"What did you do?"

She turned away. "I can't tell you. You will, you'll hate me and loathe me."

"Maggie, I never could do that."

"I don't believe you!" To his amazement he saw she was trembling, and he touched her arm.

"Maggie, tell me. I won't be angry, I swear it."

"Well . . ." With a shudder she gained control again and turned back to him, but her forehead was puckered with anxiety. "Daisy was so sweet and so dying to see me and to meet you, I *couldn't* be so cruel as to—I mean, Daisy's a sensitive person, Steve, and so dependent on the friends who love her, *you* wouldn't want me to be hard toward her either—anyway, I told her we might—just might—be able to drop in—oh, only for a few minutes, maybe before dinner, not more than a second or two. We won't, of course. We *do* have our evening all planned to be alone. But—oh, Steve, I just dread thinking of how little Daisy's going to feel."

"Of course."

"Well, that's my tough luck." Margaret sighed impatiently. "It's my own fault for not knowing how to handle situations the ways you always can."

"I understand how you felt, Maggie," Steve comforted her.

She grabbed his hand. "Do you? Oh, then you won't hate me!"

"Of course I won't hate you. It's a perfectly natural jam for you to have got in, I guess."

"But what about Daisy? She *is* going to be hurt. I don't know that I'll ever be able to explain."

"Oh. You mean you *do* think we should go there tonight."

"A few minutes wouldn't make that much difference to us,

would it? God, we're going to have our whole lives together, aren't we? And it's going to be such a beautiful life with you, my darling: it seems selfish to begrudge Daisy a few minutes——"

"Okay, okay, Maggie. I don't begrudge her anything. We can stop by for a few minutes, if you think it's important."

"Oh, my angel, thank you! I have the best husband of anybody on earth!"

But suddenly the drink he held had gone flat, and the evening stretched flat before him.

When they arrived half an hour later, the Fergusons' house was already crowded with friends celebrating the family's homecoming from Germany. Steve had met many of the guests before, and he was drawn at once into conversation, so suddenly he was unaware that Margaret had left him and gone off to find Daisy Ferguson.

She came back with her in ten minutes and introduced Steve.

"Congratulations," Daisy smiled, offering her hand. She was a rangy, well-groomed girl; Steve failed to see how Maggie had come upon her "poor little thing" description of her. Nor did Maggie show any signs now of her distress at having interrupted their evening in order to come to the Fergusons'. She was flushed and exhilarated as she gossiped with Daisy, and Steve realized with a turning-over of his heart that this would be no brief and hurried call. She finished one drink and began another. In despair Steve followed suit. With a murmur to Daisy he turned and moved away into the depths of the noisy throng.

In an hour he was drunk. He sat alone in one corner of the room, a glass half-empty in his hand, listening to the babble before him, catching only snatches of intelligible conversation. He did not know where Maggie was; he hoped she was miserable. If she wanted that much to come to another party, he thought, why the hell couldn't she have told him outright? Why did she have to indulge in a shabby and ugly little scheme to hoodwink him? Perhaps he was being too hard on her; perhaps it was his own fault; if she feared his displeasure, she would feel forced to deceive him; if she hated to disappoint him, maybe she simply couldn't bring herself to do it except piecemeal. Was that the way women's minds worked? Well, if he was going to spend the rest of his life married, he would have to come to terms with the fact. Did anyone ever really understand anyone else? Maybe he didn't have any kick coming at all. But he thought of their lost evening together and cursed under his breath.

"They had less than a month's supply of food on hand," someone near him was saying. "There wasn't a bit of food allowed into the American sector."

"Fergie says it was the most dramatic thing he's ever seen. The planes fly in, and the Berlin people know we're breaking our backs to keep them alive. I tell you, no kind of Russian propaganda is ever going to beat the Berlin airlift."

"Why the hell should we go to the trouble? Why don't we pull out of Berlin entirely?"

"The attitude of the Berliners is your answer to that. We're in too deep. We can't ever abandon them."

". . . The Democrats will never get Eisenhower, take my word for it. They're out of their minds if they nominate Truman, but Eisenhower isn't the one who's going to come to the rescue."

"Fergie says if the Russians hold out till winter, the airlift will have to get bigger still. . . ."

"General Harris says he knows from his own association with him that Eisenhower is definitely a Republican. Where do the Democrats get off?"

"Did you know the power plant is in the Russian sector, and we had a fifty per cent loss of power. *Fifty* per cent, mind you."

Steve went on drinking.

"Darling, *there* you are!" He looked up and blinked. Margaret was standing before him. "I've been looking everywhere for you. Time has just flown by. I'm so sorry. Steve, please forgive me. But if you're ready now, I am too."

He stood up, wondering if he looked as drunk as he felt. "Yes, let's go," he said, without enthusiasm. They made their way through the crowd to where the Fergusons stood, and with a hurried good night, made their exit.

In the car Steve was silent until Margaret said, "You're furious with me. Oh, Steve, I feel awful."

"You're too late. Shut up."

Margaret flinched and shrank back from him, dismayed. A

long moment, and she said, in the smallest of voices, "You hate me."

"I don't hate you." Steve sighed. "I'm disappointed in you, and I'm ashamed of you. Well, the evening is fucked good and proper, so forget it. I won't think a thing or feel a thing till the wedding is over and I've got you alone in New York. Maybe then we'll be the same again."

"We will, darling," Margaret assured him plaintively. "After the wedding we'll be by ourselves and all our obligations to other people will be over with."

"I wish I could feel sure of that."

"You *can,* Steve. Aren't we going to do exactly as you said? No honeymoon trip, because that's the way you want it: off to New York and back to work? Darling, my only reason for living is to do what my husband tells me." Her hand came to rest on his leg.

"I'm not hungry any more," said Steve. "Do you still want dinner?"

"Not especially. No, I'm not hungry at all."

"I rented a hotel room for us."

"What?"

"A hotel room for tonight. Let's get ourselves a bottle and go there."

Her hand pressed down on his thigh.

"Yes, let's," she said quickly. "That'll make up for everything that went wrong—at least a little bit, won't it?" She took a breath. "Steve, let's not stop for a bottle, let's go right there, wherever it is; I want to feel your arms around me. Really around me again."

In their intercourse Steve's anger and resentment were washed away, and he could believe again that the girl he lay with was the same who had loved him in the quiet days of the *garçonniére.* He chided himself for having forgotten, if only momentarily, the contentment he had known with Margaret then. It would come again, he was certain now, and Margaret's subsequent behavior supported him in this belief. In the following days she was calmer than he had seen her since coming to Washington, and at the parties they went to that weekend she stayed close to his side. Perhaps she had needed, he thought, to be dragged off to bed by him as she had been—without consultation, demandingly;

perhaps unconsciously she had needed all along that reassurance of his love for her.

On Monday his mother and father arrived from Houston by plane. At his mother's instruction, Steve met the plane alone. She wanted a chance to get to the hotel and freshen up before meeting her intended daughter-in-law. Their reunion was happy, and during the drive to the hotel, his parents told him the news from Houston. When they were settled in the hotel room, Steve went down to the lobby to wait for them while they dressed. In half an hour they were down. Steve stood up when he saw them coming from the elevator.

Steve's father was a tall and deeply sunburned man. Like Steve's, his hair was black and his eyes a blue that showed no sign of dimming with age. His hands were knobby and scarred: strong hands that suited the reserve of manner he had acquired as a boy growing up in the back country.

His mother, short and round, kissed him again when he came up to them. Behind her bifocals her bright eyes smiled at him shyly.

"Honey, we look all right, don't we? If you're afraid you'll be ashamed of us——"

"Mom, cut that out. You look beautiful. Dad, did you dip into the till to get her that dress?"

"Now, now." His father chuckled.

"Does it really look all right, Steve?"

"It's perfect."

"If it were wintertime, I could wear my neckpiece; that'd make me feel dressed up. Well, Maggie will just have to take us as we are."

"You'll love her, Mom. And they're waiting for us, we'd better go on."

On the way to the Cowan house he tried with delicacy to prepare his parents for the unaccustomed affluence they would see there. They listened but did not at first reply. In the midst of his uneasy exposition his mother touched his arm, and he abruptly stopped talking.

"Children are always nervous about introducing their parents," she said in her soft, crooning drawl. "It's harder for you than it is for most boys because *my*, Stevie, you've grown up into such a nicer world than what you knew in Houston. Now, hush, honey, and listen. Your father and I talked about it all before we left. There's no reason you should feel anything but proud of us; and since your father didn't raise you to be silly, I think that's what you will be. Either back home or out with the important friends you have now. The thing for us to do is be pleasant and just not cause anybody any trouble. Any more than we have to, being here."

There was no false humility in her statement, and their arrival at the Cowan house proved her to be right. Judge Cowan greeted them warmly and Margaret showed them a deference Steve had seldom seen her show to anyone. As they sat in the drawing room, Steve studied his parents, relieved and warmed by the quiet flow of conversation. They were not of the Cowans' world, it was true, he thought; but in their simplicity was a dignity Steve prayed he had inherited from them. His mother chatted gaily and easily with Margaret about her trousseau, and Judge Cowan drew his father into talk about the automobile models of the past year. It was a subject that fired his father's interst, and he showed no trace of awkwardness or discomfort as they talked. At one point Judge Cowan said, "We have a shoot over in Virginia. Not much of a place, but I'm very fond of it. And of course it will be Steve's and Margaret's after me. Perhaps before the wedding we could take a day for me to drive you over and show it to you."

Margaret found an opportunity later to draw him aside. "Darling, they're heaven, I love them already!" she cried.

His heart gave a pound of gratitude and he took her arms. "Do you really, Maggie? I can tell they like you."

"Could we go to Houston often to visit them, Steve?"

"Of course we will. Maggie, it's the damnedest thing. I love my parents very much, but I haven't seen much of them since the war. Now, getting married, I feel like I'm—closer to them again. The way I was when I was a boy. Does marriage do that to other men, do you think?"

"I think it probably does, darling. Oh, I hope they really approve of me! If they thought you were getting gypped, I'd die: they're so devoted to you, they must want only the very best for you."

"That's what I'm getting." Steve smiled at her.

After the meeting of his parents with Judge Cowan and Margaret, obligatory parties filled their schedule until the day of the wedding. Saturday dawned clear and blistering hot, and at ten o'clock Mike Cowan arrived at the Knudsens' house to help Steve get ready.

"I'm not a hysterical bridegroom, Mike," Steve said to him in the guest room, standing before the mirror and adjusting the boutonniere on the lapel of his morning coat. "Why don't you get Peggy to fix you a drink and wait for me in the garden? How's Maggie?"

"Radiant," said Mike. "Raging with curiosity about the stag dinner I had to subject you to."

"Oh." Steve smiled. "I hadn't thought of that."

"I put her at her ease. I also explained you were sound asleep by ten."

"I hope that was all right, Mike. I was pretty bushed."

"*Everybody's* bushed. If I ever do lose my mind and get married, I'm going to make sure Aunt Hermione is six months dead before the subject even arises. I'll wait for you in the garden."

It was noon. In the rear of the church Mike broke from his conference with the minister and came over to Steve.

"It's time, our friend says. Still calm?"

"Reasonable."

"I checked all the ushers," said Mike. "Homely guys, every last one of them, but the bloodlines are impeccable." Then, turning to them, "Come on, you people, here we go."

The sight of the throng in the church caused Steve to catch his breath, and for an instant he feared panic would claim him at last. The organ was playing softly as he took up his position behind Mike. In the first pew on the farther side, leaving a place for Judge Cowan, sat Hermione Cowan Pierce in an overlarge hat and a manner of businesslike interest in the scene that proclaimed her responsibility for its staging. Beside her was a sister of Margaret's mother, a thin, tall woman with equine features, and behind them, other representatives of the Boston branch of the family. In the next pew Steve recognized Senator O'Harra and his wife sitting next to Mr. Dulles, Thomas Dewey's adviser, but the rest of the church was packed with people in whose mass Steve could detect no individual face: a glittering gulf of flowered garden-party dresses, summer hats, and cutaways. His eyes came to rest on his parents in the pew before which he stood. His mother smiled once and bent to her handkerchief, and his father, with a wink at Steve, took her hand and patted it gently. The organ paused as though to draw a mighty breath, and then the music of the processional blasted through the church; with an answering roar the congregation turned to watch the entrance of the bride.

The bridesmaids moved down the aisle with the smoothest grace, the wide brims of their hats gently bobbing as they walked. Behind them at last Margaret appeared, and Steve gave a start at the sight of her loveliness: on her father's arm, a shimmering vision of white lace who came toward him, smiling at him from behind her veil, her chin uplifted.

When they reached the foot of the aisle, Steve stepped forward to receive her from her father. Margaret whispered through the veil, "Good morning, husband."

25

PUBLIC OPINION, THE NEWSPAPERS ASSERTed through the months of that summer, was firmly behind a return of the Republican Party to the White House, and the men seeking the Republican nomination seemed convinced that the election in the coming November would accomplish this fact. On the eve of the Republican national convention in Philadelphia, Harold Stassen formed a partnership with Robert Taft of Ohio to wrest the nomination from Thomas E. Dewey. All three, together with Earl Warren of California, were placed for nomination at the convention; and on the third ballot Thomas Dewey won. Governor Dewey's lead was strong in spite of the determined efforts of the others to stop him, and the predictions that the next President would be a Republican rang on the ear more convincingly than ever. Wags asked to be told who could ever vote for a man who looked like the bridegroom on a wedding cake, but the majority shook their heads over the impossible ambitions of Harry Truman when in June he set out on a transcontinental speaking tour to rally the people of America to his support. This, they said, was pitifully reminiscent of old-time politicking, no longer suitable to a rich and powerful United States, and typical of the small-time political-machine thinking of Roosevelt's hapless successor.

To many the President seemed not to have read the newspapers. In the face of a crippling revolt on the part of the Southern Democrats and the strength-sapping defection of Henry Wallace and his supporters, the whistle-stop campaign went on, and in July the President was nominated for a full term by the Democratic national convention. The following day a rump convention of the Southern Democrats held in Birmingham, Alabama, nominated J. Strom Thurmond of South Carolina and, as candidate for Vice-President, Fielding L. Wright of Mississippi.

Through August, September, and October the contest was hotly waged, and the interest of the people centered excitedly on its outcome. At town meetings and state fairs, at rallies and clambakes, the politicians fought for the support of the voters. The newspapers of the nation continued to take for granted the success of Thomas Dewey's campaign, but in restaurants and barrooms, wherever men gathered, the issues were quarreled over and the betting was feverish. The intensity of the circus excitement grew to its peak as Election Day approached. Lower-echelon party-workers labored unstintingly for their causes, and among private voters parties were arranged where friends might get together to hear the returns on the radio and find within their own circle the best last-minute odds they could.

Marvin Kaufman was to attend a party given by a former medical-school classmate of his in an apartment on East Fifty-first Street in New York City. An emergency appendectomy delayed him, and at ten o'clock he had just turned the corner and recognized the sedate marquee of the apartment building. He did not hurry; the pace at which he had been working in the last few months had slimmed his long body, and when at last the working day was over, an insupportable tiredness would come over him. In an hour it would be gone, but while it remained, his movements were lethargic and his thoughts somber. Walking toward the apartment house now, he thought of Gwen, the nurse he had been sleeping with more or less regularly for the last six months. He had thought of bringing Gwen with him to the party tonight; without knowing the cause, he had found the prospect strongly distasteful. There had never been any question of serious romance between them, and Marvin supposed his growing indifference toward her resulted from his childish, irritating feeling of guilt that his parents, though they presumed he had some sort of girl-friend arrangement, would be disappointed to know that someone like Gwen could afford him even a fleeting physical pleasure. She was, on one hand, a Gentile, and Marvin knew his father would be pained by even the possibility of any permanent relationship growing up between them. His mother, on the other hand, would despise her for her undisguised and unregretted vulgarity. By his mother's stringent standards, there was no recognizable distinction in the social position of a registered nurse and, for example, a beautician. Gwen had never been exposed to his mother's judgment. Perhaps the affair was drifting to an end, perhaps it was best that way, he mused as he walked. Eventually he supposed he would find some girl, suitably Jewish and rich by at least two generations, to satisfy his parents' ambitions for him. Until he did, he had his work, his growing and demanding private practice, his endlessly prolonged off-hour studying. Halting momentarily at the entrance to the apartment building, he adjusted his thick glasses with an automatic gesture, checked the number on the marquee to make sure it was the right one, and went in.

A number of election-night parties were in progress, Marvin diagnosed from the sounds of laughter and music he heard coming from various directions inside the building. Other people were waiting for the elevator to reach the lobby, and one or two of them looked as if they had already had more than a few drinks. When the elevator arrived, Marvin followed the others in and gave the operator the number of the floor he wanted.

The door to 7-D was at the end of the narrow corridor, and Marvin could hear clearly the noise of the guests inside. He pressed the buzzer, and almost immediately the door was opened to him by a smiling young man he did not know.

"Looking for Doctor Kelly's apartment? Come on in; I don't know where the host is, but you'll probably turn him up somewhere."

Marvin went in. The body of the roar that met him was reinforced by the blasting voice of the radio commentator analyzing the election returns from the New England states. The living room and dining room of the apartment were crowded, but Marvin could not see Kelly anywhere.

A hand grabbed his arm.

"Kaufman, you big lovable sonuvabitch, where's Gwen?"

It was Don Biel. Marvin was glad to find someone he knew, and Don's energetic good humor was always a happy antidote to his tiredness.

"Here, take off your topcoat and put it in the bedroom. This way. I'll show you."

Don, with his catlike grace and febrile aggressiveness, pushed a way open for them through the crowd of guests to the bedroom.

"Where's Kelly?" Marvin asked.

"How the hell should I know? Have you heard the news?" His acne-scarred cheeks were red; beneath his thick eyebrows his eyes, deep blue, were burning with excitement.

"No, is Truman in?" Marvin returned.

"Truman, your ass. He's ahead at the moment, but those returns aren't reliable. Every commentator on the air is convinced Dewey's going to make it; *that's* the news. Here, just throw your coat down here. Come on, I'll get you a drink. Where's Gwen?"

"She—I just came alone. I had an emergency appendectomy, that's why I'm late."

"Oh, you poor sap." Don groaned for him extravagantly. "Oh, you dedicated creeps depress me."

"I'll depress you even more," said Marvin. "I voted for Truman."

"Stabbed in the back by a buddy!" Don cried. "Are you trying to ruin this country? Don't you know boom times when you see them coming? We need the Republicans *in*: lower taxes, screw the poor and subsidize the rich, bring on the dancing girls! Here, the bar's over this way." Marvin docilely followed the short, bouncing young man, only half-listening to his stream of talk. "You're just not with it, Kaufman, you don't dig the Republicans. Hi, Dave, did you get Kaltenborn on yet? I've got a wad on Dewey's nose: not that I have any personal liking for the stuffed shirt, but the Democrats are *behind* the times. They're being Christians in catacombs when this is a fucking *Em*pire we've got. Sorry, dearie, didn't realize I was shouting. Hey, you're cute, wanna make room at the bar? Here we are, Kaufman, you poor dedicated slob, what're you having?"

The showgirl stepped aside, tugging the Dior collar of her tan moire dress into place as she did so, and Marvin ordered a Scotch and water as he stepped forward to Don's side. Don for his own part put his empty glass down and flicked a hand at the bartender. While they waited, Don chattered on. He had been having his troubles, Marvin knew. With his ruthless determination to succeed and the charm of his boyish, well-assembled features, he cornered a certain specialized market among motherly and, Marvin presumed, rich women with indefinable ills; but his prodigality kept pace with his earnings and often managed to outstrip them. Marvin did not care so much about Don's difficulties with overdrafts at the bank. Don, he was sure, would always find a way out if he were trapped in a really serious problem, but he sometimes wondered if his professional exploitation of other human beings ever bothered his friend's conscience; he supposed that it did, and attributed to that fact Don's boisterous manner and juggling of whisky and benzedrine. He would not, he thought, want to be Don Biel.

Still, he envied him: to a long, awkward man with bad eyes, living in a world made for people of average height who could see, Don's monkeyish appeal was enviable, and Marvin felt, even against his better judgment, that Don's friendship eased the burden of physical awkwardness he himself had to live with. In Don's company he was gayer, less hemmed in, courtlier to women and less intimidated by the aggressiveness of most other men.

From the bar he glanced out into the room. To his astonishment he found someone looking at him. He blinked, looked away, and looked back again. She was still looking at him. A slim and lovely girl, sitting on a sofa over against the wall on the right, her head turned in order to look his way. One foot was tucked up under her and her wide skirt spread out around her like the widest petals of a nosegay. Her softly curling gold-brown hair was short on the neck but beautifully arranged and drawn back by combs from her vivid face. The well-defined expression in her eyes momentarily confused him: she looked puzzled and somewhat anxious. Then he realized with a start that she was not looking at him at all, but at Don Biel. He blushed to have flattered himself that such an attractive girl would ever have noticed him in the bellowing throng. He nudged Don.

"I think there's someone trying to catch your eye," he said.

Don looked and with a smile waved to the young woman. "That's Helen," said Don.

"Your date?"

"I was on my way to get a drink and got sidetracked when you came in. Come on, I'll introduce you."

They made their way, cautiously balancing their glasses, through the overlapping circles of guests to the sofa. The girl smiled with relief as they came up to her.

"I thought maybe while my back was turned *you'd* been nominated by still another party," she said. The rippling in her voice was like the rustle of silk.

"Helen, this is Marvin Kaufman, my old buddy. Marvin, Helen Maclean."

"Hello," she said.

"Hi, Helen."

"Oh, no." She hesitated. "What was the name? It's *Doctor* Kaufman, isn't it? We've met before."

"Good Lord," said Marvin. "Yes, we have. Now where the hell——"

"Ladd Dorn, I think," Helen suggested. "A patient of yours. I forget where it was."

Don said, "Oh, fine, and *my* date, too."

"Oh, Don," she said gently.

"I'm sorry if——" Marvin began.

"You gotta watch this one," Don told her, nodding toward Marvin. "He's vicious with women. Lousy reputation. Right, Kaufman?"

To the girl Marvin sputtered, blushed violently, "Please don't pay any mind to——"

"I don't." She smiled. "Sit down, Marvin. Don, are you coming or going? Don't let me hold you," she teased. "The place is squirming with models."

"Ouch. Just for that I'll *leave* you with this body-snatcher. Then you'll be sorry."

"I'll bet I won't be at all," she said. Don remained standing. Helen turned to Marvin as he sat down beside her on the sofa. "Don's drinking too much because he knows I'm going to win our election bet," she said, "and he can't bear the loss of all that money."

"Screw you," said Don cheerfully. "My bet with you hardly makes a ripple in the pot I'm cooking. Well, I've been pillaged by my own best buddy, and I know when I'm licked. Hey, darling . . ."

The term of affection was addressed to someone else. Weaving, gingerly handling his glass, Don moved off into the crowd. Marvin and Helen laughed with a friendly pity as he disappeared.

"Oh, what a guy!" Marvin shook his head. "You know him well?"

"Not really." Helen smiled at him. "He's greatly given to dating fashion models, you know. I met him through one of the girls I've worked with at the agency."

"Oh, that's right, that Dorn guy is in some kind of fashion business," Marvin remembered.

"Modeling," said Helen. "Ladd and I are both executive assistants to Jules Fischel, the head of the agency. The title's silly, I guess, but it cost me a terrible hassle; I won a fight and they called me back, and oh, it's warm in the winter." She took a breath and looked at him. "It's nice to meet you again, Marvin. It makes New York seem small and friendly all at once."

Marvin cleared his throat. "I always think New York is small and friendly," he said. "Or at least I don't mind its being anonymous. Seriously, you don't know Don well?"

"What do you mean, seriously?"

"I just wondered, you understand."

Helen shrugged. "This is my second date with him, but I don't think one would call him complicated or difficult to understand in any way."

"Mmm."

His reaction provoked her laughter. "Oh. Oh, no, I'm not —committed; God, how nice to find delicacy in a doctor. Do you remember when we first met you told me about wanting to be a general practitioner? To minister to the whole man?"

"Oh, Jesus," Marvin said, "did I?"

"Yes, you did, and I liked it." Helen beamed at him, and suddenly he wanted to touch her hand.

Soon Marvin was telling her that he also had voted for Truman, and they chortled over their mutual membership in a patently lost cause. They finished their drinks, and Marvin fetched another for each of them. A number of young men stopped by them and engaged Helen briefly in conversation, but Marvin made no move to go. He enjoyed the banter of this stylish, cheerful girl. Don was nowhere to be seen, and Helen herself seemed not to mind that he stayed beside her.

Someone yelled, "Listen! Listen, it's H. V. Kaltenborn!"

And the voice from the radio in its donnish way announced that Truman was over a million votes ahead but would still undoubtedly be beaten. At this analysis Don Biel was heard to crow loudly into the breast of a flaxen-haired girl over by the windows overlooking Fifty-first Street, and the Democrats in the room released a volley of catcalls. The Democrats seemed to Marvin to be in the majority in this particular apartment; he wondered if it were symptomatic.

The returns continued to come into the networks and to be relayed by commentators to the gathering in Doctor Kelly's apartment. Consternation grew as the cumulative results were heard from Ohio and California: the bias fluctuated maddeningly.

"Is it possible he——"

"No, it couldn't really be possible!"

Marvin said, "Helen, I think maybe our boy is actually going to do it. . . ."

In another hour those in the apartment who were backing Truman to win began to feel more confident of victory, and Don Biel frantically began to hedge his bets. When he could find no takers, he drank more quickly, and soon after midnight he was moaning, to anyone who would listen, about the idiocy of placing faith in the intelligence of the American public.

"The man's a notorious Barnum!" he roared to those around him. "Here we are the richest, strongest, goddamnedest country on earth, and we're hiring a carnival tout to lead us? Bull-shit! Screw the whole lot of you boobs!" Marvin suspected the loss of his bets affected Don more deeply than the betrayal of his cause by the populace.

He held a match for Helen's cigarette.

"I like Truman," said Helen. "And I don't give a damn about the opinion of people who're so sure they're better than he is. Whatever happens tonight, I hope people remember it was under Truman those eleven Communist bigwigs got indicted. What's the name of that act they were indicted under?"

"The Smith Act."

"Yes, that's it—not that I know anything about it yet. I didn't start thinking about the election and all the issues in it till I heard so many people being snide about Truman because he had ambition enough to run a haberdashery. Did *you* ever run a store?"

"No, I haven't," said Marvin, straight-faced.

"My father runs a hardware store in Charter Oak, so I'm not entirely without knowledge of the field. Maybe that's why I'm inclined toward Truman. Besides, what other President has had to contend with this kind of election? God, *four* parties running."

"Oh, that's happened before." Marvin shrugged.

"What?" Helen turned back to him. "You're kidding me. Really? When did it?'

"Well, to begin with, they didn't use to have even conventions. In eighteen hundred twenty-four, I think it was, Tennessee put up Jackson and Kentucky put up Clay, but the Congressional caucus—the old system—nominated William Crawford. Then Massachusetts nominated John Quincy Adams. Can you imagine what a mess it was?"

"But that must've been only once. When the country was young and mixed up and——"

"Hell, no. Do you know that later on the Democrats had a convention where they couldn't agree enough to pick a candidate?"

"Marvin, that can't be true. Why——"

"But it is," he asserted. "The whole damn thing broke up. The Southern Democrats—sound familiar?—nominated one guy, the Northerners nominated Stephen Douglas——"

"Little Giant!"

"Right. And a whole other group nominated John Bell. Guess who won!"

"I can't!"

"Abraham Lincoln!"

"Oh, I'm so glad!"

They laughed together, without reserve, affectionately.

Don Biel stumbled up to them, a new drink splashing over his hand, his boyish face flushed with injured conviction.

"The bastards won't get away with it!" he cried.

"Don, listen to the returns . . ." Marvin palliated.

"It doesn't mean a goddamned thing. You know why? Even

if Truman splits his gut, he won't get a majority of electoral votes."

"Will Dewey?"

"Hell, maybe not; but Truman won't!"

Helen asked Marvin, "What would happen then?"

"The election would have to go to the House of Representatives."

"Great God, you know all *about* history," said Helen.

Don Biel moved off again into the shifting mass of the other guests, and Marvin and Helen leaned back with their cigarettes and drinks. They talked together spontaneously now, and Marvin felt no tug of shyness holding him back. Wise to the instability of comradeships initiated in the atmosphere of of Manhattan drinking parties, they kept the subjects of their conversation inconsequential, but beneath the even flow of questions and answers and opinions and shared amusements ran a companion stream, subtly but strongly bearing them along, carrying Marvin's interest in the girl into unfamiliar depths and twisting ways. He tried to remind himself she was Don's date, but already her attractiveness had left that point behind as a pale consideration. Marvin knew there was no girl Don had ever met that he really cared about as much as he cared about, say, his sports car or the finer pieces of his wardrobe; they were a necessary adjunct to his sex life, no more. This girl, Marvin thought, was in no such position with Don, though there was no telling what plans Don might have. Marvin felt without knowing why that she never would be, there was too much fiber to her, too much good sense and too grave a tone of spirit.

Someone near the radio, sweating, was shouting his amazement. "Truman's leading, he is honest-to-God leading——"

"I didn't know there were so many people as bright as I am——"

"Truman's got to win now. Even if he loses California or Texas or Illinois, the wonderful little bastard's still going to win!"

And in a corner the chorus was breaking out:

"Oh, I'm just wild about Harry,
And Harry's wild about me!"

Don Biel allowed himself to get spitefully, blindly drunk.

When late into the morning the astounding knowledge that Truman had indeed been elected could no longer be blinked away, he was too far gone to care.

Marvin and Helen toasted their victory with a final drink and went to find Don to take Helen home. He was in the bedroom, sprawled across a mound of anonymous topcoats, unconscious, beyond recall. Marvin saw his host for the first time when he came up to assure them he would see about Don if Marvin would escort Helen. Helping her on with her coat, Marvin led her out to the elevator.

On the cold and windy walk to Helen's flat on Forty-sixth Street, they happily congratulated one another over again on the outcome of the election. They wondered aloud what the peppery little man would do with this gigantic, dynamic, and unpredictable country in the next four years. They were both taken aback when they found they had reached the door of Helen's apartment building. The walk seemed to have taken only a moment.

"May I see you again?" Marvin asked.

"Of course, Marvin. I'd love to."

"Tomorrow?"

Helen pursed her lips. "Not so good for tomorrow. I'll be worn out from tonight, for one thing. . . ."

"Suppose I call you at your office tomorrow or the next day, and see what night would be good for dinner."

"Isn't it kind of tricky for you with dates—I mean, emergency calls coming up and such?"

"Sometimes it is."

She smiled and gave him her hand. "I'll be prepared for it so you won't feel bad if something does pop up at the last minute. Thanks for bringing me home."

"Oh, my God!" Marvin gaped. "I didn't think: I should've gotten you a taxicab, this cold——"

Helen laughed gently at his confusion. "Believe it or not, I prefer walking. Especially in New York. Especially in the cold. Good night, Marvin. Thank you again."

She turned and disappeared into the lower corridor of the old building.

"It's almost dawn," said Margaret.

Steve looked up from the manuscript spread out haphazardly on the desk.

"God, I'm sorry to have gotten so involved with this. You shouldn't have waited up."

"I wanted to." Margaret smiled.

She was half-reclined on the couch by the fireplace, in which only embers burned now.

The brownstone building they lived in had been converted into four sprawling, comfortable apartments that commanded high rents in return for a good address and quiet, pleasant, in some cases theatrically or literarily prominent, neighbors. The apartment had been found for them by a connection of Judge Cowan's who was familiar with New York real estate. Steve's and Margaret's apartment was on the second floor of the building.

"I'll stop now," Steve said, capping his fountain pen and standing up. He went over to Margaret, bent to kiss her, and then let himself drop down to the floor beside her. She stroked the back of his neck.

"How's the story going?" she asked.

"It's not going at all at the moment. I keep getting stuck on Sinde's accent."

"Is it about Sinde?"

"Somewhat. She told me about some of the crazy things that happened to her when she first came here from India to work for the U.N. She said I could use them if I wanted to."

"What's the accent problem?"

"I can't figure out a way to catch that British precision she speaks with, except to say so baldly."

"Is it really that important to the story?"

Steve sighed. "I guess not. Maybe I'm just fooling myself with it."

"Poor thing, you're tired out, that's all," said Margaret.

He turned to look at her, and they were silent. He refreshed himself in her quiet sleepy smile, and reaching out, lay his hand on the soft, pitifully vulnerable roundness of her hip. Her vulnerability, her softness, it was true of every part of her, permeated her thighs and her breasts as completely as it did her soul, and Steve wondered at the fact that she was unaware of it. The pervasiveness of her femininity strengthened his instinct to protectiveness.

"I shouldn't have kept you up all this while," he said. "It's not good for you. I'm sorry."

"Oh, Steve, I've sat up till dawn half the nights of my life.

I'm used to it." She pushed herself up, yawning. "But the dawn's early light does send me scurrying. Are you coming to bed now?"

Steve got to his feet, and taking her hands, drew her up into his embrace. He kissed her again.

"It's funny you should be writing about Sinde," Margaret said. "So different from stories about Houston. All that Indian musk and mystery——"

"I've used up Houston. For the time being, anyway," said Steve.

"Sinde's so reeking of glamor. That'll be good for your story; you ought to sell it at the first crack." She pressed her cheek against his shoulder briefly. "Come to bed. I promised to go antique-hunting with Sinde tomorrow afternoon. If I don't have the advantage of being able to wear a sari and sandals, I have at least to look clear-eyed."

"I love you," Steve whispered.

She looked up at him and smiled. "You don't feel trapped, being married?"

"Hell, no. Do you?"

"Not really. Sometimes I think that—oh, no, it's too late at night. I love you insanely. Now let's get to bed before you have to carry me there."

Taking her hand, Steve led her to their bedroom, where the light of dawn already brushed the windows overlooking the street.

Marvin called Helen the next day at the agency, and over the phone her voice was as friendly, he was relieved to hear, as her manner had been the night before. They arranged to dine together on Friday.

At seven o'clock Marvin arrived at the flat. Helen led him down the long stemlike hall to the clover leaf of her rooms. Small as the rooms were, Helen had obviously spent a healthy portion of her income and considerable ingenuity in decorating them. The general effect was sleekly modern, both sophisticated and comfortable. Marvin was surprised at the size of Helen's book collection. There were two low bookcases in the living room, and an entire wall of the small study next to it was lined with crowded bookshelves.

"There's a pitcher of Martinis," Helen said, indicating the

coffee table that stood under the room's only window. "Would you mind pouring while I finish getting ready?"

She left the room but was back by the time the cocktails had been poured. Marvin was afraid he might be flattering himself, but he had distinctly the sensation that she had taken more than the usual amount of trouble with her dressing. Her expressive face was carefully made up, and her eyes were additionally brilliant with whatever kind of cosmetic she had used. Her dress was strikingly effective and looked expensive to Marvin's untrained eye. He conceded to himself it was a subject about which he knew nothing.

"This is a wonderful place," Marvin said as Helen gestured to him to sit down. "Do you sublet?"

"No, it's mine." Helen smiled.

"I thought—all the books——"

"They're mine, too," she said.

"Do you have time to do anything *but* read?"

"Oh, yes. I read a lot, but not that much."

"Novels?"

"Not very much. I study things—it's my hobby."

Marvin raised his eyebrows. "Really? What kind of things?"

"Whatever preoccupies me at the moment. History, anthropology—right now it's comparative religions."

"You impress the bejesus out of me," Marvin said. "Is this some kind of hangover from college?"

Helen sipped her cocktail. "I didn't go to college. No, when I first left home and went to live in Chicago, I wanted to learn everything there was to learn. I wanted to make myself fit to meet what I thought were the brainy elite of the world. Oh, don't laugh, I had dozens of ideas like that. Then time did its work, and I found I was interested in the things I studied for their own sake."

"Did you ever get to meet the brainy elite?"

Helen laughed. "I've gotten too embroiled in earning a living. And I've found plenty enough brains among the friends I've made in New York. Young career people like myself. Like you."

"I wish I could say *I* had." Marvin shook his head.

Concern flooded at once into her eyes. "You haven't? God, how could you help it in New York?"

"Oh, I know a few bright people from medical school.

Kelly, for instance. And Don, in spite of his monkeyshines, is as bright as they make them. But that's about the limit. The only really intelligent girls I seem to meet are all muscular types from the Village. Till now."

He winced inwardly at the blunt sound of the compliment, but was reassured when Helen smiled at him. She did not speak, but looked at him with new interest, as though her curiosity were prompting her to a more careful appraisal. He smiled back at her. No, he thought, this was not the same kind of girl he had known. He had slept with many women. With a handful of them he had had affairs lasting several months; he had been genuinely fond of them as well as sexually drawn to them, but none of them had tapped that deeper spring of regard, had challenged his emotional self-sufficiency as this intelligent, good-looking young woman was doing.

They had a leisurely, talkative dinner in a shabby, very expensive restaurant on a crumbling West Side street. Marvin had thought he would take her dancing someplace later, but when the time came, they were too involved in their conversation to disrupt it. They had a drink at Sardi's and another at the Blue Angel. Their conversation followed no pattern, but probed half a dozen of their interests, revealing as it did so salient features of their characters, each to the other. Marvin was repeatedly brought up short by unexpected comments of Helen's. She was forthright; she seemed never to accept a common point of view without an exhaustive dissecting of it; she showed in her opinions both passion and originality. Moreover, she was nearer to being beautiful, he discovered, than any girl he had ever befriended. He could not suppress the sensual fantasy in which, as her lover, there was delivered over to him her slim, supple body, her soft and golden-glowing hair, the benignity of her expressive face. Twice he found himself smiling tenderly at her when the conversation had long since died. At other moments he talked rapidly to fend off the attacks of sexual ardor Helen's nearness provoked in him.

It was one o'clock when he brought her home. At the door of her apartment, Helen said, "I haven't had so much fun since I came to New York. Thank you, Marvin."

"When can we do it again?"

"Any time. But next time I'll cook the dinner. I want you

to tell me all about medicine, and I can't concentrate with Musak going on."

"It's a deal," said Marvin.

He kissed her. He did not draw her to him or take her into his arms, but bent down to her lips in an unself-conscious and tender salute. When he lifted his head, Helen smiled, but said nothing.

"I don't want to go home," he confessed.

"Would you like to come in for a nightcap? I have some rye."

"It's after one. Maybe I better hadn't."

But he knew the hour had nothing to do with it. By the familiar pattern he would have accepted her invitation. They would have had another drink, and he would have made love to her. By three o'clock they would have been in bed together: it had happened that way often enough before. He knew he would not make it happen this time. He told her good night and left.

On Second Avenue he hailed a taxi. He settled deep into the back seat for the ride uptown, but he did not relax. Why had he behaved so unaccountably? Years before he had been shy of women, clumsy, and confused by the power of the sexual attraction they held for him. But that had been long ago. He was still often shy, but that did not prevent his following the ritual that almost invariably provided himself with a sexual outlet and the girl with a tender and solicitous, if temporary, protector. What was there about Helen Maclean that made him behave in such an unlikely way? Fear that she would turn him down? That was always a possibility. He did not have good looks to offer, and Helen was as beautiful as she was bright; she might well have long ago become bored by hot-breathing males trying to seduce her. But that was not the answer. He wanted to lay her, he ached with the physical frustration he had brought upon himself; but as violent as was his desire was the cautioning command of his instinct: not yet. Not yet: there was more he wanted of this girl. More than the others had given him, more than he had ever wanted any of them to give. What was it he wanted of her? To be his wife? In the darkness of the taxi he twisted uncomfortably. For God's sake, he'd only met the girl a few days before. Well, once almost a year ago, but that hadn't counted. They had had only one evening together, properly speaking. It was damned foolishness even thinking of the subject of marriage under the circumstances. Helen, he suspected, would laugh outright if she knew such a consideration had cropped up in his mind. Yet the subject *had* occurred to him. What had it to do with sleeping with Helen? Even supposing they might fall seriously in love, was that any deterrent to their having sex together now? Why the hell should it be? Because—his mind groped—because when you sleep with a wife, it is a graver pleasure, a sacramental delight, a symbol with a significance unknown in a friendly roll in the hay. He sat upright suddenly. This sign of conservatism in his own thinking shocked him. Had all his education, all his rationalism, all his dislike of superstition come to nothing? When the issue grew serious, was he going to revert to creeds even his parents had rejected? He shook his head, mystified. Apparently he was.

Helen cooked a dinner the complexities of which threatened to undo all her labor. Revolted by herself and her too obvious bid for Marvin's approval, she managed nevertheless to get it on the table in approximately the state it should have been. Marvin had brought wine, and their sparkling glasses further enhanced the picture Helen had strived to create. For no reason they knew, their mood was a soberer one than had been the case on their first evening together. Marvin talked about his life as a general practitioner and told her his most intimate feelings about that kind of practice as opposed to the more popular and more remunerative business of specialization—not that this represented very serious financial sacrifice for him. As a matter of fact, in general practice he was doing better than he had expected.

Helen was flattered by the seeming ease with which he confided in her. From time to time she interjected a comment or a question, but for the greater part of the evening she listened with attention to the points he was making, but also noting with pleasure that he had an unaffectedly beautiful voice and, when once or twice he took off his distorting glasses, exquisitely shaped eyes with a soft, almost caressing gaze. Before he left, Helen had invited him back to dinner on Saturday night.

Marvin was now almost continually in her thoughts. His awkwardness, his gentleness, his almost ludicrous excitement when she made clear she was enjoying the things he had thought up for them to do their first evening out together, the strength in his wide, sinewy hands: all these made up a recurring reverie. At the office she time and again lost the sense of a letter or memorandum she was dictating when Marvin's image intervened between herself and the problems of business. Jules Fischel found her absent-minded in their conferences and wryly suggested she take a few weeks' vacation. Ladd Dorn said, "I know the feeling, doll. Only too well. Absolutely the only thing to do is pack a bag and go to France."

In her subsequent meetings with Marvin Helen managed to hide her feelings, except in her acceptable efforts to please him as a companion. Half a dozen times she expected him to try to seduce her, but he never did. Still, when he kissed her now, it was warmly and lingeringly, with no pretense at chasteness. She could not tell herself he found her unattractive. They dined together, they went dancing, they went to the theater. One Sunday Marvin drove her out to the country. It was patent he delighted in her company, but when once their conversation touched on love, Marvin did not pursue the subject, and Helen allowed it to die. She could not understand what was going on in his head and felt deeply troubled when she remembered her own maxim, the foolish and defensive motto that had led her into the mire of her relationship with Sprague Burrell: *men don't want to marry you.* Knowing as little about him as she did, knowing nothing of him as a lover, she longed for him to want her enough to win her. The work at the office began to bore her painfully, and with longing she dreamed of what life as Marvin's wife would be like—tending his house, refreshing him in his weariness, raising the children who, to Marvin, would be as essential an element of life as labor or affection. Little Jewish children, she thought, and the thought made her smile: her own little Jewish children.

On the first Thursday night in December they went to see *Life With Mother* and sought out each other's hands in the darkness of the theater. At the first intermission Marvin said regretfully, "Those seats aren't the best in the house, I'm afraid."

"They're the best in the world," Helen said. "Isn't she lovely? She absolutely shimmers."

"Yes, you do."

"Monkey," said Helen. "I meant Dorothy Stickney. Oh, how I envy her that fragile air. What a lovely woman."

"Too bad I missed the performance." Marvin smiled. "But I couldn't take my eye off *yours*. Are you always so excited when you watch a play?"

"A good one, yes," Helen answered. "I can't help it."

"Then I was right. You were the one shimmering. I could have read my program by the light in your face."

"Didn't you pay any attention at all to the play? And I thought your grandfather was such a dedicated theater man."

"He was a fine actor, that's true," said Marvin, "and I guess maybe my sister Zeeda's pretty good when she takes the trouble to do a part; but the rest of the Kaufmans—we've grown away from the theater, except as audience. And if I'm a poor audience, you have to shoulder the blame."

After the play they went to Sardi's for a drink. The restaurant was noisy with the after-theater crowd, but Helen, though no celebrity, was known to the staff by her frequent appearances there with business people and the young men who had taken her out in the past. It was suggested to them that they have a drink at the bar until a good table downstairs was available. Stuttering with diffidence, as though Helen might take offense, Marvin said, "No, we'd—we'd like a sort of side table, off somewhere, please. Not a good table the way you mean. If you know what I mean."

They were led to a table obscurely situated in the rear of the room. Here, Helen observed, smiling to herself, still puzzled by Marvin's request, they would certainly be undistracted by the arrival and departure of celebrated theatrical faces. Helen was grateful for that when, after their drinks had been put before them and they had lit cigarettes, Marvin faced her gravely.

At first he said nothing. Helen smiled in mock anxiety. "What's the matter, Marvin, do I have something on my face?"

"No." He licked his lips. "I don't know why I worry about your not understanding something when you're the most understanding woman I've ever met."

"If I don't understand the first time, you can tell it to me over again."

Marvin studied her a moment, then looked away. "This is no place for it, but the longer I put it off, the greater beating my coronaries are going to take. I don't want to inflict a mess on you, but if I'm ever going to get you to marry me, I'll have to."

Helen felt her throat go suddenly dry, and the palms of her hands grew damp.

Marvin went on, "I want you to marry me, Helen. I think you're happy when you're with me, and I think you'd be happier still as my wife."

Helen's voice was small when she answered, "I think so, too, Marvin."

"The mess is this: when I get married, I want to do so with my parents' approval."

"Your parents?" She found it difficult to concentrate on the details of what he was saying. A wild caroling inside her made the actual words he was using seem suddenly remote.

"Damn it, I know how unreasonable it sounds in this day and age, but—I suspect other families aren't as closely tied up together as Jewish families are. My father has given his life to make mine, Helen, and I've got a duty to consider his feelings. Even his prejudices."

"I think it's nice you're a dutiful son." Helen smiled. "It's just like you."

"My father's always wanted me to marry a Jewish girl," he plunged on. "Someone who could—in his words—understand me. My mother is a complete jerk on the subject. She doesn't care if the girl I marry is Jew or Gentile, so long as her social position is supposed to be better than mine. Not too much better, you understand, just enough to make Momma think things are looking up."

Helen chuckled. "Go on, Marvin," she said. "I'm not horrified."

Suddenly he took her hand, and he was serious again. "I want you to meet them, Helen. I'm sure when they've met you and seen how much I love you, they'll agree with me nobody else could possibly be a more desirable daughter-in-law for them. It's a hell of an ordeal to ask you to go through——"

"I don't think so. I'd *like* meeting them."

"Helen, you don't know how my mother can——"

"Maybe I'll be able to bring her around. We have to give it a chance, anyway."

"It's a screwy damned way to propose to a girl," Marvin

muttered. "But will you marry me, if everything works out all right?"

She hesitated only to look at him, to devour with her eyes his stammering, loving embarrassment. For a moment neither of them spoke. They held each other's gaze. They tried to breathe steadily. When Helen felt tears brimming in her eyes, she leaned forward abruptly and kissed him.

Helen's public kiss brought a furious blush to his face, and he bent his head against the imagined staring of the other patrons. He swallowed.

"Come on, let's get the hell out of here."

"All right, darling," Helen said.

On their way out Helen wanted to notice nothing until they were someplace where Marvin could hold her and tell her how much he loved her; and Marvin in his red-faced panic, now that at last he had proposed, was incapable of looking another human being in the eye. Had they looked in on the crowd at the little partitioned-off bar as they left, they might have seen Warren Taggert, Mike Cowan, and Wynn Bargmeister standing there.

Warren had already had a number of brandies, and in his roistering humor was starting in on another. On either side of him the two more cautious young men stood stiff with anger and embarrassment.

"Screw it, I've been on my best behavior for two days, haven't I?" Warren was demanding of them.

Between taut-drawn lips Mike whispered, "Keep your voice down please."

"I tell you it's our last night in New York, and *I* want to see the bars on the goddamned Bird Circuit."

Wynn interjected, "Listen, Warren. That's all very well in New Orleans. New Orleans is a million miles away."

"You're not in Washington now . . ." he retorted.

"We might just as well be." Mike was firm. "Oh, Christ, can't anyone make you understand?"

With Wynn he exchanged a look of real worry, and with Warren tried a conclusive note. "You've had too much to drink, Warren, that's all. You ought to go back to the hotel and go to bed."

"Bed. Ha. With what?"

"*Will* you keep your voice down."

"I'm going to the Bird Circuit," Warren answered with finality. "You two queens can do what you like."

Wynn temporized. "I don't see why you want to go to places like that anyway, Warren. The people there are nothing but trash."

"Because it's fun," Warren declared. "I've lived with polite people all my life, and it was never anything but a pain in the ass. I don't see one grain of sense in my acting like a stuffed shirt now. Or in you two doing it either."

In another place their conversaton might have attracted attention, but the other people in Sardi's bar seemed to be more interested in what they themselves were saying. In the clamor, Warren's assertions were not widely overheard, nor did they elicit any signal of astonishment from those close enough to hear.

Warren downed the remainder of his brandy. "Polite society," he grumbled. "I know, I know. The state Department. Clean noses for everybody, if you don't mind. My parents're the epitome of polite society, and I loathe them. Then what do I do? I take up with you. Big change that was. Why the hell doesn't the State Department join the Junior League?" His voice threatened to break, and he frowned at his empty glass.

"You don't know what you're saying, you poor sap."

"Do you remember Mardi Gras, Mike? The Quatre Chevaux? A gay bar was the first place you ever took me. Come on, the Bird Circuit will be hilarious. At least the faggots there won't mind admitting that's what they are. Come with me, Mike——"

"No."

Warren stepped back.

Without a word he put his empty glass down on the bar and, turning pushed off into the crowd jamming the space between the bar and the door to the street. Hurriedly Mike and Wynn downed their drinks and went after him. They caught up with him on the sidewalk as all three were struggling into their topcoats.

"Warren, honestly," Mike said. "Let me take you to the hotel."

"I'm doing the Bird Circuit if it kills me," said Warren.

They argued all the way across Times Square. Warren was sober enough to know what he was saying and drunk enough to say what he felt. For eight months he had put up with Mike's strictures. No sooner had the door of the gay life been thrown open to him than Mike had slammed it shut again, except for the narrow handful of fellow sufferers they knew in Washington. It had taken half as many months for Warren in his inexperience to realize what had happened: he was no more a free agent than he had been before. He was as shackled by Mike's fear of public disapproval as he had been by his parents' aspirations for him or his own surreptitious throttling of desire.

In the middle of the block beyond Times Square, Mike stopped. "Wait for us at the next corner, will you, Wynn?" he asked. "I want to talk to Warren alone for a moment."

"All right," Wynn said, and went on ahead.

Warren was standing there waiting, not looking at him, his fists plunged deep into the pockets of his topcoat.

"Warren," he said. "Take my advice and come back to the hotel with me. The gay bars don't have anything to offer you but sordid stuff. I'm trying to be patient about it, because I'm responsible for bringing you out and because you're a wonderful guy, but when are you going to learn there's a penalty for flaunting your sex tastes before the whole damned world?"

"Why shouldn't I flaunt them?" Warren demanded. "I don't have *you* any more, do I? I guess I was indiscreet just once too often for your goddamned standards, but if I don't have you——"

"You would, if you'd play it my way. Haven't I told you a hundred times——"

"You're kidding yourself, Mike."

Warren turned and walked on, Mike following, and in a moment they had caught up with Wynn. None spoke as they continued eastward toward the Shelton Hotel.

It was not the first time Warren had chafed beneath the restrictions his friendship with Mike put upon him, and now again he felt it was high time he bolted. Nothing about Washington attracted him, and living there, he was forced to spend too much of the time alone. Mike was continually obliged to show up at places Warren found intolerably boring —political-social gatherings of his father's; all the hullabaloo with his sister Margaret's wedding last summer—and on the other hand he was not left free to seek out friends of his own: there again a son of Judge Ellis Cowan was in a too vulnerable position. Warren was fed to the teeth with the situation, and the waning of his sexual relationship with Mike completed his dissatisfaction. In Mike he had found an attraction for all the romantic urges, the sentiment and capacity for concern he was capable of. He loved Mike, or rather he wanted desperately for his feeling to grow into love as love should grow through years of shared happiness and trouble. But where was the solution to the secret, unmentioned, tormenting problems they faced? He had been drawn to Mike physically with a relentless and taunting hunger, and at first Mike had responded. But it was changed now; Mike despised the very appetite that had drawn them together in the first place. Despised him because he was the very thing he had to be in order to be Mike's lover: a queer. What years of shared experience could ever bring their linking to the maturity of love? No laws held them together, no child could ever mirror for them the nonexistent sweetness of their hopeless mating. No two homosexuals in the world, he was convinced, could buck the conspiracy between the organized world and their own mangled natures.

To the silent pair as they waited on the Park Avenue island for a break in the uptown flow of traffic, Wynn Bargmeister said, "Is a friend allowed a word?"

Mike shrugged. Warren said nothing.

The young man went on, "Warren, you're having fits because Mike's hemmed in by having friends in State and having the father he has as well. If you two want to stay married——"

"Do you know what I think?" Warren cried. "I think the whole gay-marriage idea is shit."

He felt Mike tense. Wynn snorted. "I've known dozens of cases; it takes wisdom and courage——"

"It takes twenty-four hours a day of pretending bat-crap," Warren asserted, and turned then to Mike. "You know why, Mike? I've been thinking about it day and night and trying to find a rebuttal for it and I can't. Because we're queer, and down inside ourselves we despise ourselves for it. No, no, not because it's morally wrong, or morally anything, but because it's an imperfect way, an injured way to be."

"Oh, now, come on . . ." Wynn began behind him.

"Listen!" Warren went on to Mike. "We sleep together, and

you know then I'm not a real man, but crippled the same way you are. It's different, isn't it, than when we first got together? Then I *looked* like a male, and you weren't sure I wasn't. Now it's different. For both of us. Because neither of us wants another queer, we both of us want the same thing, the impossible: an honest-to-God man to love us. And that is the impossible."

He was shuddering with the pain of the unwelcome understanding. A couple scurrying against the cold wind passed and hurried on; the uptown traffic had lessened.

Mike said, "Wynn, go on to the hotel, we'll be right behind you, but we want to talk."

"Sure, Mike." And hesitating on the curb until another car had passed, Wynn Bargmeister went on across the street.

Mike turned to him. "Two sensible guys can learn to share their loneliness," he declared, his eyes burning like those of a fanatic who has nothing but faith to hold to.

Warren shook his head. "And be content with it? No, Mike," he said. "Never if it's me involved. We're lost to one another, Mike. Because that's the most basic fact about us, and anybody who says different is a fool. I'm fond of you, Mike. I can say I love you because my idea of what love is has kind of got watered down recently. But I'm not happy the way things are, because there's nothing between us strong enough or meaningful enough to make me give up my needs for yours."

Mike snapped, "I don't even know what needs you *have!*"

Warren grabbed the lapels of his topcoat, not in violence but insistence, his jaw trembling.

"I've got the right to be what I am and not pretend to other people that it isn't true. In that respect at least I'm like every other fairy in the Bird Circuit bars, and that's where I'm going. For the last time, are you coming with me?"

Mike held fire an instant. "No," he said.

"Okay." Warren released him.

They crossed the street, went on to Lexington Avenue, and turned up Lexington toward the Shelton. On the bright avenue, with its garish restaurants and hotels, were pub crawlers and theatergoers hurrying home. Warren did not see Wynn Bargmeister anywhere ahead. Neither he nor Mike spoke. A few feet before the entrance to the hotel Mike stopped, stepping back from the sidewalk's traffic to the wall of the building. Warren tarried before him questioningly.

"I'm going back to Washington tomorrow," Mike said.

"Yes."

"Are you coming back?"

Warren could not look at him. A dozen conflicting emotions contorted his heart. He knew that the words had to be said, but he could not sound them. His lips moved convulsively, and he shook his head.

"You're sure about that?" Mike asked.

"Yes. I hate it, Mike. But hell, it's been coming."

Mike nodded. Only in that moment did Warren realize how thoroughly he had finished it. He looked at Mike and saw the tiredness in the way he held his head, the set of his shoulders. Warren's voice made a searching sound before the words came. "Mike, I'll miss you very much."

"Not after a while."

"Maybe—maybe sometime we can get together someplace like New Orleans. Where the State Department isn't breathing down your neck quite so much. It's funny to think you don't even work for them."

"What about the hotel room?"

"Yah," said Warren. "We'd better leave it in my name. I'll need it for a few days, anyway. I guess I'll see about a room someplace, and then come down to Washington to clear things away there."

"Then," said Mike, "you won't be back tonight."

"Maybe later." Warren shrugged uneasily. "I don't know. Go on, you'd better get to sleep." Tears were struggling to reach his eyes again, and he fought them back. "You'll be freezing to death."

Mike put out his hand, and Warren took it. Mike said, "Please come back later tonight, or tomorrow before we leave, so I can tell you good-by again."

"I will." Gently he pulled his hand back. "Okay, Mike. Good night."

He turned and walked away.

He did not see the people he passed. He kept his head bent down, his eyes swaying from the little soiled mounds of snow in crevices here and there to the eddies of steam he came upon. He had been battling back his most candid thoughts for months, but now as he walked away from the situation he'd caught himself in, as he walked away from Mike, standing rigid-faced and sad outside the hotel, and did not look back to him, they poured up into his head, bouncing, inspired, on the brandy fumes. He could not find it in himself to be ashamed of being a homosexual, not as one understood shame in other cases. And it wasn't that he was callous in his morality, coated over with vice. He wouldn't be ashamed of what he was, he refused to be: he hadn't chosen it for himself, had he? He had nothing to be ashamed of. He was trustworthy and he thought he was honest. As far as he knew, he'd never been cruel to anyone knowingly. Why should he be ashamed that the hunger of his body was for men and not women, for whatever deep-buried and tortuously-related reasons? In his confusion and torment he had let his family's money make his life easier from time to time; that wasn't admirable, but it wasn't depraved, either, was it? Why should he be ashamed that he longed to be held by someone with the strength and confidence and power he had never owned, the virile man with the arms that could buoy him up, whom he in turn could repay with a faithful comforting, a steadfastness and loyalty not even very many women could offer a man? He would not be ashamed and try to justify his hunger in such a relationship as he had had with Mike, imitating respectability, aping monogamy. He would not be ashamed.

But it was bull-shit pretending that the discovery of such a hunger in yourself was anything but a catastrophe. If you were queer, you could consider yourself royally gypped of the very satisfaction your loused-up nature demanded. No man could have anything to do with you and still be your idea, or anybody else's idea, of a man; you were left to pick and choose among others like yourself, as he and Mike had chosen one another in haste, before reason could light up their self-deception, and another like yourself was the very thing you didn't want. You were caught, weren't you?—on the flying horses in a children's park. "All right!" he cried, almost aloud. If the very essence of you put aside any chance you had at a lasting happiness, you could have to the full whatever satisfaction your body with its incompleteness offered you: you could have a ball—and by Christ, he swore, he was going to.

He turned the corner and found the bar he was looking

for. A weak spotlight pointed up the dark canopy. He went up to it and stopped before the black-painted door. He knew what he was going to do. He was going to go in, he was going to order a drink, he was going to make a pass at the first guy he liked the looks of. He was going to go home with him. He was not going to bother about him again. He was going to come back the next night, to this bar or another, and the night after that, and he would feel under no compulsion to seek out with his being the same body twice.

Beyond the canopy and the heavy black door was the darkness of the barroom, darker than the night of the street outside. He stopped as the door closed behind him, momentarily taken aback by the scene. There was hardly space in which to advance from the door: laughing, chattering young men, a few somber, sulking ones, crowded between the bar and the wall four or five feet opposite it. There was illumination behind the bar, but little discernible elsewhere, and the pall of cigarette smoke was impenetrable. Warren was aware that a few nearest the door had stopped their talking and turned to stare at him, and he flushed when he heard a voice mumble, "Hmm, the upper classes."

He avoided their eyes. What had brought out that kind of remark? He could see at a glance there were other crew-cut red-blooded-looking types in the place, and in the darkness it was damned sure no one could tell that the clothes he wore were especially expensive. A new face, he concluded; it was at a premium in a place like this one. He didn't think it would last. A week or two in New York, enough touring of the Bird Circuit places, they'd consider him indistinguishable from themselves. And they'd be right, wouldn't they?

With wordless sounds of casual apology he made his way through to the bar. A figure moved aside to make room for him, and to the bartender he said, "Scotch on the rocks."

The stranger beside him had put his elbows on the edge of the bar. Standing a half-step back, Warren surreptituously glanced at him. An older guy, perhaps forty, not good-looking, but not effeminate. Warren knew the stranger was aware of the scrutiny. He was looking vaguely into the middle distance, but his gaze was turned slightly so that he could see out of the corner of his eye. He would not be likely, thought Warren, to get into a huff if a pass were made at him. Warren took his pack of cigarettes out of the inside pocket of his jacket, pulling a cigarette from it, and turned to the stranger, smiling with wry directness.

"Got a match?" he asked.

•

26

AT THREE O'CLOCK THE NEXT AFTERNOON Steve Williams was sitting in Rachel Pemberton's office, in the handsome and comfortable chair that kept visitors on a lower level than Rachel's own and made it necessary for them to look up to her. Steve had been reading an editor's report rejecting two of his latest short stories. Having read it, he sighed and put the two typewritten pages back on Rachel's desk. He sat back in the chair.

"I'm sorry, Steve," Rachel said. "This is the third editor to send them back, and I'm afraid I agree with their judgment."

"I do, too." Steve shrugged. "The material is too new to me, I guess. But it's valid material, and it's fresh. I'm sorry I wasted your time on these two scripts before I'd digested it."

Rachel waved a hand. "It's an interesting new lode for you, certainly far different from the stories you wrote about Houston. Did you know anyone from India before you moved to New York?"

"No. I've only met a handful of them, people connected with the United Nations."

"And you find them attractive?"

"It's a quietude of spirit they have," Steve thought aloud. "I wish I knew where they find it. I've read something about their religions—not very much. It's very attractive. On San Angelo Street there used to be old Mrs. Tooley who believed in something called Soul-Wholeness. I think of her often, talking to Indian friends about religion."

"Do you find their strangeness glamorous? The stories indicate you do."

Steve frowned. "One of the things wrong with the damned stories, probably. No, once you get used to the saris and the very correct accents, glamor isn't what they have. The glamor exists only in the extraordinary situation of their being dropped down into the American milieu. The contrast is something I just can't leave alone. It's touching, and sometimes it's funny. Don't you think so?"

"Yes, I can see," Rachel said. "That feeling comes through in these stories." In her approach to a new subject she folded her hands together on the top of her desk. "Do you want to go on mining this material, or do you think you'll be going back to some of the things the editors seem to want from you?"

Steve sighed again. "I don't know. I'm—in kind of an uncertain position at the moment."

The sweetness of her smile appeared. "You're busy learning about marriage, too." Steve wished she had not been so quick to point it out. "that's always work if you want to do a good job of it," Rachel went on. "And after all, there's no need to push yourself right now. How much do you have in the bank at the moment?"

"Three or four thousand, thanks to the stories about San Angelo Street—cut into by payments on bank loans. The furniture, all the rest of it. I didn't think about saving up much—we were married pretty quickly."

"But hell, Steve, that's not bad at all. Are you worried about money?"

"My—" He stopped himself. He could not let himself discuss it with anyone. He shrugged. "I should be thinking about the future," he said.

"Look, let *me* worry about your future," Rachel said, "*you* worry about your art. The money you have should last at least a year, a good deal more for someone who can cope with a budget."

"Yes, it should."

Rachel thought for a moment, her lips pursed primly, then consulted a packet of file cards before her. "You may realize some additional income from subsidiary rights. There's a producer in Hollywood still interested in the film rights to that first story we sold to *The New Yorker,* even though he hasn't been able to fit it into his life yet. And television prices are getting to be more worth while. Before long we should be able to find a good market for some of the other stories there. I wouldn't rush into it now, though. All in all, Steve, the picture isn't as black as it may seem from where you sit."

Steve sat forward in his chair, grimly earnest. "Rachel, these two Indian stories: just for the hell of it, could we keep them circulating? Just to see what reactions we'd get?"

He saw Rachel take a breath and fold her hands together again. She faced him unflinchingly.

"No, Steve," she said, regretfully but conclusively. "It could only hurt the name you're trying to build up with the editors around town."

"I see."

A pause.

"You're not bound to follow *my* advice, of course."

"I know. Well, you know what you're talking about."

He stood up and took his leave of her, picking up his topcoat and muffler as he passed through the waiting room. He walked down the hall to the elevator. Riding down, he told himself he had known the stories weren't ready. They were awkward and uncertain gropings after new ideas; they lacked both density and insight, but they'd been the best he had been able to do since coming to New York.

The wind was sharp in the street. Fixing his muffler and buttoning his topcoat against the biting cold, he started to walk to Fifth Avenue, where he could catch the uptown bus. For two cents, he told himself, he would ignore Rachel's advice and send the stories around himself. Maybe they weren't as good as they might be; none of his others had been as good as they could have been, had they? But instinctively he rejected the idea. Why did it cost him so much to do so? Why was he plummeting angrily and resentfully down the street, scowling at the sidewalk, fist pushed deep into his pockets? There *was* some money in the bank, he was less hard up for cash then he'd ever been. It wasn't money he had needed from the stories, from Rachel and the editors: it was reassurance, a reassurance that would still the gnawing sensation that his work was going sharply to hell. Why, he demanded of himself now, was he having so much trouble with it? He had survived dried-up periods before, why should he feel starved for reassurance and encouragement? Was it that before he had been alone, a bachelor, responsible only to himself when things went bad? Was he frightened of the unaccustomed responsibilities he bore now as a husband? No, it wasn't that. He grimaced against the admission: it was himself and Margaret. Nothing more.

He had reached Fifth Avenue. The bus was pulling to the curb as best it could, blocked on one side by a parked car and threatened on the other by the traffic. Steve dodged the passing cars as he rushed to board the bus.

Once on it, he found a seat and fell back into it. As the bus drove on, he looked vacantly out the window at the pretty, crowded, expensive shops of Fifth Avenue. After the wedding was over, when they were alone together in New York, they had been inordinately happy. It was an echo of the days in the *garçonnière* in New Orleans: those days of Lent that seemed to Steve now priceless, irreplaceably remote, and not entirely credible.

But the first days in New York had been an approximation, and compared with the misadventures of Washington, the experience of being alone together had transported them. He did not know when the sour note had first sounded. Even now, among the people they had met in New York, they had a reputation as a devoted young couple still bathing in the happiness of the honeymoon, the impossible happiness. In his mind Steve looked at the worn-out phrase and sneered, Impossible, all right. His work was worthless because he had been hopelessly distracted from it, his emotions drawn almost totally into his worry about Margaret. It wasn't *unhappiness* in her that worried him, he reminded himself once again; it came and went too erratically, too violently, to resemble the long and draining melancholy unhappiness comprised—it was something to be dreaded more. Hadn't she had the most cheerful of dispositions in the beginning? Wasn't she often happy still? Decorating their apartment, choosing the furniture, delighting in the business of going to market as she had back in New Orleans, delighting in it more because now the meaning of everyday chores was richer and more subtly faceted. But often now, unexpectedly, coming away from his desk after a day's work or coming back to the apartment after a meeting with Rachel or somebody else he had to do business with, he would find her unaccountably tight-lipped, petulant, morose. Invariably she denied that she felt anything but her usual self. But there was a certain suggestion of cement in her expression, her smile had a wobbly, unconvincing look, and slowly he had come to realize that she had been having a drink or two by herself while he had been working or away at an appointment. When he tried to find out what perturbed her—trying always gently; never, he hoped, really questioning—she laughingly reassured him. But the laugh was sickly, and if he remained unconvinced, she would break into tears and accuse him of being unnecessarily quarrelsome. As often as not they would end in one another's arms, tenderly reaffirming their allegiance, each comforting the other, but at the end of it Steve would find himself exhausted, and the next day, when he had planned on getting a comparatively large amount of work done, he would be disastrously preoccupied, the echo of recriminations festering, still unresolved, in the air.

Margaret seemed, he thought now, to be in the highest spirits when she was given some well-defined role to work at: the coffee-brewing wife of a writer; the clever girl of the privileged classes who knew more about comparison shopping at the A & P than any other housewife on the block; the tremblingly lovely bride in the early mysticism of possessing a loving and lustful husband. But should the role become indefinite in outline, in any way hazy or ill defined, Margaret would not know whether she could perform it or not, and, in her lack of surety, chagrin and a sense of humiliation would sweep over her.

Steve felt the stab of bafflement in his stomach: what could he do to help her, to make her happy? What could he do about his own life, the life he was tempted to throw away into the service of Margaret's? Had he the right to put his own needs in a secondary place, knowing he had no assurance that even that would be of help to her? Margaret in her nature, he suspected, would never be able to find a patterned life anything but drab and unendurable; yet that was exactly what he himself needed so badly. If he was to grow as a thinking man, as a writing man, he knew he could not endure very long without the quietude, the stability of pattern. So it would be a stultifying backwater life, so what? There was a time for that kind of life, once in a rare while, for every man. He had had enough of the unpredictable hard-drinking young veteran bit. He had had enough of letting the devil care, enough of the helling around and the swilling of his vitality as if it were an inexhaustibly replaceable commodity. For once he almost wanted to be the kind of guy who took out insurance. He nearly laughed aloud at himself, so that the man sitting next to him in a great thick overcoat and an ash-marred fedora glanced unpleasantly at the way his shoulders were silently shaking with their bitter mirth. Oh, God, he thought, that *was* almost what he wanted. As unstable, as prone to sudden violence as his life before had been, even in meeting Margaret, even in coming to love her and marrying her: now the situation was altered, and he needed peace.

He recognized the apartment-house marquee that signaled his stop. He got up and moved to the rear of the bus. The bus stopped, and he jumped out. With half a dozen steps he was into Ninety-second Street, the green of Central Park at his back. His steps grew halting. Now he must face her with the news of Rachel's regrets about the stories. Face her with his own humiliation. How would she be feeling when he opened the door to the apartment? Willing to sniff confidently at Rachel's misgivings? Or would she be in another funk, unable to keep from his eyes the fact that she thought herself a fool for casting her lot with a man who had neither money nor position nor the ability to win them.

Margaret was on the phone when he came in. She had already dressed for the evening, and kneeling on the outsized sofa in the living room, she waved to him and blew him a silent kiss while he dropped his topcoat and muffler on the chair in the entrance hall. She hung up the phone as he came into the living room.

"It was Sinde. She and her fiancé say Yes, they'd love to be with us Christmas Eve, so it's all settled. They've never been to an American Christmas Eve before." As he came over to her, she put her arms around him and kissed him. With relief Steve noted she looked in untroubled humor, clear-eyed and smiling. "Has Rachel made a mint of money for you?"

"Afraid not," said Steve.

"Oh, poor baby! What's wrong with that woman? Those stories were superb."

Steve shook his head and answered quietly. "No, Maggie, they weren't really. No agent in the world could sell them."

"Oh, Steve, my angel. Come sit down. Let me get you something to drink."

He sat on the sofa, stretching his legs out along its length, and in a moment Margaret was putting a drink into his hand. She sat down on the edge of the coffee table, and Steve could feel her studying him with concern.

"Do you want to talk or do you want me to go away?" she asked.

"Don't go away," he said. "I missed you today."

"I did you, too," she answered. "But you understand I wouldn't be a bit hurt if you asked me to go away, if you're tired or anything——"

"Maggie, please, okay——"

"You're not telling the truth." She frowned. "Please tell me the truth—Steve, *do* you want to be left alone?"

"No, Maggie. Don't you have a drink?"

"Oh," she said, taken aback by his sharpness. "Yes, right here."

"I'm sorry," Steve said. "Of course I want to be with you. I said so, didn't I?" He sighed. "I'm sorry, I'm feeling kind of beat because I'd hoped Rachel would have some good news. She didn't, and now I'm kind of worried about—oh, money." He shrugged.

"Are we broke?"

"No."

"Then what're you worrying about, silly?"

He uncrossed his legs and sat more erect. He looked at her carefully.

"Maggie. This is serious, so listen. I want to go on working with this material, but it means an investment on our part. In time and in lack of income. We have some in the bank, but not enough to splurge with."

"We aren't splurging now, are we?"

"No. But I'd been hoping that—maybe we could a little."

"Well, so we can't." Margaret shrugged. "Darling, I'm with you all the way. We just won't *have* any Christmas."

"Oh, for God's sake, *sure* we'll have Christmas. Just nothing too extravagant or——"

"Darling, we've got to be firm if we're to survive! *No* Christmas presents, not even between ourselves."

"Maggie, I wasn't talking about Christmas presents," Steve said pointedly. Then, with an effort, he went on more quietly. "A few less invitations accepted, a few less party debts we'll have to repay. Drawing in our horns a little, that's all. Darling, it'd be fine with me if I were alone, but I'm disappointed because I know you've been hoping we could—oh, break out of our shells more, have more fun than we've been able to afford since we got married."

Margaret turned her drink in her hand.

"Steve, if you went on working on this material, as you say —well, you can work any place, can't you? I mean good writers should be able to do their work wherever they are, shouldn't they?"

"What's your point, Maggie?" He felt himself waiting.

She made a gesture with one hand. "Who needs New York? What money we have is being so *drained* by our living here. The apartment, the furniture, the cost of everything——"

"What would you suggest?" Steve asked, really puzzled.

"Oh, Lord, any number of things. If we were in Washington, it wouldn't cost us a cent. Daddy's shoot in Virginia will be left to us sooner or later, and nobody ever uses it now. Darling, the money you make is perfectly all right for living in New York, don't misunderstand me, but we could live so much better on the same income in Washington or Virginia. I *hate* to see you grinding your life away with no real fun."

Steve was on his feet.

"Maggie, I'm *used* to living on a modest income. I've never in my life been able to afford a great deal of 'fun,' and I don't think I want very much of it."

Margaret looked shocked. "Oh! and you told me yourself about partying away every cent you had when you were in California."

"Damn it, that was different! I was a kid, and I was half out of my mind!"

Margaret stood up, her face in an instant rubbery with the threat of tears. "Now that you've got a wife, you're going to settle into your cocoon and vegetate? And expect me to do the same?"

"I want you to learn to live as the wife of a man with a modest income."

"I want to live with a man who loves me!" she shouted. She threw herself onto the sofa and hid her face from him.

Steve stood, shocked into silence. How had it happened? How *did* these scenes of hers materialize from nowhere? And what the hell *had* they been talking about that had suddenly provoked this one? Instinctively he went to her. He sat down beside her and touched her shoulders.

"Maggie. Maggie, what in Christ's name have I ever done to make you think I didn't love you? Come on now. You're imagining things. Jesus, you've *got* to be——"

"You write, write, write, all the time," Margaret wept, "even if you don't sell the damn things. You never have a word to say to me!"

"That's a goddamned lie!" He pulled back his hands.

"It's true, it's true, you can't pretend you ever loved me!"

He pulled himself up and plunged out of the room, down through the little hall and into the kitchen. He slammed the kitchen door shut against the sound of her crying. Trembling, he poured another shot of liquor into his glass. He sat down on the wire-legged stool next to the vegetable bin and tried to steady himself. He took a deep breath, closed his eyes, and let his sigh melt the sudden tension in him. He must swallow it, he told himself. Whatever was bothering Margaret now had nothing to do with his being a thoughtless husband—he knew damn well it couldn't. He had worked too hard at trying to please her. Nor did he think Margaret could resent him for clinging to his notions about not wanting to live at the Cowan house in Washington or the Judge's Virginia place. He could think only that she must be tired, exhausted from learning her new duties, adjusting to being a married woman and under not very attractive circumstances at that. After all, in marrying him, she had given up the ease of servants to tend the details of her living, the surety of the paternal nest. Maybe she needed a vacation. Maybe they both did. A change of scene, a trip somewhere. The hell with it, he told himself: they weren't penniless. What the hell was a guy like him doing worrying about security, money in the bank, clipping coupons? They both needed a break; they'd have one while there was dough to have it with. Time enough later to worry about making a goddamned living. He was not, he could never be the guy who worried about what insurance policy to buy. He would take Margaret to Europe on whatever money they had and provide for her whatever fun he could.

He went back into the living room.

Margaret was sitting bolt upright on the sofa now, her make-up marred by her weeping. He noticed that the fingers of her hands were rigid and her expression was wary. He did not sit beside her, but in the chair opposite.

He spoke gently, casually. "Did Mike get off all right?"

"Yes, thank you." She did not look at him, and her voice had the familiar fake politeness.

"Was he able to come by before leaving?"

"For a moment." Less guarded now, her fingers eased into a normal posture.

"That's one of the things hard on us, Maggie," he said. "Not being able to get around like Mike does. Like you used to. A change of scene once in a while."

Margaret looked at him inquiringly.

Steve went on, "We keep having explosions about nothing much at all. I think living with me is too rough on you. Why don't we take a vacation, a trip somewhere?"

She answered in a whisper, "Oh, Steve. You'd do that for me, even when things are tight for you?"

"What the hell, why shouldn't we? We've got money in the bank. When it's gone, then it'll be time enough to figure out how to make some more. How about going to Europe?"

"Europe? Oh, Steve!" With a cry of delight she jumped up and ran to him, kneeling down into his happy and relieved embrace.

"We can go any time," Steve said. "I bet I could find someone who could fix us up with a really exciting passage. A cargo ship, that'd be really interesting, Maggie. . . ."

Margaret's eyes widened momentarily. Her tongue flicked over her lips. "Oh, darling, I've got a birthday present due from Daddy. He'd be in heaven if we'd use it for a trip to Europe——"

"Baby, a birthday present wouldn't make that much difference——"

"But Daddy always gives me a *huge* check," she explained.

Steve held tightly to her hands.

"Maggie, maybe he won't now that you're married. I mean, since your father and I understand one another about large hunks of money being offered to us."

"But Steve, if you let him do it, we could have a really nice trip with——"

"Maggie, cargo passages can be the most fascinating things in the world. Everybody I know who's ever been on one has said so."

"For you!" she spat. She pulled herself away and got abruptly to her feet. "A cargo ship! You offer me a lovely, lovely present and then you ruin it in the next breath! There'd be no fun, no one to *talk* to, no . . ." She began to sob convulsively.

Steve felt suddenly frightened. "Maggie!" he cried. She fell forward, collapsing into his arms as abruptly as she had torn herself away. The sobs racked her, and her fingernails dug into his arms, her storm of emotion beyond control.

Steve held onto her, but this time he had no opportunity to invent perplexed words of comfort. Margaret cried into his shoulder, "Steve, I'm sorry, sorry, I didn't mean to cry. There's a reason you don't know, and I've been scared to tell you or Mike when he was here today or anybody—oh Steve, oh darling——"

"Tell me, Maggie."

She rasped out, "Steve, I'm pregnant."

After a motionless, endless instant, his arms were around her and he was pressing her against his chest with all his strength. Stunned, he did not notice that her sobs had run out, and she wept quietly now, delivered from the pressure of hysterics. He held her. He buried his face in her soft hair. His legs drew her closer still to him. He clung to her until his mind could clear.

"Maggie," he said. "Maggie. Really pregnant?"

"It's been on my mind for weeks, and I didn't dare——"

"How sure are you?"

"I'm sure, darling. I don't know how the hell it could've happened but——"

"Don't say that! It did. Oh, Maggie. It's wonderful——"

"You really don't mind?" she asked. "I know you want children, but I thought maybe right now, so soon and all——"

"Listen," said Steve. "As long as I've known you, I've wanted you more than could ever be satisfied. I've wanted to drink you, all of you. I've wanted neither of the two of us left, but only somebody who was both of us, in love. And so. And so that's what by Christ this baby will be, won't it? The two of us in love, in one little human."

In a freshening ecstasy Margaret hugged him.

"A little baby," she said. "Oh, God. Steve—will you help

me to be a good mother? I don't know an earthly thing about it!"

"Honey, neither of us does yet."

As quickly as had come the squalls of tension and vituperation, so quickly they vanished. And Margaret's fine-featured lovely face was filled with the light of excitement and anticipation.

"There's a course, I heard about it, on natural childbirth."

"Maggie, natural childbirth is——"

"I want it! If this little baby is going to be you and me, I want to know everything that's going on. Colic! Oh, God, I have to find out what the hell *that* is. And clothes—oh, Steve, what fun buying baby clothes! How can we possibly go to Europe—I'll have entirely too much to do! Steve, the storeroom back beyond our bedroom—it could be a heavenly nursery."

"Sure, darling——"

"Shelves, great God, but we'll need shelves!"

"I've known babies, too, who have to be fed in the middle of the night," Steve suggested blandly.

"I'll love it. Oh, Steve, I'm going to be a wonderful mother, I can feel it! And of course with something extraordinary like a baby, Daddy or Aunt Hermione will want to kick in with a temporary maid or something, you know, just something part time for a little while——"

"Oh, what the hell. Okay. Sure, darling."

"Oh, Steve, hold me. Hold me."

Snow fell over Manhattan on the night shortly before Christmas when Helen Maclean was to have dinner with Marvin Kaufman's parents. Helen had been preparing herself for the meeting for days, and still felt unready for it. Engaged to marry Marvin, she knew a happiness and pride that brightened her view of the world immeasurably, and the knowledge that Marvin's parents were the last obstacle in the way terrified her. She reminded herself of her critical meeting with Nancy Burrell, Sprague's wife, just before she had left Chicago to come to New York. That had been a humiliating and frightening encounter, yet she had handled herself comparatively well throughout it. Why, she demanded of herself, couldn't she do the same thing now? Marvin certainly expected her to be assured and unruffled; she owed him her good behavior, didn't she? But her self-lecturing accomplished nothing. She was sick with nervousness when Marvin arrived to take her to his parents.

As though God were playing a heartless joke on her, in getting out of the taxi in front of the apartment building on East Seventy-sixth Street Helen stumbled into a pile of snow and stained her stockings with a damp. A half-sobbing "Damn!" exploded from her, and Marvin comforted her as though she had been gravely injured. She was still trying to toss melting snowflakes off her hair when Bevey opened the door to them and waved them into the apartment.

Marvin moved like a man whose fate had been decided by forces beyond his consultation or control. He had not told his parents anything about wanting to marry Helen, only that she was an attractive friend of his whom he wanted them to know. Giving Bevey Helen's fur coat and his own overcoat, he wondered now, too late, whether he had been fair to Helen in doing so. Already he had seen the looks of surmise on the faces of his mother and father, and he was certain Helen would be subjected to the most suspicious scrutiny. He was surer of it when he led Helen into the living room. His parents had arranged themselves there in ceremonial tableau.

Stopping momentarily on the threshold, he tried to see them as Helen must be seeing them, wondering what Helen would think of them. His mother sat at the end of the sofa farthest from the fireplace, primly erect. Her face, carefully painted to preserve the handsomeness of her straight small nose and her uncommonly large eyes, smiled with faint arrogance. Her shoulders were straight and broad, her entire aspect imposing. His father stood behind her, tired-looking and melancholy. The plumpness of his face had been sagging steadily in encroaching age, and the brown-stained flesh around his speculative eyes had darkened perceptibly.

His father was the first to speak as he stepped forward from the picture they presented.

"Good evening."

"Momma, Poppa, this is Helen Maclean."

Helen did not betray her nervousness as she was presented. She shook hands with his father and went forward deferentially to exchange the formalities of introduction with his mother.

"Sit here, dear," Myra Kaufman said, her smile still strained. "Bevey will have Martinis for us in a moment. Marvin, dear, it's snowing—where are your overshoes?"

Helen threw Marvin a compassionate glance, and Marvin could feel his cheeks flaming. His father waved him to one of the two large chairs facing the sofa the women occupied, and himself took the other. Over in the corner by the window Bevey's frail black hands deftly measured ingredients into the Martini pitcher, and presently she served them, her mouselike face drawn with her usual preoccupied look. Marvin stiffened when he saw that Helen's fingers were trembling as she picked the glass up from the tray, so much so that she was forced to balance it with her other hand. Yet her face showed only easy composure, and he marveled at her ability to control her features when her hands revealed such tension.

Bevey withdrew, and his mother turned to Helen. After an exchange of pointless remarks about Bevey's remarkable loyalty in the face of so much servant trouble, she asked, "Marvin says you work with a modeling agency?"

"Yes, I do."

"You've been to Paris then?"

"Paris? No. No, I've never been abroad at all."

"But Helen, that's where the best of the models are. Oh, France is a beautiful country. I spent a lot of time there when I was young. I've always loved it. And when I go to the showings, the models—oh, there's no comparing these American sticks with Parisian models. You must go see them before you're a year older—if you're serious about the modeling business."

"Helen's fascinated by the business," said Marvin.

"Oh, yes," said Helen. "I've been in it ever since I came to New York. And right now I'm saving up vacation time so I *can* take that trip to France."

"You are not from New York?" Mrs. Kaufman inquired.

"No. I grew up in the Midwest. Farm country."

Marvin's father asked, "Your father, he was a farmer?"

"No, Daddy has a hardware store. His own hardware store."

"Hardware?" Mr. Kaufman echoed. "He should keep such a business and welcome."

"Oh, he loves it, the store's his whole life. In a small town like Charter Oak, the hardware store is a key business, and a man like my father likes the feeling of being in on everything going on in the town."

Marvin wished they had not started on Helen's Midwestern background. His father, he knew, comprehended little of America outside of New York, and by some logic, the steps of which he could never follow, his mother would turn farm life, as a concept, into something detrimental about Helen. They went on discussing Charter Oak. Why didn't they get back to Helen's connection with the fashion industry? At least there Helen and his mother might have an area of mutual interest. He wondered whether he should try to guide the conversation back, but felt himself restrained by an instinct he could not identify.

As the women went on talking, he realized what it was that held him back. Helen, in that honesty he was already familiar with in her, was emphasizing her country-girl background deliberately, refusing to bid for his mother's favor by skillfully highlighting what was admirable or glamorous in her present job. Marvin got up and, from the box kept on the mantlepiece, offered Helen a cigarette. When she took one, he lit it for her.

Marvin watched the easy grace with which she sat there, the unquestionable good taste of the clothes she had chosen to wear and the sophistication and good humor with which she kept the conversation with his mother bantering and relaxed in spite of the obvious tension both of them were enduring. She had learned a lot since leaving Charter Oak, as she had told him, but she had not learned to give over honesty to expedience. Marvin was glad of it. Helen probably knew as well as he did how impressed his mother would be to know the degree of authority she exercised in her job, how fast she had risen in the field, the grand people she knew. But Helen did not cater. If she was going to win his mother's approval, she obviously meant to do it the hard way.

At the dinner table his father grew more articulate, but his conversation was studded with specific Jewish references that caused Marvin's appetite to shrivel. Helen plainly understood nothing of the references. Was she ill at ease being with a Jewish family? She didn't seem so, and later on, over dessert, it occurred to him that Helen might never before in her life have been in a Jewish household, even a Reform one. Did she find them in any way strange? Joel Kaufman was no synagogue-goer—his wife had seen to that—but his prejudices and customs were there still, and Helen could not possibly be expected to share them. He cursed in his heart the demon that made his father test her this way, cursed his own embarrassment and the paralysis that prevented him from breaking in on the discussion. But if Helen was ever going to be his wife, she would have to put up with exactly what was going on now. He had no right to disguise the truth to her.

When two or three after-dinner drinks had been finished, Marvin took Helen home. They stood at the door of Helen's apartment, hands clasped. Neither of them was certain what impression Helen had made on his parents.

"I can't really have much hope that I made a good one," Helen said. "How can you show people in a single evening that you'll be a good wife to their son?"

"They've got to see you're wonderful, they've *got* to," said Marvin.

"Marvin, I hope they like me, but if they don't——"

"Oh, God, don't even think about it." He locked his arms around her. "I love you. I've never loved anybody before. Helen, when we have children, let's never put them through the kind of scrutiny you got put through tonight."

"We won't, my darling," Helen promised. "When are you going to tell them about us?"

"The first thing."

"Tonight?"

"They'll probably be asleep by the time I get back."

"Will you call me as soon as you have, if it's tomorrow?"

"Yes. Don't worry, sweet."

"I won't."

But in consternation Marvin saw that she was about to cry. "Helen, my God, don't cry, what's wrong?"

Smiling, she shook her head. "Nobody ever called me 'sweet' like that before. You haven't ever before, either."

"For you special names I've got," he mimicked.

"Good night, my beautiful young doctor."

His parents were still up when Marvin re-entered the apartment on Seventy-sixth Street. In the living room his mother sat on the sofa as she had earlier, but now a hand of solitaire was laid out on the coffee table before her. Her expression was calm, except for the two pinched lines that ran from the corners of her mouth downward, as though to meet beneath her chin and bear it up. His father stood with his back to the fire, his aging face a battleground of loyalties and demands.

Marvin came into the room but did not sit down. First he kissed his mother's uplifted cheek.

"It was a delicious dinner you had, Momma. Thank you. Helen was terribly flattered you went to so much trouble for her."

Mrs. Kaufman shrugged and played another card. Joel Kaufman said, "Who needs to take trouble? Bevey knows how to cook a chicken."

"Yes, Poppa." He stayed on his feet. He could not delay it. "You were both very nice to Helen, and I appreciate it. I wanted you to meet her and see how nice she is, because I'm asking her to marry me."

He was aware that his father caught his breath, receiving news anticipated with agony, but his eyes were on his mother. The lines from her mouth to either side of her chin tightened, and she put her remaining cards aside. She, too, took a breath, but she lifted her liquid eyes to him with on indulgent smile.

"She's a charming girl, Marvin." She waved a powdered hand. "Pretty. And you're a grown man; why shouldn't you have an innocuous little affair?"

"Myra——"

"Joe, I'm telling you it's an affair only."

"Momma, I'm not having an affair with Helen, I want to marry her."

"Foolish," said his mother complacently. "If you're not having an affair now, you should. Then you wouldn't be so keen on getting married. And dont tell me you're serious, Marvin darling. You can't be serious. She's a nobody."

"Momma, I love her, and what the hell do you mean by a nobody?"

"A farm girl," she answered distastefully. "With airs, I grant you, but at heart a farm girl."

"She's not a *farm* girl, she's from a small *town*——"

"At heart she's a nobody."

"Maybe it's at heart I love her," Marvin snapped. "Maybe I *do* love her because she's a basically simple girl who's worked very hard to develop the qualities she has."

"Qualities? Who is her father? What would being married to his daughter do for you, a brilliant young doctor?"

"Momma, I don't want to marry Helen because her father's some kind of New York wheel. I want to marry *Helen.* Poppa, can't *you* see?"

Joel Kaufman chewed his bottom lip.

"Joel, darling?" prompted his wife, picking up the cards she had still to play out on her solitaire game.

"Marvin, these feelings pass," the old man said at last. "She *is* pretty, like your Momma says. But she is not for you, Marvin."

"Why the hell not, Poppa?" Marvin demanded.

"She doesn't understand us, she won't understand you."

"Poppa, she doesn't know anything about being Jewish. She would learn——"

"Ha!" His father's eyes beseeched the ceiling of the room. "The cases I have seen. The pretty Gentile girls, the schemes of——"

"Goddam it, you're talking about tramps who got married to a lot of crusty old buddies of yours. All right, they deserve what they get. You can see with your own eyes Helen isn't that kind. Poppa, we're Jewish, but that doesn't mean a row of beans to me. One great big *bar mitzvah,* that's all *I* know about being Jewish. Helen understands me because she loves me."

His father's face went suddenly red, and Marvin's heart constricted when he realized it was not the red of anger. His father blinked at him like a cat in pain.

"You don't know what you're doing to us, to Momma and me," he said.

"Poppa, can't I fall in love? My God, can't I marry the girl when I do?"

"She will turn you away from us," his father declared. "Don't make me speak——"

"Of what, Poppa? Of what?"

His father's hand cut the air. "Your sister." He fired the words like bullets. "Zeeda. Hasn't your Momma been through enough?"

"What the hell has Zeeda got to do with my getting married to Helen?"

"Because one irreverent child is enough!" the old man snapped.

Marvin felt the rage rushing through him, sweeping beyond his control. He looked at his mother's carefully made-up face, becomingly contracted by imagined sorrow, and the rage broke. He swung first to face his father.

"Irreverent!" he cried. "You stupid old sonuvabitch, why do you think I'm asking your permission at all? You, Momma. I know about you and Zeeda. Don't look for sympathy from me. Oh, God, God, you're my parents and I love you. But what do you do to me? What do you do to yourselves?"

His mother's eyes, like buffed stones now, shone at him. "You'd defend your sister to me? To me? When she cast me off?"

"Cast *you* off? Oh, Jesus! It's a wonder to me she would bear to live with you as long as she did!"

The strong and handsome face was the color of the ashes in the fireplace. "What do you mean by that? What do you mean?"

"Look at you!" Marvin shouted. "I've found a girl I want love, and I tell you about it like a good son and ask you to bless the idea, and what do I get? Do you know what Helen and I are going through hoping for your approval? Do you know anything about anybody but yourself? You don't, Momma. You know why, Momma? Because you're a vain money-crazy vulgar Yid!"

In shock his mother half rose from the sofa, and the cards she had taken up spilled from her hand. After one tottering instant she collapsed, but Marvin did not see it. He had fled the room.

In the morning the apartment was silent. Marvin's message service had no important calls for him, and he was able to drink a cup of coffee leisurely in the kitchen before going to his office. He sat at the kitchen table to drink it, smoking a cigarette and wondering whether his father would appear to tell him he was no longer welcome to live there. He did not know what to expect because he had never had a quarrel with his parents, not of the dimension of the quarrel they had

had the night before. And even Zeeda had never been guilty of the language he had used. But no one appeared.

In the extended silence of the kitchen, the point of their quarrel assumed its primary position at the top of his rattling, disconnected thoughts. Whatever he had said to them the night before, he loved his parents. And he knew he was himself the essence of their life. With his sister's early escape from the family, unavoidably the essence. "Zeeda," he thought wryly, "why couldn't you have stayed? Why couldn't you be here now to share the burden of being devoted to?"

He thought of how his mother had looked the night before when he had shouted at her. She had not been arrogant then. A beautiful woman, a rich woman, a spoiled woman—all these. But Marvin knew that with one sentence he could break her life like a kindling stick. And his father's as well. The realization and the supplication had been in their eyes, hidden there behind the waiting eyes. And Marvin saw clearly what he had always known: he could not do it. He could call himself weak, he could call himself worthless, he could suffer Helen's disappointment and loathing and resentment, but he could not do it.

At ten o'clock he called Helen from his office. Shame sat like a stone in his chest, and he prayed Helen would not detect in his voice the lifelessness he felt.

"They had already gone to bed when I got home," he told her. "I thought they probably would have. I'll talk to them tonight."

"Will you come over after you do? I won't be able to sleep not knowing."

"Sure, of course, sweet," he said. "Look for me around eight-thirty or nine. We—Helen, we can make some plans for Christmas, too. What we'll do to celebrate and all. You *will* spend Christmas with me, won't you?"

"Marvin, who'd you *think* I'm going to spend Christmas with? Marvin, are you all right?"

"Sure I am. I'll—I'll see you tonight then."

"Good-by, darling."

"Good-by."

Later that night Helen sat erect, almost wooden, listening to what Marvin had to tell her. He had been there an hour, sitting across from her in the apartment's miniature living room, his body crumpled under the force of admitting, confessing, detailing his inadequacy. His voice as he spoke was little more than a whisper, and from time to time Helen had to strain, her rigidity increasing, to hear him clearly. His overcoat hung on the back of the chair he sat in, and he bent forward over the clasped hands between his knees. Helen watched him with a dazed stillness, not hating him for what he had to confess, but feeling as though it were a palpable thing, the barrier that separated him from her love for him.

"There's nothing I can say to make it better," he muttered, miserable. "It's horrible for you, of all people, to be subjected to it."

"No, not horrible . . ."

She looked back at the long, long road and felt the accrued weariness of every bone of her body. A little girl born in Charter Oak had fought and figured and driven her way along that road: for this? To be told by people she knew nothing of that she was, first, a Gentile, as if that were some kind of inadmissible deformity, and second, that she had nothing to offer the son of a well-kempt bitch married to a jewelry merchant? What in God's name sense did it make? She had fallen in love with Marvin, and now she was paying the toll. Why did she love him? Because he was brilliant? Because his eyes were lovely and made her good sense melt inside her? Because her legs ached to hold him? Because he was clumsy and made her feel gracious? Because he was kind and made her feel, by comparison, hard-hearted? Why do you do everything possible to live sensibly and then senselessly fall in love with someone who won't marry you? The answer blazed in her head: because it was right, because her loving Marvin was right, because he belonged to her. From the moment he had asked her to marry him, the contract had been made in her mind.

"I want you—now," she said aloud. "I don't want to wait, I can't."

It might not take so very long," Marvin argued, "Once we convince them we're going ahead with it, if we're sure of ourselves and determined and leave a door open for them to accept the idea finally——"

"No!" Helen cried. Feeling the sudden thrust of tears behind her eyes, she jumped up and turned away from him.

"I love you. I've agreed to marry you. I won't wait, Marvin, or be put off. I won't."

"Helen, if only for a few——"

She spinned to face him. "Are they so goddamned important? You're a grown man, why should you ace like some sniveling little Mama's boy?"

Marvin stood up, flushing angrily. "You know damned well that's not the way it is——"

"Then marry me!" Helen challenged him. "We could wait and wait and hope and hope and your parents might *still* not accept me."

"They will, they need time——"

"No amount of time is going to change them. I'm not dependent on them and neither are you."

"Helen, they've *lived* for me. Even in her sterile, stupid way my mother's lived for me. I'm committed to them even if I never asked to be, because they're my family. I can't ignore that commitment without damning myself to remorse the rest of my life."

Helen ran forward and grabbed his arms, shaking him. "I can't let you go! Marvin, it can't happen!"

"Don't then," he answered, breaking free from her grip with a movement of his arms. "Give me time to bring them around." He touched her shoulder. "Please, Helen."

Helen looked away from him, frowning at an unexpected and repugnant notion. "If you loved me, you'd marry me anyway," she said faintly. "Right this minute."

"It's not true, I tell you. Helen——"

She pulled back. "No. I don't know. Maybe you do love." She went back to her chair and sat down, her face turned from him. "I—I can't think right now."

Marvin sighed. "Okay. Okay, it's my own fault, and I don't have any room for complaint. Maybe after a while you'll understand how trapped I am."

But he did not leave. He stood there, waiting for what reply, Helen did not know. She thought suddenly of Ladd Dorn's supercilious remark, "Absolutely the only thing to do is pack a bag and go to France."

Aloud she said, still with her face averted, "I need a break from New York. I have some vacation time due me from Jules. And I've never been to Europe."

"I see."

"When I get back—well. Let's see what's going on then."

"Helen . . . ?"

"Good night," Helen whispered. "Right now, please."

She heard the rustle as he picked up his overcoat, and then his slow, uneven footsteps down the long narrow tunnel of the hallway to the door. Cold fingers of desolation closed over her throat as she sat in her chair, listening for the sound of the door. It opened, and then it closed.

She heard the racking sobs before she realized it was herself who sobbed. She covered her face with her hands and bent her head over until it touched the arm of the chair. The sobs continued, and she drew her legs up until her knees touched her chest, and she lay huddled in the chair like a shuddering infant; powerless to do otherwise, she surrendered herself to the passion of heartbreak.

27

DURING CHRISTMAS WEEK, AT COCKTAIL parties, at family gatherings, at church socials, throughout the country, there was an undercurrent of tension, increasing talk of serious trouble with the Russians as well as the United States' native Communists, and few thought another war was out of the question. They waited in dread, no one wishing for it. Even the younger men who had not been to war, who might in another time have been expected to thirst for the adventure and glory the naïve conceive war to be—even the young did not want it. They wanted stability, they wanted a world in which they could know what to expect, they yearned for the one condition now hopeless of attainment, not understanding that insecurity was the inescapable price of leadership.

Under this unspecific load they pursued their lives. In the Northern states winter deepened with the passage of January and the beginning of its bleak successor. New York had seemed to Margaret and Steve Williams bitterly cold.

Outside in East Ninety-second Street one morning before dawn, the February wind whistled shrilly, but Margaret felt herself choking as she came awake. She coughed convulsively and kicked her heavy blankets off. The room an hour before sunrise was dark and stifling hot. From the other side of the bathroom door a fraction of an inch of light spilled out, but it was no comfort in her torment: it reminded her only of how much she had drunk the night before and how sick she had been afterward and how disappointed and troubled Steve had looked, watching her stagger out of her clothes into a nightgown and collapse, shuddering, into bed. Now in the darkness she heard his heavy breathing. She turned over on her side, her back toward him. Once, long before, she had heard his breathing as he slept, and it had seemed male and lovely. But not now. The sound repelled her: he slept his oafish sleep while she endured the misery, the humiliation of her sickness. She squinted at the luminous dial of the clock on the dresser across the room. Four-twenty. Well, she had had something to drink at four-twenty often enough before, hadn't she? What the hell difference did it make that it was near morning and she was just waking up instead of just turning in? She'd slept hardly a wink, she told herself bitterly, she deserved a drink. She listened grudgingly to the inner word of caution—liquor made her sicker than ever; but at least for a moment it always made her feel herself again, and it was worth it. She sat up and slipped out of bed. This was the handful of minutes in which she could count on feeling comparatively well: the first few after getting up. When she had been to the bathroom, she found her dressing gown, and pulling it on, slipped out of the bedroom. She drew the bedroom door soundlessly shut behind her.

At the end of the short passage she found the living room cooler than the bedroom had been, less strangulating with closeness. She poured herself a drink, laced it with flat soda, and carrying it to the sofa, sat down and lit a cigarette. She stretched herself out on the sofa, luxuriating in the ease of being in cooler air, away from the maddening pendulum of Steve's breathing. It put her in mind of the sweet and gentle days at home in Washington: a nightcap in her own suite of rooms close on dawn after a wild and hilarious party. She would recount to herself the flirtations she had had that evening and speculate on what lay behind one or two unfamiliar faces she had met. . . . Pleasantness. That's what she'd lost from her life. The pleasantness of that late-night drink alone when you could muse over the happenings of the day, the luxury of someone coming in late the next morning and soundlessly drawing the curtains open and relighting the fire. She groaned aloud. What a fool, what a priceless ninny she'd been!

Even after she knew she was pregnant, she had been excited about the baby: oh, God, what had she been thinking of? Had she lost her mind? Had she forgotten how one was supposed to live? With some grace, with some basic comfort? Morning sickness! She spat the cigarette smoke out into the room. She'd been sick constantly, unrelentingly, and Steve's solicitude had made her sicker: what did the damn fool think *he* could do about it now that she had the thing inside her? She couldn't even think of it as a baby. She put her drink down on the coffee table and pressed the palms of her hands hard against her abdomen. If I could press and press, she thought, if I had the strength of a hundred men, I could press and press and press and finally drive it out, away from me, away . . .

Her eyes filled with tears, and she wiped them angrily away from her cheeks. It didn't feel like a baby; nothing alive, nothing anyone could care about. It was an illness, some disease that was attacking her, that she couldn't fight back against. She gulped at her drink and set her teeth against the queasiness she knew would start at any moment now. If she could bring herself to consult a doctor, he might give her something to offset the awful nausea. But she had not yet consulted anyone. Neglecting to do so did, after all, stave off the time when her pregnancy would be official.

Later, when she had finished throwing up in the bathroom again, she came back to the living room and lay down on the sofa. She fell asleep. She was still there when she awoke to the sound of Steve fixing breakfast in the kitchen. She could hear in the stillness of the apartment the clicking of the time mechanism in the toaster. Then the odor of fried bacon assaulted her.

With a gasp she sprang up from the sofa and hurried into their bedroom. She threw open a window to the knifing of the cold air in the street outside. Steve had preached at her about the efficacy of open windows at night, but she hated them open, and she didn't know why warm air should be such an agony to her now. She threw herself down on her bed, and teeth chattering almost in relief, pulled the blankets up over her. The fresh February wind poured through the opening of the window. She breathed deeply two or three times; at least the cold had driven the odor of bacon out of her head.

She wondered momentarily if she should call to Steve, to warn him to close himself off from the draft. The hell with it, she thought. The effort was too great. She sank back into sleep.

At ten o'clock she awoke, fully this time, and lay in despair as she contemplated living through another day. The dim whir of the electric clock was the only sound in the apartment. For a long time she lay unmoving, listening for some clue to Steve's presence, but there was none. Then she remembered he had an appointment with Rachel Pemberton that morning. Some California person had taken an interest in a story he had published long ago. Well, if it had taken them this long to do anything about it in pictures, nothing would ever come of talking to them.

Yet her conscience nagged her. Steve had had breakfast, bathed and dressed and gone out, and she had not said a word to him. He would have seen the empty glass on the coffee table. She knew he would not reproach her about it. He had never been anything but solicitous and concerned about the rotten time she was having, but something within her cringed at the thought.

It was just as well he *had* had to go out. She hated being seen this way. By Steve, by anyone. Vomiting every hour, her face drawn and flushed by turns, her entire appearance wrecked by what she'd been going through. How could he bear to look at her? How could he stand coming back to the apartment, facing for still another day the frowzy bleary-eyed creature her sickness had made of her? Then the thought stung her: maybe he couldn't. Maybe he faced up to her as a responsibility, a burden he was forced to carry but secretly wanted no part of. "Christ!" she cried to herself. Who could blame him?

She pulled herself out of the bed and scurried into the bathroom, closing the door against the wintry bedroom. Once inside she paused, out of her current habit, to see whether she was going to throw up again. But at the moment she seemed to be safe. She faced the full-length mirror on the bathroom door. She pulled her nightgown up over her head and threw it aside. Sullenly she studied the reflection of her body. Was there already a thickening in her waist? It couldn't be, not this early. But so it looked to her. So it must certainly look to Steve. She felt her breasts and thought she could detect already a heaviness in them. Oh, God, she breathed; already, and all the months to go. What would it be two months from now, four months from now? She looked like hell as it was. How could she let Steve see her like this? How could she hope to hold him, looking as she would look in a matter of weeks?

She turned abruptly away from the mirror and clung to the edge of the washstand. She'd lose him, she'd surely lose him. No man could want to live with her looking so ugly, so fat, like every common *hausfrau* you saw in the streets. He'd been sweet, she knew that, he'd go on being sweet. Steve was tough on himself when it came to anything he thought of as duty, but it wasn't real: it wouldn't be him loving her, not him wanting her; it would be a fake, a pretense. And, unwanted and unloved, she would have to go through the horrors of delivery. She knew little about it outside of old wives' tales picked up in boarding school, but it was bound to be terrible. The terribleness of it was the whole point, wasn't it? Like dying. Like suffering humiliation and agony until you're certain you must die, and still you don't: you go on suffering, with a roomful of strangers to watch you do it.

Now the tears rushed forth and she sat on the icy edge of the bathtub and bent her head into her hands, letting the weeping shake her. If Steve could love her, then she might bear it. But he couldn't love her, she was certain he couldn't. It was hard enough for anyone to love her at her best of times. Why should they? What had she to offer anyone? A pretty body, a carefully disguised face. Not even her brother or father had ever loved her, not as herself, only as a decorative adjunct to their lives. You had to work for love, and fight, and exploit every small advantage you possessed over the men. And oh God, even then you couldn't win! . . . You got the man, you got yourself married, and then a damned trick made you sick and swollen and ugly and you lost him.

"Don't let gallantry fool you," she told herself. "They're gallant because they feel like pigs after what they've done to you. But in their hearts they think you're loathsome, all swelled-up and clumsy and vomiting."

She couldn't let it happen.

The words spoke themselves in her head before she had quite grasped their meaning. Then she looked up into the mirrored reflection of her naked, ungainly self sitting on the edge of the bathtub. "I won't let it happen!" she said aloud.

The truth was, she didn't dare to. She had given up too much, had assumed too great a burden in marrying Steve to risk losing him now when they were both still young and life held a chance of excitement and fun for them. She couldn't lose him, she couldn't let some accident destroy everything she'd sacrificed herself for.

There were ways to do it. Somehow, somewhere you could find the people who tended to things like that, couldn't you? Steve would never consent to an abortion, she knew that much, but surely she could figure some way for it to happen without his understanding what the real point was. A miscarriage, anything of the kind: if he didn't know about it ahead of time, there'd be no question he could ever ask. And it was perfectly safe now—the miracle drugs, they removed all the risks that had used to frighten people. And she would not, after all, be one of those brutal kitchen-table victims.

She imagined to herself how it would be: something very simple—you found a doctor, God knows you had to pay him; you went some place for a day or so, some nice little clinic or infirmary off someplace; and it was all over. All over. She felt faint at the thought. Yourself again, with no nasty unwelcome growth making you misshapen and sick. You came home and told your husband how you had had the miscarriage, and he commiserated with you and cherished you. Yourself again, life as it should be again. Your husband without his anxieties and moods, yourselves a young and happy couple again.

She waited until noon before placing the call to Michael in Washington. When he was on the wire, she said, "Lookit, what's the chance of your running up to New York? It's urgent."

"Darling, whatever's happened?"

"Don't be campy, Michael, it's really urgent!" Her tone supported the statement.

"A hint?"

"Expectant."

There was a pause on the wire. "What do you want me to do about it?"

She could have screamed in irritation. "Is Daddy in the house?"

"No."

She tried to keep her voice calm. "Michael, it's got to be—

corrected. I've got no one who can help. Michael, *can* you come?"

"Oh, God. Oh, my baby, this is more than your usual speed——"

"Michael, I'll kill you if you don't come help me!"

Another pause. "Give me a day or two," he said. "I can do some inquiring around here. It may help."

"It had better," Margaret warned.

"Darling? Can't—can't it be let go on?"

"No! No, Michael, for God's sake, I'm in hell!" she shouted into the phone.

"Baby, stay calm," Michael urged. "We'll talk about it when I get there. You may feel different about it then. I'll be there day after tomorrow in any case, at the latest. And nary a whisper at this end."

"Nor this—that you're coming, I mean." The tears were streaming down her cheeks. "Oh, Michael, thank you. I knew I could count on you. Yes, hurry. Thank you. . . ."

28

TWO WEEKS LATER A ONE-CLASS PASSENGER ship, one of those converted World War II transports, was the scene of noisy festivity. In minutes it was to set out for Europe from its dock on the West Side. Helen Maclean stood on deck with Jules Fischel and Ladd Dorn, accepting their best wishes and shifting back and forth in her arms the flowers they had brought. Near them was Marvin Kaufman. He had arrived after the other two men and had been too shy and too depressed to invade their bantering, pauseless conversation. Once or twice Helen tried to draw him into the group, but Jules and Ladd obviously had no interest in him at the moment. It was clear that Marvin wished they would go away and leave him alone with Helen.

At last, amid a flurry of good-by kisses, Jules and Ladd were gone. Marvin and Helen were alone together, neither knowing now what could be said. From the rail they watched other passengers boarding the ship.

Marvin said limply, "Your flowers are very pretty."

"Thank you," said Helen. "The ones you sent are in my

room. They're breathtaking. It was very sweet of you, Marvin."

"I wish I'd sent more of them," he said. "I was so grateful to you for letting me come see you off."

Helen frowned. "Don't be grateful, Marvin, not to me. I can't bear it when you are."

"I'm sorry. If—if the work end of it doesn't get you too tied up in Paris, how soon do you think you might be back?"

"I don't know. I honestly can't tell at this point."

"Oh."

"Your glasses are slipping," Helen said. And automatically she reached up with her free hand to slide them back to the bridge of his nose.

"Thank you."

Marvin looked at her. The clothes she wore, the way she'd brushed her hair, even the gesture of pushing his glasses back in place, everything about her bespoke the sophisticated young career woman. But Helen had let him know her. He knew the girl from Charter Oak, and he thought of the wonder Europe would be to her, how much this trip meant to her growth. He tried to concentrate on that viewpoint, to distract his mind from the bitterness he felt against himself for having let her go.

"You'll be meeting some fascinating people," he said. "The whole deal is wonderful for you."

Quietly: "Yes."

But the distraction didn't work. There *would* be wonderful, clever, brilliant men she would meet. How could he hope she'd come back to him? Even if in the months to come he could cajole his parents into accepting the idea of their marrying, how could he hope she would want to come back to a gangling, myopic, book-smart jerk like himself, especially after the pain he'd brought to her?

He threw his arms around her clumsily, heedless of the flowers, not caring how laughable he might look in his unhappiness.

"Helen, try not to be in love with anybody else when you get back," he beseeched her. "Please try and believe me when I say I'll make everything right for us by the time you get back. I will."

Helen's eyes searched his face. She asked, "What'll you do, where will you be going?"

"I don't know," Marvin said. "To the office, I think—no, I forgot. When I was leaving the hospital this morning to come here, I got a call from Don Biel. I'm supposed to be at his place sometime around noon, whenever I can after the boat pulls out. I don't know what about. Helen, I love you——"

"Marvin, kiss me good-by . . ."

They kissed as though drawing from one another a store of love and hope for future sustenance. Then there was a cacophony around them, and milling crowds, and in a moment Marvin was being pushed down the gangplank by the hurrying throng behind him. He called back to her frantically and heard Helen shouting good-by to him again. At the foot of the gangplank he pulled himself out of the stream of people, and turning, searched for her on deck. At the railing Helen stood alone, looking, to his eyes, like a lost child, despite the acquired elegance she had. She did not wave or call again, but smiled down at him. The ship began to pull away, and he felt his throat constricting. His knotted fists called him six kinds of an ass for having let his parents get away with this kind of tyranny. He forced himself to keep smiling, and he rushed with the others to the end of the pier. The ship veered and Helen was lost to sight.

He tarried there; he tarried after the ship was gone and while the others who had come to see it off were dispersing. He stood alone at the end of the pier, deserted by the other well-wishers, feeling useless and bereft. He stood alone a long time. Then he walked away, telling himself contemptuously he had no right to cry.

Outside on the street, he reminded himself that Don Biel was waiting for him.

For once he was able to park his car in front of Don's apartment building on Riverside Drive. He sat behind the wheel for a moment, trying to collect himself. He knew that if Don had called him to his apartment at this hour of the day, it could only be about something unpleasant. Don would be on another drunk, or losing his pride and mind over some girl, or something equally foolish. He didn't know why he bothered to answer his friend's summons at all, except that Don had a special place in his life; his vivacity, the boundless energy and grace of his small, lithe body, so unlike the deviling sprawl of his own ungainliness. He envied and, worse, admired Don Biel—worse, because he had no illusions about him. It was an animal admiration only.

Don himself admitted Marvin to the apartment's living room. It was not large, but it had been decorated expensively and, Marvin thought to himself, repulsively. At the moment the curtains were drawn, and the room was dark. Don was drunk. He wore only a T-shirt and shorts.

"Hey. Well, finally," he said. "Siddahn." He waved an arm at a chair and threw himself down on the end of the sofa. The room was choked with cigarette smoke, and, feeling useless—any interview with Don in liquor was apt to be futile—Marvin sat down.

"I've done it, Kaufman, old son," Don said, his speech badly blurred. "This time I've done it."

"What've you done, Don?" Marvin asked calmly.

Don ignored the question. He shouted into the gloom of the room, his voice anguished, "How do they find you out? The bastards always find you out, don't they?" Then Don sat up and turned to him, and even in the semidarkness his eyes blazed. "You're my friend, you're smarter than me. Smart! If you weren't such a fucking dedicated type you could make twice what I do. Okay, Marvin, okay, I need somebody smart now."

He's drunk, yes, Marvin thought, but he's worse than that. He's crazed. He tried the light approach: "What's she doing, suing for breach of promise in this day and age?"

"What?"

"Is this girl trouble, what?" Marvin spread his hands.

"You think I got you up here about some cunt? Oh, brother. Marvin, Marvin, this time I'm in *trouble.*"

"Okay." Marvin swallowed. "Begin from the beginning."

"You won't interrupt."

"Promise."

Don took a breath.

"The real start was me and the Chase Manhattan. I've been —oh, having a few yaks, playing around, a lot of dough has gone out the window. You know how it is?"

"No," said Marvin gently.

"You sonuvabitch. Well, I do. I got strapped. Then this deal came up."

"Deal?"

Flatly: "This abortion."

Marvin started involuntarily.

"I told you not to interrupt, goddamn it!" Don screamed. "This was special. This guy came *to me,* this guy from Washington, an internist."

"Healy," Marvin prompted.

"Screw Healy. I didn't say any name, did I? Now shut up your big Yid mouth and listen to me. The price was high because this dame's father is some big muckety-muck in the Government, I don't even know who. The setup is perfect: obscure little infirmary on Long Island, I never see her before or after, she never sees me, she hasn't consulted anyone else before me, and it's a thousand bucks into Chase Manhattan's lap. For God's sake, why *shouldn't* I take the job?"

Marvin sat rigid, speechless for a moment. Then he said tonelessly, "You're asking me because you know."

Don was cowering on the end of the sofa, and now his voice was no more than a whisper. "I haven't done a curettage every day of the week, but I knew how to keep the infirmary fooled. I hadn't ever had any trouble in surgery much before——"

"She ruptured." Marvin sighed. "You ruptured the uterus."

"No, meningitis. For Christ's sweet sake, Marv, the woman's dead!" And the small-boned lively, laughing young man he had known for years was stretched out on the sofa then, sobbing, beyond consolation.

Marvin sat unmoving. The sobbing went on. He lit a cigarette and waited in the darkness. In five minutes the sobs were dry and racking, and then their energy had run its course. The young man he had so envied, for so many years, lay still, and there were silence.

"So," said Marvin.

"I had to tell somebody." His voice was hollow now and disembodied as it came out of the shadows. "There won't be any business with the police, I don't think. Her brother was on deck and knew all about it. He was the one with the money, as a matter of fact. I'm as clear as the infirmary is. She was admitted because of irregular menstruation, and the nurses, I imagine, are all sending dough home to mother this week."

He was silent. For a long while he did not stir. Then he muttered, "Kaufman, there's nothing you can say to me. But I had to tell somebody. You're the only one I could trust."

"How do you know you can trust me?"

"Are you going to do anything about it?"

There was a deeper question in the darkness. Perhaps in his heart Don wanted him to do something about it, Marvin thought, wanted to be punished for his crime, wanted the idealistic, ethics-conscious Marvin to be the agent of his punishment. Marvin sighed. He felt, he noted, no whit of outrage, no instinct to condemnation. Maybe because Helen was gone, maybe because all life was too twisted and complicated for the simple people who had to live it, he felt only a bottomless sadness. He said, "No. I don't think I am."

He heard Don's groan, but he did not receive it as a communication. His mind was on Helen again, on Helen and himself. In the same clumsiness that had tortured him from his childhood onward, he had bollixed up his immediate hope of marrying Helen. What a fool he'd been! Of what account, when you had at last to face the making of your own life, were the decisions of others, however close to you, who would never have to lead it? He disliked selfishness in himself, but the time had come. The friendly, amusing image of Don Biel lay in dust around him, the last Pompeii of a doubt-ridden, stumbling, too-hesitant growing up. Before Don fell, all else had fallen. He faced whatever life he, and not Don or Zeeda or his mother or his father, had to live. He would get Helen back. Whatever he did, he would make up to her the wound of his foolishness. He would not attempt to disguise from her the clumsiness and the idiocy that, combined, had resulted in his actions. Helen knew them. When she had time to think about it, she would give them their value, but no more than their value. In spite of any wall of hurt or disillusion that stood between them.

Over in the darkness Don moved. His voice said, "Get the hell out, Marv."

"Sure. Good-by, Don."

He put his cigarette down, and getting up, found his way out of the apartment.

For the greater part of two days Steve had been working almost without a break. Rachel Pemberton had still not been able to persuade Hal Capbern to buy the film rights to the story about Hilda, but they had discussed the project at length, and Steve felt reasonably sure of the producer's sincerity. He had suggested Steve try his hand at a treatment, and Steve, though he knew nothing of writing for that medium, decided to do so. "For the exercise, if nothing else," he had told Capbern.

With Maggie off to a weekend visit with some family connections on Long Island, the apartment was soundless and at least for the moment free of the immediate crises of pregnancy. He had not minded these last. Indeed, his concern for Maggie, his searching out of unobtrusive and imaginative ways to pamper her in the trouble she was having—these were his only means of participating in their parenthood. He relished them, but he was not enough to a sentimentalist to assert that he could give full concentration to his work under the circumstances, and concentrate was what he had to do, not only for his own sake and Maggie's, but for the baby's. He had to start earning again, and earning well; no baby of his and Maggie's was going to have anything but the best its father could provide.

Maggie had said she might be back that afternoon, and at twelve o'clock he stopped working. The apartment, he saw for himself, was a mess. He could not let Maggie come back to it looking this way. Not all the disarray was of his doing—Maggie had left precipitately—but, even so, he was sure it would depress her to come back from some decorous party on Long Island to unkempt, unswept rooms on Ninety-second Street. He gobbled a peanut-butter sandwich and went to work straightening the place. By three o'clock he had done a fairly thorough job; he shaved himself and showered and got into fresh clothes so that his own appearance would be as inoffensive and comforting to her as he hoped the apartment's would be.

At four o'clock the doorbell rang, and Steve hurried to the door. He gave a start when he found himself looking at Mike Cowan.

"Mike," he said. "For God's sake, come in."

He led Mike into the living room.

"I didn't know you were coming up from Washington. Maggie's off at some do on Long Island—a cousin of yours, I think she said—but she should be back in a little while. Sit down, Mike, sit down. How are you?"

"Fine, Steve. Thanks."

"Christ, I'm sorry to say I haven't got a thing in the house to offer you outside coffee. While Maggie was gone, I was just working and didn't do anything sensible about shopping."

"Could I have some coffee with you, Steve?"

Steve hung fire a moment. What had Mike said? Could I have some coffee *with you*, Steve. There was a note amiss.

"Sure, right away," he answered, "Sit down, I'll be back with it in a second."

He went to the kitchen and turned on the flame beneath the coffee, already mixed with milk. What had been wrong with Mike's saying *"coffee with you"*? Because that was not their relationship. Steve's thoughts groped. They had never done anything together, except that Maggie was Mike's sister, and Mike had been kind enough to be his best man at the wedding. Mike didn't have coffee "with him." Mike had coffee. Or, more usually, a drink. Steve sighed as he poured the coffee into a cup and arranged cup and sugar bowl on the small tray. Oh, Jesus, he thought, maybe he's in some kind of queen trouble and has come to weep on Maggie's shoulder. Well, I'm no help to him, and it's the last thing Maggie needs right now. He frowned. Mike had looked pretty damn worn out.

Back in the living room he served Mike's coffee and sat down opposite him. Mike sipped from the cup once, and then set it down as though that were the end of it.

"Steve," he said. "I didn't just arrive."

"Oh? No?"

"No. I was— I was at the party on Long Island. Steve, this is horrible, and I want you to get hold of yourself."

Steve blinked. In embarrassment he realized his brother-in-law was threatening to break into tears.

"What's it to do with me, Mike?" he asked, puzzled, but trying to sound kind.

Mike looked at him. "I'm sorry. I didn't make myself clear. Steve, it's Maggie."

Steve did not move. Lightning was cutting through his head, but at the same time, on some gentler plane, he registered the fact that his brother-in-law had said "Maggie," his own name for her. What a good man this is, Steve thought. Then the lightning blistered out all other thought, and his fingernails were digging through his trouser-legs into his thighs.

"Maggie?" he said.

"She's had a miscarriage. At the weekend party. Everything possible was done, Steve."

Steve tried to swallow. "Mike, we lost the baby?"

Mike bit his lip and did not answer. Steve got to his feet.

"Mike, where's Maggie? Where?" He started toward the closet where his coat hung, behind the sofa where Mike was sitting.

"Steve, oh God, sit down, sit down."

"What the hell do you mean? Maggie will . . ."

Even then he knew he was lying. Maggie wouldn't anything. He had his coat off the hanger, but he did not put it on. He held it, looking over at the unmoving figure of Maggie's brother on the sofa. He knew he would have to hear the words. Silence filled the apartment. "Where is she?" he whispered.

Mike did not turn to face him. "I'll take you there," he said.

"Maggie's dead."

Mike nodded. "My little sister's dead."

The numbing shock of grief carried him through the events to follow. The first viewing of Maggie's dead body, the notifying of her father, the confused and terrible long-distance conversation with his own parents, the details of arranging for the body to be moved to Washington for the funeral.

Steve's mother begged him to come home to Houston after the funeral.

"I will, Mom," Steve said over the phone, his voice metallic, "but maybe—you know—maybe not right away."

"Of course, honey," and again there was the snuffling sound as she tried not to wail aloud. "But soon, Stevie?"

"When things have settled down a little, Mom, then I will."

"She was so pretty, Stevie, so—wait, I'd better give this to your father." The sound of weeping faded from the telephone.

"Son?"

"Yes, Dad."

"It's me again. Son, your mother and me could get there in time for the funeral if you wanted us."

"Dad, I want you. God, I want to see you, but—it's all going to be very quick. It wouldn't do any good for either me or the two of you, and it'd be too sad for Mom. I want you two to stay there, and as soon as I can, I'll come, or maybe you can come up here and visit me. After a while. After a few weeks."

"All right, son, I'll explain to your mother when we're off the phone. We'll do what you say, Steve. You know more about these things, being—so far away from us now. And all."

"Dad, I love you, I'm not so far away," Steve said. "I'll call you tomorrow. And the next day. And—in a few days we can make plans."

"All right, son. And his father sounded satisfied, reassured. "Here's your mother to say good night. . . ."

Steve and Mike went down to Washington on the train that carried Maggie's body. No word passed between them; Steve sat looking blindly out of the train window, paralyzed by the aching effort it cost his mind to absorb the fact that she was dead—his impetuous, vivacious, mercurial girl, cold and insensible in a box somewhere on the train.

It was sundown when they arrived in Washington. Judge Cowan, his face drawn and ashen, met them at the station, and the three men drove together to the Cowan house. Steve nodded, mute and uncaring, when Judge Cowan told him he had arranged for a quick and simple service, hoping to protect both himself and Steve against the importunities of well-meaning strangers or the brutal sordidness of vicarious mourners. Maggie's closest friends would be there, and her Aunt Hermione Pierce, but few others. Hermione, he was told, had been inconsolable since she had heard. At the house, Judge Cowan gave Steve three stiff drinks and firmly directed him to bed.

He did not sleep, but lay rigid and unblinking with his thoughts. Had he expected it? Dimly somewhere in the back of his mind had he known Maggie would never be with him for long? In the very tempestuousness of her spirit were the seeds. Sometimes she had seemed to him almost insubstantial, a creature made of dancing lights, not human at all. Had that feeling in himself made him less than the husband he had wanted to be to her? Had it rendered her unhappy with their life together? He tried to push the tears back into his eyes with his fists. He had loved her with his soul, he had cherished her and worked for her. The only unhappiness he had known in their marriage had been his concern about her, his hunger to have her feel loved and content, stabilized at last against the whipping tides of the erratic emotionalism that had plagued her. There could be no answer to the questions that fired up in his brain, but he continued to writhe under the frustration of his bafflement. *Why* had he lost her? Why did his beloved girl have to die?

He turned over in the bed and sobbed into his pillow until he was drained once again of strength and the merciful numbness returned.

At midnight he got up and put on a shirt and trousers. He went downstairs—he was not sure for what reason, wondering only if anyone was still about. He found Mike alone in the Judge's study, and when their eyes met, Steve realized why he had come down.

Mike looked up from his whisky glass and blinked his eyes, trying unsuccessfully to focus them.

"Steve?"

"Yes."

"You want a drink?" Mike asked.

"No, thanks," he said, and paused. "Mike, the friends Maggie went to see. On Long Island. She said something about their being family connections. Who were they?"

"Oh—distant cousins. The kind you see every five years or so."

"I sort of wondered why I hadn't heard anything from them—you know, condolences and so forth."

". . . I don't know why you didn't, Steve."

"Mike, it was a doctor on Long Island. Wasn't it? No distant cousins, no weekend party. Wasn't it a doctor, Mike?"

Mike turned his head away. "It doesn't matter, does it, Steve?"

"Yes. I think Maggie had an abortion and died."

Silence. Then Mike, with a visible effort, turned back and faced him.

"I did everything I knew to stop her, Steve. Maggie always got her own way in the end. You know that as well as I do."

"Yes," said Steve. "The doctor was a butcher?"

"No. He was a good doctor. It was meningitis. It can happen to anyone. Any time, Steve."

"I see." Steve nodded.

Mike waved a despairing hand.

"Maybe she wasn't responsible," he said. "Maybe I should

have come to you and told you what she wanted to do. Except I don't think I could've."

"No," said Steve. "You couldn't have, if Maggie was determined."

"You married a houseful of wrecks, Steve."

Steve did not answer, but went slowly out of the room again.

The next morning, when the funeral was over and they had left the cemetery, Steve no longer felt in a state of shock, but rather one of boundless lethargy. He was enervated, wrung out. A drizzle began to fall. He sat beside Judge Cowan in the back of the limousine, his heart a ball of chill and aching iron.

After a long silence Judge Cowan said, "Steve. I'm going out to the place in Virginia for a few days. I wish you'd come. Neither of us feels up to hunting, but it's a quiet, restful place, a good place for each of us to get his bearings. It would be a kindness on your part if you'd come with me. We'd just be ourselves, no servants or such, not even Michael."

"Thank you, Judge. I'd like to," Steve said. "Very much."

There had never been time for him to get to know his father-in-law well, he thought, but the Judge had always been warm and generous to him. He was glad now he could in part repay with a kind act—the kindness of not revealing to him the way in which Maggie had died. The loss of her had perceptibly aged the man. It would be criminal if anything more were done to him.

Steve said, "I haven't had a sane thought since it happened. I'm afraid I haven't been very helpful to you through all this."

Judge Cowan looked out the window, his worn eyes squinting at the slate-colored sky and the sogginess of the street they were driving through.

"When you're as old as I am," he said, "there seems no point to dissolving into misery. I've made my blunders, I've had a large share of drama and interest in life. I go on mechanically now, like a toy you wind up. Margaret—Margaret wasn't meant to last." Still looking out the window, he reached over and took Steve's hand. Steve gave a start at the iciness of his grip. "I shouldn't babble and say things that upset you. I'm sorry, Steve."

"No, don't be, Judge," Steve said quickly. He sighed. "The truth is, I had the same thought myself, the other night."

Judge Cowan pressed his hand once more and released it.

Night had long since fallen when they reached the little house set in a dense stretch of woods. They had come in rough clothes suitable to the informality of the place and the cold of the weather, and Henry had made up a picnic basket for them to have as supper their first night. From the car Steve unloaded this and a considerable supply of his father-in-law's liquor, while the Judge busied himself getting an outsized blaze going in the fireplace. When the unpacking was done, they fixed themselves drinks and sat down in two chairs drawn near to the fire's warmth.

For a while they sat in silence, sipping from their glasses and smoking their cigarettes. Then Steve said, "I guess I'm a damned fool to try to work up light subjects of conversation. I'm sorry, but I can't think of anything but Maggie, and how much I hate what's happened."

"That's all right, Steve. My ear is at your disposal, as it's always been, and I hope always will be. Don't hold back out of any mistaken regard for me."

Steve stared into the fire for a long moment before he spoke.

"I never thought the fact of losing Maggie could be made worse than it is," he said. "But it's worse because—she never had a chance to be happy, married to me. No time to learn, no time to—I think I made her miserable."

Judge Cowan smiled sadly. "I doubt it, Steve. Maybe she let you think so."

"No, it's true. That's why I feel this way, as though Maggie's dead someplace and resenting me for everything I did to her."

Judge Cowan said nothing, but listened. After a moment Steve went on, sitting back in his chair and massaging his forehead with driving fingertips.

"I don't know, I was a stupid jerk who'd never met up against that kind of thing. Like you and Maggie and Mike and the life you've always led. It's been a world away from anything I ever knew, but I didn't used to think of that. I was too busy loving Maggie, I thought. Christ, I was so busy loving her, I never took the trouble to understand what our life together looked like to *her*. Family money. Oh, how often Maggie used that phrase. And I never knew what it meant to her."

Judge Cowan put in, "Remember, I thoroughly approved of your demanding that Margaret learn to live on your income."

Steve looked at him uncertainly. "But family money, the way she meant it, that was in a subtle way hers by right. It didn't have anything to do with me; she must have thought it was outrageous of me to prevent her having something that was her own, that had always been her own, when it might have made life—more diverting for her."

Judge Cowan frowned and pursed his lips. "Was money that much of a bone of contention between you two?"

Steve sighed. "No. But it acted as a virus does. Maybe as something wrong with me rather than Maggie. Was I maybe worshiping the Great God Dollar too much myself in denying Maggie the benefits her own heritage could've given her?"

"Steve, she is dead," said her father. "You didn't know she would die this way. In time, under your standards, she might have lived to be a mature and responsible woman. I think then you would have allowed her material things you could not in conscience have allowed her at the start. You wanted to help her make the most of herself as a woman. You didn't know she'd die. The distressful thing, it seems to me, is that you should have doubts like that biting away at you now."

Steve shook his head slowly from side to side, glowering into the light of the blazing fire.

"I think I could have been gentler," he said.

Still, he thought, the errors of judgment he had made must have been implicit in the situation. The social classes. All over the country the arrangements of groups of human beings had grown increasingly fluid. Since the war you moved from one group to another with unprecedented ease. He had, hadn't he? Thousands of others had. He had always thought this a good thing, as a theory, but now he wondered. You moved in a strange world of confusing and unfamiliar values. If you had risen to a class more privileged than the one you were native to, you loved the feeling of security your new role represented to you. Security. What fools they'd been, himself and all the others like him, to think of security! The very fact that the boundaries were no longer even remotely impenetrable robbed them of the advantage of security. You rose and fell at the same time. Now there was no security anywhere but in your own destiny and your courage to pursue it. You fell in love with a sweet and tantalizing girl, and your world changed dizzyingly. Then she was taken away from you, and you were neither where you were nor where you had been before. You had nothing but your own destiny to guide you.

After the judge had excused himself and gone to bed, Steve mused in the silence of the firelit room. His destiny, his goal, his aim. What destiny did he have? He had never thought of a destination. He had been glad to be able to live from purpose to purpose. He had no religious convictions to point out an end in heaven. No dedicated interest in whose cause he could expire. What the hell *was* his destination? His brain clouded over in his exhaustion, and his last fumbling thought was: what the hell did he care now *what* it was. . . .

The unfolding year brought violence to other lives as well. In China, the Communist forces were putting to rout the crumbling, decay-ridden government of Chiang Kai-shek, whose listless armies disintegrated before the advance of the zealous, determined soldiers of the north, and the United States prepared to declare that it had abandoned hope of saving that vast country from the sweeping grasp of Mao Tse-tung. In the maturing of nations as of persons must come the occasion for digesting the knowledge of past stupidities. The United States with a gulp swallowed whole the history of its support of an intractable and corrupt regime and, as though in expiation, turned raging upon men and women within its own borders who it fancied, accurately or not, had betrayed their country. Whittaker Chambers and Alger Hiss attained a humiliating prominence. The marshaling of public opinion against Communism was by turns hysterical and sober. Judith Coplon, an analyst in the Internal Security section of the Department of Justice, was arrested on charges of trafficking in secret defense information. Soviet sympathizers were found everywhere, it seemed, in pragmatic government as well as in antic Hollywood. No one knew who would be accused next. The trial of eleven openly professed officers of the Communist Party, U. S. A., struck a blow to the strength and organization of the Party, the impact of which few ordinary citizens were in a position to appreciate.

Through the months of the trial of the Party leaders, Zeeda Kaufman was living in an unpretentious, ill-furnished basement apartment in a building on West Eighteenth Street in New York. Since coming to New York, she had received no assignment of the importance of the agitation scheme she had carried out in New Orleans. Instead she was directed to go to work as a dance-instructor, the same work she had done in California. The financial support she received from the Party was withdrawn, and she was appointed to a number of advance-study groups. Her functionary assignments were myriad: she collected dues, she brought a mimeograph machine into her apartment and, for hours every day, was kept busy running off bulletins, study papers, schedules, delivering them to the necessary people, attending meetings of the club to which she had been attached, dunning endless lists of other members for special donations. It was a constant and unrelenting drive that burned up the hours of her day, so that there was no single moment when she could question the worth of the automaton tasks she performed. At the instruction of the Party, she put away the clothes she usually wore and dressed herself in innocuous machine-made housedresses that would attract no attention. She affected a church-mouse coiffure.

With the arrest of the leadership of the Party, everything had changed with a violent lurch. Many of the clubs had been disbanded; those remaining had been broken up into smaller and smaller groups. Members with whom Zeeda had contact in New York were in a torment of indecision as the struggle to give birth to a new leadership went on. Many members vanished from the city, going into the customary deep-freeze of hiding and isolation. Joseph Murray's occasional noncommittal notes to her from California ceased altogether.

The most unfamiliar thing to Zeeda was the shatteringly sudden crackdown within the membership itself; she had seen nothing like it before, and a dozen sessions of the club and her study groups were needed to wash her clean of doubt. No member went without a rigorous check by security squads. Loyalty and steadfastness were tested and questioned at every turn. The doubtful by the dozens were expelled from the Party, communication with them abruptly cut off, and even the merely inept or inefficient found themselves unrecognized where they had always before sought comradeship.

To Zeeda, fighting for a clarity of understanding in her meetings with older and more seasoned members, there came to be nothing strange in having her superiors question her loyalty. She was a Communist, yes, and had established an enviable record since Ozzie Lubin and Joseph Murray had midwifed her return to Party activity as an adult; but she was the product of a capitalist background, the daughter of a well-to-do man who, on top of it all, was the shameful victim of a narrow Jewish nationalism. If she had been bred in corruption, who knew what stains of it remained inside her? She knew well enough herself the momentary drifting of her thoughts to a family who should have meant nothing to her, who were diseased with every loathsome sickness of the enemy system. When she'd first come back to New York, she had been tempted to go to see her brother Marvin. That inclination revealed a taint if anything did. What other corruption might not be lurking in her, ready to weaken the spot that would give way under the terrible pressures of the torturous time the Party was enduring? She must, she degermined, work harder still. At every cost she had to prove her worth to the Party. She drove herself mercilessly to get her work done in record time. When a special collection for the defense of the eleven leaders was going on and her own club fell short of its goal, she donated what money she had and for two weeks subsisted on a number of cans of peaches and a rocklike Pullman loaf of bread that happened to be in the cupboard. She could not afford to smoke or to drink much coffee; she walked to work at the dance studio every night, from Eighteenth Street to Forty-third Street, and back again. After doing her job at the dance studio, she would keep the mimeograph machine running until near dawn. Then, hungry, exhausted, tense as a strip of steel, she would try to sleep, and could not: the alarm clock might not work, she might not get the stacks of mimeographed sheets delivered in time; she might be censured by the Party because she didn't think of more things that she could do; she might not be given more important assignments that would allow her to prove once and for all that she was of value to the people who made up her life. She lay awake, wide-eyed and hungry in the dark apartment.

On the night he appeared at her front door, she had not seen Ozzie Lubin for two weeks. He had relieved her of club meetings so that she could give her time to the mimeograph work. She showed him in quickly and closed the door, dropping onto a table the knot of waste on which she had been wiping her ink-dripping hands.

Ozzie came into the large low-ceilinged room. Turning around, he glanced momentarily at the mimeograph machine set up on a table near the utility-kitchen alcove. He was a nattily-dressed little man with white hair and thin motionless eyebrows. His was a face never in repose: tenacious, pencil-sharp eyes, lips pursed to an invariable whiteness. To the world, he was a successful patent attorney, and Zeeda thought to herself that if he had been an actor, he could not have looked the part more than he did. She almost smiled her approval of him every time she saw him, and now she did so again.

Except that Ozzie Lubin was sweating.

"I thought for a while there was someone on me," he explained. "I've been dry cleaning on the subway for two hours, trying to ditch them. Actually, I don't think there was anyone. But so."

He turned and went over to a chair, dropping his hat onto the floor next to his bright-shod foot. Zeeda came over to him and stood before him.

"Nothing's wrong, I hope," she said, unable to mask in her voice the anxiety she lived in. "This last material's all ready to roll."

Ozzie flipped an impatient hand.

"No, no," he said. "It's new business."

Zeeda hurried to pull up a wooden kitchen chair. She sat down, facing him at a slight angle.

"Tell me, Ozzie," she said evenly.

"Have you got a cigarette?"

"Well, as a matter of fact——"

"Here, I have some, have one of mine."

"Thanks."

She accepted it, and he lit it for her. She succeeded in masking her gratitude for this momentary relief. It wouldn't do, she knew, for Ozzie to suspect that she thought of the sacrifices she had been making as especially severe.

Ozzie puffed on his cigarette a moment before going on. "They've got Chasen," he said.

Zeeda started. "Not the cops, for God's sake. Why?"

"No, not the cops, not yet, anyway. But the fucking New York Labor School has."

"How?"

He flipped a hand again. "I guess this is from while you were away," he said. "The Demo-Socialists and the Feds have a deal. It scares the piss out of them to think of us infiltrating the school without wearing hammers and sickles on our foreheads, so the F.B.I. digs up what it can about anybody joining the staff there. The other side of the deal is that Shagley or Mills or Henderson feeds them on whatever they hear, which is a damn sight too much."

"They use just one Fed contact?" asked Zeeda.

Ozzie nodded. "A new one, name of Les Vernon, got Chasen," he said. "So the school canned him. We've got to get somebody in there and keep them in there."

"Me?" Zeeda brought herself to ask.

"You. We've talked it out till it's coming out my ears, but I'll give you a brief pitch. The last time you were around in any obvious way, you were a kid; nobody around the Demo-Socialists is apt to remember you. Mills and Henderson?—absolutely not. Shagley?—damned unlikely. Or any of the rest of their bunch. Their links with the coast are feeble. But if we use you, Les Vernon will be smelling out everything he can, to warn the Demo-Socialists off you if he thinks you're hot. What about New Orleans?"

"New Orleans. Let me see." Zeeda drew again on her cigarette and tried to think back through the endless piles of mimeograph paper her mind had been subsisting on for so many months. "New Orleans. A lot of publicity. The party, the thugs—all of it. Will Vernon go that far afield?"

"Could you convince the school you were a dupe in that incident?" Ozzie asked.

Again Zeeda thought for a moment. "Yes," she said with finality. "All the others were. There's no way I know that Vernon could put the finger on me instead of the fifty-odd other people involved in it."

"But go slow, I think, as regards the school," Ozzie said.

"Confidence-gaining, buddying up with members of the staff before you make a move."

"I see," she said. "How about I enroll first, get some friendly staff backing before I make pitch for a job?"

"That's what we had in mind. Don't rush. We want somebody there, and we don't want it screwed again." He nodded toward the mimeograph machine. "Are you clean here?" he asked.

"I'm sure of it," said Zeeda. "Look, at the school, what's it to be when I manage to get on the staff? What field?"

"Folk music? Dramatics?" Ozzie offered.

"Folk music, make it," said Zeeda. "I can weed out the types more easily that way. When I enroll, what should I enroll in?"

"Graeme's lecture-course on economic history," said Ozzie. "You can branch out later on. When you think they'll find it acceptable, you might arrange some folk-music recitals: open-house basis, no fee involved. It'll get them acquainted with you as a singer, as somebody knowing about folk-music history and literature, so forth."

"I understand." Zeeda nodded. "Clothes?"

"Go back to whatever you like. You *want* to attract attention now. At the school, branch out into any course that looks helpful from our viewpoint, but stick with Graeme's lectures all the way."

"Oh? How come?"

"The Demo-Socialists have an up-and-comer studying under Graeme. For you he might be a good in. His name's Rizzuto. You'll get to know him, and do your establishing of confidence through him. He's a kid, no crusty old veteran like the others. But they're sweet on him. Keep one eye open for any recruiting work that might be done on Rizzuto, by the way. He's just an opening flower, there's no telling."

"I go on with my other assignments?" she asked.

Ozzie lifted his eyebrows when he looked at her, and her heart froze.

"Certainly." He shrugged. "Would you rather not?"

"No, hell, no, I only wanted to know. I can handle everything I'm given to handle."

"Good. Keep that in mind, Zeeda."

Zeeda swallowed, but did not answer. Ozzie said, "We've already taken you off club and study meetings. You'll need that time to be at the Labor School. A tighter security arrangement all around."

"Starting when do I go to the Labor School?"

"Tomorrow. Too late to be an actual student for the summer course, but you can arrange to audit Graeme's lectures. They also need someone to take the phone evenings—no pay, of course. I'm presuming you can pay the school's tuition fee yourself, out of your dance-studio salary."

Zeeda put a hand out quickly. "Never mind, I'll find a way."

"Good girl. At the Labor School tomorrow, see a colored girl named Edith Mackey. She'll arrange the auditing. She's a D.S.P. girl, and no fool. Watch your step with her."

When he was gone, Zeeda stood leaning against the door she had just closed. She was afraid to believe what had happened. An assignment: a *real* assignment, a chance to prove herself to the Party that almost nobody but the important ones ever got these days, a chance for vindication. She could not fail. She *had* to get herself onto the Labor School staff and stay there. Moving back into the room, biting the tips of her fingers, she tried to figure out the angles of the job while going on with the errand-running, the mimeographing, the collecting. Suddenly she groaned: how could she do that also and not risk the Vernon guy finding her out? Ozzie had lost his mind!

No, the answer came quickly. Men like Ozzie knew what they were up to. In times like this they damn well had to know. Maybe they wanted to make it as tricky as possible in order to test her reliability. All right, if that's what it was, she'd find a way, by God she'd find a way to get away with it. The greater part of her salary was already committed to defense funds, but money for schooling could always be found. She'd get it, she had no fear. She could probably talk the school itself into a cut rate and at the same time get herself known to them and win their interest. A young girl eager for knowledge, desperate because she couldn't afford to pay the full tariff to hear Graeme lecture on economic history? She'd have them adoring her. She looked at the alarm clock. The attack was tomorrow. Tonight she was certain she would sleep.

In the midst of the nation's clamoring accusations against Communists, rudimentary politics went sometimes awry, and in New York the power of Tammany Hall was thrust against a Democrat. Franklin Delano Roosevelt, Jr., the third son of the late President, campaigned to fulfill the vacancy in the House of Representatives left by the late Sol Bloom. Liberals in the labor movement supported him, and active in bringing its influence to bear upon the campaign was the Demo-Socialist Party. The work Tom Henderson and Driscoll Mills were doing was an exacting education for Tiger Rizzuto, who assisted them tirelessly.

He had been an employee of the Demo-Socialist Party since the time that Henderson and Mills, getting to know him, had become indignant at the fact that a young man interested in the labor movement was being held down by the menial position of janitor of the New York Labor School. That was a year ago.

They had hired him away from Shagley. They had introduced him to leaders of the labor movement, to ward heelers of Tammany Hall, to campaign hirelings of every party, and, more recently, to the candidates themselves. Tiger's own work was functional, but it afforded him the opportunity of listening, of conjuring with the things he heard and the things he learned in his more formal study. He did so with unflagging interest.

Shortly before the election Tiger was at work one evening until midnight in the offices of the Demo-Socialist Party. His desk was in a narrow cubicle off the conference room on the third floor, and his desk lamp cast outsized shadows on the walls. For an hour he had been poring over his check list of pre-election chores, marking beside each item the name of the volunteer campaign workers he would assign to it, setting aside many for himself to oversee. He finished, and sitting back in his chair, rubbed his reddened eyes. The room was hot and filled with the smoke of the cigarettes he'd been puffing on, but he was too tired to get up and open the window. He was sitting there, half-asleep, when he heard the tapping on the door.

"Yes? Sollie?"

The door pushed open, and Mills put in his head.

"Nope. Sollie, like a good janitor, has gone down to his room and gone to bed."

"Hi." Tiger pulled himself erect in his chair.

Mills ambled over to open the window. "Don't you ever go

home to Juney any more?" he asked, wandering back with his usual stooping easiness, his long scholary face serene and contemplative.

"I just finished up," Tiger said. "I had to get the goddamned check list organized tonight or never. I had an economics lecture. Couldn't get up here till ten-thirty."

"How'd the list work out?"

"Fine. I'm still looking for a volunteer to take the switchboard nights."

Mills let his lank form down into the straight chair next to Tiger's desk. His graying hair was mussed, and the knot of his tie askew. His eyes were as red as Tiger's. He sighed and pulled a cigarette from Tiger's pack on the desk. "We're *all* going to need two weeks in a hospital when this is over."

"Not me," Tiger said. "Hell, I'm having a fucking ball." He felt suddenly wide awake and curiously exhilarated.

Mills grinned sleepily. "You're getting to be quite the power behind the throne, you know. Everybody keeps asking: Who's the young guy you got handling the office paperwork? What're you grooming him for?" He blew smoke into the light of the desk lamp, and his face grew thoughtful. "You're doing a damn good job on all this routine stuff, Tiger."

"Don't it beat hell?" Tiger asked. "I never seriously thought in my whole life I'd end up at a desk with a lot of paper clips. I guess I handle the stuff okay because I'm interested in it."

"How long've you been studying at the school?" Mills asked.

"One year while I was the janitor here, another year since I've been working for you."

"I wish to hell we had funds enough to utz your salary up a little."

"So do I," Tiger snorted. "But Juney and I manage. I'm so busy here, I never need money for painting the town or anything. And I've got enough to keep the rent on the apartment up and the baby in shoes, more or less. I realize what money the D.S.P.'s got has to be used for political action."

"Well, it won't be long before we step you up in the ranks. The pay will be better there." He stood up. "Come on, let's get you home and to sleep."

"I'll go home," Tiger said, standing, "but I don't promise to sleep. I'm getting too hopped up about the campaign."

"The neophyte syndrome," said Mills.

"The hell you say. It's just I'm getting to be a fanatic about work."

"Tiger, this is a local campaign," Mills pointed out. "I'm glad you're hopped up about it, but Roosevelt Junior is a local campaign. Remember it. Remember the waters may get a lot deeper ahead."

"I know. But don't mind my enjoying the campaign while it's the main thing going on."

Tiger Rizzuto's wakefulness did not leave him on his way home, and when Mills let him out of his car, Tiger walked away from it with a step that was almost jaunty.

When he had joined the Demo-Socialist Party's staff a year before, he and Juney had taken an apartment in a co-operative on the East Side. As he walked up to the building now, he saw the light burning in the kitchen window of his own second-floor apartment. He smiled to himself and quickened his step. Juney would have left sandwiches for him in the refrigerator, and he realized now how hungry he was. He hurried into the building, up the service stairs, and through the door that opened directly into the kitchen.

Juney gave a start, then smiled at him.

"Surprise," she said.

"Juney, what are you doing still up?" he asked, bending to kiss her. She had not yet put cold cream on, but she had washed the make-up from her face. Her lips against his own were curiously dry and soft; the kiss tasted faintly of the coffee she'd been drinking.

"Elizabeth was having the horrors," she told him as he sat down opposite her at the kitchen table. "A bad dream, I guess. It was twelve-thirty before I could get her to sleep again, so I thought I'd give myself a treat and have night-lunch with you."

She got up and from the refrigerator brought a platter of sandwiches and a bottle of milk. Tiger fetched two glasses from the cupboard.

"Have fun today?" Juney asked.

"Busy as hell. That's why I had to stay on at the office after my class."

"Did you know that if Rita Hayworth marries Aly Khan, she'll be *Princess* Rita? Really officially?"

"Boy, *you*'ve had a fascinating day, I can see that," said Tiger.

"That was just to get your attention," Juney said. Then she asked, "What's with the Chinese Communists—does Doctor Graeme think they're going to win?"

"Hell, yes, and do you know why?"

"Now just keep your voice down, dear, you'll wake the baby. . . ."

Tiger went on in a fierce, grimacing whisper, "Because *we* flubbed the dub."

"You don't have to whisper, Tiger. Just don't shout," Juney said. "Goodness but you're charged up."

"We keep supporting Chiang's regime when everybody on earth knows it's rotten. The Communists are going to win at every turn because, whether it's right or wrong, they've got something to sell, something they believe in. What have we got to sell? . . . A lot of platitudes we never even attempt to live up to. If we were a socialist country, maybe somebody would believe we lived according to our ideals. But *this* way?"

"Don't snarl at me, dear," Juney returned mildly. "I'm not a capitalist, I'm a housewife."

Tiger gave an explosive sigh and bit into another sandwich. Then he realized Juney was smiling at him, almost wistfully.

"You could rave on all night, couldn't you?" she asked. "It's so wonderful to see you fired up about something. I can hardly remember how it used to be."

Tiger reached across the table and took her hand. "I can," he said, his voice soft again. "I'm always going to."

"It's wonderful for you, and it's wonderful for Elizabeth and me, too."

"Juney? You know why things are working out so well for us? Because these are real guys, Mills and Henderson and the others, nothing snotty about them, but they're crazy for politics. I'm getting to be, too, and they encourage me. When I'm encouraged, I can do anything."

Juney stood up. "And you need some sleep if you're going to keep up with them," she said firmly.

While Juney returned the remaining sandwiches to the refrigerator, Tiger rinsed out the glasses at the kitchen sink.

They turned out the light and tiptoed past the open door of the baby's bedroom to their own room beyond. The lamp on the bedside table lit the room gently. Juney climbed into bed, and Tiger started to undress. He stopped in the midst of arranging his trousers on their hanger, and stood looking thoughtfully out the window to the glow of the street lights beyond.

"What is it?" Juney asked gently, lifting herself up on one elbow.

Tiger glanced back at her. "I was thinking how quick life helps you when you really try to do something about yourself. You forget, when things are bad, and put the blame on anybody or anything you can think of."

He hung up his trousers, and moving around to Juney's side of the double bed, sat down beside her.

"You know what I am now?" he asked. "A family man. When I first thought that was what I wanted to be, there was hardly a prayer of its working out that way."

"When was that, Tiger?"

"When it first occurred to me to see if I could work in with Mills and Henderson. I thought: Wouldn't it be a hell of a note if I could end up being a real stodgy family man?"

Juney laughed. "Oh, Tiger, stodgy?—*you?*"

"Just a little. I want to be. Like—I want us to have turkey for dinner on holidays and have waifs come join us."

"Waifs?" Juney frowned doubtfully.

"Well, you know, lonely people, friends of ours who might not have any dinner invitations for a holiday. We've been so busy settling in New York——"

"We'll have someone, Tiger. I think you're right. It'll make somebody feel better, seeing how happy we are."

"You're a terrific wife, Juney," he said. "You're the one who brought me luck."

Juney smiled. "I have a terrific husband, Robin."

Tiger frowned. "Why do you call me Robin only sometimes?"

"Because you're Robin only sometimes. Except more and more times nowadays."

"I feel like a better man when you call me Robin."

"What I call you means so much?"

"So much," said Tiger. "It even makes my nightmares ease up."

"What nightmares?"

He hesitated. He wished he hadn't brought it up, but the distress in Juney's expression told him he could not back out of it.

Softly: "I keep having nightmares—about before—about Chicago. If I ever made a million dollars, I could buy cars for all the people I stole from. But even then I couldn't find the people so I could give them the cars. In my dream I keep buying cars and keep walking up and down Chicago, trying to find the people I stole from. . . ."

"Oh, Robin. Robin, you shouldn't feel that way. Not now. If you'd go to confession, you wouldn't feel all that any more. . . ."

He patted her hand, but his answer was determined. "I don't want anybody stroking my head and telling me everything will be fine now. I want myself to make up for what I did."

"I know"—Juney nodded—"I know. Maybe, somehow, in some way you can't expect, you'll be able to one day. It happens. Now come to sleep, Robin. And no nightmares. And dearest?"

"Yes?"

"If Roosevelt loses, you won't have a nervous breakdown, will you?"

"No, Juney. Not over that, anyway." He kissed her. "Good night, dearest."

"Good night."

29

IT HAD BEEN FEBRUARY, THE MONTH OF drizzle, when Maggie was buried. Steve had spent those few days in Virginia with Judge Cowan and then had come back to New York, to the apartment he and Maggie had lived in since their marriage. His parents had arrived shortly from Houston for a visit, Steve persuading his father to let him defray at least a part of their expenses. They stayed a week and then went home. It was with relief and a rueful affection that he saw them onto their plane. He went home to the empty apartment. Somewhere in the next day or so he began to drink heavily.

He had plenty of money, he argued with himself, now that there was no trip he could give to Maggie. Why shouldn't he drink if he wanted to? . . . He did not have difficulty convincing himself. He drank alone at home; he drank in the bars on Third Avenue; he drank in the most expensive night clubs. He drank, not repeatedly, but constantly. He poured liquor down the throats of assorted faceless prostitutes he would bring to the apartment in the hope that the smell of other women in passion would drive the ghost of Maggie's smell and voice and touch from the rooms that had seen their love-making and their despair. From the beginning of the binge and through its full duration he knew that what was happening to him, the violence he was exercising on himself, destructive and ugly, was without justification, but he did not know where to turn for rescue, or whether indeed it was rescue he wanted at all.

The debauchery lasted three months, and when it was over, a substantial part of his money was gone. Gone with it, he persuaded himself, was his agony, and now he was only exhausted, lonely, and emotionless. . . .

It was June. He could no longer afford the apartment, and he looked about for another place to live. He found a studio on Forty-seventh Street and moved his things into it. He did not drink again. He did not inform any of the friends Maggie and he had made in New York of his new address. They had been friends of his and Maggie's, and those friendships, reasonless as it might seem, were in the earth with her. He wanted to see no one; he was incapable of giving of himself to anyone or anything; he was a structure molded of sawdust. He did not call Rachel Pemberton to let her know where to find him. For a long time he could not bring himself to write even to give his parents the new address. He slept at any hour. He awoke and went down to the corner lunch counter for a tasteless, mechanical meal. He came back to the apartment and sat. For hours he sat smoking cigarettes, thinking of nothing but the puzzle of Maggie that he could not really solve.

The weather warmed and one day he decided to go for a walk. The soot-filled air of the neighborhood was at least more refreshing than the sour air of the studio. He walked until sundown. It was an automatic, pleasureless exercise. As he passed, no sights arrested him, no minor incident penetrated his shell of apathy. He walked. Up one street, down another. He traversed a long avenue, and what was before him was gray and featureless. He went home at a plodding pace, neither hurrying nor tarrying.

The next day, after breakfast at the lunch counter, he did not go back to the studio, but went walking again without relish. His mind was as dulled as ever, but the blind movement of walking comforted him. If he could walk forever, he must eventually, inescapably, walk out of his stupor.

Walking became all of regimen he knew.

On one such walk, in the early hours of the morning, he found himself on a strange street, one of the countless little villages, entire to themselves, that huddle unknown and unseen inside the larger make-up of the city. Rain began to fall, at first lightly, but then with increasing insistence. He did not stop to take shelter, but continued dull-wittedly, though his clothes were getting uncomfortably wet. He went on and on. Soon he came to a large stone building whose broad steps afforded a narrow shelter from the rain. He stepped out of the downpour. The rain fell harder still, and its spashes edged him farther back. He turned to look at the door, and realized it was the entrance to a church. Faintly through the colored glass panes he could see a warming glow of candlelight. He pushed open the door tentatively an inch, and then went in.

It was, he supposed, a Catholic church. Up on the brightly lighted altar a priest in modestly grandiose vestments was being assisted through the unfamiliar ritual by two rangy schoolboys. After a time of watching Steve concluded it must be the Mass. But it could not be Sunday, he thought. There were no more than a dozen people in the forward pews—shabby middle-aged women with rags tied over their heads, a younger woman who looked like a lawyer's secretary, well but oversedately groomed, and a single old man bent into his kneeling position overemphatically, a caricature of piety. There was no music, no sound in the place but the unintelligible murmuring of the priest and the boys assisting him. The Mass continued, and no one turned to look at him.

Steve found himself moving forward slowly. He came to the pew farthest back in the church, and moving gingerly over the lowered kneeling-bench, afraid to make a noise, he sat down. He was aware of the velvet easingness of the candlelight, the stroking softness of its gleams. Most other elements of the scene eluded him: the movements of the man and the two boys on the altar ahead of him were without meaning; the people in the church, mere shifting, coughing shadows as they stood or sat or kneeled, apparently by prescribed practice, in unison.

Steve watched listlessly. Soon the priest and the altar boys descended. They turned and knelt down, facing the altar, to say a prayer in what sounded like English. He could not understand the words clearly, but they weren't Latin. Then the priest and the altar boys were gone, and the few people in the church, except for one very old woman in the foremost pew, shuffled out. . . .

Steve felt dimly that something was wrong. Was that all there was? Somewhere—he could not remember—somewhere he had heard that the ritual of the Mass was the foundation of Catholic belief. Was it Waugh? Somewhere. Well, maybe this hadn't been the Mass. Some simpler observance. Or maybe he had come in late and had missed all but the last of the show. The show?—he grimaced to himself. That was a hell of a way to think about it. Even a heathen should have some respect for the beliefs of others. What made a lawyer's secretary get up early enough to come to church before going on to the office?

Suddenly something snapped in him, and he realized how his thoughts, jumbled but active, had been running on. It was as if he had come awake. His clothes felt oddly heavy on him, as they might have if he had been wearing them for days without changing. He twisted a little to adapt his body to their sharpness. He felt the wetness around his ankles, the clamminess of his shoes. Awake, a little: this Catholic Mass, if that was what it was, was the first thing he'd given any real thought to in months.

The next day he got up early again. Over his breakfast at the lunch counter he debated going back to the church. He felt no enthusiasm for the idea, but he had nothing else to do. Why the hell not? he thought. But he did not know the name of the church or its location in any exact sense. He went back to the studio and read the list of churches in the Red Book. He could vaguely define the area he had walked in the day before, and soon he found the name of a church whose address looked likely. He called the number and learned at what time Masses were begun on weekdays.

He went to the eight o'clock Mass at the address shown in the directory and found his guess had been right. He had taken care to arrive well ahead of time, and this day he sat and watched the entire progress of the Mass in the glowing, warm, almost deserted little church. It was no more comprehensible to him than it had been before, but there was one moment, one especially arresting moment: a tinkling of bells held by one of the altar boys, a sudden almost contortive movement of the priest as he lifted a white wafer high above his head, the abrupt small crouching of the handful of people in the pews. He didn't know what, but something had happened.

Through the Masses that he went to in the days following Steve did not try to find out what it was. His curiosity was not acute, but only slowly stirring. Something in what regularly took place in the little church made him blandly curious, which could be said of nothing else he had seen or done for an extended time. He found himself returning repeatedly to its mystery, not wanting to understand it, actually, but beguiled by the advent of a mystery in his world, a mystery that could do so much as stirring up his previously paralyzed attention. For a week he went to Mass every morning, sitting nearer and nearer to the altar and its priest, knowing he could never understand the Latin, but wanting to see in greater detail what went on and straining to understand the English words of the prayer at the end of the Mass. At last he caught a few.

The priest's voice was young, and gently timbered. ". . . Be our recourse against the malice and snares of the Devil, who roams through the world, seeking the ruin of souls . . ."

The words as they met his ear had an unexpected and terrible pungency for him.

After the Mass that morning the participants dispersed as usual, the priest to his sanctum with his helpers, the faithful to the increasingly summer-warm streets. Steve sat still in his place for a time, looking idly at the ornate altar, so pitiful in its hope to attain grandeur, and wondered. At length he got up and walked out of the church through the glass-paneled doors. He gave a start when he saw on the front steps the young priest. He was wearing a cassock, and he looked at him, half-smiling. "Hi. Good morning," he said.

"Good morning," said Steve.

He was a scant five years older than Steve himself, neither muscular nor thinly made. His face was attractive—its muscles had the subtle tension of the disciplined ascetic's. His eyes had the diamond brightness and shape of a fox's. His jaw was shadowed by the heaviness of his beard.

"I'm sure as I can reasonably be that you're not a parishioner," the priest said, "but I can't help seeing you here morning after morning, sitting there so alone when everybody else comes to Communion. My name's John Davis."

"How do you do?" Steve said, and shook his hand. "Steve Williams."

"Hi, Steve."

The priest said nothing more, but looked at him with an unwavering pleasantness, as though that would be sufficient, and Steve stammered, "No, I'm not what you said. A parishioner. I just come by, in the morning. It happened by accident, you see. If you know what I mean. One day when it rained."

"Keep coming here." The priest smiled mildly. "It's nice having you. By the way, there's a rack in the back of the church with some pamphlets. Most of them are pretty awful, but there's a good one explaining all about Mass. Unless, of course, you know all about Mass."

"No—no, not a thing," Steve said.

"Good, then. Try it and see if you don't find it interesting. If you don't understand anything in the pamphlet, or want to know more about something in particular, call me up. Or any of the other monks will be happy to answer questions. Nice talking to you, Steve. Boy, can you smell the rain in the wind? I've got to get back to the parish house. Good-by."

And, like an apparition, the young priest was gone.

Steve returned to the church regularly. He took the pamphlet John Davis had recommended from the little table in the back of the church and read it at home. It seemed to him to be pious nonsense. He could not, however, simply dismiss what he learned from it. There had been intelligence and humanity in those fox eyes. After several days of rereading the pamphlet, he called up the priest and made an appointment to see him.

They sat that night in the ludicrously Victorian parlor of the parish house, facing each other across a central marble-topped table.

Steve showed the young priest the pamphlet he'd been studying.

"I can't convince myself people believe everything it says in here," he explained. "I mean—you talk like an educated, intelligent guy——"

"I'm educated," John Davis conceded. "Jesuits are."

"And you go along with this understanding of the Mass?" he asked, tapping the pamphlet.

"Suppose you tell me the particular points that floor you," the priest suggested.

"All right." Steve started to flip through the pages of the pamphlet, but hesitated. "This is uncomfortable. I have all due respect for your calling, et cetera, but you're practically my own age and I feel like a damn fool calling you Father. Do I have to?"

"My name's John. Mister wouldn't do very well, either."

For an hour they argued the points the pamphlet made to which Steve felt he had objections. John Davis unfolded for him the history of the ritual, and as the exposition went on, he spoke with increasing excitement, a fervor made up of intellectual comprehension and the gift of wonder. When Steve became lost in a forest of symbols, traditional and minute points of logic, John cut his explanation short.

"The Mass is only one moment—just one, Steve," he said. "That's when the bells you spoke of ring. It's the moment when a piece of vegetable matter becomes God. That's why you felt what you did when it happened. You felt my belief, I wouldn't be surprised, and the belief of the people around you."

He was to insist on the meaning of the Consecration again and again in their discussions. For Steve returned to the parish house often in the following weeks, and he and John Davis became friends.

"Transubstantiation," John asserted, "is literal. Familiar vegetable matter can't become the body and blood of Christ in a rational world. It needs a miracle to effect it. And a miracle is what God has given us."

"It's all very nice to believe, John but——"

"Nice? It's horrible. It's terrifying. Are you listening to

what I'm saying? Do you think I'm spouting lyrical poetry?"

"Okay, okay, I didn't mean just——"

The ascetic face grew stern and oddly remote. "Christ comes back. Every day. Many times every day."

"But a little bit of flour paste, a drop of cooking sherry . . . ?"

"Any sillier vehicle than the patchwork bacillus-ridden body of man?" John returned.

"Vehicle? What man?"

"The historical Christ," John said casually.

Steve respected John Davis' conviction, a conviction that made him able at every turn to block the objections of such a watery agnostic as Steve knew himself to be. Slowly the priest began to make his impression. He made no move to make Catholicism as an espoual attractive to Steve. He offered no rewards for the virtuous, nor recriminations for the evil or the ignorant. He contented himself with explaining, both with clarity and the passion born of his terrifying belief, the idea of transubstantiation, the miracle and the mystery of the daily Mass he celebrated.

Soon Steve learned of John's habit of going for long walks each day after lunch. Steve invited him to stop off at the studio sometime during his outing and have coffee with him. John accepted the invitation, and before long it had become their customary time of meeting and discussion. He knew, of course, that John's kindness and generosity with time were justified only by his calling: it was his business, and he said as much, to save Steve's soul, to deliver Steve Williams intact one day to heaven. But he did not ask questions about Steve's personal life, and Steve told him very little. He explained that the portrait over the mantlepiece was of his dead wife; once he referred to the despairing grief over her death that had held him in paralysis until he had become interested in the history and meaning of the Mass. John knew Steve was a writer, had gone to the trouble of seeking out a few of his stories in back issues of magazines at the public library, but he learned little else.

About himself, John was open. He had grown up in an intellectually snobbish family of academic men. "Dad is still being the awesome doctor of physics and involved in a lot of government work none of us is allowed to know anything about. He was a very loving father; he didn't mind my becoming a priest, at least not a Jesuit. He was just horrified that I didn't want to be a teacher especially, but a parish man. Of course we all do everything, the society keeps bouncing us around, but Dad has yet to reconcile himself to the fact that I *like* parish work. I was ordained only three years ago, and I've been in this parish ever since, finishing tertianship. I love it, and Dad feels vaguely that he's been betrayed."

"Why do you like it, do you think?" Steve asked. "More opportunity to win converts?"

"I guess it probably is. Something like that."

"It's a hell of a position to find myself in: on the other end of a conversion stick."

John held his gaze. "Saints are made out of people, Steve," he pointed out quietly. "Don't let it make you feel awkward."

"But if I never got to be more than an—an interested observer—I'd feel I had gypped you in some way."

John laughed. "I can't be gypped out of anything—I don't own anything. Not even my time or, really, my friendship. Look at it this way. I can explain this and that to you now, and let's say you don't respond. Not like a convert, anyway. It doesn't mean my words have lost their chance. They won't have lost their chance until you're dead and buried. You absorb what you hear, you're that kind of man; being that kind of man is part of your profession. Nothing I say or do is lost on you forever."

As the weeks passed Steve found himself drawn more and more irresistibly to John Davis' religious concepts. He could not yet believe that God was physically born anew when John said certain formulated words in the Mass, he did not believe it had much to do with himself even if such a thing occurred; but the beauty of the idea, the legacy of a God to his beleaguered children, this image of the miracle put out warm and reassuring tentacles that embraced him.

The tentacles had no sooner done so than John Davis hacked them off.

"Steve, don't be a fool," he said. "Religion doesn't give you reassurance, that isn't its business. Oh, I could. I could tell you the Lord provides and to consider the lilies of the field. He doesn't, not in a way a man like you thinks, and by all means consider the lilies of the field if you get a kick out of it. But don't call it religion. The only thing religion can give you, Steve Williams, is your life."

"My life?"

"I see your studio, I talk to you, I can guess how you live."

"How is that?"

John spread his hands. "Emptily," he said. There was a pause. Steve abruptly skirted the subject, and they did not mention it again.

"Paris 8e
June 12, 1949

Dearest Marvin:

Your letters are a joy, and I only hope you're not neglecting your practice by taking so much time to write to me.

The summer here is beautiful, though I'm told the city gets hellish later on. Everybody does a rats-from-the-sinking-ship act in August. I don't know whether I'll be here when that time comes or not. I've asked Jules to keep me on the payroll. In return, I can set up some spreads for him here. He's been very nice and hasn't fired me, and I've secured my future by finding him a wonderful new girl for the agency. Her name is Betsy, and I wouldn't dream of telling you anything more about her. She's an American—her family have been living over here—and she's coming to America to make her fortune via Fischel and his resourceful assistant, Miss Maclean. I think she'll make *our* fortunes as well. As a result of all this, my schedule is still undecided.

Elise Chambon, the girl I'm sharing this apartment with, has been very kind about introducing me around, and I've met some fabulous people—a group of Englishmen, in particular, and two or three Mexicans who work at UNESCO. I don't think I like the French people so much. The men are all very gallant, but women are kept in a very definite place and are not supposed either to know or care about anything but fashions and, possibly, the arts. Not a position I'd enjoy on a permenant basis.

I think of you often, and look forward to your letters constantly. Enjoy your week at Long Beach and get very, very tanned. Write me from there if the sights on the beach don't distract you completely from the thought of me.

Love,
Helen"

"Long Beach, New York
I don't know what date

Darling Helen:

The beach is filled with a lot of barbarians, and natch I haven't done anything but think about you. And think and think about you.

Congratulations on finding a new model for the agency. But how can you get her started when she's over here and you're over there? Or does Jules Fischel take care of that?

Being away from New York has done me good, I'm glad to report. I've had more time to think about things nonmedical than I've had in years, and I suppose you can call it 'good' to have churned up a lot of mistakes that I've been presuming were something other than mistakes. I've been giving a lot of thought to my mother, Helen, and my conclusion is that I couldn't in my wildest dreams have handled the situation with her more stupidly. Do you mind my going into this when this should be simply a pleasant letter?

She won't change, my dearest. She's not the changing type. I've always tried to excuse her behavior, and maybe there are excuses for it. But the fact remains that, once set on her course, there's no dealing with her. My sister, Zeeda, knew that. That's why Zeeda's never come back to try, I've decided. Zeeda was more perceptive about the case than I have been, and there's nothing to do but admit as much to myself. She won't ever willingly let go of me, any more than she would ever have accepted Zeeda.

I can't let her have her blind, unreasoning way any more than Zeeda could, and I've resolved not to. Unfortunately, it's too late now for that to keep you from canceling your plans and going to Europe. You were right to do so, of course. No one should be asked to take the handling you got from my parents and, thanks to my own bumptiousness, from me. Forgive me, Helen.

I'm sorry none of this is very cheerful. I'll do better in my next letter. Be good to yourself.

Love,
Marvin"

"Long Beach
Day after weepy letter

Darling Helen:

This is nerve and gall, but I can't put off writing to you about it. I have decided something I hope you will be pleased to hear, but if you are simply out of patience or annoyed, I will understand very well.

A. I was a fool to let my worry about my family cause the trouble between you and me. *B*. I love you, and as long as I live, I know I will never find another girl as marvelous. *C*. I am asking you again to marry me, and the hell with my parents. If they ever come to their senses, it will be fine with me; but if not, it's their loss. *D*. If there is anything, anything I can do to bring you back soon from France, tell me what it is.

Helen, please say you'll at least consider marrying me, and try to put from your mind the memory of what a jerk I've been in the past. I love you, I love you, I love you.

M."

"July 5

My darling:

It was a beautiful letter, and I know what it must cost you to ask me to marry you even if your parents do object. I love you more than ever, and every instinct I've got tells me to get on the next plane and come back to you at once. I *will* be back by August 15, but I'm afraid if I go rushing off now, I might get my toe stubbed. I know you will understand and not be hurt by my fearing that. Keep writing to me, keep me in your thoughts as much as you'll be in mine, and when I get back, let's see what we can do about your mother and father. The situation may not be past rescue.

May I tell you something confidentially? I have to because if I don't, my conscience will bother me. My coming over here at all was at least partially in the hope that my being away from you would give you time to think and in the end make you more determined about our getting married. Darling, I hate to cause you pain where the family is concerned, but having been away for a while, I have the feeling I may be able to help you with them, as I didn't help before. I *will* try, Marvin.

I'm so excited by your letter I can't think much of what else to write. Do you want to hear about what I've been up to here? Well, it's dull compared with what I feel now. I've been doing more party-going in the last several weeks than I thought possible. Yesterday, of course, the American Embassy had a jam-packed open house, and Elise and a group of her friends took me along. All very impersonal and official (nobody gets invited, anybody can go), but we had a wonderful time. I had dinner afterward with Elise's aunt and uncle, who turn out to be terribly rich. How they manage to do it with France in its present shape, I can't imagine. They're a good-looking couple, and brilliant talkers—in English, thank God, it's all I can do to buy a loaf of bread in French—and told me some of the goings-on during the occupation. He did some work in the underground and got a medal for it. The medal lends authority to his conversation; there are an awful lot of after-thought members of the underground around.

The Louvre is a horror. All those beautiful things, and they cram them up against one another as if they were a wall full of potholders. I figure they took whoever it was dreamt up the placement of the Winged Victory and shot him.

What else. Yes, I know. I've fallen victim to the affectation of studding my talk with the easier French phrases. It will bore you silly, but it is inevitable and I'm sure won't last forever.

What can I write except I love you? The next few weeks I'm here will be agony, but I can keep going knowing you really want to marry me after all.

More later, my sweet.

All my love,
Helen"

"134 East 47th Street
New York

16 July 1949

Dear Ben and Hilda:

And now all the way around the world to Paris—what a terrific time you must be having.

Let me tell you right off that your letters arriving with such faithful regularity since Maggie's death have meant more to me than I can express. In fact, aside from the two families, you're the only ones I've been in contact with since it happened. My parents came up some time ago to make sure I wasn't going to go off the deep end, and of course Maggie's father and brother have been kinder than anyone could wish. But your letters have been specially cherished; maybe it's because you don't have either blood line or marital connection prompting, but only our friendship to involve you. I will always remember and appreciate your loyal concern.

Enough of that. I don't know how to answer your question about what I'm doing. It's been almost five months now, but it seems much less, and I haven't been very energetic about getting organized again. The lucre in hand must be made to last, since I haven't been able to write anything saleable, so I'm somewhat out of circulation. (Incidentally, make a note of the new address. It's a studio-room on a garden behind a converted brownstone. Away from the street, and very comfortable in its damned individual way.)

It seems every time I answer a letter of yours it's the same thing—I just don't have anything much to write about. Forgive my lack of inventiveness for the moment, and we'll talk about everyting at length during your few days passing through New York. It's been too long; I'll keep the Martinis on ice for you.

Affectionately,
Steve"

"The U.S.A., in case it
slipped your mind"

Helen my sweetest:

Come home already. Nothing has improved with Mother and Father Kaufman, but I need you and want you. So does your boss.

If you can go around playing footsies with Englishmen and Mexicans, the least I can be allowed to do is have dinner with your boss. So I did. My evil plan was to persude him he had a hundred reasons for demanding that you get back to work over here. But other things came up. I know what you're going to say, and I admit it was all very presumptuous of me, but there it is.

What I did was to see how Jules—I call him that 'cause that's his name now—thought of you as a prospective partner. Before I could make myself clear, the conversation got out of hand. For one thing, Betsy has arrived in New York, and Jules has flipped over her—and flipped about you for finding her over there. Some photographer named Chester Gibson cried all the way through a two-hour sitting with her, he was so inspired. Jules is going gray because he says Betsy's acting abilities cries out for TV modeling and he hasn't enough hands to get the agency into TV as well as the fashion-mag gambit.

Marvin Kaufman deposes and says: Why don't you give Helen her head and leave TV to her?

Your boss, quote: It means additional personnel in the office and we can't afford them.

Me: What if Helen footed the salary for her own secretary-cum-booking-girl for a year? After all, she has the money to do it. She does? The poor guy really looked mystified.

No, you don't have the money, and I know it, but I do have, and I believe in community property even without the laws about it. If you want to go on working until babies start arriving, it'll be nicer for you to be a partner with Jules; you can walk out without explanation when I call you up and tell you to come home and make love unexpectedly. And when we're into the baby-raising business, you might find it nice to have some advisory capacity at the agency so you won't feel inclined to dissolve yourself into the milk along with the pablum.

Now don't snap your cap. I am better aware than anybody on earth that we haven't even set a date for a wedding, that you still have perfect freedom to suddenly take an intense dislike to the way I strike matches or something, or that on second thought a doctor's midnight calls are something you'd rather not have to put up with. But Helen, if I live, I'm going to be married to you. So I took this liberty with Jules. Naturally nothing is even remotely concrete until you're here to ask questions and satisfy yourself about what you want. But I thought—oddly enough—that the prospect of being a partner with Jules might make you feel more married to me already. Maybe if I were writing in Swahili, this would sound more sensible. It will have to stand as it is.

Please come marry me before I tell all my patients to go die and come over there after you.

Love,
M."

STEVE WILLIAMS 134 E 47 NYC ARRIVING SATURDAY ILE DE FRANCE BRING RACHEL IF YOU CAN REGARDS VERGES

Steve Williams closed the door on the narrow lightless hall and turned to read the cable by the sunlight pouring into the kitchen from the windows that looked out on the garden. The aislelike kitchen was actually an extension of the hallway and wide enough to allow only one person at a time to walk past the china closet, the stove, and the refrigerator into the studio-room beyond.

The studio was uncommonly large and high-ceilinged by New York standards, and Steve had informally divided it into areas by the placement of the uncrowding furniture. To one side of him now, beneath the outsized windows looking out on the garden, were the dining table and its four chairs; at his other hand, the washstand and drainboard, hidden from view when they were not in use by a curtain of green flannel. Over near the fireplace in the middle of the longer wall, he had grouped a deep sofa and a number of easy chairs and assorted small tables. His eyes, glancing that way, met the portrait of Maggie that hung above the empty fireplace—a gift from Judge Cowan when Steve had given up the apartment on Ninety-second Street and come to live here. The portrait showed Maggie as a glowing eager-mouthed girl of sixteen, the expression of her eyes managing to hint at the emotional uncertainty that lurked behind the coquettish smile. The presence of the telling picture had not comforted, but it had companioned him since he had moved into the studio.

He came forward into the room. Against the back wall was a studio couch that served as his bed, next to it the door to the bathroom, and the fourth wall was made up of an assortment of closets and open shelves, including the built-in desk that held his typewriter. The room had not been painted in several years, and its furnishings were shabby, but at the moment it was bright with the summer sunlight, and through it now moved a moist noontime breeze. Steve sat on the chintz-covered sofa and picked up the iced tea he had left to go to the door. He rattled the melting ice in his glass, and drained it.

He had expected—reasonable, he thought—the news of the Vergeses' arrival would delight and excite him. Now that it had come, he had to face the unwelcome fact that it meant little to him in any serious way. They were his friends, and he would be glad to see them after so long a time, but their arrival was a matter-of-fact occasion. All of life had become a matter-of-fact occasion for him. His glance lit on the volume of Charles Peguy on the table near him; he remembered that John Davis would be passing by shortly.

The studio was midway in John's after-lunch itinerary, and Steve had invited him to make it a custom to stop there for a cup of coffee. He would be ringing the doorbell soon. Steve went over to the washstand, pulled back the green flannel curtain, and stripping off his shirt, went into the habitual business of shaving.

He knew that he alone had blocked the return to personal ground of his conversations with the priest. The unexpected strength of the pull in John's evangelism frightened him. He was not prepared to commit himself to a surrender of his mind's pride, however much he might wish to be able to make such a commitment. To John, he could not unburden his mind of the insoluble emotional problems it wrestled with, he could not put aside his instinctive guard, his schooled habits of deportment, to tell John everything he thought of himself, of Maggie, of all the circumstances that had led to her death and his present emptiness. But he did not know how long he could go without a word of reference to it, and each time Steve felt the waiting more keenly. Sooner or later, he knew, he would have to tell him, as awful as it might be, as shocking as it would probably be to a perfectly inoffensive guy who had leaped from a comfortable, secure family life into the priesthood. Yet John, he knew, would not weigh friendship against confession. It was only himself who did so.

The doorbell rang. Stuffing his shirttails inside his trousers, Steve went to press the buzzer that would release the latch on the front door of the house.

John hailed him as he came back through the narrow blackness. "Hi, Steve, I've got a surprise for you."

"What's that?"

"Some money. I can buy coffee for *you* today."

He came in, his lean blue-shadowed cheeks flushed by the heat, his Roman collar sodden from the exertion of his walk.

"How about it?" he asked.

"Let me have a rain check," Steve suggested. "It's too hot even to think of going out the front door."

The two worked together assembling cups and saucers cream and sugar, and when the coffee was ready, sat down opposite one another under the portrait that hung over the empty fireplace. Even as he looked at John over his coffee cup, Steve could feel against his glottis the words that strove to pour themselves out to that comprehending ear. He checked them.

"I didn't go to your Mass today," he said. "I went to another one, up on Lexington, where they had the *Missa Recitata.* The kind you told me about. I like it much better, if that's a criterion."

John smiled and gave a deprecating shrug. "Audience participation never hurt anybody." His eyes remained—calmly, waiting—upon Steve's.

Steve made a nervous sound of response to the remark: Why wouldn't the bastard at least stir his coffee, or light a cigarette? "It's a fine feeling you get at the *Missa Recitata,*" he went on. "I mean, you don't know what you're saying, much. You just mouth Latin you don't understand, but today —today, I pretended. It was quite a game. I pretended I believed all the things we've talked about so much. The section for the catechumens being a good idea once, the Offertory, the Consecration; it threw every smallest movement into a new dimension. When you believe in it, it isn't drama, it's history right now, the most searing kind of history there is. When the Consecretarion came, I thought my head was going to split."

"And after?" John asked.

Steve shrugged, avoiding his eyes. "After, I stopped pretending, and it was another ritual. Beautiful, and movingly symbolic, but a ritual. I sat for a long time afterward, thinking about prayer, the way people pray. Dumb people, bright people . . ."

"Did you form a conclusion?"

Steve frowned. He wants so much to hear the right conclusion, he thought, and I don't have it. I'm not a convert. I'm the most prejudiced kind of examiner, but he's spent so much time on me. What can I give him? . . . My faith doesn't exist. Maybe a lesson for him to carry in the future about unhappy jerks like me who waste the time of priests? He decided to say the little he could say honestly.

"Only a tentative conclusion, John," he said. "I don't think prayers are heard. Not even by a God, if there is one. Not mine, anyway. But I think, when people pray, it—it enlarges them so that their—their consciousness of self includes forces and ideas we can't or don't really comprehend." The words sounded fake, and he felt his tension double. "That's why it's good. Not because it's heard by anyone's ear, in the way noise or music is heard by a human ear."

Why should they suddenly ring false? Because he was hedging? Like sour wine, he tasted on his lips all the griefs and guilts he wanted to tell the waiting, patient man across from him. If anybody could ever talk straight to him, John could, he told himself. But he could not be disloyal to his wife. He bit down on his lips, and then he heard John asking, "And if *you* prayed, would it enlarge you?"

He was on his feet impatiently. "I can't if I don't believe in anything!" he snapped. "Look, John. I *want* to. God, I'd love to have something to believe now that would explain and arrange all the things I don't understand. Maybe it's because all my life I've been responsible for myself and to myself——"

John Davis no longer waited calmly. He was ready. "Start talking, Steve!" he demanded.

And he obeyed. He was amazed himself by the extent to which he talked. Into the listening priest's mind he poured everything he had ever known about himself or Maggie. The ineffable appeal she had had for him before marriage, the twisted-up joyousness of their love affair, the miserable frustration of their period of engagement, the aching shambles of their married life. He held back nothing: neither Maggie's petulance nor his own despair; neither her physical infastidiousness in the last weeks of her life nor his own straightlacedness in the face of it. They drank coffee, they smoked, Steve paced the length of the studio as the afternoon grew on to darkness, and still John sat listening.

At the end of his raving, his eyes unable to focus, his hands trembling, Steve slammed down his empty coffee cup. "Why!" he shouted. "Why did we find one another? Why did we get married? Why did she die?" And he threw himself down into one of the chairs, utterly depleted, and there was silence, and John regarded him with eyes that observed but did not communicate reaction.

It was only after a long while that John began softly, but with meticulous care of enunciation, to speak. "You didn't *find* one another," he said. "And what do you write for, by the way? *Redbook?*"

"God no," said Steve.

John leaned forward, frowning, bony hands clasped together as he tried to pin the history down. "You met a girl who physically excited you and whose off-beat personality appealed to your esteem for the unusual. Am I right? You got married for the same reasons, in addition to a decent wish to render unto society what is society's, like children. But in your heart, Steve, you're not concerned about any of that. You demand to know why *she* died: *she,* not some Bowery character who fell in front of a subway train last night, not some old lady in Peoria who had a stroke. Just *she*. Why do you ask the why about one death out of so many deaths? Because you don't want the answer to be that you killed her, that's why."

Steve swallowed, his eyes screwed shut. "All right. All right, go on," he said.

"Why should you think the answer would be that? . . . Because your guess is she wasn't happy as your wife? . . . Stop me when I get the background wrong."

"I will," Steve said.

"You thought having sex with Maggie was the most fun in the world, and you didn't see what she wanted of you that you weren't providing. This, mind you, Steve, is all guesswork on my part. The thing that makes it rough on you is you won't ever know, not for sure. Now I never met the girl, but you—you, Steve Williams—can tell youself the truth. Was it maybe that she wanted of you things no one man can give? An inhuman adoration, maybe? An inexhaustible reassurance?" John took a breath. "I can put it bluntly because I deal in death and because you're no weakling. I think she was a spoiled brat, a terrible waste of brains and beauty, and you personally are well rid of her. Don't hit me. I know how to fight. I've seen all the best Pat O'Brien movies."

Steve drew the priest's words into a stunned mind. He tried to catch his breath. "I thought the meaning was in Maggie and me!—and the children we could have. Christ, that's a classic enough immortality! But for Maggie and me? Maggie and I were a joke of our own making, and don't think I don't know it!" His voice was shaking again.

"Steve!——"

"Even so!" he shouted. "Even so we had a kind of life, and we had every day at least the chance that we'd make something out of it——"

"Steve, listen——"

Steve was shouting now: "But she died, and when that happens, you look around you and nothing is the same, and nothing is the way it was before! Everything shifts all the time, and you've got nothing to hold to but a destiny, and a destiny's what I don't have! John, John, tell me if there *is* any place I'm going, and tell me what the fuck I care about it!"

He was on his feet, but he did not know it. He did not know that John had jumped up and caught him in his arms as he fell forward, sobbing. John held his erupting shoulders tightly, and then gave him a single terrible shake.

"Steve, you're a wreck. Listen! Now listen to me! Look, do you know a doctor I can get?"

Steve was gasping. "No, no——"

"A sedative might—"

"No, John. . . . Thank you. No doctors. I'll sleep easily. Now I've said all that. You've been here almost all day; I haven't talked to anybody that much in . . ."

"It's all right, boy. . . ."

"I know." Steve nodded. "I know you won't mind. But you see—" He forced himself to look up at the drawn, troubled young face above the gray and sodden Roman collar. "You see how much I want to believe in the things we talked about. That's why I keep reading, and thinking, and trying . . ."

"Sleep, Steve. We can talk another time."

Steve wiped his eyes with his fingers and caught his breath. "I'm okay now."

"Shall I see you into bed, or just get the hell out of here?" the priest asked.

"I'll get to bed all right. Thank you."

"I'll be back at the parish house in five minutes," John said. "Call me for anything you need."

"Sure, John. Thanks."

The priest stood erect and studied him a moment. "Steve."

"Yes?"

"Because you *want* to believe something doesn't make it so. For a lot of people, but not for you. Never believe cheaply, not you. Believe at the top of the mark."

"All right, John," Steve said, "I won't believe except at the top of the mark, whatever the hell that means. Thank you, thank you. I'm passing out on coffee. Thank you, John. Good night. . . ."

But John had already gone, and he was alone in the studio, heavily asleep on the sofa. He slept far into the next morning. When he awoke, he did not feel so much refreshed as cleansed. He lay still for a long time on the sofa, looking at the hot summer sunlight on the tall windows in the far wall, wondering if somehow, from somewhere, some kind of faith would be granted to him, the ability to trust beyond his sight, the ability to hope for anything. . . .

30

NEIGHBORHOOD NOISES BEGAN TO COME into the studio. Down the back yards someone was kissing for a cat, and in a neighboring apartment the television set was sounding piercingly. He got up and placed a call to Rachel Pemberton.

"Mr. *Williams,*" the secretary said. "Well, of all things. Yes, just a moment. For heaven's sake."

And shortly Rachel's own incongruously motherly voice. "Steve? Steve, shame on you, why haven't I heard from you?"

"Hello, Rachel. I'm sorry, it's been—complicated. You know. Look, I got a cable from Ben and Hilda. They're arriving on the *Ile de France* and want you to meet them if you can. Saturday."

"Saturday," said Rachel. "I'll certainly try. Look, Steve, you're all right?"

"Yes, thank you."

"What's your address now? I *have* to reach you from time to time, you know, but if you really are in seclusion or something——"

"No, it's all right. It's One-thirty-four East Forty-seventh

Street. I'm not writing much, Rachel. Not for the last few months."

"It's all right, Steve. I thought of you then, and ever since; very warmly and lovingly. I know you'll be all right." She laughed. "But when I feel like telling you what an important talent I think you have, I like to know the phone number and be able to do so."

"It's—still got your pencil?—it's Plaza, six, five-one-nine-eight. See you Saturday if you can make it, Rachel. It was nice talking to you."

"Steve—you'll try to be easy in your mind, won't you?"

"Yes, Rachel. Thank you."

"Good-by, Steve."

He put the telephone back on its hook.

Helen Maclean had promised the Vergeses that as soon as she had her trunk safely back in the apartment, she would join them for a drink at the bar in the Plaza: Ben and Hilda, that is, and the young man who was to meet them, and Dr. Paletta, the eminent Romanian who had made the crossing with them. She had not told Marvin in advance of her arrival, and once on land again she regretted not having asked him to meet her. She called his office as soon as she arrived at the apartment, but she could not reach him. Furious with the delay of their reunion, she thought momentarily of canceling the date with the Vergeses, but they had been so nice to her on the voyage home. They had told her how they made such a ritual of the first drink at the Plaza, and she could not bring herself to cancel it. She had, moreover, grown fond of Hilda. The hoarse-voiced woman, whose skin was sun-tanned to a leathery texture and whose cropped white hair was growing thin under the punishment of too many permanents, was clownish and frivolous, but Helen suspected this was a tactic serving a character more diverse and more problematical than Hilda would want anyone to know. Helen was obliged to keep their appointment. She left a message with Marvin's secretary telling him where she'd be.

The Vergeses had not yet ordered when she came into the bar off the Oak Room. She found them at a table next to the windows that looked out onto Central Park.

"At last you're here; I was going to give up and order in

another minute," Hilda barked. "Helen, this is Steve Williams, the friend we told you about."

Helen gave her hand to a pale young man who smiled gravely at her. She thought he looked like a strapping type who was in the middle of an unaccustomed illness. His clothes were shabby, but he did not look poor; he looked like he didn't care about them.

"Please sit down, Steve," she said to him. And to the others as she settled into the chair he held for her: "I'm a nervous wreck. Marvin's out on a call somewhere and I can't reach him."

"What a shame," said Dr. Paletta, his prodigious Slavic jowls quivering with sympathy. "But I told you you should have let him know ahead of time."

"I know," said Helen, "I was a fool." She turned her head to Steve. "This is my fiancé we're talking about. I got cold feet and didn't let him know what boat I'd be on coming back."

They gave their order, and presently their cocktails were put before them. Helen raised her glass to Dr. Paletta: "Doctor, welcome to America, and I hope Romania *does* get a government-in-exile for herself."

"Thank you, Helen, my dear."

Dr. Paletta's appreciation of Helen's good wishes was sincere. He had been a long time reaching America, and his itinerary had carried him through a term in a Communist prison, an escape to Trieste, another interment, and a nightmarish flight to France.

"Steve," said Hilda Verges, "it was simply a devastating trip. Of course we had a world of fun, but it was *miserable* being an American. You simply can't realize how loathed we are everywhere."

"Really? I suppose it's hard for people to love the top dog," Steve averred.

"But we're so gauche about it. Paris is filled with the most deplorable American tourists, and even out of season you keep tripping over a lot of young alcoholics going to school under the G.I. Bill of Rights. I swear I'm going to write to the President the minute I get home."

Steve turned to Helen. "Did you find it so bad being an American, Helen?"

"There's a lot of resentment toward us," Helen considered.

"At least in France—that's the only place I was. Of course there are a lot of Communists there to keep the resentment on the boil, as it were. It's so funny, it's quite respectable to be a Communist there."

"I'll say it to my dying day," Hilda declared, "there's nothing wrong between us and the Communists that those boobies we keep in Washington couldn't have prevented if they'd had a modicum of talent."

"For Pete's sake"—Steve laughed—"you haven't changed a hair."

"I'm frank, that's all," said Hilda. "Now Dr. Paletta here is violently anti-Communist——"

"They threw me out of the house I was born in. They took my family fortune away. Certainly I'm anti-Communist——"

"Yes, and I'm sure it was a very sweet house, dear, but would you be such an anti-Communist if you hadn't had a fortune?" Hilda demanded, wide-eyed.

Dr. Paletta chuckled. "Mrs. Verges, you are the only lovable Communist I have ever met."

"I'm not a Communist, but I call a spade a spade. The kind of anti-Communist propaganda we go in for is immoral——"

"Immoral?" Dr. Paletta challenged. "Would you not say, perhaps, merely impolitic? What has morality got to do with it?"

"Everything!" Hilda cried with fervor.

Dr. Paletta, chuckling, shook his head. "You Americans," he said. "In America there are as many shades and variations of opinions as there are Americans, in spite of your homogenized press. But you are never content to have an opinion. You must convince yourself that God Himself is on your side." He looked musingly at each of them in turn, still chuckling. "Each one of you thinks it is he who fights on the side of the angels. What a marvelous new race of men. . . . Impossible, but marvelous."

"You're being snide," said Hilda in mock affront.

"If you would listen to other people, you would hear the way they sound." The doctor shrugged. "Am I not right, Mr. Verges?"

"I don't have the faintest idea," said Ben, with a smile. "I don't think Jews feel that way, about necessarily having God on their side no matter what the issue is. It's more in the American Protestant tradition, I would guess."

Dr. Paletta glanced away with faint discomfort. Helen caught the movement. She had suspected before that Ben Verges was the first Jew Dr. Paletta had allowed himself to be friendly with. She felt like kicking him. In every other way he was such a sensible man, and she had grown fond of him. Anyway, if he *were* anti-Semitic, why had he befriended Ben and Hilda Verges? Was it a gesture toward the values of the New World, the camp he would now have to rely on for sanction and support? Even if that were the case, it was a shabby situation. How on earth would he react to Marvin? The consideration made her impatient with herself: what the hell did she care how Dr. Paletta would react to Marvin? If *only* Marvin would get her message and come find her.

The conversation turned to the Vergeses' adventures in North Africa. This was primarily for Steve Williams' benefit —Helen had heard it all before, and through the next round of drinks she kept her eyes on the door. She knew Marvin would be there fifteen minutes after learning where she was, and she was feeling slightly sick with anticipation and anxiety. A third round was done, and he had not yet appeared.

"I'm afraid I'm going upstairs to take a nap, my children," Hilda said. "Helen, don't look distressed, Marvin will be along any minute now. Now look, all of you, we'll be here a week or so more. What night would be good for all of you to have dinner with us? Oh, Dr. Paletta, I forgot you have to get on to Washington. Oh, damn. Try to stave it off. Steve, what about you?"

"Any night's fine."

"Helen, I know you don't know your plans yet, so call me. I *must* meet Marvin, so be sure you bring him with you to dinner."

Amid the general farewells Helen said to Steve, "I've been distracted this afternoon, waiting for Marvin to show up, but I'll be more myself at Hilda's dinner party. I want to hear about your work—Hilda and Ben are so enthusiastic about it."

"That's very kind of you," said Steve. "I'll look forward to seeing you again, and meeting the lucky bridegroom, too."

Turning from him, Helen was glad she had gotten through

that moment of social necessity with a degree of neatness. Dispirited, struggling against depression, she hurried away from the group as they hovered near the door of the bar. On the street she debated about taking a taxi and decided to walk, despite the heat of the waning afternoon. She crossed over from the hotel to the opposite pavement. She walked slowly, and had not yet reached the corner of Fifth Avenue when she heard the voice from behind her: "Helen! Helen, wait!"

At first she could not find him, then she saw the long gangling figure halfway down the block, running toward her, arms waving, glasses slipping off-kilter.

"Marvin!"

She laughed, and an unexpected sob caught at her throat. She started to put up a hand to wave to him, but before she could do so, she realized she had started to run to meet him.

When her heartbeat returned to normal, she was sitting with Marvin's arms firmly around her in the small boxlike living room of her apartment, her trunk open in the middle of the room, devouring the available floor space.

"When?" asked Marvin. "How soon?"

She sat back to look at him. His glasses off, his eyes had their look of caressing tenderness, and his smile suggested joy and pride.

"Six weeks?" she suggested, almost timidly. "God knows I can't get a television department going for Jules in that time, but I can at least get accumulated office work cleared away."

"Do you like the idea of the television department, the partnership with Jules?"

"Oh, Marvin, I don't really know, I don't care; the only thing I care about is that we're going to be married. You knocked my eyes out with the partnership thing, but then I already knew you were an incredible man."

"It's a good investment for us. We could invest in thousands of other companies and not have one of ourselves at the helm to see about it."

"Oh, sure, it'll be something for us to fall back on if good health suddenly overtakes everybody in New York. Face it, Marvin, you're a wonder."

He squeezed her shoulder. "Happy partnership!" he said. "Darling, how's the practice?"

"Bustling."

"Any entire-family deals?"

"A dozen or so."

"Oh, I'm glad. I bet they worship you." Then: "Marvin, before the wedding, there are other things I have to get done."

"Oh? What others?"

Helen shrugged. "Nothing important," she said, and changed the subject. "You won't be disappointed about it's being just a weekend honeymoon?"

"Not if you're not," Marvin answered. "We'll have a proper honeymoon soon. Niagara Falls, if you like." Helen laughed. "What d'you want, for God's sake, Grossinger's?"

"Wherever you are, darling," she said. "Lord, how much I mean it. I didn't realize till now how much I'd missed you, Marvin. It's trite as hell to say, but promise me: don't ever let anything take us away from each other again."

"I won't," he said. "I promise you."

Helen kissed him quickly and stood up, hoping to shake off the thought of how close she had come to losing him before she had gone away. "I brought you some cognac," she said, "and don't laugh—they're really beautiful—a few ties."

"How about some of the cognac now and the ties later?" Marvin asked.

"Drunkard. All right. Come help me. I don't even remember whether I own any brandy glasses."

They found two in the kitchen cabinet, and Helen presented the bottle to Marvin for serving. After Marvin had filled the glasses, they stood in the kitchen, sipping the cognac and smiling foolishly at each other.

"How are your parents?" Marvin asked.

"Fine from what they wrote to me," said Helen. "They don't know about any impending nuptials yet."

"Do you want to be married in Charter Oak?"

"Oh Lord, no. My family will be only too glad for an excuse to come to New York. They'll be at our wedding in their dandiest, some of which I brought back with me."

"You brought back their dandiest?" Marvin looked confused.

"Presents." Helen shrugged. "I hardly had room for all the presents I wanted to bring back. For Jules and Ladd Dorn, and your mother and father——"

"What? Why them?"

"An opening wedge is what I hope, who knows?" Helen

said. "Don't worry, there's nothing you have to do, darling. I'll take care of it. What are we standing here for? The living room's cooler."

In the living room Helen sat down, but Marvin remained standing. He studied her thoughtfully.

"You've changed somehow," he said.

"Have I?" Helen asked. "For the worse?"

"Oh, no. Something about you has—smoothed out. You're so assured, I guess it is. On you I like it."

She laughed. "I hope to heaven you mean that."

"I do," Marvin said. "You're a very beautiful and very spirited woman and I'm damned lucky to get you as my wife. You've completed your metamorphosis, Helen. From the little girl in Charter Oak."

She stood up and went into his arms.

"Not yet, Marvin," she said. "Not until I can call myself a successful wife. I'm untried so far. In every way that's important. I'm terrified to think how untried I am."

But she knew she was ready to be proved, and she knew how she intended going about it.

In the following days she did not mention again the gifts she had brought back for Marvin's parents, and Marvin seemed to have forgotten about them. On Thursday they dined with the Vergeses and Steve Williams, and on Friday morning, when she had cleared away the office mail for the day, she telephoned Myra Kaufman.

"Mrs. Kaufman? This is Helen Maclean."

"Helen?" There was a baffled pause. "Hello, Helen. Marvin isn't here. He's at the office."

"Yes, I know. I was phoning you."

"Oh. . . . What—what is it?"

"I wondered if I might call on you this afternoon, Mrs. Kaufman. Will you be free?"

Mrs. Kaufman almost stuttered in her astonishment. "Free? Why—of course. I'll be here."

"Shall we say about four o'clock?"

"All right, Helen. . . . Fine. Four o'clock."

"Thank you so much, Mrs. Kaufman. I'm looking forward to seeing you again. Good-by."

She hung up. She had, she thought, struck the right note. Not fawning, but blandly pleasant, as though to an acquaintance you think well of but do not know very well.

When she arrived at the Kaufman apartment, the neat oblong package in her hand, Marvin's mother had had time to recover from her surprise, but she had not solved her puzzlement. She greeted Helen with reserve, but not with coldness.

"Sit down, Helen," she said. "Marvin told me you had come back from Europe. Did you have a nice time?"

"Very nice." Helen smiled. "I was terribly homesick, but Marvin's letters kept me cheered up."

As they sat across from one another, Helen told her of the places she had visited and the people she had met. The two amusing anecdotes she had been hoarding against the day of this meeting went well when she told them, and Mrs. Kaufman, if she did not drop her guard, laughed sincerely.

"But the pom-pom on the trip," Helen said, "was a find I made—that's what I wanted to tell you about." She picked up the oblong box she had placed beside her on the sofa when she came in. "I found an artist buried away near Saint-Germain-des-Près who's working with ceramics. For income he makes ceramic jewelry, and he had some pieces that I just couldn't resist. I don't have the eyes needed for wearing these, but you do. I thought of you the minute I saw them. I—I took the liberty of bringing them to you." And giving her the box: "I hope you like them. I can't wait to see them on you."

Mrs. Kaufman stared at the box she had taken as if it were a living thing; the muscles of her face were thick struggling knots. Before she could decide how to respond, Helen went on, gently closing the last way out: "You must know what a fascinating blue your eyes are; I don't know much about colors, but I can see. Quite aside from being Marvin's mother and my wanting to bring you something from France—you remember how fondly you spoke of it that night I was here?—aside from that, I *had* to see these particular pieces on you, who have the extraordinary eyes."

Mrs. Kaufman watched her, eaglelike, as she spoke. She did not answer, but her face muscles seemed to have eased a little. Helen was glad she was able to compliment the older woman truthfully, to throw the weight of the gift on her beauty rather than her motherhood; it helped to prevent the jewelry's becoming a blatant token of beguilement between them.

With the opening of the box the pieces of ceramic tile

gleamed up from their tissues. Dominant within their whiteness was a blue that received and shone back the color of Mrs. Kaufman's eyes. The craftsmanship was of a high degree of excellence, and Mrs. Kaufman was not unaware of the fact. She said, "Oh, Helen, these are beautiful. . . ." She gestured with a hand, not looking directly at Helen, her eyes still on the diminutive tiles. "But of course I knew when I first met you that you had taste. Thank you very much for this present. . . ." She hesitated, and slowly she replaced the cover on the box. "I'd better not put them on now," she said, "this dress isn't right. We—we must ask you over some evening so I can wear them for you to their best advantage. . . ."

But her forehead was still marked with her inner debate. She put the box gently aside, and folding her hands on her lap, studied the powdered fingers. "You're very odd to bring me a present. Me, of all people. When it's out in the open between us about your marrying Marvin. It makes this difficult."

"Please don't let it, Mrs. Kaufman," Helen said. "We can discuss Marvin, if you like, quite separately from the ceramics. Actually, they're a present I gave myself. I wanted to see the right person wearing them, that's all. I know Marvin's told you we're going to be married. In spite of anything, as Marvin puts it."

"Yes."

"We regret it," Helen went on "—having to go ahead without your good wishes. But it was Marvin's decision. I didn't pressure him after I left for Europe, and I have to do what he thinks best. Maybe that isn't the best kind of woman to be, but it's the kind I am."

The blue eyes narrowed as Mrs. Kaufman weighed the implication. She did not return to it, but instead introduced a new viewpoint.

"You must understand that with a young man's mother—a young man as promising, as brilliant as my son—there are many considerations for his happiness. The girl herself, personally, isn't necessarily the whole picture."

"No, of course not." Helen assured her agreement.

Mrs. Kaufman pursed her lips, thinking for words. "I don't have anything at all against you as a person, Helen. I mean, you're hard-working and successful and rising all the time—oh, Marvin has told me. My husband, of course, feels very strongly about the religious difference."

"Yes, that is a problem." Helen nodded, attentive.

"Not to me." Mrs. Kaufman shrugged. "But there are other things. Marvin's attitude towards my opinion is one of them, I don't mind telling you." The large eyes twisted in hurt. "No, that I can never accept. You and he can go ahead with this if you like, but—I'm sorry, I can't tell you I approve of it."

Helen answered gently. "Of course you can't, Mrs. Kaufman. Especially if Marvin has hurt you, even though inadvertently. I understand." She took a breath. "But if we get married—" she let the *if* hang on the air a fraction of a second—"you know how much a girl needs advice and guidance to make her husband happy. I will need it. I have my mother, of course, but you're the one who knows all about Marvin. You're the one who's done such a wonderful job turning out such an admirable son. I'll need you so much, and I know with your sophistication you won't let the fact that you disapprove of our marriage separate us entirely."

"Why—no, there's no need for that," Mrs. Kaufman retreated. "But Marvin's turning against me this way——"

"I'm sure if he behaved offensively it was—oh, a passing thing, frustration, fatigue. I know you understand the men of your family, so you surely understand that better than I do." She got to her feet and took Mrs. Kaufman's hand. "I've already taken up too much of your time. Thank you for letting me come, and do let me come again to see you wearing the ceramic pieces."

"Yes. Thank you, Helen. And . . . oh, well."

Helen left quickly.

Alone again in her office, when she had returned the several telephone calls she had missed, Helen was able to give thought to her visit with Mrs. Kaufman. The fact that the meeting had taken some degree of deceit on her part, and would take more, rankled in her. It had accomplished as much as she had hoped it would, as much as it could be expected to. The woman would never wholeheartedly accept her, or anybody else like her, as a fit wife for Marvin. But perhaps if in this way Helen made plain she was not armed on the opposite line of battle, she would succeed in disarming Mrs. Kaufman as well. Mrs. Kaufman would, if Helen were careful, and lucky, eventually find herself resigned if not jubilant about the marriage. In the end it might mean she had won a small area of peace of mind for Marvin. That was what was important.

Two days later Mrs. Kaufman sent word through Marvin that the family would be glad if she came and had a cocktail with them on a certain day.

"You know, you're assertive as hell," said Marvin, "taking her that present without telling me."

"But I did tell you," Helen defended herself.

"Except then you let me forget it. You must have broken through to her somehow. She still says we shouldn't get married, but she's all set on being civilized and modern and still having you up for drinks."

"I think your mother is a very civilized woman."

Marvin's narrowed eyes caught the flickering smile. "I can see right through you," he said. "Well, I hope to God you know what you're doing."

Mrs. Kaufman, Helen discovered with relief, was enjoying the delicacy of the shading in her new policy toward her son's fiancée. On her return visit to the Kaufman apartment no word was mentioned about the proposed marriage, and Mrs. Kaufman treated her with an only slightly restrained good will. It was as though Marvin had brought home an attractive and interesting acquaintance to whom he was in no way committed. Marvin contributed little to their conversation. He sat, broodingly watchful, wishing his mother no ill but wondering if Helen knew the extent of jeopardy his mother represented. Helen had to a degree succeeded in altering the official family attitude toward their marriage, but Marvin did not have the faith needed to lower his guard against his mother. His stand for independence was not yet an accustomed posture.

Helen, with the same bland pleasantness she had shown his mother, turned her attention to Marvin's father.

"I had spent Seder with a French family while I was there," she said. "It was delightful, especially the questions and answers with the youngest of the family, and they were such a loving family. I promised myself I would memorize the answers, if only in English, it's such a charming part of the feast."

With a polite gesture of facetiousness Mr. Kaufman asked her the first of the ritual questions, and Helen was able to answer. She had seen to it that she would be able to answer all the others, if need be, but Mr. Kaufman in his pleasure went on to talk of other things.

"These ceramics you brought Myra," he said, "they are very nice. You found an artist who does them, Myra tells me?"

"Yes," Helen said.

"Joel, why don't you have anything as unusual in your store?"

The old man chuckled. "Oh, I don't bother with costume jewelry."

"But this young artist has genuine talent," Mrs. Kaufman went on. "Tiles by Picasso wouldn't be lumped with costume jewelry, would they?"

He looked for a moment at the necklace and earrings his wife was wearing. "They're not the usual thing you see in that line."

"Are they something you might be able to use, Mr. Kaufman?" Helen asked. "If you like, I'd be happy to put you in touch with the artist."

Marvin laughed. "You be careful, or Helen will have you fixed up in the import business."

"There might be a market," his father mused.

"It would be wonderful for the artist," Helen pointed out.

Mr. Kaufman began to explain to her some of the complications of importing, and his appreciation of the possibilities involved in the work of the artist Helen had found began to warm. He continued to pre-empt the conversation for the greater part of the time Helen stayed with them.

That night, on the way to her apartment, Helen and Marvin agreed on a date for their wedding. His parents might still be disapproving, they realized, but there was now an outside chance they'd show up for the ceremony.

31

THERE WAS A COLD DRAFT CUTTING ALONG the floor, coming into the dusty apartment from under the door to the hallway. Warren Taggert slept again.

Time passed, and he heard from a distance Spanish voices screeching somewhere in the rooming house. A sickly light was falling on the windows in the main room of the apartment. He realized he was lying across the sill of the door connecting the kitchen with the main room. He tried to stir, but his head fell back to the floor, and he gave a moan of self-disgust.

He lay still, letting the day creep on, listening to the busier sounds whispering and thudding through the rooming house as the Puerto Rican wives went about their chores and children fought in the hallways and television sets blared on, unheeding of their audience, and cooking odors accumulated through the dingy building. He didn't think any of his bones were broken, but the bruises were painful, and his muscles, sore after a night on the cold rugless floor. He wondered whether this time his eyes would again be blackened, swollen shut. He could feel the stiffness of the dried blood from his nose across his upper lip and down along his cheek.

With a gasp he was able to stagger up. He leaned against the door to steady himself, then groped his way along the covered bathtub until he came to the washbasin to consult the mirror above it. . . .

There was a cut above his eye, but it wasn't black, and there was a visible lump on the back of his head from his fall. The fall, he supposed, he could share the blame for: he had as much passed out as been knocked out, though the aching told him he had been hit hard in the stomach. He felt in the pockets of his trousers. The money, of course, was gone, but there hadn't been much on him. He was growing cagier.

He made his way to the cluttered, dirty main room of the apartment and threw himself down on his bed. A fraction of his mind registered the bitter fact that it was still neatly made. He covered his aching forehead with his hands, and it was some time before he was able to think again. When he did let his hands drop to his sides and stared out frankly at the room, he thought gratefully that the guy had not been his size. There wouldn't be any clothes missing this time.

He'd been mugged before. In a couple of months he had run through such men in the Bird Circuit bars as he had wanted. His face then was familiar, he was a fixture, and his nightly rounds were watched with boredom by those who had been to bed with him or those whom he had never attracted. He had had to carry the searching farther afield, and twice he had made the mistake of picking up rough trade.

The lusty young hoodlums who managed to fool him in his stupidity, who would come to the apartment and indulge themselves in his passionate ministrations and then would turn on him in violence. He would be left a bleeding wreck, clothes gone, money gone—a wrist watch, a phonograph, a typewriter. One by one they had all gone. But that was not what made him feel his present self-disgust.

The robbings were bad; the beatings were worse; but in his mind they did not speak with the loathsome eloquence of the physical filthiness of the young men who had enjoyed his offices. Tears of hatred and contempt for himself ran down his dried-out cheeks, and Warren twisted over on his side to hide from his sight the dinginess of the accusing room.

He slept the hangover through, but when he awoke, his body was more sore than it had been before. The telephone was ringing. It took both concentration and determination to get up to answer it, but he succeeded in doing so.

"Hello?" His voice had its usual smoothness and depth of tone. It did not give him away.

"Go ahead please."

"Warren, dearest?"

"Yes. Hello, Mother." He sat down heavily in the chair beside the telephone table.

"Well? How are you, darling?"

"Fine, Mother. It's nice to hear you. How are you?"

"Oh, darling," she said with a small sigh of impatience, "I'm having one of my spells again. You know how they've been coming and going lately."

"I'm so sorry, Mother. You've had a doctor?"

"Oh! He's had me confined to bed three days now. I wanted to call you before, but I hated to bother you——"

"Is there anything I can do?"

"No, of course not, Warren. You're an angel to ask. I'll be all right, for your sake. Darling, did you get my last little check?"

"Yah, it was a godsend, thank you. I'm looking for another job. It's—it's hard finding something here I'm really interested in. But I'm still trying."

"No mother could ask for more," said Mrs. Taggert. "And I don't *want* you to settle for just any little clerk's work, you know that. Look, darling, I have business to talk about, I shouldn't dawdle."

"What business is that, Mother?"

"Your father is going to be in New York for a few days. I wanted so *much* to come with him, but this doctor——"

"When is he getting in?" Warren asked.

"Some time this afternoon. He'll be at the Sherry-Netherland. I told him I'd tell you to call him late this afternoon, and you'd go up to see him for cocktails and dinner."

"Oh."

"Now, angel, you must be very careful and understanding, the way you always are with me. Your father hasn't been feeling well, and he's very upset about this spell of mine. Well, as much as he can be what with fretting over Truman and the Russians and God only knows what else."

"The Sherry-Netherland?" Warren was trying to register despite the pounding of his head.

"And, darling. *Please* accept my present of a trip home as soon as you can. We all miss you so much and—oh, now I'm moistening up. Anyway, Mrs. Wade is dying to spoil you a little, after so long. But Warren, do try, and you know the money doesn't mean an earthly thing——"

"It isn't the money, Mother. It's just that I've been busy. Have—have you seen Sue at all?"

"Sue? Oh, Sue: why on earth should you ask about her?" Mrs. Taggert asked.

"I wondered, that's all," Warren said.

"Oh, well, I see her from time to time, but I don't know any news of her. If you mean about your coming home for a visit, I don't think you'd have to worry about running into her. Now darling, you concentrate on New York and don't let old shades bother you."

"Yah. Thanks for calling, Mother. I'll put in a call for Dad right away. Take care of yourself, Mother."

"Well, darling, you know if poor health happens to——"

As though he had not heard the words, he called, "Good-by!" and put the phone back on its hook. In a moment he regretted the cruelty of the gesture, but he could not hold back a sigh of relief.

He was able to repair his appearance. On his way to the Sherry-Netherland he stopped off at a bar on Sixth Avenue to brace himself with two stiff shots of rye. The booth he sat in sheltered him partially from the view of the few people standing at the bar itself, and he was able to think of the coming meeting. He wished his father hadn't come to New York. He despised the blatantly mendacious talks, the occasional cynical allusion to his imperfectness—never a candid allusion—the lying assumption of any warmth between his father and himself. He was sick of masking appearances. What satisfaction was there in a fake respectability, a lying imitation? It wasn't his father's respect he wanted, it was his own.

He could not go on as he had since leaving Mike, he told himself. He had to have point to his New York life or wither irretrievably into a mincing auntie of the antique shops and the ballet openings. He couldn't let that happen. Other men, however little they might consider it, had a natural purpose. Oh, sure, they wailed as loudly as he did about dilemmas doubtlessly as baffling and frustrating as his own, but nature, as well as law, gave them fortification. They procreated; they extended the race; they held their place in the historical pattern.

No calmer for the whisky he had drunk, he paid his tab and went on to the Sherry-Netherland.

Jim Taggert, in the middle of his fifties, had missed a step. His blond hair was more discolored than before with those yellow streaks that come with aging. His face still had its slightly swollen look, to be expected of a part-time hedonist, but now it had faltered under its own weight. The harpoon eyes were blunted, too. Their regard was as intense as ever, but they did not wound. As he watched his father hang his overcoat up meticulously in the closet, Warren did not know whether the change of aspect was in his father or in his own grown-older vision.

"I haven't found anything to work at yet," Warren was saying in answer to the very jovial question. "I talked to Mother when she called this afternoon—I mean, about the job hunting." To Warren his father seemed to be on edge, unaccustomedly lacking in assurance.

"I've already had them bring us some Martinis," he said, leading Warren into the sitting room of the suite and waving him toward one of the overstuffed chairs grouped around the coffee table. "I'm sorry you're having so much trouble keeping a job." Some of the old sternness flickered behind his amiability. He handed Warren the brimming cocktail glass.

"It's my own fault, really," said Warren. "I haven't exactly been pushing myself."

"Oh? That's funny, coming from you," his father said, the smallest curling in his lips. "I thought you'd have a string of excuses a mile long."

"I did, for Mother," said Warren.

"Leveling with me all of a sudden?"

Warren faced him wearily. He knew now he'd been a fool to hope for a real change between them simply because they had each of them grown older. "No, not especially," he answered. "I just don't think you give a damn about it."

Jim Taggert flushed. "That's a hell of a thing to say."

"It's true, isn't it?"

"No!" the older man snapped.

"Well, I've got no reason to excuse myself to you."

Abruptly, desperate, Warren gave it up. "Look," he said, "suppose I leave—you'd just as soon I would, wouldn't you? You can still tell Mother you saw me. . . ." He was on his feet.

"Warren, wait!" his father gasped. "I meant us to have a pleasant, convivial visit. We're—we're being joined later by a friend of mine I wanted you to meet. Son, I didn't mean to hector you that way, and I'm sorry. Anyway, why should that make you suddenly walk out in a huff?"

"I don't know," he said, frowning. "I've been away a long time, Dad. I just don't feel like carrying on the old routine with you."

"What routine?"

"*You* the fond parent, *me* the respectable son."

His father came up and gripped him by the shoulders. "Why are you saying all these crazy damn things? What did your mother tell you?"

"Nothing," said Warren. "But since I talked to her—knowing I was going to see you today—I couldn't help wondering why the hell you wanted to bother about me. I've got nothing to say to you. We never have anything really to say to one another. I think you're doing it because she made you promise you would. I think everything between us is something she makes us do. And I'm tired of letting her get away with it."

Jim Taggert sighed. "I see. You don't find me interesting

enough in any way, I take it . . . to want us to be friends on your own."

"I don't like being Mother's patsy, even if you've gotten used to it," Warren answered evenly. "You know in what way we're not alike. You know yourself what makes it impossible for us ever to understand one another . . ."

His father turned sharply away. "No, never mind," he snapped.

Warren shrugged. "So the best thing I can do is beat it, now you've seen me."

As he turned to leave, his father's voice, suddenly anguished, stopped him. "Warren!" he said.

"Yes?"

His father threw the words out into the room. "If you're queer, it's your own business."

Warren did not move. His father was behind him. As he faced the door, he didn't know if he would ever be able to move again.

"You think I haven't been to people?" his father was saying. "You think I haven't asked doctors what I could do? All I can find out from them is that in some way it's my fault because I—I let your mother take too much of a hand in rearing you. For what it's worth." He stopped again, his breathing harsh and rasping in the stillness between them. "Maybe all that's so," he said. "But you're a grown man now, and as far as I'm concerned, what a man does for sex is something he shouldn't have to account for to his father or to anybody else." He stopped, and was silent. Warren turned in time to see him shuffle, trembling, back to the coffee table, and lift his cocktail glass and drain it. For a long moment neither of them moved.

"Well, it's out, anyway," Warren said.

"I wish we'd gotten it over with a long time ago," his father muttered. He seemed unable at first to look at Warren, but presently he said, "Now that we have, we might as well give it a try—you and I not being at one another's throats all the time. Could we, Warren? *I'd* like to try. I don't know how you feel about it. I don't know if you give a damn one way or another. But I wish you'd stay."

Warren said, "All right, Dad. If you want to try. I'll stay."

They were to be joined for dinner by a friend of Jim Taggert's, a fraternity brother named Phillip Houghton.

"A good man for you to know," Warren's father said when the two of them sat facing each other calmly again. "He publishes a magazine called *American View*. A lot more substance to it than some of these pink rags you see put out."

"Why for me to know especially?" Warren asked.

"You've always spent a lot of time on books, things like that, you might enjoy knowing somebody in the journalism business. Houghton's a brain, and he's made a great success of himself. You might even find a place for yourself in his business—if you'd be interested in working for a magazine."

"Sure, I might well be."

"I never could understand all those clerking jobs with banks you've had. I don't think you have any real interest in banking. Do you?"

"No, I don't," Warren said. "But they were convenient. I never thought of working at something I really cared about. Not until recently. There were—there were too many other things on my mind. Until recently."

"I'll bet you'll like Houghton," said his father.

Warren passed a hand over his eyes. "If I'm going to make a halfway decent impression, Dad, I think maybe I'd better have some coffee before he gets here."

"Yah." His father nodded, gruffly now. "I guess both of us had better."

Phillip Houghton was a short man with a head of sable hair, thick-growing but sternly shorn. He wore horn-rimmed glasses that looked too large for his face. He was informed, affable, and didactic in conversation. After another round of cocktails, the three of them dined at the St. Regis Hotel. In the sharp lighting of the dining room, Phillip Houghton's appearance asserted itself as that of an inexhaustibly energetic, opinionated man.

"Nothing could have made the corruption and subversion in the government plainer than the Hiss case," he declared. "Nothing could have made the corruption of our entire society plainer than the fact that the bastard has to be tried *twice*. If it were my kind of government, he'd have been taken out and shot the minute the truth was known."

"Still, it shouldn't come as any surprise to you," said Jim

Taggert; "we all know the Roosevelt group was riddled with Communists."

"And what about the Truman boys?" said Houghton.

"You mean Commies in the government even today?"

Warren said, on a tentative note, "A Republican President wouldn't waste much sympathy on them, I shouldn't think."

"There are fools in the Republican Party, too," said Houghton. "The brains of this country shy away from politics—that's why the country's in one mess after another. If we have to have this so-called democracy, it's unavoidable. The blessed *people* will always be a pushover for charlatans. A strong country needs strong men, and it can't have them being bothered about what the masses think. The masses make me sick."

"Do you think we could ever have it any other way?" Warren asked.

Houghton tapped the tines of his fork on the tablecloth. "This is the time for it," he said. "It's a time of upheaval everywhere, and the United States is no exception. Mark my word, the struggle's already beginning. The Hiss business is only the start. No damned democracy is going to be strong enough or tough enough to beat the Russians. We'll *have* to change and accept this country's obvious destiny as the leader of the free world. Russia is the enemy; why don't we learn from them? Do you know what the beloved masses are fed in Russia? Nothing—I mean nothing—that isn't designed to implement the policies of the government. Our kind of democracy is just as silly to a Russian workingman as it is to me. Why shouldn't the United States whip its own people into shape in the same way? The individual people never know the difference. Madison Avenue is there to tell them that they're good guys and the Russians are bad guys. What matters is keeping every small-time jerk in line behind the policy we know is going to bring us out ahead."

"What's the policy?" asked Warren.

Phillip Houghton gave him a look. "Does this interest you, Warren?"

"Yes, very much. I'd say an enlightened plutocracy."

"Right. It's the only moral policy. Government is supported by taxpayers. Those who pay the highest taxes should have the strongest voice in government—through a reformed voting system. Isn't it the same way in a corporation's structure?"

"I think you're right, sir, but is it a policy that can ever be adopted?"

Houghton looked at Jim Taggert. "This boy is bright," he said. He turned to Warren again. "England won't do it. France won't do it. All of them are too decrepit. We're not. We *could* do it, and I think we're going to. The time is here, isn't it? This, by God, is America's turn at the helm."

The words were in themselves exciting to Warren, and he wondered how much substance there was in Houghton's point of view. He had seldom thought of his country in such broad terms. The last few years his thinking had been occupied by the problems of his personal life to the exclusion of everything else; it was an almost physical refreshment to have his attention turned elsewhere. Houghton talked on through dinner, painting a view of a future America that was dazzling and seductive: a nation governed by the intellectual and social elite, a nation rock firm in its loyalties, clean of the strife of factionalism, unhesitating in the extension and solidification of its empire, a nation that did not pretend—except to the mass of the ignorant who needed pretense—that it was anything other than what it appeared: the new might of the West, as unchallengeable as Rome at its height had been.

"That's the point I could never make clear to Scanlon. He was my assistant, until last month. A disciple, I suppose you might say, but he never grasped the extent of what I intend. He was watery. Too bad I was so late in discovering it."

"He quit?" Warren asked.

Houghton's expression was that of a man betrayed. "Yes," he said. "His going leaves a vacuum."

The next day Jim Taggert had a number of appointments to keep, but they met in midafternoon at the Sherry-Netherland bar. Neither referred to the outburst of the night before, and Warren was grateful that his father had the sense to realize there was nothing more that could be said. They talked instead of Phillip Houghton.

"I've never read the magazine," Warren said, "but I bought a copy of the current issue this morning. You didn't say anything to him about me, did you?"

"Do you want me to?"

"No," Warren answered. "I don't want to get any job as a favor a friend of yours is doing. It may have been different before with the bank jobs and all that, but not now. If I decide to try the magazine, I want to do it on my own."

"He'll know who you are," his father said.

"Don't you think he's probably got somebody to do the hiring and firing for him? If I get a job there, he's likely not even to know it until after it's happened."

"I guess you're right." His father smiled. "Good luck to you."

"I'll let you know what happens."

The day after his father left New York, Warren presented himself at the office of *American View*. After half an hour's waiting he was taken in to the desk of the magazine's business manager, Mr. Hayes. He stated succinctly his desire to join the magazine's staff and told the rotund, sharp-eyed man of his past experience as a clerk. When he had finished, the business manager sat silently chewing on his bottom lip.

"As you can see, we don't have a very large staff here," he said, indicating with a nod the dozen people before him at desks around the room. "And I don't need anyone at the moment. There's one possibility, though." He looked at Warren piercingly, weighing what he saw. "You're not interested in editorial work, are you?"

Warren did not know what to answer. He said only, "I don't know anything about it."

"Just as well. We like to keep the business and the editorial departments here strictly divided. Too many young kids try to use clerking as a steppingstone to the glamor end. What I need is business people, not writers."

"I understand," said Warren.

"Have you had any accounts-payable experience?"

"Yes, sir; not very extensive; as much as you'd expect in a not very large bank."

"The accounts-payable clerk I have now is a young lady," Mr. Hayes said. "She's leaving us in a month to get married. I hadn't thought to hire a replacement just yet, but the extra couple of weeks' breaking-in might be just as well." He inquired further into Warren's educational background and business experience, and at the end of the inteview gave him the job.

Warren wrote to his parents that he had the job, and that his salary would be enough for him to live on. His mother need not bother sending him any more checks. Mrs. Taggert wrote back, enclosing a check, that she was sure he would need new clothes in order to be decently dressed at the office. Warren returned the check with a note insisting as gently as he could that he meant to earn his own keep, and his own clothes. No further checks arrived.

It was a week before Phillip Houghton discovered that Warren had been taken onto his staff. In that time Warren learned much about the activities of *American View*. It was not, he discovered, the only magazine Houghton published, though it was the most well known. A newsletter on current business trends and problems brought in a larger revenue, and Houghton also produced and moderated a television panel series which broadcast his views on politics and economics. None of these activities brought in impressive profits, but Houghton was backed by a small number of very affluent men—an almost fabled oil speculator and rancher in Texas, a Massachusetts industrialist, and the Florida-based owner of a coal–real estate–communications complex. Warren had begun to feel the first confidence in his understanding of what his work in accounts-payable was to be on the day he was called into Phillip Houghton's office.

"For God's sake, Warren," Houghton greeted him. "Why didn't you tell me you were coming to work for me? I'm sure your father would want me to keep a protective eye on you for a while. What does the business department have you doing?"

"Accounts-payable," Warren said, taking the seat Houghton gestured him to. "I'm being broken in to replace the present clerk."

When Houghton looked dubious, Warren explained why he had chosen not to make use of his acquaintance with the publisher to find a place for himself on the magazine's staff.

"What made you want to come to work here at all?" Houghton wanted to know.

"Talking with you when Dad was in town, frankly," said Warren. "Since I came to New York, I've been batting back and forth between one job and another because I couldn't find anything I really cared very much about."

"You care about accounts-payable?"

Warren shrugged. "I'm working for *American View,* which is what I want to do."

Houghton shook his head, frowning. "You're too intelligent to be happy with bookkeeping, and if you really feel that way about the magazine, you're not going to be content with accounts-payable for very long. At any rate, I'm glad to know you're on my payroll. Let's talk about it again later on."

Two days later Mr. Hayes, the business manager, called Warren to his desk.

"Mr. Houghton seems to have other plans for you. So now I'm back where I started."

"I'm sorry," Warren said. "But there may not be any change after all. I don't know what Mr. Houghton has in mind. It might be something I can't do, you know, for any number of reasons."

"The hell with it. He's waiting for you in his office."

Houghton described his offer straightforwardly. "I need another pair of hands," he said, "a kind of glorified secretary. I've got Ann to handle the stenographic end, so don't let that scare you off, but I need a man to help with some of the less routine chores, taking care of the V.I.P.'s when they're in town, doing some of the leg work for the TV show, odds and ends. It's a position of responsibility, and it needs a man with executive ability. I had Scanlon, but he's gone. It'll be interesting work for you, and if you're good at it, you'll be earning more than you can in the business department if you stay there the rest of your life."

"I see," Warren said. He took a breath. "I don't think I'd better accept, Mr. Houghton. But thank you."

"What? Why won't you accept?"

Warren licked his lips. "For one thing, when I took this job, I assured Mr. Hayes I was interested only in the business end."

"The hell with Hayes. You're both my employees, don't forget."

"Yes, sir, of course. On the other hand, I don't want to take a job that's offered to me because of your friendship with my father."

Phillip Houghton slapped his hands down flat on the top of his desk. "Will you talk sense to me? I need a replacement for that fair-weather Scanlon, and your father's got nothing to do with it. You share my views. You could be very valuable to me. *Now* will you take it?"

Warren swallowed. "Maybe my father wouldn't realize he had nothing to do with it. That's what matters. I'm sorry, and I'm very thankful."

"Warren."

"Yes?"

Houghton studied the calendar pad on the far edge of his desk. "The job is tough. As my assistant I need a man whose life *is* his job: no wives, no brats, no special interests."

Warren wondered how much the man was meaning to imply. Did he suspect the truth? Was he delicately declaring himself as a homosexual or only as a man unperturbed by being associated with one? Warren knew he had a wife, but he knew how little that could mean.

At the end of the interview he had accepted, and after a few days of orientation at the hands of Phillip Houghton he was ensconced in the position. Working with him, he found Houghton to be impressively intelligent and disarmingly sensitive. Houghton showed no shyness about his growing affection for Warren, and Warren found himself waiting for Houghton to declare a more intimate interest. The declaration did not come because the interest, as Warren came to discover, did not exist. Phillip Houghton in his unshakably virile nature could grow fond of an appealing youngster, such as Warren was to him, and a trustworthy disciple, but he was resolutely heterosexual and, in addition, devoted to his wife. Warren was surprised by his own ability to accept the fact and be grateful for Houghton's friendship. Often enough he found his glance lingering on the publisher's fine-boned wrists and muscular fingers, but he was not disarmed by the occurrence. In the hunger that set his life off-balance there was as much need for identification as for sexual release, he knew. If he could not make a love relationship endure—such a relationship as he had had with Mike Cowan—perhaps he could find in Phillip Houghton the lover who was not a lover, the *maître* who answered his need for identification with a man, even if there was involved no sexual link between them. And Houghton was at least of his own class.

He was thrown headlong into a round of activities that allowed him no time for private thought, no time to realize fully how far he had yanked himself up from the morass that had been poisoning his life only a month before. The extraordinary brought extraordinary response. His father telephoned to say that Houghton had written enthusiastically to him about the quality of Warren's work.

Warren became the overseer of Houghton's complex and exacting schedule, the link and buffer between Houghton and his business staff, the reservation-maker and plane-meeter, the host of the coffee-break between the television show's technical rehearsal and broadcast every Wednesday evening. His variegated labor needed no specialized training but an over-all intelligence, and, in his interest in the work, Warren found himself capable of an unusual degree of efficiency.

One of Houghton's most active interests was Funds for the American Way, Inc., an agency whose assets, elicited from private donors, were used to implement an extensive campaign to educate the public to the authoritarian standards of the conservatives. Houghton was frequently the principal speaker at fund-raising dinners, and Warren attended them as well. On a certain one of these occasions the hotel banquet room was not really adequate for the number of tables that had been set up there, but to Warren it seemed just as well. The closeness emphasized the rally element of the dinner, and the people who had paid fifty dollars to Funds for the American Way for the privilege of attending would not mind. At the moment they heeded only the voice from the dais—that of Congressman Campbell Robinson.

"Among the guests who will address us tonight," the Congressman was saying, "are two of what I can truly and factually call the great Americans of this era. The first, a distinguished publisher and television personality, has labored in our mutual cause with a dedication worthy of our forefathers, the founders of this great country and the inventors and perfectors of the American way of life. A truly great American in the tradition of great Americans. It is my privilege as Chairman of our Funds for the American Way campaign to introduce, ladies and gentlemen and fellow citizens, that outstanding citizen, Phillip Houghton."

The applause was generous, and Houghton had reached the lectern long before it died. He addressed the banqueters without use of a manuscript, but he had committed his notes to memory in advance of the occasion. Warren followed the speech closely but could detect no instance of departing from the scheme of the address the notes had outlined. His language was of a fuller texture than Congressman Robinson's, and Warren felt a vicarious pride when he noted the intensity of the silence with which the room listened.

The speech lasted twenty minutes, but the vigor of Houghton's delivery and the diversity of anecdote he included made it seem shorter. At his conclusion the applause was louder than before, and Congressman Robinson had jocularly to signal for attention before he could introduce the next speaker.

It was during the following speech that Houghton's glance, moving across the room, met Warren's, and he smiled. Warren acknowledged the smile with a brief lifting of his head, and with the exchange they congratulated themselves on how well the speech had gone. Houghton turned his attention to his successor on the dais.

In the taxi driving away from the hotel two hours later Houghton said, "You must be tired. I know I am; this has been a difficult week."

He leaned his head back and closed his eyes. Warren looked at his face, more sensitive in repose than when his driving energy enlivened it, and then at the hands resting lightly on his crossed legs. They were spatular hands, lean, the knuckles prominent, and his wrists were modeled as exquisitely as a boy's. Warren drew his gaze away and looked out the taxi window. If he lingered too long over those hands, he wanted to touch them, and he could never touch them. The affection and the paternal protectiveness Houghton gave him had grown too important to him to be jeopardized.

They rode on in silence.

In February Houghton was arranging for the appearance of Senator Joseph McCarthy on the television program.

"Have you met Senator McCarthy?" he asked Warren.

"No, I haven't."

Houghton chortled. "You'll be fascinated by him. Curious type: a vulgarian, but he's got a certain crude appeal. He first got into the news in a little way by trying to get death sentences commuted for some German S. S. men involved in the Malmédy massacre during the war. Wrong kind of publicity, all wrong, but McCarthy's convinced the Army's investigators used improper methods. For the television show, we'll have to make it a Wednesday after the ninth."

"Conflicting commitments?" Warren supposed.

"He's scheduled for some speeches over the Lincoln's Birthday weekend, one before some clubwomen in West Virginia and a couple more of the same out West. The Senate Campaign Committee is going to have him say something about Communists in the government, which is the only reason he's of any use to us. I thought he and Ted O'Harra would do well for the panel."

"Is O'Harra any less a vulgarian then McCarthy?"

"A cut above, I think. Why do you ask that?"

"You say so often that your aim is to remove just those types from a position of influence——"

"That doesn't mean they can't be made use of, Warren," Houghton cautioned. "We're in a meaner fight than that. If they can be used as channels to spread the right kind of thinking among their constituents or the public generally, then I'll use them. It's not as though a junior Senator like McCarthy can do us any harm. He'll be a perfectly innocuous mouthpiece."

But it was at the meeting of the Ohio County Women's Republican Club in Wheeling, West Virginia, that on February 11, Joseph McCarthy broke sharply forward from the ranks of less colorful legislators to launch his lone-wolf campaign against Communist subversion in the Government of the United States. The State Department, he declared, suffered not only the scars of infiltration that had occurred in the days of the United Front, as had been the case with Alger Hiss; it was at the present moment corrupt with subversive influence. "While I cannot take the time to name all of the men in the State Department who have been named as members of the Communist Party and members of a spy ring, I have here in my hand a list of two hundred and five that were known to the Secretary of State as being members of the Communist Party and who nevertheless are still shaping the policy of the State Department."

Word of McCarthy's charges reached the State Department quickly, and through an employee of the department, were relayed to Phillip Houghton. The publisher was taken completely by surprise.

"A list of *names?* In the State Department? God, when he

said Communists in Government, I didn't know he was going after State. This is better than I hoped."

Warren hesitated to believe the assertion. "Where would he get any kind of list like that? The F.B.I. couldn't have given it to him, and the State Department certainly wouldn't have."

"Who cares?" Houghton waved the question aside. "I wonder if this is the boy I've been waiting for. . . ." He turned McCarthy's possibilities over in his mind gloatingly. "He's got that naughty-boy charm, he's more than usually greedy about publicity. . . . Warren, see if you can get Ted O'Harra on the telephone for me."

On the night of February 20, McCarthy met the demand of the Senate that he explain his charges against the State Department. Both Warren and Phillip Houghton flew to Washington to hear the debate, and sat in the press gallery from late afternoon until nearly midnight as the disorganized battle of charges and demands grew increasingly incomprehensible. Warren could understand little of what was said, but vividly clear to him was the dramatic power of Joseph McCarthy's performance. Its very incoherence was awesome when Warren considered this barking, flush-faced man's scheduled appearance on Houghton's broadcast.

On the day of the broadcast it fell to Warren to escort Ted and Ethel O'Harra to their hotel from the airport and to deliver O'Harra to the studio on time. He was not introduced to Senator McCarthy until after the technical rehearsal. During the general coffee-break he listened while Houghton and McCarthy again reviewed the primary points the televised discussion would touch on. Afterward, there was time for McCarthy to tell them what he had been going through since the speech at Wheeling. The forces ranged against him in his new prominence were formidable, and McCarthy was prepared to believe they were ruthless. Under the powerful lights of the studio he sweated, and his smile was strained as he spoke. Warren was still uncertain of his opinion of McCarthy. In two weeks he had become the most controversial man in America. No one, Warren thought would place him among the elite whose interests Houghton represented, but his vividness of personality was magnetic and the personal strength of the man, the extent of the confusion he was capable of stirring up, would indeed be use ful, even if it was to a class to which McCarthy himself clearly did not belong.

Senator O'Harra, who from time to time had contributed articles about the Washington scene to *American View,* came over to them. McCarthy greeted Ted O'Harra cordially.

"I only wish this panel discussion could be repeated every night for a month," O'Harra said to him. "You're doing a great job. I've been wanting a club to use against the State Department for years, and you've given me one. I'm against this country taking any kind of Munich attitude toward the Russians and their friends over here. They're too damned dangerous for that kind of treatment. Count on me for anything, anything at all."

To Warren later Houghton said, "Ted may think McCarthy is God's gift to Americanism, but I suspect he's thinking more in terms of the next election. I've watched O'Harra change in the last couple of years. He likes the Senate—there's nothing he won't do to get the voters to keep him in."

To McCarthy, to O'Harra, to all the other politically active men with whom he was thrown in contact, Warren listened, and his espousal of Houghton's vision of the American future hardened into conviction. The sweep of history had made an imperial power of the United States. Why shouldn't the United States openly assert its imperialistic nature? Who but sentimentalists ever decried imperialism for its own sake? A benevolent colonialism was certainly still possible to the world; at the very least there was still room in America for the dedicated conservative.

And it was with the most conservative of thinking political men that Warren wanted to be allied. As forceful a motive as his political conviction was his personal need. A secret outcast in his aberration, he could in his work be associated with the most conformist of men. Once, when he had broken away from Mike Cowan, he had vowed he would not let decorum shackle him. He had paid heavily for that vow, and assuming conformity like a uniform, he turned his back forever on the lawlessness of a homosexual's desperate existence.

The call to Texas had been put through, and while Houghton talked, Warren, at the refrigerator in the corner, was pouring out the buttermilk that his employer had to be reminded to drink every hour. He carried the glass and its coaster to the desk and set it before him.

Houghton covered the mouthpiece with a hand to say, "Thanks; good boy."

He was about to go out again when Houghton signaled him to wait. The call was completed presently and Houghton hung up the phone. He smiled at Warren, eyes glinting.

"Can you go to Texas with me?"

"Of course."

"Do you *want* to go to Texas with me, I should say."

"Hell, yes. What's it about?"

"To meet our benefactor. I'm flying down to discuss the possibility of expanding *American View*—new departments I want to add. Got your book?"

Warren pulled the notebook from his coat pocket.

"If we can get reservations for tonight, I'll be happy. Otherwise tomorrow night; no morning flights."

"Right," said Warren. "Mrs. Houghton going?"

"Just you and I—it's only two days," he answered. "We'll want to take the Turner clippings, to prove he's worth the price of hiring him over to our side."

"All of them?"

"Make a selection of the best. And plan on having dinner at my house if the flight schedule allows. We can leave from there."

It was time for his next outside appointment.

He was on his feet, and drawing Warren with him. "Are you cleared away here?"

"Yes," said Warren.

"Better come along with me, then. I may need you."

He stopped then, and looked at Warren quizzically.

"When the hell do you have time for your private life?"

"What kind of question is that? You're my private life. Tha was the original deal, remember?"

Houghton's hand clapped his shoulder.

"I've gotten twice the work done that I used to, since you'v been here. I'm grateful for that."

Warren said nothing, but committed to memory the con tour of Houghton's smile.

"We won't be back for an hour," the older man said. "D you think I should have an extra shot of the buttermilk?

"I'll let you off this time," Warren answered. "Now we'r five minutes late, let's move."

He had thrown himself wholeheartedly into his work an

found in it an emotional engagement that made it possible for him to give up the bitter searching for sexual satisfaction. He had no time for pursuing love. The conflict and the drama of the arena of public affairs stood open before him, and the years to come were fat with the promise of participation. He felt himself a part, at last, of the moving world.

In the bright sunlight of a Sunday afternoon in June, Tiger Rizzuto walked down the avenue, his daughter straddling his shoulders and holding herself aloft by two fistfuls of her father's black hair. Across the avenue from the housing development where Tiger and Juney had their apartment were long rows of older buildings, shops and tenements, crowded and noisy, and Tiger enjoyed walking up and down the narrow streets dividing them. In their dirt and smelliness was a richness of humanity lacking in their housing development and reminiscent of the streets he'd grown up in. He liked to take Elizabeth with him on these walks in the unarticulated hope that she would not grow up entirely a stranger to his kind of world, unattractive as it had been.

He crossed the avenue holding tight to Elizabeth's legs, and on the opposite sidewalk set her down and took her hand. They strolled into the nearest of the tenement streets. Elizabeth kept up her usual babbling monologue, a conscientious imitation of polite conversation, and Tiger interpolated brief automatic noises to encourage her. But his eyes were drinking in the scene before him. In the summer heat, the tenement windows were thrown open, and the smell of Italian cooking—tomato paste and wine and simmering ground meats—was heavy in the street. An old woman with a combative snarl sat on a stoop they passed, gossiping over her shoulder with another woman propped by pillows in a first-story window.

"My boy not gone go," she declared for everyone to hear. "They want, I tell 'em myself, my boy not gone go fight nobody."

She was not the only one worried about war. The tension of fear was everywhere, it seemed to Tiger. He nodded to the woman as he passed, smiling, although he did not know her. Other voices were sounding excitedly through the tenement windows, and from several of them he could hear the crackling of a radio newscaster's report. Farther down the steaming block some teen-agers in rowdy horseplay were yelling and spilling off the sidewalk into the street and back again.

"We'll go over and murder the bastards!" cried one as Tiger neared them.

"They ain't gonna make me go. What the fuck do *I* care about a lot of chinks?" said another.

Tiger's step momentarily faltered. Now that the Commies had successfully declared their People's Republic of China, what was going on in the Orient that would concern these young hoods on a hot afternoon in New York City? He didn't know what they were talking about. As he hurried Elizabeth past the group, two of them were loudly imitating machine-gun fire, and another boasted in graphic slang of the prowess he would prove with Oriental women.

"Come on, beautiful," Tiger said to Elizabeth, "I'll buy you some candy at the drugstore." He hustled her out of earshot.

They went into the Rexall store, and Elizabeth chose the candy bar she wanted. Tiger asked the clerk, "Is anything going on? I heard some people outside talking about war."

"Search me, buddy," said the clerk. "I had it. I just don't pay no attention no more. Mounds is ten cents."

"Oh." He gave the clerk the extra nickel and taking Elizabeth's hand, hurried out to the street again.

On the sidewalk he paused, listening to the sounds of the tenement. It hadn't, he realized, been a current of tension, but of activity, that he had felt along this street. He had spent all Saturday reading, and he hadn't bothered to turn on the radio. The loudmouthed teen-agers were drifting away from the particular stoop they had occupied, but two sullen members of the band remained. Tiger went up to them.

"Hey, you guys, excuse me, I'm from Mars," he said to them.

"Don't you know, Mac? They're saying we're going to war again."

"Who?"

"I don't know—everybody."

"I mean who're we fighting?" Tiger asked.

"The Commies, Mac. That's all I know, Mac."

"Which ones? No, never mind. Come on, Elizabeth. Thanks, you guys." He picked the child up in his arms and hurried back down the block.

In five minutes he had reached the apartment.

"Juney, can you take Elizabeth? Something's up. I've got to call Mills."

Juney called back from the kitchen, "Sure, dear. Elizabeth . . . come help Mother set the table. You can put the forks down on top of the napkins. I'll show you how, baby."

The child ran off to the kitchen, and Tiger grabbed the telephone to dial Driscoll Mills' number.

"Hello?"

"This is Tiger," he said. "What the hell is this about war?"

"Where've *you* been?" Mills groaned. "It looks like it, Tiger. You just heard?"

"Christ, I haven't heard *any*thing. What happened?"

"The North Koreans are busting over the border; they're invading South Korea."

"They've been doing that for months."

"Border incidents," said Mills. "This is a big push. Naturally we're caught with our pants down. Truman is ordering MacArthur in."

"What?" Tiger shouted.

"As far as I can make out, it's to be a United Nations police action," he explained. "I could murder Truman with my bare hands."

"What the hell are you talking about?" Tiger cried, jumping up. "Don't you want the U.N. ever to have any muscle? Nobody likes wars, but I'm glad the U.N. is hitting back fast."

"A war never solved anything," Mills snapped, his scholar's calmness gone.

"It *isn't* a war if it's a police action," Tiger insisted.

"Words, words. Do you know where Korea *is?* Snuggling up *China's* rear end, that's where it is. One false step and China's going to blow up in our faces. . . ."

"The Commies wouldn't want that any more than we would," Tiger argued. "Not if they see we're not going to take it lying down."

"Maybe not," Mills' voice sneered through the phone. "Have you asked General MacArthur what *he* wants? Just give that baby a few days to digest what's happened, and you'll see. Oh, Jesus, it's Napoleon 'I shall return' Bonaparte all over again. Balls. I'm going to bed with a bottle."

"Wait, Driscoll. What about the political-action committees? What're the unions going to say?"

"Who knows? Henderson and everybody else in the Demo-Socialists are going to override me, but any influence *I've* got with the unions is going to back up whoever says we ought to get the hell out of the mess as soon as possible."

"For God's sake don't do anything too fast," Tiger urged. "Wait till you talk to Tom. Wait till I can talk to you tomorrow."

He hung up, and saw Juney in the kitchen doorway, her vivid blue eyes frightened and concerned.

"Tiger, what's happened?"

"As far as anybody knows," he said, "the U.N. is going to war against the Communists—in North Korea."

June came swiftly to him. "*We* belong to the U.N. Tiger, are we declaring war?"

"No, no, it's not done the same way any more, Juney."

"It amounts to the same thing, doesn't it? Tiger, you're not going to go away to a war again?"

Tiger took her in his arms, and Elizabeth in a burst of childish sentiment charged forward to them both. They fell sprawling onto the sofa, but Juney did not laugh.

"Tell me. Are you?" she demanded. "Is everybody going away again just when we're beginning to get settled?"

"Juney, there's a whole new generation to fight this one," he declared. "By fighting standards, I'm getting on in years, you know."

"Don't joke," Juney rebuked.

"Listen, I mean it," Tiger said. "This could be a great thing happening."

"A war?" Juney exclaimed, recoiling.

"It's horrible, Juney, but it's not as bad as it would be otherwise. The police sometimes have to shoot down a dangerous criminal, don't they? That's what this is, on a bigger scale. The Commies have committed a criminal action and the police force of the world is calling them on it. That's what the U.N. was meant for. That's what nobody ever thought they'd have the guts to do. And for once we're carrying out a moral action when it can do some good, instead of babbling about it until it's too late."

Unconvinced, Juney gathered Elizabeth into her lap.

"Why can't they stop?" she asked. "Why every time you turn around do they have to kill people? If you don't have to go, I don't care so much. I just won't think about it."

"Juney, don't be that way——"

"I can't help it. I'm not political like you are. I have Elizabeth, and I hate and despise everything that's going to hurt her when she's older. I hate it." She set the child down suddenly. "Oh, my God, the chicken!—Tiger, can you lend a hand? Zeeda will be here any minute."

"Zeeda Kaufman?"

"How many people named Zeeda do you know?"

"I mean, I didn't know she was coming."

"I asked her after the recital last week," Juney said. "She looks like she can use a good meal. I don't think her salary at that dancing school can be very high. Damn it, why doesn't everybody just stop having armies? The trouble with men running things is that men aren't really practical if you look it in the face."

Juney busied herself rescuing the chicken.

Through the handful of occasions Zeeda Kaufman had come to dine with them, Tiger had grown to like her. She sometimes frightened him when she got overly dramatic about something political, but she had the reputation of being a hard-working student, faithful to Dr. Graeme's lecture series, and Tiger liked to listen to her sing when she would consent to do so.

When the doorbell rang, Tiger went to let Zeeda in. Her braids of dark hair were caught up into loops behind her ears, and each sported a bright ribbon.

"I don't want to hear a word about MacArthur," she announced as she came through the door.

"Don't yell till you're hit," said Tiger. "Come on in, Juney's in the kitchen. *Why* don't you want to hear about MacArthur?"

"I'm sick over the whole thing, Tiger," said Zeeda. "Who the hell wants to go back to another war when we've hardly caught our breath after the last one? Can't we find any other way to avoid a goddamned depression?"

Tiger did what proselytizing he could while they waited for dinner, but Zeeda refused to listen or to discuss Korea in any way. When Juney started to serve dinner, Zeeda took charge of minding the baby. She played with her on the floor, talking recipes with Juney over her shoulder.

Dinner was served and they gathered around the table.

Juney placed the roast chicken on its platter in front of Tiger, and he made a show of carving—only a show, because the chicken was so well done, it delivered itself from its skeleton without help. But distributing the pieces pleased Tiger because it was a business reserved entirely to a family man. A family man—except that they had yet to have an outsider in for a turkey dinner on a holiday. Now if this could have been turkey—Zeeda! he realized unexpectedly. At last they would have someone fairly lonely to share their blessings with them. Next holiday—that would be Thanksgiving—they would ask Zeeda to come have dinner with them.

"Tiger," Zeeda began. "Do you really like Tom Henderson?"

"He's a wonderful guy," Tiger assured her. "Nobody'll ever know how much I owe him—him and Mills both."

"I just wondered. I mean, I don't know anything about him. I'm new to the D.S.P., but I wondered if maybe he wasn't—oh, exploiting your talent a little."

Tiger laughed outright. "Exploiting!" he crowed.

"Tiger, wait till you swallow," said Juney.

He wiped his lips with his napkin. "Do you know what I was doing when Henderson found me?" he began.

"I know that, being the janitor there and all," said Zeeda. "But still—well, everybody knows how good you are in your job. Shouldn't you be getting a boost up the ladder soon? Anybody would think so."

Tiger looked at her in puzzlement then, but he did not speak. What could she be driving at? It was an incongruous note, coming from her.

She went on as though in superficial conversation. "Well, you do work for peanuts, Tiger. Maybe the D.S.P. thinks you ought to be kept where you are so you won't go lousing up the budget. Don't you think so, Juney?"

Juney looked as though she were as puzzled as Tiger. "I'm the last person who'd know about their budget, Zeeda," she said.

"I just don't think they really appreciate you, Tiger," Zeeda said. "You know? A lot of other organizations would give their eye teeth for you, I'll bet."

"The Demo-Socialists aren't that hard up for money, Zeeda," Tiger said.

"It just seemed to me—well, God knows I don't want to put any doubts in your mind, but Henderson looks like the opportunist type to me. He just *looks* it, physically. That bull neck. That aggressiveness. And I don't think all is quiet behind Driscoll Mills' thoughtful drawl, either. *You* know."

"I do?"

"Sure you do." Zeeda waved a hand. "I suppose you'll say I'm too quick to draw conclusions——"

"I suppose so," Tiger said gently.

Zeeda dropped the subject.

After dinner Tiger sat with Elizabeth on his lap at the table in the kitchen while Zeeda helped Juney with the dish-washing.

"Oh, what a wonderful way to spend Sunday," Zeeda said. "You two don't know how much I appreciate it. The only trouble is, it makes going back to that damn dance school tomorrow harder to bear than ever."

Juney asked, "Isn't there some other kind of job you could find, Zeeda? I'd hate it, all those men, you don't know where they come from . . ."

"Don't think I don't try to find something else," Zeeda said. She smiled then, like a child with a secret that is trembling to escape. "Mr. Shagley is my target for this summer."

"Shagley?" Tiger asked, surprised. "How Shagley?"

"I've been thinking. The open-house recitals I've been giving every month, they're going pretty well. People *come* to them at least. I've been wondering if a course in folk music wouldn't fit the curriculum next year. In September."

"Why wouldn't it?" Juney agreed. "It might not pay very much——"

"I don't need much to live." Zeeda shrugged. "And believe me, *any*thing is better than that damn dance studio. Do you think Shagley would like the idea, Tiger?"

"No telling," Tiger said. "It can't hurt to try him on it."

"Tiger, if I did, would you put in a good word for me? I don't know Mr. Shagley terribly well. Your saying something about me to him would make all the difference."

"Sure I will, Zeeda. Glad to."

"If Zeeda gives the course," Juney put in, "I want to enroll."

Zeeda laughed. "My first customer!"

The work of the kitchen was finished, and they moved into the living room. Zeeda took Elizabeth onto her lap and began to sing to her. Holding hands, Tiger and Juney sat listening to the unfamiliar song. The vibrance of Zeeda's voice seemed to fill the apartment and yet was tender. It had not the liquidness Tiger thought of when he remembered his father singing Italian songs to him in his babyhood, but a timbre, that was almost harsh, palpably unsettling, penetrative as the sounds of priests chanting life into a requiem. . . .

On Monday and the day after, Tiger was able to learn in greater detail of the events in distant and obscure Korea. On June 25 the People's Democratic Republic of Korea, a government recognized by neither the United States nor the United Nations, had invaded South Korea with an armed force of some seventy thousand troops. Secretary of State Dean Acheson had informed the President of the invasion by a telephone call to Independence, Missouri, and the President had promptly directed Douglas MacArthur to speed military assistance to the South Koreans. An emergency meeting of the Security Council of the United Nations was called on Sunday afternoon, and the Council declared the invasion to be a breach of the peace. On Monday, MacArthur was ordered to send air and sea forces into action.

A few days later the Security Council adopted a resolution that all United Nations forces in Korea should be under a single command. The blue and white banner of the United Nations flew beside the flags of sovereign peoples.

Through that summer it became clear that the action in Korea had, on the domestic scene, lent authority and conviction to the private crusade of Joseph McCarthy against Communist influence in Government. McCarthyism became recognized as a national phenomenon of religious intensity.

One day Tiger Rizzuto was in his office at the headquarters of the Demo-Socialist Party when Tom Henderson stormed in.

"There's no stopping the man! *No* one is safe from that sonuvabitch McCarthy!"

"Who the hell now?" Tiger asked.

Henderson threw himself down into the chair beside Tiger's desk, snorting, and wagging his overlarge head. "Who knows? I ought to stop teaching. I'm being driven too hard. I've just come from a forum: do you know that even those people are permeated by this kind of thinking? I never thought

I'd hear the phrase 'red-blooded Americanism' used in *this* school, not even by a student. If there are Commies in Washington—and you know damn well there are—it isn't him who's going to find them. But all he has to do is open his big fat yap, and anybody he's got a grudge against is smeared with filth for life. Tell me who your friends are and I'll tell you what you are, yet. What a black bunch of years to live in!"

"Hardly any time for you to stop teaching, then," Tiger pointed out.

Henderson looked up. "What did I come in here for?"

"To yell at me?"

"No. Oh, I remember. Shagley told me about Zeeda Kaufman wanting to run a folk-music history course this semester. Do you know anything about her that might militate against our putting her on the school's staff? In plain English, is there any chance the Commies sent her here?"

"I don't think so," said Tiger. "No, she's pretty Bohemian, and dramatic as hell, but I think she's sincere. Has Les Vernon done a check?"

"Not yet," said Henderson. "Probably won't get to it till after the classes are started."

"I don't think he'll find anything." Tiger shook his head. "Of course I don't really know Zeeda that well, except from around here."

At first the investigator found nothing that indicated any connection between Zeeda Kaufman and the Communist Party.

In September Zeeda's class was inaugurated, and Juney Rizzuto enrolled in the course. Zeeda quit the dance studio where she'd unhappily been working, and gave herself wholeheartedly to her new enterprise. It was not until the day of the season's first snow that the revelation came.

Tiger had walked through the snow with Zeeda that day, laughing over something Elizabeth had done the last time Zeeda had been to their apartment, and they had parted with a mutual promise that she would have Thanksgiving dinner with them.

"Tell Juney I'll bring a sweet-potato casserole," she said. "And thank you for asking me, Tiger. It'll be so wonderful spending Thanksgiving with a family instead of—oh, a lot of single friends as miserable as I would be."

Tiger beamed. Zeeda left him feeling generous and appreciated. Her appreciation of the Thanksgiving invitation proved him to be, he told himself, a solid and reliable type, a dependable member of society's framework. He decided he liked Zeeda Kaufman better than ever.

Tom Henderson was waiting for him when he reached the apartment that afternoon, and Juney left the two of them alone, going out of the room with a formal air and an expression of puzzlement on her pretty features.

"I'm sorry, Tiger, this is unpleasant," said Henderson, scowling. "We only just found out, and we have to know if you can tell us anything more."

"About what?" Tiger wanted to know.

"You know Zeeda Kaufman lived in New Orleans a while back?"

"Sure, so did you know."

"That's where the break came. Tiger, she's a Commie."

Tiger stepped back, the breath knocked from him.

"I don't believe it," he said flatly.

"It's true. She was a paid agitator down there. She's buddy-buddy with Joseph Murray, Ozzie Lubin, the whole pack. She's an infiltrator."

"But she's a friend of ours——"

"She's a Commie, Tiger," Henderson repeated. "They've got her cold."

Tiger wavered where he stood. "I feel sick," he said. "Let me sit down."

He did, and Henderson stood over him, his thickset figure strung tight, his incongruously sensitive face showing pain.

"You never suspected?" he asked. "No clue at all?"

"No," said Tiger. He gave a sigh. "Shit. . . . How did they find her out?"

"A girl she had helping her in New Orleans defected, and told the whole story. Elaine Crosley, a youngster apparently, a real kid. Before we found out that much, Zeeda might just as easily have been one of the dozens of other well-meaning half-wits she duped."

Tiger found a cigarette and lit it. He blew smoke at the button of Henderson's suit jacket. "I just left her. We've gotten to be friends—Zeeda and Juney and me. I just asked her for Thanksgiving."

"She's no stray," said Henderson dryly. "We'll have to get her off the school's staff."

"Sure."

"Look, Tiger. Zeeda's pretty arty. What do you three have in common? I mean—you never had anything to do with her, did you?"

Tiger looked up. "What? Oh. No."

"I just wondered. I couldn't think of why you should be friends with her."

Tiger said, "I guess it was something *Zeeda* did, Tom. I guess we were her best bet for getting onto the staff at the school. I guess that was all it was. . . ."

32

ZEEDA STOOD STUNNED, IN THE MIDDLE OF her room. Shagley had just left, his high-pitched voice still reverberated in her ears. Caught. She could not believe it, it couldn't be happening after all the work, the months and months of work she'd put into it. Damn them, damn them all! the whole rat-pack bunch of polite reformers, rotten with the mold of sneaks like Les Vernon; she wished with her bare fingers she could rip the balls off every one of them! She caught her breath when she thought of the force of Ozzie Lubin's fury when he found out. Not at her, God knew she'd done everything imaginable to infiltrate the damned school, including befriending that fool Tiger Rizzuto and his silly, brainless wife. But Ozzie wouldn't take the news well: it had to his mind been a foregone conclusion that he had a member back inside the Labor School.

Ozzie arrived at the apartment near midnight. She told him what had transpired that afternoon. He did not blink. He did not lose his temper. His eyes pierced her, and for a long moment he said nothing.

"It's terrible," Zeeda said, "but I did everything I could, everything was going perfectly till that sonuvabitch Vernon got his report from New Orleans."

Ozzie did not answer.

"How did they find out?" Zeeda asked. "I tried to tell Shagley I'd just been a dupe, just like all the others. He knew better. Ozzie, what're you going to do about the Labor School now?"

He took a breath. He did not raise his voice, nor did his stare waver.

"That's the end of you, sweetheart," he said.

"What?"

"You're out."

"Out? Ozzie, in what way do you . . ." She stopped. Ozzie Lubin nodded. "No! No, you can't!" Zeeda gasped. "I didn't do anything——"

"You——"

"I didn't fail. I didn't let you down! Ozzie, I've got the right to appeal!"

He barked, "You're not being expelled, you're being dropped. At *my* word, on *my* authority. There isn't any appeal."

He turned to go, and Zeeda grabbed his arm with both hands.

"Ozzie, not just like that!—Ozzie, you're my friend, you're —oh, God, my *only* friend! Ozzie! *It wasn't my fault!*"

He wagged his white head and moaned his indifference. "Zeeda, Zeeda——"

"Listen to me!" she shouted, distraught now. "It wasn't my fault they found out about New Orleans. We knew there was an outside chance."

"You were supposed to've been covered in New Orleans. You were supposed to have been a dupe. Vernon isn't the type to jump to conclusions. If he pinned you, it's because somehow or other you tipped your hand down there. Vernon *knows* you're a member, he's not guessing."

"I didn't do *any*thing wrong down there, the security setup didn't have a flaw! Ozzie, it was the best job I ever did; I won't let you ruin the best thing I ever achieved in my life!"

"You silly cunt, do you know what you're talking about? If they've pinned you, do you know how many people in this very city are pinned with you, at least by implication? None of us is safe today, not one, and my skin is too serious a business for the Party to worry about the likes of you!"

"You must be kidding, Ozzie; I can't believe anything but that you're kidding. . . . A loyalty check!" She grasped at the inspiration. "Is this some kind of loyalty check? Oh, thank God for that! I *knew* you wouldn't throw me out."

She had released his arm.

"It's no joke. Good-by, Zeeda."

He turned, and before she could move to stop him, he was gone.

With the closing of the door and the sound of the latch clicking into place, she knew she would never see him again. There had to be an explanation. It hadn't been a joke. He'd meant the things he'd said—but it couldn't be possible. She'd worked too hard; she'd given up too much. There hadn't been an hour of her time in the last two years that hadn't gone to the Party's work; rarely a dime she'd earned that hadn't been at the instant call of a crisis of one kind or another in the Party; not a real friend had she made except inside the membership. They couldn't be jettisoning her like this.

Tell her she was through? Say good-by and turn and walk away and disappear? Could it happen this way? Could it be happening now? And she didn't even know why. What had she done wrong in New Orleans? What misstep had she made that she couldn't recognize or remember? She couldn't stand not knowing. She'd go crazy if she couldn't remember what mistake she'd made.

Suddenly she was aware that she felt hungry. She'd skipped lunch because—why had she?—because there had been too much mimeographing she'd had to get done, and after Shagley's appearance, there'd been no dinner. Mimeographing! She was late, late! It would make a bad impression if she were late getting the material delivered. Without thinking of a coat, she ran over to the stacks of mimeographed sheets, the day's entire output. She was halfway to the door with the gathered stacks when she realized what she was doing, and then, like ribbons, her arms collapsed. The fresh white pages spilled into a heap on the floor, and Zeeda fell down upon them, sobbing.

It was an hour before the sobbing had stopped and she could breathe again. She could feel the shock to her mind as though it were a thing of the senses, a physical thing. Her thoughts could not progress, but only sluggishly revolve one about another. Her arms and legs felt numb, and her vision was not blurred but strangely blunted. As though a boulder were strapped across her back, she pulled herself up from the wreckage of the mimeographed sheets and staggered over to her bed. She sat down heavily on the edge of it and clasped her hands between her knees.

She knew now what it meant. Everything it meant. She had been on the other end of the line often enough. When you were dropped, it was the end of you. People you'd given your love to all your remembered life no longer spoke to you or so much as caught your eye on the street. Oh, it had happened to plenty of them in the last year, and it was always the same. You gave everything you had or believed or hoped for to the Party, and when the Party was taken away, you were left with nothing—a wrung-out, shriveled, sun-bleached husk, a discard. It couldn't happen to her, not to Zeeda Kaufman—but it had.

Where could she turn now? Where? To the fools and the schemers on the other side, the likes of a Tiger Rizzuto? Her own brother? Oh, that was rich, all right. They'd have her in prison without batting an eyelash—Conspiring to advocate the violent overthrow . . . The Fifth Amendment . . . Vernon . . . The Fifth Amendment . . . The F.B.I. . . .

For a long while her thoughts unresolvedly twisted about. Then suddenly Zeeda jumped up from the bed. If Les Vernon had found out about her, how much more did he know? How much was there that she could be prosecuted for? Fingers of terror reached out of the apartment's darkness and gripped her. Her brain reeled sickeningly, and she started to gag. Was anything she had done really that important to the government, important enough for them to punish her? No, but she knew the important men, knew too much about them. Joseph Murray and Ozzie Lubin might be more dangerous to the government than she had ever thought, and she was their accomplice and their intimate. She plunged toward the bathroom, expecting to vomit, but the seizure passed, and she stood panting, steadying herself against the doorjamb.

A wave of hysteria smote her. What were they waiting for? Shagley had known since this afternoon. It was after midnight now. Were they on their way for her now? Would there be a ring at the doorbell in a minute—half an hour—an hour? She couldn't let them find her, not the witch hunt. Not the rats she'd given her life to fight against. She couldn't let them get at her.

With the chill of fear upon her, she grabbed her coat from the closet. She had to get out of the apartment. She had to start walking. She had to walk until it was impossible for them ever to find her.

On the dark street the snow was falling in driving sheets. Zeeda wrapped her woolen scarf over her head, twisted it under her chin, and held it fast beneath the collar of her coat. They were after her, she was sure now. She walked. She wandered aimlessly through the snowy, icy streets, not knowing where she was going. Where could she go? For years, for as long as she could remember, whenever there was trouble, the Party had been there to help her, to advise her, to protect. Now there could be no one, inside or out of the Party. There was no one alive who cared about her, who gave a damn whether or not the police caught up with her, whether or not she was frightened, or lonely, or broken. The cold of the streets was a pain against her face, but worst of all was her cold and hopeless knowledge. *Outcast. Rootless.* The words repeated themselves in her head like a madwoman's liturgy. *Outcast. Rootless.* Finished.

She walked all night. First to Columbus Circle, then up and down the streets of the West Side in a broken pattern, bound nowhere but away from whatever lay behind her. She passed an all-night restaurant whose clock told her it was four in the morning. A block beyond the restaurant she came to Central Park again. She turned down Central Park West, confusedly trying to figure out how many blocks she would have to go before reaching Columbus Circle again. Lacking an answer, she could only push on blindly toward it.

At dawn the snow still fell, and the wind was blowing at blizzard force. She was staggering with exhaustion, dazed, worn out and hungry, but she did not dare to stop. They were bound, she supposed, to find her, but not yet, not yet. Around her there was no light but that of the driving snow. Shivering uncontrollably, she came suddenly to a stop in her destinationless ambulation. She had passed Columbus Circle long before. There was no reason for her not to seek shelter in some unoccupied public place, was there? To rest for an hour, before there were people out to see to the business of the day? She stood on Fifth Avenue now, deserted in the storming early hours. The library wouldn't be too far away.

She made her way downtown, pressing close to the shop fronts to find whatever protection she could against the storm. When she had reached Forty-second Street, she could make them out dimly through the snow—the lions in white coverlets. She headed for them. At the height of the snow-covered steps the portico would be shelter from the cutting wind. There she could rest, could get her breath back.

Inside the portico there was only the shrill whistling sound of the storm, little direct assault of the wind. She pulled her coat more tightly about her and sat down on a cement bench next to the building's entrance. As time wore on, no sun appeared, only the sleet and snowfall, grayly glowing with the start of the day. Later she could not tell how long she had huddled there. Perhaps only momentarily she had slept. She sat up with a start when a voice at her shoulder said, "Are you all right, miss?"

She jumped up. A man she did not know was peering at her. She could not tell if he were solicitous, a stranger, or danger given face. Without answering, she started to run down the steps of the library. She tripped and caught herself against the stony, gritty base of one of the lion statues.

There were people on the street now, and a bus was laboring through the snowstorm. At the foot of the library steps, two men in drab-colored clothes were standing, their heads bent against the force of the wind. Her heart stopped. Les Vernon's men, she told herself. They might be; they could easily be. How did she know they weren't? She cut quickly over to the other side of the broad stone stairway and ran down the remaining stairs and off down the avenue, letting the driving snow close like a curtain behind her. When she had run three blocks, she looked back, and the men were not in sight. She had eluded them, at least for the moment. She slowed her pace in order to attract no attention, huddling within the coat that had ceased to contain warmth against the snow. Unless she could think of some place, they would find her. Sooner or later one of the packs would find her. She couldn't hope to escape them forever, but where was there for her to go? She couldn't give in yet. She turned off the avenue into a side street.

In the middle of the lightless, wind-whipped block she was arrested by a choking spell of coughing. She realized her face was burning with fever, and beneath her clothes, between her breasts, there was a hot moistness. Sickness: that was all she needed now, a good solid messy damnable sickness to betray her. Well, she wasn't going to let it; she wouldn't be sick; she would pay no attention to it, whatever her treacherous body did to her. She trudged on through the snowing streets, turning her course frequently, up one block and down another, doubling back again and again, cleaning herself of pursuers as she had never done before. Drive yourself, drive yourself, make your will power function, go on, go on, don't stop, don't get sick, don't let anything stop you. . . .

By noon, a blustering, sunless noon the color of ashes only partly whitened by the unrelenting snowfall, she was delirious with fever.

She did not know where she was now. Somewhere on the East Side. Was there something she recognized about the neighborhood? Something vaguely familiar about it as it crouched over the East River? She had to decide what she was going to do. She had to make up her mind where she would turn. Her brother? She wondered what Marvin was like now, a successful, kind of elegant young doctor. Was he married? Did he have children? She told herself it was asinine to think of Marvin, to wonder anything about him. All that had been too long ago.

She forced herself to go on walking, back over to Third Avenue, up Third Avenue past the barrooms and stores with dust-covered violins in their windows. Where was her guitar? she asked herself. She had left it behind. At the apartment? No, she had left it at the Labor School after her last class. She squeezed her eyes shut against the thought of humiliation, the terrible deprivation of having lost her guitar along the way. What good was Zeeda Kaufman without her guitar? That was why no one would ever consent to hide her, to help her. She had no value without her guitar. She didn't exist without her guitar, to smile, to sing to them.

The snow was piling up in great drifts that made walking treacherous, and she fell repeatedly. God, would she ever be warm again? Wasn't there some warm place she could go to sit for a while, sleep for an hour or two? She stepped back against the glass window of a shop on a corner, fighting off a wave of dizziness. She was somewhere in the Seventies. She knew this place. . . . But how? What was so familiar about this lifeless shop, two or three tenement buildings? In the middle of the block, on the other side of the street, was a more recently built, more expensive apartment building.

"Oh, no! Oh, Jesus!" Zeeda cried to herself. She gnawed at her raw knuckles and tears bit at her eyes. How had she found her way here? Had she known what she was doing all along? Had something buried deeply, deeply inside her led her here for help? . . . It was the street she had known as a child: Marvin playing handball with other boys on the block on Saturday afternoons; herself walking down that street demurely to music lessons, her mother waving to her from the sidewalk in front of the apartment house until she had reached the corner and safely boarded the bus. Her mother.

Mothers didn't change, did they? . . . Even the awful ones? . . . The ones who were vain and stubborn, who resented the fact that you lived—even they could be touched sometimes. You came to them cold and wet and not having eaten: they were impatient and annoyed with you and you were a cruel embarrassment to them, but they saw about you, didn't they, until you asserted your puny self. Even then they waited, and the door to the apartment was open to you always, maybe only somewhat, but open that little somewhat. That was what was important now.

She pulled herself up from her propped position against the drugstore window and lunged through the drifts across the street. On the opposite corner was the dimly lighted kiosk, and she saw the story because the ancient vendor had turned the papers wrong side up. The bottom of the front page was all that showed, and the subhead read with bleeding indifference:

RED LEADER ARRESTED
POLICE SEEK SINGER

She squeezed her running eyes and opened them again. In the last paragraph before the continuation note she read, "Zeeda Kaufman, a folk singer familiar in Greenwich Village circles . . ."

She stepped back, and turning sharply, reeled out of the kiosk's sickly light.

Ozzie caught, caught because she had made a mistake two years before, a mistake she didn't even know about. Oh,

Ozzie, oh, Murray and Vinnie and Elaine—oh, all of us! She wept. Cold. She could never be so cold again. And her mother was there, wasn't she? She wouldn't have read the papers, not such ugly stories. Her mother never had read tabloids like that one, had she? But of course someone might have brought them to her. There were always those who were eager to spread grief, to carry shock and scandal. But even so, she would be there as always, looking so pretty and smelling so nice. Disappointed in her. What mother wouldn't be disappointed in a heavy-eyed dark Jewish-looking child when she herself was so delicate, so blonde and fragile? But she was there, wasn't she? She would see about her, wouldn't she?

She would say, "Zeeda, you mustn't yell so much and act so much like a boy, you must come and lie down, lie down and cover up, and be warm, and calm yourself, and calm yourself, and have something to eat, and sleep and sleep a long, long time under the warm covers. . . ."

Her feet were already beginning to move, willing their own movement. She navigated some five yards down Seventy-sixth Street. Day was ending, she sensed remotely, even if the afternoon had been the color of midnight through the storm. The wind and the snow were abating. People would be coming home. She wanted to see her mother before the others got there: her mother alone, so they could talk. One foot before the other, it was all she could manage now. Her face was flaming, and her upper lip was heavy with sweat that quickly beaded and iced in the wind from the river.

There was the gentle lamp over the entrance to the apartment building. Erect, trying with every effort of will not to stumble, she made her way up the walk to the door. Inside the lobby there was a stifling warmth. She did not heed it. *My mother,* she thought. *If I can get to my mother. . . .*

Then there was the self-run elevator; the impersonal inoffensively patterned carpeting of the hall upstairs; the smallish cream-colored door—the doorbell; the long wait while she tried to put her feet together the way her grandfather, the actor, had taught her to do; the long wait while she blinked and tried to relax the knotted muscles around her eyes.

The door to the apartment opened, and she was looking into the face of a sweet-featured young Negro woman.

"Is this the Kaufman apartment?" she croaked.

"Yes," said the maid, blank-eyed.

"Is Mrs. Kaufman home? Is she here?" She was breathing heavily, and she probably didn't look very attractive, she thought, but her feet were rigidly in place.

"May I know who's calling, please?"

Zeeda swallowed, a sharply painful convulsion of her throat. "Her daughter."

The maid's face shifted, but otherwise betrayed no reaction. She went back into the apartment, leaving the door only an inch ajar. Time passed, and Zeeda stared at the waiting door. There was no place else to stare without risking having her feet come out of position. If that happened, she knew she would fall. She aged as the minutes crept along, and presently the door opened again. The maid's face was disorganized with her suppressed compassion. She spoke gently, but firmly.

"Mrs. Kaufman is out, Miss."

"My mother?"

"I'm sorry, Miss. Mrs. Kaufman is out."

"When—when will she be back? Can't I come in and wait?"

"I'm sorry. Mrs. Kaufman is really out."

Zeeda had grabbed the door. She screamed in disbelief. "Mrs. Kaufman is my *mother*, you black arrogant bitch!"

The maid stiffened and said nothing. Then Zeeda saw. Over the maid's shoulder, beyond the entrance hall, the pretty living room with the fireplace and, she remembered, the lovely cigarette box on the mantelpiece. Beyond the maid's shoulder, in the middle of that warm and pretty room, she saw her mother appear. Straight, handsome, her blue eyes as clear and as expressive as they had always been, across that distance she looked at Zeeda once, directly, piercingly—a long, unwavering look—and then she moved out of sight.

Zeeda said nothing. The maid closed the door quietly.

Zeeda began to giggle. She was moving to the elevator. Presently she was descending. She was in the air again, but now she did not feel the cold, neither the coldness nor the wetness of the snow that was falling more gently now. Her feet went forward automatically. She was only half-aware that she was directing them eastward.

Her intention was fully clear to her only when she could see the cold brown-gray water far down in the darkness, past the tips of her sodden shoes. The giggling had stopped. She was crying now, but her handkerchief had long before been used up. In her pocket it was a soggy, leaking ball. Her nose ran, and the phlegm fell unheeded from her lips down to the front of her coat. On the bridge, car lights moved, and the opposite shore of the river twinkled with the lights in the houses of living people. She could not really believe that she was going to end, but she edged closer until only her heels held her. She might scream once she was in, but she did not think so. She thought she would drop endlessly down, and she remembered the joke when she had been a child about digging a hole through the world to China. She would drop down the water mile after mile after mile and come up in China, wouldn't she? Childhood was gone. The happy jokes of childhood were all gone, she counseled herself with sudden seriousness. She had stayed too long behind. As she fell, she thought, Good night, pretty Mama, good night. . . .

33

ZEEDA KAUFMAN'S BODY WAS RECOVERED from the river four days after her suicide. Since she was wanted for questioning, her identity was quickly established and officially confirmed in the barren atmosphere of the morgue by her brother, Dr. Marvin Kaufman. New York's tabloid newspapers described her as a beautiful actress well known in Bohemian circles for her stormy temperament.

Steve Williams could not believe what he had read. The newspapers—all that had been available at the newsstand on the corner—lay now in a heap about his feet, and Steve stared sightlessly ahead, silently shaking his head from side to side. He had planned, more or less, to call on John Davis today. He had been on the verge of asking John to start him on more formal instruction in Catholicism, and had thought the parish house a more fitting scene for this particular commitment than his own apartment. He knew now he could not go; the news of Zeeda's suicide had turned his mind around.

It was, in its way, a grotesque and capricious extension of

Maggie's death. He could almost believe he had known it was coming. He had seldom thought of Zeeda since he had met Maggie, but he discovered there was a place a mistress holds in her lover's memory that remains for an extensive time reserved, a room whose door flies open at her evocation. Zeeda's name spread across the newspapers assaulted the door and splintered it. He could recall the touching fragileness of her body, the grace of her movement, the haunting gypsy mournfulness of her voice when she sang. He did not remember that he had ever been aware of her being a Communist. There had been a book in her apartment the night she had taken him there—*The Iskra Period.* And the guy the papers mentioned, Ozzie Lubin—had he been that friend of hers who had driven them into Los Angeles from Beach Cove that night? No. That name had been different.

He remembered clearly now that she had talked about a brother, a medical student: why had it never occurred to him to connect Zeeda with the doctor Helen Maclean had married? He had seen Helen and Marvin half a dozen times last winter, he had even gone to their wedding, though more as an emissary of Hilda and Ben Verges than as a gesture of intimate friendship on his own part. For Zeeda he felt a dull-throbbing repetition of grief now, but he knew he had no right to it. It behooved him to do something about the legitimate mourners. He hesitated. In Houston in his boyhood you called on a grief-stricken family and offered to be useful in some way. For all he knew, New York would look askance at the practice, but he had a notion Marvin Kaufman and his wife might appreciate at least the effort. He decided to go to see them.

He found their address in the telephone directory and had started to dress when the telephone rang.

It was Rachel Pemberton's secretary, saying, "Mr. Williams, Mrs. Pemberton asked me to call you. Hal Capbern's office on the Coast wants to set up a telephone appointment with both you and Mrs. Pemberton for this afternoon at two o'clock. Can you be here then?"

"At the office? Oh, damn."

"If you'd rather, we can set up a conference call between your home phone and here."

"Yes, that'd be much better," Steve said. "If it isn't too much trouble."

"No, sir, not at all. I'll tell Mrs. Pemberton you'll be on the phone at home."

The idea of talking to Hal Capbern today was distasteful enough. Going to Rachel's office to talk business was more than he could face with Zeëda Kaufman's death foremost in his mind. In any case, it would be the same story, he felt sure: Hal wanting to make his independent film version of the story about Hilda, Rachel icily holding to her terms, Hal enumerating all the details delaying his acceptance of them. Steve had no stomach for commerce today. He finished dressing and went out of the house.

The ending of the blizzard weather had left the streets full of melting snow, and muddy rivulets hurried down the gutters. The December wind was sharp against his face. On Third Avenue he hailed an uptown bus. In twenty minutes he had reached the Kaufmans' address. Marvin and Helen Kaufman were living in a relatively new apartment house on Seventy-ninth Street, near the corner of Second Avenue. The wizened old man in uniform who ran the elevator gave Steve the number of the apartment and carried him up. Alone in the hall after the elevator had gone down again, he hesitated diffidently before pressing the buzzer beside the door. He did not really know what he was going to say to the Kaufmans, or even whether his coming had been a good idea. He knew he was not thinking clearly. He was behaving according to the prompting of instinct, and he would have to rely on it. He pressed the button and heard the buzzing sound from inside the apartment.

Helen Kaufman opened the door, and Steve gave a start when he saw that she was pregnant.

"Steve Williams, as I live and breathe," she exclaimed after a puzzled moment. "Steve, how nice to see you. Come in. What a surprise. Come in."

When he was within the apartment, he stood awkwardly trying to explain. "I read about Marvin's sister. It came as a complete shock to me but—I knew her, you see. Oh, a long time ago. I didn't know about the connection, though . . ."

"Sit down, Steve, won't you?" Helen invited, leading him into the living room.

Following her, he went on, "Look, this must all be rotten

for both of you. I wondered if there wasn't anything I could do to be useful or——"

"Oh, Steve, you *are* the Texas gentleman. I didn't know there were any more. You're so sweet to stop by; Marvin will be disappointed that he missed you."

They sat down in a long living room that had been decorated, he guessed, by a resourceful professional. A curious mating of colors gave the room both charm and drama. On surfaces here and there were porcelain roosters of assorted sizes and postures, and much of the furniture, though new, had a Federalist air. It was, Steve thought vaguely, exactly the living room he would have expected Helen Kaufman to preside over, a mixture of the chic and the conventional, the simple and the colorful.

Helen told him as much as she knew about the details of Zeeda's death, speaking quietly as she smoothed the straight-cut maternity skirt over her knees, the pleated yellow-green jacket billowing about her.

"It's been rough on Marvin," she said. "Especially right now, with the baby practically here and himself already in a swat."

"Is Zeeda's mother still alive?" Steve asked. "I remember they were—what does the family call it? Estranged?"

"To put it mildly," said Helen. "Yes, she's alive. It seems Zeeda went to see her the day she committed suicide. Just before, as far as anyone can make out. Zeeda came to the Kaufmans' place. Her mother refused to let her in or to talk to her. Quaint, right?"

"My God," said Steve.

Helen shuddered. "I feel frightened every time I think of it. Knowing she's Marvin's mother, too. Knowing how easily it could have been Marvin instead of Zeeda who had his life poisoned by her and finally cut off by her. Of course Marvin's mother didn't realize the extent of what she was doing at the time. You can imagine how she's feeling now. It wouldn't surprise me one bit if she followed the poor girl right into the briny—I'm sorry for being flippant, I forgot you'd known her. It's tricky when you're related by marriage to someone you've never met. I don't feel anything about it at all except Marvin's grief."

"Of course."

"I don't know how they do it to themselves. Mrs. Kaufman

is a complicated woman. I don't even pretend to understand some of the things she does."

"You know, it was at the Verges that I first met Zeeda."

"At Ben and Hilda's?" Helen looked up in surprise.

"Yes. I think it was the day the war ended. I'm sorry, I guess it's bad manners going on about it. . . ."

"No, that's all right."

Steve shrugged. "It's odd, the pointless things you start to remember when someone dies."

"Do you know anything about the Communist business?" Helen asked.

"No, only what the papers said. Of course I remember her getting very overstimulated about the underdogs, the masses, and so forth."

"People from Washington have been after poor Marvin hammer and tongs. He can't tell them anything, of course. He hasn't seen her in God knows how many years. Apparently she was neck deep in it."

Steve said, "I guess in a way it's nice for Marvin there's a baby coming. The future to look for, as it were; take his mind off the past. Am I making an ass of myself?"

Helen smiled at him. "No," she said. "But tell me how *you've* been all these months. What have you heard from Hilda?"

"Not a hell of a lot," Steve said. "She's well, and Ben, too." His face broke into a grin. "I can't help asking about it. Are you excited about it, the baby being on the way?"

"God, yes," Helen said. "I'm so preoccupied with the baby, I finally had to give up even gestures of interest at the office."

"You're still working there?" Steve asked.

"Leave of absence. Marvin and I have money invested in the agency now, you know. It's not so difficult for a part-owner to take time-out having babies."

Steve searched for and found a scrap of paper and wrote down his name, address, and telephone number. "I know you'll both be terribly busy with more important things, but if he can, ask Marvin to let me know when the baby's ready to receive visitors, will you?"

"Oh, brother, I can't wait," said Helen. "It's going to be wonderful getting into a size nine again."

Steve studied her a moment, half-smiling, and walked to

the door. "Don't be in such a rush. Women always look their most beautiful when they're pregnant."

There was an unexpected gravity in his observation that made Helen blush.

"Thank you, Steve," she said, and he left the apartment.

In the dressing room down the hall from surgery, Marvin Kaufman sat on the bench before the open door of his locker, unmoving. He was staring listlessly at the black oxfords and grey woolen socks on the floor of the locker Last fall he had asked Helen to pick out some clothes for him, and these had been among the accessories she had decided upon for his new winter suits. Mutely they congratulated him on his marriage—on the fact that he had perceived in time the extent of his mother's power over others, the rigidity and impact of her will.

He tried to stir himself. He knew his first two appointments were already waiting at the office, but he was sore from lack of sleep, and he had wanted to avoid taking a pill if he could. He had sat up with his mother and father till three o'clock. His father had said no more than a word or two in the entire session, but his mother's recitation had raged on—her horrified disapproval of Zeeda's history as a Communist, her indignation that an innocent family should be disgraced by the actions of a cast-off and forgotten member. Behind her speech there was the unrelenting pressure of a savagely masochistic guilt—the guilt of a murderer once the passion that has provoked him has dissolved before the awesome definiteness of death. Her tardy bafflement tore at her, and mere garrulity was ineffective to answer, soothe, or cover it.

How far could the ability to forgive be stretched? His own ability had never been tested much, he thought. How grievous was the wrong that marked the point beyond which he could not really forgive? Was this beyond it?

He had comforted his mother and tried to assure her, pointing out that she had known nothing of Zeeda's other problems on the day she killed herself. But the words, like wooden blocks, clacked unfeelingly together, and he felt no pity for the woman.

He stood up, pulled on his shirt, and started to fasten the

cuff links. He would have to search far into himself to find where pity hid.

Steve did not go directly home. On the bus ride down Third Avenue a permeating depression weighed on him. His forehead leaned near the vibrating windowpane as the bus lumbered on, but he was unaware of the street's cluttered, panoramic façade. Two women who had been part of him had died in so short a space of time. One he had made love to, one he had loved. Both were dead now before their lives had even begun, dead without point or purpose, capriciously erased from the living scene they had helped to swell a moment before. He could not believe there was no sense to it. It was too cruel, too ugly, too wasteful of life to be without meaning. He recognized that he was parroting John Davis' argument, even if the meaning was something he could not fathom, an answer only the believing could capture. Still, it had to exist, and if it existed, he could not rest until he had in the deepest reaches of his mind and feeling directly perceived it. Torment was the scourge of the unbelieving, the tortuous nagging of the mind that demanded, groped for, stretched and grasped at, but could not grab or hold. Why did men struggle to live in order in the end to be blotted out? Why did he himself go on living, producing nothing, useful to no one, surviving only from day to day and week to week? It was impossible there should be no answer.

He stayed on the bus when it passed the street he lived on. He did not get off until it had reached the corner near John Davis' church. There would be no services at this time of day, he knew. He would be alone in the church—alone to beg of that incomprehensible sacramental presence an explanation. He walked quickly down the tenement street to the old church building, but by the time he had reached it and was inside, there was no demanding left in him. What business of his was the arrogant demanding of answers from God? . . .

A dim glow lighted the altar ahead. His footsteps echoed through the deserted place as he moved into the rearmost pew. He went down on his knees.

"Dear God, make me believe. Make me believe anything at all as long as I don't have to live in darkness any more.

Make me believe in you. Go on, go on, for Christ's sweet sake send me *some* kind of belief."

He knelt for a long time, thinking nothing, letting his prayer lift itself toward whatever ear it would. He wished he could cry out to relieve the tension in his chest; he wished he could shout out loud, but he could not. He could only wait. Time passed, and in the silent church he knew that nothing was changed. Whatever he tried, belief would never come to him. He gave a sigh and stood up. In the aisle he gazed about him. The awesome quiet, the loving tastelessness of the church's décor—these no longer impressed him with their sweetness or stimulated his emotions to dwell on matters of the soul. They were physical features only, ugly and hard and unyielding, like all the physical world. He hesitated. Should he go around to the parish house and see John now? Tell him how much he wanted to believe a logical thing, an explanatory thing, tell him how he had failed to achieve belief? He did not think so. What good could it do anything? Belief had failed him, or he had failed belief. He would have to find his way without it. He walked, lagging, out of the church, knowing he would never come back to it again.

"Steve? It's Rachel," the voice said. "I have Hal on the wire."

"Fine," Steve said. "Hello, Hal?"

From California Hal Capbern's voice crackled over the wire excitedly. "Steve, baby, listen. It looks like at last we're coming into our own. I've got the money I've wanted, and from just the sources I'd hoped would come through. I've already told Rachel I'm willing to meet all her demands, if you'll kindly meet one or two of mine."

Hal Capbern's enthusiasm stayed locked within the instrument in Steve's hand. He felt untouched by it. "What are they, Hal?" he asked.

"First, we want to use the screen-treatment you wrote originally, but we want your permission for the polishing up to be done by somebody else in collaboration with you—you know, somebody with a solid background of experience in the medium."

"Okay by me," Steve said.

"God, *that* was easier than I expected."

"Nothing's final till the contract is signed," Rachel pointed out with terrible pleasantness.

"Rachel, why don't you hang up?" Hal asked. "Steve baby, the other thing is that we want you here. Mostly to keep your fine Italian hand in the script, but also to follow through in the production itself if you want to. How soon can you come out?"

"I don't know," said Steve, surprised. "Look, Hal, is everything really going ahead this fast?"

"Fast!" Rachel broke in again. "I've been working on this for two years now. Steve can come out right away, Hal."

"Wonderful."

"Now hold on, both of you," Steve interrupted. "Hal, for a number of reasons I want—I want to be able to come out there at my own pace. Maybe drive out. You'll have enough on your hands to keep you busy for a couple of weeks, won't you?"

"Sure, sure, I didn't mean you'd have to be here for breakfast tomorrow."

"I'll come out, then," said Steve.

"Expenses?" Rachel pinpointed.

"Advance the money to Steve, Rachel, as much as he wants, you and I can settle up by mail."

"Fine, Hal," she answered. "Steve, I'll send the check over by messenger before five today."

"Hal, look," said Steve, "I'll wire you when I'm within a day or two of Los Angeles, all right? I really want not to hew to much of a schedule."

"Fine, baby. Drive carefully. I need you."

"You *are* sure this movie is going to be made at last." Steve still wondered.

"For God's sake, call the bank, ask *them* if you don't believe me. Details when you get here: the cast is going to make you cream your jeans, I don't know how I've ever done it."

"By taking two years," Rachel chorused.

Hal Capbern drew a great breath. "Steve, I want you seriously to consider going over to M.C.A."

"Not on your life." Steve laughed. "Don't have a break-down, and don't worry about me. I'll keep you posted on the progress of my safari."

"Anything else, Rachel dear?"

"No, Hal, that's fine," Rachel said. "I'm very happy for both you and Steve. I know you don't mind my kidding you."

"I love you. Pack, Steve."

"Thanks, Hal. Rachel, thanks for everything."

There was a confusion of good-bys, and the conference was over.

He sat by the telephone without moving, hesitant to believe that he would be going back to work in earnest at last. Not writing maybe, at least not turning out new work, but earning something in any case, busying himself, carrying on the motions of productivity. He leaned his head into his hands. He wished almost it hadn't happened now, not when so much else troubled his mind. But the progress of life did not care what was most important to you; it beckoned at its wish, and you responded or not as you saw fit. He had responded; he was committed now, at least for that little much.

A while later he called John Davis at the parish house.

"John, guess what? I'm going to California," he announced.

"What's happened?"

"Some people out there want to make a movie out of an old short story of mine. It's been hanging fire for an eternity, but now it really looks set."

John chuckled. "My only source of coffee vanished. But I'm glad for you, Steve. Steve—how are you feeling about it, the opportunity?"

"I'm not sure yet," he said. "Grateful, anyway."

"Will you be staying out there?"

"Oh, no, I don't think so. I'll let you know as soon as I'm back."

"Good, don't forget it."

"John . . ."

"Yes?"

"If I *don't* let you know . . ."

The young priest did not answer at first. Then he said, "If not, I'll understand. Sure, Steve. But let me hear from you anyway, even if it's not about your soul."

"I will," Steve promised. "Thank you for being such a good friend to me through all this."

"Good luck out there, Steve."

For two days Steve was preoccupied by the activity of departure—paying the rent in advance, arranging for a car, notifying his parents of where he would be, buying a few clothes that he had been in need of for a long time, packing. In the feeling of movement he found not only distraction but a momentary protection from his haunting turmoil. He began to understand why he had agreed with such alacrity to go out to California: it was the small pursuit of business that kept you alive from day to day when you felt yourself disintegrating. It was an armor against death, an escape from the pain of a fruitless contemplation. He threw himself into activity with relief, and in the car he had rented for the purpose, began the drive across-country with what he would a few years before have described as hopefulness.

He restrained himself from giving his hopefulness credence, he refused to dwell too much upon the inclination of his thoughts; instead, as he drove he turned his vision outward to the people he met and the things he saw. From New York to Cincinnati there was the leaden chill of the Eastern winter, but then the weather began to break. He drove, drinking in the images, through manufacturing towns and farmlands, through the low-hanging smoke of busy factory regions and the wine-bright sunlight of the Middle West in the beginning of December. He took his time, as he had told Hal Capbern he wanted to do. He looked. He listened. He lived outside himself in a fresh new world of shimmering impressions. He stopped often on his journey; he tarried to talk to gas-station attendants, lunch-counter waitresses, groups of wry old men on town-hall steps. In one small city he went to the local high school's basketball game, in another he bought a ticket to a dance being staged in the American Legion hall for a local charity. He realized, as though for the first time, that the country was at war, that the Korean conflict was intimately real to the people whose young men were serving in it. At one of the long series of lunch counters where he stopped to have a sandwich and a Coke, he met three soldiers bound to the nearest city on furlough. They huddled over the jukebox drinking from a bottle of Old Crow and singing songs Steve had never heard before:

"I was dancing with my darling
To the Tennessee Waltz,
When an old friend I happened to meet . . ."

This and a song of Piaf's that had at last reached the general public in the United States and a tinkling lyricless melody whose appeal to the soldiers with their bottle mystified him. When he fell into conversation with them, they told him this last was called "The Third Man Theme," and his mystification was no less. They asked for a ride as far as St. Louis, and Steve took them on. They armed themselves with sandwiches and two dozen cold cans of beer. In the course of the trip he listened, bemused, to their rambling chatter, as vigorous and boastful and young as the sailor gab he could recall from the previous war. Beside him in the front seat of the car was the recruit with the Southern accent, a product of rural life. In the back were, he judged, two city boys, but one of them was markedly more intellectually ambitious than the other. All three of them, huddled in their G.I. overcoats, talked of the mambo and Arthur Godfrey and water skiing and Johnny Ray and Dagmar.

"You-all know what I'm gonna do when I git out?" the Southerner next to him mused. "I'm gonna get me a little ole truck to haul timber in and I'm gonna get me a little ole gal to shack up with. I'm gonna spend all the rest of my days foolin' around with that little ole gal and listening to Grand Ole Opry on my TV. 'I was dancin' with my darlin' . . .' " And the song wound on beneath the others' talk.

"Who says you're *ever* going to get out, Cornpone?" one of those in the back seat asked. "The way the war's going, we're all gonna be freezing our asses off fighting the Commies the rest of our lives."

"If those sonsabitches would let MacArthur have his way, there might be some hope of getting the damn thing over with," the third declared.

"You'd rather freeze your ass in China than in Korea?" his buddy returned. "No, thank you, not this boy."

"Who's keeping MacArthur from having his way, for once?" asked Steve.

"Whaa? You kidding, man? Where've you been?"

"Well, who is?"

"Everybody, that's who. They say we ought to keep the war in Korea and MacArthur says, shit, the war's coming from *China*, isn't it? Go *there* and blow the bastards up. Those ass-wipes in the U.N.——"

"You think MacArthur's wise?" Steve asked. "What if it's just the excuse the Chinese need to throw in everything they've got? I wouldn't want nice guys like you to be in that kind of fix."

"The fix we're in now ain't no bed of roses. What the hell do I care if an atom bomb blows me up or a rifle bullet does the job? You don't think MacArthur knows what he's talking about? Don't you read the papers, man?"

If the new recruits of the Korean War, Steve thought, had taken to defending MacArthur about anything at all, he had indeed been away a long time. In his own service days, MacArthur had been the living symbol of the stiff neck of authority, and servicemen had bellowed their loathing and resentment of his Prussian manner. Were these three young men of some different breed? Had it become respectable to hold a good opinion of *any* brass? The soldiers went on talking as the highway carried them west—of the *Kon-Tiki* adventure and the death of the movies at the hands of TV.

"Hey, watch your language," said Steve. "I'm on my way to make a living out of the movies."

"Man, no, don't do a stupid thing like that," came a voice from the back of the car. "Who the hell wants to go to movies?"

"What're you doing in the movies, Steve? Here, ready for another beer?" The apparently brighter of the two city boys sat forward to hand him one.

"Thanks." Steve took the dripping can, drank from it, and put it down beside him on the seat. "I'm going to write one, in a way. Nothing special."

"What d'you mean? You write stuff? You read *Kon-Tiki?*"

"No, I haven't," said Steve.

The Southern soldier next to him in the front seat had placidly switched tunes and, slumped over against the window, was softly crooning:

> "Good night, Irene,
> Irene, good night . . .
> Good night, Irene, good night, Irene,
> I'll see you in my dreams . . ."

"Those guys in TV make fortunes, man," the loudmouth was saying from the back seat. "Who goes to the movies?

With TV you can sit on your sofa and drink a beer and play with your girl friend's boobies and be entertained all at once."

"For Christ's sake, you're as bad as Cornpone," said the other. "Don't you ever think of anything but your sex life? Did *you* read *Kon-Tiki?*" He sat forward again to say over Steve's shoulder, "You stick to movies, Steve. Remember what they say: 'Movies are better than ever.'"

As the soldiers sang their songs and chaffed one another and downed their beers, Steve felt intensely his strangeness in their midst. But the pulsating of life in the roisterous young men had taken hold of his mind and given it a sudden twist, more direct and less resistible than the twist given it by his being forced to leave New York and see a facet of existence from which he'd been too long retired. He asked the soldiers about their families, their Army assignments, their plans for the future. They answered volubly; their dreams for their future lives did not seem to him to be as colorful as those he might have expected in such young men, but their aims were as charged with energy and determination as any he had ever known. He did not think, in the long run, that Americans in their first manhood had changed very much. He felt almost defiantly glad of it, remembering his own.

He dropped the soldiers in St. Louis, and after a night in a hotel, continued westward, his senses like pores still opening to the countryside he sped through: behind him now was the galeful and stern New England coast, the great nerve-racked cities of the Eastern seaboard, the Greenbrier Mountains, the Blue Ridge Mountains, the Cumberland Mountains, the names tasting like cinnamon on his tongue as he repeated them silently to himself.

At one point he pulled to the side of the road and got out of the car to look around him. A stiff ice-touched wind was blowing. He stood, he reminded himself, the geography of school years coming back now with a fierceness of meaning he had never suspected lurked there, in the Mississippi Valley. Around him were the limitless fields of Kansas: the flat-blue winter sky over him was visible, on his right, in Nebraska and the Dakotas, Minnesota and Iowa, and on his left in the snaking Ozarks of Arkansas, Oklahoma, over whatever place in Houston, Texas, his own parents were at the moment. The awesome consideration came to him as he watched the sky that in all those regions, states, and neighborhoods lived men and women he had met in his own face-beclustered life, or from them had come the people he had known in other face-beclustered places.

Helen Kaufman was from the Middle West, wasn't she? He wasn't sure which state. And Maggie's family from Massachusetts, and Cornpone, who had sat singing next to him, from someplace off on the left, Louisiana or Alabama, the Carolinas; innumberable men he had lived with in the war from Arkansas and Oklahoma and New Mexico and Wisconsin. Before him was the slow surging of the earth just into Colorado; beyond that would be the Rocky Mountains—the rigid torsos of contending giants. And the Rockies' richness of divisions—the Great Basin, the Bitter Root Mountains, the Park Range district, the canyons and plateaus, the Cascades and the Sierra Nevada, the majesty of the desert, the lush valleys of the West, the coastal range and then at last the beaches' sand. And this was the country that had, without always knowing it, wrested to itself the attention of the world. He laughed at himself as his imagination reached out to comprehend the fact. He could not write? He had told himself he could not work? Oh, you fool—he shook his head—men can't exist outside their labor, and what a sap you are if you don't realize that compared with other men you've been handled gently. He had been, he knew. The griefs he had could be put to the service of his work. There was no greatness in his art, he thought, but it was work he could do with interest and with dignity.

His resources, if he had had the sense to see it before, were beyond number: he had known so many people, from the Vergeses to the Cowans to John Davis to the three young soldiers he had driven to St. Louis. And then there were the places he had seen: the Pacific, Los Angeles, the farms and the ranches of California, the dusty towns of Texas, moist-soft New Orleans, hard-working New York, tale-tattling Washington, the civilized decorum of expensive drawing rooms, the cold homelessness of lost men's bars: how could he have wasted his time so much when he had so abundant a creation to labor in?

His life had twice fallen in pieces about him, and perhaps it would again and again in the future. He had picked them up before; he would go on picking them up forever, and never again, he thought, would he doubt his ability to do so. Life in its energy did not allow even your private sorrows to go to waste. No man's sorrows: everywhere under the vault of the sky his eyes were searching now were the people who inhabited, worked, exploited, and loved the places whose names he had been able to call up, the stretch of the variegated continent; the colorful, cantankerous, kindly, slovenly, ambitious, passionate people who made up its hodgepodge wonder, all of them living griefs that shadowed their joys, all of them fighting in a history whose ends they did not know and whose meaning even at the present they did not care about save to lend their sweating and their happiness and their complaints to its purpose.

How in God's name could he have been such a fool as to flounder in his grief for so long? he demanded of himself, hot with outrage at his own self-occupation. Life had always been dynamic, a thing of eternal conflict and balancing; perhaps the world he lived in was unique in the intensity of that dynamism; all the better to see it by. Grief and tragedy existed, you could say no more for them, and he tried to deny it by understanding their purpose and fathoming their source. You did not deny tragedy, you embraced it and made it your own, because you could not escape the recognition that it carries within it the seed of good, the seed of balance, the seed whose growth through the conflicts of infinitely multiplied human beings must mean, small step by clumsy step, in the sum of men an advancement for all the world in its infinitely determined course. . . .

It was time to go on.

Back inside the car he was not surprised to find that the things he had thought had left him shaken. It was just as well, he considered. In the depths of his body he suspected there lay—though he could not feel it at the moment—the beginning, not of lassitude, but of a pervading peace of spirit. Nothing ahead could dismay him. He was as whole as any man could expect to be. He released the brakes and pulled back onto the highway.

34

THE VOICES ON THE INTERCOM WERE fading in again and the surging pain was subsiding. Helen took a breath and opened her eyes to look once more at the impersonal colorlessness of the labor room, one of five little cubicles connected by a rubber-floored hallway with the delivery room. Reciting to herself all the things Marvin had taught her to prepare her for the birth, she prayed she would be prepared at least for the next seizure of the pain. She heard a footstep and looked up as Marvin came into the room.

"Hi, darling," she said softly.

"Hi." Marvin smiled.

"You had some lunch?"

"Down the block," he said.

He came up to the bed and took her hand in both his own. Neither of them spoke, but each tried to smile at the other reassuringly, until Helen could smile no more and the returning onslaught took her mind away again. . . .

Marvin stroked her hair back from her forehead. "Not much longer, sweet," he said. "Doctor Miller says practically any time."

"Your mother came in earlier," said Helen.

"She's waiting outside now. She won't go home." Marvin grinned at her frown of incredulity. "It's not our child being born, you know. It's Mother's grandchild."

They had seen Mr. and Mrs. Kaufman regularly since their marriage, but their relationship was accepted by everyone concerned as a gesture on behalf of appearances. Mr. Kaufman had warmed to her increasingly in the passing months, but Marvin's mother had steadfastly maintained her position of accepting, but essentially disapproving of, the match. Nothing had changed her. The manner of Zeeda's death had made it more urgent than ever that she maintain her hold on Marvin, but Marvin had been cautious with her, and her fortress of disapproval of his marriage had not been shaken.

"It'll help her to have the excitement of her first grandchild," Helen said. "It'll ease things."

For a while they did nothing but look at one another. Then Helen asked, "Did you call Jules at the office?"

"Yes. He made me promise to call him as soon as we knew anything. Darling, do you want to hear business stuff?"

Helen nodded.

"If it's good," she amended.

Marvin told her, his voice still soft, caressing in its gentleness. "Jules said that Betsy celebrated the baby by going to Phillip Houghton and knocking his eyes out of his head. Anyway, the people who handle the Houghton show *do* want her for the commercials."

"Oh, that *is* good news," Helen said. "I was sure I could break into that show with Betsy."

"Tell me about it after," said Marvin. "I'm nowhere about it myself."

"I will, darling."

She started to speak again, but the pangs returned before they had entirely subsided. After a moment of blinding impact had passed, she felt Marvin's lips brush her forehead.

"Marvin, they're coming awfully fast now, I think."

"Hold tight, sweet," Marvin said. "I'm going for Miller."

The darkness of another spasm rose up around her, and as it receded, Dr. Miller came into the labor room. She listened to his quiet voice of encouragement, and then he asked her to move to the delivery table. Settled upon it, a moment later she felt her body striving, struggling, contorting in its efforts to deliver the baby. As the gas mask was placed across her face she saw clearly Marvin's thick glasses above his silly-looking surgical mask. She wanted to tell him how funny he looked, but her words were choked off by a tearing apart within her, and she was walking through fog-strewn blackness . . .

Her mother's voice directed her on an errand, and she was tearfully protesting that it was Saturday afternoon and why couldn't Danny go instead. She tasted the sweetness of rum and Coke and the frightening interest of the feel of a young man's hand on her thigh. Books spilled through her mind in choking numbers, and the cultivated, patient voice of Sprague Burrell told her she must get the baby born, that young women of character gave babies to their husbands and didn't make a lot of commotion about it. If Sprague were here to tell me, she thought, I would know how to do everything right; but Sprague's gone—he was the grave mistake of another life; I'm somebody else now—I'm Marvin's wife—and I must do it all well so Marvin will be proud of me. Sprague hadn't really cared about her learning anything, had he?—her delirium ran on. No, he had exchanged learning for whatever nourishment she had given his warped nature. Was she sorry about Sprague? Was she sorry that when she was a respectable old woman she would still know that as a girl she had been kept by a rich man with a penchant for young girls? No, she wasn't. It was so long ago, but if it had not been, nothing else would have been, and she wanted what she had now—her husband, her baby if it would only co-operate and come out when she was summoning it with all her strength. Please, baby, hurry up, I'm frightened in the fog. . . .

The voices of New York came harshly to her ear, and the gentler laughing voices she had known in Europe. Marvin's mother's voice with its hard gentility, and over and over again Marvin's voice as it was when he made love to her, kind and demanding, caressing and angry, by turns the voice of the swain and the voice of the master. In the darkness she reached out for his succor now, but could not find him.

Suddenly panic struck her, and she thought that she was dying. An agony tore through her bodyless mind, and she was convinced that she had died. She began to weep quietly, not that she was dead, but that she had failed to achieve a woman's achievement. She had failed everyone. She gave herself over to her weeping.

"Helen," the voice said. "Helen. . . . It's Doctor Miller, Helen. . . ."

She tried to open her eyes, but the effort needed was too great. She sensed that she was in a different room now. Her hands felt cool as they lay relaxed on fresh, smooth-folded sheets.

"Helen . . ."

Her mouth was dry, her tongue wooden and thick. She licked her lips, and taking a breath, succeeded this time in opening her eyes. The room was half dark, and there was light spilling in through the partially opened door to the corridor.

"Doctor Miller . . ."

"She's all right now, Marvin," Dr. Miller said over his shoulder. "Come on in."

Dr. Miller was withdrawing and Marvin was coming in to the side of her bed. He took hold of her hand as he had before. He still wore his surgery garb, and the mask hung down about his neck.

"Darling?" he whispered.

"Marvin, is the baby all right?" Helen asked faintly.

"It's a boy, Helen," Marvin said. "He's perfect."

"Oh, thank God." She took another breath and licked her lips again. She blinked tired, aching eyes. She could see more clearly now. "A boy. . . . Marvin, did I behave all right?"

"You were wonderful. The best delivery I ever saw. One grind and a bump, and there he was."

Helen laughed weakly and whispered again, "A nice little Jewish boy. . . . Oh, I'm so glad."

"You'll go to sleep now, sweet," said Marvin. "I'll be back by the time you wake up."

Helen moved her head on the pillow to look at him more directly.

"Is your mother still here?" she asked.

"She hasn't budged," said Marvin.

"Marvin—could I see her, just for a minute? Does she want to see me?"

"Only for a second, now," Marvin warned. "I guess it'd be all right."

"Oh, good. Good-by, darling. I'll see you when I wake up. Go have a ball someplace. I love you."

He kissed her lingeringly, then slipped away. He left the door ajar. Helen could hear faintly from the hall the voices of Marvin and his mother, and presently the door opened wider. Myra Kaufman came in.

Neither of the women spoke, and Mrs. Kaufman hesitated by the door. Looking at her, Helen was able even in her weakness to marvel at how greatly she had changed since Zeeda's death. She was still strikingly handsome, but her carriage had lost its intimidating rigidity, and facing Helen now, she looked like a chastened child, uncertain of her reception.

"Come in, Mrs. Kaufman," Helen said. "I'm so glad they let me see you for a moment."

The older woman came forward then, and when she was nearer, Helen could see how tired she looked. Her skin shone without its customary make-up. She had been waiting in the hallways of the hospital for hours.

"How do you feel, Helen?" Mrs. Kaufman asked.

"Wonderful, thanks. Faintish, but that's all. Marvin told you it's a boy? You've seen him?"

"By the window," Mrs. Kaufman said. "He's beautiful, Helen. All—oh, you know, shriveled up and red—but oh, what shoulders, what long hands. Like Marvin to the life, but I think he's going to have the shape of your head. He's beautiful." She hesitated, and Helen waited. "I—I wanted you to know I called your parents right away to tell them. In Charter Oak. I hope that's all right."

"Oh, Mrs. Kaufman, how sweet of you——"

"The least," she stopped her, "the least I could do. They were very nice to me on the phone. And so happy."

"I don't know how to thank you. I really don't."

"Don't, Helen. I wouldn't have missed it for anything."

The proud, self-bereft old lady hesitated as though she would say more. She frowned. "I have to leave now so you can sleep. Later, when you're stronger, I have some things I want to discuss with you about bringing up the child. Not that it's any of my business, he's yours and Marvin's, I realize that, but if you won't take offense, I have some things to say."

"Of course, Mrs. Kaufman. Try to come tomorrow. We can talk then. And bring the proud grandfather."

"Yes. I will." She pulled herself erect, the muscles of her face drawn into knots, her gaze averted from Helen's. The time, Helen thought, was not entirely yet, only the difficult beginning of the breakthrough. But Mrs. Kaufman struggled to smile as she patted Helen's hand, and turning, went sedately out of the room.

35

The attention of the American public in 1951 was to be engaged by a great conflict between two national leaders, and the seeds of this conflict had been inherent in the very start of the Korean War. The invading North Koreans had captured Seoul on June 28, 1950. For weeks the forces of the United Nations, taken by surprise from the beginning, could engage only in defensive actions. Through the summer the slow, climaxless, grinding war went on. Then those in the United States to whom Douglas MacArthur was a hero of intimidating proportions found their allegiance justified. In September MacArthur had created the brilliant amphibious landing at Inchon, the first major counteroffensive. The Northern forces fell back and the troops of the United Nations under MacArthur recaptured Seoul on September 26. By late October they had swept victoriously across the testy parallel to the Manchurian border. But the United Nations were not to enjoy their superiority for long. Shortly against their determined thrust was thrown the most explosive of counterattacks: two hundred thousand fully equipped and trained Chinese Communist troops broke into the war as voluntary defenders of North Korea. The general enthusiasm shown by the public in regard to MacArthur's early success paled for many into apathy, and then into impatience and disgust. Many ordinary men unconcerned about the morality of international relationships realized only that in a United Nations police action American men could die, and such men as these could see little sense in that distant and now doomed warring effort.

Others reacted differently. The fact that, through volunteers, the China of the Communists could wage war and remain free from international blame frustrated and enraged many of the Americans who read of it in their daily papers and weekly news magazines. MacArthur declared it was now a different war altogether and must be approached with different notions. All over the United States his supporters began to call for carrying the war to Manchuria, from which the Communist strength was now derived—the step toward war in China that the original swift and decisive police action had meant, in part, specifically to avoid. MacArthur asked to be allowed to attack by air the staging ground of this, the major enemy. He was refused. His superiors were determined to prevent the war's spreading to Korea's already sulphurous neighbors, not only into China but also into the other stirring countries in that region of the world. It must at any cost be contained, they said, within the fractured Korean boundaries.

Since November the bridges over the Yalu River from Manchuria had thundered with the inpouring might, in troops and supplies, of Communist China, and MacArthur's counteroffensive had ground to a standstill. Few among private men who debated the issue were clearly aware of the unique character of the personal elements involved. In newspaper records names were names, and it was only the more thoughtful who considered what strong wills were drawing into opposition, or what subtle but steely reins the practices of government had imposed upon the individuals involved.

Douglas MacArthur was commander not only of the forces provided to the United Nations by his own government, but of those of other governments: the troops of the Republic of Korea itself, ground forces of the Philippines, Australia, and England; naval strength from France, the Netherlands, and Norway; a Swedish hospital unit. The nature of MacArthur's unified command could be comprehended by many Americans only with effort in the light of the past jealous singularity of the United States' endeavors. It was the United States in a new relationship with the world: leading, but no longer the familiar unlicked braggart; a nation with a grimmer purpose, a purpose encompassing more than its most immediate interests.

Clearly troubled in lacking a precedent for his position was Douglas MacArthur himself. No one but the foolish denied that in assembling and organizing his supranational army MacArthur had succeeded to a degree befitting his reputation as a military giant. But that he was conducting a war of essentially diplomatic character was never clear in his public statements, which themselves indicated his misconception. So uncertain was his political understanding that the pronouncements from MacArthur's headquarters frequently differed sharply from the statements of those who were, by any law or understanding, his superiors. To the President his openly defiant stand on political matters was a torment. Still worse for the Western nations, it was a danger more perilous than MacArthur could comprehend in a conflict whose essences were not those of military power and opportunity, but of, to the idealist, morality, and to the more practical-minded, the fierce in-fighting of political advantage.

On November 24, 1950, MacArthur had launched a major attack, announcing as he did so that his purpose was to end the war, and promising his troops that they would be home for Christmas. Americans whose faith was committed to his military pre-eminence believed it would be so. Others, with grief, recognized a hell-for-leather bravado: the flow across the bridges of the Yalu River showed no sign of thinning. In the face of the discouraging abortion of this new attack, the Government of the United States and its President maintained its policy as it had from the beginning: governments must balance forces generals know nothing of.

MacArthur was determined in his opinion: he should be allowed to blockade the coast of China and bomb the Chinese mainland, whence came the enemy's strength. His support in certain areas of the American press was fervid: that this press was, like him, prepared to face the general outbreak of global war was seldom manifest to its readers. Again and again the President was called upon to request that his subordinate refrain from public statements of his personal opinions regarding his country's international policies. By March, 1951, the North Korean forces had been pushed back to the starting point of their aggression. This situation made it possible to negotiate for peace in Korea without the loss of world esteem. The governments whose combat forces served in Korea prepared to do so, only to find their preparations violated without warning by a statement MacArthur saw fit to release to the public of all nations:

"Operations continue according to schedule and plan," the announcement stated. "We have now substantially cleared South Korea of organized Communist forces. It is becoming increasingly evident that the heavy destruction along the enemy's lines of supply, caused by our round-the-clock massive air and naval bombardment, has left his troops in the forward battle area deficient in requirements to sustain his operations. This weakness is being brilliantly exploited by our ground forces. The enemy's human wave tactics have definitely failed him, as our own forces have become seasoned to this form of warfare; his tactics of infiltration are but contributing to his piecemeal losses, and he is showing less stamina than our own troops under the rigors of climate, terrain and battle. . . . Of even greater significance than our tactical successes has been the clear revelation that this new enemy, Red China, of such exaggerated and vaunted military power, lacks the industrial capacity to provide adequately many critical items necessary to the conduct of modern war. He lacks the manufacturing base and those raw materials needed to produce, maintain, and operate even moderate air and naval power, and he cannot provide the essentials for successful ground operations, such as tanks, heavy artillery, and other refinements science has introduced into the conduct of military campaigns. Formerly his great numerical potential might well have filled this gap, but with the development of existing methods of mass destruction, numbers alone do not offset the vulnerability inherent in such deficiencies. Control of the seas and the air, which in turn means control over supplies, communications, and transportation, are no less essential and decisive now than in the past. When this control exists, as in our case, and is coupled with an inferiority of ground fire power, as in the enemy's case, the resulting disparity is such that it cannot be overcome by bravery, however fanatical, or the most gross indifference to human loss.

"These military weaknesses have been clearly and definitely revealed since Red China entered upon its undeclared war in Korea," MacArthur continued. "Even under the inhibitions which now restrict the activity of the United Nations forces and the corresponding military advantages which accrue to Red China, it has been shown its complete inability to accomplish by force of arms the conquest of Korea. The enemy, therefore, must by now be painfully aware that a decision of the United Nations to depart from its tolerant effort to contain the war to the area of Korea, through an expansion of our military operations to its coastal areas and interior bases, would doom Red China to the risk of imminent military collapse. These basic facts being established, there should be no insuperable difficulty in arriving at decisions on the Korean problem if the issues are resolved on their own merits, without being burdened by extraneous matters not directly related to Korea, such as Formosa or China's seat in the United Nations. . . ."

That he had been instructed to avoid public political utterances was the least extraordinary aspect of MacArthur's statement. Within the statement lurked a challenge to the policy of the United Nations and to the Constitution of his own country, a challenge not unawaited by vocal forces in the United States. Phillip Houghton's magazine *American View*, for one, began immediate preparation of new articles in support of MacArthur against Truman, and a speaker on Houghton's television program was given half an hour to demand eloquently that the reins of national government be withdrawn in such a time of military crisis from the hands of elected executives and given over into those of the General.

The controversy stormed across the country. For those who thrilled to the declaration that there was no substitute for victory, there were others who agreed that the victory in MacArthur's mind was the wrong kind of victory.

Pained to bring rebuke upon a military leader of his own appointment, the President hesitated as long as he dared to in the face of the world's unblinking gaze. On April 11 his announcement was released. "With deep regret I have concluded that General of the Army Douglas MacArthur is unable to give his wholehearted support to the policies of the United States Government and of the United Nations in matters pertaining to his official duties. In view of the specific responsibilities imposed upon me by the Constitution of the United States and the added responsibility which has been entrusted to me by the United Nations, I have decided that I must make a change of command in the Far East. I have, therefore, relieved General MacArthur of his commands and have designated Lieutenant General Matthew B. Ridgway as his successor."

It was upon his arrival at the National Airport in Washington April 12 that Steve Williams saw in the afternoon papers the news of MacArthur's recall.

At the end of March, he had completed the work on his screenplay. There would be revisions, he understood, but these were left to the discretion of his collaborator and the film's director. He did not himself want to become involved in them; now that his long disorientation was past, he had too much new work he wanted to do. Hal Capbern agreed to give him his way, and Steve, turning in the rented car, booked space on an airplane bound via Washington to New York.

It was only at the last moment that he seriously considered a stopover in Washington, and the plane was going that way anyway. Feeling himself a fellow among the living again, he was curious to see Maggie's father and the house that had been witness to so much of his most intimate life. Perhaps, he thought, he needed to know that he could again move through those rooms untouched by past remembrance, see members of Maggie's family. If he were to remain a working professional bound from one job to the next, engaged in the commerce of daily existence, he must be proven immune to melancholy even in its shrine. He did not know what his reaction would be like. He wanted to find out. He telephoned Judge Cowan and found himself warmly welcomed.

"Steve, check your baggage through to New York and come have dinner with me here," Judge Cowan said on the long-distance telephone. "I confess I have no idea whether anybody else has been asked for the night of the twelfth, but I know there's nothing major planned. Do you mind that atmosphere of uncertainty?"

"No"—Steve laughed—"not at all."

"I feel deprived that you can't stay over for the night, but I'll take the responsibility of delivering you to a New York plane after dinner. There's one that leaves at about midnight."

"Perfect for my plans," Steve said. "I can't wait to see you, sir."

An hour after his arrival at National Airport, the Cowans' butler Henry, as wan and wiry as ever, was ushering him into the entrance hall of the Cowan house.

"It's the study at the moment, Mr. Williams, if you don't mind," Henry said. "Judge Cowan will be in presently."

"Thank you, Henry."

He followed the white-jacketed little man into the leather redolent handsomeness of the study. Henry hesitated at the door to say, "The staff are all very sorry you won't be staying awhile, Mr. Williams. It's been so long."

The compliment both startled and touched him. He turned to face the butler. "Thank you, Henry. It's very kind of all of you."

Henry withdrew. To Steve's eyes the Judge's study looked unchanged. He imagined that Maggie's being dead would have little affected the appearance of the house; she had never pretended to take much of a hand in the managing of it. In its way this thought was as saddening as any patent change would have been, but he had not time to dwell on it. Judge Cowan came in.

The Judge's face was marred by his increasing age, and his blue eyes had grown lusterless; but his bearing was as military as ever and his handshake still vigorous.

"Steve, Steve, what a blessing this is to me," he said.

"It's good seeing you again, Judge."

"I had Henry show you in here because we're being joined for dinner by Ted and Ethel O'Harra. Do you remember them?"

"Very well," said Steve.

"They're already here, in the drawing room, but I wanted to see you alone first."

"Thank you, I appreciate it."

"How are you?" the Judge asked seriously.

"Fine, sir. And you?"

"You're really well? Working, carrying on, and all the rest of it?"

Steve nodded, and Judge Cowan made a sharp sighing sound.

"I'm very glad of it," he said. "I was somewhat worried when you didn't answer my last several notes."

"My mail is probably very mixed up. A story of mine is being filmed," he explained, "I've just finished working on the screenplay out on the Coast. Now I'm going back to New York to start up the assembly line again."

"How gratifying, Steve. I'm proud of you."

"But you, Judge?"

Judge Cowan hesitated, and his old eyes dimmed slightly. "With Margaret gone, I'm glad I have you as a link to her. Even if you are a wretched correspondent. I'm getting too old too fast to suit me, but I don't want to bore you with that. Come along, I think we'd better get in to the O'Harras and get a cocktail into you. Whenever I travel, I'm never offered a cocktail fast enough when I get there."

Ted and Ethel O'Harra greeted him with enthusiastic friendliness when the Judge led him into the drawing room. Steve stopped for a moment when he came in, a pang of heart arresting him. The yellow-glowing lamps suffused the room, but with a gentle light. He rested his eyes in a lingering glance on the gleaming depth of mahogany colors, the richness of the upholstery's shade of apricot, the delicate working of a remembered silver ash tray.

"Steve, it's great seeing you again, boy," said O'Harra. The Senator, it seemed to Steve, was beginning to grow fat, though he looked still robust. Ethel O'Harra's chic had not faltered, and her first words warmed him with their presumption of his intimacy.

"Steve, it's a real old family night." She smiled ruefully. "Ted and the Judge have been fighting like cats and dogs ever since we arrived tonight."

"Good." Steve smiled at her. "What about?"

"Argue—that I can do endlessly, Ethel," said Judge Cowan. "Fight—I never do. Henry, let us see what Mr. Williams would like to have."

"Henry, are those Martinis over there?" Steve asked.

Henry poured one for him. Sitting with the coffee-table group, sipping the bitingly cold Martini, Steve felt an errant sense of homecoming. He knew if he were not careful he would get maudlin before dinner could be served. He asked, "What's the argument about?—MacArthur?"

"Is anybody talking about anything else today?" asked Ted O'Harra.

Steve answered with a grin, "Yes, some people are talking about Senator McCarthy, for one. You, for another."

"At this moment," the Senator declared, with a shake of his head dismissing Steve's remark, "MacArthur is all that matters. When the history of America gets written, he may be the only man in it who matters."

"Ethel, your husband's hysterical," said Judge Cowan. And to O'Harra: "Ted, Douglas MacArthur may be everything you say—I have always in the past had the highest opinion of the man—but in a history that includes Lincoln, Monroe and——"

"And Truman?"

"You've always been very temperate in your disapproval of Truman before," the Judge pointed out.

"Not any more, not after this," said O'Harra.

"It pains me to be in a position of saying anything good about Mr. Truman, but here I'm afraid I must."

Steve laughed. "Am I dreaming this, Judge?"

O'Harra put his glass aside and leaned forward to the Judge.

"No, wait, Judge. Listen to me. MacArthur was given a job to do. How can anyone expect him to do it when he's hamstrung by his own bosses? Anyone with common sense knows that the first move to make against an enemy is to disrupt his staging ground. MacArthur wasn't allowed to do that——"

"It would be suicide," Judge Cowan retorted.

"What is it otherwise? People in the United States may talk of a stalemate, but a stalemate subsists on the blood of the men maintaining it. Do you think MacArthur or anybody else can defeat those hordes just by mowing them down as they pour in? I fought with Orientals, and I can tell you there're just too damn many of them, and they don't care quite so much about sacrificing a few thousand lives here or there as we do. MacArthur is absolutely right in wanting to bomb China, if we want him to win the war."

"But it isn't a war, is it?" said Steve, glad at last to have someone to ask questions of, "—not in any sense that we've ever thought of war before. Police action they call it: policy action is more like it, isn't it?"

"Exactly," said Judge Cowan. "Steve, isn't it stimulating for us to be in agreement politically for once?" To the Senator he went on, "The war in Korea is totally bound up in the world's political life, and it is fraught with political booby traps. We have the entire globe to convince of the rightness of our actions and the goodness of our intentions. If China uses 'volunteers' instead of being openly and offically at war, we still don't dare bomb their mainland. It is entirely too great a risk to run with world opinion. Not to mention the danger of igniting a global holocaust. No, Ted. And in any event MacArthur's behavior is beyond toleration. No one would argue about the man's being a military genius, but his Caesarean instincts are terrifying. He knows next to nothing of his native country; no one's been able to seduce him into visiting it since the thirties. And in Japan he is regarded, bless Pete, as little less than a god. Gods cannot err. MacArthur has apparently taken that to heart. The fact of the matter is that he is as much a hireling of the American people as you are, and it seems to me regrettable that he's forgotten it. If recalling him is what is needed to bring that fact back to mind, good for Truman. I'm not worried about MacArthur's personal future, incidentally. I understand a number of corporations in which I own stock are offering him jobs on rarified planes." The Judge took a breath and finished his cocktail. "This country can no longer go to war like a group of fraternity brothers on a weekend spree."

"Nor," O'Harra returned, "can we go on sacrificing our great men on the altar of the moment's expedience."

Judge Cowan lifted his white eyebrows, and Ethel O'Harra's face was suddenly drawn as though with veiled pain.

"As your friend Senator McCarthy has done?" Judge Cowan said, and Steve held his breath.

O'Harra winced. "Judge, I've had my say about McCarthy to you as well as the newspaper people. Can't you drop it? Guilt by association means me, too, you know."

Judge Cowan laughed. "I only hoped, Ted, to remind you to be tentative about condemning those who sacrifice great men."

"This is something I don't know about," said Steve. "Have you and McCarthy fallen out, Ted?"

O'Harra looked at him sardonically. "If it hadn't been for the firing of General MacArthur, I would have been all over the papers today."

"What happened?"

"I think we'd all better have another cocktail," said Judge Cowan.

"Let me get them," said Ethel, rising. As she went across the room to fetch the pitcher of Martinis, no one spoke.

"Was that something I shouldn't have asked?" Steve inquired, certain that he had inadvertently put O'Harra in an awkward position.

"Not really, Steve." O'Harra waved a hand. "Yesterday I was being interviewed about some damned innocuous chore of mine, and the subject of Senator McCarthy came up. As you know, I've always supported him in his effort to root out Communists in the Government. But I've been having second thoughts, a lot of us have, both about him and his methods of working. It hit me that I should repudiate him publicly, since that's what I was doing in my own mind. So I did."

Ethel came back with the Martini pitcher and refilled their glasses. Steve asked, "Ethel, what do you think of this?"

She held the empty Martini pitcher gingerly as she returned his look. "Well, if you must know, I thought it was naïve of Ted, and very dangerous politically."

O'Harra flushed. "I'm sorry, I couldn't help it. And if I live to be a hundred, I'll never see why I should say one thing when I believe another. . . ."

There was an edge to his wife's voice. "What will people think when you believe one thing one moment and another thing the next?"

"I hope they'll think I'm honest," the Senator said.

"Don't hope they'll think you know your own mind."

"Children," Judge Cowan cautioned gently.

O'Harra stood up and, fists rammed into his pockets, paced to the empty fireplace. When he spoke, it was Steve he addressed. "In Congress I'm supposed to represent the people who voted for me, and by and large they're simple, honest people who expect a guy will admit it when he makes a mistake." With an intake of breath he tried to regain his composure. "It wasn't altogether an innocent mistake. I might as well admit that, too. Ever since I came to Washington, I've disliked the tradition-regulated methods of the State Department's men. When McCarthy went after them, I couldn't wait to beat the drum for him. It hasn't worked out the way I expected. He has no proof of anything. The F.B.I. has the only proof about Communist agents in this country, and as far as I'm concerned, those are the hands the proof belongs in. I took the bad example of making noises when the people concerned had already done the job. I've been hating myself for it for a long time."

"It's what's going to get you re-elected, though," said Ethel.

"No," the Senator answered softly.

Steve could see the woman stiffen. She looked up at her husband inquiringly.

The Senator said, his voice still soft, without looking at his wife, without looking at anyone, "When I campaign, I'm going to tell them the exact truth about my motives. I wanted to get re-elected, and I needed an explosive popular issue. I'm going to tell them how I backed up McCarthy even after I was convinced he was wrong."

"What!" Ethel gasped.

Judge Cowan said, "Ted, that would be foolhardy in the extreme. Can't you let the matter drop?"

"No, sir," said O'Harra, his voice turning almost harsh. "Hell, if I was wrong about McCarthy, maybe I'm just as wrong about Truman's recalling MacArthur from Korea. Who the hell knows? But I know one thing: if people vote for me, I want them to do it because they think I'm good at the job, and they can't decide that if they don't know the vital details of how I've performed it in the past."

Judge Cowan blew out his cheeks. "Talk about naïveté . . ."

"McCarthy's only just getting started, Judge. His greatest day is still to come, and nobody's yet found a way to muzzle him. When they do, I don't want to feel that after I'd broken away from him I'd just stuck my head in the ground and pretended he didn't exist any more. He exists, and the people who make use of his popularity exist."

"Shall we discuss this some other time, Ted?" Ethel offered. "I'm sure we're boring Steve."

"Ha," said Steve.

O'Harra turned to him. "You're the youngest of us, Steve," he said. "What do *you* think?"

"Why ask me?" Steve returned. "I'm not a politician. Also, I'm the Judge's guest."

"What the young feel today is a tip to what the future will be, that's what they tell us."

"Thanks heaps," said Steve. "I still don't see that my opinion counts a damn."

"Surely you *have* an opinion, Steve," said Judge Cowan.

"Yes, I do. A very unseasoned one. It's only lately I've started paying any attention to what's been going on outside my own bailiwick."

"Then what's your offhand impression about all this?" O'Harra asked.

Steve looked at his still-brimming Martini in some embarrassment. "In that case," he said, "I think you're right about telling your people at home that you tried to steal the F.B.I.'s thunder the way McCarthy's done."

"Oh, Steve . . ." came from Ethel, but she let him continue.

"I think you'll have to look for a new job if you do," he went on to O'Harra, "but I think it's what they call a right action. All of us keep so busy with our plans, our ambitions, the rest of it, and suddenly we're hit smack in the eye with that consideration: right action. At least to me it's a damned unfamiliar consideration. It must be tough as hell for you, Ted, but I think what you want to do is right." No one answered, and Judge Cowan was looking at him as though waiting to hear more. Steve did not immediately know what else there was to be said. The words delivered themselves only because he felt warm in the circle of their good will and friendship for him. "McCarthyism is a disgrace to us. I think we all feel that," he continued quietly, feeling his way through his own thoughts. "And this *is* only the beginning of it. It's sordid, unbelievable, and outrageous. I'm glad you've decided that too, Ted, because I always liked the sincerity you had—I liked it even more when I heard Washington people laughing behind your back because of it."

"Go on, Steve," said the Senator.

"Is there some kind of link between McCarthyism and what's happening with General MacArthur? It seems to me that the people who are pro-McCarthy and pro-MacArthur are the same people, in too many cases. And if you really want me to go on, I think they're a dying core of everything that went wrong with the United States in its growing up. They're like an adolescent's acne. They can scar, but they won't endure. It seems they were almost bound to happen in the course of things, but the country is older now, maturer now. It may not always slough off the designs of a really evil man at some point in the future—a Hitler, say, if there were one with the cleverness to win American sentiment—but it'll slough off acne. Job or no job, you're smart to jump off the witch-hunt bandwagon, because sooner or later the nation itself will dump you off—along with all the other nearsighted little fascists." He screwed up his eyes and opened them again to smile. "Father-in-law, you serve very strong Martinis."

Senator O'Harra laughed. "Strong Martinis make strong words? But I'm flattered that you haven't minded saying them to me, Steve. Especially that last particular jibe."

"You know in what way I meant it." Steve shrugged.

"Yes, sure I do." He had evidently taken no serious offense.

Ethel O'Harra's eyes were narrowed. At first Steve thought she had, quite naturally, been angered by his remarks. But then he saw she was deep in thought.

Henry came in to announce dinner, and finishing their drinks, the four of them moved toward the dining room.

"What were you thinking about?" Steve asked Ethel lightly. "Just then when Henry came in?"

"Nothing." She glanced up at him. "Yes, I was," she said. "I was wondering if maybe we *could* get Ted re-elected on the sort of regenerated-sinner platform you two were talking about."

36

THE WELCOME AFFORDED DOUGLAS MACArthur by his native country after his recall from service in Korea was tumultuous. Thousands of cheering people greeted his arrival in San Francisco, and a large and vocal group in the city began a MacArthur-for-President agitation. The shock of the realization that a great war hero, a national symbol, an idol in the conquered country he had governed since the end of the Second World War, could be summarily deposed from his high office, even by a Chief Executive worn out and exasperated by his subordinate's assertiveness, stunned the nation. In reaction to this shock the people erupted with a clamorous emotion. Everywhere there were demonstrations in favor of the General. Wherever he appeared, shouting hordes screamed their adulation. The President who had opposed him was burned in effigy. Impeachment of the President was demanded by the General's incensed defenders. When MacArthur addressed a joint session of the Congress his words were carried to the farthest and most obscure extents of the land, and listeners heard, many with surprise, a deeply moving, dramatically rendered peroration:

"The world has turned over many times since I took the oath on the plain at West Point, and the hopes and dreams have long since vanished, but I still remember the refrain of one of the most popular barracks ballads of that day, which proclaimed, most proudly, that old soldiers never die; they just fade away. And like the old soldier of the ballad, I now close my military career and just fade away, an old soldier who tried to do his duty as God gave him the light to see that duty. Good-by. . . ."

The tunesmiths were at work before the ovation had died out.

On the day MacArthur was to be welcomed in New York, Helen Kaufman had an appointment to look in on the filming of a television commercial that would feature Betsy Polk, who was still her star offering in the modeling industry. Helen had given the baby his breakfast, changed his diapers for the second time, and put him down with his bottle by the time Mrs. Kostmayer, the woman Marvin had hired to help her through her first months of motherhood, arrived at the apartment. Before going to dress she called Jules Fischel at his office.

"Jules, it's Helen," she said. "I'm going to drop in on the film session for the Houghton series this morning. Anything special you need to have done?"

"No, I don't believe, Helen. Ease Betsy into it."

"Yes, that's why I thought I'd go. Jules—I want to start back full time next week."

"Next week? Are you sure? What about the baby?"

"Mrs. Kostmayer does fine with the baby, and I can't call myself much of a partner if I'm on the scene only a few hours a day this way."

"Whatever you decide is fine with me, baby," Jules said. "It's your own money you've got tied up here. Naturally all of us will be glad to see you back in business."

"Good, we'll make it definite then?"

"Helen—nothing's wrong, is there?" Jules asked.

"Not a thing," she answered firmly. "Not an absolute thing." She told him good-by and hung up the telephone.

The studios where the commercial was to be filmed were on the second floor of a converted brownstone building, and when she came into the waiting room outside Studio B, it was filled with a milling group of interested parties—members of the firm's clerical staff, film technicians, and representatives of Houghton's sponsor. The confusion of the place was greater than usual, and it occurred to Helen that outside on the street there had seemed to be a special quality to the hectic way in which people were going about their business. In one corner of the waiting room two of the secretaries were huddling over a telephone like tittering adolescents. "Has it reached your office yet? Did you see him? Gosh, yes, I can hear the people yelling where you are. . . . When do you think they'll get up here?"

Helen sought out a young woman she had met on previous calls. She found her behind her desk, next to the doors to the studio.

"Lookit, where's Betsy?" she asked her. "I want to take a second to check her, if she's dressed."

"She's behind some flats at the back of the studio, Mrs. Kaufman. Go on in. Did you cross Fifth Avenue on your way here?"

"I always do——"

"Then they must not have gotten this far uptown yet. . . ." Before Helen could ask for clarification the girl had scurried over to her confreres by the telephone.

Helen picked her way through the noisy gathering and found the studio beyond electric with activity. The crew were still trying to resolve the lighting plot for the sequence, and a special-effects technician was barking instructions at everyone in sight. The first person in the studio Helen recognized was Warren Taggert.

"Hi, Helen," he greeted her as he came up. With his blond crew cut and in his severe Brooks Brothers clothes he looked like a magazine advertisement's representation of a successful young assistant-to-the-producer.

Helen gave a mock-rueful groan as she gave him her hand. "Oh, God, are you back with us again?" she said.

"Just for a visit," Warren assured her. "Mr. Houghton was getting perturbed about dignity in the commercial." The young man's smile was wide and easy-going, and Helen liked the casual correctness of his manner. When she had first come back to work after having the baby, she had met him at another filming session, and they had struck up a pleasant, undemanding fellow-professionals' acquaintance. Helen knew that from time to time Phillip Houghton sent him over to insure that the commercials used on his television program were sufficiently acceptable to the taste of his probable viewers, and the notion irritated her.

"I'm perfectly willing to believe your boss is a genius of some kind," she said now, "but if he wants the commercial to have dignity, I wish he'd get Prudential or somebody to sponsor his dreary panel."

"Calm down, calm down, a little softening of the sales pitch won't do your client any harm either, you know."

"True. And the ruckus *you* stir up practically guarantees her two hours' extra pay."

"You see, you should be grateful to me instead of taking cracks at the show," said Warren. "How's the crowd outside?"

"What crowd?" Helen asked.

"To welcome MacArthur, of course."

"Was *that* what all that was?"

She had taken a step away, but his sudden peal of laughter stopped her. "For God's sake, don't you think of anything but how your girls are going to look to the nation's television viewers?"

"I think about a lot of things," Helen retorted lightly. "You're a rude little snot."

She turned her back on his grinning and went to search for Betsy. When she found her, the young model was dressed and putting a finishing touch to her hair with a trembling brush. Helen scrutinized her from every angle and saw nothing amiss except the line of her lipstick. After a minor adjustment and several words of friendly encouragement she was able to release the girl to the studio's staff. Walking back through Studio B, she called "hellos" to those she knew and stopped abruptly at the door when Warren Taggert touched her arm.

"Are you rushing back to the office?" he asked.

"No, I'm going home," Helen said. "I'm working only part time till next week; I just wanted to give Betsy some moral support today."

"Come see the parade with me," he invited her. "Come on,

I've given the damn commercial script my blessing. Let's go see the fun. You probably won't be able to get through the traffic anyway."

Helen moved on through the crowded waiting room, into the hall and down the stairs, Warren at her side. She realized she was having to speed her pace to keep up with him.

"You're really excited about MacArthur's coming back, aren't you?" she said.

"Aren't *you?* What have you got against MacArthur?"

She threw him a glance. "Now really, Warren."

"You've buried yourself in domesticity," he asserted. "Don't you know what's going on in New York today? People by the thousands are turning out because he's a symbol of everything that's newest and most vigorous in this country. Sometimes I'm ready to call the people of this country a hopeless collection of jackals, but not today."

Coming out into the street Helen was saying, "I don't see that much difference about a ticker-tape parade——"

"It's for a man you'd expect to be considered in disgrace. But not MacArthur: *he* turned the tables fast enough. If this keeps up, they won't be able to avoid impeaching Truman." He took her arm as they hurried along, and through his fingers Helen could feel his excitement. "God, it's wonderful," he said, his eyes on the jostling crowd visible ahead of them. "It's everything we could want."

"It's an enormous collection of fools kowtowing to an imperialistic old——"

"Imperialistic?" Warren cried. "Is that a dirty word? Helen, come off it. Imperialism is in the air, hotter than ever with MacArthur back now."

Helen stopped suddenly and frowned at him. They were an obstruction in the thickening stream of people on the street. Except for the battering of passing elbows, the stream parted, passed them, and flowed together again as people hurried toward the parade route.

"I'm really shocked at you," Helen told him as other pedestrians jostled past.

"Why shouldn't imperialism be the new note in America?" Warren spread his hands. "We *are* an empire, as much as any empire that lived before us. From Japan to Germany it's ours, and sentimentalists are the only ones too self-deluded to admit it."

"What do you think MacArthur's going to do about it?"

"I hope and pray he'll unite the realists in this country. You know, I don't think you've ever *watched* our program." He stabbed an upturned palm with an index finger. "With MacArthur at the helm the really intelligent leaders could be made up into a governing cadre like this country's never had before, and the first thing they'll do is impeach that haberdasher Truman. Oh, but I hope they'll do it!" Turning, he took her arm. "Come on, Helen, he'll *be* there!"

The waiting crowds were impassable on Fifth Avenue. The din of cheering, even though MacArthur had not yet appeared this far north on the avenue, made the simplest sentences difficult to project.

"Can we get across the street?" Helen found herself shouting to Warren as they squeezed into the mass.

"What? I can't——"

"Can we *get* across the *street?*"

"I don't even know if they'd *let* us across," Warren shouted back.

"Warren, this is awful, I never thought that——"

"Here—Helen! here, step back this way——"

"How the hell long is this going to go on?"

"You don't want to miss it, no matter how long!"

They were pushed back against a store front by the shouting throng. Peppering the crowd were the Brooks-Brothered or doe-eyed denizens of this area of Manhattan; here and there an unbrushed intellectual sulked in the press, but the vast body of the mass were ordinary men and women who had called a halt to their pursuit of business in order to join in the welcome.

"Look at them!" Warren was exulting at Helen's side. "You think they're here for kicks? I tell you, every educated man you meet is an imperialist at heart. At least he knows that what MacArthur stands for is the dignity and the power of this country!"

In the fever of the celebration, swept by its force. Helen could almost imagine that what he said was true. Nearer now she could hear the wild cheering, and the storm of confetti falling from the windows above the street thickened like heavy snow. The cheering grew deafening, and then the motorcade came into view. She heard the slogans shouted near her, across the street, and down the block, repeatedly:

"Impeachment for Truman!" "MacArthur in the White House!"

The deliberate slogan-shouters seemed to her to be more plentiful and more active than was usually the case in a parade's crowd. "There he is, there he is!" Warren was shouting, as was everyone else around her. Even the few surly types she could pinpoint were straining on tiptoe to see him.

Helen herself could at first see nothing very clearly through the paper blizzard. But then suddenly there was an opening in the mass of waving arms, and beyond the striding plainclothes bodyguards flanking the car she caught an impressively clear glimpse of Douglas MacArthur. He was sitting up on the back of the car he was riding in, the famous cap set dashingly on his head, the gloved hand aloft to respond to the deafening welcome. She was surprised he looked so old. Photographs had always made him seem a man in the fullest vigor of his maturity, but now there was a tiredness in that handsome and intimidating face, familiar, as it was, as the face on postage stamps. Caught up in the jubilation in the street, she found herself joining Warren's cries and could not imagine why she did so. Blushing, she stopped herself. The motorcade drew past and vanished, but the cheering went on.

Breathless, Helen gasped, "My God, Warren, it's contagious. This is a riot!"

"You hear that?" Warren shouted. "These people will make MacArthur President. It's the note of the times we live in, Helen. Wouldn't it be terrific?"

"No!" said Helen.

The cheering was subsiding now, and the crowd was churning around them, trying to disperse.

"What can you object to in him?" Warren demanded. "Helen, you're no fool, you're the kind of person who's going to make the difference in what happens to us in the future. What has democracy ever done for this country but earn us the contempt and loathing of every other civilized country on the globe? Face it, the world's changed too much."

The crowd was thinning out at last. Helen breathed a sigh. "Come on, spearhead," she said. "See if you can get me through this. I've got to flag a taxi."

Warren took her arm firmly, and shouldering their way, it was just possible for them to maneuver through the moving mass of people.

"Isn't it so?" Warren insisted. "Well, isn't it?" They pushed toward the corner.

Helen tried to make herself heard. "What you've got in mind are the oldest concepts there are. Granted, I don't fancy myself a political brain. I just have the prejudices of the lower class."

"You?" Warren laughed. "Helen, there's a vulgar word for you. You've a camp."

"Because I say I've got lower-class prejudices?" Helen stopped to look at him. Then she laughed, delighted. "Warren, you are my friend for life. Come for cocktails."

"What the hell are you talking about?"

"I hope, I just hope, that I'm never tempted to tell you."

"Cocktails!" Warren slapped his forehead. "Look, I'm going to be busy as hell till we find out what MacArthur's going to do. Houghton is waist deep in work. But after everything clears, I want to give a party. Just a small one; I never have in New York before, and I feel like it'd make an official citizen of me. I meant to ask you before, would you and your husband come?"

"A party? We'd love to, Warren, thank you. It's just——"

"Oh?"

"My husband's a doctor——"

"Yes, I know. You mean about emergency calls? If he's got calls, you come along and have him follow when he's able. It'll really be a very small party, so nobody's got to sweat about details——"

"I'll tell Marvin," Helen said. "And you let me know when."

"Great. Here's a taxi."

He whistled shrilly and ran across the street to get it.

"See you at the party." He smiled as Helen caught up. She got in, and Warren closed the door. "Don't forget!" With a wave of his hand he had disappeared into the throng.

She wasn't certain how much Marvin would like going to any party of Warren Taggert's, but it would be worth a try if the invitation materialized. She liked Warren's eagerness and youngness, even if she looked askance at his political ideas. And she and Marvin hadn't been to a party since the baby had been born. She sighed and tried to relax against the musty leatheriness of the taxi as it crept its way through the crosstown traffic. She loved her little boy, she knew, and loved taking care of him, but something was wrong with the way she was feeling—the way she had felt ever since his birth. She knew she was in an especially privileged position, thanks to Marvin's success in his practice. Whenever she wanted to go out, there was money enough for nurses and baby sitters, in addition to Mrs. Kostmayer's daily services. She was not chained to the duties of a mother and wife. But she felt uncomfortable in the new role the baby's existence had settled on her shoulders.

Soon after coming home with him from the hospital, she had started going to the office a few hours each day, in the hope that this activity would restimulate her usual involvement with the things around her, her world beyond the nursery and its formulas and the sterilizer and symmetrical stacks of diapers. Even with Marvin's encouragement, it hadn't. Her interest in the agency, much as she enjoyed the work, proud as she was of the position she had attained with Marvin's help and backing, was not enough to distract her from a gnawing inner nervousness, more distressing still because she could not pin down a comprehension of its nature. Then Marvin had become preoccupied with his practice to an extent that riled her vanity and made her jealous of the mid-dinner ringing of the telephone. Was it because the birth of a son had overstimulated his drive to succeed? Or had her own withdrawing left him lonely and unattracted? Perhaps she was getting older. Perhaps motherhood made her too officially a matron, and some vain instinct in her was rebelling against the trap.

She did not know. She chided herself an ingrate. She had a lovely baby. She had her husband's unquestioning loyalty. She simply didn't know what to make of her restlessness, and she didn't know how to stop. At any rate she would be looking forward to a party—Warren Taggert's or anybody else's, for that matter—to break the disturbing and undefined spell that was binding her.

The baby was just awaking from his nap when she reached the apartment, and Mrs. Kostmayer greeted her smilingly, heaving her bulk up from one of the chairs in the living room.

"Just waking up," Mrs. Kostmayer said, nodding toward the nursery. "I'll change him."

"No, let me do it," said Helen. "You could be warming the formula, if you will, Mrs. Kostmayer."

The nursery was in semidarkness, and the baby was bellowing in his crib. He tuned himself out with a few petulant sobs when Helen picked him up. Dank as he was, she held him against her for a long moment, crooning comforting sounds into his ear. She was still intimidated by his smallness, the wobbling of his neck, and the headlong leaps he would suddenly attempt. She rocked him gently in her arms as she carried him to the changing table she had arranged against the opposite wall. She turned on the light. While she changed him, the baby made hideous faces against the new glare in the room; then, growing used to it, he began to gurgle.

She stayed alone in the nursery to give the baby his bottle while Mrs. Kostmayer went out to brew a pot of coffee for the two of them. "Oh, you beauty," she cooed to the heedless infant. "Why is it so nice to have you, and at the same time so sad? You know why, little Marvie? Because it makes Mama be stuck. Nothing will ever happen now but what I don't know about it ahead of time. Now it'll be you and your beautiful father and a job for me so my goddamned horizons will stay broad. But oh, Marvie, now I'll *never* go on a safari to Africa. I'll *never* get presented at the Court of Saint James. So I'm silly to let it bother me, but there it is. Oh, Marvie, please stay as lovely as you are now so I never have an excuse to resent you." She looked up from the baby with a click of her tongue, ashamed of herself for feeling such things.

The baby's name wasn't Marvie at all, but Joshua. She called him after his father only in such secret colloquies as this, and they were, she knew, a bad habit to get into. It'll pass, she asserted to herself. The discontent would fade away, and she would have a wonderful, useful life as a loving wife, dutiful mother, and successful businesswoman. She was a spoiled bitch to be complaining, even to a baby who could be trusted not to understand a word.

Helen had freshened up and changed her clothes when Marvin arrived home for dinner. He would have to go back to the hospital after dinner, and Helen determined to protect the hour or so they could be together. Mrs. Kostmayer played with the baby in the nursery, and in the living room Helen served Martinis.

Marvin threw himself down on the sofa and stretched his long legs out under the coffee table. "No one would believe, looking at you right now, that you're a wife and mother." He smiled. "You look like one of your own models."

Helen glanced at him sharply. She had wanted to do nothing that would betray her frame of mind, but Marvin returned the look ingenuously. Helen smiled at him.

"If I were one of my own models, you might not be running back to the hospital after dinner," she said.

"Now, now——"

"I know, I'm sorry. Your patients need you more than I do."

"How was the agency?" Marvin asked.

"I didn't go. I had to stop by where they were filming the commercial on the Houghton show."

"Did you see the parade?"

"Lord, yes," Helen said. "With Warren Taggert. He's Houghton's first lieutenant, sort of. Big MacArthur buff. MacArthur looked wonderful, I must say. Marvin, how old is he?"

"I haven't the faintest idea."

"He looked older than I expected, impressive as he was."

"A certain number of wars take it out of you," Marvin said. "He's looked older without the cap, I've noticed."

"I don't think I've ever seen him without the cap."

"Good public relations on *some*body's part." Marvin shrugged.

"Marvin—do you think he's going to start something? I mean, like a political movement or something? Having Truman impeached?"

Marvin sipped his drink. "Everyone seems to expect something of the sort," he said. "An awful lot of people are out for Truman's scalp. It's as though he'd desecrated the shrine, firing the man."

"Is MacArthur really a fascist?"

"He's a soldier." Marvin waved a hand. "I don't think there's anything much else he knows about, or cares about."

"In Japan he was a dictator," Helen pointed out.

"Japan lost the war, remember," Marvin returned.

"But I mean if he was so good at being a dictator, maybe he thinks it's the best way for *any* country." She looked at her wrist watch. "Time to heat dinner. Come keep me company?"

They stood, but Marvin held her back. "Wait," he said. He drew her into his arms and kissed her. Smiling quizzically, he studied her face a moment. "You know I *have* to go to the hospital, don't you?"

"Of course I do, Marvin. Please forget what I——"

"I don't want you to be unhappy. About anything."

"Unhappy? I have everything a woman could wish for. I just . . ." She slipped inoffensively from his embrace. "For heaven's sake, you're spoiling me. Come on, darling."

37

THE WAR OF ATTRITION IN KOREA WENT ON through that summer, a grinding and glamorless enterprise necessitated by a responsibility and sustained by a conviction. In the United States there was lacking the excitement, the sense of melodrama, that had marked the behavior of civilians through other wars. The conflict in Korea was watched with caution, but there were few armchair generals, and civil life pursued an approximately normal course because the war was something that America was committed to pursue but could not be waited upon. It was a gray engagement.

On a fetid June night in New York, Tiger Rizzuto attended a conference of Demo-Socialist leaders in the offices on the third floor of the New York Labor School. The drawling Mills reviewed for the group the background that had led to the calling of the meeting.

"In spite of the Wage Stabilization Board," he said, "this has so far been a damned good year for labor. We've moved ahead on every front, and we're digging away at the Taft-Hartley Law. I've talked to a number of you about this and I think most of us are in agreement: the time is coming to think of consolidation in the strongest terms." There was a stirring sound in the room, and Mills went on. "Labor needs the merger of the two giants, the C.I.O. and the A.F.L. It isn't going to get the merger until we use our influence to get the ball really rolling. Tonight we want to hear your ideas, my ideas, any ideas, about the obstacles we can expect to find in our path."

There were many, the ensuing discussion revealed. Seven months before, the United Labor Policy Committee had been formed to resolve defense mobilization problems. The fact that it was a co-operative venture on the part of the C.I.O. and the A.F.L. had led union leaders to hope that it might outlive its temporary basis and provide the foundation for an area of inter-union activity presaging a merger of the organizations. But already trouble was plaguing the committee, and in the opinion of Henderson and Mills it was only a matter of time before the A.F.L. would withdraw, leaving the committee in a shambles.

"If they do, how the hell are we ever going to get the C.I.O. to work with them again?" one of the older men asked.

"We won't," said Tom Henderson, "not until it can be done on terms of absolute equality. What we face is an arduous and God-knows-how-long campaign of propaganda. Working within the union leadership won't be enough for this kind of deal. We're going to have to sell the membership, each and every man in each and every little outfit."

"We don't have the manpower for that."

"Then we'll have to break our backs doing the job ourselves."

Another sounded his objection: in the past the Demo-Socialists had restricted their influence to advising and guiding the unions' leadership; the leadership would resent any effort made on the part of the Demo-Socialists to carry their ideas directly to union members.

"I don't think so," Henderson answered. "They know how important a merger is. But neither side can afford to look overeager. They've got to see how the wind blows, and so far they're leaving it up to us to do the blowing of it."

Mills outlined for the group an intensive program of speeches, forums, and pamphleteering. At the end of it, he added, "And for my money we need some new blood to help out with the speech schedule."

"A new man? Have anybody in mind?"

"Yes. Tiger here."

Tiger gave a start. "Me?" he asked incredulously.

"Why not? You'd get a bang out of it."

Another began: "I think in view of the good work Tiger's——"

"Hey, wait a minute," Tiger interrupted, "with this kind of program scheduled, I'm going to be up to my ass in the office work."

Henderson dismissed the objection: "We'll bring in some additional office help."

"But I don't know anything about giving speeches. . . ."

"You're very persuasive when you're convinced," Mills contradicted.

"No, no. Listen, I mean it——"

"Just what've you got against the idea?"

"Look. Oh, Christ; well, look at it this way," Tiger stammered. "Five years ago I would've been cock enough to sit down and have a little chat with the Supreme Court, for God's sake, but now—I just couldn't, you guys. I like the job I have. I don't want any fucking limelight."

"Let's table it for the moment," Henderson began.

"Hell, no," Tiger moved quickly. "I know you. Tabling it just means I won't be able to get you off my back till I give in."

"Listen, Tiger," Henderson said sharply then. "We've put time and money into training you. Now's the time for you to start paying off the investment, and I don't mean by just sitting in your office licking stamps."

"I'd just make a mess of it, I mean it."

"You're on the team. Now that's final. Shut up."

"Oh, God."

He said nothing more, but sat in dull-headed consternation through the closing minutes of the meeting. Afterward he drew Mills aside. "Look, who's going to write my speeches?"

"You are," said the lanky ex-Southerner.

"I wouldn't know how to begin. Couldn't one of you guys help me?"

"I'm afraid not, Tiger. We'll be busy enough with our own work. If you can find somebody to help you, it's okay with me."

"Somebody good would have to be paid. *I* don't have any goddamned money to hire help."

"I'll make a deal if it makes you feel better. You find somebody you think is good, and we'll set aside some dough for his efforts. Not much, you understand. You can have him only until the ice-breaking gets done."

"It shouldn't take much money, I don't guess," Tiger said. "All I want is somebody to straighten up what I write, give it some punch. I'd want the speeches to be my own except for that."

"See what you can find."

When the others had gone, Tiger went to sit alone for a while in the cubicle that was his office. He did not turn on the desk lamp. Sufficient light spilled in from the adjoining room, and half-light was comfortable for the vague pondering he wanted to do after the shock of what had transpired in the meeting. He sat with his hands clasped together on the desk blotter, his legs wrapped back around the base of the decrepit swivel chair. He was frightened of the new responsibility given him, but flattered and stimulated by it as well. He had wondered before if perhaps his knowing Zeeda Kaufman better than the others had would prove a hindrance to his advancement with the Demo-Socialists. These were not men given to witch-hunting, but everybody and his brother were jumpy about the Commies. He had never tried to sound any of his Demo-Socialist superiors out about it, and the subject had never since been referred to, but he realized now he had been, if only half-consciously, very much concerned about his standing in the organization. He could rest easy now, and in spite of his diffidence about taking up work as a public speaker, a debater, a rouser of rallies, he could enjoy his contemplations of this evidence of his success.

His thought went back fleetingly to the arid, acrid little world he had known when he had been a little boy—a battering, threatening, ugly Chicago. He thought of his parents, and his ruined father, who had thrown over the dignity Old Worlders sometimes kept and yet had never made sense of the New World he'd come to. They corresponded regularly, Tiger and his father, but Tiger knew that when the time came to go to visit his parent, he would be marvelously inventive of excuses to avoid it. They were neither pleased nor impressed with what he had done with his life, because they did not understand it. They had never found a way out of their graveyard of small wants, no matter how hard he had tried to show them a way to share with him his happiness and his ambitions for the future. He had come too far from them; he had come too far not from their material but their spiritual poverty.

It was that poverty of spirit he'd battled against all his life, even when he had battled stupidly and futilely. But the advantage had turned to him now, he thought. With the help of the people around him, all those who'd been generous and believing and kind, he was beginning to find inside himself a lode of spirit, the resources of loving and hope and self-respect. It was a mystery to him: why should he have been rescued in this way, handed such a good life, when he had done less than nothing to deserve it, when he could not claim, looking coldly at the doings of the world, that he had a native right to it? It could only be, he thought, because the work he was giving himself to was necessary and good, that his energy and abilities were being preserved, not for his own sake, but for the sake of others whose lives would indirectly benefit from his efforts as a political man, however modest his dimensions.

He chuckled to himself. In the days when he had first gone in with Al Gustineo, he had been just as certain he was fighting the good fight—for Juney, for the baby who had been beginning at that time to grow its way toward birth, for himself and his mother and father. And if he had been just as certain then as he was now, how could he know that now he was any nearer the truth? Well, he couldn't, he answered himself. He could only feel it, all through the new and widening soul that had been given him.

The search for someone to help with the writing of the speeches began the following day. Tiger and Juney reviewed their list of acquaintances but found no one who knew of any writers except surrealist poets in the Village. Mills and Henderson talked to friends of theirs connected with the newspapers and on the third day turned up one possibility: a down-and-out rummy whom Tiger talked to, rejected, and lambasted Mills and Henderson for suggesting. A week passed, and the time was drawing short. Mills had scheduled Tiger for a speech in the second week of July. When he told Edith Mackey of his problem, she suggested he see Vasil Stolorow, a magazine writer currently conducting a literary-appreciation course for the school.

To Stolorow that night, standing near Edith's desk in the

bookstore on the first floor, he explained the situation. "I don't need anybody who's an authority on labor problems. Just somebody who's intelligent and knows good English. If he can coach me for the actual speaking, so much the better."

"Why don't you try a literary agent?"

"I don't know any."

"They're in the Red Book." Stolorow shrugged.

"Don't *you* know any? Somebody who'd understand?"

"Rachel Pemberton belonged to the Demo-Socialists once. Her office handles my feature stories for me. Would you like me to give her a call?"

He did so, and when he had her on the phone, turned her over to Tiger. Again Tiger explained his needs. "I don't know what kind of fee is usual," he said, "but my boss has given me a hundred dollars to use. Maybe that's just enough for one speech, but I'd like to get maybe a couple or three out of it if I could."

The voice on the other end of the wire hesitated. "I don't know if I have anybody who'd be interested. There's not much money involved. . . ."

"It's all I've got, I'm afraid, Mrs. Pemberton," said Tiger.

"There just might be. . . . Let me see, Mr. Rizzuto. Would you call me at my office tomorrow at eleven? I'll see if I can think of any way to help you."

"Oh, thanks a million, Mrs. Pemberton. You don't know what—well, eleven o'clock. I'll call you then. And thank you again."

The next morning, when she had reached her office, Rachel Pemberton called Steve Williams.

"Good morning, Steve. I hope I didn't wake you."

Steve's voice came chortling over the wire. "For God's sake, Rachel, I've been up since seven."

"I got a note from Capbern yesterday," Rachel said. "He's very pleased with the way the shooting is going. And we have your new story, but I haven't had a chance to read it yet. As a matter of fact, I'm saving it for the weekend in Connecticut, where I can read in peace. Are you starting on anything else?"

"I'm trying to, let's say."

"How's it going?"

"Sticky right now," Steve said. "I'm still edging up to it. Why do you ask especially?"

"Steve, do you know anything about the labor movement?"

"The labor movement? No, not anything much, Rachel."

"I wondered if you might be interested in finding out a little about it—from the inside out, as it were."

"What's the pitch?"

She repeated in detail the conversation she had had with Tiger Rizzuto the night before, concluding, "The money will mean but nothing to you now. However, I thought as possibly fresh material for you——"

"It might be fun," Steve said. "I don't believe there *is* anybody named Tiger Rizzuto, but I'd like to meet him."

"He's calling me at eleven. Shall I set up an appointment?"

"May it be here at my place?"

"I don't see why not."

"When you talk to him, give him my number and ask him to call me. We can fix a date between the two of us."

At seven o'clock the next evening Tiger Rizzuto arrived at the studio on East Forty-seventh Street. Steve gave a start when he opened the door to him. He had expected a more mature type, but the dark-haired diffident young man standing in the doorway could not have been older, he judged, then himself.

"Steven Williams?" the caller asked, almost truculently.

"Yes. Come on in."

He led the young man through the narrow kitchen to the studio, inviting him as he did so to take off his jacket. On his return from California, Steve had undertaken to repaint the studio himself, and although the job he had done was not expert, the place looked far more clean and comfortable. He had bought bright-colored slip covers for the sofa and the chairs, several more lamps, and a number of plants to help dispel the grayness of the city that otherwise easily invaded such a room. It was an informal, cheerful place to live and work in.

Steve took Tiger's jacket from him and hung it up in the closet.

"Sit down, won't you? I've got the icebox stacked with some beer. How about one?"

"Thanks. It'd be nice in this heat," Tiger Rizzuto said.

Steve opened the beer cans and came back into the studio.

He plopped himself down on the sofa opposite his visitor.

"Shall we get this on a first-name basis?" he offered. "I'm Steve, and where the hell did you ever get a handle like Tiger?"

Tiger laughed. "In Chicago. A kid's name; it just stuck to me."

"You don't look to me like you were ever very tigerish."

"You didn't know me in Chicago."

Steve noted the brilliance of his smile, and waited for him to continue. He did not prompt him. "I guess I told you on the phone all you need to know about this deal," Tiger said. "I brought a couple of pages with me, part of the first speech. . . ."

He drew the folded sheets from his shirt pocket and passed them over to Steve. Spreading them out on his crossed knees, Steve read what Tiger had written. It would be more accurate to say that he tried to read. Through the process he could feel Tiger's gaze uneasily on him, could sense the young socialist's cringing shyness. In addition, Tiger's composition was so tortuous, Steve wasn't certain what the speech was about. He set the pages aside when he had done the best he could.

"Suppose we start by your telling me in your own way what you want to tell these guys in the unions," he suggested. "And, incidentally, fill me in on the current union situation and what the hell the Demo-Socialist Party is."

Tiger did so, haltingly at first, then fluently, then heatedly as he was caught up in the train of his thought. Steve listened with an interest engaged as much by Tiger himself as by Tiger's convictions. The fire of the young rabble-rouser's beliefs, the way his passionate interest in his subject purged him of embarrassment and gave him not only poise but dynamism: Steve tasted the salty flavor of an unexpected encounter with a legitimately dramatic personality. He began to interrupt Tiger's flow of talk with brief questions, and then with argument. The more hotly Tiger argued, the more Steve learned. They talked fervidly, loudly, often angrily, through a second beer, and then a third. When Steve got up to get the fourth, Tiger gave an explosive sigh.

"It's too damned hot to be arguing. If you don't want to help write my speeches, I'll go home and stop wasting your beer."

"Oh, I'm going to help you write the speeches," Steve tossed over his shoulder.

Tiger gave a jump and grabbed the arms of his chair. "Then what the hell are you baiting me about?"

Steve shrugged as he opened the door of the refrigerator. "I have to find out how you feel about things."

"Christ, you take the hard way."

"Oh, it's going to get worse if we work together," Steve assured him.

Fresh beers in hand, they set aside the subject of Tiger's projected speeches. Gingerly, trying to avoid scaring him off, Steve angled for more information about Tiger himself. Tiger was at first reticent, but as the evening passed he talked more easily about himself, and slowly Steve pieced together the story: the background of Chicago tenements, the Army, Juney, his hoodlum associates, the brief but traumatic limbo that swallowed him whole and spewed him out upon the steps of the New York Labor School, the months as a janitor trying to recoup his life. Steve listened to all of it with fascination. Tiger himself was apparently unaware of the drama in his story, and Steve found himself moved by his lack of self-consciousness. It was midnight before either of them was aware of the time.

Each night for a week they worked on Tiger's speeches, tacitly accepting that Steve's studio was the most convenient workshop for them. There were to be three basic speeches, with introductions and perorations appended to suit specific occasions. Enjoying the work, Steve gave more and more of his time to it. Tiger took him to the Labor School, and in the library there Steve found much to study about the work to which Tiger was so fanatically devoted. He coached Tiger in his delivery of the speeches, and cheered him through his maiden harangue in a dingy, airless meeting hall near the waterfront. They worked on the speeches intensively, altering and tightening them after each of the tryout-like speaking engagements. When they would finish an evening's work, they would sit around the studio, or out in the garden, stripped to the waist, fighting off the burden of the summer's heat with beer. Tiger did not succeed in convertng Steve to socialism, but he won Steve's high regard; on the other hand Tiger felt complimented that a man of Steve's type—educated, higher class, he analyzed—should take an interest in him. When the pressure of work on the speeches lessened, they continued to see each other, Steve dining with Tiger and Juney at their apartment on occasion, or the three of them driving out to the beach at Neponset on Sunday mornings. From time to time Steve recommended an additional rehearsal in the deserted library or one of the unused classrooms at the Labor School. The day Juney took all her maternity clothes out of their boxes, Steve helped Tiger through a mammoth drunk and later acted as a palliating agent between the badly shaken young husband and the hurt and angry Juney.

Tiger's speaking engagements were judged a success by his superiors within the Demo-Socialist Party, and by the coming of autumn the D.S.P. was beginning to receive specific requests for his appearance. When Tiger expressed discomfort that Steve's hundred-dollar fee had long since been paid him, Steve dismissed the concern. He had more than enough time for his own writing, he was earning more money than he needed, and most importantly, he had begun to sense—joyously, saying nothing to Tiger that might jinx it—the birth of an exciting political career for Tiger Rizzuto. He determined he would follow that career intimately.

On the first chilly morning of the autumn Helen Kaufman was late reaching her office. She postponed reading her mail. Already waiting to be interviewed by her were three new models whose photographs had met with Jules Fischel's approval. She took the photographs and notes of pertinent information from her files and arranged them on her desk. She flipped the intercom switch to tell her secretary to send the first girl in. The first, like the second and the third, proved to be new to New York. They were of the type Helen had worked with most successfully, their fresh quality of innocence and frequent baths still almost visible as an aura about them. Ordinarily Helen would have been delighted with at least the second one, an intelligent young actress with a fine complexion who wanted only occasional stints of modeling. Even this morning she knew she could make use of No. 2 and probably No. 3, but she scribbled her hieroglyphic notes to herself without enthusiasm. Only when the last girl was gone had she an opportunity to wonder why the interviews left her feeling so listless. She flipped the intercom switch.

"Take messages for me, please, till I let you know," she said. "Except Doctor Kaufman or Mr. Fischel."

She got up from her desk and walked away from it. She needed the time alone, she felt. It had been too breakneck a morning: discovering the nursery had grown icy cold in the night, rushing the baby through a warm bath and into heavier clothes, hurrying through the morning feeding and at the same time having to try to deceive the baby with a manufactured calm in order not to give him indigestion, tearing through her own dressing and the hectic trip across town, the three interviews each on the heels of the other. She luxuriated in a sigh, and lighting a cigarette, dropped onto the small couch against the wall opposite her desk.

The trouble with the models, she reasoned, was that they were getting to look younger and younger to her. Like the old joke about traffic cops beginning to look like college boys. She was getting, not old, but older. Nor was it a physical aging. It was far too early for her to worry about her looks losing their youthfulness, but an era of her life was sealed off now, first by marrying Marvin, then by the coming of the baby. Yet she had still to make the change-over in her own way of thinking; she was fighting it, and she knew it was a fight impossible to win.

Dwelling on the notion depressed her, and she wished she had an excuse for having a real crying jag. She should have seen the signs before in the frequency of her trips to the beauty parlor, but she had gone there blindly, expecting by some cosmetic magic to dispel the mournfulness hanging over her. Since Warren Taggert's cocktail party early in the past summer, she and Marvin had been going out regularly—to other parties, or by themselves to dance, to the theater and concerts, to picnic outings with the baby. None of it returned to her the sense of adventure and satisfaction she was certain she had known in the past.

The thought of her collection came to her. It was in the desk across the room, an accumulation of brochures from adult-education institutions around town. She had no idea how she had gotten on the mailing lists, but the brochures and pamphlets and curricula announcements came regularly in her mail, and the most interesting of them she had held on to. She had thought that when the combination of the job and the baby demanded less, she would take a course in something new to her—she didn't know what. Perhaps that was what she needed to jerk her out of her morass: a new field, a fresh interest, some kind of challenge that wasn't, like Marvin and the baby, bound up in her emotional life. She remembered the zest with which she had gone about educating herself when she'd first left home, the fever with which she had devoured the lecturing of Sprague Burrell. Dear Sprague—that was the electric excitement of youngness she lacked now. Who was to say there was no way of getting it back?

She pushed herself up from the couch and went back to her desk. She pulled the brochures out and spread them before her. Some of the covers mentioned the courses offered: history, economics, handicrafts, sculpture, music. . . . She still didn't have the time, did she? Marvin needed her, the baby needed her, the office needed her. God, she cried to herself, putting her head in her hands. Did they need the humorless mess she was now? Maybe it would be better in the long run for Marvin and the baby to put up with her having an outside interest, hoping to gain a wife and mother they could bear to have around later on. Marvin would be happy to provide extra household help, she knew; time and again he had asked her to hire someone besides Mrs. Kostmayer to help take the pressure off. She had not wanted other women doing the work she counted as a privilege; she had never really gotten used to the help Mrs. Kostmayer gave her with Joshua, as dependent on it as she had grown. But perhaps for the sake of a badly needed rejuvenation it would be worth it. She picked up the brochure nearest her hand. Sculpture. . . . That could be fun, learning to create something with her hands, a good antidote to nervous tension, at least. She looked through the brochure for details. Three nights a week, 7:00 to 9:00 P.M. An instructor's name that meant nothing to her. Two dollars per class, staggered courses beginning the second Monday of alternate months. The second Monday of the month would be next week. She could start the course next Monday if Marvin agreed to it. She flipped the intercom switch.

"Would you see if you can reach Doctor Kaufman at his office please? If he's at the hospital, don't bother him."

To Marvin that evening she explained it as boredom, the need for distraction from the round of diapers and formulas and office hours that had exclusively occupied her for the last ten months. Marvin's response was not heatedly enthusiastic, but he agreed to her taking the sculpture course and was even encouraging about what she might be able to accomplish as a Sunday sculptor. Helen registered for the course by telephone and sent the school a check to cover a semester's tuition.

The first meeting of the class proved to be an introductory lecture with the promise that on the second meeting they would start some basic modeling work with clay. Helen listened to the lecture with interest, but she felt still no fervor for the instruction to come. In the time that elapsed between the first class and the second she forgot to buy herself a smock to work in. The fact that the school had modeling clay for sale to enrollees was all that allowed her to profit from the second meeting of the class. The clay stuck to her fingers, the other men and women in the class were distractingly noisy, and the instructor's advice made no sense to her. With an inward sickened groan she prepared to face another failure to bring herself back to life again. At the end of the class she went to the women's washroom and scrubbed her hands as though she meant to wear the skin away.

She dawdled in the fourth floor hall of the school until most of the others had gone. She did not want to leave the building with that chattering, jovial pack of weirdies, and she did not want to face the subway ride alone just yet. In the forsaken mustiness of the hall there was a lonely comfort. Smoking her cigarette, waiting there idly, she found herself looking at a bulletin board, and the announcements pinned or stapled there arrested her attention. An open letter called for contributions to some Communist-sounding cause: the Defense of the Seven Minors. A smudge-edged card announced a series of admission-free concerts by an interpreter of primitive dances. A poster had something to say about the merging of the two giant labor unions.

The bulletin board fascinated her. She had thought this was another of the many organizations catering to adults wanting new hobbies, new interests, fresh friendships; she had not realized it had a political coloration. The Jefferson

School she had heard of, and she knew damn well she wasn't *there;* she couldn't tell *what* this outfit's coloration was. . . .

She wandered down to the next floor. There another bulletin board hung: the same labor union poster, but different notices. She read them all. She heard a class dispersing on the floor below. She looked over the balustrade to watch the students leaving. Young people, middle-aged people, shabby clothes, eccentric clothes: they were all talking volubly. The school, she thought, had an extremely garrulous student body. Soon they were gone out of the building, and Helen went down another flight. She could hear a single voice in the distance someplace; all else was still. On the second floor were two glass doors, and on one of them was gilded the word LIBRARY. A faint light shone within. She did not know whether the place was still officially open, but she realized that the disembodied voice she had dimly heard was coming from there. Perhaps a lecture, she thought. They probably wouldn't mind if she slipped in to listen, if she were quiet about it. She touched the knob diffidently. Venetian blinds hung on the other sides of the glass panels, and she could not tell whether there was a group of people inside or not. Gingerly she turned the knob. Its turning made no sound; she opened the door cautiously and stepped inside.

There was no one there. Reading lamps burned on the tables, but what looked like the librarian's desk was unoccupied. The shelves blocked her view except for the area immediately before her. Beyond them she heard a voice crying passionately, "And I tell you guys unless you make yourself heard, every damn one of you——"

Another voice from the opposite end of the library, equally masked by the shelves, called out, "Now wait a minute! Don't get so jived up yet, you'll wear the bastards out."

Helen realized she was interrupting and turned quickly to make an escape. Her heels clicked sharply on the floor, and and the second voice that had spoken said, "Hello?"

She threw her voice, as it were, over the barrier of the shelves. "I'm sorry, I didn't mean to barge in." She was aware of the figure moving into view to investigate the disturbance, but she did not stop to face him. She was halfway through the door when the voice said, "Helen? Helen Kaufman?" She stopped sharply. "For God's sake, that *is* you, isn't it?"

Helen turned back, astonished. Standing looking at her

from the library's aisleway was Steve Williams. She blinked a moment before she clearly recognized him. Then he was coming forward to her, smiling, his hands outstretched for hers.

"Helen Kaufman, what on earth are you doing in the New York Labor School? Looking for an earnest model?"

Helen laughed and gave her hands to him. "Steve, I didn't know what was going on," she apologized. "I just stumbled in, I didn't mean to screw anything up. You're busy."

"Hell, no." Steve laughed. "Not too busy for you." Over his shoulder he called, "Tiger? Take five. Come on out and meet a friend."

From around the barrier of bookshelves the sweating tousled-haired young orator appeared. Steve introduced him to Helen and again demanded to know what she was doing there. Helen, her composure not yet recovered, explained about having enrolled in the sculpture course, and Steve in turn told her of his project with Tiger.

"It's taken my attention away from my own work," he admitted, "but if I keep at it, I'll bet I make this guy the governor of New York one day."

"I didn't know you were a socialist," Helen said, more clearly understanding now the bulletin-board notices she'd read.

"I'm not," said Steve. "That's the damnedest thing about it."

Tiger laughed. "You two just don't dig how broad-minded we are around here."

"Could I listen in on the speech?" Helen asked Tiger.

Tiger blanched. "Why, you understand we're just practicing and——"

"I know, but—would it be all right?" She looked at her wrist watch. "I'm not in any rush, and I'd love to hear. Who knows, you might make a convert of me. Oh, please, let me. I'd like to so much."

Steve and Tiger consulted for a moment and with some hesitation agreed to let her stay. They took up their former positions at opposite ends of the long library, and Helen sat at one of the reading tables halfway between them. She sat back out of the light in the hope that Tiger would not be intimidated by her presence, but she soon realized her concern had been unnecessary. Tiger launched into his address with no thought for anything but the way he spoke and

Steve's occasional semaphoric directions from the other end of the room.

Helen listened to the speech with a mingled interest and amusement. The young Italian earnestness was vaguely funny at first, but as his oratory grew more passionate, she realized how strong an emotional pull he exerted. She found herself gripped by his arguments as his words defined the inexorable growth of labor's forces into a monolith. At the end of the speech she could imagine how spellbinding his burningly intense, unmannered method of speaking must be. Her applause when Tiger had finished sounded loudly in the room, and Tiger gave a start as though he had forgotten her presence. The three of them came together again in the middle of the library.

"Wow," Helen breathed, shaking hands with Tiger. "You had me mesmerized."

"What did I tell you?" Steve grinned.

"The really rough part," said Tiger earnestly, "comes later. When they start throwing questions at me from the floor."

"Lord, how I'd love to see you with a full house," said Helen. "That was terribly exciting."

Steve bragged, "Governor in ten years, President in twenty!"

But the bragging did not seem to please the young man. He glanced sharply at Steve, unsmiling. The tension lasted only a moment before he turned to Helen. "I'm going to have to high-tail it home. Juney's feeling lousy. I won't even get to be a state representative if that baby doesn't hurry up and get born."

He was pulling on his jacket. Helen asked, "Is this going to be your first baby?"

"Second," he answered. "It seems to take longer the second time. It isn't due until Christmas, and both Juney and I are already worn out with the idea. See you again if you're going to be around the night school."

"Oh, I will be."

"So long, Steve. Call you tomorrow."

"Fine, Tiger. Night."

He left Steve and Helen alone in the silent library. Steve invited Helen out for coffee, and after a moment's hesitation she accepted. He took her to the lunch counter in the next block from the Labor School.

As they walked down the street toward it, he explained, "This place is practically an annex of the Labor School, Tiger tells me. I wish to hell they'd air it out, but the coffee's good."

There were no other customers in the lunch counter. They sat down at an inadequate, shaky-legged table next to the plate-glass windows looking on the street, and Steve called their order over to the girl behind the counter.

Over their coffee, while they waited for it to cool, they exchanged disjointed reports of their activities since their last meeting. Steve told her of the film being made and the marvelous time Hilda Verges was having butting into it.

"It's all about Hilda," he explained. "So she's something of a technical adviser on the set, I gather. Self-appointed, you understand."

"Hilda's hardly the one to stand around waiting for somebody to appoint her," Helen observed. "Having a movie made must be doing you good, Steve. You know, I almost didn't recognize you. Last time I saw you, you looked—sort of haggard, or something. The day you came over, when Marvin's sister killed herself."

"I'm glad if I'm less repulsive now."

They drank their coffee and left.

When she was telling him good night at the entrance to the subway station, Helen said, "I hope I'll be seeing you around the school. It's so nice running into you again."

"In that case I'll just dovetail the practice schedule with Tiger to make sure we *do* meet."

"You're a terrible flirt!" She smiled at him.

"I'm sure Marvin could never find it in his heart to blame me."

At home that night Helen told Marvin about her having run into Steve, and passed on the news about the motion picture of Steve's story and Hilda Verges' activity in connection with it.

On the occasion of her fifth class, she met Steve again; the library was dark when she passed it on her way downstairs after her class, but in the hallway on the first floor she saw Steve talking with a young Negro girl. She made as if to pass them with a smiling nod, but Steve called out, "Hey, Helen, wait a minute." He said something to the Negro girl, and came over to her. "Nice to see you again. Tiger had to take off early. Would you let me buy you another cup of coffee?"

"Of course, Steve. I'd love it."

They went to the same place down the street. Sipping leisurely at their coffee, they talked easily, pleasantly, about Helen's work at the agency and the progress of the sculpture class, about the Labor School, Steve's new stories, and eventually about his plans for the future.

"I take it you're not going to make Tiger's speeches your career," Helen said.

"No. Only my hobby. You know about Robert Sherwood and Roosevelt? That's me and Tiger. Now that I've had a taste of it, I'd like to work on another screenplay sometime. Maybe I'll get the chance if everything goes all right with the present one. . . . I'm out of my shell." Steve smiled. "But I'm not rushing anything."

"I hope you marry again someday," Helen said.

Suddenly her cheeks fired. She had not expected the conversation to take so personal a turn. What business of hers was it to say anything about his marrying again? She changed the subject, but as the conversation went on, she found herself wondering about the man across the table from her. Not only was he handsome, he was talented as well, and he seemed to have taken a genuine liking to her. Was it an accident that this evening she had found him in the school's hallway after Tiger had already gone? She felt a warmth of pride that someone as nice as Steve Williams would find her attractive at a time when she felt herself a miserable specimen.

When they were ready to go, he gave her his arm as they walked to the door. She had grown used to Marvin's funny clumsiness; she had forgotten how pleasant it was to be seen being escorted by a really graceful man. Steve's movements were smooth, disciplined, assured. The masculine authority with which he ushered her through the door of the lunch counter made her feel queerly vulnerable.

Steve walked with her to the subway entrance.

"I'm going to hike home. I'm still too wide awake," he said. "So I'll leave you here."

"Good night, Steve. Thank you for the coffee."

"Thank you for joining me. Tell Marvin hello for me, won't you?" He touched her arm. "Good night," he said, and walked quickly away.

Helen found herself lingering at the entrance to the subway, watching where Steve had gone, smiling to herself. She gave a sigh, and a hint of shame began to nag her. Was she allowing herself to think too tenderly about him? He was certainly physically attractive, but that was no reason for her to stand mooning where he'd left her.

Turning, she hurried down the stairs.

On the subway ride, the nagging temptation stayed with her. She could not drive from her mind the image of Steve's sensitive eyes, not gentle, as Marvin's were, but filled with a brooding liquidness. Oh, God, she thought, this is awful. It wasn't as if she didn't know plenty of attractive men; she couldn't seriously entertain the possibility of being attracted to anyone to the point of unfaithfulness to Marvin, with Steve or with anyone else. She couldn't bring herself to be so unfair to Marvin even in her thinking when he'd always been so good to her. Besides, how did she know that Steve had any such thought in his head? He'd probably laugh out loud if he knew what she was thinking.

Chiding herself didn't help: sex didn't always stay where you put it; it jumped up and hit you in the face at the most unexpected, the worst of times. Surely Steve *did* find her attractive. It was his finding her so that made her enjoy their two meetings so much. Perhaps on his walk home he was thinking of her, too, wondering if . . .

"Look, stop it!" she told herself sternly. "This is dangerous as hell. Who do you think you are?" She wasn't really serious about him. She was only being tempted toward an affair that might, possibly, take her out of her maddening lethargy, a love-making that did not have the deadening comfort of social sanction, a relationship that existed for its own sake. She wasn't falling in love with him, was she?

A sickening thought shook her: she had only just met Steve when she'd married Marvin. Had they missed each other? Had she lost by such a hair the man she should have married? Oh, Christ, how could she be such a romantic? People weren't "meant" for each other, they chose each other, and she had chosen Marvin. She must put the thought of

Steve Williams out of her mind completely. She mustn't risk wrecking everything she and Marvin had created for themselves. . . . She bent her head into her hand. When the train reached her stop, she was trembling in her effort not to cry.

She told Marvin about the class as they dressed for bed.

"See anything of Steve?" Marvin asked.

"Steve Williams? No. No, he didn't seem to be around there tonight."

The bedside light turned out, she lay awake a long time, listening to the sound of Marvin's breathing. "You feel guilty," she told herself, "just for *imagining* being disloyal to Marvin. But you're enjoying it, too."

Having a secret, harboring a knowledge that no one could wrest from her, for the first time in months she felt adventurous, tremulously aware, awake again.

38

IN INTRODUCING TIGER TO HELEN, STEVE had boasted that Tiger would be governor in ten years, President in twenty. Tiger's unamused reaction to the remark bespoke a flaw in their friendship that ripped wide suddenly on a certain evening in November. Steve had been talking to Edith Mackey while Tiger tended to a piece of business in the party's offices upstairs. Tiger joined them, and in the bantering that preceded their departure Steve had made a similar, only half-joking remark about Tiger's future.

Once out on the street and out of Edith's earshot, Tiger turned on him angrily. "Will you do me a goddamned favor and stop saying things like that to people?"

Steve was sincerely baffled.

"You make jokes like I was some kind of character, somebody you think is pretty hilarious because I'm getting ahead and I'm not the guy you would've thought could do it."

"Tiger, I didn't—Jesus, whatever gave you the notion I had anything but admiration?"

"I'm *not* a character. Get that straight, Steve, and don't forget it again. And I'm no toy of yours, either, to amuse yourself with in your goddamned high-handed way!"

"High-handed! Tiger, look. I'm sorry if I've done anything——"

"*Don't* be sorry," Tiger shouted. "Be different. Get it through your head that I'm your equal in every way either of us cares about, and I don't like being treated as if I weren't." He turned and started down the street.

"Tiger. Wait!" Steve ran after him.

Tiger stopped, but he did not look ready to accept amends.

"I'm sorry," said Steve. "If I did anything patronizing, it was stupid on my part, and you're right to be angry. Tiger, I don't want our friendship to get messed up this way."

"Well, now you know how I feel, anyway. I gotta get home. I'll see you."

But for two weeks thereafter Steve heard no word from him or from Juney, and he was too ashamed of himself to risk calling them. He realized well enough that Tiger's accusation had been founded on fact. He *had* found the intense young radical something of a character. His mistake had been not to realize that Tiger, with his personal dignity and sensitiveness, would never stand for such treatment. He had had to turn on Steve if their relationship was ever to have anything about it that was not ludicrous.

One night Steve had gone to bed early and had been asleep an hour when he was awakened by the sound of someone banging on the kitchen door. He got up, turned on the light, and stumbled out to see who was there.

It was Tiger. "You were asleep," he said. "I'm sorry, Steve, but it's important."

"Sure." Steve waved him in groggily. "How'd you get in the building?"

"I rang somebody else. Your doorbell's not loud enough."

"I'll have it seen to, I assure you. For God's sake tell me. What's wrong?"

They settled themselves near the still-glowing ashes of the evening's fire, and Steve, now more awake, lit a cigarette.

"I've been at a meeting of some men," Tiger said, "with—no, I won't tell you the name of the union yet. It's an independent, a rich one. Steve, I stumbled right into a stink that's gonna gas this whole state. . . ." His eyes were shining like black coal.

"You don't look disturbed about it," Steve observed. "You look jubilant."

"I am"—Tiger shrugged—"for personal reasons. Otherwise I'm mad as hell about the whole stinking deal."

"Go on."

"This independent's been talking A.F.L. affiliation for months now—that much I happen to know—and the rank and file seem to want it. There's an election for them coming up, and a new strong man is rearing his Ginzo head. One, guess who?—Al so-help-me-God Gustineo!"

"Who's he?" Steve yawned.

"Don't you remember, for Christ's sake? I *told* you about him. He's a crook, a criminal. I didn't even know he was in New York, but if he is, it can't mean but one thing: he's turned into a syndicate-boy. That's what Al always wanted. And if he's muzzling into this union, he's providing a front for Weingard and Giagharelli."

"Racketeers?"

"The lousiest. I'm glad to say I never met 'em. That's a long story. Steve, I gotta stop 'em, I gotta keep 'em out of that union!"

"So?"

"I need your help. I need speeches. I need speeches like crazy, I need a whole fucking campaign to back up the legit people running in the election. I been years waiting for this chance——"

"What're you talking about?"

"Steve, are you listening or not? Al Gustineo's the guy I used to clout cars for in Chicago!"

Steve uncrossed his legs sharply, and his foot hit the floor with a thud. All of a sudden he was completely awake, remembering the first interviews they'd had.

Tiger was going on excitedly. "Even back when I knew him Al was talking about the unions as the big payload of the future. The rackets are nothing new in unions, but this independent has as clean a slate as you can find in the business. I ain't gonna let Al Gustineo go fucking it up when they're on the brink of an affiliation!"

"You got it in for him personally?" Steve asked.

"For Al? Why the hell should I? Al's a menace, but he was always good to *me*. He helped me every way he could."

"Then why is this a personal crusade?"

Tiger was on his feet then, pacing. "I've been haunted, Steve, for years. I've been having nightmares about the things

I did when I was working for Al." He turned to face Steve, and his eyes were anguished. "There's no way I can make up, except go straight. I can't return the cars. I can't restore to the people what I clouted from them. But I *can* keep Al and his kind out of the labor movement. I can, because I've got the goods on them. I don't want to see Al behind bars, nothing like that. But I want to keep this independent clean and any other union he tries to muscle in on." He moved quickly toward Steve. "It's like what you'd call poetic justice, you know? I'd feel clean again myself if I could swing that election out of the rackets' hands. Will you help me, Steve?"

Steve contemplated the fevered, earnest face, trying to imagine the years that must have had to be suffered by anyone as earnest as Tiger Rizzuto: the nightmares of crimes committed that many another would have felt were satisfied by repentance and reform. The temperament of a Tiger Rizzuto clearly thirsted for a greater expiation than that and trembled before the sight of it when it was offered to him.

"Are you free tomorrow morning?" Steve asked.

"Any time, any time."

"Come over and have breakfast with me around nine. We can talk more then, and my head'll be clearer."

"But you'll help me, Steve? . . . Oh, Christ, thanks, I'm your friend for life."

"Now get the hell home," Steve said, standing up. "I'm going back to bed."

Steve saw Helen often in the weeks following, but the pattern of their meetings was unvaried. He would take Helen out for coffee after her class and, after an hour's conversation, would escort her to the subway. The variation occurred in the nature of their talks together. As they saw more of each other, their conversation grew more intimate. Steve found Helen easy to talk to: she could banter and she could be serious; she responded to his moods deftly and smoothly. She was as chic and as charming as Maggie had been, he considered, but she was simpler, earthier, even in a way more womanly. One evening, leaving her, he had been thrown off guard by a sudden impulse to kiss her good night. He recovered himself in time, but afterward he wondered if Helen had not been hoping he would kiss her.

In a letter to Hilda Verges he had mentioned seeing Helen

again, and on the morning of Christmas Eve there arrived at the studio, along with a scattering of Christmas cards, a letter addressed to Helen in care of himself.

He called Helen at her office.

"There's a letter here for you from Hilda Verges. I guess she doesn't know your address. Shall I bring it by the agency?"

"Oh, Steve, that'd be far too much trouble," she said. "I'm leaving in a few minutes to do some last-minute shopping. Will you be home in about—oh, half an hour, if I stopped by then?"

"Sure, all day."

"*May* I stop by then? I didn't mean to invite myself."

"Of course," Steve said. "I'll give you a holiday wassail."

"Wonderful!" Her voice smiled over the wire. "I'll see you in a little while."

Steve hung up, but his hand rested on the phone, and he sat deep in thought. Maybe he was jumping the gun, but he had increasingly the feeling Helen wanted him to make a pass at her. She was such a sweet girl—could she seriously think of doing something like that to such a nice guy as Marvin? He wished he had insisted on bringing Helen's letter to her office. She was much too attractive to have alone in the apartment, and he had been too long continent. If she actually wanted to play around behind her husband's back, he was not certain he was anyone to resist the offer. "Damn!" he said, aloud, and jumped up to distract himself from the erection the thought of intercourse brought on.

He made sure there was some liquor to serve and filled an ice bucket with cubes from the refrigerator. A friendly holiday drink, that's all it would be—a half-business visit from a happily-married woman who was a friend of his. There would be no nonsense, he told himself. She was going shopping, wasn't she? The whole thing was the product of his imagination.

Helen did not hurry as she walked up Lexington Avenue toward Forty-seventh Street. The avenue was crowded with Christmas shoppers, and from stores along the way carols called out into the icy air. Approaching she knew not what, Helen felt an unnatural quietness inside herself. There was a presence of fatality, she felt, in a letter for her having been sent by Hilda to Steve's care. That he should have called her today, when everyone was expected to be busy with assorted holiday preparations, when odd hours of the day did not have to be accounted for to anyone—so small a circumstance conspired to arrange the setting. The rest could only be her responsibility, and Steve's, if anything happened between them.

It *would* happen, it was certain now, and she refused to regret it. Why should she fear it? A passing adventure, nothing permanent, nothing that need disrupt, and it would feed her hunger once and for all. It had been the first thought of the possibility of an affair with Steve that had defined for her her hunger and her restlessness. If Steve wanted her, she would not put him off.

She turned into Forty-seventh Street. In the little vestibule she found his name beneath one of the buttons. Her ring was answered by a buzzing sound, and she pushed the door open. From somewhere in the rear on the ground floor she heard Steve call, "I'm back here, Helen. Just follow the hall when it turns."

She picked her way carefully through the twisting of the unlighted corridor. Then, at a turning, she saw Steve standing in an open door.

"Hi, Merry Christmas, come on back."

"It's a long way, isn't it? Merry Christmas, Steve."

"The studio's tacked on to the back of the house," he explained as she came toward him.

He showed her in. She followed him through the kitchen into the studio proper. Steve took her coat and hung it up. Before she could speak, he said, "I'll fix us a drink, if you have time."

"Thanks, I'd love one."

"Rye is all that gives, I'm afraid."

"That'd be fine," said Helen.

She moved forward into the room. It was a comfortable, charming place, arranged with masculine casualness, filled with and warmed by the glow of the fireplace and . . .

She stopped abruptly. On the wall above the fireplace was a portrait. A girl. Steve's dead wife, she concluded. Slowly she released the breath she had caught, when her eyes had fallen on the picture. Behind her in the kitchen she could hear Steve fixing the drinks; he would not have noticed her surprise, or now her chagrin. She studied the face of the girl in the picture. She was delicately lovely, eagerly young. She was not, Helen suspected, examining the portrait more closely, the kind of girl any man could lightly love. In the expression of the eyes, the painter had caught a dancing, tantalizing glint of something unpossessable. And Steve still kept her portrait here? . . .

She heard him coming in and turned to force a smile. She indicated the portrait as he handed her the drink.

"That's exquisite," was all she said.

"It's a portrait of Maggie," said Steve. "My wife. She wasn't much more than a child when it was painted. Won't you sit down, Helen?" He sat down in the chair across from her. "Season's greetings," he said. He drank deeply from his glass. "Did you get your shopping done?"

"Not yet," Helen smiled. "It's only odds and ends. The hefty stuff is done." She put down her glass and in her bag found a cigarette. Steve got up to light it for her. "Thank you," Helen said, and her eyes moved to the picture again. "How extraordinarily lovely she must have been."

"Yes," he answered somewhat sharply.

Helen realized she had touched something sore in him and regretted it. She swallowed some of her drink. Angrily, desiringly, frustratedly, she watched him as he sat across from her. His features were strong, but finely drawn, and beneath the curve of his dark eyebrows, the deep blueness of his eyes lent to his aspect a shattering sensuousness. She noted the muted stylishness of the clothes he wore and tantalized herself about the clothes underneath—the odd gracelessness of boxer shorts, the general roughness of men's underclothes that was so foreign, always, to a woman. Despite her nearness to the fireplace, her hands felt like lifeless slabs of ice.

"Drink up," Steve was saying. "No one slug ever got Christmas on its feet."

Did he want her to get tight? Did he want to prime her to be seduced? she asked herself. If only he wanted her, if only he would show a sign she could be sure of. . . .

"What about Hilda's Letter?" Helen asked. If that was the excuse for being there, the least she could do was make a show of interest in it.

"Oh, I almost forgot it. I'm enjoying having company so much," said Steve.

He fetched it from the bookshelf. "Please don't mind my presence, Helen, go ahead and read it."

With a practiced flip of her fingernail she had the envelope open and the letter in hand. She pretended to read the scrawled lines, but could not take them in. She made a smiling, meaningless comment and stowed the perfumed page in her bag.

"Come on, won't you have another drink?" Steve asked.

Helen hesitated. "All right, Steve."

He took the glasses and disappeared into the kitchen. She wished he knew how unnecessary it was for him to soften her up with drinks. There was something ugly about his plying her with liquor in the classic game, something unworthy of the idea she had formed of Steve, of the two of them as an entity. She got up and stepped over to the fireplace. She stood looking down into its shimmering flames. How sweetly he could do it, if he really wanted to, how gently invite her to his love. Well, it apparently wasn't to work that way. They would drink, if only to blind themselves to guilt, and when their hearts were blunted sufficiently, he would be coming over to her, embracing her, and there would be a violent grappling and a hungry, loveless, willful coming together of their bodies, her legs around him on the bed over there, his weight pressed on her, arrogant and affectionless.

She forced herself to look up at the portrait of his beautiful dead wife. She would be watching them. She would be looking, mute, upon their drinking and their intercourse. Her head reeled, and she had to look away from the picture. Oh, God, what kind of mess had she brought herself into now? Perhaps it wasn't wrong to have an affair with him; perhaps adults should feel free to mate as they ate and drank and slept, but the shabbiness of it was more than she could stand.

I'm bourgeois, she said to herself then, and screw the whole shooting match. Had she lost her mind, coming to his apartment this way, proclaiming to him her availability? If that was the case, why was she waiting, what was the value of coyness, why didn't she take his hand and put it on her breast herself, offer herself to him openly, unblinkingly?

Her face was hot with the shame she felt, and she thought suddenly of her mother and father. Had she forgotten who she was? Her grandfather's face loomed suddenly in the prospect of her mind. What would *he* have thought of her? He was no prude, but a strong, just man. He would have put her down for a fool. Helen caught her breath.

She *had* forgotten who she was, and now, dismayed that she should ever have been able to forget, she began to remind herself grimly, as a stern mentor might have made her repeat over again forgotten multiplication tables: a Maclean, and on her mother's side a Bergson and a Lyle and from far, far back in the past, a Smithfield. These had not been shabby people. It was because she was all of them that she had started out so determinedly on her life, wasn't it?—because she was all of them, condensed into the end product of the lines, that she had fought to make something of herself, to learn, to establish herself in the world, to grow. For this?—to mar and dirty what she had accomplished with a messy little sex party behind her rightful husband's back?

The tears burned themselves through her eyes. She should have learned long ago that that notion of sophistication was a fake. Sprague Burrell had done his inadvertent best to teach her. What was the meaning of studying and working, of all the years she had been through, if she ended without goodness or rightfulness of even so much as a spine in her character? All that time she had been preparing herself for her role. She had her role now, in Marvin and in Joshua. The preparation was over. Her attention should be on the role itself now. Nothing else could hope to make any sense.

Behind her Steve said, "Helen. Helen, are you all right?"

She gave a start, but quickly recovered. She shook her head without turning to him. "No, not really," she said. "God, I think your whisky went to my head. I—I suppose it's too early in the day for me."

"Oh, I'm sorry. I know what a miserable feeling it is when it hits you from behind that way. May I get you anything?"

She pressed her eyes with her fingertips, and when she decently could, she turned to face him.

"I really—" she began, but stopped. "I really should get on with the shopping," she concluded.

"It was nice having you come by." Steve smiled. He put

the newly mixed drinks aside. "Let me help you with your coat."

He brought the coat to her and helped her into it.

She gave him her hand and held his gaze a moment. She wondered if he knew all that had been happening to her since she'd come into the studio. His smile was reassuringly bland, and Helen gave a sigh.

"Merry Christmas, Steve," she said.

"Merry Christmas, Helen."

As soon as she reached the apartment, she sent Mrs. Kostmayer off for the holiday and spent the afternoon tending the baby herself. Chattering with the infant, she found little trouble in cooking dinner as well, and she took the baby with her when she went to get ready for the evening. They bathed together gleefully, and when he had been dressed Helen propped him up in the middle of her bed. He watched her gravely while she got into a new dinner dress and finished putting on her make-up and brushing her hair. Her nonstop patter distracted the baby from the temptation of crawling to the edge of the bed and falling off it onto the floor. They were both ready when Marvin came in from work.

For the first time since his birth, the baby stayed with them through cocktails and dinner. Conversation was not easy, but their fractured exchanging of gossip and holiday plays had a cheerfulness and excitement that brought to Marvin's expression a smiling placidity Helen realized had been long absent. When the baby had been put to bed, they busied themselves decorating the Christmas tree, and while they did so, Helen bragged about her banishment of Mrs. Kostmayer and the efficiency with which she had cooked dinner as well as readied herself and baby for Marvin's homecoming.

The medium-sized Christmas tree did not take long to finish. They sat together on the sofa to admire their handiwork and the twinkling of the colored lights. Helen's arm slipped through Marvin's, and she leaned her cheek against his shoulder.

For a long while they were silent; then Marvin said, "Helen?"

"Yes, darling?"

"It's curious as hell. . . ." He stopped.

"What is?"

"Nothing. I shouldn't have started it."

"It's all right, Marvin. Go on."

"Well, I apologize for starting it. Hell, I shouldn't ask questions—a woman's got a private right and a husband shouldn't go bungling into it."

"Tell me what you have in mind, Marvin," she insisted gently.

"I was thinking. In the beginning I had a devoted, beautiful young wife. Then suddenly, in some way I can't put my finger on, she disappeared. Some twelve months or so go by, and just as unaccountably she's back again. Is it because it's Christmas? Am I nuts? Am I way off the beam?"

Helen looked up at him and smiled. "No, you're not, Marvin. You're too smart a man, and you know me too well to make that kind of mistake. I have been away, I guess —oh, Marvin, I've had the longest postpartum blues in history. I'm so grateful to you for putting up with it."

They both knew there would be no need to say anything more, and the telephone rang.

"Damnation," Marvin said. "If that's a call——"

"If that's a call, you'll take it like a good boy."

"I could get someone else to go instead."

"Nobody's as good as you," Helen said. "I can wait up for you."

"Are you sure, Helen?" he asked.

"I'll wait up as long as you want me to, Marvin. It's high time I started behaving like a doctor's wife without crying in my beer about it. Go answer the phone and tell them you're on your way."

His arms went around her, and his kiss was no longer the dutiful husbandly salute, but a happy masculine seeking.

Hours later, after Marvin had come back, after they had talked and danced to the music of the phonograph awhile, they lay together in Marvin's bed, their bodies damp with the sweat of loving, their voices cotton soft in the darkness.

"Helen."

"Darling?" her voice returned.

There was a pause. The whisper came through the darkness hesitantly.

"Helen," he said, "I'm going to love you deeper and deeper

the longer we live." He drew a breath. "But I don't think I'm ever going to love you any more thankfully than I do right this minute."

Her lips were against his moist chest; she smiled in the darkness.

"I thought the same thing," she said. "Earlier today. I never thought of it that way before. Not until today."

After a time had passed, she got up to go to the bathroom and find her bobbypins and comb. When she came back into the room, Marvin had turned on the light and was reading. She stood in the doorway watching him. For a long time he had not read anything before going to sleep, with or without their having had intercourse. It was a comfortable, married, pleasant thing for him to do, she thought, and out of his own sensitive instincts he had done without it while he had done without the wife that was his by right. Helen felt a sense of deliverance that he was able to read comfortably in bed again.

On the dressing table a magazine lay. She took it with her to her own bed and propped it on her knees to read while she put up her hair. There would be desultory talk, she knew, comment on the things each of them was reading. It was a warm and splendid time of night.

"Marvin, you know what's nice about marriage?"

"Yes, but what's *your* notion?"

She acknowledged his leer with a click of her tongue against her teeth, and then she said, "What's nice about marriage is that if you're just on a date, you have to shake hands or kiss good night and you go home and the party's over. But when you're married, the evening isn't over. You can go home with your husband and swap ideas about how somebody was looking and what somebody said about Proust or Senator McCarthy. The evening doesn't end at all but draws out into love and into a glass of milk and crackers, and cold cream on your face, and lazy talk, and before you know it, you're asleep and still the party hasn't ever really ended. You've never had to close the front door and go up alone to your room. It's no wonder people take marriage so seriously."

"No wonder at all," said Marvin.

When the article she was reading made her think of it, she said, "Darling?"

"Yes?"

"I'm not really disturbing you? I'm sorry I'm so garrulous."

"You're not disturbing me, sweet. What did you want to tell me?"

"Let's not see *Guys and Dolls* on New Year's Eve. We have the record, and I like it so much. I don't want to risk seeing the show itself."

"They say it's a great show."

"I know," Helen said. "I just want to spoil myself."

"Go ahead."

A silence while they smoked their cigarettes. "Marvin. You know what I want to do instead of going to see *Guys and Dolls?"*

"What?"

"I want to have just a handful of friends in for a drink with us. Really a handful, maybe three or four. Would you like that?"

"There're so few friends I see any more——"

"I could ask people *I* see that I think you'd like. How would you like that?"

"Better than anything else in the world." Marvin smiled over at her sleepily. "Except these last two hours."

In the bouyant, joyous day that followed, after the presents were exchanged and breakfast eaten and games played with the baby, who was suitably awed by the spectacle of the clumsily assembled tree and the general eruption of tissue paper and Christmas ribbon around the room, Helen asked Marvin again about New Year's Eve, and again, on his way out to see his patients, he agreed. Helen put the baby down for a nap after his noontime feeding. Alone, she poured herself another cup of coffee. Then she carried the telephone into the living room and called Warren Taggert.

"Hi, Helen," Warren's voice answered over the phone. "A large shot of Noel to you. Did you have a good one?"

"Oh, the finest. And you, Warren?"

"I had Christmas breakrast with some friends of mine, and I came out on top with a magnificent lithograph for a present."

"Warren, Marvin and I are going to have a sane New Year's Eve here at our place," Helen said. "I wondered if you'd spend part of it, at least, being sane with us."

"Why, sure, I'd love to."

"And bring a date, of course."

"Oh, I won't I don't think," Warren said.

"Warren. Not on New Year's *Eve?*"

He chuckled. "I regret it, but I'm a sorry old bachelor, and no one would have me."

"Oh—well, bring yourself then. We'll be ready from nine o'clock on, so any time that suits you, show up."

"I will," he answered. "And thank you, Helen. Tell Marvin and the baby Merry Christmas for me, won't you?"

She debated inviting Jules Fischel and his wife, but decided against it. Ladd Dorn wouldn't be a very good idea, either. She was tempted to postpone calling Steve for a few days, but she knew the sooner she got it over, the easier it would be. She dialed his number.

"Hello?"

"Steve, it's Helen," she said. "Merry Christmas."

"Merry Christmas, Helen. It's a gorgeous day, isn't it? Have you been out?"

"Not yet. Look, Marvin and I want you to come have a drink with us New Year's Eve. Can you?"

"I'd like to very much," he said. "You having a real blow-out?"

"No, just a handful," Helen said.

"Fine. I can't tell you how glad I am you're asking me. I was faced with subjecting some poor unsuspecting female to a round of pub-crawling. What time do you want me to get there?"

"Any time after nine. It's really a very offhand party."

"Wonderful. By the way," he told her, "Tiger's wife had another girl this morning."

"Really? On Christmas!" Helen exclaimed in a tone of mock regret. "Now the poor little thing will never have her own birthday. Is Tiger furious it wasn't a boy?"

"No I don't think so," Steve said. "He's too busy being grateful it finally got here. Look, I don't know whether Juney will still be in the hospital, but if she is—I know this is presumptuous, Helen, but—could I bring Tiger with me to your house New Year's Eve?"

"Certainly, we'd love it," Helen answered. "I'll call him a little later to ask him. Would that be all right?"

"You're a good woman, Mrs. Kaufman."

"Thank you. Good-by, Steve," she said.

Warren, Steve, Tiger, and Marvin: herself and four men, just like that. What, she thought, could be more heavenly? She'd be damned if she'd invite another soul. She left the telephone and went to make sure the baby was sleeping soundly.

With Edith Mackey's help, Steve traced Tiger to the union hall a few days later.

"Steve, we're winning it! We're creaming Gustineo. He hasn't got a chance! The legits are already celebrating, and Tom Henderson says the affiliation is in the bag—Steve, you stupid sonuvabitch, why aren't you crying like me?"

"I'm happy for you, Tiger. I'm glad you did it," Steve said.

It was ten minutes before he could quiet Tiger enough to ask if he had accepted the Kaufmans' invitation.

"Hell, yes, Helen called me on Christmas Day. Look, I gotta get up to the hospital and tell Juney about what we did. Shit, her complications are gonna go right out the fucking window when she hears about this; I haven't told her a word yet about Al being in the picture and——"

"Fine, fine," said Steve. "Give her my love, and tell her I'll be up to see her tomorrow afternoon."

"I'm taking deep breaths," Tiger said over the phone. "You know how many years it's been since I could take a really deep breath? I'm breathing again, Steve, just like everybody else who never clouted a car. You got yourself a crown in heaven, you heathen, and you'll probably need it, too. G'bye!"

Helen spent the day of the party cleaning the apartment and replacing the burned out lights on the Christmas tree. At four o'clock her hair was up in curlers and cold cream covered her face. "Damn!" she said when the doorbell rang. She hurried back through the apartment to the nursery. Mrs. Kostmayer, whom she had called in to help her with the preparations for the party, was playing with the baby.

"Mrs. Kostmayer, would you mind answering the door for me?" Helen asked. "I don't know who it could be at this hour of the day; I don't dare answer it looking like this."

"Sure, Mrs. Kaufman, be glad to," the nurse said. She waddled heavily out of the room, leaving the baby with Helen.

In a moment she was back again, grinning with her announcement.

"It's a young soldier," she beamed. "He says he's your brother, Mrs. Kaufman."

Helen cried out, incredulous, "Danny?"

"I showed him into the living room," Mrs. Kostmayer said.

"Danny's *here?*"

Her heart leaped inside her, and tears of surprise stung her eyes as she gave the baby over to Mrs. Kostmayer again. Forgetting her appearance, she had flung out of the nursery and was running down the hall.

"Danny!" she shouted. "Danny, what are you doing here?"

He stood up when she came into the room. She hesitated only an instant before she ran forward into his open arms.

"Oh, Danny! My own brother! What a wonderful Christmas present, my own little brother here!"

"Did I really surprise you?" Danny laughed. "I surprised myself, finding you without any directions."

"Danny, Danny, for God's sake, how long are you here for?" she demanded.

Danny's face fell. He did not look into her eyes but at the cap he held awkwardly in his hands.

"Don't be angry, Helen," he said, "but I only have a couple of hours. I'm on my way to a new post. In Texas, natch."

Helen wailed. "You're going to spend New Year's Eve on a *train?* Oh, Danny!"

"I'm afraid so," the young man shrugged. "It won't be too bad, Helen; a couple of buddies of mine are getting on at Washington. If our wires don't get crossed, we'll celebrate New Year's Eve like crazy on the train. Hey, can I see my nephew?"

"Joshua!" Helen remembered with a laugh. "Of course. I've never thought of him as being your nephew before. Come on back, Danny."

She led him to the nursery and presented the baby to him. As he bounced the wide-eyed Joshua gently in his arms, Helen studied her brother, trying to accustom herself to the thought that the dreadful little brat from Charter Oak had grown into this bass-voiced gangling young man. His features had coarsened with maturity, and his hair was several shades darker. He was not handsome, but the straightness of his nose and the strong line of the jaw were attractive. He had, Helen thought, turned out well; she felt a swell of pride in him.

Remembering her appearance, she found a towel and wiped the excess cold cream from her face. There was nothing she could do about her hair, it would have to stay up in curlers.

When they were alone in the living room again, Helen mixed a drink for her brother, and they sat down to talk. The family was all well, Danny reported, and their mother seemed resigned to the fact that he would be going on to Korea after his additional training stint.

"You know who I saw at home?" he offered. "Of all people, she wanted to know how you were. Ione Nelson. Remember old Mrs. Nelson, the one who was always sick, lived down the street from us?"

"Of course I do." Helen chuckled. "I should've thought she'd be dead by now. I'm glad she remembers me." She laughed. "Oh, Lord, but it's good seeing you again, Danny. Marvin is going to be mad as hell that he missed you. We're having some friends over for drinks tonight—it would've been so much fun if you could've been with us."

"I wish I could," her brother answered, with patently genuine regret. He lit a cigarette. "Helen, are *you* getting along all right, huh? I mean, you're really happy and all?"

"Very much so," she nodded, touched by his concern.

"Last time you were home—well, you'd turned into such a nice girl, not so snotty as you were before," he explained. "The main reason I came to New York was—I wanted to make sure you were happy. Before leaving the country and all."

Helen smiled at him and put her hand on his. "Thank you, Danny," she said. "You *will* be coming back, you know. The peace talks might come to something before you even get to Korea."

"It does look like it might be grinding to a halt."

"Hold the thought," said Helen.

They talked for an hour more: of the war, of the training Danny had been through, of Marvin and the baby. When, after another drink and a tender, embarrassed farewell kiss, he had left, Helen sat for a long time by herself in the living room, thinking of the stick-legged sullen little boy Danny had been in Charter Oak. So much time had passed. . . . She gave herself a shake and applied her attention to the work remaining for her before the party would begin.

39

THERE WAS A GLOW OF LEMON LIGHT and greenery in the living room of the Kaufmans' apartment, and in one corner the Christmas tree twinkled. Around the room were vases of poinsettias, and the gleaming glass ash trays and scattered bowls of nuts and pumpkin seeds bespoke the beginning of a party. Helen and Marvin were both dressed and ready for their guests. Helen put records on the phonograph and adjusted the volume to an unobtrusive level. Show tunes, lively and popular, awoke the attractive room to its full readiness, and the first of their guests, Steve Williams and Tiger Rizzuto, arrived.

Helen introduced Tiger to Marvin.

"Helen's told me a lot about you," said Marvin. "Run for office soon so I can vote for you. And congratulations on the new daughter, by the way."

"Congratulations would not be amiss," Steve said, "for another small item. Tiger has single-handedly rescued a pet union of his from the encroachment of mobsters."

Helen caught but did not understand the sudden look of chagrin Steve threw at Tiger, as though he realized he had said something regrettable and hadn't meant to. As little did she understand Tiger's answering half-smile.

"Relax, friend," he reassured Steve.

"What union?" Helen asked. "What did you do, Tiger?"

"Steve and I did it together," Tiger said, "if the truth were told. We're a vaudeville team, you know."

"I want to hear every detail," said Helen. "But let me see what you two will have to drink first. Marvin's spreading himself tonight. We've got everything but benedictine."

"We can always send out for benedictine." Marvin shrugged broadly.

Marvin mixed the drinks, and Helen took their coats. When they were reassembled, Helen asked after Juney and the baby, and Steve and Marvin fell into conversation about Steve's film.

"It should open in New York around June," Steve said. "I want all of you to come and hold my hand through the premiere. Or hold my head is maybe more to the point."

To Helen, Tiger was saying, "She looks just like Elizabeth did when she was born. I wish I knew a diet that could get us a blond baby. Boy or girl, I don't care, I just wish we could have a blond in the family." He lowered his voice then. "Helen, I feel like a jerk asking this but—I didn't catch your husband's first name when you introduced us."

"It's Marvin."

"Marvin. That's what I thought, but I wasn't sure. Oh, a fine politician I'm going to make."

At Helen's insistence he told her about the union election in which Al Gustineo had been roundly defeated and Gustineo's future opportunities in the labor movement crippled. Helen listened to the story with marveling attention. When, soon after, she had to excuse herself, Tiger found himself alone beside a low bookcase whose upper surface held a trio of brilliantly colorful porcelain roosters. Marvin Kaufman, he thought. When first he'd heard it, when he had been introduced to Helen's husband at the door, he had thought it sounded familiar. Now he was sure. That had been the name of Zeeda's brother, the young doctor who had identified her body. Marvin Kaufman. Well, it was no time to bring up the fact. Forget it. The poor guy deserved to have it left behind. All of them deserved it. . . . He moved over toward Steve's and Marvin's conversation.

Helen watched the three men as they talked, wondering how much Marvin had guessed of what had happened—or almost happened—between herself and Steve. If he knew anything, he did not show it. She said a silent prayer of gratitude.

When Warren Taggert arrived, there was a moment of clumsiness while Marvin began to introduce Tiger. He stumbled even with the names he knew, and gave it up. "Hell, I don't know any of you that well yet." They introduced themselves.

"Tiger Rizzuto?" Warren repeated when Tiger mentioned his name. "Haven't we ever—no, I guess not, People are always saying that at New York parties. It's enough to drive you wild. How do you do."

Helen fixed Warren's drink while Marvin freshened the others. Presently she put the recording of the *Guys and Dolls* score on the phonograph, and when the brash, vigorous music became danceable, first Marvin, then Warren, asked her to dance. She had never danced with Warren Taggert before, and his ability delighted her. They spoke to one another very little while they danced, and Helen thought bemusedly of the irony of his presence in her home. She was well aware that for all his typical-American-youth steeliness of wrist and spine there was a lack of crude ore in him, but he was plainly a member of that unmentionable elite, the American priviledged class. She could not help considering that, when she had been a little girl and her brother Danny the primary cross she'd had to bear in life, Warren Taggert or anyone like him would have been social universes away from her attainment. The world had turned over in those few years so contortively, so reasonlessly, that now he was a guest in her apartment, and she was the wife of a brilliant young Jewish doctor, and nothing was as she had anticipated. Everything was different, everything was surprisingly, unpredictably better.

Later Helen and Marvin and their guests were sitting in a loosely organized circle around the room. Nearest to Helen, on the sofa, were Warren and Steve. They were discussing Phillip Houghton's television show.

"I believe I met him once," Steve said to Warren, "at some do in Washington. My wife—she's dead now—was a Washington girl."

He frowned at Steve wonderingly. "You said your name was Steve Williams? Yes, that was the name. Oh, Lord. You were married to Margaret Cowan, weren't you?"

"Yes, I was," Steve replied.

"I'll be damned," Warren said. "I knew Margaret. Not very well, you understand. I knew Mike Cowan better. He was a great friend of mine."

Steve registered the connection, but in his own mind reined in the supposition. Was this guy one of Mike Cowan's pansy boy friends? He didn't look it. But then neither had Mike.

Steve lifted his glass and with a twist of his head said, "Small world, all right."

"Do you ever see Mike any more?" Warren asked.

"No, I haven't in a long time."

"We—lost track of one another long ago," Warren said.

"If you're with Phillip Houghton," said Steve, "you should get to know your competitor over there."

Tiger looked up at the remark. "Meaning me?"

"Tiger's a professional radical," Steve explained to Warren. "The white hope of the Demo-Socialist Party."

"You're really a socialist?" Warren asked Tiger.

"Yes, I am."

"It seems old-fashioned somehow, as though you had said you were a Whig. Don't you think the D.S.P. is on its way out?"

"Hardly. At the moment we are busily engaged in promoting a merger of the two largest labor organizations in the world. Does that sound as though it were—were—oh, hell, Steve!"

"Moribund," Steve provided.

"Thanks."

"I hate to think of what it's going to be like when they're merged. Frankly, I find their audacity appalling enough as it is."

"Audacity? Is it audacious for workingmen to stand up for their rights? Tell me what you think—I really want to know."

"Labor has no right to assume control of industries that were conceived and nurtured by businessmen with more sense of adventure and more guts than ordinary men. Ordinary men have to work for a living—hell, *I* have to work for a living. But I don't feel that gives me the right to dictate to Phillip Houghton what the policies of his magazine must be or whom he shall or shall not invite to be on his television program. The unions are heading straight for a pratfall."

Tiger answered banteringly, unoffended, "Got your brown shirt all cleaned and ready for the occasion?"

Warren's glance was skeptical, and smiling, he shook his head. "All the labels you've got," he said. "Don't you know Hilter lost the war? You're beating a dead horse."

"McCarthyism is no dead horse," said Tiger.

"Hey," Marvin said, "this is New Year's Eve, you two, and it's supposed to be a party!"

"It's all right, darling," said Helen.

"No, it isn't," Warren admitted. "I'm sorry I opened my big mouth. Both of us are."

Steve could sense the real anger, which had risen to just beneath the surface of their dispute, subsiding now. Neither Tiger nor Warren, he thought, was uncivilized enough not to be able to accept their differences. Steve raised his glass. "What do we drink to? To your intellectual elite, Warren? To Tiger's high regard for ordinary men? For the moment, how about to both?"

"Fair enough," said Warren.

Marvin danced with Helen a second time, and when the others were paying no attention to them, he said, "They're a fine group, Helen—I didn't know you had such nice friends. We ought to see more of them. With the practice—I don't know, I don't think we see enough really interesting people."

"Would you really like to, Marvin? You're as busy with medicine as I am with the baby and the agency, but if I knew you *wanted* us to see more of people——"

"I do," Marvin said. "These are good people. They're poles apart in some ways. I should have known you'd have catholic tastes to the point of wildness."

As the evening passed, the talk was free-flowing and diverse, and Helen noted the drinking was moderate for a New Year's Eve. It was, she thought, exactly the kind of party she had wanted, her secret celebration that she was a happy woman, rich in love, eager for the years ahead of her, the two or three babies more she hoped now she would have, the friendships she and Marvin would know, the deep-abiding contentment that would replace the younger yearning for excitement. After midnight, she reminded herself, she had better see to it that everyone got fed.

Some time later Helen found herself momentarily alone near the serving bar. She had been adding fresh ice cubes to her drink, but she stopped to contemplate—warmly, almost possessively—the scene before her. Steve and Marvin were standing together at the other end of the room. Near the phonograph Tiger was telling Warren about some eccentric incident of life at the Labor School. Helen stood thinking, not only of these four, but of herself: five of them, how distinct they were, one from the other, in their accomplishments, in their convictions. Tiger, the radical; Steve, the easy-going liberal; Warren, who wanted to turn history back to what he thought of as a nobler time; Marvin and his dedication to advancing himself for his progeny, as his father had been dedicated before him; herself and her long battle to build something substantial and good out of an ignorant, prurient little Midwestern girl. Different as they were, they had each of them—to the extent of his or her ability—rendered his life as an achievement, each assured of the rightness of the cause he labored in.

She remembered then the odd little anti-Communist man who had been on the boat on the way back from Europe. Dr. Paletta. Had that been his name? . . . Yes, Dr. Paletta. Their arrival celebration at the Plaza hadn't been as long ago as it seemed, but his words came to her mind as from a great distance.

"You Americans," he had said, ". . . each one of you thinks it is he who fights on the side of the angels. . . ."

It was true. And now it was as if she could see, in her own medium-sized apartment in New York, on a New Year's Eve, a microcosm of the mystery and the vigor of her country.

Outside through the city the sirens of midnight sounded. Helen waited a moment to make sure that was what she heard. Then she saw Marvin disengage himself from his conversation with Steve. Warren and Tiger were shaking hands and wishing each other good luck, and Steve was drifting over to where they stood. Marvin was coming across the room to kiss her. He was smiling. Helen put her glass aside and moved forward to meet him.

ABOUT THE AUTHOR

Alexander Fedoroff was born thirty-three years ago in New Orleans and like many of its natives, cannot pull himself entirely away from it. Mr. Fedoroff's outlook on the material in THE SIDE OF THE ANGELS reflects a certain contradiction in his family lines. His paternal grandparents were Russians, escapees from Siberia, where they were imprisoned as Nihilist revolutionaries. His maternal grandparents were American-born Scots: a Presbyterian schoolteacher and a fire-eating and fire-drinking newspaper man. His education was by the Jesuits for whom he has great admiration. Mr. Fedoroff has a wide background in the theatre and has been encouraged by Howard Lindsay and the late Bretaigne Windust and Theresa Helburn. He has been Leland Hey-ward's production assistant and has also been secretary to Anton Dolin and Alicia Markova and playwright Marc Connelly. His play, "Day of Grace," with Ben Gazzara, Macdonald Carey and Albert Salmi, was produced at the Westport (Connecticut) Country Playhouse and he is currently writing television films and planning a new play. In 1954 Mr. Fedoroff and Constance Burke of New Orleans were married. In 1960 they moved, with their two sons, to Los Angeles.